"Who says you can't bottle experience? Between the covers is a wealth of information that clearly demonstrates how to take a logical approach to finding and eliminating bugs. This is an absolute must-have book for anyone who develops, tests, or supports software for Microsoft Windows."

**—Bob Wilton, Escalation Engineer, Critical Problem Resolution Team, Microsoft Corporation**

"I have been fortunate enough to personally work with the authors on extremely demanding systems projects for more than eight years. This volume contains the kind of stuff we all wish we had known back at the beginning of those projects—the kind of stuff that the debugging guru tells you over a coffee-spilled keyboard on February 29 only because an extra day showed up and he has the afternoon free; the kind of stuff that only comes from actually building and then debugging complex systems projects instead of just reading about somebody else doing it.

Most books leave the advanced cases as 'exercises to the reader' or to 'other, more advanced books,' and those never seem to materialize. This book is one of those very rare 'other' books. Get two copies. You will always be lending the other one out."

**—Raymond McCollum, Architect, Microsoft Forefront Security Products**

"This book by Microsoft authors Mario and Daniel is an excellent reference for both intermediate and advanced debuggers. In-depth examples showing how to debug intricate problems, such as stack and heap corruptions, make this book stand out among current available literature on debugging Win32 software on Windows. The book is highly practical and is filled with numerous debugging tricks and strategies."

**—Kinshuman, Development Lead, Windows Core OS Division**

"I am pleased to see this guided tour through a comprehensive set of clever debugging techniques. It does not only tell how to deal with tough diagnosis problems, but it also explains the mechanisms behind the techniques used. The pragmatic approach taken in *Advanced Windows Debugging* makes it a good resource to understand several key Windows areas."

**—Adrian Marinescu, Software Architect, Microsoft Corporation**

"*Advanced Windows Debugging* fills the need for good documentation about debugging and fixing software defects. The book is based on the authors' valuable experience of tracking down the cause of various classes of software bugs. It includes representative examples of typical defects, the tools used to investigate these defects, and step-by-step instructions for using these tools. Software developers and testers will greatly benefit from becoming familiar with these examples."

**—Daniel Mihai, Software Design Engineer, Developer Productivity Tools, Microsoft**


"I wrote the WinDbg symbol handler, Symbol Server, and Source Server. Even so, I can't get my own wife to use WinDbg. She thinks it is hard to use, and, consequently, she hasn't learned of the potential of this toolset. I am buying a copy of this book, so she can learn it. The chapters on postmortem debugging and memory corruption are essential reading that provide real insight into the internals of the runtime and OS in the context of a program fault. Mario and Daniel's understanding of debugging comes from being asked to resolve completely unexplained bugs in unfamiliar target programs. This is what industrial strength debugging is all about."

**—Pat Styles, Microsoft**

# ADVANCED WINDOWS DEBUGGING

# ADVANCED WINDOWS DEBUGGING

*Mario Hewardt*
*Daniel Pravat*

✦Addison-Wesley

Upper Saddle River, NJ • Boston • Indianapolis • San Francisco
New York • Toronto • Montreal • London • Munich • Paris • Madrid
Cape Town • Sydney • Tokyo • Singapore • Mexico City

Many of the designations used by manufacturers and sellers to distinguish their products are claimed as trademarks. Where those designations appear in this book, and the publisher was aware of a trademark claim, the designations have been printed with initial capital letters or in all capitals.

The authors and publisher have taken care in the preparation of this book, but make no expressed or implied warranty of any kind and assume no responsibility for errors or omissions. No liability is assumed for incidental or consequential damages in connection with or arising out of the use of the information or programs contained herein.

The publisher offers excellent discounts on this book when ordered in quantity for bulk purchases or special sales, which may include electronic versions and/or custom covers and content particular to your business, training goals, marketing focus, and branding interests. For more information, please contact:

> U.S. Corporate and Government Sales
> (800) 382-3419
> corpsales@pearsontechgroup.com

For sales outside the United States please contact:

> International Sales
> international@pearsoned.com

**Editor-in-Chief**
Karen Gettman

**Acquisitions Editor**
Joan Murray

**Senior Development Editor**
Chris Zahn

**Managing Editor**
Gina Kanouse

**Copy Editor**
Rhonda Tinch-Mize

**Indexer**
Brad Herriman

**Proofreader**
Karen A. Gill

**Editorial Assistant**
Kim Boedigheimer

**Cover Designer**
Chuti Prasertsith

**Composition**
TnT Design

**This Book Is Safari Enabled**

The Safari® Enabled icon on the cover of your favorite technology book means the book is available through Safari Bookshelf. When you buy this book, you get free access to the online edition for 45 days.

Safari Bookshelf is an electronic reference library that lets you easily search thousands of technical books, find code samples, download chapters, and access technical information whenever and wherever you need it.

To gain 45-day Safari Enabled access to this book:

- Go to http://www.awprofessional.com/safarienabled
- Complete the brief registration form
- Enter the coupon code VJKK-KILI-JE-6MJ7-CN78

If you have difficulty registering on Safari Bookshelf or accessing the online edition, please e-mail customer-service@safaribooksonline.com.

Visit us on the Web: www.awprofessional.com

Library of Congress Cataloging-in-Publication Data:

Hewardt, Mario.

  Advanced windows debugging / Mario Hewardt, Daniel Pravat.

    p. cm.

  Includes index.

  ISBN 0-321-37446-0 (pbk. : alk. paper) 1. Microsoft Windows (Computer file) 2. Operating systems (Computers)—Management. 3. Debugging in computer science. I. Pravat, Daniel. II. Title.

  QA76.76.O63H497 2007

  005.4'46—dc22

2007030163

ISBN-13: 978-0-321-37446-2
ISBN-10: 0-321-37446-0

Text printed in the United States on recycled paper at Edwards Brothers Malloy in Ann Arbor, Michigan.
Eighth Printing, October 2012.

*To my wife Pia, whose support, patience, and encouragement helped make this book a reality. To the familia who taught and encouraged me to follow my dreams and passions.*
*Mario Hewardt*


*To Claudia, Alexis, and Edward*
*Daniel Pravat*

# CONTENTS

Foreword . . . . . . . . . . . . . . . . . . . . . . . . . . . . . . . . . . .xiii
Preface . . . . . . . . . . . . . . . . . . . . . . . . . . . . . . . . . . . . .xv
Acknowledgements . . . . . . . . . . . . . . . . . . . . . . . . . . .xxvii
About the Authors . . . . . . . . . . . . . . . . . . . . . . . . . . . .xxviii

**PART I: OVERVIEW** . . . . . . . . . . . . . . . . . . . . . . . . . . . . . . . .1

**Chapter 1:**   **Introduction to the Tools** . . . . . . . . . . . . . . . . . .3
Leak Diagnosis Tool . . . . . . . . . . . . . . . . . . . . . . . . . . .4
Debugging Tools for Windows . . . . . . . . . . . . . . . . . . .7
UMDH . . . . . . . . . . . . . . . . . . . . . . . . . . . . . . . . . . . .9
Microsoft Application Verifier . . . . . . . . . . . . . . . . . . .9
Global Flags . . . . . . . . . . . . . . . . . . . . . . . . . . . . . . .16
Process Explorer . . . . . . . . . . . . . . . . . . . . . . . . . . . .21
Windows Driver Kit . . . . . . . . . . . . . . . . . . . . . . . . . .23
Wireshark . . . . . . . . . . . . . . . . . . . . . . . . . . . . . . . . .26
DebugDiag . . . . . . . . . . . . . . . . . . . . . . . . . . . . . . . .27
Summary . . . . . . . . . . . . . . . . . . . . . . . . . . . . . . . . .27

**Chapter 2**   **Introduction to the Debuggers** . . . . . . . . . . . . . .29
Debugger Basics . . . . . . . . . . . . . . . . . . . . . . . . . . . .30
Basic Debugger Tasks . . . . . . . . . . . . . . . . . . . . . . . .45
Remote Debugging . . . . . . . . . . . . . . . . . . . . . . . . .109
Debugging Scenarios . . . . . . . . . . . . . . . . . . . . . . . .117
Summary . . . . . . . . . . . . . . . . . . . . . . . . . . . . . . . .121

**Chapter 3**   **Debuggers Uncovered** . . . . . . . . . . . . . . . . . . . .123
User Mode Debugger Internals . . . . . . . . . . . . . . . . .124
Controlling the Target . . . . . . . . . . . . . . . . . . . . . . .168
Summary . . . . . . . . . . . . . . . . . . . . . . . . . . . . . . . .178

**Chapter 4:**   **Managing Symbol and Source Files** . . . . . . . . . . . . . .**179**

Managing the Symbols for Debugging . . . . . . . . . . . . . . . . . . . . . .180
Managing Source Files for Debugging . . . . . . . . . . . . . . . . . . . . . .188
Summary . . . . . . . . . . . . . . . . . . . . . . . . . . . . . . . . . . . . . . . . .196

**PART II: APPLIED DEBUGGING** . . . . . . . . . . . . . . . . . . . . . . . . . . . . . . .**197**

**Chapter 5:**   **Memory Corruption Part I—Stacks** . . . . . . . . . . . . . .**199**

Memory Corruption Detection Process . . . . . . . . . . . . . . . . . . . . .201
Stack Corruptions . . . . . . . . . . . . . . . . . . . . . . . . . . . . . . . . . . .209
Summary . . . . . . . . . . . . . . . . . . . . . . . . . . . . . . . . . . . . . . . . .258

**Chapter 6:**   **Memory Corruption Part II—Heaps** . . . . . . . . . . . . . .**259**

What Is a Heap? . . . . . . . . . . . . . . . . . . . . . . . . . . . . . . . . . . . .259
Heap Corruptions . . . . . . . . . . . . . . . . . . . . . . . . . . . . . . . . . . .281
Summary . . . . . . . . . . . . . . . . . . . . . . . . . . . . . . . . . . . . . . . . .314

**Chapter 7:**   **Security** . . . . . . . . . . . . . . . . . . . . . . . . . . . . . . . . . . . .**317**

Windows Security Overview . . . . . . . . . . . . . . . . . . . . . . . . . . . .318
Source of Security Information . . . . . . . . . . . . . . . . . . . . . . . . . . .328
How Is the Security Check Performed? . . . . . . . . . . . . . . . . . . . . .334
Identity Propagation in Client-Server Applications . . . . . . . . . . . . .334
Security Checks at System Boundaries . . . . . . . . . . . . . . . . . . . . .338
Investigating Security Failures . . . . . . . . . . . . . . . . . . . . . . . . . . .340
Summary . . . . . . . . . . . . . . . . . . . . . . . . . . . . . . . . . . . . . . . . .378

**Chapter 8:**   **Interprocess Communication** . . . . . . . . . . . . . . . . . . . .**379**

Communication Mechanisms . . . . . . . . . . . . . . . . . . . . . . . . . . . .380
Troubleshooting Local Communication . . . . . . . . . . . . . . . . . . . . .382
Troubleshooting Remote Communication . . . . . . . . . . . . . . . . . . . .396
Additional Technical Information . . . . . . . . . . . . . . . . . . . . . . . . . .422
Summary . . . . . . . . . . . . . . . . . . . . . . . . . . . . . . . . . . . . . . . . .426

**Chapter 9: Resource Leaks** . . . . . . . . . . . . . . . . . . . . . . . . . . .**427**

What Is a Resource? . . . . . . . . . . . . . . . . . . . . . . . . .427
High-Level Process . . . . . . . . . . . . . . . . . . . . . . . . . .428
Reproducibility of Resource Leaks . . . . . . . . . . . . . . . . . .433
Handle Leaks . . . . . . . . . . . . . . . . . . . . . . . . . . . . .434
Memory Leaks . . . . . . . . . . . . . . . . . . . . . . . . . . . . .460
Summary . . . . . . . . . . . . . . . . . . . . . . . . . . . . . . . .492

**Chapter 10:   Synchronization** . . . . . . . . . . . . . . . . . . . . . . . . .**493**

Synchronization Basics . . . . . . . . . . . . . . . . . . . . . . . .493
High-Level Process . . . . . . . . . . . . . . . . . . . . . . . . . .505
Synchronization Scenarios . . . . . . . . . . . . . . . . . . . . . .510
Summary . . . . . . . . . . . . . . . . . . . . . . . . . . . . . . . .550

**PART III: ADVANCED TOPICS** . . . . . . . . . . . . . . . . . . . . . . . . . . . . .**551**

**Chapter 11:   Writing Custom Debugger Extensions** . . . . . . . . . . . . .**553**

Introduction to Debugger Extensions . . . . . . . . . . . . . . . . .553
Example Debugger Extension . . . . . . . . . . . . . . . . . . . . .556
Summary . . . . . . . . . . . . . . . . . . . . . . . . . . . . . . . .594

**Chapter 12:   64-Bit Debugging** . . . . . . . . . . . . . . . . . . . . . . . . .**595**

Microsoft 64-Bit Systems . . . . . . . . . . . . . . . . . . . . . . .595
Windows x64 Changes . . . . . . . . . . . . . . . . . . . . . . . . .602
Summary . . . . . . . . . . . . . . . . . . . . . . . . . . . . . . . .629

**Chapter 13:   Postmortem Debugging** . . . . . . . . . . . . . . . . . . . . . .**631**

Dump File Basics . . . . . . . . . . . . . . . . . . . . . . . . . . . .632
Using Dump Files . . . . . . . . . . . . . . . . . . . . . . . . . . . .645
Windows Error Reporting . . . . . . . . . . . . . . . . . . . . . . .653
Corporate Error Reporting . . . . . . . . . . . . . . . . . . . . . . .682
Summary . . . . . . . . . . . . . . . . . . . . . . . . . . . . . . . .690

**Chapter 14:** **Power Tools** . . . . . . . . . . . . . . . . . . . . . . . . . . . . . . . . . . .**691**

    Debug Diagnostic Tool . . . . . . . . . . . . . . . . . . . . . . . . . . . . . .691

    !analyze Extension Command . . . . . . . . . . . . . . . . . . . . . . . . . .699

    Summary . . . . . . . . . . . . . . . . . . . . . . . . . . . . . . . . . . . . . . . .708


**Chapter 15:** **Windows Vista Fundamentals** . . . . . . . . . . . . . . . . . . .**709**

    Chapter 1—Introduction to the Tools . . . . . . . . . . . . . . . . . . . .710

    Chapter 2—Introduction to the Debuggers . . . . . . . . . . . . . . . . .711

    Chapter 6—Memory Corruptions—Part Heaps . . . . . . . . . . . . . .717

    Chapter 7—Security . . . . . . . . . . . . . . . . . . . . . . . . . . . . . . . . .723

    Chapter 8—Interprocess Communication . . . . . . . . . . . . . . . . . .736

    Chapter 9—Resource Leaks . . . . . . . . . . . . . . . . . . . . . . . . . . .736

    Chapter 10—Synchronization . . . . . . . . . . . . . . . . . . . . . . . . . .737

    Chapter 11—Writing Custom Debugger Extensions . . . . . . . . . . .741

    Chapter 13—Postmortem Debugging . . . . . . . . . . . . . . . . . . . . .741

    Summary . . . . . . . . . . . . . . . . . . . . . . . . . . . . . . . . . . . . . . . .745


**Appendix A:** **Application Verifier Test Settings** . . . . . . . . . . . . . . . . .**747**

    Exceptions . . . . . . . . . . . . . . . . . . . . . . . . . . . . . . . . . . . . . . .747

    Handles . . . . . . . . . . . . . . . . . . . . . . . . . . . . . . . . . . . . . . . . .747

    Heaps . . . . . . . . . . . . . . . . . . . . . . . . . . . . . . . . . . . . . . . . . .749

    Locks . . . . . . . . . . . . . . . . . . . . . . . . . . . . . . . . . . . . . . . . . . .757

    Memory . . . . . . . . . . . . . . . . . . . . . . . . . . . . . . . . . . . . . . . . .760

    ThreadPool . . . . . . . . . . . . . . . . . . . . . . . . . . . . . . . . . . . . . . .762

    TLS . . . . . . . . . . . . . . . . . . . . . . . . . . . . . . . . . . . . . . . . . . . .764

    FilePaths . . . . . . . . . . . . . . . . . . . . . . . . . . . . . . . . . . . . . . . .764

    HighVersionLie . . . . . . . . . . . . . . . . . . . . . . . . . . . . . . . . . . . .765

    InteractiveServices . . . . . . . . . . . . . . . . . . . . . . . . . . . . . . . . . .767

    KernelModeDriverInstall . . . . . . . . . . . . . . . . . . . . . . . . . . . . . .768

    Low Resource Simulation . . . . . . . . . . . . . . . . . . . . . . . . . . . . .769

    LuaPriv . . . . . . . . . . . . . . . . . . . . . . . . . . . . . . . . . . . . . . . . .771

    DangerousAPIs . . . . . . . . . . . . . . . . . . . . . . . . . . . . . . . . . . . .774

    DirtyStacks . . . . . . . . . . . . . . . . . . . . . . . . . . . . . . . . . . . . . . .775

    TimeRollOver . . . . . . . . . . . . . . . . . . . . . . . . . . . . . . . . . . . . .775

    PrintAPI and PrintDriver . . . . . . . . . . . . . . . . . . . . . . . . . . . . . .776


**Index** . . . . . . . . . . . . . . . . . . . . . . . . . . . . . . . . . . . . . . . . . . . . . . . . .**777**

# FOREWORD

Software has one goal: simplify. If there's a workflow that can be optimized or automated, data that can be stored or processed more efficiently, software steps in to fill the job. While simplifying, software must not introduce undo complexity, and therefore should install with minimal user interaction, seamlessly integrate services and data from other applications and multiple sources, and be resilient to changes in its software and hardware environment. For the most part, software magically just works.

However, while software strives to simplify the experiences of end users and administrators, it has become more and more complex. Whether it's the amount of the data they work with, the number of applications with which they communicate, their degree of internal parallelism, or the APIs they import directly and indirectly from the software stack upon which they run, most of software's apparent simplicity hides a world of subtle timings, dependencies, and assumptions that run between layers of software, often across different applications and even computers. Just determining which component is at fault—much less why, for a problem that surfaces as a crash in a library, a meaningless error message, or a hang—is often daunting.

The reason you're reading this book is that you develop, test, or support software, and therefore face breakdowns in software's myriad moving parts that you are charged with investigating through to a root cause and maybe fixing. Success in this endeavor means identifying the source of a problem as quickly and efficiently as possible, which requires knowing what to look with, where to look, and how to look. In other words, succeeding means knowing what tools are at your disposal, which ones are the most effective for a class of failures, and how to apply the tool's features and functionality to quickly narrow in on the source of a problem.

Learning how to troubleshoot and debug Windows applications on the job has, for the most part, been the only option, but when you debug an application failure, knowing about that one obscure tool or scenario-specific debugger command can mean the difference between instantly understanding a problem and spending hours or even days hunting it without success. That's why a book like this pays for itself many times over.

*Advanced Windows Debugging* takes the combined knowledge and years of hands-on experience of not just Mario and Daniel, but also the Microsoft Customer

Support Services and the Windows product and tools development teams and puts it at your fingertips. There's no more authoritative place to learn about how the Windows heap manager influences the behavior of buffer overflows or what debugger extension command you should use to troubleshoot DCOM hangs, for example. I've been debugging my own Windows applications and device drivers for over 10 years, but when I reviewed the manuscript, I learned about new techniques, tools, and debugger commands that I'd never come across and that I've already found use for.

We all earn our pay and reputations not by how we debug, but by how quickly and accurately we do it. Whether you've been debugging Windows applications for years or are just getting started, Mario and Daniel equip you well for your bug hunting expeditions. Happy hunting!

Mark Russinovich
Technical Fellow, Platform and Services Division
Microsoft Corporation

# PREFACE

Not long ago, we were reminiscing about a really tough problem we faced at work. The Quality Assurance team was running stress tests on our product, and every four or five days, a crash would rear its ugly head. Sure, we had debugged the crash as far as we thought possible, and we had done extensive code reviews to try to figure it out, but alas, not enough information could be gained to get to the bottom of it. After several weeks of unfruitful attempts, we started looking for alternative approaches. During a random hallway conversation, someone happened to casually mention a tool called gflags. Having never heard of this tool before, we set out to do some research to find out how it could help us get to the bottom of our crash. Unfortunately, the learning process proved to be somewhat difficult. First, finding information about the tool proved to be a real challenge. There was a ton of great information in the reference documentation that came with the tools, but it was hard to figure out how to actually get started. We quickly realized that without some basic guidance, there was little hope for us to be able to utilize the tool. Naturally, we decided to ask the person who had happened to mention the tool if he knew of any documentation or pointers. He gave us some brief descriptions of the tool and, perhaps more importantly, the names of other people who had worked with the tool extensively. What followed was a series of long and instructive conversations, and bit by bit the basic idea behind the tool started falling into place.

Did we ever get to the bottom of the crash? Yes—we did. As a matter of fact, enabling the correct tool while running our stress tests pinpointed the problem to such accuracy that it only took an hour of code reviewing to locate and fix the misbehaving code. Had we known about this tool and how to use it from the start, we would have saved several weeks of work. From that point on, we dedicated quite a lot of time to furthering our understanding of the tools and how they can help while trying to troubleshoot misbehaving code.

Over the years, the Windows debuggers and tools have matured and grown and become increasingly powerful. The amount of timesaving features now available is truly mind-boggling. What is equally mind-boggling is that after several years, the native debuggers and tools are still relatively unknown to developers. The few developers who do find out that these tools exist have to go through a similarly painful learning process as we did years ago. We were fortunate to have the luxury of working with engineers at Microsoft (some of whom wrote the tools), but without this luxury, many hopeful developers end up at a dead end and are never able to reap the benefits of the tools. This unfortunate problem of a lack of learning material also turned out to be a great opportunity for a solution, and thus the idea for this book was born. The key to enable developers to gain the knowledge required is to provide a central repository of concise information that fully explains the ins and outs of the debugging tools and processes. The book you are holding serves as that key and is the net result of three years of writing and over 15 years of collective debugging experience.

We hope that you will enjoy reading this book as much as we enjoyed authoring it and that it will open up the door to a truly amazing world of highly efficient software troubleshooting and debugging. Knowing how to use the tools and techniques described in this book is a critical part of a computer scientist's work and can teach you how to very efficiently troubleshoot some of the toughest problems in software.

## Who Is This Book For?

The short answer to this question is anyone who is involved in any facet of software development and has a strong desire to learn what is actually happening deep inside Windows. Although the technical nature of the book might make you believe that its content is only intended for advanced system engineers, this is absolutely not true. One of the key points of this book is the *removing of the magic*. For various reasons, a lot of software engineers believe that there is a *magical* relationship between the software they are working on and the operating system. When a problem surfaces that requires the analysis of operating system components (such as RPC/COM or the Windows heap manager), this preconceived notion of magic prevents them from venturing *inside* Windows to gain more information that can potentially help them solve the problem. To make effective use of this book, you will have to learn how to remove this preconceived notion and truly be of the mind-set that there is no *magic* behind-the-scenes. The core Windows components should be viewed as an extension of your product and not as a separate and magical layer. After all, it's all just code—some of which just happened to be written by other people. If you can adjust your mind-set to accept this, you will have taken your first steps to mastering the art of Windows debugging.

### Software Developers

Anyone from a low-level system developer to a high-level RAD developer will benefit from reading this book. Whether your preference is writing Windows-based software in assembly language or by using the .NET framework, there is a ton of useful information to be learned about the tools and techniques behind Windows debugging.

Over the years, we've had several discussions with higher-level RAD developers who claim that they really don't see the need to learn about these low-level topics. After all, the beauty of writing code at a higher level is that all of the low-level intricacies are abstracted and *hidden* away from the developer. We couldn't agree more. However, our claim is that although abstractive programming allows the developer not to have to focus on low-level details, it *does not* negate the need to know how the abstraction really works. The substance behind this claim is simple. What you are working with is really just that—an abstraction. Usage of this abstraction in a design that it was not suited for can cause serious problems in your software; and, in such a case, without a solid understanding of how the abstraction works, it can mean the difference between shipping your product on time and slipping the release date by several months.

Another key factor when considering mastering the Windows debuggers and tools is related to the debugging of live production servers. While every attempt should be made to fix bugs before shipping a product, we all know that some bugs might slip through the cracks. When these bugs do surface post release, it can be a real headache tracking them down. Customers who encounter the bugs on live production servers are typically very sensitive to downtime and configuration changes, making it impossible to install a complex debugger package. The Debugging Tools for Windows, on the other hand, enables live debugging with no server configuration change and no installation requirements. In short, it enables customers to keep a pristine server during the troubleshooting process.

## Quality Assurance Engineers

Just as software developers will find the information in this book useful in their day-to-day tasks, so will quality assurance engineers. Quality assurance typically runs a battery of tests on any given component being tested. During this time, any number of bugs can surface. Whether they are memory corruptions, resource leaks, or hangs, knowing what extended instrumentation to enable during the test run can dramatically reduce the time it takes for root cause analysis. For instance, imagine that quality assurance is tasked with stress testing a credit card authorization service. One of the goals is that the service must be capable of surviving one week of continuous and simultaneous hammering by client requests. On day six, the service starts reporting errors for all client requests. At this point, the developers responsible for the service are called in to analyze the problem. It doesn't take long for them to figure out that the server has run out of memory, presumably due to a small memory leak that accumulates over time. After six days of accumulated leaks, figuring out the source of the leak, however, is a much bigger challenge that can take days of debugging and code reviewing. Had the correct extended instrumentation been enabled while running these tests, the time it would have taken to analyze the leak could have been greatly reduced.

## Product Support Engineers

In much the same way that quality assurance uses the Windows debuggers and tools to make root cause analysis more efficient, so can the product support engineers. Product support faces many of the same problems that quality assurance and software developers face on a day by day basis. The key difference, however, is the environmental constraints that they work under. The constraints can include not having full access to the server exhibiting the problems, having a limited amount of time available for troubleshooting the server, having limited access to customer source code, and other issues.

The information presented in this book will give product support engineers a great deal of ammunition when tackling these tough problems. Knowing how to debug customer problems with minimal downtime and minimal system configuration changes enables product support engineers to much more efficiently and nonintrusively gather the required data to get to the bottom of the problem.

# Where There Is a Will, There Is a Way

It should come as no surprise that the material presented in this book is highly technical in nature. We are not going to try and convince you that you don't need to know anything about Windows internals to benefit from the book because the simple truth is that you do. As with any technically oriented book, a certain amount of knowledge is assumed.

## Curiosity and a Will to Learn

While writing this book, we came to the realization that some of the areas of Windows we were writing about had been taken for granted. Sure, most of the time we knew that those areas *worked* a certain way, but we did not know exactly *what made them work* that way. We could have simply accepted the fact that they *just work*, but curiosity got the best of us (as it usually does). We spent quite a lot of time researching the topics and trying to connect the dots. The net result was a more in-depth understanding of Windows, which, in turn, allowed us to more efficiently debug problems.

The basic principle behind learning anything is that there must be a will to learn. Depending on your background, some of the high-level material in the book might feel intimidating. Embrace this intimidation, and you will be in a stronger position to fully grasp and understand the contents of this book.

If you possess the will to learn and have a great deal of curiosity, you will be well on your way to becoming an expert in Windows debugging.

## C/C++

All the sample code throughout the book is written in C/C++, and as such a good understanding of the language as well as its object layout is required. If some of the language concepts in the book are unfamiliar to you and you want to brush up on your C/C++ skills, we recommend the following books:

> *The C++ Programming Language (3rd Edition)*, by Bjarne Stroustrup, Boston: Addison-Wesley, 2000.

> *Inside the C/C++ Object Model*, by Stanley B. Lippman, Reading, MA: Addison-Wesley, 1996.

## Windows Internals

This book is about advanced Windows debugging, and as such parts of the book are dedicated to describing the internals of several integral Windows components (for example, heap manager, RPC, security subsystem). Our intentions are not to fully explain all aspects of these components but rather to give a brief but in-depth summary of how the component functions in relationship to the debugging scenarios being illustrated. If you want to take your knowledge of the internals of Windows even further, we strongly recommend reading

> *Microsoft Windows Internals, Fourth Edition: Microsoft Windows Server 2003, Windows XP, and Windows 2000*, by Mark E. Russinovich and David A. Solomon. Redmond, WA: Microsoft Press, 2004.

## Organization

The book consists of three major parts. In this section, we provide a short description of the contents of each chapter.

## Part I: Overview

Part I lays the groundwork. It provides an overview of the tools and debuggers and lets you familiarize yourself with the fundamentals of the debuggers. Even if you are already familiar with the Windows debuggers, we strongly encourage you to, at the very least, skim through these chapters, as they contain a ton of valuable information.

Chapter 1, "Introduction to the Tools," provides a high-level introduction to the tools used throughout the book. Topics such as download locations, installation instructions, and usage scenarios are detailed.

Chapter 2, "Introduction to the Debuggers," introduces the reader to the fundamentals of the Windows debuggers. Basic concepts such as what debuggers are available, how to use them, and how to configure them are covered.

Chapter 3, "Debuggers Uncovered," provides a more in-depth examination of user mode debuggers. A minimalist implementation of a debugger is provided, as well as looking at more advanced topics such as how the exception dispatch mechanism works.

Chapter 4, "Managing Symbol and Source Files," discusses how to maintain two of the most critical pieces of information during debugging: symbol files and source files. It gives a brief description of what symbol and source servers are, how to use them in association with the debuggers, and how to effectively manage them by setting up symbol servers and maintaining source servers for your organization.

## Part II: Applied Debugging

The focus of Part II is to provide the reader with the opportunity to analyze common programming mistakes using the Windows debuggers. Each of the chapters in this section is focused on a particular category of problems, such as memory corruption, memory leaks, and RPC/COM. Each chapter begins with an overview of the Windows component(s) involved followed by one or more scenarios that illustrate common programming mistakes in that area.

With the exception of Chapters 5 and 6, the chapters in Part II are standalone and can be read in any order.

Chapter 5, "Memory Corruption Part I—Stacks," and 6," Memory Corruption Part II—Heaps," take a close look at a very common problem that plagues developers on a daily basis: memory corruptions. Chapter 5 focuses on stack corruptions, and Chapter 6 on heap corruptions. Each chapter begins by explaining the overall concept behind the type of memory being examined (stack and heap) and is followed by a number of common scenarios under which the corruption can occur. Each scenario has associated sample code and a walk-through of the process that is used during debugging and root cause analysis.

Chapter 7, "Security," discusses common security-related problems that often surface during development. Quite often, developers face situations in which an API returns an access denied error code without any more in-depth information, making it hard to understand or track down where the error is coming from. This chapter will show several security-related examples of code and how to use the debuggers and appropriate tools to get to the bottom of the issue.

Chapter 8, "Interprocess Communication," focuses solely on interprocess communication debugging. Arguably perhaps the most used interprocess communication protocol in Windows but also the most magical is RPC/LPC. Knowing how to troubleshoot this important component is paramount when working with most applications. Using the debuggers, this chapter will show how you can track identity, analyze RPC failures, and much more.

Chapter 9, "Resource Leaks," details a very common problem with software today: resource leaks. The most common form of resource leaks is related to memory but not limited to it. Other examples includes registry keys, file handles, and so on. This chapter takes a look at the resource leak problem by showing a number of scenarios and associated sample code, as well as how to use the debuggers and tools to efficiently track them down.

Chapter 10, "Synchronization," discusses the topic of application hangs and how to most efficiently make use of the debuggers to track down synchronization problems such as deadlocks and lock contentions. A number of different synchronization scenarios are examined with associated debug sessions that give an in-depth view of the analysis process.

## Part III: Advanced Topics

Part III is an advanced section that consists of chapters that discuss topics such as postmortem debugging 64-bit debugging, Windows Vista fundamentals, and much more. The goal of these chapters is not to provide an exhaustive examination of each area, but rather provide just enough fundamentals for the reader to get started in the topic explained.

Chapter 11, "Writing Custom Debugger Extensions," talks about custom debugger extensions. Even though the Windows debuggers pack an extremely powerful set of commands and tools, there are times when you want to automate certain aspects of your own application debugging sessions. This chapter details how the extensibility model of the debuggers works and describes an example of a sample custom debugger extension.

Chapter 12, "64-Bit Debugging," introduces the basic concepts of debugging 64-bit architectures. Basic concepts such as stack traces, function calls, and parameter passing are discussed to enable the reader to get started on debugging these powerful architectures.

Chapter 13, "Postmortem Debugging," discusses postmortem debugging, which is an incredibly useful way of troubleshooting problems when there is no means of debugging a problem at the point of occurrence. This is a very common form of debugging once the product has shipped and problems surface on the customer site.

Chapter 14, "Power Tools," discusses two powerful tools that can be used to automate the debugging process. The first tool is called DebugDiag, and it provides an excellent way of automating resource leak debugging. The other tool is a command called analyze, which automates the initial fault analysis process.

Chapter 15, "Windows Vista Fundamentals," details some of the fundamentals behind Windows Vista. With the introduction of the new generation Windows platform, certain aspects of the operating system have changed dramatically, and some of the key changes are outlined in this chapter.

## Required Tools

All the tools required to make full use of this book are available as downloads free of charge. The new Windows Drivers Kit contains a complete command-line C/C++ development environment and a great set of associated development tools.

## Sample Code

As software engineers, we spend a great deal of our time hunting for the ultimate treasure of writing perfect code. While writing this book, we were faced with quite the opposite chore—the need to write not-so-perfect code to illustrate common programming mistakes.

The sample code is structured to achieve one goal: present examples of common programming mistakes in the shortest and most concise fashion as to not pollute the basic principle of the programming mistake being examined. To satisfy the goal of short and concise examples, we had to, at times, concoct examples rather than use real-life examples. Even though the sample code is "made up," it serves to simulate real-life examples, and every effort was made to ensure that the example stays true to the problem being examined.

All sample code is written in C/C++. We chose this language for two simple reasons:

- C/C++ is predominantly used in Windows development.
- In order not to obscure the debugging concepts discussed with higher-level abstractions, we chose the language that is most commonly used and also closest to the core.

All sample code is compiled and tested using the Windows Drivers Kit. The WDK was chosen so that readers would be able to enjoy learning the art of Windows debugging without being required to purchase a complete developer suite.

The source code assumes a Unicode environment, and as such Win32 API calls, as seen in the debugger, will be illustrated using the Unicode version of the API. For example, the sample code might show a call to the CreateProcess API, but when working in the debugger, the `CreateProcessW` API will be utilized. The API shown in the debugger is prefixed by the module name implementing the API. One example is the `CreateProcessW` API, which is implemented in kernel32.dll. It is often required to specify both the module name and the API name separated by the (!) character (`kernel32!CreateProcessW`).

All sample code and binaries are available on the book's Web site (http://www.advancedwindowsdebugging.com). In addition to source code and binaries being available, the site acts as a symbol and source code server for the book's binaries. When you try out the debugging sessions illustrated in the book, there is no need to download all the symbols for the binaries; rather, point your debuggers symbol path directly to the book's symbol server, and you can debug with remote symbols. The sources are also retrieved by the source servers from the book's Web site.

To provide a consistent learning experience, the binaries on the book's Web site have been built as nonoptimized and checked releases for the x86 architecture using the Windows XP platform. We chose to use Windows XP as the common denominator due to its widespread usage. If you choose to build the samples on your own using a different target platform, there might be minor variations in the debug output.

To build the samples on your own, simply open a WDK build window and type `build /ZCc` from the directory containing the makefile. If the source code being compiled requires additional steps, those steps will be spelled out in the chapter discussing the sample code.

Throughout the book, it is assumed that all binaries have been downloaded from the Web site and copied to the local hard drive (keeping the folder structure intact) to the following location: `C:\AWDBIN`, and the sources have been downloaded to the `C:\AWD` folder.

## Conventions

Code, command-line activity, and syntax descriptions appear in the book in a `monospaced` font. Many of the examples and walk-throughs in this book show a great deal of what is known as debug spew. Debug spew simply refers to the output that the debugger displays as a result of some action that the user takes. Typically, this debug spew consists of information shown in a very compact and concise form. In order to effectively reference bits and pieces of this data and make it easy for you to follow, the boldface and italic types are used. Additionally, anything with the boldface type in the debug spew indicates commands that you will be entering. The following example illustrates the mechanism.

```
0:000> ~*kb
.  0  Id: 924.a18 Suspend: 1 Teb: 7ffdf000 Unfrozen
ChildEBP RetAddr  Args to Child
0007fb1c 7c93edc0 7ffdf000 7ffd4000 00000000 ntdll!DbgBreakPoint
0007fc94 7c921639 0007fd30 7c900000 0007fce0 ntdll!LdrpInitializeProcess+0xffa
0007fd1c 7c90eac7 0007fd30 7c900000 00000000 ntdll!_LdrpInitialize+0x183
00000000 00000000 00000000 00000000 00000000 ntdll!KiUserApcDispatcher+0x7
0:000> dd 0007fd30
0007fd30   00010017 00000000 00000000 00000000
0007fd40   00000000 00000000 00000000 ffffffff
0007fd50   ffffffff f735533e f7368528 ffffffff
0007fd60   f73754c8 804eddf9 8674f020 85252550
0007fd70   86770f38 f73f4459 b2f3fad0 804eddf9
0007fd80   b30dccd1 852526bc b30e81c1 855be944
0007fd90   85252560 85668400 85116538 852526bc
0007fda0   852526bc 00000000 00000000 00000000
```

In this example, you are expected to type **~*kb** in the debug session. The result of entering that command shows several lines, with the most critical piece of information being *0007fd30*. Next, you should enter the **dd 0007fd30** command illustrated to glean more information about the previously highlighted number *0007fd30*.

All tools used in this book are assumed to be launched from their installation folder. For example, if the Windows debuggers are installed in the C:\Program Files\ Debugging Tools for Windows folder, the command line for launching windbg.exe will be shown as

```
C:\>windbg
```

## Supported Windows Versions

Windows XP or higher is required to fully make use of this book. All sample code and debugging scenarios have been run on Windows XP SP2 or Windows Server 2003 SP1, depending on the requirements of the specific scenario. Please note that service packs or even specific patches can change the result of various commands, although these changes will not affect the overall outcome of what is being illustrated with the debug session.

Chapter 15, "Windows Vista Fundamentals," covers the most important changes made in Windows Vista and includes debug sessions that must be run on a machine running Windows Vista.

Furthermore, all samples and debug sessions were run using the 32-bit version of Windows. Samples used in Chapter 12, "64-Bit Debugging," were run using the 64-bit version of Windows XP.

## Support

While every attempt has been made to make this book 100% accurate, without a doubt errors will be found. If you encounter an error in this book, feel free to contact us using any of the following resources:

Email: `marioh@advancedwindowsdebugging.com` or
`daniel@advancedwindowsdebugging.com`.

Alternatively, the book discussion forum at http://www.advancedwindowsdebugging.com is monitored and can be used to report erroneous information. As corrections are made, they will be posted to the errata section of the Web site.

# ACKNOWLEDGMENTS

Writing a technical book is a large-scale effort, far more substantial than we had originally anticipated. As authors, we provided the raw material and the first draft of the book, but throughout the project, a number of people shared their insights and expertise to make this book worth the time spent reading it.

Thanks to all the team members at Addison Wesley, especially Elizabeth Peterson, Jana Jones, Curt Johnson, Joan Murray, and Gina Kanouse. Chris Zahn also played an instrumental role in editing the book and in correcting our self-styled syntax.

As with any technical publication, technical accuracy is of utmost importance. We were fortunate to have great engineers (many of them own the specific technology areas discussed in the book) look at the material and provide feedback. Thanks go to Mark Russinovich, Ivan Brugiolo, Pat Styles, Pavel Lebedynskiy, Daniel Mihai, Doug Ellis, Cristi Vlasceanu, Adrian Marinescu, Saji Abraham, Kamen Moutafov, Kinshuman Kinshumann, Bob Wilton, Raymond McCollum, Viorel Mititean, Andy Cheung, Saar Picker, Drew Bliss, Jason Cunningham, Adam Edwards, Jen-Lung Chiu, Alain Lissoir, and Brandon Jiang.

Special thanks go to Mark Russinovich for not only reviewing the book but also writing the foreword. Mark's remarkable body of work is well known among software developers and has been a great influence on us and countless other engineers.

Ivan Brugiolo was also instrumental in reviewing and providing in-depth feedback. Ivan was incredibly generous with his spare time, sharing knowledge that has added considerable value to this book.

We also want to extend our gratitude to Alexandra Hewardt for designing and implementing the book's Web page.

# ABOUT THE AUTHORS

© www.BrookeClark.com

**Mario Hewardt** is a senior design engineer with Microsoft Corporation and has worked extensively in the Windows system level development arena for the past nine years. Throughout five releases of Windows (starting with Windows 98), he has worked primarily in the server and desktop management arena, focusing the majority of his time on ensuring the reliability, robustness, and security of the product.

Photo by Eduard Koller

**Daniel Pravat** is a senior design engineer with Microsoft Corporation and was actively involved in releasing several windows components in multiple Windows releases. Prior to joining Microsoft, he developed telecommunication software for computer-based telephony servers. He expects all software applications to be reliable, predictable, and efficient.

# PART I

# OVERVIEW

**Chapter 1**    Introduction to the Tools . . . . . . . . . . . . . . . . . . . . . .3

**Chapter 2**    Introduction to the Debuggers  . . . . . . . . . . . . . . . . .29

**Chapter 3**    Debuggers Uncovered . . . . . . . . . . . . . . . . . . . . . .123

**Chapter 4**    Managing Symbol and Source Files . . . . . . . . . . . . . . .179

# INTRODUCTION TO THE TOOLS

Many books and articles have been written about the importance of proper software design and engineering principles. Some of the publications take a very balanced approach between methodology and practice, whereas others focus mostly on methodology. Books written about the importance of object-oriented design and programming, design patterns, or modular programming are all great examples of methodologies that help us write better software. Without a doubt, proper software methodologies are the precursors to all successful software projects. However, they are not the sole contributors to the success of the software. Regardless of how well we think that we can design software and regardless of how accurate we believe our scheduling to be, mysterious problems always plague us during the development process. Hectic schedules, complex component interactions, and legacy code are just some of the reasons why we cannot practically anticipate and solve all the problems by simply employing good development methodologies. In addition to the methodologies, we have to know how to troubleshoot complex problems in a cost- and time-efficient manner.

This chapter introduces you to invaluable tools that will be of great aid in the troubleshooting process, as well as help reduce the time and money spent on handling a wide range of common problems. A lot of the problems that we discuss in this book leave developers feeling frustrated because of their complex nature. Even if a developer has an idea of how to manually approach a particular problem, the effort of tracking it down is typically very costly. Unbeknownst to many developers, help is out there; the help comes in the form of incredible tool sets that aid developers in tracking down and solving a lot of these types of problems. Not only does it help with the problem solving, but it does so in a very efficient manner.

This chapter provides an introduction to the tools used throughout the book. Each tool is discussed in detail, and the coverage includes important information, such as common usage scenarios, install points, and background information on how the tools do their work The tool descriptions are not exhaustive sources for all the various usage scenarios; rather, they serve as high-level overviews of the tools. Each of the tools listed is used in other parts of the book to illustrate the usage of the tool to solve a real problem. This chapter can be viewed as an introduction to the tool set that complements its practical usage scenario in subsequent chapters in the book.

Note that the tools this chapter describes are the latest versions of each tool available at the time of writing. Newer versions might have been published by the time you read this chapter. This does not constitute a problem, as the general tool behavior generally stays the same.

## Leak Diagnosis Tool

| | |
|---|---|
| Usage Scenarios | Memory leak detection |
| Current Version | 1.25 |
| Download Point | ftp://ftp.microsoft.com/PSS/Tools/Developer Support Tools/LeakDiag |
| Analysis Mechanism | Log Files |

The Leak Diagnosis tool (LeakDiag) is a tool used during the memory leak detection process. It goes well beyond the basic capabilities of showing how much memory a process has leaked to detailed information, such as the exact stack trace that resulted in the allocation and allocation statistics.

The installation process for LeakDiag is trivial. Download leakdiag125.msi from the download point and use the default settings during the install process. The application is, by default, installed into C:\LEAKDIAG and can run in two modes. Specifically, it has a command-line version and a graphical user interface (GUI) version. The command-line version is called ldcmd.exe, and the GUI version is called leakdiag.exe. Both can be executed from the command line or by going to the Start button and selecting All Programs, LeakDiag.

Diag includes a superset of the capabilities of UMDH.exe (see the later section "UMDH") in the sense that UMDH is only capable of showing allocations coming from the standard heap manager. LeakDiag extends this functionality to include not only the standard heap allocations, but also COM allocations (external and internal), virtual memory allocations, and much more. All in all, the current version of LeakDiag supports six different allocators:

- Virtual Allocator
- Heap Allocator [DEFAULT]
- MPHeap Allocator

- COM AllocatorCoTaskMem
- COM Private Allocator
- C Runtime Allocator

The capability of LeakDiag to support all these allocators makes it a very flexible tool to be used for memory leak detection. Another significant difference from most other memory leak detection tools is the way in which LeakDiag collects memory-related activity. Rather than relying on the operating system support for recording memory allocation stack traces, LeakDiag uses Microsoft's Detours technology to intercept calls to the memory allocators. By doing so, LeakDiag eliminates the need to enable stack tracing support in the operating system.

Figure 1.1 shows the start screen of the GUI version of LeakDiag. The LeakDiag interface has two main sections: the list of all running processes and the available memory allocators with associated action buttons. To start memory allocation tracking, simply select one of the running processes followed by the memory allocator that you want to track. Click the Start button, followed by the Log button. Reproduce the memory leak and click the Log button once again. When you are finished tracking, click the Stop button. LeakDiag outputs all the information into log files in XML format. By default, the log files are written to `C:\LeakDiag\logs` and the log files are named by LeakDiag itself to guarantee a unique filename for each run.

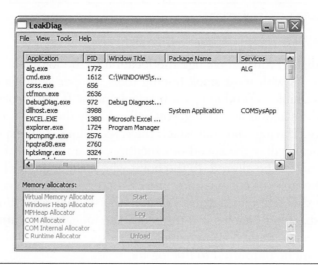

**Figure 1.1**   Start screen of LeakDiag

As with most memory leak detection tools, LeakDiag works on the basis of snapshot comparisons. By taking snapshots of all the memory allocations at regular intervals, LeakDiag is capable of taking a delta between snapshots to describe allocations that have not yet been freed (potential leaks). The Log button is the mechanism by which you take the snapshots.

LeakDiag has a few options that allow you to customize the default behavior. By selecting the Options menu item on the Tools menu, you are presented with the Options dialog, as shown in Figure 1.2.

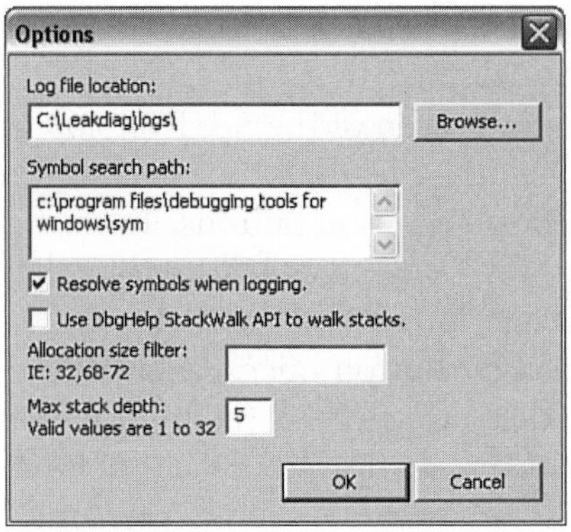

**Figure 1.2**   LeakDiag customizations

In the Options dialog, you can change the location of the log files, as well as specify the symbol path. As with most stack tracing tools, proper symbols are required for LeakDiag to be capable of producing useful stack traces. If you incorrectly specify the symbol path or the symbols are wrong, you will see only the addresses for each frame in the stack trace. Having said that, stack trace recording is an expensive operation that can dramatically alter the speed of execution. As a matter of fact, at times, the speed of execution can be altered  to the point where the memory leak will not even surface (if it is because of concurrency and/or timing related issues). Fortunately, a check box also exists that allows you to disable the symbol resolution while logging. The Allocation size filter enables you to specify the range of allocation sizes that you want to track. Finally, stack depth enables you to specify the number of frames per stack trace that will be outputted to the log file.

For a detailed description of the command-line mode of LeakDiag, as well as the log file format, see Chapter 9, "Resource Leaks," where we use LeakDiag to analyze and nail down a real memory leak.

### *The Microsoft Detours Library*

Microsoft Detours is an innovative solution to the problem of instrumenting and/or improving existing code at the binary level. Historically, instrumenting and/or improving code involved simply changing the source code and recompiling. However, in today's world of commercial development, you will rarely (if ever) have access to the source code for a component or product. Microsoft Detours allows you to intercept binary functions and provide your own detour function that can either completely replace the original function or add some code and then call the original function (via a trampoline). It does this seeming magic by replacing the first few instructions of the original function with an unconditional jump to the new function. It is important to understand that this process happens at runtime and is not persisted, which in essence means that you can detour different instances of the same application independent of one another.

For more information on Microsoft Detours, please see http://research.microsoft.com/sn/detours.

# Debugging Tools for Windows

| | |
|---|---|
| Usage Scenarios | Collection of debuggers and tools |
| Current Version | 6.6.0007.5 |
| Download Point | http://www.microsoft.com/whdc/ddk/debugging/ |

Debugging Tools for Windows is a comprehensive, freely available package that contains powerful debuggers and tools to aid developers in becoming more efficient in their day-to-day jobs.

The download point allows you to choose between the 32- and 64-bit (Itanium and x64) versions. Setup is straightforward, and the express setup is sufficient to get all the necessary tools installed. One caveat exists; if you plan on developing custom debugger extensions (as we will show in Chapter 11, "Writing Custom Debugger Extensions"), you must do a custom install and elect to install the SDK as well. Table 1.1 shows all the tools that come as part of this package.

**Table 1.1**   List of Tools That Are Part of the Debugging Tools for Windows

| Image | Description |
| --- | --- |
| agestore.exe | Handy file deletion utility that deletes files based on last access date. |
| cdb.exe | Console-based user mode debugger. Virtually identical to NTSD. |
| dbengprx.exe | Lightweight proxy server that relays data between two different machines. |
| dbgrpc.exe | Tool used to query and display Microsoft Remote Procedure Call (RPC) information. |
| dbgsrv.exe | Process server used for remote debugging. |
| dumpchk.exe | Tool used to validate a memory dump file. |
| gflags.exe | Configuration tool used to enable and disable system instrumentation. |
| kd.exe | Kernel mode debugger. |
| kdbgctrl.exe | Tool used to control and configure a kernel mode debug connection. |
| kdsrv.exe | Connection server used during kernel mode debugging. |
| kill.exe | Console-based tool to terminate processes. |
| logger.exe | Tool that logs the activity of a process (such as function calls). |
| logviewer.exe | Tool used to view log files generated by logger.exe. |
| ntsd.exe | Console-based user mode debugger. Virtually identical to CDB. |
| remote.exe | Tool used to remotely control console programs. |
| rtlist.exe | Remote process list viewer. |
| symchk.exe | Tool used to validate symbol files or download symbol files from a symbol server. |
| symstore.exe | Tool used to create and maintain a symbol store. |
| tlist.exe | Tool to list all running processes. |
| umdh.exe | Tool used for memory leak detection. |
| windbg.exe | User mode and kernel mode debugger with a graphical user interface. |

Not surprisingly, the most important tool is the debugger itself. Chapter 2, "Introduction to the Debuggers," and Chapter 3, "Debuggers Uncovered," are dedicated to explaining how the debuggers work, how to set them up, and how to most effectively use them.

The tools introduction in this chapter details the most interesting tools we use throughout the book. When the download point specifies 'Part of Debugging tools for Windows' for each tool, it is required that Debugging Tools for Windows be installed.

Please note that at the time of writing, the most recent version was 6.6.0007.5. It is quite possible that a new version of the Windows debuggers will be released by the time you read this book. Even so, there should be relatively minor changes in the debugger output, and all the material in the book should still apply and be easily followed. The debugger download URL also keeps a history of debug versions (going back two to three releases) that can be downloaded. If you want to follow the same version, you can download the Debugging Tools for Windows corresponding to version 6.6.0007.5.

## UMDH

| | |
|---|---|
| Usage Scenarios | Memory leak detection |
| Current Version | 6.0.5457.0 |
| Download Point | Part of Debugging Tools for Windows |
| Analysis Mechanism | Log files |

UMDH is another form of memory leak detection tool that includes a subset of the functionality of LeakDiag. Whereas LeakDiag is able to track memory from a variety of allocators, UMDH is only capable of tracking memory that originates from the heap manager. In addition, it requires that user mode stack tracing is enabled in the operating system (see the "Global Flags" section of this chapter) to work properly.

Chapter 9 shows examples of how to use UMDH to track down memory leaks.

## Microsoft Application Verifier

| | |
|---|---|
| Usage Scenarios | General application troubleshooting |
| Current Version | 3.3 |
| Download Point | http://www.microsoft.com/downloads/details.aspx?FamilyID=bd02c19c-1250-433c-8c1b-2619bd 93b3a2&DisplayLang=en |
| Analysis Mechanism | Log files and debugger |

Every serious developer needs to be aware of the Application Verifier tool. Enabling Application Verifier for your process allows you to catch a whole range of common programming mistakes. Examples include invalid handle usage, lock usage, file paths, and much more. It is good practice to always have Application Verifier enabled for all the processes involved during development time. Having said that, some test settings in Application Verifier can dramatically alter the speed of execution in your application and, as such, can cause timing-related issues not to surface. One common solution to this problem is to always have Application Verifier enabled, and at select milestones turn it off and run the entire test suite again to make sure that timing issues are not a problem. Another good time for Application Verifier to be enabled is when the product is in bug fixing mode. By running with Application Verifier enabled, you can make sure that regressions are not introduced when fixing bugs.

Installation of Application Verifier is straightforward using the default install settings. After the installation completes, you can start Application Verifier by going to the Start button and then selecting All Programs, Application Verifier. Figure 1.3 shows the start screen presented when launching Application Verifier.

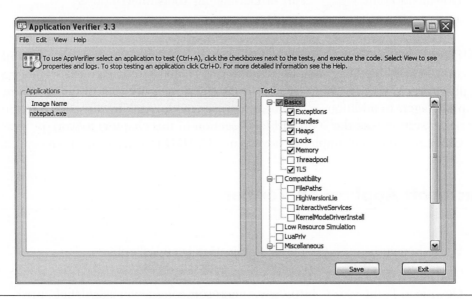

**Figure 1.3**   Start screen of Application Verifier

The Applications pane shows all applications currently enabled for verification. You can add applications by selecting the Add Application option from the File menu. Reciprocally, you can also remove applications by selecting the application and selecting the Delete Application menu item from the File menu.

To change the settings for a particular application, select the application in the left pane and choose the Property Window on the View menu. This adds a property section to the bottom of the start window that allows you to control the following behaviors:

- Propagate: Controls whether the test settings of this image will be propagated to child processes. Enabling this property causes the test settings to propagate.
- AutoClr: If enabled, causes Application Verifier to disable all test settings of this image once it starts running.
- AutoDisableStop: If enabled, causes Application Verifier to report a given problem only once.
- LoggingWithLocksHeld: If enabled, causes Application Verifier to log the DLL load and unload events. Note that this might cause problems in the application since logging requires I/O that is performed during the execution of the DllMain code path.

To get a brief description of each test setting, you can hover over the test setting to open up a balloon tip. The balloon tip will also tell you whether a debugger is required to see the results of the tests.

To get more details or for configuration settings for each test setting, you can right-click on the test setting and choose from one of two options.

- Properties: Allows you to control the properties of the selected test. For example, choosing properties on the Handles test allows you to control the number of traces that will be recorded for handle tracking. Note that the Properties selection is not available for all test settings.
- Verifier Stop Options: Allows you to control the options for the selected test. Figure 1.4 illustrates the verifier stop options menu selection when used on the Handles test setting.

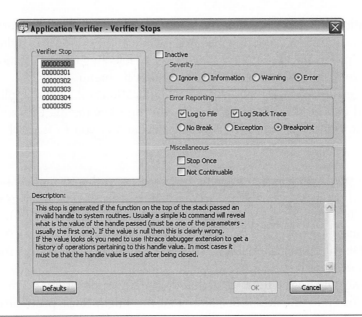

**Figure 1.4**   Handles Verifier Stop options

The Application Verifier Stop options are further divided into several sections:

- The Verifier Stop Section contains a list of all the verifier stops that the test setting is capable of performing. In Figure 1.4, the Verifier Stop section shows that six stops are available when verifying handles. All other sections in this window work on the basis of a selected stop code.
- The Description section gives a detailed description of the selected verifier stop.
- The Inactive check box controls whether the selected verifier stop is active or inactive, enabling you to control the granularity of the test setting.
- The Severity section allows you to control how severe you consider the stop code to be. Depending on what choice is made, it will have a direct impact on how the stop is surfaced. For example, setting the verifier stop 00000300 to Ignore causes the stop, when triggered, not to break into the debugger.
- The Error Reporting section allows you to control in more detail what should happen when a verifier stop occurs. The check boxes control the logging actions taken (such as whether it should be logged to a file) as well as whether

it should log the stack trace for the stop. The radio buttons control the debugger behavior when the stop occurs. You can set it to execute a breakpoint, throw an exception, or not break at all.

- The Miscellaneous section controls the frequency of the stop. If the Stop Once check box is selected, the stop will only occur the first time it is encountered. If the Non Continuable check box is selected, the debugger will break in when a stop occurs, and you will not be able to recover from the stop—in essence, preventing you from continuing process execution.

The next section of the start screen (refer to Figure 1.3), the Tests pane, shows all available test settings. Selecting the check box enables that particular test setting for the selected process. Right below the Tests pane is a short description of the test setting itself.

After an application has been enabled for verification, you can simply run the application, and Application Verifier will work in the background. Depending on how each test setting is configured, there are two primary ways to see the results of an Application Verifier run. The first way is to view the associated log file by selecting the Logs menu item from the View menu and then selecting the application log you are interested in. It is important to note that not all test settings report their results using log files. Some of the test settings require a debugger to get the desired results. To see which test settings require a debugger, simply hover over the test setting to get the context-sensitive help. If a test setting requires a debugger, you must run the application under the debugger to see the results.

When Application Verifier requires a debugger to be attached, the output of a violation observes the following general outline:

```
VERIFIER STOP <stop-code>: <process-PID>: <message>
parameter-1: <description>
parameter-2: <description>
parameter-3: <description>
parameter-4: <description>
```

The stop-code indicates the particular violation that occurred, the PID shows the process ID of the faulting process, and the message gives a brief textual description of the fault. The parameter list is dependent on the type of test being performed.

For example, the following output shows the violation as reported by the Application Verifier when trying to close an invalid handle:

```
========================================
VERIFIER STOP 00000300 : pid 0xFF0: Invalid handle exception for current stack trace.

        C0000008 : Exception code.
        0007FBD4 : Exception record. Use .exr to display it.
        0007FBE8 : Context record. Use .cxr to display it.
        00000000 : Not used.


========================================
This verifier stop is continuable.
After debugging it use `go' to continue.


========================================
```

Using the GUI mode to enable tests for an application is quite convenient, but sometimes it is necessary to enable tests in an automated fashion. Let's say that the product you are working on is built every night, and automated tests are launched right
after the build completes. As part of this test suite, the quality assurance team has
requested that Application Verifier be enabled during testing. Rather than having an
engineer manually use the GUI mode version of Application Verifier and enable the
tests each night, he can simply write a script that uses the console mode version to
enable the tests. The default installation path for application verifier is

```
C:\windows\system32\appverif.exe
```

When you launch the appverif.exe executable with the /? switch, you will see the
following:

```
Application Verifier 3.3.0045
Copyright (c) Microsoft Corporation. All rights reserved.

Application Verifier Command-Line Usage:

    -enable TEST ... -for TARGET ... [-with [TEST.]PROPERTY=VALUE ...]
    -disable TEST ... -for TARGET ...
    -query TEST ... -for TARGET ...
    -configure STOP ... -for TARGET ... -with PROPERTY=VALUE...
    -verify TARGET [-faults [PROBABILITY [TIMEOUT [DLL ...]]]]
    -export log -for TARGET -with To=XML_FILE [Symbols=SYMBOL_PATH]
[StampFrom=LOG_STAMP] [StampTo=LOG_STAMP] [Log=RELATIVE_TO_LAST_INDEX]
    -delete [logs|settings] -for TARGET ...
    -stamp log -for TARGET -with Stamp=LOG_STAMP [Log=RELATIVE_TO_LAST_INDEX]
```

```
-logtoxml LOGFILE XMLFILE
-installprovider PROVIDERBINARY
```

Available Tests:

```
Heaps
Handles
Locks
Memory
TLS
Exceptions
DirtyStacks
LowRes
DangerousAPIs
TimeRollOver
Threadpool
LuaPriv
HighVersionLie
FilePaths
KernelModeDriverInstall
InteractiveServices
PrintAPI
PrintDriver
```

(For descriptions of tests, run appverif.exe in GUI mode.)

Examples:
```
    appverif -enable handles locks -for foo.exe bar.exe
        (turn on handles locks for foo.exe & bar.exe)
    appverif -enable heaps handles -for foo.exe -with heaps.full=false
        (turn on handles and normal pageheap for foo.exe)
    appverif -enable heaps -for foo.exe -with full=true dlls=mydll.dll
        (turn on full pageheap for the module of mydll.dll in the foo.exe
    appverif -enable * -for foo.exe
        (turn on all tests for foo.exe)
    appverif -disable * -for foo.exe bar.exe
        (turn off all tests for foo.exe & bar.exe)
    appverif -disable * -for *
        (wipe out all the settings in the system)
    appverif -export log -for foo.exe -with to=c:\sample.xml
        (export the most recent log associated with foo.exe to c:\sample.xml)
    appverif /verify notepad.exe /faults 5 1000 kernel32.dll advapi32.dll
        (enable fault injection for notepad.exe. Faults should happen with
         probability 5%, only 1000 msecs after process got launched and only
         for operations initiated from kernel32.dll and advapi32.dll)
```

To enable all Application Verifier tests for a given executable, you could use the following command line:

```
appverif.exe -enable * -for myexecutable.exe
```

In addition to enabling tests for a given application, it is also possible to control Application Verifier from the debugger. The extension command used to control Application Verifier from the debugger is `!avrf`. For a complete listing of all the available test settings, see Appendix A, "Application Verifier Test Settings."

## Global Flags

| | |
|---|---|
| Usage Scenarios | Configuration |
| Current Version | 6.6.0007.5 |
| Download Point | Part of Debugging Tools for Windows |
| Executable | gflags.exe |

The Global Flags application (gflags) is installed as part of the Debugging Tools for Windows, and the executable (gflags.exe) can be launched from the default installation path. For example, on my system, I would use the following command line to start gflags:

```
c:\>gflags.exe
```

Many of the tools we use in this book rely on support from Windows to function properly. For example, UMDH requires that the Create user mode stack trace database option be enabled. Global Flags (or gflags) is the one-stop configuration tool for all the various options available.

### GUI Mode

Most of the available options can be enabled for the entire system (that is, all processes running) or on a per-process basis. Figure 1.5 shows the main screen of gflags.

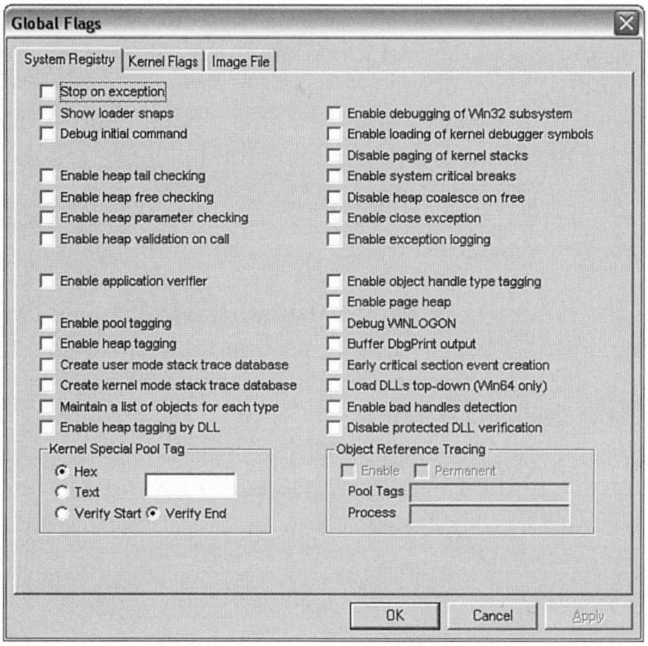

**Figure 1.5**   Main screen of gflags

The System Registry tab shows the options available on a systemwide basis, and the Image File tab shows the options available on a per-process basis. If you change any of the systemwide settings, a reboot is generally required. The Kernel Flags tab shows the options that affect the running kernel only. For a per-process setting, the process must be restarted before the settings will take effect.

Because the options available in gflags configure various aspects of the operating system, where are the settings stored, and how are they interpreted? The answer: the Registry. Depending on whether you change systemwide settings or per-process settings, they are stored in different locations in the Registry:

- Systemwide settings: HKEY_LOCAL_MACHINE\SYSTEM\
  CurrentControlSet\Control\SessionManager\GlobalFlag
- Per-process settings: HKEY_LOCAL_MACHINE\SOFTWARE\
  Microsoft\Windows NT\Current Version\Image File Execution
  Options\<Image File Name>\GlobalFlag

The per-process Registry path has some interesting properties associated with it. In addition to storing the global flags in the GlobalFlag value, other useful settings can be stored there. For example, if you are trying to debug a process not directly started by yourself (such as a service started by the service control manager), you can enable debugging of that process by specifying the following registry value:

```
HKEY_LOCAL_MACHINE\SOFTWARE\Microsoft\Windows NT\Current Version\Image File Execution
Options\<Image File Name>\Debugger
```

You can specify the debugger of choice that you want launched when the process starts. We will see how this feature can be used in more detail in Chapter 2.

The Image File tab allows you to enable instrumentation on a per-process basis. Figure 1.6 shows the available options.

When you first navigate to this tab, all the options will be grayed out until you specify an image name in the Image text field and press the Tab key.

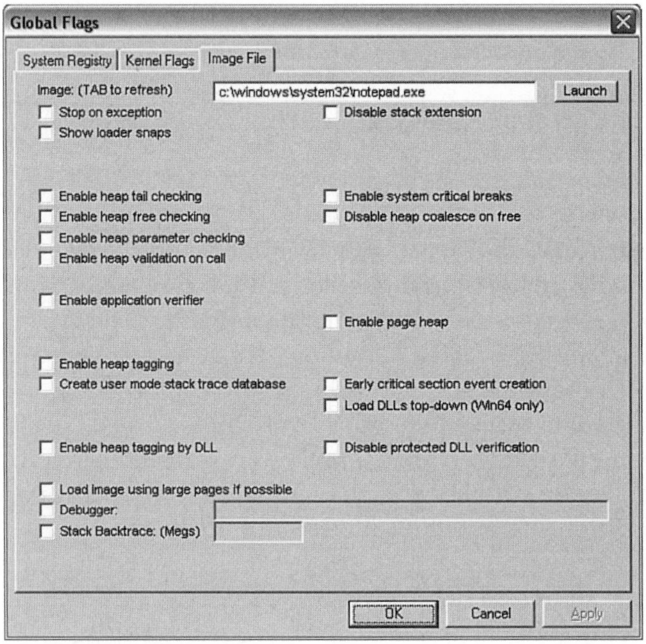

**Figure 1.6**   Per-process instrumentation

## Command-Line Mode

In addition to the GUI mode, gflags can be run on the command line. The options available on the command line mimic the options in GUI mode:

```
usage: GFLAGS [-r [<Flags>]] |
              [-r +spp TAG | -r +spp SIZE | -r -spp |
              [-k [<Flags>]] |
              [-i <ImageFileName> [<Flags>]] |
              [-i <ImageFileName> -tracedb <SizeInMb>] |
              [-p <PageHeapOptions>] (use `-p ?' for help)  |
```

Each of the options is explained a bit more in the following list:

- -r controls the persistent options for the entire system (analogous to the System Registry tab in GUI mode).
- -k controls current kernel options (analogous to the Kernel Flags tab in GUI mode).
- -i controls options on a per-image basis (analogous to the Image File tab in GUI mode).
- -p controls pageheap options (analogous to the Verifier tab in GUI mode).

Each of the preceding switches can either display the current settings for the particular switch or modify the settings according to the flags specified. If you simply want to see what the settings are, specify the switch (such as -i notepad.exe) without the flags. If you want to enable the settings, the flags can be specified as either a hexadecimal number or an abbreviation that represents the gflags option. Table 1.2 shows the available abbreviations.

**Table 1.2**  gflags Option Abbreviations

| Abbreviation | Description |
|---|---|
| soe | Stop On Exception |
| sls | Show Loader Snaps |
| dic | Debug Initial Command |
| shg | Stop on Hung GUI |
| htc | Enable heap tail checking |
| hfc | Enable heap free checking |
| hpc | Enable heap parameter checking |

*(continues)*

**Table 1.2**   gflags Option Abbreviations *(continued)*

| Abbreviation | Description |
| --- | --- |
| hvc | Enable heap validation on call |
| vrf | Enable application verifier |
| ptg | Enable pool tagging |
| htg | Enable heap tagging |
| ust | Create user mode stack trace database |
| kst | Create kernel mode stack trace database |
| otl | Maintain a list of objects for each type |
| htd | Enable heap tagging by DLL |
| dse | Disable stack extensions |
| d32 | Enable debugging of Win32 Subsystem |
| ksl | Enable loading of kernel debugger symbols |
| dps | Disable paging of kernel stacks |
| scb | Enable system-critical breaks |
| dhc | Disable Heap Coalesce on Free |
| ece | Enable close exception |
| eel | Enable exception logging |
| eot | Enable object handle type tagging |
| hpa | Enable page heap |
| dwl | Debug WINLOGON |
| ddp | Disable kernel mode DbgPrint output |
| cse | Early critical section event creation |
| ltd | Load DLLs top-down |
| bhd | Enable bad handles detection |
| dpd | Disable protected DLL verification |
| lpg | Load image using large pages if possible |

To set a specific option, use +<abbreviation>; to deselect a specific option, use -<abbreviation>. For example, if you wanted to enable the user mode stack trace database for notepad.exe, you would use the following command line:

```
C:\> gflags /i notepad.exe +ust
Current Registry Settings for notepad.exe executable are: 00001000
    ust - Create user mode stack trace database
```

Reciprocally, if you wanted to disable the same option, you would use

```
C:\> gflags /i notepad.exe -ust
Current Registry Settings for notepad.exe executable are: 00000000
```

If you simply wanted to find out what the settings are for a particular image, you would use the following:

```
C:\> gflags /i notepad.exe
Current Registry Settings for notepad.exe executable are: 00000000
```

To see what options are available for pageheap and Application Verifier, you can use

```
C:> gflags.exe /p /?
```

and

```
C:> gflags.exe /v /?
```

The final switch of importance is the `-tracedb` switch, which allows you to specify the size of the stack trace database. If enough activity exists in the system, the max size can easily be reached. This switch allows you to customize the size of the database.

We will not discuss the meaning behind all the different gflags options in this chapter, as this discussion is intended to merely serve as an introduction to the tool. Throughout Part II, "Applied Debugging," we will use the various settings exported by gflags to show how they can be leveraged to track down some really interesting and tough problems.

## Process Explorer

| | |
|---|---|
| Usage Scenarios | Analyze overall system and process health |
| Current Version | 10.2 |
| Download Point | http://www.microsoft.com/technet/sysinternals/ ProcessesAndThreads/ProcessExplorer.mspx |
| Executable | procexp.exe |

Process Explorer is a tool originally developed by the team over at SysInternals that is now part of Microsoft TechNet. Process Explorer is most easily described as a powerful alternative to the Windows Task Manager. It gives detailed information about all the processes currently running on the system. Features include

- Detailed handle usage, which includes the handle type as well as its name. It also provides detailed information per handle, which includes reference count, signal state, and more.
- Powerful search capabilities allow you to search for handles by name or type across all processes or, alternatively, search for any process that has a particular file loaded.
- Detailed process information, such as thread utilization, performance history, security, and much more.

The tool is so powerful that most users who use it end up never going back to the traditional Windows Task Manager. As a matter of fact, one of the Process Explorer options is Replace Task Manager.

Installation of the tool comes in the form of a zip file from which you simply extract the contents to a location of choice. The executable name is procexp.exe. Figure 1.7 shows how Process Explorer looks when you first start it.

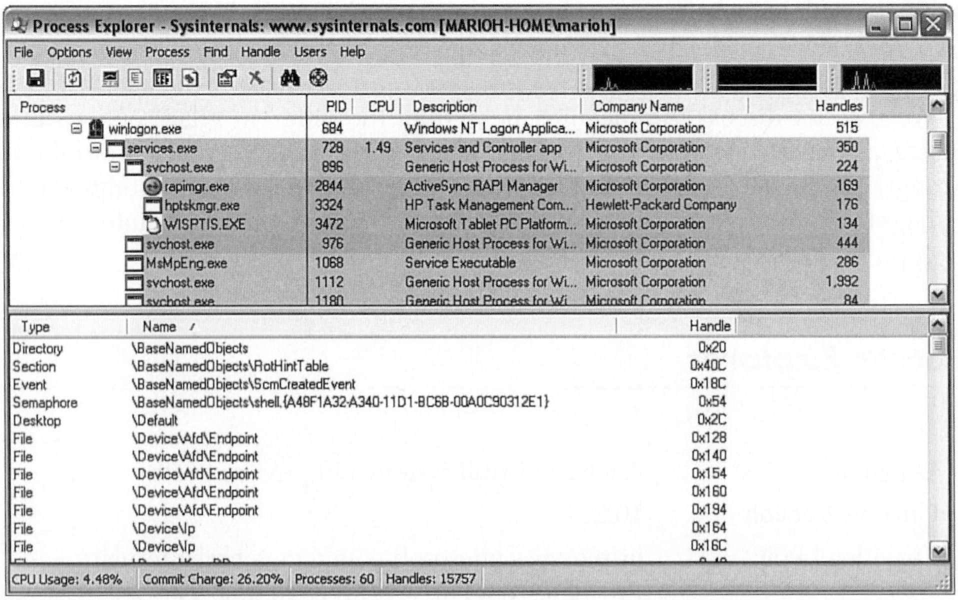

**Figure 1.7**    Process Explorer GUI view

By default, Process Explorer consists of two main views. The top view lists all the processes currently running on the system, and the bottom view shows all handles that the process has open (as well as the name of the handle). The columns of the top view can be customized by right-clicking on the column status bar and selecting the Select Columns menu. The bottom view can be changed from listing handles to listing DLLs by choosing DLLs from the Lower Pane View menu on the View menu.

We will be using Process Explorer in Chapter 9 to illustrate how the tool can be used to aid in tracking down resource leaks.

### Process Monitor

Process Monitor, which is another recently released tool, is related to Process Explorer. Process Monitor is an advanced monitoring tool that shows file system, registry, and process/thread activity. We use the tool in several chapters in the book. The tool is free of charge and can be downloaded from http://www.microsoft.com/technet/sysinternals/utilities/processmonitor.mspx.

# Windows Driver Kit

| | |
|---|---|
| Usage Scenarios | General development |
| Current Version | WDK 6000 |
| Download Point | Can be downloaded from http://www.microsoft.com/whdc/DevTools/WDK/WDKpkg.mspx |

The Windows Driver Kit (WDK) is a powerful and complete build environment that can be used for production development. This development environment is truly remarkable because it includes a large number of powerful development tools (including the compiler and linker) and is available free from Microsoft.

The WDK supports building for all Windows versions starting with Windows XP up to and including Windows Vista. This allows development targeting the x86, x64, and Itanium architectures.

Installation of the WDK is straightforward, and typically, choosing the default settings is sufficient. When the installation begins, you will be asked to install the prerequisite setup packaged (packages such as the .NET framework 2.0). Once the installation of those packages is complete, you can select to install the WDK.

Figure 1.8 shows the various options available during installation.

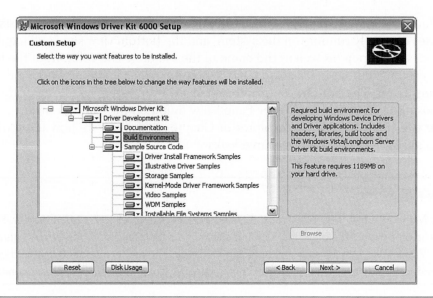

**Figure 1.8**   WDK installation options

By default, the build environment, documentation, tools, and samples will be installed.

The default installation path for the WDK is

```
%systemdrive%\WINDDK\6000
```

As mentioned previously, the documentation node is selected by default. Unless you have hard drive size limitations or know the WDK inside out, you should always keep this selection.

Finally, the Tools option allows you to select specific tools you want installed. Most of the tools in this selection are very specific to device driver developers, but some (such as command-line Registry tools) can be very useful not only for device driver developers, but also across all types of development.

After the installation process completes, all you need to do to start building source code is to open a WDK command-line window by going through the Start, All Programs, Windows Driver Kit, WDK 6000, Build Environments menus and choose the target platform of choice. The WDK build environments come in two flavors: free and checked. The free version is typically the final version of the product and contains highly optimized code. The checked version, on the other hand, is used during development to smooth the troubleshooting process. Checked versions typically have minimal or no optimizations turned on, making it much easier to debug code.

Open a Windows XP Checked x86 Build Environment window and navigate to the following directory:

```
C:\AWD\Chapter1
```

This directory contains a sample of a very small console-based application. To build this application, type build /ZCc:

```
C:\AWD\Chapter1>build /ZCc
BUILD: Adding /Y to COPYCMD so xcopy ops won't hang.
BUILD: Object root set to: ==> objchk_wxp_x86
BUILD: Compile and Link for i386
BUILD: Examining c:\awd\chapter1 directory for files to compile.
BUILD: Compiling (NoSync) c:\awd\chapter1 directory
Compiling - sample.cpp for i386
BUILD: Linking c:\awd\chapter1 directory
Linking Executable - objchk_wxp_x86\i386\sample.exe for i386
BUILD: Done

    2 files compiled
    1 executable built
```

The net result of this successful compilation is sample.exe, located in

```
C:\AWDBIN\WinXP.x86.chk
```

Running this sample application yields

```
C:>C:\AWDBIN\WinXP.x86.chk\01sample.exe
Welcome to Advanced Windows Debugging!!!
```

An important note is that the resulting output directories are named according to the following convention:

```
obj<flavor>_<platform>_<architecture1>\<architecture2>\<target executable>
```

The flavor can be one of the following:

- chk: Corresponds to checked builds
- fre: Corresponds to free builds

The `platform` can be one of the following:

- wnet: Corresponds to Windows Server 2003
- wxp: Corresponds to Windows XP

The `architecture1` can be one of the following:

- x86: Corresponds to Intel 32-bit processors
- amd64: Corresponds to AMD 64bit processors

Finally, `architecture2` can be one of the following:

- I386: Corresponds to Intel 32-bit processors
- AMD64: Corresponds to AMD 64-bit processors

All the samples in this book are built using the freely available WDK; however, the samples should build correctly using the Visual Studio environment; but no testing has been done using this build environment.

This book does not aim to detail every aspect of the WDK but rather just use the basic build mechanism to provide realistic samples of tough debugging problems that occur frequently in the software world. For more in-depth information on the WDK, refer to the documentation.

## Wireshark

| | |
|---|---|
| Usage Scenarios | Network Protocol Analyzer |
| Current Version | 0.99 |
| Download Point | http://www.wireshark.com/download.html |
| Analysis Mechanism | Network traces |

Wireshark is a powerful, open source network protocol analyzer that can be used to help the troubleshooting of cross machine calls. Wireshark allows you to capture and analyze data from a live network or analyze previously created capture files.

When installing Wireshark, choose the typical installation option.

Chapter 8, "Interprocess Communication," gives examples of how to use Wireshark to help analyze and track down interprocess communication issues in your code.

## DebugDiag

| | |
|---|---|
| Usage Scenarios | Process troubleshooting (memory leaks and crashes) |
| Current Version | 1.0 |
| Download Point | Part of the IIS Diagnostics Toolkit http://www. microsoft.com/downloads/details.aspx?familyid=9BF A49BC-376B-4A54-95AA-73C9156706E7& displaylang=en |
| Analysis Mechanism | Debuggers, log files |

DebugDiag was originally designed to help analyze performance issues with IIS, but it can be used equally well with any process. It combines the following troubleshooting features:

- Process crash data gathering: Much like the Windows debuggers, DebugDiag attaches to a process and generates dump files when a crash or exception occurs.
- Memory leaks: The DebugDiag tool injects a DLL into the process to be monitored for leaks and monitors memory allocations over time. A dump is then generated, which can be analyzed to find the leaking code path. Depending on the allocation pattern of the application, the tool calculates a leak probability.
- A powerful extensible object model (COM based): This surfaces the information needed to analyze the memory leaks and process crashes.

When installing the IIS Diagnostics Toolkit, choose the typical installation option.

Chapter 14, "Power Tools," gives examples of how to use DebugDiag to help analyze and track down memory leaks and process crashes.

## Summary

The tools described in this chapter constitute a developer's best friend. Rather than relying on expensive trial-and-error approaches to navigate your way around tough problems, these free tools will not only reduce the amount of time you spend on identifying and tracking down difficult bugs, but they will also surface bugs that otherwise might not be found during testing. Considering the fact that these tools are available free of charge as simple downloads, there should be no reason not to fully integrate these tools into the development process (making them a great complement to integrated development tools). Mastering these tools is a key ingredient to becoming highly efficient in the debugging process.

Throughout the remainder of this book, we will show you how to master these tools by utilizing them to track down tough and common problems.

# INTRODUCTION TO THE DEBUGGERS

The software debugging process has different meanings, depending on the programming language used to create the product, as well as the situation at hand and the developer's experience. Although some developers are still debugging by using extensive console printouts or analyzing verbose logging files, most are using a specialized tool: a debugger.

This chapter focuses on the Debugging Tools for Windows, freely available from Microsoft Corporation. It contains several debuggers, which we describe shortly. Why are those debuggers so important?

The Windows debuggers are enhanced in parallel with the Windows development process since they are used to debug each operating system version. As a result, they are always in sync with the latest operating system version or service pack. Since the same tools are also used to debug previous versions of the operating systems, debugger developers work hard to ensure that the current debuggers are compatible with existing systems. When a specific piece of functionality is not available in the older operating systems, the debuggers fail gracefully. To realize the backward compatibility level of these debuggers, it is enough to mention that the latest Windows debuggers work with Windows 9x/Me, Windows NT, Windows 2000, Windows XP, Windows 2003, and Windows Vista.

Other qualities of these debuggers are not obvious, such as the extensibility, the minimal install, and runtime requirements. The Windows debuggers' functionality can be enhanced with domain specific extensions, running simultaneously with the existing debugger commands. But they are also very flexible because they do not require any local registration, making them the true xcopy "installable"; they can run from any location (such as a USB thumb drive, where the debugger folder has been copied from another installation), and the memory they require is very small.

In a parallel development, the 64-bit family of the Windows operating systems is the first step of introducing 64-bit computing into the mainstream, and many development companies are already planning to convert 32-bit applications to 64-bit. Debugging Tools for Windows offers an excellent debugging environment for the 64-bit platform.

All this makes the Windows debuggers the perfect set of tools—powerful and usable in any situation. In this chapter, we explore

- The basics about the Windows debuggers
- How to set up the Windows debuggers
- How to work with symbols and sources
- Basic commands available in the Windows debuggers
- How to use the Windows debugger remotely
- Several debugging scenarios

This chapter uses 02sample.exe, which is specially handcrafted to help introduce the Windows debuggers. The source code and binary for 02sample.exe can be found in the following folders:

Source code: `C:\AWD\Chapter2`

Binary: `C:\AWDBIN\WinXP.x86.chk\02sample.exe`

## Debugger Basics

This section describes the types of available debuggers, when to use each debugger, and the most effective way to use them. User mode developers represent the main audience for this section even if some sections have references to kernel mode.

## Debugger Types

The two basic types of debuggers discussed here are user mode and kernel mode debuggers.

### User Mode Debuggers

The simplest form of a debugger is capable of debugging a single target user mode (UM) process. User mode debuggers are capable of examining the program state (running threads, memory content, registers, and kernel objects opened in the process space) representing the debugger target. The capabilities are similar to what the target process is capable of doing if it can execute code similar to the code executed by the debugger.

User mode debuggers are also capable of modifying the state (changing the thread execution order, changing registers' content, and changing the memory content) and being notified of special events happening in the target process. This scenario is commonly known as live debugging because the debugger can interact with the debugger target as long as the target process is running.

User mode debuggers can also examine a dump file that contains a snapshot of a given process, also known as postmortem debugging. Chapter 13, "Postmortem Debugging," describes in detail various ways to create user mode dump files. Because these snapshots represent the process state, they are a good representation of the original running process and can be successfully used to investigate various problems with minimal impact on the application.

Debugging Tools for Windows come with three user mode debuggers: cdb.exe, ntsd.exe, and windbg.exe. These three are built around the same debugger engine but go about exposing the same functionality in different ways. All three are capable of debugging console applications, as well as graphical Windows programs. All three can be used to perform source-level debugging, if the sources are available, or straight machine-level debugging. A short explanation of each one will help you decide which one is the most appropriate to use.

- cdb.exe (CDB) is a character-based console program that enables low-level analysis of Windows user-mode memory and constructs. CDB is extremely powerful for debugging a currently running or recently crashed program and is simple to set up. CDB can attach to vital subsystem processes that run during the early boot phase (such as WinLogon or CSRSS), whereas a graphical debugger does not work that early in the boot process, since the graphical subsystem is not yet initialized. If the target application is a console application, the target will share the console window with CDB. To spawn a separate console window for a target console application, use the -2 command-line option.
- ntsd.exe (NTSD) is identical to CDB in every way, except that it spawns a new text window when started. More precisely, CDB is a console application, whereas NTSD is a GUI application that can create its own console. Like CDB, NTSD is fully capable of debugging both console applications and graphical Windows programs. The only time they are not interchangeable is when you are debugging a user mode system process. In that case, errors or breaks in the process might cause all console applications to work improperly. In such cases, it is possible to configure NTSD to run with no console at all.
- windbg.exe (WinDbg) is a powerful graphical interface debugger with the same debugging capabilities found in console mode debuggers, enhanced to automate routine tasks such as examine the current call stack, view variables (including C++ objects), show the current registers, and a lot more. WinDbg also provides convenient, full, source-level debugging when the symbol files are properly configured, as we explain later in this chapter. At startup, some WinDbg settings are retrieved from workspaces, which can be changed and saved during the debugging session. All these capabilities make WinDbg the preferred tool for interactively debugging user mode applications.

### Kernel Mode Debuggers

In contrast to user mode debuggers, kernel debuggers can inspect the computer system as a whole, with nearly the same view as the system processor. For kernel debuggers, each process or thread is just a collection of data structures, the memory addresses have a direct relation with the physical memory installed on the system, and the paged out memory is not accessible without loading it in the physical memory. The kernel mode debugger can change the state of the entire computer and can be notified of special events. This model of debugging is known as live kernel debugging.

Kernel debuggers are mainly used by device driver developers, but they can also be very useful when debugging user mode applications. Several scenarios described in this book make use of the kernel mode debuggers, even if the debugged code runs entirely in user mode.

Much in the same way user mode debuggers can load user mode dumps, a kernel debugger can load kernel mode dumps and perform offline debugging of an existing system or a postmortem analysis of the bug checks. The Windows debuggers contain two basic kernel mode debuggers: kd.exe and windbg.exe.

- kd.exe (KD) is the kernel mode character-based debugger. It enables in-depth analysis of kernel-mode activity on Windows and can be used to debug kernel mode programs and drivers, to debug user mode applications, or to monitor the behavior of the operating system itself.
- windbg.exe (WinDbg) is also capable of kernel mode debugging. WinDbg provides full source-level debugging for the Windows kernel, kernel-mode drivers, as well as user mode applications running on the system. It allows you to debug any application or kernel module in a friendly user interface by tracing the source code, setting breakpoints based on the source content, and much more.

Kernel debuggers are capable of debugging a target computer running a platform different from the host platform. The debugger automatically detects the platform on which the target is running.

## Debugger Commands

The Windows debuggers support a set of commands that are natively implemented in the executable file and are entered without any special prefix at the command prompt. Most short commands, such as kP, are built-in commands. Meta-commands are another set of commands implemented by the executable file that starts with a dot (.). For example .help is a meta-command that displays all meta-commands implemented by debuggers. Also, the Windows debuggers enable the use of debugger extension commands. Extensions add power and flexibility to the debugger by extending the range of functions that can be executed against the debugger target, extending the ease by which target data and structures can be parsed. Extension support enables a model in which additional extensions can be added to the debugger for component and driver-specific debugging. The debugger extensions are sometimes called 'bang' commands to indicate that they are all prefixed with the exclamation point (!).

Debugger extension commands are used much like the standard debugger commands. However, although the built-in debugger commands are part of the debugger binaries themselves, debugger extension commands are exposed by DLLs separated from the debugger. A number of debugger extension DLLs are shipped with the debugging tools themselves.

The syntax used to call a debugger extension is !module.extension [arguments], where the module name is the name of the debugger extension DLL and the extension name is the function exported by that DLL. The extension function can also accept parameters through arguments on the command line. These extension commands are entered at the debugger prompt in the same way as other commands.

Various DLLs that ship with the kernel debugger provide default kernel and user mode extensions, including kdext.dll and exts.dll. When an extension is called without a module name specified, these DLLs are always checked unless another extension DLL has been loaded containing that command. Example debugger extensions supported by these DLLs include !teb to get the tread environment block using a thread from any debugger and !thread to get information on the current or a specific thread from the kernel mode debugger.

An extension DLL can be implicitly loaded by calling a function in that DLL with the full !module.extension syntax. An extension DLL can also be explicitly loaded using the .load debugger command, specifying the full path to the DLL. When loaded, all other extension functions can be called without specifying the extension DLL unless the same function is implemented in two loaded extensions. In this case, the full syntax must be used to resolve the name collision.

## Setting Up the Debuggers

Even in their basic usage, the Windows debuggers provide exceptional and valuable flexibility, while also forcing you to choose among their various options. This section details those options that enable you to configure the debugger for all cases presented in this book.

### User Mode Debuggers

Debuggers need at least two key ingredients to perform at full capacity: the target image being debugged and the symbol information associated with that image. In this section, we focus on setting up the debugger target. The later section "Setting Up and Using the Symbols" shows how to load the associated symbols for the debugger target. Some examples from this section use cdb.exe, but they work similarly with windbg.exe or ntsd.exe.

In the most common situation, the debugger starts a new process, and the target image is loaded in the newly created process that becomes the debugger target. Using the tlist.exe executable (located in the debugger installation folder), you can see the debugger as the parent of the debugged process. The executable name is passed in as a parameter to the debuggers, as you can see in Listing 2.1. The command line starting the debugger shows as `cdb 02sample.exe`. The debugger cdb.exe having the process identifier `2428` is the parent for the process 02sample.exe having the process identifier `2816`.

**Listing 2.1**    Listing all processes as task tree

```
C:\> REM tlist with -t parameter displays the process tree
C:\> tlist -t    tlist will display the process tree
System Process (0)
System (4)
  smss.exe (756)
    csrss.exe (836)
    winlogon.exe (864)
      services.exe (908)
        svchost.exe (1080)
        svchost.exe (1152)
        svchost.exe (1216)
        svchost.exe (1348)
        svchost.exe (1408)
        spoolsv.exe (1748)
        svchost.exe (572)
        svchost.exe (1688)
      lsass.exe (920)
explorer.exe (3552) Program Manager
  cmd.exe (2856) C:\WINDOWS\system32\cmd.exe - tlist -t
    cdb.exe (2428) cdb 02sample.exe
      02sample.exe (2816)
    tlist.exe (268)
```

When debugging a process in which the actual process lifetime is managed by an external entity, one approach is to attach the debugger to the running process. The "Debugging Scenarios" section toward the end of this chapter describes additional options to debug such a process. This is the approach used when debugging Windows services, DCOM servers, IIS filters, and so on. Listing 2.2 shows the list of switches that can be used when attaching to an already running process.

**Listing 2.2** Options for attaching the debugger to a running process

```
C:\>cdb -?
cdb version 6.4.0004.3
usage: cdb [options]

Options:
...
  <command-line> command to run under the debugger
  - equivalent to -G -g -o -p -1 -d -pd
  [ more]
  -p <pid> specifies the decimal process ID to attach to
  -pn <name> specifies the name of the process to attach to
  -psn <name> specifies the process to attach to by service name
  -pv specifies that any attach should be noninvasive
  -pvr specifies that any attach should be noninvasive and nonsuspending
...
```

Although most options displayed by the command help are self-explanatory, we will stress a few helpful parameters to use when you are attaching the debugger to a running process. `cdb.exe -p <pid>` is the standard command used when the process identifier is known. If the image name is known (as is the case with DCOM servers or with SCM services), `cdb.exe -pn <image name>` does an excellent job in finding its process identifier and attaching to it. However, if multiple processes are started with the same image, the command bails out, as shown here:

```
C:\>cdb -pn svchost.exe
```

```
There is more than one 'svchost.exe' process running.  Find the process ID of the
instance you are interested in and use -p <pid>.
```

In this case, we find the target process identifier using tlist.exe and use it as parameter for the `cdb -p <pid>` command. Special for service writers sharing the same host image name, it is possible to specify a service name as a parameter: `cdb -psn`

<service name>. Last, but not least, –pv can be used with all other options to attach nonintrusively to a running process. This allows you to access process information even if another debugger is attached to that process or if the previous debugger hung (bad extensions, long symbols resolution, and so on). Listing 2.3 shows the command line used to attach nonintrusively to the dnscache service, as well as the output generated by the debugger.

**Listing 2.3**   Debugging a service nonintrusive

```
C:\>cdb.exe -pv -psn Dnscache
...

*** wait with pending attach
Symbol search path is: SRV*c:\symbols*http://msdl.microsoft.com/download/symbols

Executable search path is:
WARNING: Process 1320 is not attached as a debuggee
        The process can be examined but debug events will not be received
.......................................
(528.52c): Wake debugger - code 80000007 (first chance)
eax=0007fc44 ebx=00000000 ecx=7c80999b edx=02160001 esi=00000000 edi=00000068
eip=7c90eb94 esp=0007fc48 ebp=0007fcb0 iopl=0         nv up ei pl zr na po nc
cs=001b  ss=0023  ds=0023  es=0023  fs=003b  gs=0000          efl=00000246
ntdll!KiFastSystemCallRet:
7c90eb94 c3              ret
```

The debugging session finishes when the debugger target ceases to exist or when you use the q (quit) command or the qd (quit and detach) command. The latter option leaves the debugger target running. WinDbg's Exit menu item in the File menu (the ALT+F4 key combination) is equivalent to the q command.

A common scenario encountered in development centers is dumping the process memory on error and restarting the test process. In this case, the memory dump can be loaded as an active target using the windbg –z <dumpname> command. Listing 2.4 shows how to load one dump file that has been previously generated from a running instance of the notepad.exe process. Chapter 13 describes multiple ways to create memory dump files and use them effectively.

**Listing 2.4**   Debugging a memory dump

```
C:\>windbg -z c:\AWDBIN\DUMPS\notepad.dmp
...
Loading Dump File [C:\AWDBIN\DUMPS\notepad.dmp]
```

```
User Dump File: Only application data is available

...

...........................
eax=7ffdc000 ebx=00000001 ecx=00000002 edx=00000003 esi=00000004 edi=00000005
eip=7c901230 esp=0091ffcc ebp=0091fff4 iopl=0         nv up ei pl zr na po nc
cs=001b  ss=0023  ds=0023  es=0023  fs=0038  gs=0000            efl=00000246
ntdll!DbgBreakPoint:
7c901230 cc                   int     3
```

### Kernel Debuggers

The kernel debugger usually runs on a different system from the system being debugged. Live kernel mode debugging requires two computers (the host computer running the kernel debugger and the target computer being debugged) since the debugger target cannot execute any code while it is stopped in the kernel debugger. The debugger target is the system that has experienced the failure of a software component, system service, an application, or of the operating system. This system can be located within a few feet of the computer on which you run the kernel debugger, or it can be in a completely different location, depending on the connection options used. The debugger target can also be a virtual machine running inside the host system.

The kernel debugger is very flexible. It can target computers running on an x86 platform, an Itanium platform, or an x64 platform. The kernel debugger automatically detects the target platform. The operating system running on the host computer does not need to be the same version as the one running the debugger target. However, it is recommended that the kernel debugger is up-to-date in order to support the latest operating system versions as the debugger target.

A portion of the debugging system lives inside the operating system and runs regardless of whether a kernel debugger is connected to the system. Because this portion is an integral part of the Windows kernel, the kernel debugger does not require any additional software to be installed on the debugger target. This functionality is configured at boot time. For example, a system enabled for kernel debugging freezes when entering CTRL-SysReq from a PS/2 keyboard. In this state, a kernel debugger can connect to this system and debug it.

On x86 computers running Windows XP, the kernel debugger can be enabled in the boot.ini file, or it can be enabled interactively, at boot time, by choosing Windows Advanced Option after pressing the F8 key from the boot console, as shown in Figure 2.1.

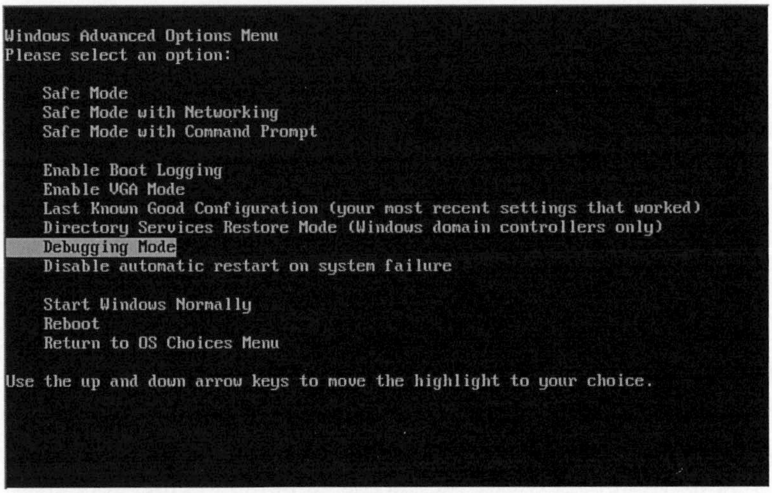

```
Windows Advanced Options Menu
Please select an option:

    Safe Mode
    Safe Mode with Networking
    Safe Mode with Command Prompt

    Enable Boot Logging
    Enable VGA Mode
    Last Known Good Configuration (your most recent settings that worked)
    Directory Services Restore Mode (Windows domain controllers only)
    Debugging Mode
    Disable automatic restart on system failure

    Start Windows Normally
    Reboot
    Return to OS Choices Menu

Use the up and down arrow keys to move the highlight to your choice.
```

**Figure 2.1**   Windows Advanced Options menu

The following shows a sample entry with several parameters controlling the kernel debugger such as `/debug` (enabling the debugger), `/debugport` (representing the serial port used by the kernel debugger), and `/baudrate` (serial port's baud rate). For a full description of all the available options when changing boot.ini, check the debugger help (help topic `Boot parameters to Enable Debugging`).

Despite the documentation available about boot.ini, the safest way of changing the configuration files is through bootcfg.exe, as it guarantees the correctness of start-up parameters. A simple boot.ini file that starts the default installation with the kernel debugger active on `COM1` port, initialized at `57600` baud rate, is shown here:

```
[boot loader]
timeout=30
default=multi(0)disk(0)rdisk(0)partition(1)\WINDOWS
[operating systems]
multi(0)disk(0)rdisk(0)partition(1)\WINDOWS="KD" /fastdetect /debug /debugport=COM1
/baudrate=57600
```

Assuming that the serial cable is connected on the serial port COM2 of the host system, the following line can be used to start a kernel debugger using that port at a 57600 baud rate.

```
C:\>windbg -k com:port=COM2,baud=57600
```

The kernel debugger is enabled if any debug parameter is found in boot.ini, regardless of the presence of the /debug switch.

## Connecting the Kernel Debuggers

In the most common case, on a live operating system, the kernel debugger connects to the target operating system using a serial null-modem cable, but faster ways to connect are already available, such as IEEE 1394 or USB 2.0 cables. Today, each connection is a physical connection, represented by a cable, as shown in Figure 2.2. But in the near future, other connection paradigms might be available, such as providing kernel debugging support over TCP/IP using a dedicated networked controller board that runs independent from the host computer.

KD Debugger                                                    KD Target

**Figure 2.2**   Connecting a kernel debugger to the target system

For target computers running Windows XP or higher, the connection from the debugger to the target computer can be established using an IEEE 1394 (FireWire) cable. The connection to target computers running Windows Vista or higher can use a USB 2.0 debug cable connection. The connection method selected is determined by the available hardware to make the connection and by the target computer characteristics. Consult the debugger help file for more information about the connection options and the command line required to use such a connection (help topic `Choosing Kernel Debugging Settings`).

Is the kernel debugger even useful if you cannot use two computers because you are restricted by the environment? In this case, you can simulate the target machine in a virtual machine environment and at least have the same options as in the two machine set-up case. Currently, most virtualization software products on the market offer a free version. Although this section uses Microsoft Virtual PC as an example, the same functionality is available on all virtualization products. With the exception of hardware-specific software, all other software components can run successfully and can be debugged within a virtual machine.

The virtual machine emulator virtualizes a serial port available in the target PC into a named pipe in the host computer namespace. In Figure 2.3, the serial port `COM2` of the Microsoft Virtual PC is accessible as a named pipe on the host PC, having the name `\\.\pipe\pipe2`.

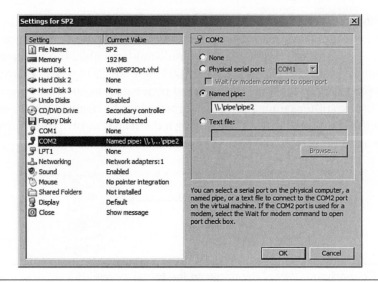

**Figure 2.3**    Enable Virtual PC for kernel debugger

The kernel debugger can then connect to the virtual machine having the settings shown in Figure 2.3 using the following command line:

```
C:\>windbg -k com:pipe,port=\\.\pipe\pipe2
```

The kernel mode debugging session finishes when the debugger target ceases to exist or the kernel debugger disconnects from the target by using the CTRL+B command. If the debugger target waits for user input before disconnecting the kernel debugger, the system state does not change until a new kernel debugger connects to it or the system is restarted. WinDbg's Exit menu item in the File menu (ALT+F4 key combination) is equivalent to the CTRL+B command.

   If using a virtual machine is not possible (because of license constrains), you can still benefit from using a kernel debugger in local connection mode (functionality introduced starting with Windows XP). You have very limited functionality in controlling the target, but you have unlimited options to view the machine status. Any memory write should be very carefully inspected because it can potentially corrupt the integrity of the operating system running the kernel debugger. As with any kernel debugger setup, the corresponding boot.ini entry must specify the /debug flag. The kernel mode debugger can start in local mode using the following command line:

```
C:\>windbg -kl
```

The kernel mode debugger can also open kernel dump files generated using the methods described in Chapter 13. Both kd.exe and windbg.exe can open kernel dumps, so choosing between them is a personal preference. Windbg.exe recognizes the kernel dump file type and starts in kernel mode debugging, without requiring any additional command-line parameter. The following command lines are capable of opening the mini dump files captured automatically by the operating system in the %windir%\Minidump folder, as well as some manually generated ones.

```
C:\>kd -z %temp%\full.dmp
C:\>kd -z %windir%\Minidump\Mini091704-01.dmp
C:\>windbg -z %wtemp%\full.dmp
```

## Redirecting a User Mode Debugger Through a Kernel Debugger

One important feature of a kernel debugger is its capability to control a user mode debugger for the kernel debugger session and synchronize the user mode debugging session with the system activity. Because the system activity is frozen while you are controlling the user mode debugger, you can use it to debug sequences expected to execute in a bound time period—time relative to the system activity. Since the kernel debugging session is already established at system boot time, you can debug processes early in the start-up phase or very late in the system shutdown phase when no interactive console is available. The kernel debugger also gives you access to information not available from a user mode session debugger, making the combination the most powerful form of user mode debugging.

By starting the user mode debugger with the –d parameter in the command line, any user mode debugger redirects its input and output to a kernel debugger, as in the following listing:

```
C:\>ntsd -d <Process Path>
C:\>ntsd -d -p <PID>
```

The kernel mode debugger must be enabled before using the redirection options. Otherwise, the user mode debugger returns to the command prompt without executing the command passed in as a parameter. However, with the kernel debugger enabled, the operating system allows low privilege users to stop the entire activity, which is not always desired.

When the debugger is in a state in which it waits for user input, either at the user mode prompt or the kernel mode prompt, as shown in Figure 2.4, the kernel activity is suspended. The exact state is clearly identifiable in the debugger input. KD shows the user mode prompt as a regular user mode debugger, whereas WinDbg, used as a kernel debugger, shows the prompt as `Input>` instead of the regular `kd>` prompt. It is not unusual to go back and forth between the kernel mode debugger and the user debugger before resolving problems involving interprocess communication.

After entering a new command at the user mode debugger prompt, the kernel mode debugger dispatches that command to the current user mode debugger and resumes the system activity, enabling the user mode debugger to perform the command. If, after executing the command, the user mode debugger prompts the user, the system goes back to the user mode debugger prompt.

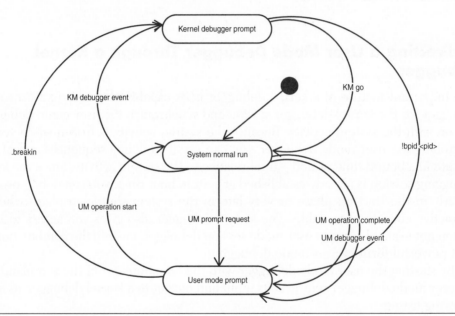

**Figure 2.4**   State transition between a kernel mode prompt and a user mode prompt

While in the user mode prompt state, it is possible to jump to the kernel mode prompt state by entering the `.breakin` command in the user mode debugger. The kernel debugger breaks in the context of the debugger process, not of the process being debugged:

```
0:000> .breakin
.breakin
Break instruction exception - code 80000003 (first chance)
```

```
nt!RtlpBreakWithStatusInstruction:
8051ac9c cc                 int    3
kd> !process -1 0
PROCESS ff7eeb38  SessionId: 0  Cid: 055c    Peb: 7ffdf000  ParentCid: 03c8
   DirBase: 03983000  ObjectTable: e1a02fb8  HandleCount:  39.
   Image: ntsd.exe
```

This command requires SeDebugPrivilege privileges for the debugger process itself, and it fails with an explicit error if the debugger does not run under an account having the debug privilege, as follows:

```
0:000> .breakin
.breakin
.breakin requires debug privilege
```

In such cases, an alternative way to go into KD is to issue a break (using CTRL+C, CTRL+break, or CTRL+SysRq) after asking the user mode debugger to perform anything long running, such as a sleep command, as seen in Listing 2.5. The key combination CTRL+C is being interpreted by the kernel mode debugger as a kernel mode event.

**Listing 2.5**  Switching from user mode to kernel mode debugger

```
0:000> .sleep 1000
.sleep 1000
Break instruction exception - code 80000003 (first chance)
*************************************************************************
*                                                                     *
*    You are seeing this message because you pressed either           *
*        CTRL+C (if you run kd.exe) or                                *
*        CTRL+BREAK (if you run WinDBG)                               *
*    on your debugger machine's keyboard.                             *
*                                                                     *
*               THIS IS NOT A BUG OR A SYSTEM CRASH                   *
*                                                                     *
* If you did not intend to break into the debugger, press the "g" key,*
* then press the "Enter" key now.  This message might immediately     *
* reappear.  If it does, press "g" and "Enter" again.                 *
*                                                                     *
*************************************************************************
nt!DbgBreakPointWithStatus+0x4:
8051ac9c cc                 int    3
kd>
```

From the kernel mode prompt, you can enter the system in normal execution mode by entering any form of the g command. If the user mode debugger prompts the user, the system moves to the user mode prompt. The transition back into the user mode prompt is difficult when there is no user mode prompt or a new debugger event requiring user prompting has been sent to the kernel debugger.

The most reliable method to regain the control of the user mode debugger is to use the breakin.exe utility installed with the Debugging Tools for Windows. Breakin.exe accepts only one parameter, the process identifier of the target process that must be stopped. In this case, the process identifier is the user mode process previously started under the user mode debugger. The breakin.exe <pid> command is executed directly on the target computer being debugged. From the kernel debugger prompt, it is possible to regain the user mode debugger prompt by using the !bpid <pid> extension command.

A useful command for suspending the user mode debugger is .sleep <time>. This command leaves the target system in a normal running state for the specified time interval—time in which the system can be used for operations, such as copying local symbols or even to attach a user mode debugger to another process.

---

**DEFAULT NUMERIC BASE IS IMPORTANT** If you ever wonder why the .sleep 1000 command feels more like four seconds than one second, we should note that the timeout is interpreted according to the current radix used by the debugger—the default base being 16.

---

## To KD or Not to KD

Most application developers are not considering using a kernel debugger, as it seems unnecessary if not too complicated. We want you to consider some cases in which the kernel debugger is the natural way of debugging a particular problem—how is detailed in the later section "Debugging Scenarios," as well as in some other chapters in this book. In such cases, all alternative solutions for debugging the problem are usually just expensive workarounds.

At the other end of the spectrum are cases in which kernel debugging is not an option at all, mostly because other components installed on the system cannot work well in its presence. In this category, we can enumerate various products that use files protected by Digital Right Management (DRM) technologies. Those products have become commonly used in our lives to store our music securely or to protect the confidentiality of our files. Unfortunately, the products capable of reading or writing DRM-protected content do not work with debuggers, including kernel mode debuggers. It is expected that all such products use all sorts of anti-debugging tricks and debugging detection mechanisms. In the most common case, they will simply refuse to work if a kernel mode debugger is detected. In this case, each scenario for which we are recommending the use of a kernel debugger should instead use an alternative, non-KD, method.

In the development phase, there are cases in which the user of the developed application sees a huge number of failures when a kernel mode debugger is enabled. In this case, the product might contain some special function calls, named asserts, that break in the debugger for specific parameters. These assert statements were introduced by developers just to validate their thinking. When the assert statement is no longer valid in the customer environment and the kernel mode debugger is enabled, the application breaks often in the kernel debugger. In this case, the correct solution should be tailored to the environment (disabling the kernel mode debugger, updating the application, or removing the assert statement).

**SECURITY NOTE** If you enable the kernel debugger on a system shared by multiple users, the debugger will not differentiate between handling breakpoints on low privileged users' processes and breakpoints in processes running under a system or administrator account. By enabling the KD this way, you allow any user to break the system and put the system's service into a nonfunctional state. Therefore, a best practice is to disable the kernel debugger on production systems.

We can now recognize some situations in which kernel debugging is not an acceptable technique in the toolbox, but we are not always sure when it can be really useful. Therefore, in the later section "Debugging Scenarios," we will reveal some typical situations in which a kernel debugger is extremely useful.

## Basic Debugger Tasks

After setting up the debugger, you should see a command prompt or a debugger window waiting for your commands. After a new command is entered, the debugger switches to execution mode, executes the command displaying the results, and switches back into the command prompt mode. If the command entered requires the target to execute code, any debugger event encountered while executing the command returns the debugger back into the command mode. In the following sections, we describe some of the most used commands and provide a brief description of the resultant output, highlighting the most relevant information from it.

## Entering Debugger Commands

Within the console-based debuggers ntsd.exe, cdb.exe, and kd.exe, the entire console window is used to display the results of the commands entered at the command prompt. In WinDbg, the output window is a special window, identifiable by the Command title. The window has an input box at the bottom that is used to enter commands in the same fashion as in the console-based debuggers. The Command menu item in the Tool menu can be used to display the command windows (alternatively, the Alt+1 shortcut).

One big advantage of the GUI interface is the capability to show multiple views of the debugged process at the same time, eliminating the need to enter a new command to display that piece of information and accept commands from the menu and toolbar. All user interface commands have one correspondent textual command and can be entered in the command window. Because the WinDbg's command window is more or less identical to the console of any text-based debugger, all examples in this book are illustrated using the command window commands.

Furthermore, one of the biggest advantages WinDbg has over the console mode debugger is the source mode capabilities. With proper access to symbol and source files, which are managed by using a process similar to the one described in Chapter 4, "Managing Symbol and Source Files," the power of WinDbg is fully realized. The user benefits from a debugger that automatically retrieves the source files, shows, and synchronizes multiple views into the debugger target while enabling fine control of the debugger target using the command prompt. This debugger can also be extended with business-specific functionality, as explained in Chapter 11, "Writing Custom Debugger Extensions."

You can use any command from the multitude of debugger commands or debugger extensions commands, but your goal is to resolve a specific problem, and we should follow some general directions. The generic workflow used to resolve a debugger session starts by identifying the current debugging environment and correct, if possible, any problem with the symbols. The next step is to understand why the debugger stopped where it did and, with the available information, create possible scenarios leading to the current stop. With each such scenario in mind, we should use any piece of information from the debugger session to try to prove that the scenario was really executed. If we find any contradiction, we should go back and try another scenario. With the scenario proven by the current state of the application in mind, the developer goes to the source code, finds the problem, and fixes it. In the next section, we explore the basic commands used to explore the application state required in the steps described previously.

## Interpreting the Debugger Prompt

Without entering any commands in the debugger and just by looking at the debugger prompt, including some of the previous console output, we can figure out a few details concerning the debugger target. We will start by examining the normal output from a user mode debugger immediately after starting a new process (for example., `c:\>windbg notepad`). The output is shown in Listing 2.6.

**Listing 2.6**   User mode debugger output

```
(2d4.23c): Break instruction exception - code 80000003 (first chance)
eax=7ffdf000 ebx=00000001 ecx=00000002 edx=00000003 esi=00000004 edi=00000005
eip=77f75a58 esp=0084ffcc ebp=0084fff4 iopl=0         nv up ei pl zr na po nc
cs=001b  ss=0023  ds=0023  es=0023  fs=0038  gs=0000            efl=00000246
ntdll!DbgBreakPoint:
77f75a58 cc              int     3
0:000> vertarget
Windows XP Version 2600 (Service Pack 2) UP Free x86 compatible
Product: WinNt, suite: SingleUserTS
kernel32.dll version: 5.1.2600.2180 (xpsp_sp2_rtm.040803-2158)
Debug session time: Mon May 28 20:21:23.486 2007 (GMT-7)
System Uptime: 2 days 18:44:45.827
Process Uptime: 0 days 0:01:04.402
  Kernel time: 0 days 0:00:00.000
  User time: 0 days 0:00:00.010
0:000> .lastevent
Last event: 2d4.23c: Break instruction exception - code 80000003 (first chance)
0:000> ||
.  0 Live user mode: <Local>
```

The first line contains the process and the thread identifier generating the last debugger event (debugger events are described in more detail in Chapter 3, "Debuggers Uncovered") displayed as (2d4.23c) along with the event description, a break instruction exception, and the exception code 80000003. The debugger handled the event on the first chance, before the normal exception handling in the user code. (Exception handling is covered in more detail in Chapter 3.) This information is not always available, but we should use it if we can find it.

The register values displayed on the next few lines are not so relevant at this point, with the notable exceptions of the instruction pointer (eip) and the stack pointer (esp). The register structure tells about the architecture under which this process runs, such as x64 or Itanium.

Immediately after the register information, there is the symbol associated with the address where the last event was raised, along with the address and the instruction at that address. As you will see in the remainder of the book, the instruction itself can explain the immediate cause of the break.

The last piece of information from the debugger output is the command prompt. The prompt (0:000>) tells that we are in the user mode debugger. (For a kernel mode debugger session, the prompt contains the kd string.) The first number indicates the active target of this debugger, and it will be 0 for most debugging sessions. The second number represents the thread "number" of the thread raising the debugger event.

---

**DEBUGGING MULTIPLE TARGETS** It is not a very well-known fact that the Microsoft debuggers are capable of debugging multiple remote systems at the same time. In this case, the debugger will change the prompt and prefix the prompt with the system name as 0:0:000>. You can read more about this in debuggers help under the "Debugging Targets on Multiple Computers" topic.

---

The kernel debugger prompts reveal information about the running environment and the stop reason. Using option '2' of 02sample.exe in the presence of the kernel debugger causes the whole system to stop. Listing 2.7 shows the kernel debugger console output while using the same commands as in the previous listing.

**Listing 2.7**　Kernel mode debugger output

```
Break instruction exception - code 80000003 (first chance)
7c901230 cc              int     3
kd> vertarget
Windows XP Kernel Version 2600 (Service Pack 2) UP Free x86 compatible
Product: WinNt, suite: TerminalServer SingleUserTS
Built by: 2600.xpsp_sp2_rtm.040803-2158
Kernel base = 0x804d7000 PsLoadedModuleList = 0x8055ab20
Debug session time: Tue May 29 20:47:16.107 2007 (GMT-7)
System Uptime: 0 days 0:11:24.844
kd> .lastevent
Last event: Break instruction exception - code 80000003 (first chance)
  debugger time: Tue May 29 20:48:23.671 2007 (GMT-7)
kd> ||
.  0 Remote KD:
KdSrv:Server=@{<Local>},Trans=@{COM:Port=\\.\pipe\pipe1,Baud=19200,Pipe,Timeout=4000,
Resets=2}
```

The first few lines indicate the cause of the current break, the amount of information being dependent of the stop type. In this example, the kernel debugger encountered a break instruction and stopped. The debugger also tells the exception code 80000003 generated by the break instruction. The next line contains the address of the current instruction pointer followed by the current instruction in assembly language. A 64-bit address for the instruction indicates that the current processor runs in 64-bit mode. In this case, the 32-bit address indicates a processor executing in 32-bit mode. The operating system version and architecture are displayed in response to the `vertarget` command.

The debugger uses `kd>` as a prompt when the debugger target is a single processor system and `n:kd>` as a prompt when the debugger target has more than one processor. The numeral denotes the logical processor number generating the current debugger event.

## Setting Up and Using the Symbols

Debugging an application break without proper symbols is difficult, and there are minimal chances to discover the problem in that application. No wonder that determining the accuracy of the symbol information is the most important step in debugging. Bad symbols can lead you in wrong directions and create unrealistic hypotheses. In this section, we discuss how to use the symbol files and discover their importance in debugging.

### What Are Symbol Files?

When applications, libraries, drivers, or operating systems are built, the compile and link procedure that creates the .exe, .dll, .sys, and other executable files (collectively known as binaries or images) also creates a number of additional files known as symbol files. To effectively debug a target image, all that symbolic information generated at compile and link time must be available to the debugger.

For various reasons, ranging from compilation performance to IP protection, Microsoft has used several symbol formats, such as Common Object File Format (COFF), CodeView format (CV), and Program Database format (PDB). Table 2.1 presents some characteristics of those formats.

**Table 2.1**  Different Formats Used by Microsoft in the Past 10 Years

|  | Embedded in PE Image | Extension When Non-embedded | Supported by Windbg/ntsd |
|---|---|---|---|
| COFF | Yes | .dbg | Yes |
| CV | Yes | .dbg | Yes |
| PDB | No | .pdb | Yes |
| Windows 9x/Me core symbols | No | .sym | No |

For example, early versions of Windows NT used symbol files with the extension .dbg. Windows 2000 and earlier versions of Windows NT keep their symbols in files with the extensions .pdb and .dbg. Windows XP and Windows Server 2003 use .pdb files exclusively. Symbols for Windows drivers can follow either model, depending on the compiler and linker version used to build them. Binary files generated by tools not conforming to either of the recognized formats cannot be debugged properly using the Windows debuggers.

Symbol files hold a variety of data not needed when executing the binaries but that is essential to the debugging process. Typically, symbol files contain

- Names and addresses of global variables
- Function names, their addresses, and their signatures
- Frame Pointer Optimization (FPO) data to aid the debugger
- Names and locations of local variables
- Source file paths and line numbers associated with each symbol
- Type information for variables, structures, and so on

The binaries are smaller due to keeping these symbol files separate. However, this means that when debugging, you must make sure that the debugger can access the symbol files associated with the target you are debugging. Both interactive debugging and debugging crash dump files benefit from using correct symbols. You must obtain the proper symbols for the code you want to debug and load these symbols into the debugger.

Errors encountered in binary images running on the customer's site can be investigated without having all this information available on the customer's site. To discourage reverse engineering, the generated symbol files, also known as private symbols, are usually kept private by the company owning the intellectual property for those binary images. However, the customer can always use another symbol file, containing a restricted set of symbols, called public symbols. Public symbol files are sufficient for the module users, without disclosing the internal structures, function parameters, or local variables.

For example, public symbols are available for download as a whole package for every version of the operating system shipped by Microsoft. In addition, each driver shipped with any version of Windows has public symbols available in the same download package. The binary file contains just a pointer to the symbols files, and the debugger loads a public symbol or a private symbol, subject to availability.

If you like to see the debug information stored in the binary file, the link.exe utility, available from within WDK build windows, is the best tool for the task, as shown in Listing 2.8. The information about the symbol file is stored in the debug directory section of each executable module.

**Listing 2.8** Using the link.exe utility to find debug information stored in the binary file

```
C:\>link -dump -headers C:\WINDOWS\system32\ntdll.dll
Microsoft (R) COFF/PE Dumper Version 7.10.2179
Copyright (C) Microsoft Corporation.  All rights reserved.


Dump of file C:\WINDOWS\system32\ntdll.dll
  ... other information about the module
  Debug Directories

        Time Type      Size      RVA   Pointer
        ---- ----  ---- ---- ----
     41107F17 cv          22 0007B6DC    7AADC     Format: RSDS, {36515FB5-D043-45E4-
91F6-72FA2E2878C0}, 2, ntdll.pdb
     41107F17 (    A)      4 0007B6D8    7AAD8     BB030D70
```

Public symbol download packages represent a convenient way to get access to all symbol files if the system does not change over time. Since it is very common to see one binary file being updated several times between service pack releases, a dynamic method of downloading the symbols just in time is much more useful. This functionality is provided by a symbol server, described in more detail in the "Symbol Server" section. The symbol server finds and downloads on demand the symbol file associated with the module debugged, using the debug directory information as the key for the symbol file.

### Symbol Path

How does the debugger know where to get the symbols required for a specific assembly? The debugger uses two pieces of information: the location of the symbols path, represented as a collection of paths, combined with the information stored in the module headers used to validate the symbol files. Each path can be a local folder, a UNC share, or a symbol server path, as described in the "Symbol Server" section.

In the simple form, the symbol path is a succession of folders separated by the semicolon (;) character entered in the interactive debugger using the following command:

```
0:000>.sympath C:\SymPath;\\mysymbols\symbols
```

The symbol filename is extracted from the CV record of the image header or manufactured from the binary filename when the header is not available. The debugger uses a heuristic algorithm to search the symbol file on the symbol path, validating each symbol file found against the module information. If no matching symbol file is found, the debugger defaults to using symbols exported by the module, as in Listing 2.9. The commands used in the listing will be explained shortly, in the "Reloading the Symbols" section.

**Listing 2.9**    Heuristic used by debugger to find the symbol file

```
0:000> !sym noisy
noisy mode - symbol prompts off
0:000> !reload -f kernel32.dll
DBGHELP: c:\SymPath\kernel32.pdb - file not found
DBGHELP: c:\SymPath\symbols\dll\kernel32.pdb - file not found
DBGHELP: c:\SymPath\dll\kernel32.pdb - file not found
DBGHELP: C:\WINDOWS\system32\kernel32.pdb - file not found
DBGHELP: kernel32.pdb - file not found
*** ERROR: Symbol file could not be found.  Defaulted to export symbols for C:
\WINDOWS\system32\kernel32.dll -
DBGHELP: kernel32 - export symbols
```

### Symbol Server

Setting up symbols correctly for debugging can be a challenging task, especially when a specific module has been released more than once. It requires knowing the names and releases of all the modules loaded in the debugger target. The debugger must be capable of locating each of the symbol files corresponding to the product release and service pack. This can result in an extremely long symbol path, consisting of a long list of directories.

To simplify the difficulties associated with coordinating symbol files, a symbol server can be used. A symbol server enables the debuggers to automatically retrieve the correct symbol files without product names, releases, or build numbers.

The symbol server is activated by including a certain text string in the symbol path. Each time the debugger needs to load symbols, it calls the symbol server to locate the appropriate files. The symbol server locates the files in a symbol store, which is a collection of symbol files indexed according to combination of parameters such as the symbol filename, the time stamp, and the image size.

The symbol path to a symbol server uses a special syntax that might contain multiple paths to downstream stores followed by the real address of the symbol server. The basic syntax for the symbol path is

```
0:000>SRV*[cacheⁱ]*toppath
```

The SRV string indicates that the path is a symbol server path, with `toppath` representing the address of the symbol server. The symbol path can contain up to 10 downstream stores, local or UNC, which are used to cache the symbols. The cache stores chain is a convenient method to implement common caches for a remote location having a limited bandwidth. The symbol server address can be the UNC to a symbol server implemented on a file system share, or it can be a URL to the symbol server. This path can be combined with other symbol paths, using a semicolon (;) as a separator, to create a symbol search path having access to all symbols required in that specific debugging session.

Within a symbol server path, the symbol server searches for the symbol file in the first downstream symbol store and loads it from this location, if found. On failure, it recursively searches each symbol store for the file until one is found. The debugger then caches that symbol file into previous downstream stores, which are writable.

Because the software runs on Microsoft Windows operating systems, the debugger should always use the Microsoft public symbol store, available at `http://msdl.microsoft.com/download/symbols` URL, as one entry on the symbol path.

It is also highly recommended that companies have a strong private symbol management policy. Chapter 4 describes the process of creating and maintaining such a symbol store. In this case, the company-wide private symbol store path will be the first entry in the symbol path, followed most likely by Microsoft public symbol store's address.

The first downstream store in the symbol path should be a local cache entry, which is usually faster than any other remote store. Listing 2.10 shows some examples of symbol paths pointing to the Microsoft public symbol store, to a company symbol store combined or not with a downstream store. The examples use `c:\`*`symbols folder`* as the downstream store for faster symbol access. Note that you can combine symbol server paths with regular UNC locations, as described in the previous section.

**Listing 2.10**   Example of symbol server paths

```
0:000>.sympath srv*c:\Symbols*http://msdl.microsoft.com/download/symbols
0:000>.sympath srv*http://msdl.microsoft.com/download/symbols
0:000>.sympath srv*c:\symbols*\\myserver\mysymbols*http://msdl.microsoft.com/
download/symbols
```

### Symbol Cache

In the previous section, you saw how the debugger uses the downstream folders as intermediate caches for the symbol files provided by the symbol server. The caching improves the response time of all operations requiring new symbol file download. However, if the symbol files are stored in a remote share but they are not organized as a symbol server, we cannot use this caching mechanism.

Later versions of debuggers solve this deficiency using the built-in support for symbol files caching. The caching feature is enabled by specifying the cache folder in the symbol path using a special format. The debugger recognizes the `cache*` directive and treats the folder following the asterix (`*`) character as a cache location. All symbols acquired by the debugger from any path following the cache directive will be cached regardless of their source. Listing 2.11 uses the cache directive to indicate a local cache for symbols downloaded from a symbol server or from a symbol share.

**Listing 2.11**   Example of symbol paths with local cache

```
0:000>.sympath cache*c:\symbols;srv*http://msdl.microsoft.com/download/symbols
0:000>.sympath cache*c:\symbols;\\farawayserver\symbols;
```

### Maintaining the Symbol Cache

The local cache created by the mechanism described in the previous sections does not have an expiration policy, and it can grow unbound if the target binaries change often.

It is a good idea to periodically purge the cache folder. The Debugging Tools for Windows provides the agestore.exe cleanup tool that can delete all files not accessed after a specific date. The built-in help is sufficient to learn how to use it efficiently. Listing 2.12 uses the agestore.exe command in list mode to evaluate how many files were not recently used. It is recommended to always use this option before the actual delete operation to confirm which files need to be deleted.

**Listing 2.12** Listing all symbol files unused since a specific date

```
C:\> agestore.exe -date=01-01-2007 -l -s c:\symbols
processing all files last accessed before 01-01-2007 12:00 AM

12-26-2006 9:43 PM   c:\symbols\02sample.pdb\5226684770524C77B6D9658E94FEA2F21\
02sample.pdb
12-26-2006 9:43 PM   c:\symbols\kernel32.pdb\04B9D5F57B154AA2BDBAB7946947DC4F2\
kernel32.pdb
12-26-2006 9:43 PM
c:\symbols\msvcrt.pdb\8A24BF4B1A05412FB0312AD4CB7867042\msvcrt.pdb
12-26-2006 9:43 PM   c:\symbols\ntdll.pdb\C0A498F0036E4D4FB5CBF69005B0F9242\ntdll.pdb

6098944 bytes would be deleted
```

### Setting the Symbol Path

At startup, the debugger reads the _NT_ALT_SYMBOL_PATH and _NT_SYMBOL_PATH environment variables and uses them together as a symbol path, in that order. If the environment cannot be set, another method of setting the symbol path from the beginning of the debug session is to start the debugger with the -y parameter. WinDbg combines the path retrieved from the workspace with the one provided through alternative mechanisms. The two sections shown in Listing 2.13 have the same meaning.

**Listing 2.13** Two methods of setting up the symbol path at debugger startup

**Using the environment**
```
c:\>set _NT_SYMBOL_PATH=c:\symbols
c:\>windbg <image.exe>
```
**Using the command-line parameter**
```
C:\>windbg -y c:\symbols <image.exe>
```

Regardless of the method used to specify the symbol path during the debugger start-up, you can overwrite it in the interactive mode. After the debugger enters the interactive mode, multiple options exist for managing the symbol paths. You can set the symbol path by using the `.sympath` command in one of the following forms. It is important to notice that the change doesn't affect the symbol files already loaded from the previous symbol path.

- `0:000>.sympath <new path>`
  Changes the current symbol path to the new path specified as the argument to the command, which the debugger uses to load symbol files from. It overwrites the existing symbol path without reloading any symbol file or discarding any symbol already loaded.
- `0:000>.sympath+ <new path>`
  Appends the specified new path to the existing symbol path.
- `0:000>.sympath`
  Displays and resolves the current symbol path. Inaccessible symbol paths are listed at the end of the output; currently, symbol server entries are not resolved.
  If you look at the previous examples using the Microsoft symbol store, you might be wondering if such a long URL must be memorized. You can keep it in a file with well-known strings to paste in the debugger console when you need it, but a better way is by using the `.symfix` command.
- `0:000>.symfix <downstream folder>`
  Changes the symbol path to Microsoft's public symbol store. The command takes a downstream folder, caching all symbols downloaded from the Microsoft public symbol store. As a result of this command, the symbol path is set to SRV°downstream folder°http://msdl.microsoft.com/download/symbols.
- `0:000>.symfix+ <downstream folder>`
  Appends the Microsoft public symbol store to the existing symbol path. The command takes a downstream folder, caching all symbols downloaded from the Microsoft public symbol store. Listing 2.14 shows the typical usage of the `.sympath` and `.symfix` commands.

**Listing 2.14**  Using the .sympath and .symfix commands

```
0:000> .sympath srv*c:\symstore.pri
Symbol search path is: srv*c:\symstore.pri
0:000> .sympath+ c:\PathNotAvailable
```

```
Symbol search path is: srv*c:\symstore.pri;c:\PathNotAvailable
WARNING: Inaccessible path: 'c:\PathNotAvailable'
0:000> .sympath
Symbol search path is: srv*c:\symstore.pri;c:\PathNotAvailable
WARNING: Inaccessible path: 'c:\PathNotAvailable'
0:000> .symfix c:\symbols
0:000> .sympath
Symbol search path is: SRV*c:\symbols*http://msdl.microsoft.com/download/
    symbols
0:000> .sympath c:\
Symbol search path is: c:\
0:000> .symfix+ c:\symbols
0:000> .sympath
Symbol search path is: c:\;SRV*c:\symbols*http://msdl.microsoft.com/download/symbols
```

Even if all the illustrated examples are used in the user mode debugger, the same options are available for the kernel mode debugger. It is important to note that all paths are relative to where the debugger engine runs; this has a direct impact in scenarios in which the user mode debugger is redirected through the kernel debugger.

### Checking the Loaded Modules and Symbol Files

The debugger loads the symbols as needed at the first attempt to resolve a symbol within a specified module. If the load operation fails, the debugger does not retry reloading the module. The symbol loading state can be viewed using the lm (list modules) command, one of the most useful commands for exploring the loaded module's information.

```
0:000>lm [option] [-a Address] [-m Pattern] [-M Pattern]
```

The general form of the command has multiple options, but only a few are used more often. This section includes several examples using the 02sample.exe binary, the book's symbols store, followed by the Microsoft public symbols store. For clarity, the symbol path is set using the environment variable, as follows:

```
c:\>set _NT_SYMBOL_PATH=CACHE*C:\Symbols;
SRV*http://www.advancedwindowsdebugging.com/symbols/symstore.pri;
SRV*http://msdl.microsoft.com/download/symbols
C:\>windbg C:\AWDBIN\WinXP.x86.chk\02sample.exe
```

The _NT_SYMBOL_PATH variable is observed by most tools used to debug software applications on the Windows platform. The same symbol path can be set into any other tool using methods specific to each tool. The symbol path shown in the previous listing is sufficient to download and cache all the symbols used in the book's samples.

lm returns information about all modules loaded in the process, along with the address range used by the module, the symbol loading results, and the symbol file path (relative to the symbol path).

```
0:000> lm
start    end         module name
00400000 00404000    02sample        (private pdb symbols)
c:\symbols\02sample.pdb\DE4335BC88FD4EA1A1714350C33B84281\02sample.pdb
76080000 760e5000    msvcp60      (deferred)
77c10000 77c68000    msvcrt       (deferred)
7c800000 7c8f4000    kernel32     (deferred)
7c900000 7c9b0000    ntdll      (pdb symbols)
c:\symbols\ntdll.pdb\36515FB5D04345E4
91F672FA2E2878C02\ntdll.pdb
```

The command accepts various options filtering the list of modules that are processed. For example, lm l processes only loaded symbols files, whereas lm e processes the modules for which no symbol file has been found.

The lm command also accepts a string pattern that is used to filter which modules are processed by the commands. The module name filtering is specified by using the m parameter, and the entire path filtering is triggered by the M parameter. The parameters can be combined to obtain the desired behavior, as shown in Listing 2.15. Listing 2.15 shows verbose information about modules whose names match the kernel* string. Note that the pattern string does not include the extension. When the extension is entered as part of the pattern, the command doesn't find the specified module.

**Listing 2.15**    Displaying information about a loaded module

```
0:000> lm v m kernel*
start    end         module name
7c800000 7c8f4000    kernel32    (export symbols)      C:\WINDOWS\system32\kernel32.dll
    Loaded symbol image file: C:\WINDOWS\system32\kernel32.dll
    Image path: C:\WINDOWS\system32\kernel32.dll
    Image name: kernel32.dll
    Timestamp:       Wed Aug 04 00:56:36 2004 (411096B4)
    CheckSum:        000FF848
    ImageSize:       000F4000
    File version:    5.1.2600.2180
    Product Version:   5.1.2600.2180
```

```
File flags:       0 (Mask 3F)
File OS:          40004 NT Win32
File type:        2.0 Dll
File date:        00000000.00000000
Translations:     0409.04b0
CompanyName:      Microsoft Corporation
ProductName:      Microsoft<< Windows<< Operating System
InternalName:     kernel32
OriginalFilename: kernel32
ProductVersion:   5.1.2600.2180
FileVersion:      5.1.2600.2180 (xpsp_sp2_rtm.040803-2158)
FileDescription:  Windows NT BASE API Client DLL
LegalCopyright:   © Microsoft Corporation. All rights reserved.
```

Despite the amount of information returned by the lm command, additional information is buried in the module header that can be explored by the !lmi extension command. This extension command dumps the entire debug directory information, as shown in Listing 2.16.

**Listing 2.16**   Displaying the module headers

```
0:000> * !lmi command accepts the module address or module's name
0:000> !lmi ntdll.dll
Loaded Module Info: [ntdll.dll]
         Module: ntdll
   Base Address: 7c900000
     Image Name: ntdll.dll
   Machine Type: 332 (I386)
     Time Stamp: 411096b4 Wed Aug 04 00:56:36 2004
           Size: b0000
       CheckSum: af2f7
Characteristics: 210e perf
Debug Data Dirs: Type  Size     VA  Pointer
          CODEVIEW  22, 7b6dc,   7aadc RSDS - GUID: (0x36515fb5, 0xd043, 0x
45e4, 0x91, 0xf6, 0x72, 0xfa, 0x2e, 0x28, 0x78, 0xc0)
            Age: 2, Pdb: ntdll.pdb
           CLSID   4, 7b6d8,   7aad8 [Data not mapped]
     Image Type: FILE    - Image read successfully from debugger.
           C:\WINDOWS\system32\ntdll.dll
    Symbol Type: PDB     - Symbols loaded successfully from symbol server.
           ntdll.pdb\36515FB5D04345E491F672FA2E2878C02\ntdll.pdb
    Load Report: public symbols , not source indexed
           ntdll.pdb\36515FB5D04345E491F672FA2E2878C02\ntdll.pdb
```

In some cases, not even the information returned by !lmi is enough. The module headers can be further explored using another debugger extension, !dh <module address> , or they can be inspected outside the debugger with your tools of choice.

---

**MORE MODULE INFORMATION** Some debugging situations require additional information about the binary images. For example, when debugging a stack overflow, it is easy to obtain the stack size used by the thread. However, this value must be compared against the default stack reserve size. This size, stored in the process image headers, is useful to understand if the thread uses more stack space than the developer intended. The following command displays the module headers, similar to the WDK tool link.exe, described in Listing 2.8.

```
0:000>!dh <module start address>|<module name> -f
```

---

### Reloading the Symbols

Because using an invalid symbol file is worse than not using any, reloading the correct symbol files is important. The basic command for fixing the symbols is .reload combined with the multitude of its available options. Despite its name, the .reload command does not load by default the new symbol files. The command discards previously loaded symbol files and relies on the debugger to reload the files on the first attempt to use them. Some common forms of the .reload command are

- `0:000>.reload`
  Discards symbol information for all loaded modules, returning the debugger back to the initial state. Any attempt to resolve a symbol reloads the symbol file from the disk.
- `0:000>.reload <module>`
  Discards the information about a specified module. Any attempt to resolve a symbol will reload the symbol file from the disk.
- `0:000>.reload /f <module>`
  Forces the debugger to immediately resolve and load the symbol file associated with the module.
- `0:000>.reload nt`
  Kernel mode debugger option. It reloads the symbol file corresponding to the current Windows NT kernel, essential for most operations in the kernel mode debugger. The command does not work in user mode.
- `0:000>.reload /user`
  Kernel mode debugger option. It reloads all user mode symbol files for the active process.

- `0:000>.reload <module>=start, size`

  All the commands shown previously use the information stored in the module header and in the process control block (PCB) to obtain the module address space in memory and the symbol file reference. If any information is missing, as is the case when the system is low in memory, you can find the starting address from different sources (build log, identical running systems) and force the symbol load by specifying the starting address, as shown in the following example:

  `0:000>.reload rpcrt4.dll=78000000,86000`

  This is also useful if you have an address for a module that has already been unloaded, and you need to reconstruct the stack for the code path in the missing module.

- `0:000>!sym noisy`

  When the `.reload` command fails, you must turn on the verbose log for the `.reload` command, controlled by the `.sym` command. `!sym noisy` enables the verbose logging after which any `.reload` command shows all the load attempts and their operation results.

### Validating Symbols

Without the correct symbols, a good developer can spend hours reading the source code, hoping to understand why the debugger shows a stack that does not make sense or why some variables have completely unrealistic values. We cannot overstate the importance of ensuring that the symbols are correct. But how can you be sure that the symbols are correct?

The first option is to use the `lml` command to inspect the possible warnings about symbol files. Furthermore, the debugger provides an extension command that can test the validity of the symbol file against the image file. This extension command takes either an address inside the loaded image or the image name. The extension tests against the symbol file specified as a parameter or against the symbol file already loaded by debugger. The following listing uses the extension command to validate the correctness of the loaded symbols for the image loaded at the specified address.

```
0:000> !chksym 01001b90

02sample.exe
    Timestamp: 461001C1
  SizeOfImage: 5000
```

```
        pdb: 02sample.pdb
    pdb sig: 52266847-7052-4C77-B6D9-658E94FEA2F2
        age: 1

Loaded pdb is +.sympath
SRV\02sample.pdb\5226684770524C77B6D9658E94FEA2F21\02sample.pdb

02sample.pdb
    pdb sig: 52266847-7052-4C77-B6D9-658E94FEA2F2
        age: 1

MATCH: 02sample.pdb and 02sample.exe
```

### Using Symbols

Almost every command uses the symbol information, directly or indirectly, but a few are dedicated to symbol inspection. The basic command to examine the symbols is **x**, which stands for "examine symbols." The command has the following general syntax:

```
0:000>x [options] module!symbols
```

Both the module part and the symbols part can contain wildcards. The wildcard support is a powerful tool when debugging unfamiliar code because it allows us to guess function names or global variables well before reading the code. Several common uses of the **x** command are listed here:

- **0:000>x *!*some***
  Search a symbol name containing the string **some** in the middle of every symbol within each symbol file for the debugger target. If the symbol is an exported function, the result contains both the modules implementing it, as well as the modules importing it (prefixed by _imp string), as in the following example:

  ```
  0:000> x *!*NtOpenThreadToken*
  77e41348 kernel32!_imp__NtOpenThreadToken = <no type information>
  7c821808 ntdll!NtOpenThreadTokenEx = <no type information>
  7c8217f8 ntdll!NtOpenThreadToken = <no type information>
  ```

- **0:000>x module!***
  If any module uses naming conventions, such as prefixing all global variables by a common prefix, these conventions can be factored into the investigation. For example, if all global variables are prefixed by g_, the **x module!g_*** command lists all global variables, along with their current value, as follows:

```
0:000> x kernel32!g_*
77ecdb74 kernel32!g_hModXPSP2Res = <no type information>
...
77e77c80 kernel32!g_DllEntries = <no type information>
```

- 0:000>**x /v /t module!symbol**

Using the /v command can help you better understand the content of the
binary file. It shows the symbol type and the size, in bytes, occupied by that
object or function in ascending size order.

```
0:000> x /v /t 02sample!*
prv global 00402004   4 02sample!__security_cookie_complement = 0xffff4134
...
prv global 004010a0   4 02sample!__xc_a = <function> *[1]
...
prv func   00401713  11 02sample!__SEH_epilog (void)
prv func   004013fa  cc 02sample!wmain (unsigned long, wchar_t **)
...
```

The symbol inspection commands are unable to work at their full capabilities when
the debugger uses the public symbol file for the image. Another helpful command
making good use of the symbols is the ln command, which stands for "list near." The
ln command shows the symbol associated with the specific address, if available.
When no symbol exactly matches the address, the debugger returns a symbol generated by pointer arithmetic on a symbol closer to that address.

```
0:000> ln 01001b90
(01001b90)   02sample!wmain | (01001bc0)   02sample!AppInfo::AppInfo
Exact matches:
    02sample!wmain (unsigned long, wchar_t **)
0:000> ln 01001b90+1
(01001b90)   02sample!wmain+0x1 | (01001bc0)   02sample!AppInfo::AppInfo
```

The exact matches are very valuable, although the calculated one should be taken
with caution, especially when the address is part of an image file that is part of the
operating system. Microsoft uses special techniques to optimize the executable
images for performance before releasing them. After optimization, a single function
can be split in multiple sections located at different addresses, adversely impacting
the pointer arithmetic performed by the debugger. The performance-optimized
image can be identified by the presence of the perf attribute into the module characteristics, as shown in Listing 2.16.

This command is very powerful when you are inspecting an arbitrary piece of data and you don't know what it represents. If the address you are examining is part of a stack, most probably you will find sequences from the calling stack, and `ln` can help you identify them. If you are inspecting a heap block, it is very possible to find fragments from original objects, which can help with identifying the block usage.

## Using Source Files

When debugging a software application, the source files are useful in two main situations: when executing the code line by line to learn or to validate its behavior, or when creating possible scenarios leading to the application failure. In both cases, the access to private symbol files is required, as they contain information that correlates each symbol with the source filename and line, as well as the location of all source files used to generate the binary file.

The debugger uses the source location information stored in the symbol file and tries to locate files in various locations as indicated by the source path location. WinDbg preserves the last source path location in the workspace. The location can be overwritten using the `srcpath` command-line switch, such as `windbg -srcpath <SourcePath>`. Interactively, the source path can be changed using the `.srcpath` command or using the Source File Path menu item in the File menu. When debugging images on the same system used to compile them, the debugger does not need any source path. The unprocessed symbol files contain fully qualified paths to the source files, which are opened directly by the debugger.

The source path is interpreted by the debuggers as a list of file paths, separated by semicolon (;) characters. The debugger then finds a source file, located in the source path folder, representing the best match for the file path originally used to build the binary. The source path is entered in the debugger command windows using a dot (.) command, as in the following:

```
0:000>.srcpath c:\;\\mycompany\sources
Source search path is: c:\; \\mycompany\sources
```

Because the source file resolution process is relatively complex and depends on a number of parameters on the local system, sometimes the debugger is unable to locate or access the correct source file for the source path retrieved from the private symbol files. The debugger provides a verbose mode for the process of locating the correct source code files. This mode can be controlled by another command, `.srcnoisy <1|0>`. When enabled, the debugger displays all locations checked for the presence of the source file, as well as the result of each operation.

```
0:000> .srcnoisy 1
Noisy source output: on
0:000> .srcpath e:\;c:\
Source search path is: e:\;c:\
DBGENG:  Scan paths for partial path match:
DBGENG:    prefix 'c:\awd\chapter2'
DBGENG:    suffix 'sample.cpp'
DBGENG:      match 'e:' against 'c:\awd\chapter2': 14 (match '')
DBGENG:      match 'c:' against 'c:\awd\chapter2': 14 (match '')
DBGENG:  Scan paths for partial path match:
DBGENG:    prefix 'c:\awd'
DBGENG:    suffix 'chapter2\sample.cpp'
DBGENG:      match 'e:' against 'c:\awd': 5 (match '')
DBGENG:      match 'c:' against 'c:\awd': 5 (match '')
DBGENG:  Scan paths for partial path match:
DBGENG:    prefix 'c:'
DBGENG:    suffix 'awd\chapter2\sample.cpp'
DBGENG:      match 'e:' against 'c:': 1 (match '')
DBGENG:      match 'c:' against 'c:': -1 (match 'c:')
DBGENG:      check 'c:\awd\chapter2\sample.cpp'
DBGENG:      found file 'c:\awd\chapter2\sample.cpp'
```

The default source file matching is not as strict as the symbol file matching because the source information is just the fully qualified source filename. As long as a source file having the same name as the name indicated in the symbol file is found in the source path, the debugger loads it. The process works reasonably well for applications in which the source files are unchanged from last compilation.

Chapter 4 explains how to address this problem using a source server that works side by side with a source control system to ensure source correctness. The debugger interprets the source server information stored in the symbol files when the SRV* string is present in the source path. The debugger extracts the source file from the source store described in the symbol file and caches it on the local system.

For the sake of convenience, the debugger accepts the .srcfix command, which simply sets the source path to SRV* in case the exact syntax of the source server path is forgotten. The process of loading the source file from the source server is illustrated in the following listing:

```
0:000> .srcnoisy 1
Noisy source output: on
0:000> .srcfix
Source search path is: SRV*
DBGENG:  Scan srcsrv SRV* for:
DBGENG:    '<token>!c:\awd\chapter2\sample.cpp'
```

```
DBGENG:       found file 'c:\awd\chapter2\sample.cpp'
DBGENG:       server path 'SRV*'
DBGENG:       local 'http://www.advancedwindowsdebugging.com/sources/AWD/Chapter2/
sample.cpp/VERSION1/sample.cpp'
```

When the source path is a combination of local paths and the source server path, the debugger uses the source server mechanism for all files that are indexed in the source server, as described in the symbol files. The debugger uses the standard path when matching all other files. Even if the sources are provided by multiple source stores, the SRV* string is required just once in the source path.

Similar to the symbol path, to simplify the process of composing the source path, both .srcfix and .srcpath provide an alternative syntax, .srcpath+ <srcpath> or .srcfix+, which append to the existing source server path. The next listing shows an example of appending a share location to the existing source path.

```
0:000> .srcpath+ \\mysources\sources
Source search path is: srv*;\\mysources\sources
```

## Exploratory Commands

As you have seen before, the message displayed by the debugger is very helpful in understanding why and where the debugger stopped. If we connect to a remote debugger after the event has been encountered, we lose precious information, which might have been previously displayed in the debugger console. In this section, we explore a few options that we have when trying to understand the state in which the debugger target stopped and the reason for the current stop.

### Why Did the Debugger Stop?

The .lastevent command displays information about the last debugger event that caused the current debugger to stop. Chapter 3 explains the origin and importance of possible debugger events. Listing 2.17 shows a sample of output generated by the .lastevent command in two cases: after the debugger stopped because of a user-defined breakpoint and, in the second output, because of an operation on an inaccessible memory location. Knowing why the debugger stopped can sometimes complete the investigation, as is the case with the initial process breakpoint or process exit breakpoint.

**Listing 2.17**   .lastevent output

```
0:000> * after a breakpoint
0:000> .lastevent
Last event: 170c.1464: Hit breakpoint 2
0:000> * after an access violation exception
0:000> .lastevent
Last event: 170c.1464: Access violation - code c0000005 (first chance)
```

### What Is the Target System?

The program you are debugging behaves differently depending on the operating system and the updates installed on it—not because it uses a feature of one of those releases, but because the operating system mechanism can change between releases. At the same time, the debugger and its extensions use components implemented in the operating system, which can behave differently across different releases, introducing limitations to the debugger tool itself.

So, except for the case in which you are debugging a component not dependent on operating system services, you most likely need to know the operating system version, the debugger version, the loaded extension version, and so on.

The vertarget command is a subset of the version command, which displays only the version of the operating system running the debugger target. The version command shows additional information about the debugger environment, the command line used to start the debugging session, as shown in Listing 2.18. If the system uses more than one processor, the first line also shows the number of active processors; otherwise, it shows the UP (which stands for uni processor) string.

**Listing 2.18**   The version output from a user mode debugger

```
0:000> version
Windows XP Version 2600 (Service Pack 2) UP Free x86 compatible
Product: WinNt, suite: SingleUserTS
kernel32.dll version: 5.1.2600.3119 (xpsp_sp2_gdr.070416-1301)
Debug session time: Sun Jul  8 14:31:35.259 2007 (GMT-7)
System Uptime: 0 days 0:10:39.826
Process Uptime: 0 days 0:00:04.356
  Kernel time: 0 days 0:00:00.030
  User time: 0 days 0:00:00.020
Live user mode: <Local>
command line: '"c:\Program Files\Debugging Tools for Windows"\ntsd notepad'
```

*(continues)*

**Listing 2.18**    The version output from a user mode debugger *(continued)*

```
Debugger Process 0x738
dbgeng:  image 6.6.0007.5, built Sat Jul 08 13:12:40 2006
        [path: c:\Program Files\Debugging Tools for Windows\dbgeng.dll]
dbghelp: image 6.6.0007.5, built Sat Jul 08 13:11:32 2006
        [path: c:\Program Files\Debugging Tools for Windows\dbghelp.dll]
        DIA version: 60516
Extension DLL search Path:
    c:\Program Files\Debugging Tools for Windows\winext;c:\Program Files\Debugging
Tools for Windows\winext\arcade;c:\Program Files\Debugging Tools for
Windows\WINXP;c:\Program Files\Debugging Tools for Windows\pri;c:\Program Files\Debug-
ging Tools for Windows;c:\Program Files\Debugging Tools for
Windows\winext\arcade;C:\WINDOWS\system32;C:\WINDOWS;C:\WINDOWS
\System32\Wbem
Extension DLL chain:
    dbghelp: image 6.6.0007.5, API 6.0.6, built Sat Jul 08 13:11:32 2006
        [path: c:\Program Files\Debugging Tools for Windows\dbghelp.dll]
    ext: image 6.6.0007.5, API 1.0.0, built Sat Jul 08 13:10:52 2006
        [path: c:\Program Files\Debugging Tools for Windows\winext\ext.dll]
    exts: image 6.6.0007.5, API 1.0.0, built Sat Jul 08 13:10:48 2006
        [path: c:\Program Files\Debugging Tools for Windows\WINXP\exts.dll]
    uext: image 6.6.0007.5, API 1.0.0, built Sat Jul 08 13:11:02 2006
        [path: c:\Program Files\Debugging Tools for Windows\winext\uext.dll]
    ntsdexts: image 6.0.5457.0, API 1.0.0, built Sat Jul 08 13:29:38 2006
        [path: c:\Program Files\Debugging Tools for Windows\WINXP\ntsdexts.dll]
```

### What Are the Current Register Values?

After we know why the debugger stopped, what operating system it runs on, and what extensions are available for our investigations, it is time to find an explanation for the current break. The process of finding the reason for the break can be compared to forensics work of collecting and questioning every piece of evidence that we can get from the debugger, exploring all unknown elements, and validating any assumption that we made while investigating the failure. The first step is to validate symbol correctness, as described in the symbol section. If the symbols are not correct, we can easily fix them, as described in the earlier section "Reloading the Symbols."

The r command, which stands for register, provides the access to processor registers. In the simplest form, it displays all register values according to the register mask active on the debugger. The r command can also load a register with a user-entered value. That option is extremely useful when you use the debugger to simulate various failures in the code execution to trigger different code paths. For example, after a call to allocate some memory using the malloc function, the allocated block address is returned from the function using the eax register. If that value is replaced with zero, the application can be tested for out-of-memory conditions. The display command can be scoped to a single register or even to a single flag from the eFlags register. WinDbg provides a register window that's updated with the current context every time the debugger stops. Listing 2.19 uses the r command to read and write register values.

**Listing 2.19**  Registers value using the default register mask

```
0:000> r
eax=00000000 ebx=00000000 ecx=00000000 edx=00000000 esi=7d61cbcf edi=00000000
eip=7d61cbe1 esp=0014fed4 ebp=0014ff0c iopl=0         nv up ei pl nz na po nc
cs=0023  ss=002b  ds=002b  es=002b  fs=0053  gs=002b         efl=00000202
ntdll!NtTerminateProcess+0x12:
7d61cbe1 c20800          ret     8
0:000> * Displaying eax register
0:000> reax
eax=00000000
0:000> * Displaying the overflow flag
0:000> r of
of=0
0:000> * Changing eax register
0:000 > reax=1
```

The register mask is a bit mask that controls what registers are displayed by the r command. The rm command can be used to display the current register mask or to change it according to the debugging needs. Listing 2.20 shows some useful examples of the rm command. In general, for a standard application, we are only interested in integer registers. If the application makes heavy use of floating point, we will set the mask to show those values as well. When debugging programs that make heavy use of Streaming SIMD Extensions, we can enable MMX or SSE XMM registers in the output using the register mask.

**Listing 2.20**  Changing the default register mask

```
0:000> * What is the current mask?
0:000> rm
Register output mask is 9:
      1 - Integer state (32-bit)
      8 - Segment registers
```

*(continues)*

**2. INTRODUCTION TO THE DEBUGGERS**

**Listing 2.20**   Changing the default register mask *(continued)*

```
0:000 > * What is the meaning of all register mask bits?
0:000 > rm ?
        1 - Integer state (32-bit) or
        2 - Integer state (64-bit), 64-bit takes precedence
        4 - Floating-point state
        8 - Segment registers
       10 - MMX registers
       20 - Debug registers and, in kernel, CR4
       40 - SSE XMM registers
0:000 > * Setting the mask to zero (nothing is displayed)
0:000 > rm 0
0:000 > r
ntdll!NtTerminateProcess+0x12:
7d61cbe1 c20800          ret     8
```

The first question we might ask is the value of the program counter register (also known as instruction pointer registers). We also might ask how the processor got to that location. An instruction pointer register name depends on the processor architecture, making it difficult for casual debugger users to remember the name on all platforms. To overcome the naming problem, the debugger's team introduced various pseudo-registers, specialized to the hardware architecture by debugger. For example, the $ip pseudo-register name represents the instruction pointer register name in the current debugger target architecture.

Pseudo-registers are symbolic names, in the form of $name, recognized by the debugger as variables holding values in the current debugging session. The debugger manages several automatic pseudo-registers representing values meaningful in the current debugger session. For example, the $ip pseudo-register is the same as the eip register from x86 processors or the rip register for x64 processors; the $tpid pseudo-register is the current process identifier (PID). The debugger provides 20 other general-purpose pseudo-registries, named $t0-$t19, in the current debugger session. As with the standard registers, pseudo-register names must be escaped using ampersand (@) characters in expressions.

You can find a detailed list with the description of each pseudo-register in the debugger (help topic Pseudo-Registers), along with their availability in various debugger scenarios. In the remainder of this book, we use the following pseudo-registers as much as possible:

- $ip: The instruction pointer register; dot sign (.) evaluates to the current instruction pointer as well. Depending on the processor architecture, $ip evaluates as the following:

$ip = eip on x86 architecture

$ip = rip on x64 architecture

$ip = iip on Itanium architecture

- $ra: The return address from the current function.
- $retreg: The primary value register; immediately after the function call returns, it contains the result of the function. Depending on the processor architecture, $retreg evaluates as the following:

$retreg = eax on x86 architecture

$retreg = rax on x64 architecture

$retreg = ret0 on Itanium architecture

- $csp: The current stack pointer; depending on the processor architecture, $csp evaluates as following:

$csp = esp on x86 architecture

$csp = rsp on x64 architecture

$csp = bsp on Itanium architecture

- $proc: The current process; it contains the address of the process environment block (PEB) in user mode or the address of the current processes' EPROCESS structure in kernel mode debugger.
- $thread: The current thread; it contains the address of the thread environment block (TEB) in user mode or the address of the current thread's ETHREAD structure in kernel mode debugger.
- $tpid: The current process identifier (PID).
- $tid: The current thread identifier (TID).

Listing 2.21 shows the typical use of pseudo-register in normal commands.

**Listing 2.21**   Pseudo-register used on user mode debugger break (x86)

```
0:000> reip
eip=00401264
0:000> r$ip
$ip=00401264
0:000> ?.
Evaluate expression: 4199012 = 00401264
0:000> reax
eax=00401264
0:000> r$retreg
$retreg=00401264
0:000> r$proc
$proc=7ffde000
```

*(continues)*

**Listing 2.21**   Pseudo-register used on user mode debugger break (x86) *(continued)*

```
0:000> r $peb
$peb=7ffde000
0:000> r$thread
$thread=7ffdd000
0:000> r$teb
$teb=7ffdd000
0:000> ~
.  0  Id: 16f8.16c8 Suspend: 1 Teb: 7ffdd000 Unfrozen
0:000> r$tid
$tid=000016c8
0:000> r$tpid
$tpid=000016f8
0:000> r$t1=0xbaadf00d
0:000> r$t1
$t1=baadf00d
```

### What Code Is the Processor Executing Now?

To find out details about the current break, we will start by analyzing the code section containing the failure, starting with the current program counter. The u command, which stands for "unassembly," is used to inspect the machine code generated from the source code. We start the executable 02sample.exe under the debugger and select the option '1' to generate an access violation. Listing 2.22 shows the debugger command window after using the u command at the break. WinDbg provides a disassembly window that's updated with the assembly code at the current instruction pointer location every time the debugger stops.

**Listing 2.22**   The u command used in user mode debugger (x86)

```
0:000> * Unassembly eight instruction as the address current $ip
0:000> u .
02sample!RaiseAV+0xd:
00401264 c6050000000000   mov     byte ptr [00000000],0x0
0040126b 8be5             mov     esp,ebp
0040126d 5d               pop     ebp
0040126e c3               ret
...
0:000> * Unassembly the entire function containing the current $ip
0:000> uf .
02sample!RaiseAV:
00401257 8bff             mov     edi,edi
```

```
00401259 55              push    ebp
0040125a 8bec            mov     ebp,esp
0040125c 6a04            push    0x4
0040125e 58              pop     eax
0040125f e8cc020000      call    02sample!_chkstk (00401530)
00401264 c6050000000000  mov     byte ptr [00000000],0x0
0040126b 8be5            mov     esp,ebp
0040126d 5d              pop     ebp
0040126e c3              ret
0:000> * Unassembly eight instructions prior to the current $ip
0:000> ub .
02sample!RaiseCPP+0x24:
00401255 cc              int     3
00401256 cc              int     3
02sample!RaiseAV:
00401257 8bff            mov     edi,edi
00401259 55              push    ebp
0040125a 8bec            mov     ebp,esp
0040125c 6a04            push    0x4
0040125e 58              pop     eax
0040125f e8cc020000      call    02sample!_chkstk (00401530)
0:000> * Unassembly two instructions after the current $ip
0:000> u . L2
02sample!RaiseAV+0xd:
00401264 c6050000000000  mov     byte ptr [00000000],0x0
0040126b 8be5            mov     esp,ebp
0:000> * Unassembly two instructions prior to the current $ip
0:000> ub . L2
02sample!RaiseAV+0x7:
0040125e 58              pop     eax
0040125f e8cc020000      call    02sample!_chkstk (00401530)
0:000> * Unassembly ten instructions between $ip and $ip plus ten
0:000> u . .+a
02sample!RaiseAV+0xd:
00401264 c6050000000000  mov     byte ptr [00000000],0x0
0040126b 8be5            mov     esp,ebp
0040126d 5d              pop     ebp
```

## What Is the Current Call Stack?

Knowing the current register values, the current executing instruction pointer, plus a few instructions surrounding it helps us to understand the current fault, but we are far from understanding the dynamic factors contributing to this fault, such as what code was executed before it, how the registers have been changed by other functions, and much more.

The processor uses stack memory areas controlled by a stack register to record the return address where the execution must continue after completing the current function call. Because each processor manages the stack in its own way, we focus on the x86 family of processors, as they are common and easily accessible, for all of our examples in this chapter. The 64-bit processor-specific aspects are discussed in Chapter 12, "64-Bit Debugging," that must be studied before digging into the 64-bit realm. The x86 processor stack always grows downward, and it is addressed by the stack pointer register, named esp.

Chapter 5, "Memory Corruption Part I—Stacks," explains in detail the differences between various calling conventions used in the x86 processor architecture and how they affect code execution. This chapter focuses on the __stdcall calling convention, as it is the default convention used by Windows APIs. This section (and the remainder of the book), ignores frame pointer omission (FPO) optimization, simply because it is not used in Windows XP SP2 and later operating systems. Since FPO optimization makes debugging nearly impossible without symbols, the current recommendation is to avoid it completely.

Upon entering a function, the compiler generates a so-called stack frame that is maintained using the frame base pointer register ebp. The function prolog saves the current value of ebp on the stack and loads the current stack pointer value that will be kept until the function executes the function epilog. Within the function, the compiler addresses input parameters using positive offsets for the frame-based pointer and negative offsets for the local variable allocated in the function. The simplest function prolog and function epilog are shown here:

```
0:000> uf .
02sample!KBTest::Fibonacci_stdcall:
00401760 8bff            mov     edi,edi
00401762 55              push    ebp
00401763 8bec            mov     ebp,esp
...
004017b3 8be5            mov     esp,ebp
004017b5 5d              pop     ebp
004017b6 c20400          ret     4
```

In the function epilog, the ebp value is reloaded with the saved value so that the register is preserved after the call. The layout of the input parameters, the local variable, and the base frame pointer are shown in the next figure. Before making a function call, the caller pushes all the function parameters on the stack. The processor then saves the address from where the execution will continue on return. The called function uses the stack to save the old ebp and allocates the necessary space for the local variable. The ebp register is then used to access the input parameters and the local variable, as you can see on the right side of Figure 2.5.

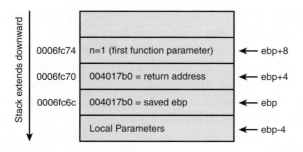

**Figure 2.5** Stack content when calling a function following the __stdcall convention

The call stack records the entire chain of function calls made by the current thread, resulting in the invocation of the current function. The stack representation starts with the current executed function displayed at the top followed by its caller, the caller of the current function callers, and so on—each calling point being identified by its stack frame. The process repeats itself until the debugger reaches the last stack frame on the call stack, or an external condition, such as incorrect symbols or a non-accessible stack, prevents the debugger from further decoding the stack.

Not surprisingly, the stack of the current fault is one of the most used pieces of information. Sometimes the thread stack is used to index and catalogue software failures.

The **k** (display stack back trace) command can be used to analyze the current stack using module symbols and formatting the information according to additional parameters passed in the command line. As with most context-dependent commands, **k** interprets the stack from the current context information. WinDbg provides a call stack window that's updated every time the debugger stops.

To experiment with **k** commands, we will run 02sample.exe under debugger and select the option to generate a normal call stack. This option recursively calculates the 32$^{nd}$ number from the Fibonacci series. The source code for the function is shown in Listing 2.23.

**Listing 2.23** Source of Fibonacci function implemented in the 02sample.exe sample

```
#define STOP_ON_DEBUGGER { if (IsDebuggerPresent()) DebugBreak();}
unsigned int Fibonacci(unsigned int n)
{
    switch(n)
    {
        case 0: STOP_ON_DEBUGGER;return 0;
        case 1: return 1;
        default: return Fibonacci(n-1)+Fibonacci(n-2);
    }
}
```

This function includes a special functionality to facilitate its debugging. When it runs under a user mode debugger, our Fibonacci function calls DebugBreak before returning F (0).

We discussed (in the "Setting Up and Using the Symbols" section) how to set the symbols, and we assumed that they are correct. Now we are ready to experiment with k commands after the program stops in the debugger. In the basic form, the k command shows a maximum number of frames controlled by the .kframes command, the default value being 20. For each frame, the command displays in the ChildEBP column stack frame information. In the RetAddr column, it displays the address where the code starts to execute, when the function returns, and with which symbol the current function is associated, as shown in Listing 2.24.

**Listing 2.24**   Displaying the call stack

```
0:000> k
ChildEBP RetAddr
0006fcb0 010017eb ntdll!DbgBreakPoint
0006fcc0 01001810 02sample!KBTest::Fibonacci_stdcall+0x2b
0006fcd4 01001802 02sample!KBTest::Fibonacci_stdcall+0x50
...
0006ff2c 0100179c 02sample!KBTest::Fibonacci_stdcall+0x42
0006ff38 01001d93 02sample!Stack+0xc
0006ff50 01001cab 02sample!AppInfo::Loop+0xb3
0006ff5c 01002076 02sample!wmain+0x1b
0006ffa0 76033833 02sample!__wmainCRTStartup+0x102
0006ffac 7734a9bd kernel32!BaseThreadInitThunk+0xe
0006ffec 00000000 ntdll!_RtlUserThreadStart+0x23
```

Each function most likely receives a few parameters with relevant values for program execution history. kp and kP are specially designed to interpret each function's information and display the parameter type, parameter name, as well as the associated parameter's value. kp shows all parameters on a single line, whereas kP uses a line for each parameter (see Listing 2.25).

**Listing 2.25**   Displaying the parameters used by the past five functions from the call stack

```
0:000> * Displays the past five function on the stack with their parameters
0:000> kP 5
ChildEBP RetAddr
0006fcb0 010017ab ntdll!DbgBreakPoint
0006fcc0 010017d0 02sample!KBTest::Fibonacci_stdcall(
```

```
                 unsigned int n = 0)+0x2b
0006fcd4 010017c2 02sample!KBTest::Fibonacci_stdcall(
                 unsigned int n = 2)+0x50
0006fce8 010017c2 02sample!KBTest::Fibonacci_stdcall(
                 unsigned int n = 3)+0x42
0006fcfc 010017c2 02sample!KBTest::Fibonacci_stdcall(
                 unsigned int n = 4)+0x42
```

Because function symbols are part of private symbols, it is common for the stack to contain a function without the parameter information. In such cases, we can use the kb command to display the first three parameters passed on the stack to that function. Using additional information, such as the function signature and its calling convention, we can interpret what parameters are valid for each function. In Listing 2.26, you can see that a real parameter is shown correctly, whereas the next two parameters have no meaning in this stack, as the function has just one parameter.

**Listing 2.26** Displaying the first three parameters used by the five functions from the call stack

```
0:000> kb 5
ChildEBP RetAddr  Args to Child
0006fc6c 004017b0 00000001 00191ffc 00000003 02sample!KBTest::Fibonacci_stdcall+0x5
0006fc80 004017a2 00000003 00191ffc 00000004 02sample!KBTest::Fibonacci_stdcall+0x50
0006fc94 004017a2 00000004 00191ffc 00000005 02sample!KBTest::Fibonacci_stdcall+0x42
0006fca8 004017a2 00000005 00191ffc 00000006 02sample!KBTest::Fibonacci_stdcall+0x42
0006fcbc 004017a2 00000006 00191ffc 00000007 02sample!KBTest::Fibonacci_stdcall+0x42
```

In the process of developing and testing reliable servers, failure to extend the thread's stack in a low memory condition represents a common failure. The solution employed in this case is limiting the stack usage to the committed stack size by carefully watching the stack space used in every stack frame and minimizing it as much as possible.

The stack usage for each frame can be calculated by subtracting the current base frame pointer from the base frame pointer of one of the functions called by the current function. The process is facilitated by a form of the k command that calculates and shows this value for each function except the current one. The kf command accepts the same parameters as all other forms of the k command, and it is used in Listing 2.27 to display the past five functions. In the first column, the command displays the stack size used by the function.

2. INTRODUCTION TO THE DEBUGGERS

**Listing 2.27**    Displaying the stack size used by past the five functions from the call stack

```
0:000> kf 5
  Memory  ChildEBP RetAddr
          0006fc6c 004017b0 02sample!KBTest::Fibonacci_stdcall+0x5
      14  0006fc80 004017a2 02sample!KBTest::Fibonacci_stdcall+0x50
      14  0006fc94 004017a2 02sample!KBTest::Fibonacci_stdcall+0x42
      14  0006fca8 004017a2 02sample!KBTest::Fibonacci_stdcall+0x42
      14  0006fcbc 004017a2 02sample!KBTest::Fibonacci_stdcall+0x42
```

In some cases, only part of the stack is available, and the debugger k command is unable to decode the stack since the address pointed to by the current base frame pointer ebp and the current stack pointer esp are not accessible. In those cases, a variant of the k command that accepts values for the base frame pointer, the stack pointer, and the instruction pointer can be used instead.

The hardest part in the manual process of reconstructing the stack is identifying a good pair of values from the memory area that represents a correct stack frame from the calling stack. One way to find them is to identify a series of values representing an address pointing to the current stack, followed by an executable address. Each address can be a potential frame, and it should be verified using the k command. The operation should be repeated with another potential frame until the stack is properly rendered and the k command shows a reasonable stack, as shown in Listing 2.28.

**Listing 2.28**    Manual stack reconstruction using the k command

```
0:000> * Dump the memory block and look for pattern
0:000> dc esp
0006fc6c  0006fc80 004017b0 00000001 00191ffc  ......@.........
0006fc7c  00000003 0006fc94 004017a2 00000003  ..........@.....
0006fc8c  00191ffc 00000004 0006fca8 004017a2  ..............@.
0006fc9c  00000004 00191ffc 00000005 0006fcbc  ................
0006fcac  004017a2 00000005 00191ffc 00000006  ..@.............
0006fcbc  0006fcd0 004017a2 00000006 00191ffc  ......@.........
0006fccc  00000007 0006fce4 004017a2 00000007  ..........@.....
0006fcdc  00191ffc 00000008 0006fcf8 004017a2  ..............@.
0:000> * Used saved ebp, the address storing it and the return address
0:000> k = 0006fc80 0006fc6c 004017b0
ChildEBP RetAddr
0006fc80 004017a2 02sample!KBTest::Fibonacci_stdcall+0x50
0006fc94 004017a2 02sample!KBTest::Fibonacci_stdcall+0x42
```

This is a common scenario encountered while debugging extremely loaded systems from the kernel mode debugger and only some pages from the thread stack are paged in.

### Setting a Code Breakpoint

The debugger is often used to validate the execution of a specific code sequence, either by stopping the execution at the sequence start or when an interesting condition is happening. This can be achieved by using breakpoint commands.

Code breakpoints are set using the bp command that takes as parameters the address to set the breakpoint, breakpoint options, breakpoint restrictions, and a string containing the command to be executed when the breakpoint is hit. The breakpoint set in the user mode debugger can be prefixed with a thread identifier; in which case, the debugger will stop only when the specified thread reaches the breakpoint. Listing 2.29 shows the usage of breakpoint commands for setting a breakpoint, listing all the breakpoints, and deleting them.

**Listing 2.29**   Using breakpoints in the user mode debugger

```
0:000> * Breakpoint only on thread 0 and execute "resp" command
0:000> ~0 bp 02sample!KBTest::Fibonacci_stdcall "resp"
0:000> * List the breakpoints
0:000> bl
 0 e 00401750     0001 (0001)  0:~000 02sample!KBTest::Fibonacci_stdcall "resp"
0:000> g
esp=0006fdc4
eax=00000012 ebx=7ffdf000 ecx=00000011 edx=77c61b78 esi=7c9118f1 edi=00011970
eip=00401750 esp=0006fdc4 ebp=0006fdd4 iopl=0         nv up ei pl nz na pe nc
cs=001b  ss=0023  ds=0023  es=0023  fs=003b  gs=0000            efl=00000206
02sample!KBTest::Fibonacci_stdcall:
00401750 8bff             mov      edi,edi
0:000> * Clear all breakpoints
0:000> bc *
0:000> * Set a breakpoint for all threads to execute"reasp;g"
0:000> bp 02sample!KBTest::Fibonacci_stdcall "resp;g"
0:000> g
esp=0006fc98
esp=0006fcac
esp=0006fc98
esp=0006fc98
...
```

Upon creation, each breakpoint gets a numeric identifier that can be used later to make changes to that breakpoint. The identifier of the breakpoint that was at the origin of the current stop is shown by the debugger immediately after the stop. WinDbg provides a toolbar button and a Breakpoints window for managing the breakpoints.

The same breakpoint can be set from the kernel mode debugger, with the main difference being that it is global for the whole system. If the breakpoint scope must be limited to a specific process or thread, the address of the EPROCESS or KTHREAD structure must be specified as an option to the breakpoint command. In Listing 2.30, the first breakpoint is set for all threads (and implicitly all processes) running on the system, whereas the second one is scoped to the process having the current process identified by the $proc pseudo-register.

**Listing 2.30**    Using breakpoints in the kernel mode debugger

```
kd> * Breakpoint on ntdll!RtlAllocateHeap will break on each allocation
kd> bp ntdll!RtlAllocateHeap
kd> * Breakpoint limited to the process
kd> bp /p @$proc ntdll!RtlAllocateHeap  "!process -1 0;g"
kd> g
PROCESS 811de7f8  SessionId: 0  Cid: 037c    Peb: 7ffd9000  ParentCid: 0240
    DirBase: 0567b000  ObjectTable: e1781770  HandleCount: 1412.
    Image: svchost.exe
kd> bl
0 e 7c9105d4      0001 (0001) ntdll!RtlAllocateHeap
      Match process data 811de7f8
```

The bm command is a convenient way to set multiple breakpoints on all addresses matching the symbol pattern specified as parameter. Listing 2.31 uses the bm command to set breakpoints for all methods implemented by the class KBTest. When the private symbols are not available for the target module, the bm command fails unless we override its behavior using the /a parameter.

**Listing 2.31**    Using breakpoints in the user mode debugger

```
0:000> bm 02sample!*kbtest*
  1: 00401860 @!"02sample!KBTest::Fibonacci_fastcall"
  2: 004017a0 @!"02sample!KBTest::Fibonacci_stdcall"
  3: 004018d0 @!"02sample!KBTest::ObjFibonacci"
  4: 00401800 @!"02sample!KBTest::Fibonacci_cdecl"
breakpoint 2 redefined
  2: 004017a0 @!"02sample!KBTest::Fibonacci"
```

The Windows operating system loads dynamic l
and we must often set a breakpoint on a module
command can set a deferred breakpoint that b
module owning that breakpoint is loaded. Fo
deferred breakpoint on the DCOM initializatio

```
0:000> bu ole32!CoInitializeEx
```

When the module containing the symbol is alr
mand sets a breakpoint immediately at the s
breakpoints are based on symbolic information
by WinDbg, which are used in subsequent debugging sessions. ₁vᴏt surprising,
often used as the preferred method of enabling breakpoints.

The bu command works with the kernel mode debugger as well. But for the kernel mode debugger, the command sets breakpoints only on modules to be loaded in
kernel space. So the user mode breakpoints must be set using a combination of techniques, as you can see later in the section "Debugging Scenarios."

### What Are the Variable Values?

Because the entire code execution is dependent on the instant values of all variables
used in that specific function, it is essential to know the values in order to understand
the execution history and predict further execution.

The dv command does exactly that, offering a large set of options for variable
inspections. The command is similar in meaning, and sometimes in functionality, to
the x command used to inspect symbol information. To illustrate the dv command
functionality, we will set a breakpoint at the Fibonacci_thiscall member function built in the 02sample.exe, which is exercised by selecting option '6.' The function
member, shown in the following listing, implements the Fibonacci functionality.

```
unsigned int KBTest::Fibonacci_thiscall(unsigned int n)
    {
        m_lastN = n;
        int localN = n + gGlobal.m_ref;
        switch(n)
        {
            case 0: STOP_ON_DEBUGGER;return 0;
            case 1: return 1;
            default:
                {
                return Fibonacci_thiscall(localN-2)+Fibonacci_thiscall(localN-3);
                }
        }    }
```

just four variables: the function parameter with the symbolic name
plicit pointer named `this`; the local variable, `localN`; and the global
`obal`. Listing 2.32 shows various uses of the `dv` command exploring vari-
s in the context of the Fibonacci_thiscall function after the code execution
n stopped with a breakpoint. The executable has been compiled without opti-
ation to minimize the discrepancies between the C++ code and the generated
sembly code. Even when the optimization is turned off, the `dv` command sometimes returns unexpected information to the user. WinDbg provides a Locals window
that's updated with the current variable value times the debugger stops.

### Listing 2.32  Use of dv command

```
0:000> * In the simplest form dv displays the local variables
0:000> dv
           this = 0x77c146f0
              n = 0x20
         localN = -1
0:000> * dv can be used to display variables matching a pattern
0:000> dv 02sample!gGlo*
02sample!gGlobal$initializer$ = 0x01002920
02sample!gGlobal = class Global
0:000> * dv /i shows the symbol type (priv) and parameter type
0:000> * on the second column
0:000> dv /i
prv local              this = 0x77c146f0
prv param                 n = 0x20
prv local           localN = -1
0:000> * dv /V shows the location where the variable is stored
0:000> dv /V this
0006fee4 @ebp-0x08            this = 0x77c146f0
0:000> * If the variable is not correct, unassemble the function
```

When the variable is a complex type, such as a data structure or a class, the `dv` command shows only its address. However, the `dt` command, which stands for display
type, can interpret a block of memory as a data type whose name is passed a parameter. The `dt` command does not require the data type name if the address is a symbolic name whose type is known by debugger. Listing 2.33 shows some examples of
using the `dt` command The `dt` command can also recursively process an embedded
object or an array of objects with the right options, well described in the debugger
help (help topic DT).

**Listing 2.33** Use of dt command

```
0:000> * dt interprets this object type when displaying the memory block
0:000> dt this
Local var @ 0x6fee4 Type KBTest*
0x77c146f0
   +0x000 __VFN_table : ????
   +0x004 m_lastN          : ??
Memory read error 0x77c146f0
0:000> * dt uses the data type passed in when displaying the memory block
0:000> dt KBTest 0x0006fee4
02sample!KBTest
   +0x000 __VFN_table : ????
   +0x004 m_lastN          : ??
0:000> * dt interpret the object type when displaying the memory block
0:000> dt 02sample!gGlobal
gGlobal
   +0x000 m_ref            : 1
```

If you are arbitrarily inspecting a heap block, it is very possible to find in the first few positions a v-table symbol, indicating the type of C++ object located (or previously located) at that address. You can then use the type information to display the object, as shown in the following listing captured at the same break as Listing 2.33.

```
0:000> dc @ecx 14
0006fee4  00401504 ffffffff 0006ff90 01002b28  ...........(+..
0:000> ln 00401504
(00401504)  02sample!KBTest::`vftable'  |  (00401508)  02sample!`string'
Exact matches:
0:000> dt KBTest @ecx
02sample!KBTest
   +0x000 __VFN_table : 0x00401504
   +0x004 m_lastN          : -1
```

In Listing 2.32, the value displayed for the this pointer variable does not look right, as that value is usually reserved for system binary code segments. By looking at the code, you can see that the object is allocated on the stack and should have a value close to the current stack pointer. Let us examine the output from the dv /V this command:

```
0006fee4 @ebp-0x08            this = 0x77c146f0
```

The `this` pointer is stored at the stack location `0006fee4` and is accessed by the function code by using the frame-based register `@ebp-0x08`. The value stored at that address is, in fact, wrong. How can that be? The member function call follows the `__thiscall` convention, meaning that the ecx register contains the `this` pointer value. The register value is later saved in the function stack frame at the location `@ebp-0x08`, meaning that the value becomes accurate after the function executes the following statement:

```
00401878 894df8            mov     dword ptr [ebp-8],ecx
```

The question now becomes this: Why doesn't the compiler generate better symbols for tracking the local variable locations? Try to imagine what will happen in code highly optimized with many variables: The registers are reused and the writes to the function stack frame are minimized, meaning that the compiler will have to generate a new symbol reference for each assembly instruction touching the variables. This means that the symbol files will be larger. This larger file must be moved around and loaded by debuggers at debug time, as well as examined much more often, resulting in poor user experience with minimal benefits.

Until a better solution is found to this problem, you must make sure that the variable value is correct before continuing the investigation. You can then inspect it using the `dt` command, as in the next listing:

```
0:000> dt kbTest @ecx
02sample!KBTest
   +0x000 __VFN_table : 0x00401504
   +0x000 m_lastN       : -1
```

---

**LOCAL VARIABLE VERSUS INPUT PARAMETERS**   Generally, most of the input parameters can be found on the stack and are addressed using the frame-based parameters with a positive offset, such as `@ebp+8`, whereas the local parameters are accessed using negative offsets, such as `@ebp-8`. At times, the compiler reuses the variable storage, which can cause difficulties when debugging.

---

### How Do You Inspect Memory?

When investigating a problem in a debugger, we often have to examine different memory blocks to understand the reason behind the problem and to later prove that the scenario is indeed valid. Because the state of various objects persists in memory, the memory content is equivalent to the object's state. The `display` command takes an address or a range of addresses and displays the content stored at those addresses according to the command arguments.

The most common form of `display` command simply reads formats and displays the data based on the types stored at the address. The debugger does not attempt to guess what data is stored in that location because it will more than likely be wrong in most cases. The user determines the format in which the data should be interpreted. `display` has the following syntax:

```
d[type] [AddressRange]
```

To illustrate various forms of this command, we use the same 02sample.exe, but we start it with multiple command-line arguments. Even if the arguments are ignored, they are still passed to the main function. The function signature is the standard main declaration, as follows:

```
VOID _cdecl wmain( ULONG argc, WCHAR argv[] )
```

In Listing 2.34, we use several forms of the `display` command to inspect the command-line parameters passed in the `argv[]` array after setting a breakpoint in `02sample!wmain` function.

**Listing 2.34** Use of d command

```
0:000> bp 02sample!wmain
0:000> g
Breakpoint 0 hit
0:000> * Get the address of argv parameter
0:000> dv /V argv
0006ff68 @ebp+0x0c              argv = 0x005f0ea0
0:000> * Dump 4 double words at argv address
0:000> dc 0x005f0ea0 14
005f0ea0  005f0eb4 005f0efe 005f0f08 005f0f12  .._..._..._..._.
0:000> dd 0x005f0ea0
005f0ea0  005f0eb4 005f0efe 005f0f08 005f0f12
0:000> * Dump one Unicode string
0:000> du 005f0eb4
005f0eb4  "c:\AWDBIN\WinXP.x86.chk\02sample"
005f0ef4  ".exe"
0:000> * Dump one Unicode string as ASCI string
```

*(continues)*

**Listing 2.34**  Use of d command *(continued)*

```
0:000> da 005f0eb4
005f0eb4  "c"
0:000> * Dump four bytes as byte array
0:000> db 005f0eb4  14
005f0eb4  63 00 3a 00                                           c.:.
0:000> * Dump four bytes in binary format
0:000> * The heading line represent the bit position
0:000> dyb 005f0eb4  14
          76543210 76543210 76543210 76543210
          ──────── ──────── ──────── ────────
005f0eb4  01100011 00000000 00111010 00000000  63 00 3a 00
0:000> * Dump four double words in binary format
0:000> dyd 005f0eb4  14
              3        2        1        0
          10987654 32109876 54321098 76543210
          ──────── ──────── ──────── ────────
005f0eb4  00000000 00111010 00000000 01100011  003a0063
005f0eb8  00000000 01000001 00000000 01011100  0041005c
005f0ebc  00000000 01000100 00000000 01010111  00440057
005f0ec0  00000000 01001001 00000000 01000010  00490042
0:000> * Dump four float numbers
0:000> df 005f0eb4  14
005f0eb4     5.3265975e-039   5.9694362e-039   6.2449357e-039   6.7040837e-039
0:000> * Dump four words numbers
0:000> dw 005f0eb4  14
005f0eb4  0063 003a 005c 0041
0:000> * Dump four float numbers with the character representation
0:000> dW 005f0eb4  14
005f0eb4  0063 003a 005c 0041                        c.:.\.A
0:000> * Dump an invalid memory address
0:000> dc 0 14
00000020  ???????? ???????? ???????? ????????  ????????????????
```

In the listing, the nonprintable characters are displayed as dots (.). This can be a bit confusing when the block really does contain dots. At other times, the debugger displays just a stream of question marks (?) that represent, well…nothing. The address is not valid, and the debugger cannot read anything from that address because the address is not mapped in the target process.

After selecting option '6,' we use thread zero to exemplify other forms of this command. The next form is used to dump the memory area, as well as to treat each element in memory as a symbol and to resolve it. There are three forms of this command, generically referred to as d*s commands: dds treats each group of four bytes as a symbol; dqs treats each group of eight bytes as a symbol; whereas dps uses the length most appropriate for the processor architecture being debugged. Listing 2.35 shows an example of using this command over some stack memory.

**Listing 2.35**   Use of d*s command

```
0:000> dps esp 18
0005fcb4  010017ab 02sample!KBTest::Fibonacci_stdcall+0x2b
0005fcb8  00000001
0005fcbc  00000000
0005fcc0  0006fcd4
0005fcc4  010017d0 02sample!KBTest::Fibonacci_stdcall+0x50
```

The last form is similar to the d*s command. The debugger iterates over the memory area considering it as a sequence of 32- or 64-bit pointers, as the d*s command discussed previously does. It uses each value read from the memory area as a pointer to a different data type, which is subsequently displayed using the type specific format. Not convinced, or confused about the usefulness of this? At the debugger prompt used in Listing 2.34, we use this option to display an array of Unicode strings representing the debugger target command-line arguments.

```
0:000> * Dump an array of UNICODE strings
0:000> dpu 0x005f0ea0 L4
005f0ea0  005f0eb4 "c:\AWDBIN\WinXP.x86.chk\02sample.exe"
005f0ea4  005f0efe "arg1"
005f0ea8  005f0f08 "arg2"
005f0eac  005f0f12 "arg3"
```

This form of command is also highly effective when acting over an unknown memory area. The s command, which stands for search, is another effective command to discover known values in the debugger target memory. The command accepts the searched type and the search value as parameters. The next listing demonstrates the usage of the s command to search an exception code in the process memory. The next listing is captured after selecting the option '1' in 02sample.exe. The s command searches a double-word value in the first 265MB from the virtual address space.

```
0:000> * Run the debugger target after the access violation exception
0:000> g
(53a8.4070): Access violation - code c0000005 (!!! second chance !!!)
eax=00000000 ebx=00000000 ecx=01003008 edx=01003008 esi=00000001 edi=0100373c
eip=010016d0 esp=0006ff34 ebp=0006ff38 iopl=0         nv up ei pl nz na pe nc
```

```
cs=001b  ss=0023  ds=0023  es=0023  fs=003b  gs=0000            efl=00010206
02sample!RaiseAV+0x10:
010016d0 66c7000000      mov     word ptr [eax],0        ds:0023:00000000=????
0:000> * Search for the exception code in the first 256Mb of the address space
0:000> s -d 0 L10000000/4 C0000005
0006fc4c  c0000005 00000000 00000000 010016d0  ................
0006ff80  c0000005 00000000 0006ff70 0006fb30  ........p...O...
0006ffc8  c0000005 76b25984 76b25984 0006ffb8  .....Y.v.Y.v....
```

### Setting a Breakpoint on Access

Not all problems can be found with code breakpoints. For example, there are multiple cases in which one memory location changes less often than the function changing that type of data, as in the case with kernel32!HeapFree API. We are interested when a specific block is deleted, and it is not practical to intercept all calls and break only when the parameter passed to the API matches the address we are concerned about. Nevertheless, the block can be changed as a result of a buffer overrun and not during the function execution.

The problem in this scenario can be solved effectively only by using the processor capability to generate a breakpoint on accessing a specific memory location. The facility is controlled by using the ba, or breakpoint on access, debugger command. The address monitored by breakpoint on access facilities must be aligned with the data size monitored by the breakpoint.

Listing 2.36 contains the Global class definition used in 02sample.exe to declare the global variable, gGlobal. The class has one member variable, m_ref, that is changed every time the constructor or the destructor of this class is executed. The class is hypothetically used in many other places besides the global static variable, but our goal is to find out which stack changes the m_ref member of the global static variable.

**Listing 2.36**   gGlobal declaration

```
class Global
{
public:
    int m_ref;
    Global():m_ref(1){};
    ~Global()
        {
            m_ref = 0;
        };
} gGlobal;
```

After a quick look at the class definition, we can try to set a breakpoint on the con-structor and the destructor of `Global` class, under the assumption that we can easi-ly understand what object is changed. Since the destructor is called numerous times, the process gets costly and prone to errors.

However, the memory address of the object, and implicitly the memory address of the `m_ref` member, is known in each debugging session. The address is then used to set a breakpoint on access, monitoring the `m_ref` memory address for writing operations. The breakpoint is set to monitor four bytes that store the `m_ref` member. Listing 2.37 shows how `ba` can be used to solve the problem in a single line. The `ba` command requires the access mode and the data size that will be monitored by the processor.

**Listing 2.37**   Typical use of the ba command

```
0:000> * Getting the address of the variable to be monitored
0:000> dt gGlobal
   +0x000 m_ref          : 0
0:000> * Setting a breakpoint when m_ref memory address is changed
0:000> * The processor monitors writes in the four bytes following
0:000> ba w4 gGlobal+0
0:000> bl
 0 e 0040301c w 4 0001 (0001)  0:**** 02sample!gGlobal
0:000> g
Breakpoint 0 hit
eax=0040301c ebx=00000000 ecx=0040301c edx=775ec534 esi=00000001 edi=003f2bd0
eip=004018c2 esp=0006fefc ebp=0006ff00 iopl=0         nv up ei pl nz na po nc
cs=001b  ss=0023  ds=0023  es=0023  fs=003b  gs=0000            efl=00000202
02sample!Global::~Global+0x12:
004018c2 8be5            mov     esp,ebp
0:000> * The break is happening after the change happened
0:000> ub . l1
02sample!Global::~Global+0xc:
004018bc c70000000000    mov     dword ptr [eax],0
```

Breakpoint on access works equally well from the kernel mode debugger.

### *What Does That Memory Location Contain?*

While debugging, there are a lot of pointers in the objects as well as on the stack for which we cannot quickly guess what they represent. Although it is easier to distin-guish kernel space addresses than user mode addresses, it is not easy to distinguish an address representing the stack from an address representing a block on the heap. The debugger team created an extension command useful to solve this problem, accessed by !address <address>. The command is extremely useful in user mode debugging. Typical output is shown in Listing 2.38.

### Listing 2.38  !address debugger command example

```
0:000> !address .
    7c900000 : 7c901000 - 0007b000
                        Type      01000000 MEM_IMAGE
                        Protect   00000020 PAGE_EXECUTE_READ
                        State     00001000 MEM_COMMIT
                        Usage     RegionUsageImage
                        FullPath  ntdll.dll
0:000> !address @esp
    00030000 : 0006e000 - 00002000
                        Type      00020000 MEM_PRIVATE
                        Protect   00000004 PAGE_READWRITE
                        State     00001000 MEM_COMMIT
                        Usage     RegionUsageStack
                        Pid.Tid   1124.1568
0:000> !address 00080000
    00080000 : 00080000 - 00004000
                        Type      00020000 MEM_PRIVATE
                        Protect   00000004 PAGE_READWRITE
                        State     00001000 MEM_COMMIT
                        Usage     RegionUsageHeap
                        Handle    00080000
0:000> !address 1000
    00000000 : 00000000 - 00010000
                        Type      00000000
                        Protect   00000001 PAGE_NOACCESS
                        State     00010000 MEM_FREE
                        Usage     RegionUsageFree
```

The first time, the command parameter is a code address (the current execution address); the second time, it is the stack address, followed by a heap address, and finally an invalid address. The extension command can process other types of memory, as well.

When no address is provided, the extension searches and enumerates all memory zones with all available details, as shown in Listing 2.39. Afterward, it computes a summary with the memory usage based on the type of section, on the access mode, and on the page sharing mode. A simplified output analyzing the process space can be seen in the following listing.

## Listing 2.39    !address command

```
0:000> !address
    00000000 : 00000000 - 00010000
                        Type      00000000
                        Protect   00000001 PAGE_NOACCESS
                        State     00010000 MEM_FREE
                        Usage     RegionUsageFree
...
7ffdf000 : 7ffdf000 - 00001000
                        Type      00020000 MEM_PRIVATE
                        Protect   00000004 PAGE_READWRITE
                        State     00001000 MEM_COMMIT
                        Usage     RegionUsageTeb
                        Pid.Tid   1124.1568
...
---------- Usage SUMMARY -------------
    TotSize (       KB)   Pct(Tots) Pct(Busy)   Usage
     1d4000 (     1872) : 00.09%    32.16%    : RegionUsageIsVAD
    7fa41000 ( 2091268) : 99.72%    00.00%    : RegionUsageFree
     266000 (     2456) : 00.12%    42.20%    : RegionUsageImage
      40000 (      256) : 00.01%    04.40%    : RegionUsageStack
       1000 (        4) : 00.00%    00.07%    : RegionUsageTeb
     130000 (     1216) : 00.06%    20.89%    : RegionUsageHeap
          0 (        0) : 00.00%    00.00%    : RegionUsagePageHeap
       1000 (        4) : 00.00%    00.07%    : RegionUsagePeb
       1000 (        4) : 00.00%    00.07%    : RegionUsageProcessParametrs
       2000 (        8) : 00.00%    00.14%    : RegionUsageEnvironmentBlock
    Tot: 7fff0000 (2097088 KB) Busy: 005af000 (5820 KB)

---------- Type SUMMARY --------------
    TotSize (       KB)   Pct(Tots)  Usage
    7fa41000 ( 2091268) : 99.72%   : <free>
     266000 (     2456) : 00.12%   : MEM_IMAGE
     1d4000 (     1872) : 00.09%   : MEM_MAPPED
     175000 (     1492) : 00.07%   : MEM_PRIVATE

---------- State SUMMARY --------------
    TotSize (       KB)   Pct(Tots)  Usage
     34e000 (     3384) : 00.16%   : MEM_COMMIT
    7fa41000 ( 2091268) : 99.72%   : MEM_FREE
     261000 (     2436) : 00.12%   : MEM_RESERVE

Largest free region: Base 00405000 - Size 75c7b000 (1929708 KB)
```

## Other Exploratory Commands

Another common question that debugger users ask is what command-line parameters have been used to start the current debugger target.

This information is stored in the process environment block (PEB) and can be easily obtained by using the !peb extension command as shown in Listing 2.40. The command interprets the PEB showing the command line, the location of all loaded DLLs, the environment variables, and much more.

### Listing 2.40  Obtaining the process PEB

```
0:000> !peb
PEB at 7ffdd000
    InheritedAddressSpace:    No
    ReadImageFileExecOptions: No
    BeingDebugged:            Yes
    ImageBaseAddress:         00400000
    Ldr                       00181ea0
    Ldr.Initialized:          Yes
    Ldr.InInitializationOrderModuleList: 00181f58 . 001821a0
    Ldr.InLoadOrderModuleList:           00181ee0 . 00182190
    Ldr.InMemoryOrderModuleList:         00181ee8 . 00182198
          Base TimeStamp                     Module
        400000 453bf190 Oct 22 15:32:48 2006 C:\AWDBIN\WinXP.x86.chk\02sample.exe
      7c900000 411096b4 Aug 04 00:56:36 2004 C:\WINDOWS\system32\ntdll.dll
      7c800000 44ab9a84 Jul 05 03:55:00 2006 C:\WINDOWS\system32\kernel32.dll
      77c10000 41109752 Aug 04 00:59:14 2004 C:\WINDOWS\system32\msvcrt.dll
      76080000 41109751 Aug 04 00:59:13 2004 C:\WINDOWS\system32\msvcp60.dll
    SubSystemData:     00000000
    ProcessHeap:       00080000
    ProcessParameters: 00020000
    WindowTitle:  'C:\AWDBIN\WinXP.x86.chk\02sample.exe'
    ImageFile:    'C:\AWDBIN\WinXP.x86.chk\02sample.exe'
    CommandLine:  'C:\AWDBIN\WinXP.x86.chk\02sample.exe'
    DllPath:
'C:\AWDBIN\WinXP.x86.chk;C:\WINDOWS\system32;C:\WINDOWS\system;C:\WINDOWS;.;c:\Debug.x
86\winext\arcade;C:\WINDDK\3790~1.183\bin\x86;C:\WINDDK\3790~1.183\bin;C:\WINDDK\3790~
1.183\bin\x86\drvfast\scripts;C:\Perl\bin\;C:\WINDOWS\system32;C:\WINDOWS;C:\WINDOWS\
System32\Wbem;'
    Environment:  00010000
    =::=::\
    =C:= C:\
    =ExitCode=00000000
...
    OS=Windows_NT
```

```
       Path=c:\Debug.x86\winext\arcade;C:\WINDDK\3790~1.183\bin\x86;C:\WINDDK\3
790~1.183\bin;C:\WINDDK\3790~1.183\bin\x86\drvfast\scripts;C:\Perl\bin\;C:\WINDO
WS\system32;C:\WINDOWS;C:\WINDOWS\System32\Wbem;
       PATHEXT=.COM;.EXE;.BAT;.CMD;.VBS;.VBE;.JS;.JSE;.WSF;.WSH
       PREFAST_ROOT=C:\WINDDK\3790~1.183\bin\x86\drvfast
...
       _NT_TOOLS_VERSION=0x700
```

The !peb extension command depends on the current process context that can be changed using one of the options explained in the later section, "Changing the Context."

Another piece of useful information is the thread environment block that can be displayed using the !teb extension command. Although it is possible to display any thread's TEB by specifying the address as a parameter to the command extension, most commonly the extension command detects the TEB address from the current thread, as you can see in Listing 2.41.

**Listing 2.41**   Obtaining the thread TEB

```
0:000> !teb
TEB at 7ffdf000
    ExceptionList:         0006ff34
    StackBase:             00070000
    StackLimit:            0006e000
    SubSystemTib:          00000000
    FiberData:             00001e00
    ArbitraryUserPointer:  00000000
    Self:                  7ffdf000
    EnvironmentPointer:    00000000
    ClientId:              000013b4 . 00001184
    RpcHandle:             00000000
    Tls Storage:           00000000
    PEB Address:           7ffdd000
    LastErrorValue:        203
    LastStatusValue:       c0000100
    Count Owned Locks:     0
    HardErrorMode:         0
```

The !teb extension command depends on the current thread context that can be changed using one of the options explained in the later section, "Changing the Context."

Win32 APIs do not always return the status code to the caller using the return value or one of the output parameters. In fact, most APIs store the last error code in a thread-specific location preallocated in the thread environment block, accessed programmatically by using the kernel32!GetLastError API.

The value can be inspected immediately after an API failure by using the !gle extension command. This command extracts the value and displays the formatted string to the user. The command also displays the last NTSTATUS error that represents the error previously returned from a system API.

```
0:000> !gle
LastErrorValue: (Win32) 0xcb (203) - The system could not find the environment option
that was entered.
LastStatusValue: (NTSTATUS) 0xc0000100 - Indicates the specified environment variable
name was not found in the specified environment block.
```

The command reads the error code from the current thread contexts.

The last useful command in this category is the simple <enter> or <CTRL>+M key that repeats the last entered commands. This is useful only when the last command changes some internal state in the debugger, as is the case with d or u commands, and the operation is repeated for the next memory block.

## Context-Changing Commands

The following set of commands affect the state of the debugger target and are normally used to watch the debugger target in a controlled execution mode or to change the view interpreted by various extension commands.

### Tracing Code Execution

t is the basic command used to execute the code step-by-step, also known as tracing. When we trace the code in assembly mode, it steps over a single assembly instruction at a time. When the debugger runs in source mode, each step executes multiple assembly instructions representing a single line in source mode. The mode can be controlled by the source option mode command, as you can see in the following listing:

```
0:000> l+t
Source options are 1:
     1/t - Step/trace by source line
0:000> l-t
Source options are 0:
    None
```

Chapter 3 explains the mechanisms used by the debugger to implement the tracing functionality in assembly mode. Source mode tracing is possible only in the modules for which the private symbols are available; otherwise, the debugger switches silently into assembly mode. Tracing usefulness is limited to cases in which the register changes must be closely watched or the code execution must step into a method call instead of executing it entirely as a single statement, as you can see in the following listing:

```
02sample!KBTest::Fibonacci_stdcall+0x4b:
004017ab e8b0ffffff     call    02sample!KBTest::Fibonacci_stdcall (00401760)
0:000> t
02sample!KBTest::Fibonacci_stdcall:
00401760 8bff           mov     edi,edi
```

When tracing a multithreaded application, any thread context switch schedules the executions of a different thread on the current processor. While executing the new thread, the debugger can encounter a breakpoint or a different event requiring user attention, and the command can return with a different active thread and stack. The engineer can prevent the context switch by prefixing the trace command with the desired thread number. For example, the ~.t command executes one statement on the current thread, while other threads are suspended.

---

**SOURCE-LEVEL TRACING VERSUS ASSEMBLY LEVEL TRACING** Many developers using tracing at the source code level have a really hard time debugging highly optimized code, as the debugger jumps back and forth between source lines. The explanation lies in the number of processor statements the compiler generates for every source line and the way they are intermixed with code corresponding to another line, to maximize processor utilization. In such cases, moving from source-level debugging to assembly-level debugging brings back the predictability of debugging tracing.

---

### *Stepping Over a Function Execution*

The p command is functionally similar to that of the trace command for all statements except for the function calls. The p command treats the entire function call as a single statement and executes it in its entirety.

```
0:000> p
02sample!KBTest::Fibonacci_stdcall+0x4b:
004017ab e8b0ffffff     call    02sample!KBTest::Fibonacci_stdcall (00401760)
0:000> p
```

```
02sample!KBTest::Fibonacci_stdcall+0x50:
004017b0 03c6              add       eax,esi
```

When debugging a complex piece of code, we want only to validate the variable's value at some important point in the code execution, such as the place where the code calls a new function. At this point, both the parameters to the function can be checked, as well as the return values from the function after it is executed.

pc is the command that executes the entirety of the code until the next subroutine call. It can be combined nicely with p when only the function results are important or with t when more careful tracing is required. With the debugger stopped right before the function call, all parameters passed to the function can be inspected. If necessary, the parameters can be changed using the e or r commands; this is usually done to simulate various failures.

```
0:000>t
02sample!wmain:
01001c90 8bff              mov       edi,edi
0:000> pc
02sample!wmain+0xe:
01001c9e e81d000000        call      02sample!AppInfo::AppInfo (01001cc0)
0:000> p
02sample!wmain+0x13:
01001ca3 8d4dfc            lea       ecx,[ebp-4]
```

## Continuing Code Execution

When the debugger waits in command mode, the debugger target does not change its state at all. To resume the execution of the debugger target, the user must explicitly tell the debugger to continue the execution. When the current break has been caused by an exception and the debugger cleared the exception condition, the continuation should be done using the form of the command telling the system that the exception has been handled. A very good description of these details can be found in Chapter 3.

g is the basic command used to release the debugger target, and it works equally well in user mode and kernel mode debugger. By far the most used command, in the simplest form, it just continues, unconditionally, the execution of the debugger target.

The second most used form, g <address>, is used to continue the debugger target execution until a specific address is hit, where the execution stops in the debugger. The command is equivalent with setting a breakpoint, executing the debug target until the breakpoint is hit, and removing the breakpoint.

gu is another common form used to continue the execution of the debugger target until the current function finishes and returns to the caller. The command is aware of the current stack pointer, so it can be used to return from a recursive function call.

In the user mode debugger, all forms of the execute command can be directed to a specific thread instead of the entire process. When the thread identifier is specified, all threads but the specified one are frozen until the debugger target stops again in the debugger.

```
0:000> k3
ChildEBP RetAddr
0006fc64 00401792 02sample!KBTest::Fibonacci_stdcall+0x50
0006fc78 00401792 02sample!KBTest::Fibonacci_stdcall+0x42
0006fc8c 00401792 02sample!KBTest::Fibonacci_stdcall+0x42
0:000> * Execute until returning from the current function
0:000> gu
eax=00000001 ebx=7ffd9000 ecx=00000001 edx=00000000 esi=00000000 edi=00000000
eip=00401792 esp=0006fc70 ebp=0006fc78 iopl=0         nv up ei pl nz na po nc
cs=001b  ss=0023  ds=0023  es=0023  fs=003b  gs=0000            efl=00000202
02sample!KBTest::Fibonacci_stdcall+0x42:
00401792 8bf0             mov     esi,eax
0:000> * Unassemble the function to find a good spot to execute to
0:000> u . 14
02sample!KBTest::Fibonacci_stdcall+0x42:
00401792 8bf0             mov     esi,eax
00401794 8b5508           mov     edx,dword ptr [ebp+8]
00401797 83ea02           sub     edx,2
0040179a 52               push    edx
0:000> * Execute until 0040179a address is reached
0:000> g 0040179a
eax=00000001 ebx=7ffd9000 ecx=00000001 edx=00000001 esi=00000001 edi=00000000
eip=0040179a esp=0006fc70 ebp=0006fc78 iopl=0         nv up ei pl nz na po nc
cs=001b  ss=0023  ds=0023  es=0023  fs=003b  gs=0000            efl=00000202
02sample!KBTest::Fibonacci_stdcall+0x4a:
0040179a 52               push    edx
0:000>  * Execute until returning from the current function, freezing all threads but
0.
0:000> ~0 gu
eax=00000002 ebx=7ffd9000 ecx=00000001 edx=00000001 esi=00000000 edi=00000000
eip=00401792 esp=0006fc84 ebp=0006fc8c iopl=0         nv up ei pl nz na po nc
cs=001b  ss=0023  ds=0023  es=0023  fs=003b  gs=0000            efl=00000202
02sample!KBTest::Fibonacci_stdcall+0x42:
00401792 8bf0             mov     esi,eax
```

All execute commands described so far have matching buttons in the WinDbg toolbar.

### Tracing and Watching a Function Execution

wt is a very useful command that can be used instead of the p command to step over a function. The command obtains statistical information about the called function, such as what functions are called inside, how many times they are called, and how many processor instructions are executed inside the function itself. The command accepts multiple parameters—the nesting level –1 being the most important. Listing 2.42 shows the output of the wt command while executing the 02sample!AppInfo::AppInfo constructor.

**Listing 2.42**   Trace and watch function execution

```
0:000> g
Breakpoint 2 hit
02sample!wmain:
01001b90 8bff            mov     edi,edi
0:000> pc
02sample!wmain+0xe:
01001b9e e81d000000      call    02sample!AppInfo::AppInfo (01001bc0)
0:000> wt -11
   13      0 [  0] 02sample!AppInfo::AppInfo

13 instructions were executed in 12 events (0 from other threads)

Function Name                       Invocations MinInst MaxInst AvgInst
02sample!AppInfo::AppInfo                     1      13      13      13

0 system calls were executed
```

Regardless of how the code execution resumes, the processor context changes each time it executes a new assembly instruction. Sometimes, the context must be explicitly set in order to evaluate register values or a local variable.

### Changing the Context

To understand how the context must be changed, we start by defining what the context is in different situations. The most common use of the term *context* refers to the set of registers representing the processor state at a specific moment, known as register context. Chapter 3 describes the use of the context as related to the exception dispatching.

The register context when the exception was generated is saved by the exception dispatcher code on the stack and can be used to restore the register values at the

moment when the exception was raised. How can that context be found? The easiest
way is to grab it from the parameters of various functions used in the exception dispatching process or by searching the stack for the context information. Regardless of
how the register context is found, it can be set as the current context using the .cxr
<context address> command, as follows. After we selected the option to gener-
ate an access violation exception, the investigation continued when the access violation exception occurred.

```
0:000> * Search for full context signature in the first 256Mb of the address space
0:000> s -d 0 L10000000/4 0001003f
0006fc1c  0001003f 00000000 00000000 00000000  ?..............
0:000> * Set the context found at this address
0:000> .cxr 0006fc1c
eax=00000000 ebx=7ffde000 ecx=00401174 edx=77c61b18 esi=7c9118f1 edi=00011970
eip=0040130a esp=0006fee8 ebp=0006fef0 iopl=0         nv up ei pl nz na pe nc
cs=001b  ss=0023  ds=0023  es=0023  fs=003b  gs=0000         efl=00000206
02sample!RaiseAV+0x1a:
0040130a c60000          mov     byte ptr [eax],0         ds:0023:00000000=??
```

After we set the context, all commands depending on the context use that information as a base. (k shows the stack for the current context; dv shows the local variable
for the current function.)

In user mode, the context used by the debugger to perform various operations
can also be changed by selecting a thread different from the current one. The debugger identifies each thread by a thread number, which is an index starting from a value
of 0. To activate a particular thread, we must use the thread number in the ~<thread
index>s command. After the change, all commands are executed in the context of
the new thread. Some debugger commands can be prefixed by the thread index to
execute in a different thread context without changing the active thread.

The thread index does not have meaning for the application. The application knows
only thread identifiers obtained from various APIs, which are usually stored in various
locations in the application. Instead of listing all threads, finding the thread index corresponding to a thread identifier, and using that index for all thread-related commands,
it is possible to use the thread identifier directly. ~~[ThreadIdentifier] is the
equivalent command that uses the thread identifier. We use the same sample, with the
option to generate a stack overflow, to experiment with those commands, as illustrated
here:

```
0:002> ~
   0  Id: 16cc.f80 Suspend: 1 Teb: 7ffdf000 Unfrozen
   1  Id: 16cc.1248 Suspend: 1 Teb: 7ffde000 Unfrozen
```

```
.  2  Id: 16cc.10e4 Suspend: 1 Teb: 7ffdd000 Unfrozen
   3  Id: 16cc.111c Suspend: 1 Teb: 7ffdc000 Unfrozen
0:002> * dot sign marks the current thread
0:002> ~0s
eax=0006fec8 ebx=00000000 ecx=0000bd09 edx=7c90eb94 esi=0006fdc8 edi=00000000
eip=7c90eb94 esp=0006fd7c ebp=0006fd9c iopl=0         nv up ei pl zr na pe nc
cs=001b  ss=0023  ds=0023  es=0023  fs=003b  gs=0000             efl=00000246
ntdll!KiFastSystemCallRet:
7c90eb94 c3              ret
0:002> ~~[f80] s
eax=0006fec8 ebx=00000000 ecx=0000bd09 edx=7c90eb94 esi=0006fdc8 edi=00000000
eip=7c90eb94 esp=0006fd7c ebp=0006fd9c iopl=0         nv up ei pl zr na pe nc
cs=001b  ss=0023  ds=0023  es=0023  fs=003b  gs=0000             efl=00000246
ntdll!KiFastSystemCallRet:
7c90eb94 c3              ret
0:000> * # sign is the thread that broke initially in the debugger
0:000> ~
.  0  Id: 16cc.f80 Suspend: 1 Teb: 7ffdf000 Unfrozen
   1  Id: 16cc.1248 Suspend: 1 Teb: 7ffde000 Unfrozen
#  2  Id: 16cc.10e4 Suspend: 1 Teb: 7ffdd000 Unfrozen
Id: 16cc.111c Suspend: 1 Teb: 7ffdc000 Unfrozen
0:000> k
ChildEBP RetAddr
0006fd94 77370190 ntdll!KiFastSystemCallRet
0006fd98 77377fdf ntdll!NtRequestWaitReplyPort+0xc
0006fdb8 760416f4 ntdll!CsrClientCallServer+0xc2
0006fea4 760415ef kernel32!GetConsoleInput+0xd2
0006fec4 75e4f529 kernel32!ReadConsoleInputW+0x1a
0006ff04 75e4f5ef msvcrt!_getwch_nolock+0xa8
0006ff38 01001d50 msvcrt!_getwch+0x1d
0006ff50 01001cab 02sample!AppInfo::Loop+0x70
0006ff5c 01002076 02sample!wmain+0x1b
0006ffa0 76033833 02sample!__wmainCRTStartup+0x102
0006ffac 7734a9bd kernel32!BaseThreadInitThunk+0xe
0006ffec 00000000 ntdll!_RtlUserThreadStart+0x23
0:000> * dv command depends on the last .frame command
0:000> .frame 8
08 0006ff5c 01002076 02sample!wmain+0x1b
0:000> dv
        argc = 1
        argv = 0x001b2d58
     appInfo = class AppInfo
```

In the previous listing, we also use the .frame command, which changes the context and affects which local variables are displayed using the dv command. The command works equally well in user mode and with the kernel mode debugger.

The frame command is internally executed by WinDbg every time a different function is selected from the Calls windows. When a different thread is selected from the Processes and Threads window, the current context is changed to that thread.

Specific only to kernel mode are register contexts captured when threads transition into kernel mode identifiable in each thread stack as trap frames. Each such captured trap can be used as a parameter to the `.trap` command. All commands used afterward are dependent on the last trap context.

Each thread has its own state whose context can be set as the current register context, regardless of its running state, using the `.thread` command. This assumes that the debugger target is stopped in the kernel mode debugger, so each thread context is fixed in time. In the kernel mode debugger, each thread can potentially be part of a different process. The debugger needs process-specific information, such as the symbol file information, to interpret the stack and execute various commands. This is called the process context. Unless the thread examined by the user is in the same process that caused the break, the process context must be switched to the process owning the thread. The process context is a page directory used to translate the virtual addresses into physical addresses required to read the virtual space content.

User mode symbols are loaded based on the current process context, and they are used until the debugger reloads the user mode symbols. As a result, each time the thread or the trap we are interested in is associated with a different process, we must make sure that the process context is correct and that the user mode symbols corresponding to the current process are loaded.

The next listing uses all those concepts on a kernel mode debugger session that has been stopped in an arbitrary location using the CTRL+C keys. The thread we focus on has been selected from the list of threads ready to run next, displayed by the `!ready` extension command.

```
kd> !ready
Processor 0: Ready Threads at priority 10
    THREAD ffb9a020 Cid 037c.04d4  Teb: 7ffa4000 Win32Thread: 00000000 READY
kd> * Setting the current thread, change the active process and reload user mode
symbols
kd> .thread /p /r ffb9a020
Implicit thread is now ffb9a020
Implicit process is now 812532d8
.cache forcedecodeuser done
Loading User Symbols
.......................................................................................
....................................
............
kd> * Debugger tells that context has been set explicitly
kd> k
```

```
   *** Stack trace for last set context - .thread/.cxr resets it
ChildEBP RetAddr
f72973f0 806f4070 nt!KiDispatchInterrupt+0x7f
f72973f0 faa0d8c7 hal!HalpDispatchInterrupt2ndEntry+0x1b
f729746c 804f82ae Ntfs!NtfsAllocateFcbTableEntry
...
kd> * Display full thread information
kd> !thread ffb9a020
THREAD ffb9a020  Cid 037c.04d4  Teb: 7ffa4000 Win32Thread: 00000000 READY
Impersonation token:  e1a54278 (Level Impersonation)
Owning Process            812532d8       Image:           svchost.exe
Wait Start TickCount      3721769        Ticks: 2 (0:00:00:00.020)
Context Switch Count      523
UserTime                  00:00:00.0260
KernelTime                00:00:06.0329
Win32 Start Address schedsvc!PfSvProcessTraceThread (0x7730a597)
Start Address kernel32!BaseThreadStartThunk (0x7c810856)
Stack Init f7298000 Current f72973dc Base f7298000 Limit f7295000 Call 0
Priority 8 BasePriority 8 PriorityDecrement 0 DecrementCount 16
ChildEBP RetAddr  Args to Child
f72973f0 806f4070 00000000 f7297484 faa0d8c7 nt!KiDispatchInterrupt+0x7f
f72973f0 faa0d8c7 00000000 f7297484 faa0d8c7 hal!HalpDispatchInterrupt2ndEntry+0x1b
(TrapFrame @ f72973fc)
f729746c 804f82ae 812943c8 0000001c e13afcc8 Ntfs!NtfsAllocateFcbTableEntry
f7297484 faa3c180 812943c8 f72974c8 0000000c
nt!RtlInsertElementGenericTableFullAvl+0x1f
f7297520 faa3c9ec f7297880 81294100 00004cae Ntfs!NtfsCreateFcb+0x20c
...
kd> * Set the context from a TrapFrame address
kd> .trap f7297100
ErrCode = 00000000
eax=ffbb7201 ebx=f7297228 ecx=ffb9a020 edx=ffb9a020 esi=ffbb71e8 edi=f7297230
eip=804f61b8 esp=f7297174 ebp=f72971e8 iopl=0         nv up ei pl nz na po nc
cs=0008  ss=0010  ds=0894  es=715c  fs=7164  gs=7228          efl=00000202
nt!CcPinFileData+0x3ca:
804f61b8 e925abffff     jmp    nt!CcPinFileData+0x3fc (804f0ce2)
kd> k
  *** Stack trace for last set context - .thread/.cxr resets it
ChildEBP RetAddr
f72971e8 8057a5a7 nt!CcPinFileData+0x3ca
f729725c faa34017 nt!CcPinMappedData+0xf4
f729727c faa35045 Ntfs!NtfsPinMappedData+0x4f
...
kd> * Make sure the current process and symbols are correct. .trap does not fix them
```

```
kd> .process /p /r 812532d8
Implicit process is now 812532d8
.cache forcedecodeuser done
Loading User Symbols
```

. . . . . . . . . . . . . . . . . . . . . . . . . . . . . . . . . . . . . . . . . . . . . . . . . . . . . . . . . . . . . . . . . . . . . . . . . . . . . . . . . . . . . . . . . . . . . . . . .

The command used to examine local variables, as well as the stacks, is reset after each context switch. When the user mode symbols are not loaded correctly, all commands depending on the symbols have unpredictable behavior.

### Entering Value

Although most of the debugger commands are not destructive, the capability to change some of the debugger target memory can be considered a dangerous one. What it does is clear enough; it allows you to change the memory content at a specific virtual address or at a series of addresses.

Most of the time, we change a global variable required for triggering a specific change in the system or perhaps a local variable that was not initialized properly as a result of some bug. The command has multiple forms that must be selected according to the type of data we want to change; the eb command is used to enter a series of bytes, but a series of DWORDs must be entered using the ed command. The next listing demonstrates the usage of the ed command to change first a local variable and then a global variable. The next listing is captured after selecting option '6' in 02sample.exe.

```
0:000> * We want to change the input parameter for testing purposes
0:000> dv /V
0006fc60 @ebp+0x08              n = 0
0:000> * Change a dword variable using its name as address
0:000> ed n 3
0:000> * Change a dword variable using its storage address
0:000> ed @ebp+0x08 5
0:000> dv /V
0006fc60 @ebp+0x08              n = 5
0:000> * Change a dword global variable
0:000> ed kernel32!g_dwLastErrorToBreakOn 5
```

The command is powerful enough to change the code being executed on the debugger target. Although this is not a common operation, we need to understand when or how to use it. In our experience, the most common case is an overactive assert function that prevents us from continuing a specific operation, and the turnaround time of making the fix in the source code relatively large. In such cases, we will patch the debugger target by replacing the assert code with a series of NOP operations so that the code will just skip over the former assert.

```
0:000> * After returning from breakpoint we examine the previous instruction
0:000> ub . l1
02sample!KBTest::Fibonacci_stdcall+0x25:
00401785 ff1508104000    call    dword ptr [02sample!_imp__DebugBreak (00401008)]
0:000> * DebugBreak call takes 6 bytes that will be replaced with opcode 90
0:000> eb .-6 90 90 90 90 90 90
0:000> ub . L6
02sample!KBTest::Fibonacci_stdcall+0x25:
00401785 90              nop
00401786 90              nop
00401787 90              nop
00401788 90              nop
00401789 90              nop
0040178a 90              nop
```

Armed with a minimal set of commands that enable memory content to be changed, any debugger session is easily accessible because it becomes controllable. In the next section, we describe some commands without an apparent connection to the debugger that have been proven to save precious debugging time.

## Other Helper Commands

Not all commands interact with the debugger target, yet they still provide useful functionality to the user. We will enumerate a few of them, along with some sample usage.

One very common situation encountered in debugging is to have an error code on the screen without having any idea what it means. The !error extension command takes an error and tries to find the message code associated with it.

```
0:000> !error 0x80070005
Error code: (HRESULT) 0x80070005 (2147942405) - Access is denied.
0:000> !error 5
Error code: (Win32) 0x5 (5) - Access is denied.
```

In some cases, it is not possible to start the full GUI just to see the registry values, as is the case with remote debugger sessions. The solution is yet another debugger extension command, !dreg, that can be used to investigate the registry values on the machine being debugged.

The command accepts multiple options, which are very well described in the debugger documentation or by the command itself running in the help mode:

```
!dreg
```

Because the parameters accepted by the `!dreg` extension command are long, they are often copied from a note or previous debugging session. It is not unusual to have some files containing a list of commands used every time before investigating each debugger session.

```
0:000> !dreg Software\Microsoft\Windows NT\CurrentVersion\AeDebug!*
Value: "Auto" - REG_SZ: "0"
------------------------------------
Value: "Debugger" - REG_SZ: ""C:\WINDOWS\system32\vsjitdebugger.exe" -p %ld -e %
ld"
------------------------------------
Value: "UserDebuggerHotKey" - REG_DWORD: 0 = 0x00000000
------------------------------------
```

While debugging a piece of code, we are faced with the challenge of performing some calculations, not too complex but hard to do manually. The built-in expression evaluator can be invoked using the question (?) character followed by the mathematical MASM expression to be evaluated. The debugger also provides a C++ expression evaluator invoked by using a double question (??) string. The usage of both expression evaluators is similar and predictable as long as no symbolic names are involved. To better understand the differences, we will examine both the object information using the `this` pointer variable and the stack information associated with the current thread. The class used has a single integer member at offset 4, as follows:

```
class KBTest
{
    int m_lastN;
};
```

The MASM expression evaluator considers each symbol equal with its memory address; in other words, each symbol is a pointer. To obtain the value from that location, we must dereference the pointer using one of the dereference expressions. Based on the pointer type, different operators must be used for this: `poi` for an architecture specific pointer size, `qwo` for a quad word pointer, `dwo` for a double-word pointer, `wo` for a word pointer, and `by` for a byte pointer.

Next, we have a simple expression used to show the value of the `m_lastN` member value folowed by an expression to calculate the stack size for the current thread, using an MASM expression.

```
0:000>dt this
Local var @ 0x6fee4 Type KBTest*
```

```
0x0006ff20
   +0x000 __VFN_table : 0x00401504
   +0x004 m_lastN        : 32
0:000> ? poi(poi(this)+4)
Evaluate expression: 32 = 00000020
0:000> ?poi(@$teb+4)-poi(@$teb+8)
Evaluate expression: 8192 = 00002000
```

The same calculation can be performed using the C++ expression evaluator, which uses the type information to perform the necessary indirections. Note that the evaluator understands the type for each pseudo-register value.

```
0:000> ?? this->m_lastN
int 32
0:000> ?? int(@$teb->NtTib.StackBase) - int(@$teb->NtTib.StackLimit)
int 8192
```

Last, the expression evaluator can be used to perform conversions of numbers in different numeric systems from decimal to hexadecimal formats.

```
0:000> ? 0y1010
Evaluate expression: 10 = 0000000a
0:000> ? 0n255
Evaluate expression: 255 = 000000ff
0:000> ? 0xFF
Evaluate expression: 255 = 000000ff
```

When more complicated conversions are necesary, the user must use the `.formats` command, which shows the parameter in various formats, as shown in the following:

```
0:000> .formats 44444444
Evaluate expression:
  Hex:      44444444
  Decimal:  1145324612
  Octal:    10421042104
  Binary:   01000100 01000100 01000100 01000100
  Chars:    DDDD
  Time:     Mon Apr 17 18:43:32 2006
  Float:    low 785.067 high 0
  Double:   5.65866e-315
```

Some readers ask how they can remember all the commands described in this chapter. The debugger team comes to the rescue by providing a simple command-line equivalent to the F1 key, the `.hh  <string>` command. This starts the debugger help in search mode with the string already entered in the search box. Just select the topic you aren't sure about and want more information for. For example, the .hh log command entered in the debugger console starts the help at the topic, describing how the user can keep logs with the debugger activity so that they can be used later as reference.

A multitude of extensions can be used in specific situations; be curious about various commands and extension commands used elsewhere in this book. Don't forget to check this book's Web site for various tips and real-life scenarios that we were unable to cover in this book.

## Examples

When debugging an application, we must combine the facilities provided by the debugger with our knowledge about the debugger target to achieve results. This section shows a few common cases demonstrating the capabilities of such combinations.

### Conditional Breakpoints

With each breakpoint, the debugger accepts a command that is executed every time the debugger target execution triggers that breakpoint. This facility can be used to create a powerful conditional breakpoint. We often have a function that fails occasionally, and we want to stop the execution in that point and perform further investigations. This can be achieved by conditionally executing the g command when the error condition is not detected after each function's execution. In the following listing, we set a breakpoint that performs these steps: It executes the current function; it tests the function result afterward; and if the result is different from the value 1, the debugger is told to execute another g command. When the function returns the value 1, the debugger waits at the command prompt.

```
0:000> bp 02sample!KBTest::Fibonacci_stdcall "gu;.if (eax!=1) {g}"
0:000> g
eax=00000001 ebx=00000000 ecx=00000001 edx=0100302c esi=00000001 edi=0100373c
eip=010017c2 esp=0006fccc ebp=0006fcd4 iopl=0         nv up ei pl zr na pe nc
cs=001b  ss=0023  ds=0023  es=0023  fs=003b  gs=0000            efl=00000246
02sample!KBTest::Fibonacci_stdcall+0x42:
010017c2 8bf0            mov     esi,eax
```

### Detecting a Reference Release

Breakpoints on access are extremely useful for catching, for example, what's holding a reference to a specific kernel object. When the reference is maintained by a user mode process, the investigation is fairly easy using tools, such as Process Explorer, available from Microsoft. If the reference is maintained by a kernel component, such as an antivirus filter driver, no tool is capable of finding out what's holding that reference. In this case, the best bet is to assume that the reference is eventually released in time or at system shutdown.

To find the culprit, start from the object and find out the object header address. The address is used as a base for a breakpoint on access, with an offset of 0, when tracking an object-only reference, or with an offset of 4, when tracking a handle reference. In Listing 2.43, we are tracking the last handle release, with the handle pointing to the process object representing an instance of cmd.exe. We start by using the !process extension command to obtain the EPROCESS structure address for the target process. Next, we use the !object extension command to obtain its header address, which is used to set the breakpoint on access.

**Listing 2.43**   Finding the stack that released a specific handle

```
kd> !process 0 0 cmd.exe
PROCESS ffba1020  SessionId: 0  Cid: 01a4    Peb: 7ffd5000  ParentCid: 05d4
    DirBase: 0567e000  ObjectTable: e17c2b60  HandleCount: 30.
    Image: cmd.exe

kd> !object ffba1020
Object: ffba1020  Type: (812ee900) Process
    ObjectHeader: ffba1008
    HandleCount: 1  PointerCount: 8
kd> dt nt!_OBJECT_HEADER ffba1008
    +0x000 PointerCount    : 8
    +0x004 HandleCount     : 1
...
kd> ba w4 ffba1008+8
kd> g
Breakpoint 2 hit
nt!ObpFreeObject+0x16c:
80563f66 5e              pop     esi
kd> k
ChildEBP RetAddr
fafb3cd0 80563ffe nt!ObpFreeObject+0x16c
fafb3ce8 804e3c55 nt!ObpRemoveObjectRoutine+0xe7
fafb3d0c 8057e5fb nt!ObfDereferenceObject+0x5f
fafb3d24 80563ff6 nt!PspThreadDelete+0xea
fafb3d40 804e3c55 nt!ObpRemoveObjectRoutine+0xdf
fafb3d64 804f9c5c nt!ObfDereferenceObject+0x5f
fafb3d74 804e47fe nt!PspReaper+0x4a
fafb3dac 8057dfed nt!ExpWorkerThread+0x100
```

```
fafb3ddc 804fa477 nt!PspSystemThreadStartup+0x34
00000000 00000000 nt!KiThreadStartup+0x16
kd> dt nt!_OBJECT_HEADER ffba1008
   +0x000 PointerCount    : 0
   +0x004 HandleCount     : 0
...
```

# Remote Debugging

Remote debugging is a popular choice in the developer community because it permits a high density of systems available for testing without the requirement to provide real estate for an application developer who might need to debug the systems. Remote debugging offers the luxury of using the personal office with the entire bookshelf around instead of debugging the system while being physically present in the remote location.

## Remote.exe

The easiest method of remote debugging is remoting the debugger console streams, STDIN and STDOUT, through the remote.exe utility (help topic `Remote.exe`). Remote.exe is automatically installed with the Debugging Tools for Windows. Remote.exe uses Windows named pipes to communicate between the remote server and the remote client. The client must be authenticated by the server to be capable of connecting to it. This utility is not specific to debugging, and it can be used to remote any interactive command-line utility, such as cmd.exe.

The command line shown in Listing 2.44 activates a remote server named `DiskPartRemote` corresponding to the console running the `diskpart.exe` command. The same `remote.exe` utility is then used to connect to the server, using the command line provided by the remote server at startup (the To Connect: line in Listing 2.44).

**Listing 2.44**  Remoting the console using remote.exe

```
C:\> remote /S "diskpart" DiskPartRemote
*************************************
**********      REMOTE    ***********
**********      SERVER    ***********
*************************************
```

*(continues)*

**Listing 2.44**   Remoting the console using remote.exe *(continued)*

```
To Connect: Remote /C AWD-TEST "DiskPartRemote"

Microsoft DiskPart version 5.1.3565

Copyright (C) 1999-2003 Microsoft Corporation.
On computer: AWD-TEST

DISKPART>
```

It is important to note that remote.exe uses the existing console to launch the command line passed in as a parameter, imposing some restrictions when you want to spawn another remote session from it. For example, assume that you have access to a remote session, running cmd.exe, and you want to create another remote session to a second-ary cmd.exe execution. You must first create a new console using `start` and pass the remote command line as a parameter. You end up with a new remote server to a new process using a different name, while the first remote is still available. The following listing illustrates the command succession required to spawn another remote session.

```
C:\> remote /s "cmd" cmdOrigRemote
****************************************
**********     REMOTE     ***********
**********     SERVER     ***********
****************************************
To Connect: Remote /C AWD-TEST "cmdOrigRemote"

Microsoft Windows XP [Version 5.1.2600]
(C) Copyright 1985-2001 Microsoft Corp.

C:\>start remote /s "cmd" cmdNewRemote
start remote /s "cmd" cmdNewRemote

C:\>
```

## Debug Server

The second option for remote debugging is the built-in support in the debugger, called debugger server. Each debugger has the option to give away its control to remote debugging clients, using different protocols, through the following form of command line (help topic `Activating a Debugging Server`):

```
<debugger> -server <protocol>:<protocol options> <debugger options>
```

If the debugger is already running, the debugger server can start at any time by entering the built-in debugger command, `.server`. This option has an advantage over the command line in that you can support multiple endpoints at once. Some examples of using the `.server` command are shown in Listing 2.45.

**Listing 2.45**   Starting the debugger server

**Command form**
```
0:000>.server <protocol>:<protocol options>
```
**Results**
```
0:000> .server npipe:pipe=notepad_%i_debug
Server started.  Client can connect with
    <path>\<debugger>.exe -remote <options>
0 - Debugger Server - tcp:Port=6000,Server=AWD-TEST
1 - Debugger Server - tcp:Port=6001,Server=AWD-TEST
2 - Debugger Server - npipe:Pipe=notepad_debug,Server=AWD-TEST
3 - Debugger Server - npipe:Pipe=notepad_2112_debug,Server=AWD-TEST
```

The remote debugger client—that is, the controller—can connect to the debugging server using the following command (help topic `Activating a Debugging Client`):

```
C:\><debugger> -remote <protocol>:<protocol options>
```

The `<debugger>` parameter can be WinDbg.exe, cdb.exe, or kd.exe, whereas the `<protocol>` parameter can be npipe, tcp, spipe, ssl, and even serial com port. You will use one or the other, depending on the debugging situation. Let's look at each protocol in more detail.

### The npipe protocol

The npipe (and its secure version spipe) protocol uses Windows named pipes managed by the SMB redirector and the Named Pipe File System (NPFS). The client must authenticate to the SMB server as any other client would, using the system provided command-line utility, as follows:

```
net use \\RemoteServer\IPC$
```

The npipe protocol requires users to have a set of credentials in the domain on which the debugger server runs.

2. INTRODUCTION TO THE DEBUGGERS

**NOTE** The debugger server can interpret up to two formatting commands, `%d` or `%x`, that replace them with the debugger process identifier and the debugger thread identifier. This capability is handy when you want to attach a debugger without human intervention and ensure name uniqueness. For example, the following command lines are expanded as shown:

```
C:\> ntsd -server npipe:pipe=pid(%d)tid(%d) notepad
C:\> ntsd -server npipe:pipe=pid(%d) notepad

C:\> cdb -QR \\AWD-TEST
Servers on \\AWD-TEST:
Debugger Server - npipe:Pipe=pid(296)tid(608)
Debugger Server - npipe:Pipe=pid(3188)
```

### TCP

TCP and its secure version SSL use the TCP/IP stack and are best used when authentication is neither possible nor desired. The debug server allows you to specify a specific port or to enable the system to select one for you. Alternatively, you can specify a range, and the debugger selects the first one from that range.

```
0:000> * remote using  a specified port
0:000>.server tcp:port=5000
0:000> * remote using the first free port
0:000> .server tcp:port=
0:000> * remote using a range and ask the debugger to pick the fist one available in
the range
0:000>.server tcp:port=5000:6000
```

The servers started on the system were in this case. (Note that the `.servers` command offers the same functionality as the `<debuggers>` `-QR` command line, but from within the debugger server console.)

```
0:000> .servers
On the client, use <path>\<debugger>.exe -remote <options>
0 - Debugger Server - tcp:Port=5000,Server=AWD-TEST
1 - Debugger Server - tcp:Port=4488,Server=AWD-TEST
2 - Debugger Server - tcp:Port=5001:6000,Server=AWD-TEST
```

The TCP protocol offers another option, `clicon=<client_host>`, useful in debugging a server behind firewalls when the debugger client accepts an inbound TCP/IP connection. The following line starts the debugger server and tells it to try to connect to AWD-TEST on port 5000, and the next line starts the debugger client to wait for the connection request on port 5000.

```
c:\> ntsd -server tcp:port=5000,clicon=AWD-TEST notepad 2
c:\> ntsd -remote tcp:port=5000,clicon=AWD-TEST
```

### Other Commands

Other useful commands in remoting scenarios are listed here. (A few have already been used earlier in the chapter.)

- `.endsrv <server_id>` stops a debugger server.
- `.servers` lists the debugger servers started by this debugger.
- `.clients` lists the current connected clients.
- `.remote_exit` exits the current debugger client.
- `.echo` is useful to send text messages to other users connected to the same debugging session.

## Process and Kernel Server

So far you've seen the remote debuggers in action, and you should have a good understanding of them and how to use them. The previous methods require having an operator with full access to the remote system to find the proper process identifier, attaching the debugger in server mode, reattaching if the process exits, and so on. In some cases, it is not feasible to have the operator doing all this, and there is a better way to resolve the problem. The solution is represented by stand-alone debugger servers: a user mode debug server, known as a process server, is implemented in dbgsrv.exe; and the kernel mode debug server, known as a KD connection server, is implemented in kdsrv.exe. We describe the user mode debug server in more detail because the same idea applies to the kernel mode debug server.

A process server runs on the target system and, in essence, does nothing more than accepting commands from the remote smart clients. The accepted commands are similar to what the debugger engine supports, and they offer the capability to debug processes on the target system similar to the way we debug local processes. The process server takes the transport option as a parameter, which is visible when querying the target system as a Remote Process Server.

```
C:\>dbgsrv -t npipe:pipe=smart_um
C:\>cdb -QR 127.0.0.1
Servers on 127.0.0.1:
Remote Process Server - npipe:Pipe=smart_um
```

After the process server starts, you can use any user mode debuggers as a smart client by using the -premote option followed by the same transport protocol used to start the process server. After the transport sequence, we specify the command line to be used by the debugger, as the debugger will run locally on the target system. In the following, there are two examples of using a smart client to start two debugging sessions: In the first case, the process server starts the new process; and in the second case, it attaches to a running process.

```
C:\>cdb -premote npipe:server=localhost,pipe=smart_um notepad
C:\>cdb -premote npipe:server=localhost,pipe=smart_um -p PID
```

Contrary to the remote server scenarios, the smart client performs all the activities that influence the symbol and source resolution. The symbol source files are accessed directly by the smart clients. Most of the extensions are unaware of the smart client environment and work normally, with the exception of a few dedicated commands—the most notable being the .send_file command.

WinDbg behaves in an extremely interesting fashion when it is started in smart client mode, without specifying a debugger target. It starts normally, but all existing menu commands, such as the Open Executable menu item or the Attach to a process menu item in the File menu, are working against the remote process server, effectively abstracting the remoteness relation.

If this is not enough, any smart client can also be started as a debugger server and can accept remote connections from ordinary clients. This last setup is known as "symbols in the middle scenario" because neither the debugger operator nor the target system has physical access to symbol or source files, but the system in the middle can have access to them.

The KD connection server works in the same way, except for the method of passing the connection string required on the server side. The option used by the kernel debugger to become a smart client is kdsrv, as exemplified here:

```
C:\>kdsrv -t npipe:pipe=smart_kd

C:\>cdb -QR 127.0.0.1
Servers on 127.0.0.1:
Remote Kernel Debugger Server - npipe:Pipe=smart_kd

C:\>kd -k kdsrv:server=@{npipe:server=localhost,pipe=smart_kd},
    trans=@{com:port=com1}
```

## Symbol Resolution in Remote Debugging Scenarios

Remote debugging success is dependent on the symbols available to the debugger and sometimes on the source's code availability. Because remote debugging involves a server and a client running in a different logon session, in most of the cases on different computers, it is very important to understand where and how the symbol resolution takes place or how the source is seen by the debugger.

Because the symbols are loaded by the debugger server engine, the engine interpreting the symbols and interacting with the image, these symbols files must be visible and accessible to that debugger server session. When the debugger console is shared using remote.exe, it is clear that the debugger server runs where the debugger process starts. For an alternative remote debugging method, where the server is started by the debugger `-server` command, the debugger server is running where the server runs. If the smart client is connected to the process server, the debugger engine runs on the smart client, and the symbol files must be accessible to them.

Figure 2.6 shows the relation between the debugger client, the debugger server, and the symbol location.

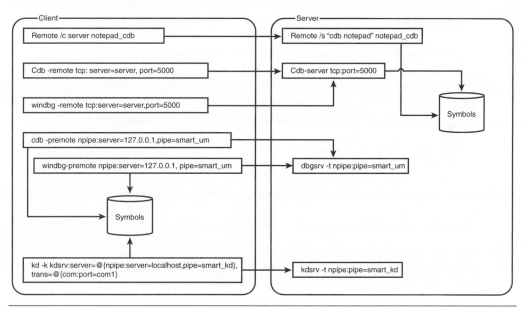

**Figure 2.6**   Remote debugging and symbol resolution

When the debugger target is deployed to the remote server without the corresponding symbol file and the symbol is required locally, we must find ways to make it available to the server. In most cases, we cannot authenticate the remote server to our client by using the `.shell net use \\client\ipc$ /U:user password` because it requires us to type the password into the shared debugger console. One solution is to copy the symbol files to a remote location visible from the server without entering new credentials.

An interesting way of combining all the remote capabilities is to use a combination of normal clients and smart clients to push the symbols on the remote box. The scenario is as before, and the client debugger is connected to the debug server.

1. Start a process server from within the debugger using the `.shell` command, using a transport different from the one used by the current debugger server.

```
0:000>.shell start dbgsrv.exe -t tcp:port=5001
```

2. Start a smart client with the command to attach none interactively to the process we are currently debugging: in this case, a process having the PID equal to 3204.

```
C:\>ntsd -premote tcp:server=AWD-TEST1,port=5001 -pvr -p 3204
```

3. Use the smart client to resolve all the symbols required for debugging and send them to the server, using the `.send_file` command, into the symbol path used by the server. The target path is local to remote debugger server.

```
0:000> .send_file -s c:\temp
Copying C:\symbols\02sample.pdb\DE4335BC88FD4EA1A1714350C33B84281\02sample.pdb
(155 KB)
Copying c:\symbols\msvcrt.pdb\62B8BDC3CC194D2992DCFAED78B621FC1\msvcrt.pdb (395
KB).
Copying c:\symbols\kernel32.pdb\75CFE96517E5450DA600C870E95399FF2\kernel32.pdb
(1.52 MB)......
Copying c:\symbols\msvcp60.pdb\3CF541551\msvcp60.pdb (489 KB).
Copying c:\symbols\ntdll.pdb\DCE823FCF71A4BF5AA489994520EA18F2\ntdll.pdb (1.16
MB)....
```

4. Going back to the original debugger, point the symbol path to the location used in step 3, and reload the symbols.

```
0:000> !sympath c:\temp
Symbol search path is: c:\temp
```

```
0:000> !reload -f
Reloading current modules
. . . . .
0:000> lml
start     end        module name
00400000 00404000    02sample        (private pdb symbols)   c:\temp\02sample.pdb
77ba0000 77bfa000    msvcrt     (pdb symbols)        c:\temp\msvcrt.pdb
77e40000 77f42000    kernel32   (pdb symbols)        c:\temp\kernel32.pdb
780c0000 78121000    msvcp60    (pdb symbols)        c:\temp\msvcp60.pdb
7c800000 7c8c0000    ntdll      (pdb symbols)        c:\temp\ntdll.pdb
```

## Source Resolution on Remote Debugging Scenarios

Sources are handled similarly to the way symbol files are handled; the system where the debugger runs must have access to the source file. Not surprisingly, WinDbg is much more powerful when working with source files. It supports the concept of a local source path used when performing remote debugging. It loads the source file on the remote client, which usually has more extensive access to the source file. The local source path is supported by an additional set of commands, .lsrcpath and .lsrcfix, or by using the Local check box on the Source File Path menu item in the File menu.

# Debugging Scenarios

What are the most common problems using the Windows debuggers? The most difficult situations seem to arise when it is not possible to interactively control the debugger target lifetime. In such cases, the debugger must be started by the system, and its configuration must be performed automatically.

When the debugger starts the debugger target, we can run the debugger target as many times as needed since it's fully controllable. What if the process we have to debug is started by another application that cannot be changed to start the process under a debugger? In this case, the parent application must be started under the debugger with the −o option that forces any new process spawned by the debugged application to start under the same debugger, as shown here:

```
C:\>windbg -o cmd.exe /c notepad.exe
```

The same debugger attaches to every new process. The current process can be switched using the process set command, |<process number>s. The current process number becomes a part of the debugger prompt, as in the following listing:

```
1:001> |
   0    id: 1dc8        create  name: cmd.exe
.  1    id: f44 child   name: notepad.exe
```

Another option implemented by the operating system requires changes in the Image File Execution Option (known as IFEO) registry key. The IFEO registry key contains multiple values influencing how the operating system starts the executable. One value in the corresponding IFEO key represents the debugger values whose content is used by the operating system to launch the executable. In the following example, Notepad starts under the debugger with the -g -G command-line options:

```
HKLM\SOFTWARE\Microsoft\Windows NT\CurrentVersion\Image File Execution
Options\notepad.exe]
"Debugger"="c:\\debug.x86\\ntsd.exe -g -G"
```

As an alternative to changing the registries directly, we can use gflags.exe, installed as part of the Debugging Tools for Windows. The previous IFEO can be set by using the following command line:

```
C:\>gflags /p /enable notepad.exe /debug "c:\debug.x86\ntsd.exe -g -G"
```

After you complete your investigation, you can revert the changes in the registry using the following:

```
C:\>gflags /p /disable notepad.exe
```

After these changes are written into the registry, each instance of notepad.exe starts under the debugger. Instead of launching the application identified by the IFEO key, the system launches the debugger and passes the application name as a parameter to it. If the application is visible to the user, the debugger will be visible as well. If the application runs on a noninteractive session, as is the case for all services, the debugger starts but is not actionable, as it is not visible.

## Debugging a Noninteractive Process (Service or COM Server)

Although IFEO represents a good option for interactive processes, most Win32 services and COM servers run in a noninteractive station. The debugger started by the system using IFEO is invisible, and we need to find methods to connect to the debugger console.

The kernel debugger is the best option in this scenario, and the easiest option is to just redirect the debugger console into the kernel debugger. The image file execution option is changed, as explained before, to use a different debugger command line, `ntsd -d`.

```
HKLM\SOFTWARE\Microsoft\Windows NT\CurrentVersion\Image File Execution Options\
myService.exe]
"Debugger"="c:\\debug.x86\\ntsd.exe -d"
```

In several cases, the process name is not a good discriminator, as in the case of modules loaded by DllHost.exe, and you want to be able to debug only your module. In this case, the debugger accepts a few commands from the command line, asking the debugger to stop on the initial breakpoint (don't use the –g option), to raise an exception on the module load, and to continue the execution. If the shared host never loads our module, the breakpoint is never hit and the system runs normally.

```
HKLM\SOFTWARE\Microsoft\Windows NT\CurrentVersion\Image File Execution Options\
dllhost.exe]
"Debugger"="c:\\debug.x86\\ntsd.exe -d -G -c "sxe ld <mymodule>;g""
```

## Debugging a Noninteractive Process (Service or COM Server) Without Kernel Debugger

When no kernel debugger is connected to the target system, the system can be debugged using the user mode debugger's remote capabilities. A debugger in server mode is used as a debugger parameter in IFEO.

```
HKLM\SOFTWARE\Microsoft\Windows NT\CurrentVersion\Image File Execution Options\
dllhost.exe]
"Debugger"=" c:\debug.x86\ntsd.exe -server tcp:port=6000 -G"
```

The client connects to the debug server, after the server process was started, using a specific connection string.

```
C:\>windbg -remote tcp:port=6000,server=localhost
```

This method does not work well when the debugger target implements a Windows service and the debugger exits without warning shortly after starting the debugging session. That is Service Control Manager, also known as SCM, standard behavior if the service does not communicate the starting status back to it in 30 seconds. Fortunately, this limit can be changed by modifying one registry setting, as shown here:

```
HKEY_LOCAL_MACHINE\SYSTEM\CurrentControlSet\Control
ServicesPipeTimeout = NewTimeoutInMiliseconds
```

What happens if the service is started multiple times on the system, as is the case for the dllhost.exe process? Since each debugger instance opens the specified endpoint, only the first process will start normally under the debugger; all the other instances will fail when the debugger tries to open the endpoint and start the debugger server. The solution is to defer the debugger server initialization until the target process loading that module is identified. The option of specifying a command to be executed when the debugger prompts the user allows us to send the command to break the execution when the specific DLL is loaded and only then starts the remote server.

```
HKLM\SOFTWARE\Microsoft\Windows NT\CurrentVersion\Image File Execution Options\
dllhost.exe]
"Debugger"="c:\\debug.x86\\ntsd.exe -d -G -c "sxe ld <mymodule>;g;.server
tcp:port=6000""
```

All techniques described here can be combined with the CLICON option mentioned in the "TCP" section to better synchronize the debugger server with the debugger client.

When multiple processes share the same IEFO key and all processes must be debugged using debugger servers, the endpoint must be dynamically created, but names must be predictable. The named pipe name can be autogenerated by the debugger, as shown in Listing 2.45, with a discoverable name that is used later on the debugger client. The next listing represents the registry value causing each dllhost.exe process to start a named pipe debugger server, using the pipe name \\.\pipe\dllHost_xyz.

```
HKLM\SOFTWARE\Microsoft\Windows NT\CurrentVersion\Image File Execution Options\
dllhost.exe]
"Debugger"="c:\debug.x86\ntsd.exe -d -G -c ".server npipe:pipe=dllHost_%i;g""
```

## Summary

The Windows debuggers are powerful tools that can be used to troubleshoot software problems throughout the whole software life cycle. In the initial development phase, the debuggers are used to validate the correctness of the code, usually with the source code available. Later, after the code is deployed, the software developers debug the dump files generated each time the application crashes on the user system.

Because of their flexibility, the Windows debuggers can be used in various combinations and can be extended to maximize the productivity of all engineers involved in the development process. To effectively use the debugger, the user should have a good grasp of some basic commands and must be willing to learn new commands or options, as required by the debugging scenario at hand. The next chapters introduce additional commands as required by the chapter scenarios.

# DEBUGGERS UNCOVERED

The Microsoft Debugging Tools for Windows package comes with very powerful tools that were designed with the goal of providing total control over the debugger target while keeping the overhead of exercising it at a minimal level. Every command entered in the command windows is executed without asking for confirmation, making the user fully responsible for the command consequences. As with any tool, the more knowledge you have about it, the more likely you are to understand the side effects and predict the final result of its application. In our experience, we encounter multiple situations in which an application is stopped in the debugger in one critical spot and any further application progress irreversibly changes the state of the debugger target. Losing a debugger session this way is not desirable, especially if the failure scenario is very hard to reproduce. In a few other cases, the process being debugged is part of a larger live system, and you must understand the effect the debugger has on that process; otherwise, you most likely need to restart the service, or, in the worst-case scenario, the internal structures are corrupted, resulting in unpredictable behavior.

This chapter reveals some of the magic offered by debuggers and explains the underlying mechanism used to provide this magic. This chapter describes in detail the interaction between the debugger and the operating system, as well as between the debugger and the debugger target. In this chapter, we explore

- How the debugger works and its relationship to the code execution.
- How the operating system and the debugger target generate the debugger events, especially software exceptions.
- How the operating system interacts with the exception handling code contained in the application.
- How the debugger controls the target and what to expect from each debugger action entered by the debugger user. This enables you to fine-tune the debugging technique appropriate to a particular debugging scenario.

This chapter uses the 03sample.exe file, which exercises the basic operations performed by a debugger in a fully automated mode. Instead of requiring user input before proceeding to the next step, the pseudo-debugger displays information about the current state and continues in a preconfigured mode. The debugger target is passed in as command-line parameter. The source code and binary are located in the following folders:

Source code: `C:\AWD\Chapter3`

Binary: `C:\AWDBIN\WinXP.x86.chk\03sample.exe`

The sample reuses the 02sample.exe introduced in Chapter 2, "Introduction to the Debuggers," as a debugger target.

# User Mode Debugger Internals

As presented in Chapter 2, the Microsoft Debugging Tools for Windows contains multiple user mode debuggers and kernel mode debuggers, all sharing the functionality provided in part by the operating system. Because user mode debuggers are the primary tool used by software engineers to validate their assumptions about a code sequence and to validate algorithms correctness, as well as to investigate unexpected failures in their application, this chapter focuses on user mode debuggers' internals.

This section, and the majority of the current chapter, describes how user mode debuggers work and highlights how to use each feature provided by the debuggers in the most efficient way.

## User Mode Debugger Support from the Operating System

Windows provides a small set of Win32 APIs exposing the debugger support implemented in the operating system. User mode debuggers combine debugger APIs with other general-purpose Win32 APIs to provide the functionality expected from them.

These Win32 APIs can be grouped into several categories based on the functionality they provide, as follows:

- APIs to create the debugger target
- APIs to handle the debugger events used in a debugger loop
- APIs to inspect and modify the debugger target, used when processing the debugger event

This section explores the usage of each group of APIs.

### Creating the Debugger Target

The live debugging session starts with the creation of the debugger target. User mode debuggers can start a new process, or they can attach to a running process started using alternative mechanisms. After this step, that process becomes the new debugger target to which all further action performed by the debugger is directed. The operating system associates the debugger target with the current debugger, which is maintained until the debugger target ceases to exist or the debugger explicitly breaks the association.

Debuggers start new debugger targets by passing the DEBUG_PROCESS flag to the CreateProcess API call used to start the new process. The 03sample.exe samples create the debugger target using the code sequence shown in Listing 3.1. The process name, passed as the second parameter to CreateProcess API, is the first command-line parameter represented by the variable argv[1].

**Listing 3.1**   Sample code used to start a process under user mode debugger

```
STARTUPINFOA startupInfo={0};
startupInfo.cb = sizeof(startupInfo);
PROCESS_INFORMATION processInfo = {0};
BOOL res = CreateProcess(NULL, argv[1], NULL, NULL, FALSE,
          DEBUG_PROCESS, NULL, NULL, &startupInfo, &processInfo);
```

A running process can enter at any time in the debug state if a debugger requests the operating system to start debugging that process, by attaching to it, using the DebugActiveProcess API. Regardless of the method used to create the debugger target, attaching to an existing process or starting it for the purpose of debugging it, further interaction between the debugger and the operating system is performed in the same way. The debugger process connected to the debugger target this way is called the active debugger. Each debugger target can have only one active debugger.

### Debugger Loop

When a process is being debugged, notable operations encountered by this process are signaled to the debugger. Dynamic library loading and unloading, new thread creation, thread exiting, and an exception thrown by the code or by the processor are all considered special events of interest to debuggers. When such an event must be sent to a debugger, the Windows kernel suspends all the threads in the process, notifies the active debugger about the event encounter, and waits for a continuation command from it.

Most of the time, the debugger waits for the kernel to return new data in response to the WaitForDebugevent API, data generated only if the debugger target encounters one of the special debugging events described previously. The

WaitForDebugEvent API returns the event information into a DEBUG_EVENT structure, which contains a union of all possible event types needed by the debugger to further interpret the event. While the debugger examines the DEBUG_EVENT structure, the process state does not change, as every thread is suspended.

After the event has been properly interpreted and processed, the debugger resumes debugger target execution by calling the ContinueDebugEvent API. In response, Windows kernel continues the process execution, taking into account the ContinueDebugEvent API parameters. Depending on the event type, the kernel might immediately dismiss the event and cancel its processing for the current event and, if the event is not an exception, resume the execution of all threads from the point they were left when the event was generated.

This sequence of operations, called a debugger loop, continues until the debugging session ends, either because the debugger target no longer exists or because the debugger detaches from the target. Listing 3.2 exemplifies such a debugger loop.

**Listing 3.2**   Standard user mode debugger loop

```
for(DWORD endDisposition = DBG_CONTINUE;endDisposition != 0;)
{
    DEBUG_EVENT debugEvent = { 0 } ;
    WaitForDebugEvent(&debugEvent, INFINITE);
    endDisposition = ProcessEvent(debugEvent);
    ContinueDebugEvent(debugEvent.dwProcessId, debugEvent.dwThreadId, endDisposi-
tion);
}
```

### Debugger Event Processing

After the debugger loop retrieves a new event, the debugger needs to interpret the information from the DEBUG_EVENT structure, possibly handing the control over the debugger target to the engineer using that debugger before returning to the debugger loop. Listing 3.3 shows a very simple processing function, ignoring any information from within the DEBUG_EVENT structure and returning DBG_CONTINUE for every type of event, except for the EXIT_PROCESS_DEBUG_EVENT type, when it returns zero. For simplicity, the return code is used both to end the loop and as a parameter to the ContinueDebugEvent API.

**Listing 3.3**   Simple debugger events processing

```
DWORD ProcessEvent(DEBUG_EVENT& dbgEvent)
{
    switch (dbgEvent.dwDebugEventCode)
    {
        case EXCEPTION_DEBUG_EVENT:
        break;
        case CREATE_THREAD_DEBUG_EVENT:
        break;
        case CREATE_PROCESS_DEBUG_EVENT:
        break;
        case EXIT_THREAD_DEBUG_EVENT:
        break;
        case EXIT_PROCESS_DEBUG_EVENT:
        break;
        case LOAD_DLL_DEBUG_EVENT:
        break;
        case UNLOAD_DLL_DEBUG_EVENT:
        break;
        case OUTPUT_DEBUG_STRING_EVENT:
        break;
        case RIP_EVENT:
        break;
    }
    return DBG_CONTINUE ;
}
```

In the following sections, several cases from the switch statement in Listing 3.3 are detailed with the automated handling code, designed with the idea of providing reasonable default action. Cases not described in the book are covered in 03sample.exe, and their understanding is left as an exercise for the reader. Please note that a full-fledged debugger allows the user to examine and change the debugger target state before calling the ContinueDebugEvent API.

### Processing OUTPUT_DEBUG_STRING_EVENT

Software engineers often use debug output commands in their code with the goal of providing an easy-to-use tracing required to troubleshoot their code. The exact syntax used differs between languages, but most syntax ends up calling one of the Windows-provided debugging APIs, such as OutputDebugStringA or OutputDebugStringW. The string output generated in such ways by the debugger target can be displayed by the debugger using event processing code similar to that shown in Listing 3.4. The

DEBUG_EVENT structure contains an OUTPUT_DEBUG_STRING_INFO structure, which in turn contains message-specific information. The lpDebugStringData member contains the address, relative to the debugger's target address space, of the string to be displayed, whereas nDebugStringLength contains the length of this string, and fUnicode tells if the characters are Unicode or ANSI characters. The code uses the handle to the process where the event originated to read the message from the debugger target address space.

**Listing 3.4**   Processing output debug string event

```
case OUTPUT_DEBUG_STRING_EVENT:
//typedef struct _OUTPUT_DEBUG_STRING_INFO {
//      LPSTR lpDebugStringData;
//      WORD fUnicode;
//      WORD nDebugStringLength;
//} OUTPUT_DEBUG_STRING_INFO, *LPOUTPUT_DEBUG_STRING_INFO;

{
OUTPUT_DEBUG_STRING_INFO& OutputDebug = dbgEvent.u.DebugString;
WCHAR * msg = ReadRemoteString(hTargetProcessHandle, OutputDebug.lpDebugString-
Data, OutputDebug.nDebugStringLength, OutputDebug.fUnicode);
std::wcout << L"OutputDebugStringEvent\nMessage:\t";
std::wcout <<<< msg << std::endl;
delete[] msg;
break;
}
```

The ReadRemoteString function used in Listing 3.4 is a helper function abstracting the character size and string length from the OUTPUT_DEBUG_STRING_INFO structure, built around kernel32!ReadProcessMemory. It reads the string from the debugger target address space and converts it to a null-terminated Unicode string as required by 03sample.exe. The ReadRemoteString implementation is listed in Listing 3.5.

**Listing 3.5**   Read a specific length string from the debugger target space

```
WCHAR *
ReadRemoteString(HANDLE process,LPVOID address,WORD length,BOOL unicode)
{
    WCHAR * msg = new WCHAR[length];
    if (!msg) return NULL;
    memset(msg, 0, sizeof(WCHAR)*(length));
```

```
    if ( unicode )
    {
        ReadProcessMemory(process, address ,msg, length*sizeof(WCHAR),NULL);
        return msg;
    }
    else
    {
        CHAR * originalMsg = new CHAR[length];
        if (!originalMsg)
        {
            delete[] msg;
            return NULL;
        }
        memset(originalMsg, 0, sizeof(BYTE)*(length));

        ReadProcessMemory(process, address ,originalMsg, length,NULL);
        for (WORD i = 0; i < length; i++)
        {
            msg[i] = originalMsg[i];
        }
        delete[] originalMsg;
        return msg;
    }
}
```

After the resulting string is displayed in the debugger console, the debugger loop continues. The debugger target continues execution after the debugger enters back into the loop. This additional activity performed by the debugger target changes the application execution timing, which can hide or expose race conditions in the application.

### Processing EXCEPTION_DEBUG_EVENT

The debugger target can generate several exceptions in the whole lifetime—each type of exception being treated differently by the debugger. Some exceptions have a special meaning to the debugger itself, whereas others have runtime meaning for the debugger target. A debugger exception handler can be very complex. This section just reveals the basics as required to understand the exception processing done by the debugger.

In the case of an EXCEPTION_DEBUG_EVENT, the DEBUG_EVENT structure contains an EXCEPTION_DEBUG_INFO structure containing a copy of the exception information packed as the EXCEPTION_RECORD structure in the ExceptionRecord member, as described in Listing 3.6. From EXCEPTION_RECORD, the debugger obtains the exception code, the address at which the exception was raised, and exception arguments. The EXCEPTION_DEBUG_EVENT second member, the dwFirstChance flag, tells the debugger whether this is the first notification about this exception. The whole aspect of first-versus second-chance (exception) notification is treated in detail later in this chapter.

From the Windows operating system perspective, the debugger must interpret the exception and use either DBG_CONTINUE or DBG_EXCEPTION_NOT_HANDLED as the parameter to ContinueDebugEvent. In the first case, Windows assumes that the exception has been properly dismissed, the condition causing the exception is no longer present, and the execution can continue at the address that caused the exception. In the second case, Windows behaves as if the debugger is not even present and continues its normal dispatching procedure.

Listing 3.6 shows the minimal handler used in the 03sample.exe sample design, so it does not affect the Windows exception mechanism for most of the exceptions. Because the Windows operating system notifies the debugger about other special operations using an STATUS_BREAKPOINT exception, our exception handler returns DBG_CONTINUE for such exceptions.

**Listing 3.6**   Processing exception debug event

```
case EXCEPTION_DEBUG_EVENT:
//typedef struct _EXCEPTION_DEBUG_INFO {
//      EXCEPTION_RECORD ExceptionRecord;
//      DWORD dwFirstChance;
//} EXCEPTION_DEBUG_INFO;

    std::cout << "ExceptiondebugEvent\nException Code:\t " << std::hex <<
dbgEvent.u.Exception.ExceptionRecord.ExceptionCode;
    std::cout << "\tFirstChance:\t" << dbgEvent.u.Exception.dwFirstChance
<<std::endl;

    switch (dbgEvent.u.Exception.ExceptionRecord.ExceptionCode)
    {
    case EXCEPTION_BREAKPOINT:
    case EXCEPTION_SINGLE_STEP:
        return DBG_CONTINUE;
    }
    return DBG_EXCEPTION_NOT_HANDLED;
```

The return code from the handling routine is returned to Windows as the last parameter of the ContinueDebugEvent API, having the dwContinueStatus name.

## Debugger Events Order

In the time interval between the moments the debugger loop returns from the WaitForDebugEvent API until the call to ContinueDebugEvent API is made, the debugger target does not run, and its state remains unchanged. While the target is suspended, a full debugger implementation would enter into an interactive mode accepting user commands and would execute them using various means. As part of the execution, the debugger can use debugger APIs to find out more information about the debugger target and the debugger event, it can examine the symbol files associated with the debugger target modules, and it can use any other Win32 API to provide any functionality the user requests. When the command entered on the debugger input lines is an execution command, the debugger calls ContinueDebugEvent and waits for the next event.

With all this information and code available in the sample, it is time to obtain the list of all events generated by the debugger target using our 03sample.exe. Listing 3.7 contains the console output generated by running the sample, which uses xcopy.exe as a parameter and debugger target.

**Listing 3.7**    Debugger events generated by a simple process execution (xcopy.exe)

```
C:\>C:\AWDBIN\WinXP.x86.chk\03sample.exe xcopy.exe
DebugEvent from PID.TID=33308.32256
EventType:       CreateProcessDebugEvent
PID:    33308
DebugEvent from PID.TID=33308.32256
EventType:       LoadDllDebugEvent
Mapped address: 7C900000
ImageName:       ntdll.dll


DebugEvent from PID.TID=33308.32256
EventType:       LoadDllDebugEvent
Mapped address: 7C800000
ImageName:       C:\WINDOWS\system32\kernel32.dll


... More LoadDllDebugEvent ...


DebugEvent from PID.TID=33308.32256
EventType:       LoadDllDebugEvent
Mapped address: 77920000
ImageName:       C:\WINDOWS\system32\setupapi.DLL


DebugEvent from PID.TID=33308.32256
```

*(continues)*

**Listing 3.7**   Debugger events generated by a simple process execution (xcopy.exe) *(continued)*

```
EventType:       ExceptiondebugEvent
Exception Code:  80000003      FirstChance:    1


DebugEvent from PID.TID=33308.32256
EventType:       LoadDllDebugEvent
Mapped address: 5CB70000
ImageName:       C:\WINDOWS\system32\ShimEng.dll

... More LoadDllDebugEvent ...

DebugEvent from PID.TID=33308.32256
EventType:       LoadDllDebugEvent
Mapped address: 5D090000
ImageName:       C:\WINDOWS\system32\comctl32.dll

Invalid number of parameters
0 File(s) copied

DebugEvent from PID.TID=33308.32256
EventType:       ExitProcessDebugEvent
ExitCode:        4
```

Listing 3.7 shows the order of events and deserves some comment. The first event received by the debugger when starting the debugger target is CreateProcessDebugEvent, followed by a series of LoadDllDebugEvents, one for each dynamic library the process depends on. Because LoadDllDebugEvent is not generated for the process image itself, CreateProcessEvent contains the information present in LoadDllDebugEvent, such as the handle to the executable file, the image starting address, the debug info pointers, and the executable image name—plus event-specific information, such as the process handle, the first thread's handle, or the start address. The event is generated after the module has been mapped to the process space, and it can be used to set breakpoints in the process code or to examine global variables.

After all modules are mapped in the debugger target, the debugger target is ready to run, and the debugger is notified that the process is ready to run. This is the best opportunity to set breakpoints before the process actually starts. The debugger is notified by the kernel using a STATUS_BREAKPOINT exception (identified by the 0x80000003 exception code).

At this point, the 03sample.exe sample application returns DBG_CONTINUE, enabling the debugger target to start process execution. Process execution continues by loading a few other dynamic libraries into the process space, generating the corresponding `LoadDllDebugEvents`.

Finally, the process executes its task, and the output is combined in the console output. After the process execution completes, the target generates `ExitDebugProcessEvent` as the last event before the process goes away.

It is important to understand the order of debugger events or to recognize the situations in which the debugger does not receive an event. For example, when the process terminates, the debugger does not receive an `UnloadDllDebugEvent` for all dynamic libraries still loaded in the process. It is also very important to recognize the meaning of each exception and the situations in which the Windows operating system raises a `STATUS_BREAKPOINT` exception to notify the debugger about a special event. Knowing the debugger events and the order in which they are received during the debugger target lifetime, we use the windbg.exe debugger with 02sample.exe as the debugger target for the remainder of this chapter.

## Controlling Exceptions and Events from the Debugger

Not all events are created equally, and not all are treated equally. The Windows debuggers intercept all debugger events, but the way these events are handled by the debugger or how they are controlled by the user varies across event types and even from event to event. Most debugger events are pure notification events that the debugger can ignore. The debugger does so and automatically continues its execution, sometimes after printing a brief description of the event. The debugger can also stop at that event if the user asks it to do so, enabling the user to interact with the system.

Although most debugger events shown previously are generated by the Windows operating system independent of the debugger target execution, the debugger target generates debugger exception events as part of normal execution. The interaction between the exception-handling code and debugger is designed to minimize the run-time execution flow impact while providing the debugger maximum flexibility. Debuggers can choose to treat exceptions in the same fashion as any other debugger event; they can ignore them, they can print exception information on the screen, or they can break into the debugger. An EXCEPTION_DEBUG_EVENT debugger exception event can be generated more than once for the same exception, as described later in this chapter. First-event occurrence, called first-chance exception, is sent as debugger aid, while the second event generated for the same exception, called second-chance exception, implies that the operating system or the application cannot handle that exception. Since second-chance exceptions become unhandled exceptions that terminate the process, it is essential to investigate and understand the legitimacy of each such exception and reevaluate the application's desired behavior in such cases.

Windows operating systems use a structured exception handling (SEH) mechanism to propagate the exceptions raised by the processor, into the kernel, and into user mode applications. Each SEH exception type is uniquely identified by an unsigned integer representing the exception code, assigned to it when the exception is raised in the system. The exceptions raised by the operating system use well-known exception codes, defined by the operating system developers (exceptions such as access violation or breakpoint exception). Other exceptions, such as C++ exceptions, are also represented in the system as structured exceptions using a specific exception code. The C++ exception information is managed by the runtime provided by the compiler.

For example, C++ exceptions have 0xE06D7363 code, access violation exceptions have 0xC0000005 code, and breakpoint exceptions have 0x80000003 code. The common exception codes, expected to be used by all software engineers developing code targeting Windows, can be found in the <ntstatus.h> headers in the WDK as constants defined having the STATUS_<NAME> form name, such as

```
#define STATUS_BREAKPOINT        ((NTSTATUS)0x80000003L)
```

You might ask why this is relevant for any engineer debugging Windows code. The answer is to be able to use the tools at maximum capacity. The truth is that software developers have been used to working only with symbolic names and ignoring the value behind the name. This indirection layer between their code and the operating system isolates them from changes in the operating system and makes their application code easy to read and understand. Because symbol files have no references to the original symbolic names, the debuggers display raw numbers represented by symbolic names in the source code. Since this situation is unlikely to change in the near future, and it does not change for the systems created today, it is important to become familiar with some of the "magic" numbers seen over and over in this book. More importantly, you need to understand how to find their meaning by yourself. Most exception-symbolic names used can also be found in the debugger help, including the source header or the raw value (help topic Specific Exception).

### Events Alias

Because it is hard to remember the exception codes, the Windows debuggers have friendly aliases mapped to them that can be used to control the debugger behavior. Alias names resemble the exception type and can be used interchangeably with exception codes in the commands managing debugger events. For example, a hard-to-remember C++ exception code, 0xE06D7363, is aliased by eh, whereas the breakpoint exception code 0x80000003 is aliased by bpe.

**DEBUGGER EVENTS AS EXCEPTIONS** Some debugger events are actually exceptions raised by the code implementing the event behavior, as is the case for initial breakpoint exceptions or for output debug string events. In those cases, we should use other hints, such as the stack, to find out the break reason.

### Inspecting Events Break and Handling

The built-in events-handling command, sx, issued without parameters, enables the user to inspect event-handling settings used in the respective debugging session (see Listing 3.8). The command output is grouped into three areas: events-handling interaction with the respective handling mode, followed by the second group with the standard exceptions interaction and handling behavior, and last, user-defined exceptions interaction and handling behavior.

**Listing 3.8** Displaying the current event-handling state

```
0:000> sx
  ct - Create thread - ignore
  et - Exit thread - ignore
 cpr - Create process - ignore
 epr - Exit process - break
  ld - Load module - output
  ud - Unload module - ignore
 ser - System error - ignore
 ibp - Initial breakpoint - break
 iml - Initial module load - ignore
 out - Debuggee output - output

  av - Access violation - break - not handled
asrt - Assertion failure - break - not handled
 aph - Application hang - break - not handled
 bpe - Break instruction exception - break
bpec - Break instruction exception continue - handled
  eh - C++ EH exception - break - not handled
 clr - CLR exception - second-chance break - not handled
clrn - CLR notification exception - second-chance break - handled
 cce - Control-Break exception - break
  cc - Control-Break exception continue - handled
 cce - Control-C exception - break
  cc - Control-C exception continue - handled
  dm - Data misaligned - break - not handled
```

*(continues)*

**Listing 3.8**   Displaying the current event handling state *(continued)*

```
dbce - Debugger command exception - ignore - handled
  gp - Guard page violation - break - not handled
  ii - Illegal instruction - second-chance break - not handled
  ip - In-page I/O error - break - not handled
  dz - Integer divide-by-zero - break - not handled
 iov - Integer overflow - break - not handled
  ch - Invalid handle - break
  hc - Invalid handle continue - not handled
 lsq - Invalid lock sequence - break - not handled
 isc - Invalid system call - break - not handled
  3c - Port disconnected - second-chance break - not handled
 sse - Single step exception - break
ssec - Single step exception continue - handled
 sbo - Stack buffer overflow - break - not handled
 sov - Stack overflow - break - not handled
  vs - Verifier stop - break - not handled
vcpp - Visual C++ exception - ignore - handled
 wkd - Wake debugger - break - not handled
 wob - WOW64 breakpoint - break - handled
 wos - WOW64 single step exception - break - handled

   * - Other exception - second-chance break - not handled
       Exception option for:
           12345678 - break - not handled
```

### Adjusting Event Break and Handling

Since the exceptions are useful if we can break the program execution when the event is happening, this section shows you how to control debugger behavior from an interactive prompt. In its most generic form, this command's syntax is the following:

```
sx{e|d|i|n} [-c "Cmd1"] [-c2 "Cmd2"] [-h] {Exception|Event|*} [parameter]
```

where,

- `sxe` (set exceptions enable) is used to enable the debugger break on the events.
- `sxd` (set exceptions disable) is used to disable the debugger break on the events. Although the first-chance exception does not break, the second chance breaks on the debugger and the message is displayed on the screen as usual for that specific event.

- `sxn` (set exceptions notify) is used to disable the debugger break (either first- or second-chance exception) but still prints the message to the screen. A side effect is that the debugger enters in a continuous loop. The operation system notifies the debugger for a first chance exception; the debugger prints a message and continues the target execution. If no handler is found, the debugger receives a second-chance notification. On continuation, the debugger again receives the first-chance exception, and the process repeats until the debugger receives another event.
- `sxi` (set exceptions ignore) is used to completely "ignore" the exception (either first- or second-chance exception); the exception is handled exactly as in the `sxn` case.
- `-c` is a parameter that contains a command to be executed when a new debugger event is received by the debugger. When this event is an exception event, the parameter affects first-chance exception only. Since the command is executed before the event is processed by the debugger, it should never contain a 'g' (go) statement.
- `-c2` is a parameter that contains the command to be executed when a second-chance exception is dispatched to debugger. Since the command is executed before the event is processed by the debugger, it should never contain a 'g' (go) statement.
- `Exception|Event|*` represents the event alias, exception alias, or exception code, such as `ct` for create thread event or `av` (or `0xC0000005` if the exception code is used instead) for access violation exception. The star (`*`) character represents all other exceptions identified by the exception code and not by an alias.
- `parameter` contains parameters specific to the event. For example, `DllLoadEvent` can be restricted to one or more dynamic libraries specified in the parameter. To break the application when `ole32.dll` is loaded, the `DllLoadEvent` event must be configured using the following command.

```
0:000>sxe ld:ole32.dll
```

- `-h` is a parameter that instructs the debugger to change the handling behavior instead of the break behavior. As described at the beginning of this chapter, after receiving an exception event, the debugger must return handling state to the operating system, so-called continuation disposition. Because no explicit option exists to specify the handling state, this is inferred from the command as follows: `sxe` means that the exception is handled; anything else means that the exception is not handled by the debugger.

Another interactive command, `sxr` (structured exception reset), must be used to reset all event breaks and handlings to the default values.

---

**WHAT IS THE DIFFERENCE BETWEEN SSE AND SSEC?** After a careful inspection of all the possible events, we can see exception pairs, such as sse (single step exception) followed by ssec (single-step exception continuation). This separation does not have support from the operating system, being interpreted only by the debugger engine, and is created just to expose the break and handling state easily on the command line as two different events.

---

### *Adjusting Event Break and Handling from the Windbg GUI*

Although the command window gives all the flexibility in the world, most people prefer to use the WinDbg UI to change the event break and handling state. The options can be accessed by selecting the Event Filters menu item in the Debug menu from any debugger session performed using Windbg, as you can see in Figure 3.1.

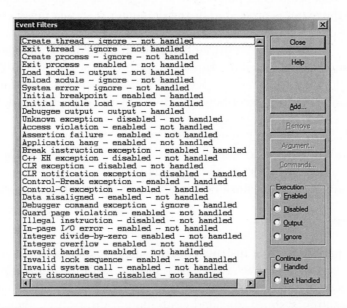

**Figure 3.1** WinDbg.exe Event Filters window

All options available on the command line are also available in the Event Filters window. Event command strings (-c and -c2) can be changed by clicking the Commands button, break status can be changed using the Execution radio buttons, handling state can be changed using the Continue radio buttons, and the event parameters can be added using the Argument button. The commands to change the event break and handling state affect the event selected from the main list. New exception codes can also be added or removed from the main list using the Add and Remove buttons, respectively, if the debugger target uses exception codes not shown in this list.

### Adjusting Event Break and Handling Defaults

Knowing how to control event break and handling state in interactive mode enables adjustment of the debugging environment to suit the debugging needs at any time. In some cases, the default event-handling settings are not adequate to the debugging situation. For example, an arbitrary module used to manage media licenses in a Digital Rights Management (DRM) system cannot be debugged using the normal debugger settings, as it uses various anti-debugging tricks, such as handled access violations, handled debug breakpoints, and so on and cannot be debugged using the normal debugger settings. Not surprisingly, such anti-debugging tricks leverage the side effects introduced in the process behavior by the debugger.

In this case, the software engineer must use other ways to adjust the event break and handling defaults to match the specific debugging needs. The most common way to adjust the defaults is through the use of the command-line parameters described in Table 3.1. The table contains the command-line option and the equivalent interactive command, along with the command description.

**Table 3.1** Command-Line Parameter Mapped to Interactive Commands

| Parameter | Interactive Command | Description |
|---|---|---|
| -g | sxd ibp | Don't break at process start-up |
| -G | sxd epr | Don't break at process termination |
| -xe <event> | sxe <event> | Break on <event> occurrences |
| -xd <event> | sxd <event> | Don't break on <event> occurrences |
| -xi <event> | sxi <event> | Ignore all <event> occurrences |
| -xn <event> | sxn <event> | Notify on <event> occurrences |
| -x | sxd av | Don't break on access violation |

To exemplify the mapping between the command-line parameters and interactive commands, the next command line has the following effect:

```
C:\>windbg -g -xe ld:kernel32* -xd av <debugger target>
```

- -g disables the initial breakpoint.
- -xd av disables access violation breaks.
- -xe ld:kernel32 breaks after kernel32.dll is mapped to the address space. The library name can contain wildcards. For example, the string ld:msvc* matches all various versions and flavors of the C runtime library.

The other option for setting the initial debugging environment for the command-line debugger is through the initialization file read by debugger on start-up. The initialization file is named tools.ini, and its folder location is indicated by an environment variable named INIT. For example, to obtain the same behavior as the previous command line for ntsd.exe, tools.ini must contain the lines shown in Listing 3.9.

**Listing 3.9**   Tools.ini content

```
[NTSD]
sxd: av
sxd: ibp
sxe: ld kernel32.dll
```

The Windbg debugger loads those defaults, as well as other runtime parameters, from the workspace file created either explicitly by the users or implicitly when the debugger session ended. The workspaces are very well covered in the debugger reference (help topic Workspaces).

**SAVING THE ENVIRONMENT** WinDbg saves the last debugger settings and reloads them when a new session starts. While this is not really a way of controlling the environment, it offers a pretty nice experience to casual debugger users.

### *Debugger Events*

This section takes a few events from Listing 3.8, analyzes them in the debugger console, notes any peculiarities, and provides tips on using them. Because the next section is dedicated to exceptions, the focus is on actionable debugger events: creating a process debug event, exiting a process debug event, loading a DLL debug event, unloading a DLL debug event, creating a thread debug event, and exiting a thread debug event.

### Create a Process Event (cpr)

The cpr event, not to be confused with the initial breakpoint event, is handled automatically by the Windows debuggers. If needed, the automatic handling can be disabled from the debugger command line. This event is raised before the dynamic libraries that the process depends on are loaded into the process address space. At this point, all global variables requiring explicit initialization are not yet initialized, while plain old data variables are filled with their default values. This is the first chance the debugger's user has to execute various commands, such as setting breakpoints or unassembling functions on the process image. This is the typical time to enable the load notification for a dynamic library the process depends on.

### Initial Breakpoint Event (ibp)

After the dependent libraries are loaded in the process, the system generates another exception signifying the initial breakpoint. The initial breakpoint is raised right before the process execution starts. At this point, we can set a breakpoint in the constructor used to initialize one global variable or set breakpoints in any function implemented in the process image, such as the main function.

If the initial breakpoint is not desired, we can overwrite event handling by using the -g command line parameter. The "Debugging Scenarios" section in Chapter 2 has a good example of how the initial breakpoint can be used to facilitate automation tasks. We should notice that the initial breakpoint does not look different from a regular breakpoint, and the event must be identified by inspecting the stack at the current breakpoint, as shown in Listing 3.10. The first two numbers displayed by the .lastevent command are the process identifier and the thread identifier raising the event.

**Listing 3.10**  Initial breakpoint stack trace for any process started under debugger

```
0:000> .lastevent
Last event: 13b4.184: Break instruction exception - code 80000003 (first chance)
0:000> k
ChildEBP RetAddr
0007fb1c 7c93edc0 ntdll!DbgBreakPoint
0007fc94 7c921639 ntdll!LdrpInitializeProcess+0xffa
0007fd1c 7c90eac7 ntdll!_LdrpInitialize+0x183
00000000 ntdll!KiUserApcDispatcher+0x7
```

### Exit a Process Event (epr)

Before the debugger target is terminated, the debugger gets a last notification in the form of the epr event, the event recognized by the .lastevent command. The .lastevent command uses the event information to display the process exit code, as illustrated in Listing 3.11. The event is not handled by default, but this can be overridden by starting the debugger using the -G command-line parameter.

**Listing 3.11**    Final event for any process started under debugger

```
0:000> .lastevent
Last event: 1674.c80: Exit process 0:1674, code 0
0:000> k
ChildEBP RetAddr
0007fde4 7c90e89a ntdll!KiFastSystemCallRet
0007fde8 7c81ca5e ntdll!NtTerminateProcess+0xc
0007fee4 7c81cab6 kernel32!_ExitProcess+0x62
0007fef8 77c39d45 kernel32!ExitProcess+0x14
0007ff04 77c39e78 msvcrt!__crtExitProcess+0x32
0007ff14 77c39e90 msvcrt!_cinit+0xee
0007ff28 01007522 msvcrt!exit+0x12
0007ffc0 7c816d4f notepad!WinMainCRTStartup+0x185
0007fff0 00000000 kernel32!BaseProcessStart+0x23
```

### Load a Module Event (ld)

ld is generated by the Windows operating system immediately after a dynamic library is mapped to process memory but before executing the library initialization code. This is the only opportunity to set breakpoints in library initialization code, including global variables initialization or to understand why this specific library is brought into the process space. The latter can be understood by inspecting the call stack of this event, as shown in Listing 3.12.

**Listing 3.12**    The stack trace after loading a dynamic link library

```
0:000> .lastevent
Last event: 43c.b18: Load module C:\WINDOWS\system32\ShimEng.dll at 5cb70000
0:000> k
ChildEBP RetAddr
0007f72c 7c90dc61 ntdll!KiFastSystemCallRet
0007f730 7c91c3da ntdll!NtMapViewOfSection+0xc
0007f824 7c916071 ntdll!LdrpMapDll+0x330
```

```
0007fae4 7c924a07 ntdll!LdrpLoadDll+0x1e9
0007fb10 7c9216b6 ntdll!LdrpLoadShimEngine+0x28
0007fc94 7c921639 ntdll!LdrpInitializeProcess+0x1079
0007fd1c 7c90eac7 ntdll!_LdrpInitialize+0x183
00000000 00000000 ntdll!KiUserApcDispatcher+0x7
```

## Unload a Module Event (ud)

The ud event is generated after a dynamic library is unmapped from the address space as a result of a call to FreeLibrary (see Listing 3.13). This event can be useful to track the dynamic link library unload order if needed.

**Listing 3.13**   Evaluating an ud event

```
0:000> .lastevent
Last event: 138c.cbc: Unload module C:\WINDOWS\System32\MSXML3.DLL at 74980000
0:000> k
ChildEBP RetAddr
0007fc28 7c90e96c ntdll!KiFastSystemCallRet
0007fc2c 7c91e7d3 ntdll!NtUnmapViewOfSection+0xc
0007fd1c 7c80aa7f ntdll!LdrUnloadDll+0x31a
0007fd30 77513442 kernel32!FreeLibrary+0x3f
0007fd3c 77513456 ole32!CClassCache::CDllPathEntry::CFinishObject::Finish+0x2f
0007fd50 77530729 ole32!CClassCache::CFinishComposite::Finish+0x1d
0007fe10 7752fd6a ole32!CClassCache::CleanUpDllsForProcess+0x1b2
0007fe14 7752fee4 ole32!ProcessUninitialize+0x37
0007fe28 774fee88 ole32!wCoUninitialize+0x11b
0007fe44 01035966 ole32!CoUninitialize+0x5b
0007ff44 0103caab WMIC!wmain+0x8af
0007ffc0 7c816d4f WMIC!wmainCRTStartup+0x125
0007fff0 00000000 kernel32!BaseProcessStart+0x23
```

## Create a Thread Event (ct)

The ct event is generated when a new thread is created (see Listing 3.14). Unfortunately, there is no useful information in this event, such as the thread creator stack or the creator thread identifier. This event, however, can be very useful for debugging thread lifetime issues in thread pool code. However, a breakpoint set on kernel32!CreateThread calls is often enough to determine the execution path leading to the thread creation.

### Listing 3.14    Evaluating a ct event

```
0:001> .lastevent
Last event: 1494.1220: Create thread 1:1220
0:001> k
ChildEBP RetAddr
0007cea4 00090178 kernel32!BaseThreadStartThunk
WARNING: Frame IP not in any known module. Following frames may be wrong.
0007cea4 00000000 0x90178
```

### Exit a Thread Event (et)

The et event is generated when a running thread is terminated. Its stack back-trace gives clues why the thread is getting terminated. For example, the thread from Listing 3.15 exits naturally when determined by the ole32.dll thread pool idle-detection mechanism.

### Listing 3.15    Evaluating an et event

```
0:003> .lastevent
Last event: 1494.11ac: Exit thread 3:11ac, code 0
0:003> k
ChildEBP RetAddr
011eff50 7c90e8af ntdll!KiFastSystemCallRet
011eff54 7c80cd04 ntdll!NtTerminateThread+0xc
011eff94 7c80cebf kernel32!ExitThread+0x8b
011effa0 774fe45d kernel32!FreeLibraryAndExitThread+0x28
011effb4 7c80b50b ole32!CRpcThreadCache::RpcWorkerThreadEntry+0x34
011effec 00000000 kernel32!BaseThreadStart+0x37
```

### Structured Exception-Dispatching Mechanism

An exception is an event that occurs during code execution either as a result of an event encountered by the CPU while executing the code, events known as hardware exceptions, or by explicit instructions to raise an exception, known as software exceptions. Hardware exceptions are the mechanisms used by the CPU to signal errors encountered while executing the instruction stream, such as encountering an invalid instruction or executing a breakpoint statement. Because no explicit statement exists to raise the exception in the code, compiler documentation often refers to such hardware exceptions as asynchronous exceptions.

On the other hand, software exceptions are raised by passing the exception information along with the desired handling mode to the user mode API kernel32!RaiseException. High-level languages, such as C++ or .NET languages, use this mechanism to throw exceptions and rely on the operating system to properly dispatch them. Because the compilers know that the throw statement introduces a discontinuity in code execution, such exceptions are known as synchronous exceptions.

The rest of this chapter uses 02sample.exe as the debugger target. The sample is a collection of bad practices; the code accesses invalid addresses, it raises exceptions and does not handle them, and so on. Each such bad behavior can be selected from the application menu. For example, by using the option '3,' the sample simulates an unhandled C++ exception situation.

### Exception Structures

To make the exception handling mechanism uniform across the entire operating system, Windows operating systems unify both concepts and treat all exceptions as structured exceptions, regardless of their source. This uniformity starts with using common data structures to pass exception record information between the operating system and exception handlers. The structure _EXCEPTION_POINTERS, defined in <winnt.h>, contains a pointer to the exception record and another one to the processor context, when the exception has been raised, as follows:

```
struct _EXCEPTION_POINTERS {
    EXCEPTION_RECORD *ExceptionRecord,
    CONTEXT *ContextRecord }
```

EXCEPTION_RECORD is defined in <winnt.h> and is listed in Listing 3.16. The same structure is later passed by the operating system to the debugger, where the information stored inside the structure is used to interpret and present exception information to the user.

**Listing 3.16**   EXCEPTION_RECORD structure, as defined in <winnt.h> header

```
typedef struct _EXCEPTION_RECORD {
    DWORD     ExceptionCode;
    DWORD ExceptionFlags;
    struct _EXCEPTION_RECORD *ExceptionRecord;
    PVOID ExceptionAddress;
    DWORD NumberParameters;
    ULONG_PTR ExceptionInformation[EXCEPTION_MAXIMUM_PARAMETERS];
} EXCEPTION_RECORD;
```

Because most exceptions are nonfatal, notably debugger breakpoint statements, the operating system needs to capture the processor state at the exception location to resume code execution if requested to do so. The processor state is stored in a processor architecture-specific structure called exception context that contains all the register values, and is defined in <winnt.h>. The first member of the structure describes the type of CONTEXT structure (see Listing 3.17).

**Listing 3.17**   CONTEXT structure, as defined in MSDN

```
typedef struct _CONTEXT {
    DWORD ContextFlags;
  ...
} CONTEXT,
```

The ContextFlags field takes a value from the constants defined in the same <winnt.h> header. For example, the possible constant values for the x86 family of processors is shown in Listing 3.18. A complete exception context for a typical application running on an x86 processor always starts with 0x0001003f, which represents the CONTEXT_ALL constant. That kind of signature is very useful when searching stack content and trying to understand the meaning of a specific memory block. We can set the context recognized this way as the current thread context to understand what the processor state was before raising the exception.

**Listing 3.18**   x86 context flags values

```
#define CONTEXT_i386    0x00010000    // this assumes that i386 and
#define CONTEXT_CONTROL         (CONTEXT_i386 | 0x00000001L) // SS:SP, CS:IP, FLAGS,
BP
#define CONTEXT_INTEGER         (CONTEXT_i386 | 0x00000002L) // AX, BX, CX, DX, SI,
DI
#define CONTEXT_SEGMENTS        (CONTEXT_i386 | 0x00000004L) // DS, ES, FS, GS
#define CONTEXT_FLOATING_POINT  (CONTEXT_i386 | 0x00000008L) // 387 state
#define CONTEXT_DEBUG_REGISTERS (CONTEXT_i386 | 0x00000010L) // DB 0-3,6,7
#define CONTEXT_EXTENDED_REGISTERS  (CONTEXT_i386 | 0x00000020L) // cpu-specific
extensions

#define CONTEXT_FULL (CONTEXT_CONTROL | CONTEXT_INTEGER |\
                    CONTEXT_SEGMENTS)


#define CONTEXT_ALL (CONTEXT_CONTROL | CONTEXT_INTEGER | CONTEXT_SEGMENTS |
CONTEXT_FLOATING_POINT | CONTEXT_DEBUG_REGISTERS | CONTEXT_EXTENDED_REGISTERS)
```

*Exception Life Cycle*

A hardware event forcefully transfers the processor control from the current executed program to system routines that handle interrupt events. Those routines are called interrupt handlers, which are installed by the operating system. After the processor state switches into kernel mode, the kernel saves the processor state into a trap context, which can be used to inspect the processor state before transition. Listing 3.19 shows the call stack of a thread immediately after it raised an exception. The process throwing the exceptions has been started under the user mode debugger using the windbg.exe 02sample.exe command line. The exception is raised by selecting option '3.' The process then stops in the debugger, which in turn waits for user input. The thread is in fact blocked while the Windows operating system dispatches the exception information to the debugger, as we can see by using the kernel mode debugger in this state. We identify the process by using the `!process` extension command and the `!thread` extension command to interpret the stack of the single process's thread.

**Listing 3.19**   Exception dispatched to the user mode debugger

```
kd> !process 0 4 02sample.exe
PROCESS ff68a020  SessionId: 0  Cid: 0a7c    Peb: 7ffdd000  ParentCid: 0a70
    DirBase: 03912000  ObjectTable: e180e158  HandleCount:   7.
    Image: 02sample.exe

        THREAD ffa7d868  Cid 0a7c.0a78  Teb: 7ffdf000 Win32Thread: 00000000 WAIT


kd> !thread ffa7d868
THREAD ffa7d868  Cid 0a7c.0a78  Teb: 7ffdf000 Win32Thread: 00000000 WAIT: (Executive)
KernelMode Non-Alertable
SuspendCount 1
    f7cf3490  SynchronizationEvent
Not impersonating
DeviceMap                e19f85a0
Owning Process           ff68a020     Image:        02sample.exe
Wait Start TickCount     14796478     Ticks: 1035 (0:00:00:10.364)
Context Switch Count     44
UserTime                 00:00:00.0000
KernelTime               00:00:00.0290
Win32 Start Address 02sample!mainCRTStartup (0x0040183d)
Start Address kernel32!BaseProcessStartThunk (0x7c810867)
Stack Init f7cf4000 Current f7cf3414 Base f7cf4000 Limit f7cf1000 Call 0
Priority 10 BasePriority 8 PriorityDecrement 0 DecrementCount 16
ChildEBP RetAddr  Args to Child
f7cf342c 804dc6a6 ffa7d8d8 ffa7d868 804dc6f2 nt!KiSwapContext+0x2e ()
f7cf3438 804dc6f2 00000000 ffa7d868 f7cf3488 nt!KiSwapThread+0x46
```

*(continues)*

**Listing 3.19**   Exception dispatched to the user mode debugger *(continued)*

```
f7cf3460 8065879b 00000000 00000000 00000000 nt!KeWaitForSingleObject+0x1c2
f7cf3540 80659903 ff68a020 00000000 f7cf3578 nt!DbgkpQueueMessage+0x17c
f7cf3564 8060fed2 f7cf3578 00000001 f7cf3d64 nt!DbgkpSendApiMessage+0x45
f7cf35f0 804fc914 f7cf39d8 00000001 00000000 nt!DbgkForwardException+0x8f
f7cf39b0 804fcbfe f7cf39d8 00000000 f7cf3d64 nt!KiDispatchException+0x1f4
f7cf3d34 804e297d 0006fe48 0006fb64 00000000 nt!KiRaiseException+0x175
f7cf3d50 804df06b 0006fe48 0006fb64 00000001 nt!NtRaiseException+0x31
f7cf3d50 7c81eb33 0006fe48 0006fb64 00000001 nt!KiFastCallEntry+0xf8 (TrapFrame @
f7cf3d64)
0006fe98 77c2272c e06d7363 00000001 00000003 kernel32!RaiseException+0x53
0006fed8 004012c5 0006feec 00401d38 004012b0 msvcrt!_CxxThrowException+0x36
0006fef0 00401471 00011970 7c9118f1 7ffdd000 02sample!RaiseCPP+0x25
0006ff44 0040196c 00000002 00262588 00262a58 02sample!wmain+0xe1
0006ffc0 7c816d4f 00011970 7c9118f1 7ffdd000 02sample!mainCRTStartup+0x12f
0006fff0 00000000 0040183d 00000000 78746341 kernel32!BaseProcessStart+0x23
kd> .trap f7cf3d64
ErrCode = 00000000
eax=0006fe48 ebx=7ffdd000 ecx=00000000 edx=002625b0 esi=0006fed8 edi=0006fed8
eip=7c81eb33 esp=0006fe44 ebp=0006fe98 iopl=0         nv up ei pl nz na pe nc
cs=001b  ss=0023  ds=0023  es=0023  fs=003b  gs=0000             efl=00000206
kernel32!RaiseException+0x53:
001b:7c81eb33 5e              pop       esi
kd> k
  *** Stack trace for last set context - .thread/.cxr resets it
ChildEBP RetAddr
0006fe98 77c2272c kernel32!RaiseException+0x53
0006fed8 004012c5 msvcrt!_CxxThrowException+0x36
0006fef0 00401471 02sample!RaiseCPP+0x25
0006ff44 0040196c 02sample!wmain+0xe1
0006ffc0 7c816d4f 02sample!mainCRTStartup+0x12f
0006fff0 00000000 kernel32!BaseProcessStart+0x23
```

The handler uses the trap information and possibly other information retrieved from the processor to create two pieces of information: an exception record, describing the exception encountered and an exception context, containing the state of the processor at the time the processor encountered that exception. Please note that the trap frame information (shown in the first kernel function from the previous stack as TrapFrame) captured at the transition into the kernel mode point can be used as context information to the .trap command, as shown in Listing 3.19.

Software exceptions are initiated by an explicit call into a kernel mode, using the undocumented API ntdll!NtRaiseException called by the public API kernel32! RaiseException. ntdll!NtRaiseException creates the exception record and captures the process state in an exception context. With the exception record and the exception context, the kernel is ready to dispatch the exception using the exception-dispatching mechanism, similar to the hardware exceptions.

The dispatching process starts in kernel mode and continues later in user mode or kernel mode, matching the mode active when the exception was encountered. All exceptions encountered in kernel mode should be handled; otherwise, that exception causes a bug check (also known as blue screen errors or BSOD), such as the following:

```
bug check 0x8E: KERNEL_MODE_EXCEPTION_NOT_HANDLED
```

With the exception information captured as described previously, the operating system starts the exception-dispatching routine. As part of this routine, the Windows operating system performs several activities, such as

- Attempts to call all registered handlers until the exception is handled
- Provides additional functionality such as exception logging
- Ultimately decides what to do with any unhandled exception

This complex functionality, provided by the Windows operating system, is performed almost silently. We use "almost" because the exception dispatching is relatively expensive when compared to normal code execution. As long as no exceptions are raised as part of the normal execution flow, the overall cost of dispatching the exception is negligible.

### Exception Dispatching

The Windows operating system takes debugger availability into account when an exception is dispatched—that is, a user mode debugger attached to the process generating the exception or a kernel mode debugger attached to the system causing the exception. The scope of this section is limited to exceptions encountered while executing user mode code.

When the Windows operating system starts to process user mode exceptions, it first asks the user mode debugger attached to the process, if any, to handle the exception. If no debugger is attached to the process, the kernel examines a global flag controlling the dispatching process and dispatches the exception according to the flag. Bit 0 of nt!NTGlobalFlag controls exception-dispatching behavior and is named StopOnException (soe). When the StopOnException flag is set, all exceptions encountered on a process, not attached to a user mode debugger, are first dispatched to the kernel debugger attached to the target system. When the flag is not set, the kernel mode debugger does not interfere with exception-dispatching code, unless the exception has special debugging meanings, such as STATUS_BREAPOINT and STATUS_SINGLE_STEP.

The best option to use for decoding the flags is the !gflag extension command, which deciphers the contents of nt!NTGlobalFlag, as shown in Listing 3.20.

**Listing 3.20**    Deciphering kernel global flags

```
kd> dc nt!NtGlobalFlag 11
80540aec  00000001                            ....
kd> !gflag
Current NtGlobalFlag contents: 0x00000001
    soe - Stop On Exception
```

This flag, just as all other kernel flags, can be changed from the debugger console. The flags can also be changed using the gflags.exe utility installed with Debugging Tools for Windows. Listing 3.21 shows an example of temporary or permanently enabling the StopOnException flag using gflags.exe.

**Listing 3.21**    Changing kernel flags using command line gflags.exe

```
c:\> gflags -k +soe
Current Running Kernel Settings are: 00000000
    soe - Stop On Exception

c:\> gflags -r +soe
Current Boot Registry Settings are: 00000001
    soe - Stop On Exception
```

However, for a better interactive experience, the user can start gflags.exe without a parameter and change the kernel flags in the graphical user interface, as shown in Figure 3.2.

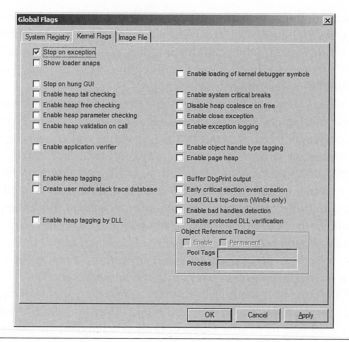

**Figure 3.2** Changing kernel flags using GUI gflags.exe

Regardless of how the `StopOnException` flag is changed, the exception behavior is affected in the same way. The next section focuses on the steps taken by the kernel to dispatch an exception, taking into consideration the `StopOnException` flag as well. The logic used to dispatch a user mode exception is described in the following. Figure 3.3 presents this logic in a flow chart format.

Dispatching a user mode exception can be summarized as follows:

**1.** When a new exception is raised, the Windows kernel tries to dispatch the exception to the user mode debugger if available. If available, the exception-dispatching flow continues from step 6. When a kernel debugger is attached to the host, the exception dispatching flow continues in step 2; otherwise, it continues from step 4.

**2.** Exceptions that have meaning for the debugger, such as STATUS_BREAKPOINT or STATUS_SINGLE_STEP, are sent as debugger notification to the kernel debugger. When the `StopOnException` flag is set, all other exceptions are also sent as debugger notifications to the kernel debugger; otherwise, the exception-dispatching flow continues in step 4. The system is "frozen," waiting for a reply to the kernel debugger notification.

3. The kernel debugger examines the exception and, depending on the debugger settings, it can handle the exception. In this case, the exception is dismissed, and the code execution continues from the exception location when the kernel debugger replies to the debugger notification. For unhandled exceptions, the dispatching flow continues from step 4.

4. The Windows kernel searches for an exception handler by evaluating all functions from the call stacks for the presence of a frame-based exception handler. Exception handler filters found in this phase are called, starting with the most recent function from the stack, until one filter returns EXCEPTION_ EXECUTE_HANDLER. Starting with Windows XP and Windows Server 2003, the developer can register additional filters to be called prior to starting the search process using a vectored exception handler mechanism. With the exception handler found earlier, the kernel starts to roll back the execution stack to the function owning the handler, executing all the final handlers registered within the functions traversed—a process called stack unwinding. Finally, the code execution continues with the exception handler in the target function.

5. What if the current thread stack contains no handler capable of handling the current exception? Each thread guards the procedure code with a built-in filter and handler designed to handle all exceptions not handled by user-provided code. This filter, generically called the unhandled exception filter, takes the necessary steps to terminate the process by calling the kernel32!UnhandledExceptionFilter API when an exception is not handled. The logic used by unhandled exception filters is described in Chapter 13, "Postmortem Debugging."

6. When a user mode debugger is attached to the process, it receives the exception notification, and it can handle it or not based on the debugger settings. (See the previous section "Controlling Exceptions and Events from the Debugger" regarding exception handling settings.) This notification is referred to in the debugger documentation as first chance exception. Handling of exceptions unhandled by the debugger continues by searching an exception handler for the exception and unwinding the stack when this is available, as in the process described in step 4. Exceptions handled by the user mode debugger, such as STATUS_BREAKPOINT, continue by executing the code from the location that generated the exception after any adjustment is made by the debugger.

7. If the debugger does not handle the exception and no handler is found in step 6, the Windows kernel makes a second attempt to have the exception handled by the debugger, a notification process known as second chance exception. If the exception is still not handled by the debugger, the process simply restarts the sequence from step 6 until the exception is handled.

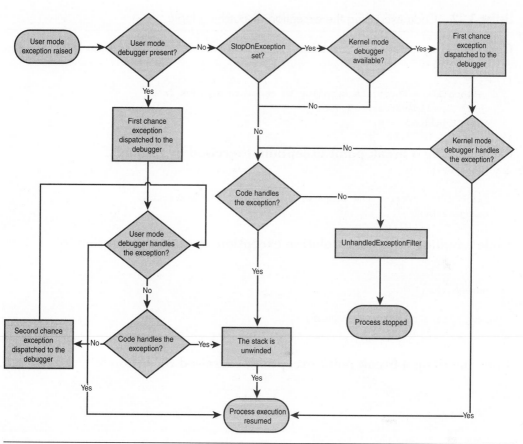

**Figure 3.3**   Exception dispatching logic

The next section shows, in practical ways, the effects of various debugger configurations for different exceptions, using the logic described previously.

### Exception Reflected in Different Debugger Configurations
The sample 02sample.exe is once again used to illustrate the user mode exception dispatching logic. Various options invoke code paths with different exception-handling behaviors. In the C language, exception handlers are created using __try/__except keywords, a Microsoft extension to the company compilers designed to generate the exception filters and handler required by the operating system. This section details several aspects of the exception-handling mechanism implemented by the Windows operating system. Listing 3.22 shows the code exercised by each option described in the subheadings, code compiled in the executable 02sample.exe.

**Listing 3.22**   Code exercising the exception dispatching logic

### Code causing an access violation exception, exercised by option '1'

```
void RaiseAV()
{
    _alloca(1); //Force the compiler to generate a stack frame
    char* invalidAddress = 0;
    *invalidAddress = 0;
}
```

### Code causing a break point exception, exercised by option '2'

```
void RaiseBP()
{
    _alloca(1); //Force the compiler to generate a stack frame
    DebugBreak();
}
```

### Code handling an access violation exception, exercised by option 'b'

```
__try
{
    RaiseAV();
}
__except(EXCEPTION_EXECUTE_HANDLER)
{
}
```

### Code handling a break point exception, exercised by option 'c'

```
__try
{
    RaiseBP();
}
__except(EXCEPTION_EXECUTE_HANDLER)
{
}
```

Each function, shown previously, runs in different environments. All relevant information pertaining to the interaction between the code and the Windows operating system (or the interaction with the debuggers if any are attached) is detailed next. The entire exercise is done under the assumption that the system configuration was not altered by any program installed on that system, especially a debugger toolkit or a development suite with debugging capabilities.

The same executable runs under four different configurations, as follows:

- The first configuration does not use a debugger, which is representative of a real user environment. We call this a normal configuration.

- The second configuration has a kernel debugger connected to the host, commonly used in software testing phase. We call this a kernel mode debugger or KD configuration.
- The third configuration has a kernel debugger connected to the host and has the `StopOnException` global flag enabled. We call this a KD with SOE configuration.
- In the fourth configuration, the executable runs under a user mode debugger, a configuration popular in the development phase. We call this a user mode debugger or UM configuration.

### Unhandled Access Violation Exception (STATUS_ACCESS_VIOLATION)

The first option generates the most familiar exception, having 0xC0000005 code representing an access violation exception, also known as a protection fault. The first function described in Listing 3.22 must be used in each of the preceding configurations. The behavior across all configurations is as follows:

- Normal configuration
  Without a debugger available, exception-dispatching code evaluates all available filters in step 4 of the "Exception Dispatching" section described previously. After not finding any, the exception-dispatching code invokes kernel32!UnhandledExceptionFilter, causing the application to report the error and exit. This process is described in Chapter 13.
- KD configuration
  With a kernel debugger connected to the system, the system behavior does not change and the application exits in the same way as in the normal configuration.
- KD with SOE configuration
  In this configuration, exception-handling code forwards the exception to the kernel mode debugger and waits for the handling disposition. The system resumes the execution after entering the g command with the exception-handling code described in the normal configuration.
- UM configuration
  The user mode debugger is notified about the exception encountered since the debugger is normally configured to stop on the first-chance exception. After entering the g command, the exception handling code searches for a frame handler for that exception, and because no handler is available, the exception notification is sent one more time to the debugger as a second-chance exception. Handling the exception in the debugger does not help because the condition causing the access violation is still present and the failing instruction is

executed again. As a result, the system again raises the exception as a first-chance exception, and the cycle continues until the condition disappears. This cycle can be seen in action by starting the faulty code under the debugger and instructing it to just notify the user about access violation exceptions instead of waiting for user input:

```
c:\>windbg.exe -g -G -xn av C:\AWDBIN\WinXP.x86.chk\02sample.exe
```

### Unhandled-Breakpoint Exception (STATUS_BREAKPOINT Exception)

As seen at the beginning of this chapter, this STATUS_BREAKPOINT exception has special meaning for the debugger, and the system behavior is changed slightly when compared to the access-violation exception.

- Normal configuration
  The system exhibits the same behavior as with an access-violation exception. Any int 3 processor instruction (executed from within the DebugBreak() or assert() statement) is perceived by the system and user as any other exception. Contrary to what we see in the debugger, the code execution does not continue immediately after the int 3 statement.
- KD configuration
  Because the exception is characteristic of the debugging process, the kernel debugger stops and handles this exception. Upon continuation, the execution resumes from the instruction following the int 3 statement.
- KD with SOE configuration
  Because the STATUS_BREAKPOINT exception is already handled by the kernel mode debugger, the StopOnException flag does not add further changes.
- UM configuration
  The debugger stops at the breakpoint instruction and handles the exception. Upon continuation, the execution resumes from the instruction following the int 3 statement.

**Handled Access-Violation Exception**   The code used in this case is similar to what we used to test unhandled-access violations, except that it provides a frame-based exception handler for the exception.

- Normal configuration
  As expected, the exception is handled, and the code continues normally after the handler is executed.

- KD configuration
  As expected, the exception is handled, and the code continues normally, without kernel mode notification.
- KD with SOE configuration
  In this configuration, the exception-handling mechanism forwards the exception to the kernel mode debugger and waits for a continuation disposition. Upon continuation (after the g command), the exception is handled in the user mode code, which continues normally.
- UM configuration
  The debugger stops at the first-chance exception notification according to the debugger default exception-handling settings. Upon continuation, the exception handler is handling the exception, and the process execution continues normally.

**Handled-Breakpoint Exception**   What is different when the exception is a debugging-specific exception, such as the STATUS_BREAKPOINT exception or the STATUS_SINGLE_STEP exception? All debuggers try to understand and handle such exceptions.

- Normal configuration
  As expected, the exception is handled and the code continues normally.
- KD configuration
  Because the exception is specially used in debugging, the kernel debugger stops and handles this exception.
- KD with SOE configuration
  In this configuration, the exception-handling code forwards the exception to the kernel mode debugger and waits for a disposition of it. Upon continuation (after the g command), the execution resumes from the instruction following the int 3 statement and the process finishes normally.
- UM configuration
  The debugger stops at the first-chance exception notification according to the debugger default exception-handling settings. Upon continuation, the execution resumes from the instruction following the int 3 statement and the process finishes normally.

After testing all such configurations using different exception codes, several interesting conclusions can be drawn and used in day-to-day work, as follows.

- By default, any unhandled exception generates, using Windows Error Reporting (WER), a crash report that can be used for postmortem debugging. The customers can centralize such reports at the enterprise level using the Microsoft Corporate Error Reporting or the newer Agentless Exception Monitoring server. The customer can also have them uploaded to the WER site to be investigated by Microsoft developers or by the participating software vendors. Chapter 13 describes how independent software vendors can participate in analyzing WER reports and provide solutions to the commonly reported problems.

- Although users of any software solution don't have a pleasant experience when encountering unhandled exceptions, from the developer perspective, these exceptions provide the necessary feedback loop required to fix all software flaws present in the applications. The alternative technique of hiding all exceptions by "handling" them, irrespective of the types or source, so the user doesn't see them, creates long-term reliability problems that are hard to diagnose and sometimes are never fixed, as there is no "visible" impact on users.

- In the development and testing phases, the kernel debugger is a very powerful tool and should be used to monitor a percentage of the systems used in product testing if it does not conflict with the application.

- Distributed applications propagating errors from one process to another are usually difficult to debug since the source of the original error is not known in advance. If the error was initially an exception raised on any constituent process, it is easy to stop the system execution in that spot using the KD with SOE configuration and the appropriate sx command in the kernel debugger.

- Good developers are usually asserting the state of the process by using various assert techniques. Unfortunately, most of the asserts are disabled in the released version of the product, the most likely target of the testing phase, and one big opportunity to make sure that the code works as expected is wasted. Really important asserts can be replaced with code that raises a breakpoint and handle intermediately. This breakpoint causes the code to stop in the debugger if present or continues the execution with a small performance hit (as the condition asserted should always be true).

Knowing how the exception is handled by the system in various configurations enables developers to understand why the code stopped where it stopped. Developers can use this knowledge to define the error-handling strategy for their product, to rely on an unhandled exception filter to collect crash data, or to handle few exceptions by themselves and collect some information from the process. In the development phase, the code can be instrumented and the testing environment can be adjusted to bring valuable feedback into the development process. Ideally, the developers should not change the unhandled exception filter behavior and rely on WER feedback mechanism.

---

**ANTI-DEBUGGING TECHNIQUES**    Please be aware that several anti-debugging techniques use the exception mechanism to check if the environment is running without debuggers and to discourage people from debugging the code protected this way. An exception raised in a product dealing with data protection, rights management, or license management is not always what it appears to be.

---

### Frame-Based Exception Handler

As we have seen in this section, the Windows exception-handling mechanism is quite flexible. It enables any function from the call stack to filter all the exceptions raised when executing the current function or any function called by it. Depending on the exception type or other factors determined by the filter, the function can handle the exception, fix the condition generating the exception and retry the execution, or ignore the exceptions. The function can also set a termination handler to be called when the current function returns. This section explains the underlying mechanism used by the applications to support the exception-dispatching mechanism. Understanding this mechanism is useful when debugging problems encountered in the exception-handling code itself.

Although the mechanism described in this section is specific to the x86 architecture, it represents a good case for learning how the system deals with exceptions and how to debug such code. The system requirements for a function to participate in an exception-handling mechanism are minimal. The application must provide an exception handler with a well-defined function signature and register it with the process-unwinding mechanism for the duration of the function execution. Each registration represents a new exception frame. This handler is invoked by the Windows operating system when the function might terminate the execution because of an exception. Although it is possible to handcraft exception handlers that interact directly with the native exception-handling mechanism, we use C/C++ compilers to build exception frames.

On x86 architectures, the exception handlers are organized in a single linked list, private to each thread, adjusted dynamically by the code running on that thread. When a new handler must be added to the list, this handler's node becomes the head of the list, which is then stored in the thread environment block (TEB). Each node stores the exception handler for the corresponding function plus the link to the next node corresponding to a caller with an exception handler. Figure 3.4 illustrates the list organization.

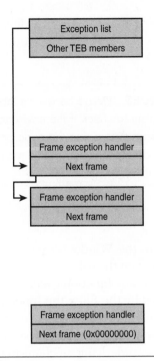

**Figure 3.4** Exception handler list

Because each function provides one exception handler at most, the list length cannot exceed the length of the call stack. Most functions do not require participation in the exception-dispatching logic and do not provide a handler into the exception chain. Listing 3.23 demonstrates the use of information described in Figure 3.4: finding the exception handler list head and printing the entire exception list using the !slist extension command. The Windows debugger team recognizes that this process is cumbersome, so they provided an extension command, !exchain, to do all this plus the necessary function handlers deciphering when possible. Listing 3.23 uses those commands to investigate the exception handler chain at the debugger stop caused in the function invoked by option 'd' of the sample 02sample.exe.

**Listing 3.23** Investigating x86 exception handler list

```
0:000> !teb
TEB at 7ffdf000
    ExceptionList:        0006ff28
0:000> * Obtain the exception chain type information
```

```
0:000> dt nt!_NT_TIB ExceptionList
   +0x000 ExceptionList : Ptr32 _EXCEPTION_REGISTRATION_RECORD
0:000> !slist $teb _EXCEPTION_REGISTRATION_RECORD 0
SLIST HEADER:
   +0x000 Alignment          : 700000006ff28
   +0x000 Next               : 6ff28
   +0x004 Depth              : 0
   +0x006 Sequence           : 7

SLIST CONTENTS:
0006ff28
   +0x000 Next               : 0x0006ff90 _EXCEPTION_REGISTRATION_RECORD
   +0x004 Handler            : 0x010020d2      _EXCEPTION_DISPOSITION
02sample!_except_handler4+0
0006ff90
   +0x000 Next               : 0x0006ffdc _EXCEPTION_REGISTRATION_RECORD
   +0x004 Handler            : 0x010020d2      _EXCEPTION_DISPOSITION
02sample!_except_handler4+0
0006ffdc
   +0x000 Next               : 0xffffffff _EXCEPTION_REGISTRATION_RECORD
   +0x004 Handler            : 0x77b88bf2      _EXCEPTION_DISPOSITION
ntdll!_except_handler4+0
ffffffff
   +0x000 Next               : ????
   +0x004 Handler            : ????
0:000> !exchain /f
0006ff28: 02sample!_except_handler4+0 (010020d2)
0006ff90: 02sample!_except_handler4+0 (010020d2)
0006ffdc: ntdll!_except_handler4+0 (77b88bf2)
...
```

In this case, each function uses the same exception handler, and the !exchain extension command does not understand the exception frame or show additional information about it. In such situations, we have to manually decode the exception frames. Because the handlers are generated by the compiler tools in most cases, the next section goes into the details of the generated code, using Microsoft C/C++ compilers as models. The compiler provides this support by a nonstandard extension in the form of the __try/__except and __try/__finally constructs.

### Generating a Frame-Based Exception Handler

We start with a simple function containing an exception handler and an exception handler filter that always evaluates to EXCEPTION_EXECUTE_HANDLER. The code protected by the exception handler accesses an invalid memory location that generates an access violation exception. The source for this function is shown in Listing 3.24.

3. DEBUGGERS UNCOVERED

**Listing 3.24**   Simple function using __try/__except constructs

```
void try_except()
{
    __try
    {
        *((int *) 0) = 0;
    }
    __except(ex_filter())
    {
    global = 1;
    }
}
```

The generated code for this function can be inspected in the debugger after starting 02sample.exe. Listing 3.26 contains the annotated code corresponding to the function shown in Listing 3.25.

**Listing 3.25**   Generated code for a simple function using __try/__except support

```
0:000> uf 02sample!try_except
02sample!try_except:
...
01001d75 6afe               push    0FFFFFFFEh                              ;Set the block counter
01001d77 68d02a0001         push    offset 02sample!_CT??_R0H+0x60 (01002ad0)
01001d7c 68d2200001         push    offset 02sample!_except_handler4 (010020d2)
01001d81 64a100000000       mov     eax,dword ptr fs:[00000000h] ;Retrieve the head
01001d87 50                 push    eax                          ;Save the old head
...
01001d99 8d45f0             lea     eax,[ebp-10h]
01001d9c 64a300000000       mov     dword ptr fs:[00000000h],eax ;Save the new head
01001da2 8965e8             mov     dword ptr [ebp-18h],esp
01001da5 c745fc00000000     mov     dword ptr [ebp-4],0          ;Block change
01001dac c705000000000000000000 mov dword ptr ds:[0],0
01001db6 c745fcfeffffff     mov     dword ptr [ebp-4],0FFFFFFFEh
01001dbd eb1a               jmp     02sample!try_except+0x69 (01001dd9)
02sample!try_except+0x69:
01001dd9 8b4df0             mov     ecx,dword ptr [ebp-10h]      ; Get old head
01001ddc 64890d00000000     mov     dword ptr fs:[0],ecx         ; restore old head
...
01001dea c3                 ret
0:000> dc 01002ad0 18
01002ad0  fffffffe 00000000 fffffffd8 00000000  ................
01002ae0  fffffffe 01001dbf 01001dc5 00000000  ................
```

The compiler splits the function into multiple regions with different handler functionality, and it generates an aggregate structure containing a filter and a handler for each region. To link this information with the standard unwinding mechanism, the compiler registers a generic handler at the beginning of the function call and deregisters it at the end of the function call. The handler common to all functions in the module evaluates the exception using the filter function and invokes the user code handling the exception matching the current executed block. The handler is implemented in the compiler runtime library, also known as the CRT.

How does the generic handler know which block is currently executing? Microsoft C/C++ compilers on x86 processors use a local counter indicating which region is currently executing. The local counter is changed by compiler-generated code when the execution crosses the region borders.

Plain assembly code limits the capability of understanding the exception-handling code and the transformation happening in the compilation process. To reduce the gap between the familiar C/C++ source code and assembly code, the compiler can generate an intermediate file called an assembly listing. An assembly listing contains the assembly code annotated with the original source code and suggestive labels instead of just addresses. This is often used to understand the role of a specific processor instruction in the original C/C++ source code. Listing 3.26 contains the assembly listing corresponding to the function `try_except` shown previously in plain assembly language.

In the annotated code shown in Listing 3.27, we can see that the exception information block, identified by the `$__sehtable$?try_except@@YGXXZ` label, contains pointers to the exception filter `$LN5@try_except` and to the exception handler `$LN6@try_except` function. The generic exception-handling function, the `__except_handler4` function imported from the MSVCRT library, is stored on the stack immediately after the exception information block at the address `0000c`. The region index, referred to using the `__$SEHRec$[ebp+20]` label, is changed from −2, meaning that the function is outside any exception region without anything to execute on exception, to 0 after starting the `__try` block execution on the offset `00035`. When the protected region execution completes, the index is changed back to −2, indicating that the code execution is outside any protected region. The exception handlers list is referred to by `fs:0`.

## Listing 3.26  Assembly listing generated for the function from Listing 3.24

```
PUBLIC     ?try_except@@YGXXZ                    ;
xdata$x    SEGMENT
__sehtable$?try_except@@YGXXZ DD 0fffffffeH
     DD     00H
```

*(continues)*

**Listing 3.26** Assembly listing generated for the function from Listing 3.24 *(continued)*

```
    DD    0ffffffd8H
    DD    00H
    DD    0fffffffeH
    DD    FLAT:$LN5@try_except
    DD    FLAT:$LN6@try_except
xdata$x   ENDS
_TEXT     SEGMENT
?try_except@@YGXXZ PROC                        ; try_except, COMDAT
...
  00005  6a fe          push    -2              ; fffffffeH
  00007  68 00 00 00 00    push    OFFSET __sehtable$?try_except@@YGXXZ
  0000c  68 00 00 00 00    push    OFFSET __except_handler4
  00011  64 a1 00 00 00 00    mov    eax, DWORD PTR fs:0
...
  00029  8d 45 f0       lea    eax,   DWORD PTR __$SEHRec$[ebp+8]
  0002c  64 a3 00 00 00  00 mov    DWORD PTR fs:0, eax
  00032  89 65 e8       mov    DWORD PTR __$SEHRec$[ebp], esp
; 29   :      __try
  00035  c7 45 fc 00 00 00 00 mov    DWORD PTR __$SEHRec$[ebp+20], 0
; 30   :      {
; 31   :          *((int *) 0) = 0;
  0003c  c7 05 00 00 00 00 00 00 00 00  mov    DWORD PTR ds:0, 0
; 32   :      }
  00046  c7 45 fc fe ff ff ff mov    DWORD PTR __$SEHRec$[ebp+20], -2 ; fffffffeH
  0004d  eb 1a          jmp    SHORT $LN4@try_except
$LN5@try_except:
$LN10@try_except:
; 33   :      __except(ex_filter())
  0004f  e8 00 00 00 00    call    ?ex_filter@@YGHXZ    ; ex_filter
$LN7@try_except:
$LN9@try_except:
  00054  c3             ret     0
$LN6@try_except:
  00055  8b 65 e8       mov    esp, DWORD PTR __$SEHRec$[ebp]
; 34   :      {
; 35   :      global = 1;
  00058  c7 05 00 00 00 00 01 00 00 00    mov    DWORD PTR ?global@@3HA, 1 ; global
; 36   :      }
  00062  c7 45 fc fe ff ff ff mov    DWORD PTR __$SEHRec$[ebp+20], -2 ; fffffffeH
$LN4@try_except:
; 37   : }
  00069  8b 4d f0       mov    ecx, DWORD PTR __$SEHRec$[ebp+8]
```

```
  0006c  64 89 0d 00 00 00 00 mov      DWORD PTR fs:0, ecx
...
  0007a  c3                   ret      0
?try_except@@YGXXZ ENDP                ; try_except
_TEXT      ENDS
```

How did we generate this code? The process is dependent on the development environment used to build the application. Within the WDK build environment, the process of generating annotated code is straightforward; the annotated code file is just another target of the compilation process, the target identified by extension .cod. For example, the file FuncAV.cpp (containing the code for this section) can be compiled to the annotated file by nmake-ing the target file FuncAV.cod, as exemplified in Listing 3.27.

**Listing 3.27**  Generating annotated assembly file from the source file

```
C:\AWD\CHAPTER2>nmake FuncAV.cod

Microsoft (R) Program Maintenance Utility   Version 7.00.8882
Copyright (C) Microsoft Corp 1988-2000. All rights reserved.

      cl -nologo @objfre_wxp_x86\i386\clcod.rsp /Fc /FC .\FuncAV.cpp
FuncAV.cpp
```

The fs:0 label, representing the exception handler list head, is evaluated to the address fs:[0], the first pointer from TEB. Because the fs selector has the same value for all threads, the question you might ask is what's happening in a multithread environment; how does the exceptions list not get corrupted when all exception handler heads are stored at the same address?

The operating system uses only the fs selector to address thread-specific information, which provides the indirection required to access different addresses using the same "handle." Although the selector value stays the same for all threads in the process, thread separation is achieved by the operating system by changing the segment descriptor pointed by the fs selector each time a new thread is scheduled for execution on a processor. Listing 3.28 shows the segment descriptor corresponding to the fs selector having the value 0x3b, for two threads in the same process. The base column represents the virtual address where TEB starts.

**Listing 3.28**  Thread environment block on two different threads in the same process

```
0:000> dg @fs
                              P Si Gr Pr Lo
Sel   Base    Limit     Type  l ze an es ng Flags
-- ---- ---- ----- - - - - - ----
003B  7ffdf000 00000fff Data RW Ac 3 Bg By P  Nl 000004f3
0:001> dg @fs
                              P Si Gr Pr Lo
Sel   Base    Limit     Type  l ze an es ng Flags
-- ---- ---- ----- - - - - - ----
003B  7ffdd000 00000fff Data RW Ac 3 Bg By P  Nl 000004f3
```

After this overview of the entire exception mechanism, you should understand what code is executed when the exception passes through your functions, and you should be able to set up the breakpoints in exception filters or exception handlers when necessary. At other times, you might be in a situation in which the source code handles the exception properly but the executable code does not, and you might discover that the handler was added after that executable was compiled and you have the means to prove it.

As a side effect, by examining the exception handler list head stored in the TEB, we can find out which functions from the current stack are using exception handlers. This information is priceless when the stack is corrupted or not available, as in some kernel debugging situations in which the stack is not resident in memory.

## Debugger Event Handling from the Kernel Debugger

The concept of using debugger events to communicate between the debugger target and the debugger client is extended in a natural way to kernel debuggers, with the main difference being the communication mechanism between the debugger and the debugger target. The communication protocol is not documented, but curious minds can see some of the communication between the kernel debugger and the debugger target after pressing the CTRL+D key combination in the debugger console and watching the verbose tracing of the entire protocol.

As discussed previously, user mode developers can rarely benefit from kernel debugger events, since there are not as many useful events for them. Without a doubt, the most useful one is the EXCEPTION_BREAKPOINT exception event, raised when any piece of code executes from user mode an int 3 statement called by `DebugBreak()` or various assert APIs. Second in importance are the exception events sent when all user-mode exceptions are funneled to the kernel debugger by using the `StopOnException` flag.

Finally, the Windows kernel can send notifications when user modules are mapped into the memory. This functionality is enabled by setting the `KernelSymbolLoad(kls)` flag in the same global variable as `nt!NTGlobalFlag` using the `gflags.exe` utility or the `!gflag` extension command.

After enabling the flag, we activate the notification by entering the `sxe ld:<module>` command in the kernel mode debugger. The debugger is notified when the module is mapped in memory, which presents a good opportunity to debug the process loading it, from kernel mode. Listing 3.29 uses the `kls` flag to detect the first instantiation of the `notepad.exe` process.

This feature is very powerful to debug modules loaded in early stages of Windows start-up or when it is hard to predict which process will load the module of interest. However, this notification is not sent if the module is already cached in the system memory.

**Listing 3.29**   Using kls flag for detecting a user mode module mapping

```
kd> !gflag +kls
New NtGlobalFlag contents: 0x00040000
    ksl - Enable loading of kernel debugger symbols
kd> sxe ld notepad
kd> g
nt!DebugService2+0x10:
8050b897 cc                  int     3
kd> k
ChildEBP RetAddr
f3b7da24 8050b8d9 nt!DebugService2+0x10
f3b7da48 805d536c nt!DbgLoadImageSymbols+0x42
f3b7da98 805d5212 nt!MiLoadUserSymbols+0x169
f3b7dadc 8057bc22 nt!MiMapViewOfImageSection+0x4b6
f3b7db38 80503a0b nt!MmMapViewOfSection+0x13c
f3b7db94 80588c21 nt!MmInitializeProcessAddressSpace+0x337
f3b7dce4 80588635 nt!PspCreateProcess+0x333
f3b7dd38 804df06b nt!NtCreateProcessEx+0x7e
f3b7dd38 7c90eb94 nt!KiFastCallEntry+0xf8
WARNING: Frame IP not in any known module. Following frames may be wrong.
0013fa88 00000000 0x7c90eb94
kd> !process -1 0
PROCESS 82f5a020  SessionId: 0  Cid: 0000    Peb: 00000000  ParentCid: 0544
    DirBase: 0de15000  ObjectTable: e1b12638  HandleCount:   1.
    Image: notepad.exe
```

# Controlling the Target

After this overview of the mechanisms provided by the operating system to debug any running target process, one step is still required to understand how the debugger is capable of doing all its magic. This section describes some of the levers used by debuggers to control the debugger target and how each lever influences the debugger target.

## How Breakpoints Work

An exception having the code STATUS_BREAKPOINT is used all through this book, especially in this chapter, without a clear explanation of the way this exception is raised. It is time to explain how the process generates this exception.

The x86 instruction set contains a special instruction named int 3 introduced to facilitate debugging by generating a STATUS_BREAKPOINT hardware exception on the processor executing this instruction. In response to the STATUS_BREAKPOINT exception, the processor executes the interrupt handler registered for the interrupt vector 3. The interrupt handler converts the hardware exception into a software exception raised at the address containing the statement. The instruction is represented in the instruction stream, representation called Operation Code or opcode, by a single byte with the value 0xCC. Without a debugger available, the software exception is treated as a regular exception; otherwise, the Windows operating system instructs the debugger to break right at the instruction's address.

The debugger uses the 0xCC opcode when setting a breakpoint. To set the breakpoint, the debugger changes the protection on the memory block containing the breakpoint address so that it can write an int 3 statement at that address. The old value, along with the information about the breakpoint number, is then saved in the debugger memory.

A breakpoint address must be the address of a valid opcode in the instruction stream, which is always the first byte of a machine language instruction. A breakpoint set to any other address in the machine language instruction changes the instruction meaning, without triggering a STATUS_BREAKPOINT hardware exception when that instruction is generated. Needless to say, running the application containing a wrong machine language instruction is dangerous and unpredictable.

The changes in memory should not be visible to the user, as those changes can influence the results of unassembling code functions. Therefore, when the debugger stops, it always replaces the original memory values for each breakpoint set by the debugger before doing any kind of processing. Regardless of the magic used to hide the breakpoints, when the debugger targets start to run again, int 3 opcodes are inserted back into the target image.

To demonstrate this mechanism, we start the favorite debugger target notepad.exe under the debugger. At the initial breakpoint, we set a breakpoint at any address, `notepad!WinMain` start address in this case, and we examine that address content from another debugger attached noninteractively to the same process. This setup allows us to find the real memory content owned by the debugger target.

While the user mode debugger waits for user input at the command prompt, the memory contains the original instruction stream. When executing the debugger target, we enter g in the interactive user mode debugger command window to change the memory, as shown in the second section of Listing 3.30.

**Listing 3.30**   Examining the process memory from a noninvasive debugger

**Before setting the breakpoint**
```
0:000> u 010028e4
010028e4 85c0            test    eax,eax
010028e6 7594            jnz     0100287c
010028e8 e8c3effff       call    010018b0
```
**After setting the breakpoint**
```
0:000> u 010028e4
010028e4 cc              int     3
010028e5 c07594e8        shl     byte ptr [ebp-0x6c],0xe8
010028e9 c3              ret
010028ea ef              out     dx,eax
```

The kernel mode debugger follows the same model when setting the breakpoint with minor differences imposed by the operating system memory-management mechanism. In the Windows operating system, most pages containing the executable code are shared between all processes using that module, a feature used by common DLL libraries loaded in two different processes. When the user mode debugger enables a new breakpoint, it changes the page protection from read-only to read-write. The new page, generated using the Copy-On-Write (COW) technique, becomes a private page for the debugged process and can be changed without impact on other processes sharing the page. Because the kernel mode debugger is unable to generate a private page using the COW technique, it directly sets the breakpoint on the shared page.

The kernel mode breakpoints are reflected on all running processes sharing the page. Furthermore, depending on the memory available in the system, the kernel mode breakpoints can persist in system memory after the debugged process finishes execution. The side effects are hard to predict in real debugging situations, as the Windows memory management is greatly influenced by memory load and by the overall system activity. However, we can draw a few conclusions regarding kernel mode breakpoints, as follows.

- Setting a breakpoint on a page shared by many processes breaks in many processes. Because the kernel debugger processes the breakpoints relatively slowly, especially over serial cables, it must never be used for frequently called functions, such as ntdll!RtlAllocateHeap. We can reduce the number of times the debugger stops by using an EPROCESS address or a KTHREAD address to reduce the breakpoint scope. Unfortunately, the debugger still gets notified for each hit, and it handles the breakpoint automatically for all nonmatching processes.
- After the process previously debugged from the kernel debugger terminates, all user mode breakpoints must be removed to avoid any conflict with other running processes. (Shared pages might remain in memory for an undetermined time period, with all breakpoints previously set, even if the process is restarted.)
- When the user mode debugger is used together with the kernel mode debugger, the breakpoints must always be set from the user mode debugger. Otherwise, the breakpoint exception is dispatched to the user mode debugger. Because it is unaware of the fact that int 3 is a breakpoint and not an explicit int 3 instruction, the execution flow is compromised. Needless to say, the instructions stream executed after entering g is completely wrong, ending most likely with a long stream of access violation exceptions or single step exceptions in one of the debuggers.

## How Breakpoints on Access Work

In addition to standard breakpoint instruction, all processors supported by the Windows operating system are capable of generating a break when a specific address is read, written, or executed from. The ba command uses this processor functionality to implement the break on access functionality. The processor capability is controlled by a set of eight registers (again, we focus on the x86 architecture), named DR0-DR7. The usage of these processor registers is well documented in the processor manufacturer documentation. In short, the first four registers DR0-DR3, known as address-breakpoint registers, contain virtual addresses monitored by the processor, and DR7, known as the debug control register, contains control information about each such address in part (the length of the block, the type of access being monitored, and the enabled state). Listing 3.31 shows debug registers before and after hitting a breakpoint in a kernel mode debugger.

**Listing 3.31**  Debug registers on a normal processor

**Before setting a breakpoint on access**
```
kd> rM 20
dr0=00000000 dr1=00000000 dr2=00000000
dr3=00000000 dr6=ffff0ff0 dr7=00000400 cr4=00000699
ntdll!RtlAllocateHeap+0x5:
001b:77f57bb3 68781cf577  push    0x77f51c78
```
**After setting a breakpoint on access (for execution)**
```
kd> ba e1 77f57bae
kd> g
Breakpoint 0 hit
ntdll!RtlAllocateHeap:
001b:77f57bae 6808020000  push    0x208
kd> rM 20
dr0=77f57bae dr1=77f57bae dr2=00000000
dr3=00000000 dr6=ffff0ff1 dr7=00000501 cr4=00000699
ntdll!RtlAllocateHeap:
001b:77f57bae 6808020000  push    0x208
kd> .formats @dr7
Evaluate expression:
  Hex:     00000501
  Decimal: 1281
  Octal:   00000002401
  Binary:  00000000 00000000 00000101 00000001
  Chars:   ....
  Time:    Wed Dec 31 16:21:21 1969
  Float:   low 1.79506e-042 high 0
  Double:  6.32898e-321
```

In this case, the debug control register has only two bits set—bit 0 and bit 8—meaning that breakpoint 0 is enabled. Based on Intel processor specifications, when there is no additional information, such as the length of the breakpoint to be watched or the access mode to be monitored, the breakpoint is considered to be an execution access breakpoint.

As with normal breakpoints, the kernel debugger access breakpoints are shared by all processes running on the system, and they will interfere with any user mode debugger running in the same system. If the breakpoint is encountered by a user mode debugger unaware of the reason for this break, that debugger raises a STATUS_SINGLE_STEP exception.

## Processor Tracing

Tracing at the assembly level, another commonly used feature in the debuggers, is achieved using the native processor-tracing capabilities. On x86 processors, tracing is enabled using the trap flag, identified as tf flags in the debugger console. When the flag is set, the processor executes only the current statement followed by raising a STATUS_SINGLE_STEP exception. For example, when we type the t command in the debugger console, the debugger sets the trap flag in the thread context and continues the thread execution. When the new thread context is loaded and the processor raises the STATUS_SINGLE_STEP exception, the debugger recognizes the exception, resets the trace flag, and stops after the last instruction. The behavior can be easily reproduced by setting the trap flag and enabling the debugger target to execute, as shown in Listing 3.32. In this case, the debugger is unaware of the "request" to perform a single-step operation, and it just shows the exception on the console.

**Listing 3.32**  Simulating code tracing after attaching to a running project

```
0:001> r tf=1
0:001> g
(608.6bc): Single step exception - code 80000004 (first chance)
First chance exceptions are reported before any exception handling.
This exception may be expected and handled.
eax=7ffdf000 ebx=00000001 ecx=00000002 edx=00000003 esi=00000004 edi=00000005
eip=77f5f31f esp=0084ffd0 ebp=0084fff4 iopl=0         nv up ei pl zr na po nc
cs=001b  ss=0023  ds=0023  es=0023  fs=0038  gs=0000              efl=00000246
ntdll!DbgUiRemoteBreakin+0x2d:
77f5f31f eb07            jmp     ntdll!DbgUiRemoteBreakin+0x36 (77f5f328)
```

In addition to single-step tracing, newer processors are continuously improving the debugger capabilities by implementing additional tracing capabilities, such as trace to next branch.

## Thread State Management in Live Debugging

Although tracing is a simple-to-use mechanism for single-threaded processes, it adds a level of unpredictability on multithreaded processes; when multiple threads are involved, the debugger enables all other threads to run free while the current thread executes the instruction expected to step over. If a thread context switch happens, the user types t in the debugger, and it hits another breakpoint already set in the debugger instead of stopping at the next instruction. The code execution no longer follows a single execution path, making it hard, if not impossible, to follow a single execution thread performing a specific scenario. We really want to see a single thread in the process, allowing us to control it using the commands we are familiar with instead of using a series of breakpoints scoped to a single thread and so on.

To minimize the chance of having multiple threads executing the same code sequence, it is possible to temporarily suspend the execution of noninteresting threads and leave a single running thread in the process. How exactly does this work?

Each time a new debugger event must be delivered to the user mode debugger, all running threads in the process are automatically suspended by the Windows kernel for the entire duration of the event processing. When the debugger decides to continue execution, after processing that event, the kernel resumes the execution of all threads in the process. The threads shown in Listing 3.33 have a suspend count associated with each thread, along with a Frozen/Unfrozen state.

**Listing 3.33** Dumping the thread state

```
0:001> ~
   0  Id: 1370.fc0 Suspend: 1 Teb: 7ffdf000 Unfrozen
.  1  Id: 1370.101c Suspend: 1 Teb: 7ffde000 Unfrozen
```

The thread's suspend count represents the value recognized by the Windows kernel, controlled by the SuspendThread and ResumeThread API. The suspend count can also be controlled from the debugger using the ~n or ~m command. The thread having a <tid> identifier can be suspended by using the following command:

```
~<tid>n
```

The thread having a <tid> identifier can be resumed by using the following command:

```
~<tid>m
```

If any such commands are used, as shown in Listing 3.34, make sure that the suspend count is balanced with the number of resumes commands before detaching the debugger from the process. A suspended thread remains suspended forever. It is also important to understand the side effect of suspending a particular thread for the entire process. For example, most graphic user interface applications use a single thread to retrieve and dispatch windows messages corresponding to user interactions. Suspending that thread practically freezes the whole application. Suspending a thread that owns a resource causes all other threads waiting on the same resource to block until the thread is resumed. As before, this unbound wait is perceived as an application hung.

**Listing 3.34**   How to suspend and resume threads

```
0:001> * Suspend the thread zero
0:001> ~0n
0:001> ~
   0  Id: 1370.fc0 Suspend: 2 Teb: 7ffdf000 Unfrozen
.  1  Id: 1370.101c Suspend: 1 Teb: 7ffde000 Unfrozen
0:001> * Resume the thread zero
0:001> ~0m
0:001> ~
   0  Id: 1370.fc0 Suspend: 1 Teb: 7ffdf000 Unfrozen
.  1  Id: 1370.101c Suspend: 1 Teb: 7ffde000 Unfrozen
```

The `Frozen/Unfrozen` state discussed previously is different from the suspend state described in the preceding section. The `Frozen` state is a pure debugger concept without support from the Windows operating system. For each frozen thread, the debugger remembers that state and increases its suspend count before resuming debugger event processing. The suspend count is later decreased when the new event is processed, so the suspend count looks unchanged.

The thread having a `<tid>` identifier can be frozen by using the following command:

```
~<tid>f
```

The thread having a `<tid>` identifier can be unfrozen by using the following command:

```
~<tid>u
```

Listing 3.35 shows an example of each command in action. Because a frozen thread impacts the normal process execution, the debugger reminds the user about the number of frozen threads each time a new event is processed. The freeze commands must be matched by unfreeze commands, in the same way as suspend-resume commands. Interestingly enough, when the last running thread in the process is frozen, the debugger terminates the target process, as there are minimal chances for any further activity to happen in that process.

## Listing 3.35  How to freeze or unfreeze threads

```
0:001> * Freeze thread number one
0:001> ~1f
0:001> * Dump thread status
0:001> ~
   0  Id: 1098.1418 Suspend: 1 Teb: 7ffdf000 Unfrozen
.  1  Id: 1098.143c Suspend: 1 Teb: 7ffde000 Frozen
0:001> * Let the debugger target run
0:001> g
System 0: 1 of 2 threads are frozen
System 0: 1 of 3 threads were frozen
System 0: 1 of 3 threads are frozen
System 0: 1 of 3 threads were frozen
(1098.15fc): Break instruction exception - code 80000003 (first chance)
eax=7ffd9000 ebx=00000001 ecx=00000002
edx=00000003 esi=00000004 edi=00000005
eip=7c901230 esp=0092ffcc ebp=0092fff4
iopl=0           nv up ei pl zr na po nc
cs=001b  ss=0023  ds=0023  es=0023
fs=0038  gs=0000             efl=00000246
ntdll!DbgBreakPoint:
7c901230 cc                 int     3
0:001> * Unfreeze thread number one
0:002> ~1u
0:001> * Dump thread status
0:002> ~
   0  Id: 1098.1418 Suspend: 1 Teb: 7ffdf000 Unfrozen
   1  Id: 1098.143c Suspend: 1 Teb: 7ffde000 Unfrozen
.  2  Id: 1098.15fc Suspend: 1 Teb: 7ffdd000 Unfrozen
```

Last, the debugger offers the capability to replace the current executing thread with any other thread within the process. This change is a temporary one, and it is in effect until the new thread loses the execution quantum by either execution preemption, by voluntary releasing the remaining of the execution quantum time, or by entering a wait state. As you can see in Listing 3.36, the current thread has a dot (.) in front of the thread identifier. If the current thread is different from the active thread (the thread generating the current event), the active thread is marked with a pound sign (#) in front of the thread identifier. The thread having the `<tid>` identifier can be made the active thread by using the following command:

```
~<tid>s
```

**Listing 3.36**   Changing the current thread

```
0:001> ~
   0  Id: 3edc.1970 Suspend: 1 Teb: 7ffdf000 Unfrozen
.  1  Id: 3edc.44e8 Suspend: 1 Teb: 7ffde000 Unfrozen
0:001> ~0s
eax=0043de20 ebx=008f0507 ecx=00420000 edx=a4011de2 esi=0007fefc edi=77d491c6
eip=7c90eb94 esp=0007febc ebp=0007fed8 iopl=0         nv up ei pl zr na po nc
cs=001b  ss=0023  ds=0023  es=0023  fs=003b  gs=0000              efl=00000246
ntdll!KiFastSystemCallRet:
7c90eb94 c3              ret
0:000> ~
.  0  Id: 3edc.1970 Suspend: 1 Teb: 7ffdf000 Unfrozen
#  1  Id: 3edc.44e8 Suspend: 1 Teb: 7ffde000 Unfrozen
```

Changing the current thread affects the scope of all the commands dependent on the current thread and is extremely useful for complex commands, such as the kb command or the !teb extension command.

## Suspending a Thread Using Kernel Mode Debugger

Currently, the kernel debugger does not offer a similar way of altering the execution pattern, such as suspending a thread, resuming a thread, or even scheduling another thread for execution instead of the current one. This is not available for multiple reasons, ranging from the complexity of providing such support to the safety of such a mechanism. Even more important, such support has limited usefulness in kernel space, as the number of threads is relatively large.

However, it is possible to simulate this functionality with the support already available in the kernel debugger, provided that several conditions are met. The scenario calling for this functionality is presented in the rest of this section.

We assume that one process of interest stops in the kernel mode debugger as a result of executing a DebugBreak() statement. The process cannot continue after the break has been encountered, and any attempt to continue the execution past the breakpoint terminates the process. The break is often a direct result of breaking one process invariant, such as heap integrity or perhaps the value of a global variable falling out of the expected range. The virtual address space containing break clues is not currently loaded in RAM but is available in the page file. The .pagein command can be used to bring the necessary pages back into memory. The debugger target must run to schedule a thread that will do the actual page-in operation. Because of the nondeterministic nature of the page-in process, the former thread causing the break can execute and terminate the process.

A solution to avoid this scenario is stopping the failing thread from executing the termination code by putting it in a waiting state. With this thread waiting, .pagein can be called countless times without fear of losing the current live debug session. The thread can be easily put in a waiting state by changing its current instruction pointer and forcing the thread to execute the kernel32!Sleep API. This API takes a single parameter representing the sleep duration in milliseconds.

The currently running thread stack must be changed to simulate the state before invoking a standard API call with one parameter. The context must be changed to match the updated stack pointer, and the instruction pointer must be updated to match the called API start address. When the thread continues its execution, it enters into sleep mode for the duration retrieved from the stack, as shown in Listing 3.37.

**Listing 3.37**  *Simulating a kernel32!Sleep call*

```
kd> r
eax=0040136f ebx=7ffdf000 ecx=004011d0 edx=00262649 esi=00000002 edi=00000000
eip=77f75a58 esp=0006fee8 ebp=0006fef0 iopl=0
        nv up ei pl nz na po nc
cs=001b  ss=0023  ds=0023  es=0023  fs=0038  gs=0000            efl=00000206
ntdll!DbgBreakPoint:
001b:77f75a58 cc            int     3
kd> ed esp-4 <time>
kd> ed esp-8 .
kd> resp=@esp-8
kd> reip=kernel32!Sleep
kd> .pagein <address>;g
. . .
```

For the entire sleep duration, the debugger can be used to page in multiple pages without fear of losing the process or having the state changed in an unexpected way. If necessary, in this state, it is possible to even start a user mode debugger and debug the failing process from within the target system if the system is accessible.

Regardless of the method used to complete the investigation, the thread returns to its initial location after the timeout has expired. Even if registers normally preserved in __stdcall are preserved in this case, the attempt to continue the process execution beyond this point is dangerous.

## Summary

In this chapter, you learned how the debugger interacts with the operating system while debugging a process and how to effectively control all debugger events and exceptions to your advantage. You then learned how the system reacts when it encounters various exceptions and how to use this information in day-to-day debugging. Last, we investigated the mechanisms available to control the thread state using both the debugger support and manual changes in the process state.

With this information, it is possible to define a clear debugging strategy for various situations and use the debugging facilities to your advantage.

# CHAPTER 4

# MANAGING SYMBOL AND SOURCE FILES

Imagine for a moment that your company flagship product experiences a problem on a small but significant set of systems, and you are asked to resolve the problem, using memory dump files sent by the customer. You load the memory dumps in a debugger to find out what is wrong. Because the debugger has limited functionality without the proper symbol files, you must find the symbol files matching the application version, generated at the application build time. If those symbol files cannot be found, the only option is to go back to the customer and provide excuses instead of solutions.

Symbol management is proven to save time for engineers debugging software systems, and its importance should not be underestimated; the timesaving continues to pay during the entire product lifetime. A carefully designed symbol management policy provides indirect business value compared to an ad hoc or nonexisting policy. With a solid symbol management policy, the company stays behind its products, it fixes the problems in a timely manner, and it releases a more stable future version.

Microsoft Debugging Tools for Windows provides the tools necessary to set up a symbol server and prepares the symbols to support source server mechanism. The cost of setting up a symbol server is proportional to the storage cost, which continues to decrease dramatically. In this chapter, we will explore

- How to set up and maintain a private symbol server on an ongoing basis
- How to set up and maintain a public symbol server on an ongoing basis
- How to prepare the symbol file for supporting the source server on an ongoing basis

All debuggers installed with Microsoft Debugging Tools for Windows use those servers. All Visual Studio .NET versions are capable of using the symbol server. The source server is supported by Visual Studio 2005 Professional and Visual Studio Team Editions. The symbols are, and should always be, understood by all debugging tools available on a specific platform. This way, the engineers can switch from one tool to another, confident that they have all the information they need.

# Managing the Symbols for Debugging

In Chapter 2, "Introduction to the Debuggers," the importance of using the correct symbol files was stressed on multiple occasions—from setting the right symbols to validating them. Easier debugging after the product has been released is the whole reason for implementing a strong symbol management policy. As a general rule, every binary installed on different systems for a period of time longer than the immediate testing should have its symbol file indexed on a symbol server outliving the binary.

The symbol management process starts from the moment of building the set of binaries that are part of your product to be installed and used for a longer period of time. If the developers are sure that there is no bug in the product, or the product does not need to be supported and the next version does not use any of the current code, the process can stop here. Anyone else starts a process of preparing the generated symbol files for long-term maintenance.

Along with the binary files, the compiler generates the associated symbol files, in PDB format, containing all private symbols. Those symbol files contain references to all the source files used to build the product. Each symbol corresponding to an executable address in the binary file contains a reference to the source code line used to generate it. Most companies, Microsoft included, believe that such detailed information discloses the intellectual property embedded in the product, so they choose to disclose only a part of it, in the form of public symbols. Therefore, those companies keep both file types in two different locations. The private symbol files are stored in a secured location, whereas the public symbol files are typically stored on a publicly accessible HTTP server. This allows application users to get a grip on why the application crashes when it does, which is sometimes enough to tell what must be done to fix the problem.

Microsoft publishes the public symbols for most applications on the symbol server located at http://msdl.microsoft.com/download/symbols.

## Generating Public Symbols

In this chapter, we demonstrate how to integrate the symbol file management into a build process—in this case, the process used to build the book sample files. We start by creating the stripped symbol files, called public symbol files, from the private symbol files. We use the binplace.exe utility, installed with the Windows WDK, which also helps us organize the binary files after building them. If the additional functionality offered by binplace.exe is not needed, you can use the pdbcopy.exe tool provided with the Debugging Tools for Windows to generate the public symbol files.

The following steps are performed from the command prompt shortcut created by the Windows WDK. Other tools, such as the debugger tool, are assumed to be present in the path, as required in the listings in the chapter. In this chapter, we will reuse the source code and binary for 03sample.exe introduced in the previous chapter.

Binplace.exe is a powerful tool that is extremely useful for large projects. It can run at the end of the build phase to move files into various locations (hence the binplace name) and to process symbol files. In this section, we use binplace.exe to place the binary files in a single location and extract the public symbol information from the private symbol, generated by the compiler. Binplace.exe uses a processing instruction file, where each line is treated as an instruction stating how to process that file. Listing 4.1 shows the content of the `placefil.txt` file, used to post process our sample binaries.

**Listing 4.1**   Binplace file content

```
C:\>type c:\awd\placefil.txt
02sample.exe retail
03sample.exe retail
```

The binplace.exe command is invoked for each binary file, which is passed as a parameter to the command. The binary filename is used as a index into the processing instructions file. The matching is done by comparing the binary name to the names stored in the first column. In our case, we have a line for each EXE or DLL followed by the special `retail` string that indicates the placement location in the output binary folder.

To help us understand all the options available, WDK help has a few topics dedicated to the binplace.exe command, describing place file syntax and all command-line options, as well as all environment variables observed by binplace.exe. A wealth of information can be found on the MSDN Web site when searching for the binplace string (without the .exe extension).

As with most command-line tools, binplace.exe behavior is affected by the environment variables—few variables being required. Other parameters are passed in as command-line arguments. In our scenario, the tool depends on the following parameters:

- The target binary location, provided through the environment variable, _NT386TREE, _NTAMD64TREE, or _NTIA64TREE, depending on the platform targeted by the binary files processed with binplace.exe. The target folder specified contains all the resulting binary files.
- The `placefile.txt` location, provided through the environment variable `BINPLACE_PLACEFILE`, contains the processing instruction for all project files.

- The private symbol files target, passed in as an argument for the –n command-line switch, represents the location holding the private symbol files.
- The public symbol files target, passed in as an argument for the –s command switch, represents the location holding the private symbol files.
- Other command-line switches—–a and –x—tell binplace.exe to remove private symbols from the public symbol file and to remove any symbol from the binary file itself.
- The binary file location we are about to process, passed in as the last parameter.

Listing 4.2 is taken from the command-line prompt used to set these variables and execute the bin place operation. In response, `binplace.exe` shows the name of a successfully bin placed file. Please note that there is no output in case of an error.

**Listing 4.2**    Binplacing the symbol files

```
C:\> set _NT386TREE=C:\AWDBIN\WinXP.x86.chk
C:\> set BINPLACE_PLACEFILE=C:\awd\placefil.txt
C:\> binplace -a -x -s %_NT386TREE%\sym.pub -n %_NT386TREE%\sym.pri
chapter3\objchk_wxp_x86\i386\03sample.exe
binplace C:\awd\chapter3\objchk_wxp_x86\i386\03sample.exe
```

The binplace.exe utility is called repeatedly for each binary. In the end, the target folder contains all binaries, all private symbol files, and all public symbol files. The entire process can be automated, as you can see in the release.cmd batch file, installed with the sample files. The target folder tree created after this operation looks similar to the one in Listing 4.3.

**Listing 4.3**    Binary folder tree

```
C:\AWD>tree c:\AWDBIN\WinXP.x86.chk /F/A
Folder PATH listing
Volume serial number is 00310030 B817:38E9
C:\AWDBIN\WinXP.X86.CHK
+--03sample.exe
|
|   +--sym.pri
|      \--retail
|          \--exe
|              \--03sample.pdb
\--
    \--sym.pub
```

```
|   \--retail
|      \--exe
|            03sample.pdb
```

During the bin-placing process, the content of the debug directory stored in the executable headers is adjusted, and the original symbol file location is removed. The debug directory can be visualized by the link.exe command, as shown in Chapter 2. Listing 4.4 shows the content of the debug directories before the bin place operation, and Listing 4.5 shows it after the operation.

**Listing 4.4**   Debug directories immediately after building the binaries

```
C:\AWD>link -dump -headers
c:\AWD\chapter3\objchk_wxp_x86\i386\03sample.exe
Microsoft (R) COFF/PE Dumper Version 8.00.50727.220
Copyright (C) Microsoft Corporation.  All rights reserved.

Dump of file c:\awd\chapter3\objchk_wxp_x86\i386\03sample.exe
...
   Debug Directories

        Time Type         Size     RVA  Pointer
        ---- ---          ----    ----    ----
     45A417D2 cv             49 00001810     C10     Format: RSDS, {B10B7ACC-81C5-4533-
AFEA-5AF20D9B7A09}, 1, c:\awd\chapter3\objchk_wxp_x86\i386\03sample.pdb
...
```

**Listing 4.5**   Debug directories after bin place operation

```
C:\AWD>link -dump -headers c:\AWDBIN\WinXP.x86.chk\03sample.exe
Microsoft (R) COFF/PE Dumper Version 8.00.50727.220
Copyright (C) Microsoft Corporation.  All rights reserved.

Dump of file c:\AWDBIN\WinXP.x86.chk\03sample.exe
...
   Debug Directories

        Time Type         Size     RVA  Pointer
        ---- ---          ----    ----    ----
     45A417D2 cv             25 00001810     C10     Format: RSDS, {B10B7ACC-81C5-4533-
AFEA-5AF20D9B7A09}, 1, 03sample.pdb
...
```

## Storing Symbols in the Symbol Store

After processing each binary file using binplace.exe, the public symbol folder contains a tree with all the public symbol files, and the private symbol folder contains a tree with all the private symbol files. Although it looks feasible to store each version of such a tree in a different location and refer to its files when debugging any module created by that build version, the process is tedious and inefficient. A lot of bookkeeping must be done to ensure that no symbol is ever lost. Any group doing daily builds on multiple platforms finds this process very laborious and will try to automate it. Fortunately, the whole process of organizing the symbol files and discovering them when needed is already automated by a set of tools and technologies called symbol server. This section describes how to organize the symbols to create the symbol server information.

Debugging Tools for Windows provides a symstore.exe tool, which scans a folder, collects all executable modules with their associated symbols, and organizes them in a structure recognized by the symbol server client running in the debugger. The symbol files are organized based on their names and the GUID stored after the RSDS string shown in Listing 4.5. The binary files are indexed based on their name and the compilation time stamp.

Because there are two categories of symbols, the tool can be used to generate two symbol stores—one having public and one having private symbol files. The tool is very rich in options, all well described in the Windows debugger help. In this section, we invoke symstore.exe with the following parameters:

- /f indicates the binary folder used as an argument to binplace.exe.
- /s indicates the symbol store location.
- /r tells symstore.exe to recursively scan all files in the folder.
- /z indicates what types of symbols to extract: pri means private symbols and pub is for public symbols.

The result of running the command twice, once for public and once for private folder, is shown in Listing 4.6. The command displays the statistics about the operation that must be analyzed for error. The files ignored from Listing 4.6 are the symbols not matching the required type: a public symbol file when only private symbols files were requested and vice versa.

**Listing 4.6**   The command to store the symbols on the symbol servers

### Creating public symbol store

```
C:\AWD>symstore.exe add /F C:\AWDBIN\WinXP.x86.chk /S
C:\AWDBIN\symstore.pub /t book /r /z pub
Finding ID...  0000000001
```

```
SYMSTORE: Number of files stored = 2
SYMSTORE: Number of errors = 0
SYMSTORE: Number of files ignored = 1
```

## Creating private symbol store

```
C:\AWD>symstore.exe add /F C:\AWDBIN\WinXP.x86.chk /S
C:\AWDBIN\symstore.pri /t book /r /z pri
Finding ID...  0000000001

SYMSTORE: Number of files stored = 2
SYMSTORE: Number of errors = 0
SYMSTORE: Number of files ignored = 1
```

As a result of executing these commands, two very simple symbol stores are created on the local file system. Even with just one file version stored in the symbol server, when you set it, the debugger automatically picks the correct symbol file. After rebuilding the project several times, it is easy to understand why the automatic symbol management is so simple compared to the manual bookkeeping process. Instead of keeping all files separated by using some manually determined keys, everything is done by the tools. The process is repeated each time we build the product—once for each processor architecture or compilation settings. All symbol files are stored in the same symbol server. The tree structure for one of the stores can be examined in Listing 4.7.

**Listing 4.7**   Directory structure on the symbol servers

```
C:\AWD>tree c:\AWDBIN\symstore.pri /F/A
Folder PATH listing
Volume serial number is B817-38E9
C:\AWDBIN\SYMSTORE.PRI
+--pingme.txt
|
| +--000Admin
|     0000000001
|     0000000002
|     0000000003
|     history.txt
|     lastid.txt
|     server.txt
|
|  \--03sample.exe
|    \--45A417D214000
|        \--03sample.exe
|            \--refs.ptr
```

*(continues)*

**Listing 4.7**   Directory structure on the symbol servers *(continued)*

```
|
|   +---45A4624314000
|       \---03sample.exe
|          \---refs.ptr
|
|   +---45A4625414000
|       \---03sample.exe
|          \---refs.ptr
|
+---03sample.pdb
|   +---A69EEFF7C43B400799E03BF7BCF55A9B1
|       \---03sample.pdb
|          \---refs.ptr
|
|   +---B10B7ACC81C54533AFEA5AF20D9B7A091
|       \---03sample.pdb
|          \---refs.ptr
|
|   +---FF76A7EC166D489C943F238F76FCB32F1
|       \---03sample.pdb
|          \---refs.ptr
```

The private and public symbol store structure is identical, but their content is different. This simple organization model works for a small to medium project requiring reasonable disk usage. For larger projects, symstore.exe has various other options that enable the symstore.exe tool to generate a more complex store, such as stores with symbol files stored in multiple locations or with compressed files. The sysmstore.exe help describes the various options supported by the tool, which can be used for creating such complex stores.

The private symbol folder can then be stored on a file share and used by all users through the share UNC, something similar to \\symserver\symbols. This UNC location becomes the symbol server used as a symbol path in the debuggers, as follows:

```
0:000> !sympath srv*\\symserver\symbols
Symbol search path srv*\\symserver\symbols
```

Each symbol indexing operation gets a transaction identifier that can be used for further symbol management operations. Normally, the transaction identifier is used to delete from the symbol store all symbol files corresponding to intermediate releases. For example, in Listing 4.8, we use the symstore.exe tool to remove the file added in the transaction 0000000001 shown in Listing 4.6.

**Listing 4.8**   The command to delete the symbol files from the symbol servers

```
C:\AWD> symstore del /i 0000000001 /s c:\awdbin\symstore.pri
Finding ID...  0000000004

SYMSTORE: Number of references deleted = 0
SYMSTORE: Number of files/pointers deleted = 2
SYMSTORE: Number of errors = 0
```

We can now publish the public symbol files on an Internet server. This process is described in the next section.

## Sharing Public Symbols on an HTTP Server

The last step is to make the public symbols really public, by making them available using an HTTP symbol server. Although it might seem to be a daunting task, it's actually quite simple. The public symbols store folder created before must be added as a virtual directory in the web server storing the symbols. The HTTP server must be configured to deliver the symbol files as `application/octet-stream`, as shown in Figure 4.1.

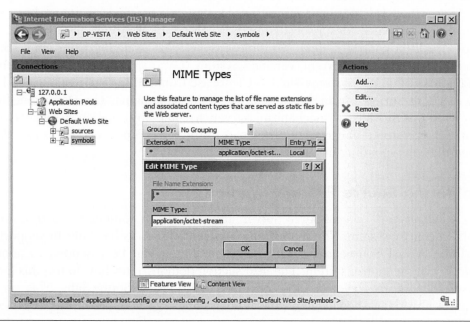

**Figure 4.1**   Configuring the MIME type (Vista IIS snap-in)

Step-by-step instructions are available in the symhttp.doc document, installed with the Debugging Tools for Windows in the symproxy folder. The new server URL, assuming that the symbols are located in the `symbols` virtual folder, can be used as follows:

```
0:000> !sympath srv*http://127.0.0.1/symbols
Symbol search path is: srv*http://127.0.0.1/symbols
```

After reading this section, you know what tools can be used to automate the symbol file management with minimal overhead. The next section goes even further and describes how to prepare the symbol files with source server information.

# Managing Source Files for Debugging

While the initial triage of most problems can be performed with access only to the correct private (or even public) symbols, engineers must validate the problem by analyzing the source files as well. When the source files in question have gone through multiple changes, it is important to find the exact file used to generate the binary file. This is exactly what we show how to solve in this section.

Unless the product is built and released just once—in which case, each binary has a single set of source files associated with it—the sources are usually managed by a source revision control system. Multiple options exist—ranging from open source products, such as Concurrent Versions System (CVS) or its successor Subversion (SVN), to commercial systems, such as ClearCase from IBM, Visual SourceSafe from Microsoft, or Perforce from the company with the same name. The Debugging Tools for Windows provides a mechanism by which some information associated with source files is stored in a symbol file as part of the build process, and it is used later, when the corresponding module is loaded in the debugger.

## Gathering Source File Information

The mechanism is called Source Server, and it works in conjunction with a source revision control system. The Debugging Tools for Windows has built-in support for Perforce, Visual SourceSafe, and Subversion, but it can be extended to another source revision control system. The next section demonstrates how to use this mechanism. The source revisions are controlled with Visual SourceSafe. This section requires a working knowledge of Visual SourceSafe to re-create the steps related to the interaction with the source revision control system. The steps are similar, if not simpler, with Perforce or Subversion. The process of generating the source information is illustrated in Figure 4.2.

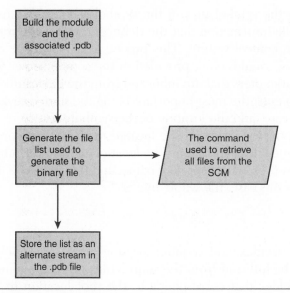

**Figure 4.2**  The process of generating source information

The source server tools are based on Perl, which needs to be installed prior to running the process. In our case, we used ActivePerl, which can be downloaded, free of charge, from the www.ActiveState.com site. The source server tools are installed by selecting the SDK option as part of installing the Debugging Tools for Windows. In the installation folder, the sdk\srcsrv\srcsrv.doc document describes the entire process in detail. The source server location, as well as the location of the Visual SourceSafe installation, must be present in the path, set by the following command line (dependent on the installation location):

```
C:\awd>set PATH=%PATH%;C:\Program Files\Microsoft Visual
SourceSafe;C:\debug.x86\sdk\srcsrv
```

The next step is to set the SSDIR environment variable to point to the Visual SourceSafe database, which maintains the project file as follows, assuming that the database is stored in the C:\AWD\VSS folder:

```
C:\awd>set SSDIR=C:\AWD\VSS
```

For simplicity, we assume that all files stored in the VSS database have a structure similar to the folder structure on disk.

Before storing the symbol files in the symbol server, we must process them to inject the source file information that the debugger will use to retrieve the file from the source revision control system. This process is achieved by running the source server indexing tool, ssindex.cmd, provided in the source server folder. ssindex.cmd requires several parameters that are inherited from the environment or are passed in as command arguments: the most important being the source revision control system name, VSS in this case, and the location of the symbol files.

To work properly, the srcsrv.ini file located in the source server folder must be updated with a single line that contains the location of the VSS database. The left side of the equals sign represents the project name, and the right side, the source revision control address. In this case, the whole line is

```
AWD=C:\AWD\VSS
```

When using VSS, ssindex.cmd requires passing a revision label as the parameter because it cannot be inferred from the source files. The command is executed from the project root folder that corresponds to the root location in the VSS database, where each subfolder is a project in the same database. The files were being labeled with a revision number using the command-line tool ss.exe provided by Visual SourceSafe, as in the following listing:

```
C:\AWD>ss cp \
Current project is $/
C:\AWD>ss Label
Label for $/: VERSION1
Comment for $/: Advanced Windows Debugging source code
```

After associating all the files with the version information manually chosen, we can launch the indexing command for all the files stored in the bin place location, as follows:

```
C:\AWD>ssindex /SYSTEM=VSS /LABEL=VERSION1 /SYMBOLS=%_NT386TREE%
-----------------------------------
ssindex.cmd [STATUS] : Server ini file:
d:\debug.x86\sdk\srcsrv\srcsrv.ini
ssindex.cmd [STATUS] : Source root    : C:\AWD
ssindex.cmd [STATUS] : Symbols root   : C:\AWDBIN\WINXP.X86.CHK\sym.pri
ssindex.cmd [STATUS] : Control system : VSS
ssindex.cmd [STATUS] : VSS Server     : C:\AWD\VSS
ssindex.cmd [STATUS] : VSS Client Root: C:\AWD
ssindex.cmd [STATUS] : VSS Project    : $/
ssindex.cmd [STATUS] : VSS Label      : VERSION1
-----------------------------------
ssindex.cmd [STATUS] : Running... this will take some time...
ssindex.cmd [STATUS] : Processing vssdump.exe output ...
```

The result of this process can be inspected using the srctool.exe command, which is capable of showing the source server information stored in the symbol file. The srctool.exe tool can also be used to extract the raw source information from the PDB file and to retrieve the source file from the version control system. It is good practice to periodically use the tool to validate the correctness of the source indexing process.

The srctool.exe tool shows the name of the original source file, as well as the command line required to extract this exact file from the source revision control system. The result of processing 03sample.pdb is shown in Listing 4.9.

**Listing 4.9**    Information stored in the PDB file

```
C:\AWD>SrcTool.exe %_NT386TREE%\sym.pri\retail\exe\03sample.pdb
[c:\awd\chapter3\spydbg.cpp] cmd: ss.exe get -
GL"C:\AWD\AWD\chapter3\spydbg.cpp\
VERSION1" -GF- -I-Y -W
"$/chapter3/spydbg.cpp" -V"VERSION1"
c:\AWDBIN\WinXP.X86.chk\sym.pri\retail\exe\03sample.pdb: 1 source files are indexed -
494 are not
```

If the source gathering failed and the previous listing is empty, ssindex.cmd can be started with the /debug parameter to find out what part of the source indexing process fails. When the source files are controlled by VSS, the vssdump.exe tool can also be used to understand what revision label is associated with the source files.

The pdbstr.exe tool is then used for extracting or changing the information stored in the symbol file. For example, the following command line extracts the source server information shown in Listing 4.10. The source server information is stored under the srcsrv stream name, which is passed as a value to the -s option to pdbstr.exe.

```
C:\>pdbstr -r -p:%_NT386TREE%\sym.pri\retail\exe\03sample.pdb -s:srcsrv
```

**Listing 4.10**    SourceServer information stored in the PDB file

```
SRCSRV: ini -----------------------
VERSION=1
INDEXVERSION=2
VERCTRL=Visual Source Safe
DATETIME=Mon Jan  8 00:04:15 2007
SRCSRV: variables --------------------
SSDIR=C:\AWD\VSS
SRCSRVENV=SSDIR=%AWD%
VSSTRGDIR=%targ%\%var2%\%fnbksl%(%var3%)\%var4%
```

*(continues)*

**Listing 4.10** SourceServer information stored in the PDB file *(continued)*

```
VSS_EXTRACT_CMD=ss.exe get -GL"%vsstrgdir%" -GF- -I-Y -W "$/%var3%" -V"%var4%"
VSS_EXTRACT_TARGET=%targ%\%var2%\%fnbksl%(%var3%)\%var4%\%fnfile%(%var1%)
AWD=C:\AWD\VSS
SRCSRVTRG=%VSS_extract_target%
SRCSRVCMD=%VSS_extract_cmd%
SRCSRV: source files --------------------
c:\awd\chapter3\spydbg.cpp*AWD*chapter3/spydbg.cpp*VERSION1
SRCSRV: end -----------------------
```

## Using Source File Information

Each symbol file processed by ssindex.cmd contains the commands required to extract each source file from the source revision control system. The command line stored in the symbol file shown in Listing 4.8 can retrieve the file from Visual SourceSafe.

This information is primarily used by the Debugging Tools for Windows that implement this functionality in symsrv.dll, accessible through the DbgHelp function SymGetSourceFile. Windbg uses the source server information to extract the source from any source revision control system. The console debuggers, ntsd.exe, cdb.exe, and kd.exe, can use only source files stored in the UNC share or HTTP server organized as a source server, as described in the next section, "Source Server Without Source Revision Control."

The source server mechanism is enabled when the debugger source path contains the SRV* string, set by using the .srcpath SRV* command at the prompt or using the Source symbol Path menu item in the File menu, in the case of windbg.exe. The debuggers examine the symbol file matching the current execution address from which extracts the source information associated with that symbol. If present, the source server information is used to retrieve a local copy of the source file cached in the SRC folder, under the debugger installation folder.

How is the file extracted? If the debugger has not been customized, it directly executes the command displayed in Listing 4.8. This requires that the source revision control system is installed and properly configured on the system used for debugging. It also requires access to the source revision control system to execute the command retrieving the file, as seen in Figure 4.3.

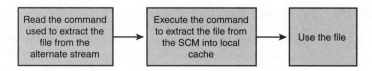

**Figure 4.3**   Using source information

Although those limitations slightly impact the productivity in some scenarios, espe-cially when the application is debugged without proper access to the source revision control systems, they are ensuring protection for the source code. Because the com-mand used to extract the file is retrieved from a file that resides on a symbol server, most likely an HTTP server, the debugger requests user permission for executing the command.

The security warning dialog box, shown in Figure 4.4, contains the command line ready to be executed. It must be evaluated before accepting it, especially when the symbol server or the PDB origin is not trusted. After the source file has been cached, no further dialogs are shown for this file version, regardless of what other components are using that source file.

**Figure 4.4**   Windbg.exe prompting before executing the source control command

## Source Server Without Source Revision Control

When the authorization to the source code is not controlled by a source revision system, the source files can be stored to a simple UNC share or an HTTP server. The access to the source code is then restricted using the authorization mechanism supported by the backend storage.

The access to an HTTP server can be restricted using different mechanisms, ranging from basic authentication to client certificate authentication, all being supported by the debuggers. Moving the source location from the source revision system to an HTTP server can be achieved in three steps, as follows:

1. We first extract all source files from the source revision control system, using the source server information stored by the source indexing process described in the earlier section "Gathering Source File Information." The file extraction is performed by using srctool.exe with the –x option for each PDB file generated. The source server tool set provides a helper batch file, walk.cmd, that can enumerate all files from a specific folder and pass each filename to another command. The following line executes srctool.exe for all symbol files we have in the public symbol folder.

   ```
   C:\>walk C:\AWDBIN\symstore.pri\*.pdb srctool -x -d:C:\AWDBIN\sources
   ```

   The extracted sources are organized similarly to the tree shown in Listing 4.11, in a structure that enables multiple file versions to be simultaneously stored in the sources folder. This tool is very powerful; it can extract all source files that were used to build the products.

**Listing 4.11** Source server file tree configuration

```
C:\AWD>tree c:\AWDBIN\sources /F/A
Folder PATH listing
Volume serial number is B817-38E9
C:\AWDBIN\SOURCES
+--AWD
|   \--chapter3
|       \--spydbg.cpp
|           \--VERSION1
|                   spydbg.cpp
```

**2.** In the next step, we change the source file information stored in the symbol files. The cv2http.cmd batch file, available in the source server installation folder, can change the source server information to the location of choice. The next line changes the source server information to the book's HTTP site, http://www.advancedwindowsdebugging.com:

```
C:\>walk C:\AWDBIN\symstore.pri\*.pdb cv2http.cmd HTTP_AWD
http://www.advancedwindowsdebugging.com/sources
```

If the desired source server location is an UNC path or an HTTPS address, this address replaces the URL used in the previous command line. HTTP_AWD is a simple variable that can be ignored in most cases. The source server documentation explains how to use this variable, if necessary.

**3.** In the final step, the folder containing all sources is added to the HTTP server as a virtual directory, enabled for browsing. A snapshot of the virtual folder settings is displayed in Figure 4.5, which was taken from the Internet Information Services MMC snap-in running on Windows Vista.

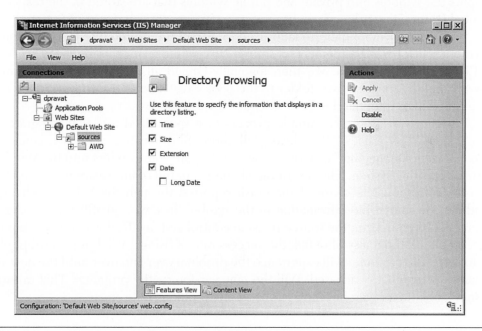

**Figure 4.5**  Source server virtual folder enabled for directory browsing (Vista IIS snap-in)

Be aware that the symbol files prepared in this way have no trace of the original source revision control system. If that is required, the original symbol files should be preserved before starting the operation described in this section.

## Summary

Debugging Tools for Windows provides additional tools, enabling all Windows platform developers to manage the symbol files and maintain the source server information for their modules. A variation on the steps described in this chapter can be integrated in the release management process of important release. This phase is important in providing support for the application.

Although it seems daunting at first glance, we want to assure you that the steps required are trivial. For example, we created an entire process for all book samples in the form of a very simple batch file, called release.cmd, that does it all. It creates the binary for the specific processor architecture used to start the WDK console, and it splits the symbols into private and public symbols that are stored in the respective symbol stores.

The private symbol files are later used to extract the source files from the source revision control management. The source server information is replaced with the HTTP server information. We then manually copied all the files from the symbol servers and the source server folder to the book's Web site. This process can be easily automated or integrated in your software release process.

Whether you use a very simple process or a specialized tool that integrates all those steps, the process of indexing all those files must be done. Chapter 13, "Postmortem Debugging," describes how to integrate your product into the Windows Error Reporting system. The rest of the chapters are full of information that will help you to understand the cause of the crash reported through the WER mechanism. Without the source file information in the symbol files, we can still retrieve a good source file version from the source revision control system. That is not great, but it is acceptable. Without a symbol file, the success rate of fixing a WER report drops closer to zero. The customer will experience the problem over and over until the next version of the product is released. Will the new version fix the problem? That question is impossible to answer, but most probably the problem will remain.

# PART II

# APPLIED DEBUGGING

**Chapter 5**  Memory Corruption Part I—Stacks . . . . . . . . . . . . . . . . . . .199

**Chapter 6**  Memory Corruption Part II—Heaps . . . . . . . . . . . . . . . . . .259

**Chapter 7**  Security . . . . . . . . . . . . . . . . . . . . . . . . . . . . . . . . . .317

**Chapter 8**  Interprocess Communication  . . . . . . . . . . . . . . . . . . . . .379

**Chapter 9**  Resource Leaks . . . . . . . . . . . . . . . . . . . . . . . . . . . . . .427

**Chapter 10** Synchronization . . . . . . . . . . . . . . . . . . . . . . . . . . . . . .493

# CHAPTER 5

# MEMORY CORRUPTION PART I— STACKS

A memory corruption is one of the most intractable forms of programming error for two reasons. First, the source of the corruption and the manifestation might be far apart, making it difficult to correlate cause and effect. Second, symptoms appear under unusual conditions, making it hard to consistently reproduce the error.

Fundamentally, memory corruption occurs when one or both of the following are true.

- The executing thread writes to a block of memory that it does not own.
- The executing thread writes to a block of memory that it does own, but corrupts the state of that memory block.

To exemplify the first condition, consider this small application:

```
#include <windows.h>

#define BAD_ADDRESS 0xBAADF00D
int __cdecl wmain (int argc, wchar_t* pArgs[])
{
    char* p =(char*)BAD_ADDRESS;

    *p='A';

    return 0;
}
```

This small application declares a pointer to a char data type and initializes the pointer to an address for which it does not have access (`0xBAADF00D`). The net result of running the application is a crash, and the dreaded Dr. Watson UI pops up. Although it's very clear that this simple application performs an invalid memory access, more complex systems can be trickier to figure out. For example, if the application allocated blocks of memory and made assumptions about the lifetime of those allocations, premature deletion might cause a memory corruption because of stale pointers. The best-case scenario for writing to memory that an application does not own is a crash. But wait a minute, you say—a crash is the best-case scenario? Yes—for memory corruptions, a crash might immediately indicate where the source of the memory corruption is. In our preceding sample code, the memory being written to is invalid, and a crash occurs. This is good news. We can very easily figure out why we have a pointer that points to invalid memory. However, consider the scenario in which the invalid pointer points to a block of memory in use by other parts of the application. The symptoms in this particular case could be one of the following:

- Application crashes: The main difference is that the crash might happen at a later time. In the original preceding sample application, the code crashed because the application wrote to memory designated as invalid by the operating system. In the changed scenario, however, the application writes to memory that the operating system considers valid, and the write is allowed to proceed without errors. Subsequently, the application might try to use the memory that was mistakenly written to, and a crash might occur (depending on the nature of the memory access).
- Non-crashing and unpredictable behavior: Much in the same way the previous item allowed the application to write bad data to the memory owned by other parts of the application, the net result does not have to be a crash. Other parts of the application might very well continue using the memory that bad data has been written to even though the state of that memory has been altered (and usually never in a good way). Let's take an example. Assume that we have a class that represents a thread pool. In addition to being capable of queuing requests to the thread pool, a method exists that sets a flag indicating that a shutdown is in progress. The thread pool periodically checks this flag, and if it ever equals true, a shutdown commences. A singleton instance of the thread pool is instantiated and used by the application. Now, let's say that the thread pool is servicing 200 requests (credit card authorizations) when a thread in the application mistakenly overwrites the shutdown flag to true. All of a sudden, the thread pool shuts down, customers start getting errors on their credit card transactions, and the phone calls start pouring in. This is a classic example of a memory corruption in which the net effect of the thread corrupting memory results in unpredictable behavior. Since the thread that overwrote the memory has already done the damage, the subsequent use of the memory can (and most likely will) be unpredictable. Finding the source of these types of memory corruptions is extremely difficult.

It should be quite clear that, when faced with a memory corruption, we want to be notified as soon as the offending thread writes to memory that it does not own rather than having to backtrack from a strange application behavior that might surface days after the invalid memory write took place. Short of getting lucky that the pointer points to truly invalid memory (causing an access violation right away), most of the memory corruptions surface in the form of strange application behaviors or crashes after the memory has already been altered.

Fortunately, with the right strategy and a powerful tool set, we can maximize our efficiency when analyzing a potential memory corruption and force the strategy of "crash immediately" to make it easier to figure out the source of the memory corruption.

## Memory Corruption Detection Process

This section outlines the memory corruption detection process. It includes a graphical representation of the process, as well as a brief discussion of each step. It is important to understand that figuring out the root cause of a memory corruption might include several iterations of the process illustrated in Figure 5.1, depending on the nature of the memory corruption.

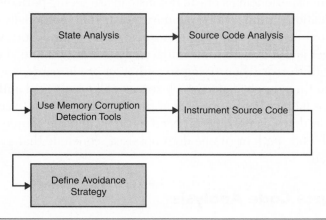

**Figure 5.1** Memory corruption analysis process

## Step 1: State Analysis

The very first step in investigating a memory corruption is to assure yourself that the failure you are looking at is indeed because of a memory corruption. This step can be further broken down, as seen in Figure 5.2.

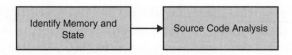

**Figure 5.2**    State analysis process

As we mentioned earlier, memory corruption symptoms fall into two categories: crashes and noncrashing and unpredictable behavior. This first step calls for an initial analysis of the behavior seen by means of analyzing the state of the corrupted memory. How do we know which state to analyze? With crashes, finding the starting point is pretty simple. The code that crashed did so because of some unexpected state, and the code is well-known at crash time. By looking at the state of the memory when the crash occurred in conjunction with focused code reviewing, we can make sound judgment calls on the origins of the state. "Valid," albeit buggy, code paths can lead to the state. If that is the case, you are not experiencing a memory corruption, per se, but rather an unexpected code path that erroneously wrote to the memory. If, however, no code paths allow for the memory to get into that state, the only plausible explanation is that someone overwrote that memory, and hence a memory corruption has occurred.

If you are not experiencing a crash, but instead are seeing periodic strange behaviors in the application, finding which memory had its state potentially corrupted is not as clear as with crashes. Typically, when unexpected behavior occurs, you would break into the debugger and start with some initial analysis. For example, if clients are experiencing error after error when trying to authorize credit cards, you might start by investigating the thread pool state (which services all credit card authorizations) and see why they are failing. If you notice that the thread pool is not accepting requests due to being shut down, you would proceed to step 2 and the source code analysis to identify a "valid" code path or (if one does not exist) conclude that a memory corruption has occurred.

## Step 2: Source Code Analysis

After you have identified (in step 1) that you are faced with a possible memory corruption bug, the next step is to do some source code analysis to see if the root cause can be identified. A memory corruption might occur when a thread writes to a memory location that it does not own. A very important observation can be made from this statement. The thread writes data to the memory block. Presumably, the data being written is of interest to that particular thread, and, as such, if we could analyze the data and make sense out of it, we could further narrow down the scope of possible suspects. Let's take an example. The code in Listing 5.1 shows a very simple console-based application that presents the user with two choices: show the application information (such as full name and version) and simulate memory corruption. Try not to look at the full source code, rather only the code presented in Listing 5.1.

**Listing 5.1**   Simple console-based application that simulates a memory corruption

```
int __cdecl wmain (int argc, wchar_t* pArgs[])
{
    wint_t iChar = 0 ;
    g_AppInfo = new CAppInfo(L"Simple console application", L"1.0" );
    if(!g_AppInfo)
    {
        return 1;
    }

    wprintf(L"Press: \n");
    wprintf(L"    1    To display application information\n");
    wprintf(L"    2    To simulate memory corruption\n");
    wprintf(L"    3    To exit\n");

    wprintf(L"\n\n> ");

    while((iChar=_getwche())!='3')
    {
        if(iChar == '1')
        {
            g_AppInfo->PrintAppInfo();
        }
        else if(iChar=='2')
        {
            SimulateMemoryCorruption();
        wprintf(L"\nMemory Corruption completed\n");
        }
        else
        {
            wprintf(L"\nInvalid option\n");
        }
        wprintf(L"\n\n> ");
    }

    delete g_AppInfo;

    return 0;
}
```

The source code and binary for Listing 5.1 can be found in the following folders:
    Source code: `C:\AWD\Chapter5\MemCorrupt`
    Binary: `C:\AWDBIN\WinXP.x86.chk\05MemCorrupt.exe`
Run the application using the following command line:

```
C:\AWDBIN\WinXP.x86.chk\05MemCorrupt.exe
```

The application consists of a class that encapsulate the application-specific information (full application name and version). The main function allows the user to print the application information, simulate a memory corruption, or exit the application.

```
Press:
        1        For application information
        2        For simulated memory corruption
        3        To exit
```

If you press 1, you will see the following:

```
> 1
Full application Name: Simple console application
Version: 1.0
```

If you press 2, you will see:

```
> 2
Memory Corruption completed
```

If you then press 1 again, you will see, not surprisingly, that the application crashes. Now comes the interesting part. How can we find out which part of the application caused the memory corruption (without stepping through the code for step 2)? First things first. Run the application under the debugger and choose the same sequence of choices as you did before. When you choose option 1 for the second time, the debugger should break into the debugger with an access violation.

```
...
...
...
0:000> g
ModLoad: 5cb70000 5cb96000   C:\WINDOWS\system32\ShimEng.dll
Press:
        1        To display application information
        2        To simulate memory corruption
```

```
     3         To exit


> 1
Full application Name: Simple console application
Version: 1.0


> 2
Memory Corruption completed


> 1(bdc.8d8): Access violation - code c0000005 (first chance)
First chance exceptions are reported before any exception handling.
This exception may be expected and handled.
eax=72726f43 ebx=7ffd0073 ecx=00000007 edx=7ffffffe esi=00000020 edi=00000002
eip=77c43869 esp=0007fa68 ebp=0007fed8 iopl=0         nv up ei pl nz na po nc
cs=001b  ss=0023  ds=0023  es=0023  fs=003b  gs=0000              efl=00010202
msvcrt!_woutput+0x695:
77c43869 66833800        cmp      word ptr [eax],0        ds:0023:72726f43=????
0:000> kb
ChildEBP RetAddr  Args to Child
0007fed8 77c42290 77c5fca0 01001208 0007ff28 msvcrt!_woutput+0x695
0007ff1c 01001448 01001208 72726f43 00032cb0 msvcrt!wprintf+0x35
0007ff30 010013b2 00032cb0 00032cb0 7ffd0031 memcorrupt!CAppInfo::PrintAppInfo+0x18
0007ff44 010015fa 00000001 00032bf0 00036880 05memcorrupt!wmain+0xb2
0007ffc0 7c816fd7 00011970 7c9118f1 7ffdf000 05memcorrupt!wmainCRTStartup+0x12f
0007fff0 00000000 010014cb 00000000 78746341 kernel32!BaseProcessStart+0x23
```

From the stack, we can see that our main function calls into the `PrintAppInfo` function of the `CAppInfo` class, which in turn makes a call to `wprintf`. Correlating what we see in the debugger with the source code, this seems to make perfect sense. The next question is why the `wprintf` function failed. If we look at what we pass to the function from the source code, we see the following:

```
VOID PrintAppInfo()
{
    wprintf(L"\nFull application Name: %s\n", m_wszAppName);
    wprintf(L"Version: %s\n", m_wszVersion);
}
```

It stands to reason that the pointers (`m_wszAppName` and/or `m_wszVersion`) we are passing must be invalid. The `wprintf` function assumes that the pointer passed in (in our case, strings) represents a wide character string that is NULL terminated. If that assumption fails, the function might crash. We now turn our attention to analyzing the state of the object in question. More specifically, let's look at the CAppInfo state:

```
0:000> X 05memcorrupt!g_*
01002008 05memcorrupt!g_AppInfo = 0x00032cb0
0:000> dt CAppInfo 0x00032cb0
    +0x000 m_wszAppName      : 0x72726f43  -> ??
    +0x004 m_wszVersion      : 0x01747075  -> ??
```

The pointer values we are interested in are wszAppName and wszVersion. Let's try to dump each of the pointers to see what they point to:

```
0:000> dd 0x72726f43
72726f43   ???????? ???????? ???????? ????????
72726f53   ???????? ???????? ???????? ????????
72726f63   ???????? ???????? ???????? ????????
72726f73   ???????? ???????? ???????? ????????
72726f83   ???????? ???????? ???????? ????????
72726f93   ???????? ???????? ???????? ????????
72726fa3   ???????? ???????? ???????? ????????
72726fb3   ???????? ???????? ???????? ????????
0:000> dd 0x01747075
01747075   ???????? ???????? ???????? ????????
01747085   ???????? ???????? ???????? ????????
01747095   ???????? ???????? ???????? ????????
017470a5   ???????? ???????? ???????? ????????
017470b5   ???????? ???????? ???????? ????????
017470c5   ???????? ???????? ???????? ????????
017470d5   ???????? ???????? ???????? ????????
017470e5   ???????? ???????? ???????? ????????
```

The question marks indicate that the memory is not accessible. Quite interesting, isn't it? The first time we asked the application to print out the information, everything worked fine. Now, the pointers seem to be pointing to inaccessible memory. Somehow, the contents of the CAppInfo instance became corrupted. The object layout of a simple C++ class instance consists of its data members, which in our case includes the two pointers. If the object layout was overwritten, we could get into a situation in which we have corrupt pointers. Based on that, it would be worthwhile to see what the actual instance pointer points to:

```
0:000> x 05memcorrupt!g_*
01002008 05memcorrupt!g_AppInfo = 0x00032cb0
0:000> dd 0x00032cb0
00032cb0   72726f43 01747075 abababab abababab
```

```
00032cc0   00000000 00000000 00040012 001c07f2
00032cd0   00500041 00440050 00540041 003d0041
00032ce0   003a0043 0044005c 0063006f 006d0075
00032cf0   006e0065 00730074 00610020 0064006e
00032d00   00530020 00740065 00690074 0067006e
00032d10   005c0073 0061006d 00690072 0068006f
00032d20   0041005c 00700070 0069006c 00610063
```

The memory dump shows us the pointer values we were looking at before. Instead of using the dd command, we can try to dump out the instance pointer as text instead:

```
0:000> da 0x00032cb0
00032cb0   "Corrupt........."
```

This looks much more interesting. It seems that the CAppInfo instance pointer was overwritten with the string: "Corrupt". We can now employ code reviewing to see if any of the code in the application manipulates strings with the content being "Corrupt". As you already suspected, when we choose option 2 (simulate memory corruption), the application forcefully overwrites the contents of the CAppInfo instance pointer with a string ("Corrupt").

How do we know in what form to try to dump data and make sense out of it? No clear rule exists, only guidelines. The following strategies work well and should be tried when analyzing memory contents.

1. Use the dc command to dump out the memory contents of the pointer. The dc command dumps out the content as double-word values, as well as the ASCII equivalent. If you see any strings in the output, use the da or du commands to dump out the string.

2. Use the !address extension command to glean information about the memory. The !address extension command tells you the type of the memory (such as private), the protection level (such as read and write), the state (such as committed or reserved), and the usage (such as stack or heap memory).

3. Use the dds command to dump out the memory as double words and symbols. This can help correlate the memory to a specific type.

4. Use the dpp command to dereference the specified pointer and dump out the double-word contents of the memory. If any of the double words matches a symbol, the symbol is displayed as well. This is a useful technique if the memory pointed to contains a virtual function table.

5. Use the dpa and dpu commands to display the memory pointed to in ASCII and Unicode formats.

6. If the memory content is a small number (in a multiple of 4), it might be a handle; you can use the `!handle` extension command to dump out information about the handle.
7. If the previous steps yield nothing, you can try searching the entire address space for references to the address of the memory block.

This technique of recognizing data in a corrupted memory block is very useful when trying to figure out the culprit code that corrupted the memory block. But, yet again, it might not always be possible to find the offender using this technique. The next step in the process is to use memory corruption detection tools that can make your life a whole lot easier.

## Step 3: Use Memory Corruption Detection Tools

Before we proceed to describe these tools, it is important to understand that the tools do not provide guarantees with regard to catching memory corruptions. The tools merely help you catch a number of very common memory corruption scenarios. Depending on which category of memory corruptions you are experiencing, different tools are available. For stack-based corruptions, the best tool available is the compiler itself, as it can inject stack verification code in your application. When it comes to heap-based memory corruptions, the best tool is Application Verifier (see Chapter 1, "Introduction to the Tools"). Application Verifier has a ton of test settings to choose from related to memory corruption. What both of these tools have in common is that they attempt to trap common memory-related programming mistakes immediately, as the memory corruption occurs, rather than later when the more troublesome side effects might appear. We will examine how the compiler can aid us in stack corruptions in this chapter and use Application Verifier when analyzing heap-based corruptions in Chapter 6, "Memory Corruption Part II—Heaps."

## Step 4: Instrument Source Code

If the previous steps haven't helped you find the culprit, you are in for some hard labor. The next step is to collect all the information you have gathered from the previous steps and theorize about possibilities. When you have come up with a few theories, you can instrument your code to prove them right or wrong. Instrumentation techniques vary from simple trace statements to operating system supported tracing.

## Step 5: Define Avoidance Strategies

Last, and arguably most important, is to take what you have learned and define a future avoidance strategy. Avoidance strategies can come in the form of utilizing tools throughout the development to help catch common memory corruption problems, as well as making sure that the code you are writing takes explicit steps to minimize the risk of potential memory corruptions.

The remainder of the chapter walks through some common memory corruption scenarios and shows you how the memory corruption process can be applied to figure out the reason behind the memory corruption. The scenarios in this chapter focus on stack-based corruptions, and Chapter 6 focuses on heap-based corruptions.

# Stack Corruptions

The stack is one of the most common and well-known data structures around. Most algorithm introductory classes begin with the study of the stack data structure. It's really a pretty simple and straightforward data structure that can be equated to a stack of papers. Each piece of paper that you put (or push) onto the stack goes at the top of the stack. Each piece of paper you take off (pop) the stack is taken from the top of the stack. As such, both of the basic operations performed on a stack (push and pop) always work from the top. Because each piece of paper put onto the stack or removed from the stack works from the top, the algorithm is said to have last in first out (LIFO) semantics.

A stack, as related to executing code in Windows, is simply just a block of memory assigned by the operating system to a running thread. The purpose of the stack, among other things, is to track the function call chain (allocation of local variables, parameter passing, and so on). Any time a function call is made, another frame is created and pushed on the stack. As the thread makes more and more function calls, the stack grows bigger and bigger. Figure 5.3 illustrates the anatomy of a stack during a function call.

We will see exactly how each element on the stack materializes in examples to follow, but for the time being, Figure 5.3 illustrates the general stack layout during a function call on the x86 architecture.

To get a better understanding of how stacks work and how they can become corrupted, let's take a look at an example. The application in Listing 5.2 shows the starting point of a new thread that makes a number of nested function calls, as well as declaring local variables in each of the functions.

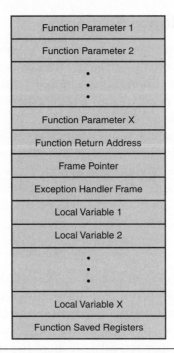

**Figure 5.3**   Anatomy of a call stack during a function call

---

**NOTE** If you are building the source code for this chapter, you need to make sure to disable buffer overrun checks by setting the BUFFER_OVERFLOW_CHECKS environment variable in your build window to 0.

---

**Listing 5.2**   Sample application showing the creation of a new thread

```
#include <windows.h>
#include <stdio.h>
#include <conio.h>

DWORD WINAPI ThreadProcedure(LPVOID lpParameter);
VOID ProcA();
VOID Sum(int* numArray, int iCount, int* sum);

int __cdecl wmain ()
{
```

```
    HANDLE hThread = NULL ;

    printf("Starting new thread...");

    hThread = CreateThread(NULL, 0, ThreadProcedure, NULL, 0, NULL);
    if(hThread!=NULL)
    {
        printf("success\n");
        WaitForSingleObject(hThread, INFINITE);
        CloseHandle(hThread);
    }

    return 0;
}

DWORD WINAPI ThreadProcedure(LPVOID lpParameter)
{
    ProcA();
    printf("Press any key to exit thread\n");
    _getch();
    return 0;
}

VOID ProcA()
{
    int iCount = 3;
    int iNums[] = {1,2,3};
    int iSum = 0 ;

    Sum(iNums, iCount, &iSum);
    printf("Sum is: %d\n", iSum);
}

VOID Sum(int* numArray, int iCount, int* sum)
{
    for(int i=0; i<iCount;i++)
    {
        *sum+=numArray[i];
    }
}
```

The source code and binary for Listing 5.2 can be found in the following folders:

Source code: `C:\AWD\Chapter5\StackDesc`

Binary: `C:\AWDBIN\WinXP.x86.chk\05StackDesc.exe`

5. MEMORY CORRUPTION PART I—STACKS

A high-level overview of the code in Listing 5.2 shows the main function creating a new thread using the `CreateThread` API and setting the starting function of that thread to a function named `ThreadProcedure`. The `ThreadProcedure` function is also the starting point of our stack investigation. According to our prior discussion about stacks, each time a thread makes a function call, a new frame is pushed onto the stack with the frame consisting of the data required to execute that function. Is the `ThreadProcedure` function frame the first item on our newly created thread stack? Not quite. Before our thread ever gets the chance to execute the `ThreadProcedure` function, the operating system executes a series of function calls as part of the thread creation. To get an idea of what is executed, build the sample application in Listing 5.2, and run it in the debugger, setting a breakpoint at the start of the `ThreadProcedure` function (as shown in Listing 5.3). After you enter Go, the debugger stops at that function, and you can look at the stack of the executing thread.

**Listing 5.3**  Displaying the call stack of newly created thread

```
...
...

...
0:000> X 05stackdesc!*ThreadProcedure*
01001210 05stackdesc!ThreadProcedure (void *)
0:000> bp 05stackdesc!ThreadProcedure
0:000> g
ModLoad: 5cb70000 5cb96000   C:\WINDOWS\system32\ShimEng.dll
Starting new thread...success
Breakpoint 0 hit
eax=00000000 ebx=00000000 ecx=002bffb0 edx=7c90eb94 esi=00000000 edi=00030000
eip=01001210 esp=002bffb8 ebp=002bffec iopl=0         nv up ei pl zr na pe nc
cs=001b  ss=0023  ds=0023  es=0023  fs=003b  gs=0000            efl=00000246
05stackdesc!ThreadProcedure:
01001210 55              push    ebp
0:001> kb
ChildEBP RetAddr  Args to Child
002bffb4 7c80b683 00000000 00030000 00000000 05stackdesc!ThreadProcedure
002bffec 00000000 01001210 00000000 00000000 kernel32!BaseThreadStart+0x37
```

As can be seen, our thread procedure is actually not the first function to execute; rather, it is a function defined in kernel32.dll named `BaseThreadStart` followed by a call to our thread function. The `BaseThreadStart` function is simply an interceptor defined by the operating system that is invoked prior to all newly created thread executions.

Now that we have reached the starting point of our thread, let's take a closer look at the stack itself to see how it is organized. As previously discussed, stack operations—such as push and pop—work from the top of the stack, and, as such, a pointer needs to be kept around that tells us where the top of the stack is. On x86 architectures, a register named esp is used for that purpose. Before we dig in and examine the actual contents of the stack, let's take a look at the first few instructions of our function. Listing 5.4 shows the assembly code starting at the ThreadProcedure function.

**Listing 5.4**   Assembly code of the ThreadProcedure function

```
0:000> u 05stackdesc!ThreadProcedure
05stackdesc!ThreadProcedure:
01001220 8bff           mov    edi,edi
01001222 55             push   ebp
01001223 8bec           mov    ebp,esp
01001225 e826000000     call   05stackdesc!ProcA (01001250)
0100122a 68b0100001     push   offset 05stackdesc!`string' (010010b0)
0100122f ff1550100001   call   dword ptr [05stackdesc!_imp__printf (01001050)]
01001235 83c404         add    esp,4
01001238 ff1548100001   call   dword ptr [05stackdesc!_imp___getch (01001048)]
```

Prior to the call to ProcA (fourth instruction from the top of the assembly code), a number of interesting assembly instructions are executed. Specifically, the following instructions are of interest when it comes to the anatomy of a call stack:

```
01001220 8bff           mov    edi,edi
01001222 55             push   ebp
01001223 8bec           mov    ebp,esp
```

The second instruction pushes the ebp register onto the stack. We will see how the ebp register is used later on, but for now it is sufficient to view the ebp register as always containing the base pointer to any given frame. Since the base pointer needs to be retained for each frame, it gets pushed onto the stack prior to any new frame creation (that is, call instruction). The next instruction moves the stack pointer to the ebp register to establish the beginning of the new stack frame. These three instructions form the prologue of a function. In general, most functions that you encounter follow a general outline:

- Function prologue
- Function code
- Function epilogue

The function prologue ensures that the stack is prepared properly for the new function code to be executed. Following the prologue is the actual function code, and finally the function epilogue makes sure that the stack is restored to the correct state prior to returning to the caller.

We are now at a point at which we are ready to call to the `ProcA` procedure via the call instruction. When a call instruction is executed, the stack also gets updated. More specifically, during the execution of the call instruction, the return address of the call (that is, the address of the next instruction after the call) is pushed onto the stack. This is necessary because upon returning from the function just called, a `ret` instruction is executed. The `ret` instruction should return to the next instruction right after the call instruction. So that we know where this location is, the `ret` instruction pops the address from the stack and jumps to that location. Figure 5.4 shows the current state of our thread stack prior to the call instruction.

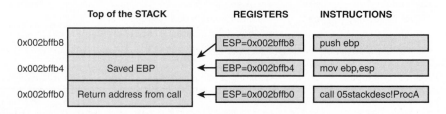

**Figure 5.4** Contents of stack prior to calling ProcA

It is important to note that the stack grows from top to bottom on the x86 architectures. From Figure 5.4, you can see how the addresses of the stack decrease as a result of pushing data onto the stack. The x86 push instructions are a two-step operation:

1. Decrements the stack pointer (`esp`) by the size of the operand
2. Transfers the source (`ebp` in Figure 5.4) to the stack

In Figure 5.4, `esp` started by pointing to stack location `0x002bffb8`. When the push instruction is executed, `esp` is first decremented by 4 bytes (`0x002bffb4`), followed by transferring the value of `ebp` into that stack location. The `mov` instruction ensures that `ebp` and `esp` point to the same location on the stack, which is also the base location for the new call frame.

At this point, the stack has been prepped and set up for the actual call instruction that will transfer the flow of execution to the next function called (`ProcA`). Positioned on the call instruction, we continue the execution by entering `t` to trace into the next function. Once in that function, we unassemble the code for the entire function, as shown in Listing 5.5.

**Listing 5.5**   Assembly code for ProcA

```
0:000> uf 05stackdesc!ProcA
05stackdesc!ProcA:
01001250 8bff            mov     edi,edi
01001252 55              push    ebp
01001253 8bec            mov     ebp,esp
01001255 83ec14          sub     esp,14h
01001258 c745ec03000000  mov     dword ptr [ebp-14h],3
0100125f c745f401000000  mov     dword ptr [ebp-0Ch],1
01001266 c745f802000000  mov     dword ptr [ebp-8],2
0100126d c745fc03000000  mov     dword ptr [ebp-4],3
01001274 c745f000000000  mov     dword ptr [ebp-10h],0
0100127b 8d45f0          lea     eax,[ebp-10h]
0100127e 50              push    eax
0100127f 8b4dec          mov     ecx,dword ptr [ebp-14h]
01001282 51              push    ecx
01001283 8d55f4          lea     edx,[ebp-0Ch]
01001286 52              push    edx
01001287 e824000000      call    05stackdesc!Sum (010012b0)
0100128c 8b45f0          mov     eax,dword ptr [ebp-10h]
0100128f 50              push    eax
01001290 68d0100001      push    offset 05stackdesc!`string' (010010d0)
01001295 ff1550100001    call    dword ptr [05stackdesc!_imp__printf (01001050)]
0100129b 83c408          add     esp,8
0100129e 8be5            mov     esp,ebp
010012a0 5d              pop     ebp
010012a1 c3              ret
```

The `uf` command is used to unassemble the entire function in one step rather than having to use the `u` command which, by default, only unassembles the first eight instructions.

The first four instructions in this function are part of the function prologue:

```
01001250 8bff            mov     edi,edi
01001252 55              push    ebp
01001253 8bec            mov     ebp,esp
01001255 83ec30          sub     esp,0x14
```

The first three instructions are identical to the previous frame and simply make sure that the base frame pointer and stack pointer are set up properly for the frame. The last instruction (`sub  esp,0x14`) looks very interesting. It seems to be subtracting 0x14 bytes (or decimal 20) from the stack pointer. Why is that subtraction taking place? It is making room for local variables. As you can see from the source code for `ProcA` in Listing 5.2, it allocates the following local variables on the stack:

```
int iCount = 3;
int iNums[] = {1,2,3};
int iSum = 0 ;
```

The total size of these variables is

```
4 (iCount) + 12 (iNums) + 4 (iSum) = 20 bytes
```

When we subtract 20 bytes from the stack pointer, the apparent gap in the stack becomes reserved for the local variables declared in the function. Figure 5.5 shows the stack contents after the `sub` instruction has executed.

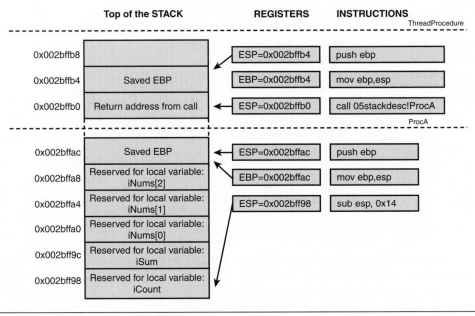

**Figure 5.5**   Contents of stack after reserving space for local variables in ProcA

After the stack pointer `esp` has been adjusted to make room for the local variables, the next set of instructions executed initializes the stack-based local variables to the values specified in the source code:

```
05stackdesc!ProcA+0x8:
01001258 c745ec03000000   mov      dword ptr [ebp-14h],3
0100125f c745f401000000   mov      dword ptr [ebp-0Ch],1
01001266 c745f802000000   mov      dword ptr [ebp-8],2
0100126d c745fc03000000   mov      dword ptr [ebp-4],3
01001274 c745f000000000   mov      dword ptr [ebp-10h],0
```

An important observation to be made with these mov instructions is that the ebp register is used with an offset to reference the stack location where the local variable resides. Why is the ebp register used instead of esp? Remember how we said that the ebp register always points to the beginning of a call frame? The reason for that is to always have a reference point from where we can access anything related to that frame. By convention, the ebp register is used for that purpose. This is also the reason why particular care is always taken to store the ebp register on the stack prior to the creation of a new frame so that it can safely be restored when the frame goes away (that is, function returns). In contrast, the esp register changes continually throughout the execution of a function, and, as such, would be difficult (or at the very least costly) to use as a base frame pointer.

### Frame Pointer Omission

Frame pointer omission is an optimization technique in which the base frame pointer register can be used as a general-purpose register rather than a reserved base frame pointer shown in the chapter. Enabling the base frame pointer register to be used in this way speeds up execution and enables the compiler to use the base frame pointer register as yet another general-purpose register.

Following the initialization of the local variables comes a series of instructions that gets the application ready to make another function call, as shown in Listing 5.6.

**Listing 5.6**   Preamble assembly code for calling the Sum function

```
0100127b 8d45f0          lea     eax,[ebp-10h]
0100127e 50              push    eax
0100127f 8b4dec          mov     ecx,dword ptr [ebp-14h]
01001282 51              push    ecx
01001283 8d55f4          lea     edx,[ebp-0Ch]
01001286 52              push    edx
01001287 e824000000      call    05stackdesc!Sum (010012b0)
```

At a glance, it seems that a lot of data is pushed onto the stack prior to the call instruction. If we look at the Sum function prototype, we see the following:

```
VOID Sum(int* numArray, int iCount, int* sum);
```

Three parameters are passed to the function:

- A pointer to an integer array, which contains the numbers we want to add
- An integer that represents the number of items in the array
- A pointer to an integer that will (upon success) contain the sum of all the numbers in that array

The way by which the parameters are passed from the ThreadProc function to the Sum function is—you guessed it—the stack. Anytime a `call` instruction results in calling a function with parameters, the calling function is responsible for pushing the parameters onto the stack from right to left (using the standard calling convention). In our case, the first parameter that needs to go on the stack is the pointer that will contain the sum (`sum`). The first two instructions in Listing 5.6 show how the parameter is pushed on the stack. Once again, we see that the `ebp` register is used to reference the local variable of interest. Because we are passing a pointer, the `lea` instruction (load effective address) is used. The remaining parameters are pushed onto the stack in a similar fashion (remember—from right to left).

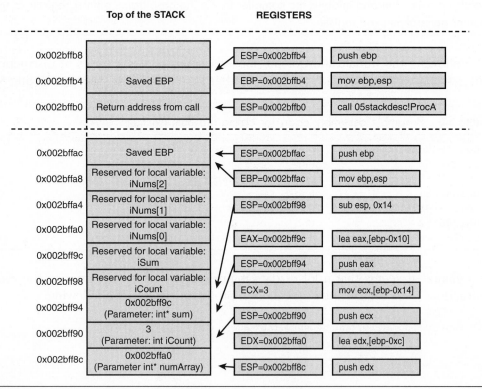

**Figure 5.6**   Call stack as we are ready to call the Sum function

I will leave it as an exercise to the reader to figure out what the stack looks like in the new frame while calling the Sum function. Here is a hint: Because the parameters are passed via the stack, an offset is used in conjunction with the ebp register to access the passed-in parameters.

After the call has returned to the calling frame (ProcA), the stack pointer esp is set to 0x002bff98, which is also the last stack slot used prior to pushing parameters for the call to Sum. How did the stack pointer get adjusted back to that position? The answer to that lies in how a frame returns from a function, as you will see when we analyze the return from the ProcA function. Listing 5.7 shows the assembly instructions right after our call to Sum.

**Listing 5.7** Assembly instructions right after our call to Sum

```
0100128c 8b45f0              mov     eax,dword ptr [ebp-10h]
0100128f 50                  push    eax
01001290 68d0100001          push    offset 05stackdesc!`string' (010010d0)
01001295 ff1550100001        call    dword ptr [05stackdesc!_imp__printf
(01001050)]
0100129b 83c408              add     esp,8
0100129e 8be5                mov     esp,ebp
010012a0 5d                  pop     ebp
010012a1 c3                  ret
```

The next call instruction on line 4 shows another call, this time to the printf function. This matches up well with our source code, as it tries to print out the result of the call to Sum (stored in iSum). Once again, before calling the printf function, the stack is set up for any parameters that might be needed during the call. More specifically, two parameters are passed:

- A string: "The sum is: %d\n"
- The value of iSum

Remember that parameters are always passed from right to left, so we push the value of iSum onto the stack first. The first two instructions of Listing 5.7 show how the value of iSum is pushed onto the stack. Because iSum is a local variable on the ProcA frame, it is accessed via the ebp register minus an offset of 0x10. From Figure 5.6, we can see that ebp-0x10 indexes the iSum local variable. The last parameter that should be pushed onto the stack is the string itself, and we can see that with the push offset 05stackdesc!`string' (010010d0) instruction. To validate that it is in fact pushing the correct string onto the stack, we can use the da (dump ASCII) command:

```
0:001> da 0x10010d0
010010d0   "Sum is: %d."
```

This does indeed validate that the correct string is being passed.

After the call instruction has executed, the final few instructions in the ProcA function ensure that the stack is restored to its original state prior to the call to ProcA, as shown in Listing 5.8.

**Listing 5.8**   ProcA function epilogue

```
0100129b 83c408          add       esp,8
0100129e 8be5            mov       esp,ebp
010012a0 5d              pop       ebp
010012a1 c3              ret
```

The first instruction adds 8 to the stack pointer esp. What is the reason behind this addition? Well, when the printf function returns, esp is set to the last parameter that was pushed onto the stack in preparation for the call. Remember that each time a frame makes a call, we need to ensure that the stack is restored to the state prior to the call. Since we pushed two parameters onto the stack in order to call printf, we need to add 8 bytes from the stack pointer esp in order to get back to the state we had prior to the call (2*4 bytes = the size of the two parameters pushed onto the stack). Once the state has been restored, we are just about ready to return from the ProcA function. Since we allocated local variables in the ProcA function, the esp register is pointing to the last local variable declared on the stack. As we return from the function, we need to make sure that the esp register is reset to the value that it was prior to making the call to the ProcA function. The key to accomplish this is to remember what took place in the ProcA function prologue. More specifically, the mov ebp,esp instruction in the prologue saved the value of the esp register into ebp. To restore esp, we simply execute the mov esp,ebp instruction, as shown in Listing 5.8. Figure 5.7 shows the current state of our stack.

Because the ebp register is used as the base frame pointer, it is as important to restore that register as it is to restore the esp register. After we have returned from the ProcA function, we want the calling function (ThreadProcedure) to be capable of using the ebp register just as it was being used prior to the call to FuncA. Because the next item on our stack is the saved ebp (that is, the frame pointer of the calling function), we simply pop that value into the ebp register. Finally, we can issue the ret instruction to return to the calling function. But, hold on—our esp register (0x002bffb0) seems to be pointing to a return address that was pushed onto the stack automatically when executing the call instruction. Do we have to do anything with that stack location prior to returning? The answer is yes and no: yes in the sense that we need the return address to know where to return to, and no because we don't explicitly pop it from the stack. When the `ret` instruction is executed, the return address is popped from the stack and control is transferred to that location so that execution can resume.

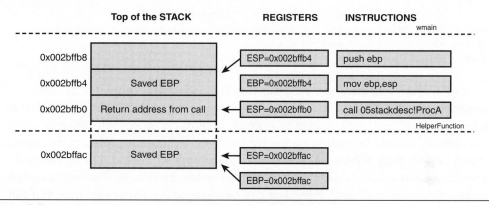

**Figure 5.7**   Call stack prior to returning from the ProcA function

As you can see, the stack is a very versatile data structure, and it is at the heart of thread execution in Windows. It enables applications to transfer control back and forth between functions in a very structured and ordered fashion. Because the compiler generates all the code that handles this control transfer (managing the stack, passing parameters, addressing local variables, and so on), developers typically do not worry too much about what actually goes on behind-the-scenes. For the most part, developers should not have to worry, but some very frequent programming mistakes can cause the thread stack to become corrupt. When it does, understanding how the stack is managed can mean the difference between a successful application launch and disaster. In the following sections, we detail some of the most common scenarios that can lead to stack corruption and ways to apply the memory corruption detection process to get to the root cause.

## The Mysterious mov edi,edi Instruction

A function prologue is responsible for setting up the current frame. As we have seen, the general structure of a function prologue sets up the base frame pointer, pushes the base frame pointer onto the stack, and reserves space for local variables. Here is an example of the `FindFirstFileExW` function prologue:

```
0:000> u kernel32!FindFirstFileExW
kernel32!FindFirstFileExW:
7c80ec7d 8bff              mov      edi,edi          ▪ Useless instruction?
7c80ec7f 55               push     ebp              ▪ Save away old base frame pointer
7c80ec80 8bec             mov      ebp,esp          ▪ Set up new base frame pointer
7c80ec82 81eccc020000     sub      esp,0x2cc        ▪ Reserve space for local
variables
7c80ec88 837d0c01         cmp      dword ptr [ebp+0xc],0x1
7c80ec8c a1cc36887c       mov      eax,[kernel32!__security_cookie (7c8836cc)]
7c80ec91 53               push     ebx
7c80ec92 8945fc           mov      [ebp-0x4],eax
```

What we have not discussed yet is the very first and mysterious mov edi,edi instruction. Every function prologue begins with this seemingly useless instruction. Most of the time, the mov edi,edi instruction is simply a NOP (no operation), but under certain circumstances, it might be used to enable hot patching. Hot patching refers to the capability to patch running code without the hassle of first stopping the component being patched. This mechanism is crucial to avoiding downtime in system availability. The basic principle is that the 2-byte mov edi,edi instruction can be replaced by a jmp instruction that can execute whatever new code is required. Because it is a 2-byte instruction, the only jmp instruction that will actually fit is a short jmp, which enables a jump of 127 bytes in either direction. This is typically not enough because chances are that you would jump to locations where existing code is already located. To bypass this limitation, we have to look at the instructions preceding the mov edi,edi instruction:

```
0:000> u kernel32!FindFirstFileExW-9
kernel32!OpenMutexW+a6:
7c80ec74 33c0             xor      eax,eax
7c80ec76 eb98             jmp      kernel32!OpenMutexW+0xad (7c80ec10)
7c80ec78 90               nop
7c80ec79 90               nop
7c80ec7a 90               nop
7c80ec7b 90               nop
7c80ec7c 90               nop
kernel32!FindFirstFileExW:
7c80ec7d 8bff             mov      edi,edi
```

The five bytes preceding the mov instruction are all 1-byte NOP instructions. By replacing the mov edi,edi instruction with a short jump to the NOP instructions and replacing those instructions with a long jump, we can easily hot patch to a location of choice.

## Stack Overruns

A stack overrun occurs when a thread indiscriminately overwrites portions of its call stack reserved for other purposes. This can include, but is not limited to, overwriting the return address for a particular frame, overwriting entire frames, or even exhausting the stack completely. The net effect of stack overruns ranges from crashes to unpredictable behavior and even serious security holes. Stack overruns have become one of the most common attack angles for malicious software, as they can potentially allow the attacker to gain complete control of the computer on which the faulty software runs. To exemplify the seriousness of stack overruns, we will look at a scenario in which a stack overrun could result in a security hole. The seemingly innocent code in Listing 5.9 shows an application that accepts a connection string on the command line and attempts to use that connection string to establish a connection to a data source.

**Listing 5.9** Application that establishes a connection to a data source

```
#include <windows.h>
#include <stdio.h>

#define MAX_CONN_LEN    30

VOID HelperFunction(WCHAR* pszConnectionString);

int __cdecl wmain (int argc, wchar_t* pArgs[])
{
    if (argc==2)
    {
        HelperFunction(pArgs[1]);
        wprintf (L"Connection to %s established\n",pArgs[1]);
    }
    else
    {
        printf ("Please specify connection string on the command line\n");
    }

    return 0;
}

VOID HelperFunction(WCHAR* pszConnectionString)
{
    WCHAR pszCopy[MAX_CONN_LEN];

    wcscpy(pszCopy, pszConnectionString);
```

**Listing 5.9**   Application that establishes a connection to a data source *(continued)*

```
    //
    // ...
    // Establish connection
    // ...
    //
}
```

The source code and binary for Listing 5.9 can be found in the following folders:

   Source code: `C:\AWD\Chapter5\Overrun`

   Binary: `C:\AWDBIN\WinXP.x86.chk\05Overrun.exe`

If we run this application and specify a few simple connection strings, everything appears to be fine:

```
C:\AWDBIN\WinXP.x86.chk\05Overrun.exe MyDataSource
Connection to MyDataSource established
C:\AWDBIN\WinXP.x86.chk\05Overrun.exe MyRemoteDataSource
Connection to MyRemoteDataSource established
```

As the code seems to be working fine, everyone in the product group gets ready for the ship party. A few weeks after the product is released, the product support group starts getting a large number of complaints about application crashes. Even worse, Internet rumors start circulating with claims that the application is vulnerable to a security exploit that allows an attacker to inject and run arbitrary code in the process.

To troubleshoot this problem, we need to gather data from product support to see if it's possible to reproduce the problem. Drilling deeper into the data set provided from support shows that long connection strings seem to be the culprit. Sure enough—specifying the following connection string seems to cause the application to crash:

```
C:\AWDBIN\WinXP.x86.chk\05Overrun.exe ThisIsMyVeryExtremelySuperMagnificantConnec-
tionStringForMyDataSource
```

As per Figure 5.1, the first step in debugging the memory corruption process is to analyze the state at the point of the crash. Let's fire up the application under the debugger and let it run until the crash occurs, as shown in Listing 5.10.

**Listing 5.10**   Crash reproduced in the debugger

```
...

...

...

0:000> g
ModLoad: 5cb70000 5cb96000   C:\WINDOWS\system32\ShimEng.dll
(f80.d10): Access violation - code c0000005 (first chance)
First chance exceptions are reported before any exception handling.
This exception may be expected and handled.
eax=0007fefc ebx=7ffde000 ecx=0007ff86 edx=00034d5a esi=7c9118f1 edi=00011970
eip=00630069 esp=0007ff44 ebp=00660069 iopl=0         nv up ei pl nz na pe nc
cs=001b  ss=0023  ds=0023  es=0023  fs=003b  gs=0000         efl=00010206
00630069 ??                     ???
0:000> kb
ChildEBP RetAddr  Args to Child
WARNING: Frame IP not in any known module. Following frames may be wrong.
0007ff40 00430074 006e006f 0065006e 00740063 0x630069
0007ffc0 7c816fd7 00011970 7c9118f1 7ffde000 0x430074
0007fff0 00000000 01001234 00000000 78746341 kernel32!BaseProcessStart+0x23
```

At first glance, the stack seems to be so broken that our inclination might be to say that we have a potential bug in the debugger. After all, how could we cause the call stack to get into a state like that? Again, the first thing we need to do is to analyze some state. Because we are experiencing a crash, it is crucial to first find out where we are crashing. Because the call stack (as shown by the kb command) isn't yielding a nice clean and readable stack, we can look at the eip register to see where we are in the code. The eip register (instruction pointer) is also called the program counter and always points to the next instruction to be executed. To find the instruction pointer, we use the r eip command:

```
0:000> r eip
eip=00630069
```

The eip register points to 0x00630069. Dumping out the memory at that location yields

```
0:000> dd 00630069
00630069 ???????? ???????? ???????? ????????
00630079 ???????? ???????? ???????? ????????
00630089 ???????? ???????? ???????? ????????
00630099 ???????? ???????? ???????? ????????
006300a9 ???????? ???????? ???????? ????????
```

```
006300b9   ???????? ???????? ???????? ????????
006300c9   ???????? ???????? ???????? ????????
006300d9   ???????? ???????? ???????? ????????
```

The contents of that memory location are a series of question marks, which we know indicate inaccessible memory. From this trivial exercise, we can hypothesize that the instruction pointer the processor uses to control the flow of execution in our application has gotten into a corrupt state. Because we do not explicitly control the `eip` register, how is this possible? The key to finding out the answer is to understand how the `eip` register is controlled indirectly. We already know that the processor takes care of updating the `eip` register automatically when executing instructions, but what happens if we encounter a branching instruction? From our previous discussion of the anatomy of a call stack, we know that when a `call` instruction is executed, the contents of the `eip` register are pushed onto the stack to enable the processor to know where to continue execution. When the calling function returns via the `ret` instruction, the return address is popped from the stack, `eip` is reset to that location, and execution continues from there. Is it possible that we somehow put a bad return address on the stack, causing the processor to continue execution from the bad address? Our first inclination might be to again say no, but knowing that our code does in fact branch makes this a somewhat plausible theory. Let's rerun the application in the debugger and this time pay close attention to the state of the stack. We begin the investigation right before making the call to the string copy function in `HelperFunction`. Figure 5.8 shows the state of the stack right before calling the `wcscpy` function.

So far, the stack looks to be in good shape. Now let's execute (stepping over using the `p` command) the string copy function call. Our expectations are that the stack looks intact and that the local variable `pszCopy` will contain a copy of the connection string. Let's dump out the local variable and take a look:

```
0:000> du ebp-0x3c
0007fefc   "ThisIsMyVeryExtremelySuperMagnif"
0007ff3c   "icantConnectionStringForMyDataSo"
0007ff7c   "urce"
```

Looks good—the contents are exactly what we expected them to be. Following the call, the remainder of the instructions is the epilogue code for the `HelperFunction`. Step over the instructions until you reach the `ret` instruction. We know that when the `ret` instruction is executed, the next item on the stack is popped off and execution resumes from the location popped off. As a sanity check, we dump the next item on the stack to see what the return address really is:

```
0:000> dd esp
0007ff3c  00630069 006e0061 00430074 006e006f
0007ff4c  0065006e 00740063 006f0069 0053006e
0007ff5c  00720074 006e0069 00460067 0072006f
0007ff6c  0079004d 00610044 00610074 006f0053
0007ff7c  00720075 00650063 7ffd0000 e4361000
0007ff8c  00000000 00000000 00000002 00034ca8
0007ff9c  00000000 00036ce0 00000000 0007ff7c
0007ffac  89e6a074 0007ffe0 01001442 010010f0
0:000> u 00630069
00630069 ??              ???
         ^ Memory access error in 'u 00630069'
```

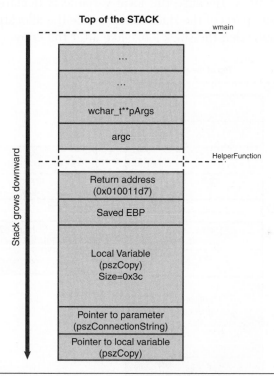

**Top of the STACK**

wmain

...

...

wchar_t**pArgs

argc

HelperFunction

Return address
(0x010011d7)

Saved EBP

Local Variable
(pszCopy)
Size=0x3c

Pointer to parameter
(pszConnectionString)

Pointer to local variable
(pszCopy)

Stack grows downward

**Figure 5.8** Call stack prior to calling wcscpy from HelperFunction

When we try to unassemble the return address on the stack, we get a memory access error. Without even executing the ret instruction, we can fairly confidently say that we now know what is causing the crash. Executing the ret instruction shows how the eip pointer is set to the bad return address, and the subsequent execution of that bad return address fails with an access violation. Because we know that the stack looked fine prior to making the call to the string copy function, something during the execution of the function caused the stack to become corrupted. A quick glance at the source for HelperFunction shows that we are trying to make a copy of the connection string passed in and place it in a local variable named pszCopy. The destination string (pszCopy) is declared to be 30 characters in length, which means that the source string we passed in, 69 characters long, will not fit. Does wcscpy respect the boundaries of our local variable? No, it does not. In fact, the only stopping point of wsccpy is when it reaches a null terminator in the source string. What happens when the wcscpy function passes the end of the local variable? The answer is that it just keeps copying characters. Because the local variable is declared on the stack, the function will overwrite parts of the stack that precede the allocation for the local variable. Figure 5.9 shows what the stack looks like after the copy.

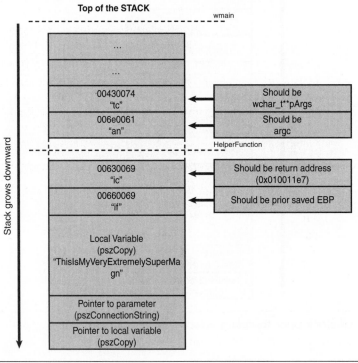

**Figure 5.9** Call stack after call to wcscpy from HelperFunction

As you can see from Figure 5.9, the seemingly simple execution of a string copy function has completely corrupted our stack. After the string copy function reaches the boundary of our local variable, `pszCopy`, it just keeps copying the string, overwriting all stack contents along the way. More specifically, it overwrites the return address used when `HelperFunction` returns with the two characters "ic" (`0x00630069`). When the processor returns from the function using the `ret` instruction, that value is automatically popped from the stack, the instruction pointer `eip` is set to that value, and execution resumes. As you saw earlier on, executing code located in the erroneous location `0x00630069` causes a crash because of the location not containing any valid code. As a matter of fact, that location points to invalid memory.

The fix for this problem is to make sure that we do not copy more than we have allotted for in our local variable. Two possible solutions exist depending on the specification of the connection string.

- If the connection string can be of variable length with no upper boundaries, allocating memory on the stack is the wrong approach. Without knowing the size of the string at compile time, it is impossible to allocate a buffer on the stack that could hold the source string. If this is the case, allocating the buffer from the heap is a better approach.
- If the connection string really is limited to 30 characters, we must make sure to respect that boundary independent of how long the string that is passed in really is. A good approach in this case is to use a string copy function that allows you to specify the size of the destination string to ensure that no more than 30 characters are ever copied to the destination. See the `StringCchCopy` API for an excellent and safe way to achieve this.

Before shipping an update that contains a fix for the crashing bug in the application, we must also pay careful attention to the rumors that were going around on the Internet: A security hole was uncovered as well, leading to a machine compromise. We have already done most of the investigative work to realize that the crash we were seeing can also lead to a security hole. Code exploits can utilize the fact that the return address can be overwritten. If an attacker was able to carefully construct a connection string that overwrote the return address on the stack with an address of his choosing, the application would execute the code at that address and potentially let the attacker take control of the application.

Because stack buffer overruns are such common problems, you might be wondering if there is a tool that can help detect these errors at compile time. The answer is yes, and the tool is called PREfast (part of the Windows Driver Kit). To illustrate the usage of PREfast, we will use the same buffer overrun sample as shown previously. Start by opening up a Windows Driver Kit build window (checked XP). Navigate to the directory containing the source code for the sample and type the following:

```
C:\> prefast /filterpreset="Recommended Filters" build /ZCc
```

This command line launches PREfast using the recommended filters setting and performs a complete build of the sources in the directory. As part of the build, PREfast also analyzes the code to determine if there are any problematic code paths. After the process completes, PREfast displays a summary of the number of defects detected:

```
----------------------------------------
PREfast reported 1 defects during execution of the command.
----------------------------------------
Enter PREFAST LIST to list the defect log as text within the console.
Enter PREFAST VIEW to display the defect log user interface.
```

To view the defects, simply enter the following:

```
PREFAST LIST
```

This is used when displaying defects in the console.
     Or enter this:

```
PREFAST VIEW
```

This is used when displaying defects in a graphical user interface.
As an example, we will use the list feature of PREfast to see what defects it detected in our source code:

```
----------------------------------------
Microsoft (R) PREfast Version 8.0.86081.
Copyright (C) Microsoft Corporation. All rights reserved.
----------------------------------------
Contents of defect log: C:\Documents and Settings\marioh\Application
Data\Microsoft\PFD\defects.xml
----------------------------------------
c:\awd\chapter5\overrun\overrun.cpp (27): warning 6204: Possible buffer overrun in
call to 'wcscpy': use of unchecked parameter 'pszConnectionString'
        FUNCTION: HelperFunction (23)
----------------------------------------
```

As you can see, PREfast notifies us that there is a possible buffer overrun in our HelperFunction because of an unchecked parameter.

PREfast contains a whole slew of different checks that can be employed during the build process. You can use predefined or custom filters to change which checks are applied. PREfast is an incredibly useful tool to use when building code, and it is highly recommended to use during the build process. After all, why spend time debugging a problem that a tool can automatically pinpoint for you?

## Asynchronous Operations and Stack Pointers

The lifetime of a local variable declared in a function is directly tied to the scope of that function. Assuming a standard calling convention, when a function executes its epilogue code, the stack pointer is reset to the prior frame and any local variables are deemed invalid. A very common programming mistake is to make wrongful assumptions about the lifetime of local variables and cause unpredictable behavior during execution.

To exemplify the problem, we investigate a reported crash in a command-line application that enumerates the first two registry values in a user-provided registry path. The basic architecture behind this application is relatively simple. The user specifies the registry path that he wants to enumerate (the application assumes that the root key is HKEY_CURRENT_USER) followed by a maximum timeout for the enumeration. Next, the application calls the RegEnum helper function that starts the registry enumeration asynchronously by calling another helper: RegEnumAsync. The RegEnumAsync function returns a handle that the application then waits for (with a specified timeout). If a timeout occurs, an error is displayed; otherwise, the result of the enumeration is printed out to the screen. To minimize unnecessary noise, the registry enumeration only returns registry values of type REG_DWORD. Before running the application, make sure to import the test.reg file that is included with the application:

```
C:\AWDBIN\WinXP.x86.chk>regedit /s test.reg
```

An example run is shown in Listing 5.11.

**Listing 5.11**  Example run of Registry enumeration application

```
C:\AWDBIN\WinXP.x86.chk\05Async.exe
Enter registry key path ("quit" to quit): Test
Enter timeout for enumeration: 5000
Value 1 Name: Value1
Value 1 Data: 1
```

*(continues)*

**Listing 5.11**   Example run of registry enumeration application *(continued)*

```
Value 2 Name: Value2
Value 2 Data: 2
Enter registry key path ("quit" to quit): Does\Not\Exist
Enter timeout for enumeration: 5000
Error enumerating DWORDS in HKEY_CURRENT_USER\Does\Not\Exist within 5000 ms!
Enter registry key path ("quit" to quit): quit
Exiting...
```

The source code and binary for Listing 5.11 can be found in the following folders:

Source code: `C:\AWD\Chapter5\Async`

Binary: `C:\AWDBIN\WinXP.x86.chk\05Async.exe`

As you can see, the application seems to be working fine. Valid registry paths successfully enumerate the first two DWORD values contained within that key, and invalid registry paths generate expected errors. The only other variable left is the timeout, which we specified to be 5000ms. When we try to pass in a smaller timeout (2000ms) for a valid registry key, we end up with a failure:

```
C:\AWDBIN\WinXP.x86.chk\05Async.exe
Enter registry key path ("quit" to quit): Test
Enter timeout for enumeration: 2000
Timeout occurred...
Error enumerating DWORDS in HKEY_CURRENT_USER\Test within 2000 ms!
```

The failure might be expected, as it could have taken more than 2000ms to enumerate the registry key (for example, during a remote registry enumeration). What is not expected is the appearance of the Dr. Watson UI. To start investigating this problem, we run the application under the debugger. Using the same registry path (Test) and timeout value (2000), the debugger breaks in with an access violation exception, as shown in Listing 5.12.

**Listing 5.12**   Access violation enumerating registry values

```
...
...
...
0:000> g
ModLoad: 5cb70000 5cb96000   C:\WINDOWS\system32\ShimEng.dll
Enter registry key path ("quit" to quit): Test
```

```
Enter timeout for enumeration: 2000
Timeout occurred...
Error enumerating DWORDS in HKEY_CURRENT_USER\Test within 2000 ms!
(bc.eb0): Access violation - code c0000005 (first chance)
First chance exceptions are reported before any exception handling.
This exception may be expected and handled.
eax=00000000 ebx=7ffde000 ecx=7c80240f edx=7c90eb94 esi=7c9118f1 edi=00011970
eip=000380d1 esp=0007fd00 ebp=00000001 iopl=0         nv up ei pl zr na pe nc
cs=001b  ss=0023  ds=0023  es=0023  fs=003b  gs=0000            efl=00010246
000380d1 006100          add     byte ptr [ecx],ah        ds:0023:7c80240f=c2
0:000> kb
ChildEBP RetAddr  Args to Child
WARNING: Frame IP not in any known module. Following frames may be wrong.
0007fcfc 7c9118f1 0007fd10 01001a7a 00001770 0x380d1
0007fdcc 7c9118f1 7ffde000 00090000 0007fa18 ntdll!RtlDeleteCriticalSection+0x72
00011970 00750074 00690064 0020006f 005c0038 ntdll!RtlDeleteCriticalSection+0x72
00011970 00000000 00690064 0020006f 005c0038 0x750074
```

The stack at the point of the access violation looks really strange. Nothing on the stack trace gives us any indication of what is being executed. All we have is a mysterious address (0x380d1). How do you approach a problem like this, when the stack is apparent garbage and there is no indication of what happened (or what was executing)? The answer once again lies in step 1 of the memory corruption process: state analysis.

Although it might seem discouraging to see a stack trace like we just did, it really is not the end of the world. To get a better picture of what is going on in the application, the key is to step back and question the debugger's capability to give you truthful answers all the time. In our case, we are presented with a stack that looks utterly useless. The debugger gave us this stack based on its own process of retrieving stack traces. This process, by which the debugger retrieves stack traces, relies on certain aspects of the stack to be intact. If the stack integrity has been compromised, the debugger will most definitely give you inaccurate results. In order to get a much better stack trace, we have to do the job ourselves. The first thing we should do is figure out what instruction was executed at the point of the crash. We can accomplish this very easily by using the u command in the debugger. (Remember that eip always points to the instruction to be executed.)

```
0:000> u eip
000380d1 006100          add     byte ptr [ecx],ah
000380d4 6c              ins     byte ptr es:[edi],dx
000380d5 007500          add     byte ptr [ebp],dh
000380d8 650032          add     byte ptr gs:[edx],dh
```

```
000380db 0000            add     byte ptr [eax],al
000380dd 00adba0df0ad    add     byte ptr [ebp-520FF246h],ch
000380e3 ba0df0adba      mov     edx,0BAADF00Dh
000380e8 0df0adba0d      or      eax,0DBAADF0h
```

A few observations can be made from this output.

First, we are trying to move data into a location pointed to by the `ecx` register, which points to the following address: `0x7c80240f`. If you unassemble this address, you will find that it actually points to code and not data, per se. As a matter of fact, the code resolves to `kernel32!SleepEx`:

```
0:000> u 7c80240f
kernel32!SleepEx+0x8a:
7c80240f c20800           ret     8
7c802412 8975d8           mov     dword ptr [ebp-28h],esi
7c802415 c745dc00000080   mov     dword ptr [ebp-24h],80000000h
7c80241c 8d45d8           lea     eax,[ebp-28h]
7c80241f 8945e4           mov     dword ptr [ebp-1Ch],eax
7c802422 ebbd             jmp     kernel32!SleepEx+0x55 (7c8023e1)
7c802424 3d01010000       cmp     eax,101h
7c802429 75ca             jne     kernel32!SleepEx+0x70 (7c8023f5)
```

Next, the address that `eip` points to does not fall into the address range of any currently loaded modules. Each module (both code and data) loaded into a process is located at a starting address. The starting address is determined either by the module itself or the operating system if a collision occurs. In either case, the instruction pointer almost always points to a location within a currently loaded module's loading address. You can very easily determine the address range of the modules loaded into your process by using the `lm` command:

```
0:000> lm
start    end        module name
01000000 01003000   05async    (deferred)
77c10000 77c68000   msvcrt     (deferred)
77dd0000 77e6b000   ADVAPI32   (deferred)
77e70000 77f01000   RPCRT4     (deferred)
7c800000 7c8f4000   kernel32   (pdb symbols)
7c900000 7c9b0000   ntdll      (pdb symbols)
```

Our current `eip` location (`000380d1`) does not fall within any of the address ranges shown.

Last, the code at the `eip` location seems to be incorrect. For example, the following instruction ORs the contents of the `eax` register with a very interesting value:

```
or      eax,0DBAADF0h
```

Armed with these observations, our theory is that a stack location containing a return address has been corrupted, causing the processor to jump to a valid memory region containing invalid code. Furthermore, we know that the address of the invalid memory region is (or is close to) `000380d1`. We say close to because the processor really doesn't care too much where it is executing code, as long as it is valid memory. As such, if the instructions that the processor is executing are benign (from a crashing perspective), it will continue executing and advancing `eip` until a real failure occurs. In our case, we are most certainly executing in a valid memory area, albeit not the right code.

In order to find the corruptor of our stack, we need to do some detective work on the stack itself. Let's begin by dumping out the contents of the stack, and then see if we can recognize what the execution flow was. We already know that the established range for our code module (05async.exe) is `01000000-01003000`. By looking at the stack contents, we can see if any elements on the stack are within that range. If so, we might have found a return address that will help us construct the call chain. Listing 5.13 shows the contents of the stack.

**Listing 5.13**   Contents of the stack at the point of crash

```
0:000> dd esp esp+100
0007fd00    7c9118f1 0007fd10 01001a7a 00001770
0007fd10    0007ff44 0100156a 0007fd2c 00000004
0007fd20    000007d0 00000001 000007d0 00650054
0007fd30    00740073 00000000 00000000 00000000
0007fd40    00000000 00000000 00000000 00000005
0007fd50    a9b81a60 a9b81a74 89e3cc00 80543dfd
0007fd60    00000000 c0000034 888b7370 00f80084
0007fd70    e44b1738 87cd0e00 888b73d0 00000000
0007fd80    00000000 00000068 c0000034 00000000
0007fd90    00000005 a9b81adc 8056a251 888b7370
0007fda0    8056a267 a9b81b98 00000000 00000000
0007fdb0    00000000 00000000 e4657bc8 00000000
0007fdc0    00000038 00000023 00000023 00011970
0007fdd0    7c9118f1 7ffde000 00090000 0007fa18
0007fde0    01001a83 7c910570 7c810665 0000001b
0007fdf0    00000200 0007fffc 00000023 8056a267
0007fe00    8056aa94
```

Note that we dump the stack contents from the current location all the way up to the current location plus an offset of 100. Because the stack grows downward, we need to add an offset in order to get a good look at the stack from start to finish. Is 100 a magic offset? Not really—it all depends on how much data is put on the stack (local variables for each frame, and so on). Generally, an offset of 100 is a good starting number. If you don't find anything useful, you can increase it and try again.

As you can see, three locations on the stack fall within the range of our module. To see where in our module these locations correspond to, we use the `ln` command:

```
0:000> ln 01001a7a
(01001a20)   05async!DisplayError+0x5a   |   (01001a83)   05async!wmainCRTStartup
0:000> ln 0100156a
(010014a0)   05async!wmain+0xca   |   (010015d0)   05async!RegEnum
0:000> ln 01001a83
(01001a83)   05async!wmainCRTStartup   |   (01001c0a)   05async!operator new
Exact matches:
    05async!wmainCRTStartup (void)
```

From the output, we can now hypothesize the following call chain:

```
wmainCRTStartup → wmain → DisplayError
```

To reassure ourselves, we look at the source code and see that this is definitely a viable path. The `wmain` function ended up calling `DisplayError` due to an error occurring while calling `RegEnum`. It is also fairly safe to assume that the error occurred because of a timeout (as we've verified in sample runs). `DisplayError` in turn calls the `Sleep` API. Now that we have a good idea of what is being called and why, we can continue our investigation and prove our original hypothesis that the stack is, in fact, corrupted. The next logical step is to take a look at the stack before the `ret` instruction that caused our instruction pointer to execute invalid code. If we dump out the contents of the stack, this time with a negative offset, we can get a historical perspective on the execution right before we returned to the invalid memory. Listing 5.14 shows the dump of the stack.

**Listing 5.14**   Walking the stack back in time

```
0:000> dd esp-8
0007fcf8   000380d0 00000002 7c9118f1 0007fd10
0007fd08   01001a7a 00001770 0007ff44 0100156a
0007fd18   0007fd2c 00000004 000007d0 00000001
0007fd28   000007d0 00650054 00740073 00000000
```

```
0007fd38   00000000 00000000 00000000 00000000
0007fd48   00000000 00000005 a8242a60 a8242a74
0007fd58   89e3cc00 80543dfd 00000000 c0000034
0007fd68   8813c708 00f80084 e44c3570 87c81800
```

Taking a bottom-up approach, the first item of interest is the return address of the call to `Sleep` (000380d0). Next, as always, the `ebp` register is pushed onto the stack (00000002) so that it can be restored prior to returning. What should follow after these two items are any items pushed onto the stack by the `Sleep` API (local variables or parameters). To get a better understanding of what the `Sleep` API actually does, we unassemble the function:

```
0:000> u kernel32!Sleep
kernel32!Sleep:
7c802442 8bff            mov     edi,edi
7c802444 55              push    ebp
7c802445 8bec            mov     ebp,esp
7c802447 6a00            push    0
7c802449 ff7508          push    dword ptr [ebp+8]
7c80244c e84bffffff      call    kernel32!SleepEx (7c80239c)
7c802451 5d              pop     ebp
7c802452 c20400          ret     4
```

It seems that the `Sleep` API pushes two more values onto the stack: a 0 and the time-out value passed into the Sleep API via the stack (ebp+0x8). Can you spot the discrepancy? The first three items seem to be incorrect. We know for a fact that the first item should be the return address, the second item the timeout parameter (ebp+0x8), and the third item 0.

Instead, what we have is a return address of 000380d0, which does not fall into our module's code range. Next we have a value of 2 for the timeout parameter, which should in actuality be 0x1770, and finally the last item should be 0 (explicitly pushed by the `Sleep` API), but rather is 7c9118f1. We have now, without a doubt, proven that a stack corruption is occurring, and all the work that went into proving it will bear even more fruit as we have almost all the needed information to find the culprit.

The next obvious step is to find out who is corrupting our stack. Because we already know the stack location being corrupted, all we need to do prior to calling the Sleep API is to somehow monitor all access to that stack location. If we could break into the debugger any time that address was written to, we could potentially get a stack trace that would uncover the corruptor. Fortunately, the debugger steps up again, this time with a command that allows us to set a breakpoint on any given address. The breakpoint can be set to trigger any time a read or write occurs at that memory location or only when a write occurs. Restart the application under the debugger and set a breakpoint in `DisplayError` right before executing the call to `Sleep`. Feed the same input parameters to the application, and after it breaks into the debugger, use the following command to set the memory access breakpoint:

```
0:000> ba w4 0007fcf8
```

The command used is `ba`. The `w` stands for write followed by a `4`, which indicates the size in bytes of the memory location. The last parameter specified is the address of the memory location to break on. Remember that the memory location specified is the location of the return address when `SleepEx` returns.

When you continue execution of the application, we almost immediately hit a breakpoint:

```
0:000> g
Breakpoint 1 hit
eax=00000043 ebx=7ffde000 ecx=77c422b0 edx=77c61b78 esi=00191ffc edi=00191fc0
eip=7c80239c esp=0007fcf8 ebp=0007fd04 iopl=0         nv up ei pl nz ac po nc
cs=001b  ss=0023  ds=0023  es=0023  fs=003b  gs=0000             efl=00000212
kernel32!SleepEx:
7c80239c 6a2c            push    2Ch
0:000> kb
ChildEBP RetAddr  Args to Child
0007fcf4 7c802451 00001770 00000000 0007fd10 kernel32!SleepEx
0007fd04 01001a7a 00001770 0007ff44 0100156a kernel32!Sleep+0xf
0007fd10 0100156a 0007fd2c 00000004 000007d0 05async!DisplayError+0x5a
0007ff44 01001bae 00000001 00034ca8 00036c80 05async!wmain+0xca
0007ffc0 7c816fd7 00191fc0 00191ffc 7ffde000 05async!wmainCRTStartup+0x12b
0007fff0 00000000 01001a83 00000000 78746341 kernel32!BaseProcessStart+0x23
```

This makes perfect sense because the call to `SleepEx` needs to store the return address on the stack. No foul play yet. Continue execution, and we get another breakpoint—this time much more interesting than the last:

```
0:000> g
Breakpoint 1 hit
eax=0007fcf8 ebx=00035598 ecx=000380d0 edx=00035598 esi=00090178 edi=00000001
eip=01001a01 esp=002bff70 ebp=002bff74 iopl=0         nv up ei pl zr na pe nc
cs=001b  ss=0023  ds=0023  es=0023  fs=003b  gs=0000             efl=00000246
05async!CRegValue::SetProperties+0x11:
01001a01 8b55fc          mov     edx,dword ptr [ebp-4] ss:0023:002bff70=0007fcf8
0:001> kb
ChildEBP RetAddr  Args to Child
```

```
002bff74 0100197d 000380d0 00000002 8882ab01 05async!CRegValue::SetProperties+0x11
002bffb4 7c80b683 00035598 00000001 00090178 05async!RegThreadProc+0xcd
002bffec 00000000 010018b0 00035598 00000000 kernel32!BaseThreadStart+0x37
```

This time, the call stack shows an entirely different thread writing to our return address location. A quick glance at the source code shows that every time a registry enumeration is performed via the RegEnum API, a new thread is created to handle the enumeration. As a matter of fact, looking closer at what that thread is attempting to store into our return address stack location, we see

```
0:001> p
eax=0007fcf8 ebx=00035598 ecx=000380d0 edx=0007fcf8 esi=00090178 edi=00000001
eip=01001a04 esp=002bff70 ebp=002bff74 iopl=0         nv up ei pl zr na pe nc
cs=001b  ss=0023  ds=0023  es=0023  fs=003b  gs=0000          efl=00000246
05async!CRegValue::SetProperties+0x14:
01001a04 8b450c          mov     eax,dword ptr [ebp+0Ch] ss:0023:002bff80=00000002
0:001> dd 0007fcf8
0007fcf8  000380d0 00001770 00000000 0007fd10
0007fd08  01001a7a 00001770 0007ff44 0100156a
0007fd18  0007fd2c 00000004 000007d0 00000001
0007fd28  000007d0 00650054 00740073 00000000
0007fd38  00000000 00000000 00000000 00000000
0007fd48  00000000 00000005 a8242a60 a8242a74
0007fd58  89e3cc00 80543dfd 00000000 c0000034
0007fd68  87df34e8 00f80084 e3d2de08 87dff700
```

The item placed on the stack matches perfectly with our prior analysis in Listing 5.14. We have now identified the culprit of the stack corruption. Are we done? Not quite yet—we still need to figure out why it is writing to that stack location. How did the thread even get a pointer to it? Did it randomly happen to choose a memory location to write to? The final piece of the puzzle is easy to put in place by employing some simple code reviewing. If we look at the RegThreadProc function (the starting function of the new thread), we see that its parameter is of type CRegEnumData. It is the responsibility of the function creating this new thread to pass an instance of that type to the thread function. In this case, the RegEnum function is responsible for making sure that everything is set up properly prior to creating the new thread. The most important member of CRegEnumData is a pointer to an array of type CRegValue. This member contains the result of the enumeration (all values enumerated). After RegEnum calls RegEnumAsync, the call returns immediately, returning a handle to the newly created thread. The RegEnum function now waits for an X number of milliseconds (as specified in the parameter passed in). When the wait returns, the operation has either finished and we can display the results, or a timeout occurred—in which case, we return to the `wmain` function, which subsequently calls `DisplayError` to indicate that an error occurred. The problematic part of this code is that the `RegEnum` function declares the array of type `CRegValue` on the stack and passes the address of that array to another thread. In the case of a timeout, the `RegEnum` call returns (invalidating the locally declared array) while the new thread executing the registry value enumeration still has a pointer to it. From here on out, any time the new thread writes a result to that stack pointer, it will be writing to a location no longer considered valid. As you have seen, the actual write does not result in an immediate crash because the stack location is still considered accessible memory. However, the write might cause undesirable results because it could be overwriting memory that is used by other parts of the code. In our case, the `DisplayError` function sets up a call to `Sleep`, which in turn sets up a call to `SleepEx`. All these calls are in need of stack space to declare local variables, passing parameters and storing return addresses. The combination of the new thread writing to that stack space and our application's further use of the stack caused the access violation because of a return address being overwritten.

## Calling Conventions Mismatch

In the introduction to this chapter, we gave a detailed walk-through of how a stack is managed throughout the lifetime of a thread. The example did a step-by-step analysis of the intricacies involved when calling functions, declaring local variables, passing parameters, returning from functions, and so on. One topic has been intentionally left out—calling conventions. A calling convention is nothing more than a contract between the caller of a function and the function itself. It specifies a set of rules that both parties must agree on for the call to be made properly. As can be seen in Table 5.1, a few different types of calling conventions are available to choose from. The main difference between these calling conventions lies in how parameters are passed to the calling function and how they are cleaned up from the stack. Listing 5.15 shows a small example that uses the two most common calling conventions: `__cdecl` and `__stdcall`.

**Listing 5.15** Examples of using the __cdecl and __stdcall calling conventions

```
#include <windows.h>
#include <stdio.h>
#include <conio.h>

void __cdecl CDeclFunction(DWORD dwParam1, DWORD dwParam2, DWORD dwParam3);
void __stdcall StdcallFunc(DWORD dwParam1, DWORD dwParam2, DWORD dwParam3);
```

```
int __cdecl wmain ()
{
    wprintf(L"Calling CDeclFunction\n");
    CDeclFunction(1,2,3);

    wprintf(L"Calling StdcallFunc\n");
    StdcallFunc(1,2,3);
    return 0;
}

void __cdecl CDeclFunction(DWORD dwParam1, DWORD dwParam2, DWORD dwParam3)
{
    wprintf(L"Inside CDeclFunction\n");
}

void StdcallFunc(DWORD dwParam1, DWORD dwParam2, DWORD dwParam3)
{
    wprintf(L"Inside StdcallFunc\n");
}
```

The source code and binary for Listing 5.15 can be found in the following folders:

> Source code: `C:\AWD\Chapter5\CallConv`
>
> Binary: `C:\AWDBIN\WinXP.x86.chk\05Callconv.exe`

The code in Listing 5.15 declares two auxiliary functions—each with different calling conventions. The `wmain` function simply makes calls to each of these functions. If we run this application under the debugger and unassemble the `wmain` function, we can immediately see how the two calling conventions differ from each other:

```
0:000> u wmain
05callconv!wmain:
01001200 8bff            mov     edi,edi
01001202 55              push    ebp
01001203 8bec            mov     ebp,esp
01001205 68a8100001      push    offset 05callconv!`string' (010010a8)
0100120a ff1500100001    call    dword ptr [05callconv!_imp__wprintf (01001000)]
01001210 83c404          add     esp,4
01001213 6a03            push    3
01001215 6a02            push    2
0:000> u
05callconv!wmain+0x17:
01001217 6a01            push    1
01001219 e832000000      call    05callconv!CDeclFunction (01001250)
```

```
0100121e 83c40c           add       esp,0Ch
01001221 687c100001       push      offset 05callconv!`string' (0100107c)
01001226 ff1500100001     call      dword ptr [05callconv!_imp__wprintf (01001000)]
0100122c 83c404           add       esp,4
0100122f 6a03             push      3
01001231 6a02             push      2
0:000> u
05callconv!wmain+0x33:
01001233 6a01             push      1
01001235 e836000000       call      05callconv!StdcallFunc (01001270)
0100123a 33c0             xor       eax,eax
0100123c 5d               pop       ebp
0100123d c3               ret
```

When wmain prepares to call the CDeclFunction, it begins by pushing the parameters 3, 2, and 1 onto the stack (remember—they are pushed from right to left) followed by making the actual call. After the call returns, another instruction is executed: add esp,0Ch. This instruction ensures that the stack pointer is set back to its original location (prior to the call). Adding 0Ch simply counteracts the three parameters that were pushed onto the stack prior to the call. It stands to reason that when calling a function declared with the __cdecl calling convention, the calling function is responsible for making sure that the stack integrity is upheld by adjusting the stack pointer. If we contrast that with the next function call made (StdcallFunc), we see that the parameters are pushed the same way (from right to left): 3, 2, and 1. The call instruction is then executed, but we see no subsequent cleanup of the stack pointer. How is the stack integrity upheld in this case? The answer is that StdcallFunc itself is responsible for adjusting the stack pointer. If we unassemble StdcallFunc, we see the following:

```
0:000> u StdcallFunc
05callconv!StdcallFunc:
01001270 8bff             mov       edi,edi
01001272 55               push      ebp
01001273 8bec             mov       ebp,esp
01001275 6804110001       push      offset 05callconv!`string' (01001104)
0100127a ff1500100001     call      dword ptr [05callconv!_imp__wprintf (01001000)]
01001280 83c404           add       esp,4
01001283 5d               pop       ebp
01001284 c20c00           ret       0Ch
```

The last instruction executed is the ret instruction, which transfers control to the calling function. Additionally, we can see that the ret instruction specified another parameter: 0Ch. Adding this parameter to the ret instruction tells it to adjust the stack pointer by the number of bytes specified. In this case, we want to adjust it by 0Ch bytes, which corresponds to the three parameters passed into the function.

The main difference between the __cdecl and __stdcall calling conventions is who has responsibility for cleaning up the parameters passed on the stack. Using __cdecl, the caller is responsible, and using __stdcall, the called function is responsible. Generally speaking, the __stdcall calling convention is the preferred way of calling functions because it reduces the size of the code generated. Instead of the cleanup code being scattered everywhere in the application where a function call is made, it's only made once—in the function being called. So why even bother with __cdecl? The __cdecl call convention is needed to support variable argument lists, a very useful feature of C/C++. In cases in which the function accepts a variable number of arguments, there is no guaranteed way for the called function to know how many parameters were passed in, which makes it impossible for it to properly clean up the stack. In these situations, __cdecl is required, and the caller is tasked with cleaning up the stack.

The Decoration column shown in Table 5.1 shows how the functions are decorated by the linker in an attempt to guarantee that the correct function is always called.

**Table 5.1** Calling conventions available

| Calling Convention | Arguments | Stack Cleanup | Decoration |
|---|---|---|---|
| Stdcall | Stack (right to left) | Called function | Function name prefixed by '_' and appended by '@' followed by the number of bytes of stack space required |
| Cdecl | Stack (right to left) | Calling function | Function name prefixed by '_' |
| Fastcall | First two arguments (<=32bits) passed in via ECX and EDX; rest on the stack (right to left) | Called function | Function name prefixed by '@' and appended by '@' followed by the number of bytes of stack space required |
| Thiscall | 'this' pointer passed via ecx register; rest on the stack (right to left) | Called function | C++ decorations |

Listing 5.16 shows a simple application that declares (but does not define) a set of functions with different calling conventions.

**Listing 5.16**   Simple application that declares a number of functions

```
extern void __cdecl Func1(int iOne);
extern void __cdecl Func2(int iOne, int iTwo);
extern void __stdcall Func3(int iOne);
extern void __stdcall Func4(int iOne, int iTwo);

void __cdecl main()
{
    Func1(1);
    Func2(1,2);
    Func3(1);
    Func4(1,2);
}
```

The source code for Listing 5.16 can be found in the following folder:

Source code: `C:\AWD\Chapter5\CallConv2`

If we were to try to build this application, the linker would generate errors (because of missing definitions for the functions):

```
C:\AWD\Chapter5\CallConv2>build /ZCc
BUILD: Adding /Y to COPYCMD so xcopy ops won't hang.
BUILD: Object root set to: ==> objchk_wxp_x86
BUILD: Compile and Link for i386
BUILD: Examining C:\AWD\Chapter5\CallConv2 directory for files to compile.
BUILD: Compiling (NoSync) C:\AWD\Chapter5\CallConv2 directory
Compiling - callconv2.c for i386
BUILD: Linking C:\AWD\Chapter5\CallConv2 directory
Linking Executable - objchk_wxp_x86\i386\05callconv2.exe for i386
errors in directory C:\AWD\Chapter5\CallConv2
callconv2.obj : error LNK2019: unresolved external symbol _Func4@8 referenced in
function _main
callconv2.obj : error LNK2019: unresolved external symbol _Func3@4 referenced in
function _main
callconv2.obj : error LNK2019: unresolved external symbol _Func2 referenced in func-
tion _main
callconv2.obj : error LNK2019: unresolved external symbol _Func1 referenced in func-
tion _main
msvcrt.lib(wcrtexe.obj) : error LNK2019: unresolved external symbol _wmain referenced
in function _wmainCRTStartup
```

```
objchk_wxp_x86\i386\05callconv2.exe : error LNK1120: 5 unresolved externals
BUILD: Done

    2 files compiled
    1 executable built - 6 Errors
```

The errors show the names that the linker uses when referring to the declared functions. Func1 and Func2 are both declared with __cdecl and are decorated by the linker by prefixing an underscore to the function name. Func3 and Func4 are both declared as __stdcall and, as such, are decorated by prefixing an underscore and appending @ followed by the number of total bytes of all the parameters that are part of the declaration. Func3 takes one int parameter (4 bytes), and Func4 takes two int parameters (8 bytes total). It is important to note that the decoration scheme used by the linker is never visible to the developer when writing the code. It is purely a linker facility. However, understanding the decoration scheme is important when trying to understand why the linker sometimes spews out errors related to unresolved external symbols.

Typically, the compiler and linker work in tandem to ensure that the correct function with the correct calling convention is called. However, at times the linker is unable to provide this mechanism for you, and careful attention must be paid in order to avoid calling convention mismatches.

Take a look at Listing 5.17, which shows the code of an application that explicitly loads a DLL (05mod.dll) and attempts to call the InitModule function defined in that DLL.

**Listing 5.17**   Application that calls a function in a DLL

```
#include <windows.h>
#include <stdio.h>
#include <conio.h>

typedef int (__cdecl *MYPROC)(DWORD dwOne, DWORD dwTwo);
VOID CallProc(MYPROC pProc);

int __cdecl wmain ()
{
    HMODULE hMod = LoadLibrary ("05mod.dll");
    if(hMod)
    {
        MYPROC pProc = (MYPROC) GetProcAddress(hMod, "InitModule");
        if(pProc)
        {
            CallProc(pProc);
```

**Listing 5.17** Application that calls a function in a DLL *(continued)*

```
        }
        else
        {
            wprintf(L"Failed to get proc address of InitModule");
        }
    }
    else
    {
        wprintf(L"Failed to load 05mod.dll.");
    }
    return 0;
}


VOID CallProc(MYPROC pProc)
{
    pProc(1,2);
}
```

The source code and binary for Listing 5.17 can be found in the following folders:

> Source code: `C:\AWD\Chapter5\CallConv3\Client` and
> `C:\AWD\Chapter5\CallConv3\Mod`
>
> Binary: `C:\AWDBIN\WinXP.x86.chk\05CallConv3.exe` and `C:\AWD-BIN\WinXP.x86.chk\05mod.dll`

As you can see, the code is pretty straightforward. First, it loads the DLL using the `LoadLibrary` API. If successful, it attempts to get the address of the `InitModule` function defined in the DLL and then calls a local helper function (`CallProc`) that simply calls the `InitModule` function. Without looking at the implementation of `InitModule`, all we are going to say is that it simply prints out the following string when called:

```
In InitModule
```

Nothing too complicated going on with this code, is there? If you run this simple application, you might be surprised at the results:

```
C:\AWDBIN\WinXP.x86.chk\05CallConv3.exe
In InitModule
In InitModule
```

The string is printed out twice. Not only that, but we also seem to be crashing, as the dreaded Dr. Watson UI is displayed. Let's run the application under the debugger and see where in the application the crash occurs:

```
0:000> g
ModLoad: 5cb70000 5cb96000   C:\WINDOWS\system32\ShimEng.dll
ModLoad: 00400000 00403000   C:\AWDBIN\WinXP.x86.chk\05mod.dll
In InitModule
In InitModule
(8bc.1bc): Unknown exception - code c0000096 (first chance)
(8bc.1bc): Unknown exception - code c0000096 (!!! second chance !!!)
eax=00000001 ebx=7ffd6800 ecx=77c422b0 edx=77c61b78 esi=7c9118f1 edi=00011970
eip=0007ffc5 esp=0007ff50 ebp=004010b0 iopl=0         nv up ei pl nz na po cy
cs=001b  ss=0023  ds=0023  es=0023  fs=003b  gs=0000             efl=00000203
0007ffc5 6f             outs    dx,dword ptr [esi]   ds:0023:7c9118f1=3359066a
0:000> kb
ChildEBP RetAddr  Args to Child
WARNING: Frame IP not in any known module. Following frames may be wrong.
0007ff7c 7c9118f1 7ffdf000 e1389408 00000000 0x7ffc5
00011970 00730069 00610075 0020006c 00740053 ntdll!RtlDeleteCriticalSection+0x72
00011970 00000000 00610075 0020006c 00740053 0x730069
```

Interestingly, the stack shown for the access violation seems to show incorrect frames. This looks strikingly similar to our previous debug session (asynchronous operations and stack pointers). As always, when we are faced with a potential stack corruption, we begin by looking at the state to see if we can extrapolate any useful information. We begin by convincing ourselves that the address in the top frame does not fall into any of the address ranges of our loaded modules:

```
0:000> lm
start    end        module name
00400000 00403000   05mod       (deferred)
01000000 01003000   05CallConv3 (deferred)
77c10000 77c68000   msvcrt      (deferred)
7c800000 7c8f4000   kernel32    (deferred)
7c900000 7c9b0000   ntdll       (pdb symbols)
```

The address 0x7ffc5 does not fall within any of the ranges displayed by the lm command. Next, knowing that the debugger is giving us incorrect stack results, we try to reconstruct a historic picture of the calling sequence by analyzing the stack ourselves. Listing 5.18 shows the process by which we dump out the stack contents and try to resolve any address that falls within our module.

**Listing 5.18**  Attempt at manually constructing the stack

```
0:000> dd esp esp+100
0007ff50    00034cb0 00036c88 01001050 01001054
0007ff60    0007ff94 0007ff98 0007ffa0 00000000
0007ff70    0007ff9c 01001058 0100105c 00011970
0007ff80    7c9118f1 7ffdf000 e1389408 00000000
0007ff90    c0000096 00000001 00034cb0 00000000
0007ffa0    00036c88 00000000 0007ff7c 0007fb7c
0007ffb0    0007ffe0 01001486 01001118 00000000
0007ffc0    0007fff0 7c816fd7 00011970 7c9118f1
0007ffd0    7ffdf000 c0000096 0007ffc8 0007fb7c
0007ffe0    ffffffff 7c839aa8 7c816fe0 00000000
0007fff0    00000000 00000000 01001278 00000000
00080000    78746341 00000020 00000001 00002498
00080010    000000c4 00000000 00000020 00000000
00080020    00000014 00000001 00000006 00000034
00080030    00000114 00000001 00000000 00000000
00080040    00000000 00000000 00000000 00000002
00080050    00000000
0:000> ln 01001050
(01001050)   05callconv3!__xc_a   |   (01001054)   05callconv3!__xc_z
Exact matches:
    05callconv3!__xc_a = <function> *[1]
    05callconv3!__xc_a = <function> *[]
0:000> ln 01001054
(01001054)   05callconv3!__xc_z   |   (01001058)   05callconv3!__xi_a
Exact matches:
    05callconv3!__xc_z = <function> *[1]
    05callconv3!__xc_z = <function> *[]
0:000> ln 01001058
(01001058)   05callconv3!__xi_a   |   (0100105c)   05callconv3!__xi_z
Exact matches:
    05callconv3!__xi_a = <function> *[1]
    05callconv3!__xi_a = <function> *[]
0:000> ln 0100105c
(0100105c)   05callconv3!__xi_z   |   (0100107c)   05callconv3!`string'
Exact matches:
    05callconv3!__xi_z = <function> *[1]
    05callconv3!__xi_z = <function> *[]
0:000> ln 01001486
(01001486)   05callconv3!except_handler3   |   (01001492)   05callconv3!controlfp
Exact matches:
0:000> ln 01001118
(01001110)   05callconv3!`string'+0x8   |   (01001128)   05callconv3!_load_config_used
0:000> ln 01001278
(01001278)   05callconv3!wmainCRTStartup   |   (010013fe)   05callconv3!XcptFilter
Exact matches:
    05callconv3!wmainCRTStartup (void)
```

As you can see from Listing 5.18, the addresses that fall within our module's range do not resolve to anything that seems correct (with the exception of `01001278`). We can't even see calls to the `InitModule` function that we know we've called. It is often useful to go back to the basics and restate what we are currently seeing: We are seeing a crash because of a badly corrupted stack with no capability to construct a historical perspective on what call sequences were made. If we stop to think about it, there is still some more room for investigation. What is the reason for the crash? Yes—we have a badly corrupted stack; but what was the instruction that caused us to crash, and can we get anything useful from that? Let's unassemble the `eip` register and see what we can find:

```
0:000> u eip
0007ffc5 6f              outs    dx,dword ptr [esi]
0007ffc6 817c70190100f118 cmp    dword ptr [eax+esi*2+19h],18F10001h
0007ffce 91              xchg    eax,ecx
0007ffcf 7c00            jl      0007ffd1
0007ffd1 50              push    eax
0007ffd2 fd              std
0007ffd3 7f96            jg      0007ff6b
0007ffd5 0000            add     byte ptr [eax],al
```

Two observations can be made from the unassembled code. First, the sequence of instructions certainly does not look like they make much sense. From that observation, we can draw up a new theory: We are executing code in a seemingly random piece of memory. To convince ourselves that the theory is plausible, we look to the second observation from the unassembled code, namely the value of the instruction pointer itself (`0007ffc5`). If we dump out the registers at the point of the crash, we see the following:

```
0:000> r
eax=00000001 ebx=7ffdc800 ecx=77c422b0 edx=77c61b78 esi=7c9118f1 edi=00011970
eip=0007ffc5 esp=0007ff50 ebp=004010b0 iopl=0         ov up ei ng nz na po nc
cs=001b  ss=0023  ds=0023  es=0023  fs=003b  gs=0000              efl=00000a82
0007ffc5 6f              outs    dx,dword ptr [esi]    ds:0023:7c9118f1=3359066a
```

The stack pointer and the instruction pointer seem to be awfully close to each other. This observation seems to imply that the instruction pointer somehow ended up with a stack location. Unless our intentions were to execute code located on the stack (which, suffice to say, is almost never the case), we have gotten one step closer. The next big question is this: How did we end up with the instruction pointer pointing to a stack location? Remember that when a function returns, we pop the stack and set the instruction pointer to the value popped off. This is normally the return address, but in our case (because of a corrupted stack), it's some other value. Either the return address was overwritten, or somehow we very incorrectly popped off a value from a different stack location. Because any number of items can be pushed onto the stack (parameters, local variables, return addresses, frame pointers, and so on), it will be nearly impossible to say which piece of this stack content was mistaken for the return address. At this point, our best approach is to rerun the application under the debugger and pay close attention to any function calls that are made (starting from the wmain function). When any called function returns, we check to see what the next value is on the stack and see if we can correlate it to the bad instruction pointer we currently have (0007ffc5). Listing 5.17 shows that the application makes the following function calls:

- LoadLibrary
- GetProcAddress
- CallProc

In order to avoid wasting valuable debugging time, we focus in on the CallProc function call, since we know by now that this function actually makes the call to the InitModule function located in 05mod.dll. We set a breakpoint at the CallProc function and step our way to the InitModule call (eip should be pointing to 01001269). Next, we trace into the function call and continue stepping until we reach the ret instruction. This is the point where we need to start looking closer. When the ret instruction executes, we know that the return address will be popped off the stack and the instruction pointer will be set to that value. Dumping out the contents of the stack and unassembling the supposed return address, we see the following:

```
0:000> dd esp
0007ff24  0100126c 00000001 00000002 0007ff44
0007ff34  0100122d 004010b0 004010b0 00400000
0007ff44  0007ffc0 010013a3 00000001 00034cb0
0007ff54  00036c88 01001050 01001054 0007ff94
0007ff64  0007ff98 0007ffa0 00000000 0007ff9c
0007ff74  01001058 0100105c 00191fc0 00191ffc
0007ff84  7ffd6000 e466e840 00000000 00000000
0007ff94  00000001 00034cb0 00000000 00036c88
0:000> u 0100126c
05callconv3!CallProc+0xc:
0100126c 83c408          add     esp,8
0100126f 5d              pop     ebp
01001270 c20400          ret     4
01001273 cc              int     3
```

```
01001274 cc                int    3
01001275 cc                int    3
01001276 cc                int    3
01001277 cc                int    3
```

The information we just got makes perfect sense. The return address on the stack does, in fact, point to the instruction right after the call to `CallProc`. Continuing the stepping of the code, the next `ret` instruction we encounter is that of the `CallProc` function returning to `wmain`:

```
0:000> p
eax=00000001 ebx=7ffd6000 ecx=77c422b0 edx=77c61b78 esi=00191ffc edi=00191fc0
eip=0100126c esp=0007ff30 ebp=0007ff30 iopl=0         nv up ei pl nz ac po nc
cs=001b  ss=0023  ds=0023  es=0023  fs=003b  gs=0000             efl=00000212
05callconv3!CallProc+0xc:
0100126c 83c408             add     esp,8
0:000> p
eax=00000001 ebx=7ffd6000 ecx=77c422b0 edx=77c61b78 esi=00191ffc edi=00191fc0
eip=0100126f esp=0007ff38 ebp=0007ff30 iopl=0         nv up ei pl nz na po nc
cs=001b  ss=0023  ds=0023  es=0023  fs=003b  gs=0000             efl=00000202
05callconv3!CallProc+0xf:
0100126f 5d                 pop     ebp
0:000> p
eax=00000001 ebx=7ffd6000 ecx=77c422b0 edx=77c61b78 esi=00191ffc edi=00191fc0
eip=01001270 esp=0007ff3c ebp=004010b0 iopl=0         nv up ei pl nz na po nc
cs=001b  ss=0023  ds=0023  es=0023  fs=003b  gs=0000             efl=00000202
05callconv3!CallProc+0x10:
01001270 c20400             ret     4
```

We use the same technique to verify that the return address we are about to pop from the stack is the correct one:

```
0:000> dd esp
0007ff3c  004010b0 00400000 0007ffc0 010013a3
0007ff4c  00000001 00034cb0 00036c88 01001050
0007ff5c  01001054 0007ff94 0007ff98 0007ffa0
0007ff6c  00000000 0007ff9c 01001058 0100105c
0007ff7c  00191fc0 00191ffc 7ffd6000 e466e840
0007ff8c  00000000 00000000 00000001 00034cb0
0007ff9c  00000000 00036c88 00000000 0007ff7c
0007ffac  89e6904c 0007ffe0 01001486 01001118
0:000> u 004010b0
05mod!InitModule:
004010b0 8bff               mov     edi,edi
004010b2 55                 push    ebp
```

5. MEMORY CORRUPTION PART I—STACKS

```
004010b3 8bec          mov     ebp,esp
004010b5 682c104000    push    offset 05mod!`string' (0040102c)
004010ba ff1500104000  call    dword ptr [05mod!_imp__wprintf (00401000)]
004010c0 83c404        add     esp,4
004010c3 b801000000    mov     eax,1
004010c8 5d            pop     ebp
```

This time, it seems blatantly wrong. We are supposed to return to wmain, but instead the return address is to the start of the InitModule function. This certainly explains why we are seeing InitModule printed twice and perhaps why we are even seeing the crash. We now proceed by stepping into the InitModule function until we once again reach the ret instruction. At that point, we dump out the contents of the stack to see where it decides to return to this time:

```
0:000> dd esp
0007ff44  0007ffc0 010013a3 00000001 00034cb0
0007ff54  00036c88 01001050 01001054 0007ff94
0007ff64  0007ff98 0007ffa0 00000000 0007ff9c
0007ff74  01001058 0100105c 00191fc0 00191ffc
0007ff84  7ffd6000 e466e840 00000000 00000000
0007ff94  00000001 00034cb0 00000000 00036c88
0007ffa4  00000000 0007ff7c 89e6904c 0007ffe0
0007ffb4  01001486 01001118 00000000 0007fff0
0:000> u 0007ffc0
0007ffc0 f0ff07          lock inc dword ptr [edi]
0007ffc3 00d7            add      bh,dl
0007ffc5 6f              outs     dx,dword ptr [esi]
0007ffc6 817cc01f1900fc1f cmp     dword ptr [eax+eax*8+1Fh],1FFC0019h
0007ffce 1900            sbb      dword ptr [eax],eax
0007ffd0 0060fd          add      byte ptr [eax-3],ah
0007ffd3 7ffd            jg       0007ffd2
0007ffd5 3d5480c8ff      cmp      eax,0FFC88054h
```

The instruction we will be returning to this time is 0007ffc0, which matches up exactly with what we were looking for; and if we step over the ret instruction, we will be at the point where a crash is about to occur.

While we were tracing through this program, the first problem surfaced when the CallProc function was about to return. Instead of returning to the originating wmain function, it returned to the start of the InitModule function. Let's take a look at the unassembled CallProc function and try to figure out how the stack should look throughout the execution of the function:

```
0:000> u CallProc
05callconv3!CallProc:
```

```
01001260 8bff          mov     edi,edi
01001262 55            push    ebp
01001263 8bec          mov     ebp,esp
01001265 6a02          push    2
01001267 6a01          push    1
01001269 ff5508        call    dword ptr [ebp+8]
0100126c 83c408        add     esp,8
0100126f 5d            pop     ebp
0:000> u
05callconv3!CallProc+0x10:
01001270 c20400        ret     4
```

Figure 5.10 shows how we expect the stack to look when the instruction pointer is about to execute the call instruction to `InitModule`.

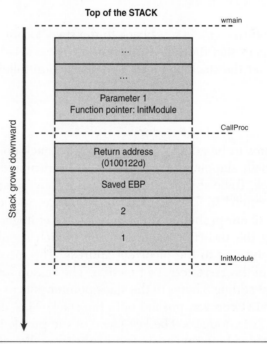

**Figure 5.10**   Expected stack prior to calling InitModule

Now, the `InitModule` function takes two parameters (both of type DWORD), and when the function returns, we would expect the stack pointer to be set to the stack location prior to the parameter list:

```
0:000> p
In InitModule
eax=00000001 ebx=7ffd5000 ecx=77c422b0 edx=77c61b78 esi=00191ffc edi=00191fc0
eip=0100126c esp=0007ff30 ebp=0007ff30 iopl=0         nv up ei pl nz ac po nc
cs=001b  ss=0023  ds=0023  es=0023  fs=003b  gs=0000            efl=00000212
05callconv3!CallProc+0xc:
0100126c 83c408          add     esp,8
0:000> dd esp
0007ff30  0007ff44 0100122d 004010b0 004010b0
0007ff40  00400000 0007ffc0 010013a3 00000001
0007ff50  00034cb0 00036c88 01001050 01001054
0007ff60  0007ff94 0007ff98 0007ffa0 00000000
0007ff70  0007ff9c 01001058 0100105c 00191fc0
0007ff80  00191ffc 7ffd5000 e46afdd8 00000000
0007ff90  00000000 00000001 00034cb0 00000000
0007ffa0  00036c88 00000000 0007ff7c 89e6a074
```

After the function returns, esp is reset back to the stack location prior to the parameter area, which implies that the called function (InitModule) properly cleaned up the stack (that is, reset the stack pointer). The instruction following the call instruction is

```
add     esp,8
```

This instruction seems to be adding 8 bytes from the stack pointer, resulting in the stack pointer essentially skipping the saved ebp and return address values that were pushed onto the stack. To be able to return to the previous frame, we need the return address, right? Absolutely! In fact, the addition of 8 bytes to the stack pointer seems to be the root cause of our problem. After we reach the epilogue code for CallProc, we end up popping the incorrect value for ebp (which should be the saved ebp value), as well as returning to the incorrect address. The incorrect address, in this case, is the address of the InitModule function. The reason for picking up that particular address is that adding 8 bytes to the stack pointer puts us at the location where the parameter to CallProc was pushed onto the stack. This also happens to be the function pointer to InitModule. The last piece of the puzzle is trying to figure out why the stack pointer is being mismanaged in this way. We already know that the CallProc function tries to clean up the stack. (That is, it skips the parameters passed into the InitModule function.) Cleaning up the stack after function calls is essential to maintaining stack integrity. However, we also saw that after the call returned from InitModule, but before the addition of 8 bytes to the stack pointer, the stack pointer already seemed correct. (That is, the stack was already cleaned up.) This seems to imply that the InitModule function already cleaned up the stack at the point of return. (If you unassemble the `InitModule` function, you can see that it does so.) It should come as no surprise that the root cause of the problem is a mismatch in calling conventions. Since `InitModule` is cleaning up the stack prior to returning, it was declared with the `__stdcall` calling convention:

```
int __stdcall InitModule(DWORD dwOne, DWORD dwTwo)
```

whereas the client code declared a function pointer to the `InitModule` with the following signature:

```
typedef int (__cdecl *MYPROC)(DWORD dwOne, DWORD dwTwo);
```

The mismatch in calling conventions caused our stack to become badly corrupted.

### NX-Enabled Systems

In the previous debug session, we showed how a calling convention mismatch could cause the application to execute code on the stack. The net result was that of a strange call chain and, ultimately, a crash. The problem can be generalized to executing code in any area that is reserved for data only. Malicious software writers often use this capability by injecting code into memory reserved for data and simply jumping to the code and executing. Processor and software manufacturers recognized the need to protect against this problem, and the net result was that of the NX (No eXecute)-enabled processor. The basic idea is to mark areas with the NX bit, which indicates that only data can be stored in that memory. If code is ever executed from this location, an immediate fault will occur. Windows enabled support for NX-enabled systems starting with Windows XP SP2 and Windows Server 2003 SP1. On systems running with NX-enabled hardware and a Windows version that supports NX, the result of executing code from data-only memory is an access violation.

## Avoidance Strategies

As you have seen, the effects of stack corruptions (much like other types of memory corruptions) do not necessarily surface right at the point of the corruption. Instead, a stack corruption might go unnoticed for quite some time before an actual crash occurs. As we mentioned earlier in the chapter, the easiest way to track down a corruption is when we can trap the corruption at the point it occurs. Several options are available to trap stack corruptions early in the development process. The best line of defense lies in the compiler itself, as it has the capability to inject stack integrity checks into your code. To enable these runtime checks, your application must be built with the correct set of options.

The first compiler option we discuss is the /GS switch. While stack buffer over-run attacks have been around for quite some time now, they have gained in popularity in recent years. A large number of viruses make use of this attack angle to wreak havoc on computers. For this reason, the Microsoft compiler team introduced a mechanism that protects the stack and serves as a safety net against buffer overrun attacks.

As you saw earlier, the basic problem of stack buffer overruns is the fact that an attacker is able to overwrite the return address of a frame and resume execution at a location of his own choosing. If we were somehow able to protect the return address from being overwritten, the vulnerability could never be exploited. The introduction of the /GS flag takes a stab at this protection by pushing a cookie onto the stack before the return address, and when the function returns, checks to see if the cookie is intact. If it is, the return address has not been tampered with and execution continues. If it is not the same, this means that there is a possibility that the return address has been tampered with and the application terminates. In order to get this added protection, the following changes must be made in the build environment:

- Sources
  The sources file must specify the /GS compiler flag by using the following:
  USER_C_FLAGS=/GS
- Build window

The BUFFER_OVERFLOW_CHECKS environment variable must be 1. If we look at the application used in the buffer overrun scenario (05overrun.exe), we can see that the function prologue for HelperFunction has some added steps in it:

```
0:000> u 05overrun!helperfunction
05overrun!HelperFunction:
01001230 8bff          mov     edi,edi
01001232 55            push    ebp
01001233 8bec          mov     ebp,esp
01001235 83ec40        sub     esp,40h
01001238 a118200001    mov     eax,dword ptr [05overrun!__security_cookie
(01002018)]
0100123d 8945fc        mov     dword ptr [ebp-4],eax
01001240 8b4508        mov     eax,dword ptr [ebp+8]
01001243 50            push    eax
```

The two highlighted mov instructions show how the function takes the unique cookie and moves it onto the stack at the location before the return address. Prior to returning, in the function prologue, the stack location containing the cookie (ebp-0x4) is checked against the original cookie:

```
0:000> u helperfunction+19
05overrun!HelperFunction+0x19:
01001249 1560100001      adc      eax,offset 05overrun!_imp__wcscpy (01001060)
0100124e 83c408          add      esp,8
01001251 8b4dfc          mov      ecx,dword ptr [ebp-4]
01001254 e87e000000      call     05overrun!__security_check_cookie (010012d7)
01001259 8be5            mov      esp,ebp
0100125b 5d              pop      ebp
0100125c c20400          ret      4
```

The __security_check_cookie call checks to see if the cookie is intact; if it's not, the call terminates the process. By default, if the cookie has been overwritten, the handler displays a dialog stating that a buffer overrun has occurred. If you do not want a dialog displayed when the check for the cookie fails, it is possible to provide your own handler.

The cookie is generated by the CRT (C runtime) during startup and is different each time the program is run to make sure that its value is not known to attackers. A few caveats exist that you need to be aware of. If applications do not use the CRT, an explicit call must be made to __security_init_cookie during startup to ensure that the cookie has been properly initialized. Also, applications that make explicit calls to initialize the CRT might inadvertently reinitialize that cookie, which will cause the security check to fail since the cookie has changed. It is also important to note that this compiler option is meant to be used with released code.

It is critical to note that the /GS safety net should be viewed as just that: a safety net. Under no circumstances should you rely on this mechanism to fully protect you against buffer overrun attacks.

The next compiler switch of importance is the /RTC switch. RTC stands for RunTimeChecks. RTC provides a number of suboptions.

- /RTCs: Stackframe runtime error checking
  This option helps protect against a number of different stack corruptions:
  - Each time a function is called, it initializes all local variables to nonzero values to prevent them from retaining old values from prior function calls.

- It verifies the stack pointer (`esp` register) to ensure that stack corruptions caused by calling convention mismatches do not occur.
- Protects against buffer overruns and underruns of local variables.

- `/RTCc`: Data loss protection
  Another common mistake made by developers is to make casts between data types that result in a loss of data. For example, casting a `ULONG` value to a `BYTE` value results in data being potentially lost. This compiler option displays an error dialog anytime a cast results in a data loss.
- `/RTCu`: Uninitialized variable protection
  This compiler option displays an error whenever a variable is accessed that has yet to be initialized. Uninitializing variables is a common mistake made while developing and can cause your variables to take on values left over from prior calls. These values can cause a lot of grief during execution.

It is important to note that the `/RTC` compiler options are designed to work with debug builds and, as such, have no impact on released builds. The `/RTC` switch is meant solely to test your code during development.

While the compiler options provide an excellent mechanism for finding stack corruption-related errors during development, they do not provide the same level of detection as other tools. Other viable (albeit not free) options include Rational's Purify or NuMega's BoundsChecker.

## Summary

As you have seen throughout this chapter, an application suffering from stack corruption can cause serious instability issues. These issues typically surface in the form of random crashes that ultimately end up leaving users frustrated and fed up. In the worst-case scenario, stack corruptions can even lead to severe security holes that can compromise the user's computer and leave him vulnerable to a number of different attacks. It is crucial for any serious developer to be aware of the causes of stack corruption and ways to analyze it. Ultimately, the developer should employ avoidance techniques to ensure the integrity of the stack and future success of his software. This chapter walked you through a detailed explanation of the anatomy of the stack. It also walked you through some of the most common forms of stack corruptions, explained how to detect the corruption, and covered how to analyze it and figure out the root cause. Finally, you learned how powerful compiler techniques can help you trap stack corruptions during development and even aid in preventing some forms of stack corruption in released software.

# CHAPTER 6

# MEMORY CORRUPTION PART II— HEAPS

In Chapter 5, "Memory Corruption Part I—Stacks," we discussed how stack-based buffer overflows can cause serious security problems for software and how stack-based buffer overflows have been the primary attack angle for malicious software authors. In recent years, however, another form of buffer overflow attack has gained in popularity. Rather than relying on the stack to exploit buffer overflows, the Windows heap manager is now being targeted. Even though heap-based security attacks are much harder to exploit than their stack-based counterparts, their popularity keeps growing at a rapid pace. In addition to potential security vulnerabilities, this chapter discusses a myriad of stability issues that can surface in an application when the heap is used in a nonconventional fashion.

Although the stack and the heap are managed very differently in Windows, the process by which we analyze stack- and heap-related problems is the same. As such, throughout this chapter, we employ the same troubleshooting process that we defined in Chapter 5 (refer to Figure 5.1).

## What Is a Heap?

A heap is a form of memory manager that an application can use when it needs to allocate and free memory dynamically. Common situations that call for the use of a heap are when the size of the memory needed is not known ahead of time and the size of the memory is too large to neatly fit on the stack (automatic memory). Even though the heap is the most common facility to accommodate dynamic memory allocations, there are a number of other ways for applications to request memory from Windows. Memory can be requested from the C runtime, the virtual memory manager, and even from other forms of private memory managers. Although the different memory managers can be treated as individual entities, internally, they are tightly connected. Figure 6.1 shows a simplified view of Windows-supported memory managers and their dependencies.

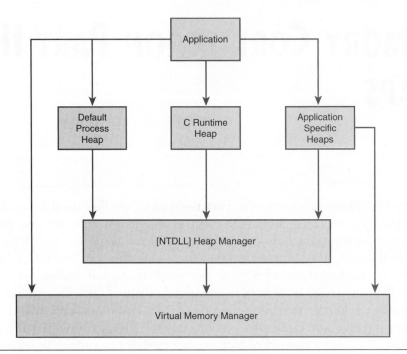

**Figure 6.1**    An overview of Windows memory management architecture

As illustrated in Figure 6.1, most of the high-level memory managers make use of the Windows heap manager, which in turn uses the virtual memory manager. Although high-level memory managers (and applications for that matter) are not restricted to using the heap manager, they most typically do, as it provides a solid foundation for other private memory managers to build on. Because of its popularity, the primary focal point in this chapter is the Windows heap manager.

When a process starts, the heap manager automatically creates a new heap called the default process heap. Although some processes use the default process heap, a large number rely on the CRT heap (using new/delete and malloc/free family of APIs) for all their memory needs. Some processes, however, create additional heaps (via the HeapCreate API) to isolate different components running in the process. It is not uncommon for even the simplest of applications to have four or more active heaps at any given time.

The Windows heap manager can be further broken down as shown in Figure 6.2.

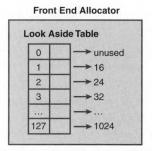

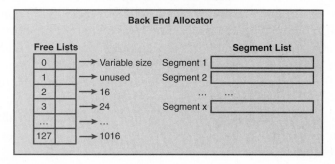

**Figure 6.2** Windows heap manager

## Front End Allocator

The front end allocator is an abstract optimization layer for the back end allocator. By allowing different types of front end allocators, applications with different memory needs can choose the appropriate allocator. For example, applications that expect small bursts of allocations might prefer to use the low fragmentation front end allocator to avoid fragmentation. Two different front end allocators are available in Windows:

- Look aside list (LAL) front end allocator
- Low fragmentation (LF) front end allocator

With the exception of Windows Vista, all Windows versions use a LAL front end allocator by default. In Windows Vista, a design decision was made to switch over to the LF front end allocator by default. The look aside list is nothing more than a table of

128 singly linked lists. Each singly linked list in the table contains free heap blocks of a specific size starting at 16 bytes. The size of each heap block includes 8 bytes of heap block metadata used to manage the block. For example, if an allocation request of 24 bytes arrived at the front end allocator, the front end allocator would look for free blocks of size 32 bytes (24 user-requested bytes + 8 bytes of metadata). Because all heap blocks require 8 bytes of metadata, the smallest sized block that can be returned to the caller is 16 bytes; hence, the front end allocator does not use table index 1, which corresponds to free blocks of size 8 bytes.

Subsequently, each index represents free heap blocks, where the size of the heap block is the size of the previous index plus 8. The last index (127) contains free heap blocks of size 1024 bytes. When an application frees a block of memory, the heap manager marks the allocation as free and puts the allocation on the front end allocator's look aside list (in the appropriate index). The next time a block of memory of that size is requested, the front end allocator checks to see if a block of memory of the requested size is available and if so, returns the heap block to the user. It goes without saying that satisfying allocations via the look aside list is by far the fastest way to allocate memory.

Let's take a look at a hypothetical example. Imagine that the state of the LAL is as depicted in Figure 6.3.

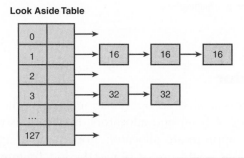

**Figure 6.3**  Hypothetical state of the look aside list

The LAL in Figure 6.3 indicates that there are 3 heap blocks of size 16 (out of which 8 bytes is available to the caller) available at index 1 and two blocks of size 32 (out of which 24 bytes are available to the caller) at index 3. When we try to allocate a block of size 24, the heap manager knows to look at index 3 by adding 8 to the requested block size (accounting for the size of the metadata) and dividing by 8 and subtracting 1 (zero-based table). The linked list positioned at index 3 contains two available heap blocks. The heap manager simply removes the first one in the list and returns the allocation to the caller.

If we try allocating a block of size 16, the heap manager would notice that the index corresponding to size 16 (16+8/8–1=2) is an empty list, and hence the allocating cannot be satisfied from the LAL. The allocation request now continues its travels and is forwarded to the back end allocator for further processing.

## Back End Allocator

If the front end allocator is unable to satisfy an allocation request, the request makes its way to the back end allocator. Similar to the front end allocator, it contains a table of lists commonly referred to as the free lists. The free list's sole responsibility is to keep track of all the free heap blocks available in a particular heap. There are 128 free lists, where each list contains free heap blocks of a specific size. As you can see from Figure 6.2, the size associated with free list[2] is 16, free list[3] is 24, and so on. Free list[1] is unused because the minimum heap block size is 16 (8 bytes of metadata and 8 user-accessible bytes). Each size associated with a free list increases by 8 bytes from the prior free list. Allocations whose size is greater than the maximum free list's allocation size go into index 0 of the free lists. Free list[0] essentially contains allocations of sizes greater than 1016 bytes and less than the virtual allocation limit (discussed later). The free heap blocks in free list[0] are also sorted by size (in ascending order) to achieve maximum efficiency. Figure 6.4 shows a hypothetical example of a free list.

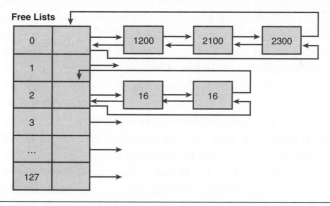

**Figure 6.4**  Hypothetical state of the free lists

If an allocation request of size 8 arrives at the back end allocator, the heap manager first consults the free lists. In order to maximize efficiency when looking for free heap blocks, the heap manager keeps a free list bitmap. The bitmap consists of 128 bits, where each bit represents an index into the free list table. If the bit is set, the free list corresponding to the index of the free list bitmap contains free heap blocks. Conversely, if the bit is not set, the free list at that index is empty. Figure 6.5 shows the free list bitmap for the free lists in Figure 6.4.

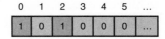

**Figure 6.5**   Free list bitmap

The heap manager maps an allocation request of a given size to a free list bitmap index by adding 8 bytes to the size (metadata) and dividing by 8. Consider an allocation request of size 8 bytes. The heap manager knows that the free list bitmap index is 2 [(8+8)/8]. From Figure 6.5, we can see that index 2 of the free list bitmap is set, which indicates that the free list located at index 2 in the free lists table contains free heap blocks. The free block is then removed from the free list and returned to the caller. If the removal of a free heap block results in that free list becoming empty, the heap manager also clears the free list bitmap at the specific index. If the heap manager is unable to find a free heap block of requested size, it employs a technique known as block splitting. Block splitting refers to the heap manager's capability to take a larger than requested free heap block and split it in half to satisfy a smaller allocation request. For example, if an allocation request arrives for a block of size 8 (total block size of 16), the free list bitmap is consulted first. The index representing blocks of size 16 indicates that no free blocks are available. Next, the heap manager finds that free blocks of size 32 are available. The heap manager now removes a block of size 32 and splits it in half, which yields two blocks of size 16 each. One of the blocks is put into a free list representing blocks of size 16, and the other block is returned to the caller. Additionally, the free list bitmap is updated to indicate that index 2 now contains free block entries of size 16. The result of splitting a larger free allocation into two smaller allocations is shown in Figure 6.6.

As mentioned earlier, the free list at index 0 can contain free heap blocks of sizes ranging from 1016 up to 0x7FFF0 (524272) bytes. To maximize free block lookup efficiency, the heap manager stores the free blocks in sorted order (ascending). All allocations of sizes greater than 0x7FFF0 go on what is known as the virtual allocation list. When a large allocation occurs, the heap manager makes an explicit allocation request from the virtual memory manager and keeps these allocations on the virtual allocation list.

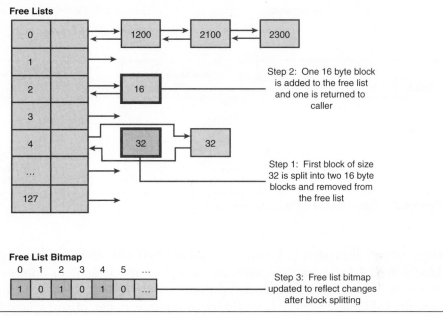

**Figure 6.6**   Splitting free blocks

So far, the discussion has revolved around how the heap manager organizes blocks of memory it has at its disposal. One question remains unanswered: Where does the heap manager get the memory from? Fundamentally, the heap manager uses the Windows virtual memory manager to allocate memory in large chunks. The memory is then massaged into different sized blocks to accommodate the allocation requests of the application. When the virtual memory chunks are exhausted, the heap manager allocates yet another large chunk of virtual memory, and the process continues. The chunks that the heap manager requests from the virtual memory manager are known as heap segments. When a heap segment is first created, the underlying virtual memory is mostly reserved, with only a small portion being committed. Whenever the heap manager runs out of committed space in the heap segment, it explicitly commits more memory and divides the newly committed space into blocks as more and more allocations are requested. Figure 6.7 illustrates the basic layout of a heap segment.

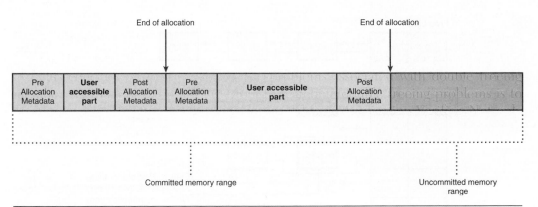

**Figure 6.7**   Basic layout of a heap segment

The segment illustrated in Figure 6.7 contains two allocations (and associated metadata) followed by a range of uncommitted memory. If another allocation request arrives, and no available free block is present in the free lists, the heap manager would commit additional memory from the uncommitted range, create a new heap block within the committed memory range, and return the block to the user. Once a segment runs out of uncommitted space, the heap manager creates a new segment. The size of the new segment is determined by doubling the size of the previous segment. If memory is scarce and cannot accommodate the new segment, the heap manager tries to reduce the size by half. If that fails, the size is halved again until it either succeeds or reaches a minimum segment size threshold—in which case, an error is returned to the caller. The maximum number of segments that can be active within a heap is 64. Once the new segment is created, the heap manager adds it to a list that keeps track of all segments being used in the heap. Does the heap manager ever free memory associated with a segment? The answer is that the heap manager decommits memory on a per-needed basis, but it never releases it. (That is, the memory stays reserved.)

As Figure 6.7 depicts, each heap block in a given segment has metadata associated with it. The metadata is used by the heap manager to effectively manage the heap blocks within a segment. The content of the metadata is dependent on the status of the heap block. For example, if the heap block is used by the application, the status of the block is considered busy. Conversely, if the heap block is not in use (that is, has been freed by the application), the status of the block is considered free. Figure 6.8 shows how the metadata is structured in both situations.

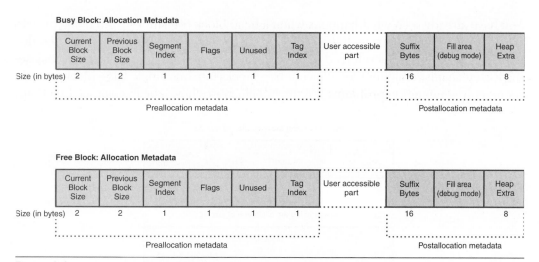

**Figure 6.8** Structure of pre- and post-allocation metadata

It is important to note that a heap block might be considered busy in the eyes of the back end allocator but still not being used by the application. The reason behind this is that any heap blocks that go on the front end allocator's look aside list still have their status set as busy.

The two size fields represent the size of the current block and the size of the previous block (metadata inclusive). Given a pointer to a heap block, you can very easily use the two size fields to walk the heap segment forward and backward. Additionally, for free blocks, having the block size as part of the metadata enables the heap manager to very quickly index the correct free list to add the block to. The post-allocation metadata is optional and is typically used by the debug heap for additional bookkeeping information (see "Attaching Versus Running" under the debugger sidebar).

The flags field indicates the status of the heap block. The most important values of the flags field are shown in Table 6.1.

**Table 6.1** Possible Block Status as Indicated by the Heap Flag

| Value | Description |
|---|---|
| 0x01 | Indicates that the allocation is being used by the application or the heap manager |
| 0x04 | Indicates whether the heap block has a fill pattern associated with it |
| 0x08 | Indicates that the heap block was allocated directly from the virtual memory manager |
| 0x10 | Indicates that this is the last heap block prior to an uncommitted range |

You have already seen what happens when a heap block transitions from being busy to free. However, one more technique that the heap manager employs needs to be discussed. The technique is referred to as heap coalescing. Fundamentally, heap coalescing is a mechanism that merges adjacent free blocks into one single large block to avoid memory fragmentation problems. Figure 6.9 illustrates how a heap coalesce functions.

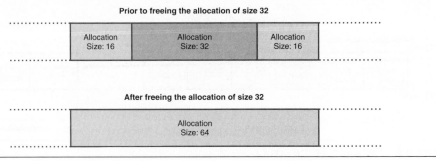

**Figure 6.9**    Example of heap coalescing

When the heap manager is requested to free the heap block of size 32, it first checks to see if any adjacent blocks are also free. In Figure 6.9, two blocks of size 16 surround the block being freed. Rather than handing the block of size 32 to the free lists, the heap manager merges all three blocks into one (of size 64) and updates the free lists to indicate that a new block of size 64 is now available. Care is also taken by the heap manager to remove the prior two blocks (of size 16) from the free lists since they are no longer available. It should go without saying that the act of coalescing free blocks is an expensive operation. So why does the heap manager even bother? The primary reason behind coalescing heap blocks is to avoid what is known as heap fragmentation. Imagine that your application just had a burst of allocations all with a very small size (16 bytes). Furthermore, let's say that there were enough of these small allocations to fill up an entire segment. After the allocation burst is completed, the application frees all the allocations. The net result is that you have one heap segment full of available allocations of size 16 bytes. Next, your application attempts to allocate a block of memory of size 48 bytes. The heap manager now tries to satisfy the allocation request from the segment, fails because the free block sizes are too small, and is forced to create a new heap segment. Needless to say, this is extremely poor use of memory. Even though we had an entire segment of free memory, the heap manager was forced to create a new segment to satisfy our slightly larger allocation request. Heap coalescing makes a best attempt at ensuring that situations such as this are kept at a minimum by combining small free blocks into larger blocks.

This concludes our discussion of the internal workings of the heap manager. Before we move on and take a practical look the heap, let's summarize what you have learned.

When allocating a block of memory

1. The heap manager first consults the front end allocator's LAL to see if a free block of memory is available; if it is, the heap manager returns it to the caller. Otherwise, step 2 is necessary.
2. The back end allocator's free lists are consulted:
    a. If an exact size match is found, the flags are updated to indicate that the block is busy; the block is then removed from the free list and returned to the caller.
    b. If an exact size match cannot be found, the heap manager checks to see if a larger block can be split into two smaller blocks that satisfy the requested allocation size. If it can, the block is split. One block has the flags updated to a busy state and is returned to the caller. The other block has its flags set to a free state and is added to the free lists. The original block is also removed from the free list.
3. If the free lists cannot satisfy the allocation request, the heap manager commits more memory from the heap segment, creates a new block in the committed range (flags set to busy state), and returns the block to the caller.

When freeing a block of memory

1. The front end allocator is consulted first to see if it can handle the free block. If the free block is not handled by the front end allocator step 2 is necessary.
2. The heap manager checks if there are any adjacent free blocks; if so, it coalesces the blocks into one large block by doing the following:
    a. The two adjacent free blocks are removed from the free lists.
    b. The new large block is added to the free list or look aside list.
    c. The flags field for the new large block is updated to indicate that it is free.
3. If no coalescing can be performed, the block is moved into the free list or look aside list, and the flags are updated to a free state.

Now it's time to complement our theoretical discussion of the heap manager with practice. Listing 6.1 shows a simple application that, using the default process heap, allocates and frees some memory.

**Listing 6.1** Simple application that performs heap allocations

```
#include <windows.h>
#include <stdio.h>
#include <conio.h>

int __cdecl wmain (int argc, wchar_t* pArgs[])
{
    BYTE* pAlloc1=NULL;
    BYTE* pAlloc2=NULL;
    HANDLE hProcessHeap=GetProcessHeap();

    pAlloc1=(BYTE*)HeapAlloc(hProcessHeap, 0, 16);
    pAlloc2=(BYTE*)HeapAlloc(hProcessHeap, 0, 1500);

    //
    // Use allocated memory
    //

    HeapFree(hProcessHeap, 0, pAlloc1);
    HeapFree(hProcessHeap, 0, pAlloc2);
}
```

The source code and binary for Listing 6.1 can be found in the following folders:

Source code: `C:\AWD\Chapter6\BasicAlloc`

Binary: `C:\AWDBIN\WinXP.x86.chk\06BasicAlloc.exe`

Run this application under the debugger and break on the `wmain` function.

Because we are interested in finding out more about the heap state, we must start by finding out what heaps are active in the process. Each running process keeps a list of active heaps. The list of heaps is stored in the PEB (process environment block), which is simply a data structure that contains a plethora of information about the process. To dump out the contents of the PEB, we use the `dt` command, as illustrated in Listing 6.2.

**Listing 6.2** Finding the PEB for a process

```
0:000> dt _PEB @$peb
   +0x000 InheritedAddressSpace : 0 ''
   +0x001 ReadImageFileExecOptions : 0 ''
   +0x002 BeingDebugged    : 0x1 ''
```

```
+0x003 SpareBool          : 0 ''
+0x004 Mutant             : 0xffffffff
+0x008 ImageBaseAddress   : 0x01000000
+0x00c Ldr                : 0x00191e90 _PEB_LDR_DATA
+0x010 ProcessParameters  : 0x00020000 _RTL_USER_PROCESS_PARAMETERS
+0x014 SubSystemData      : (null)
+0x018 ProcessHeap        : 0x00080000
+0x01c FastPebLock        : 0x7c97e4c0 _RTL_CRITICAL_SECTION
+0x020 FastPebLockRoutine : 0x7c901005
+0x024 FastPebUnlockRoutine : 0x7c9010ed
+0x028 EnvironmentUpdateCount : 1
+0x02c KernelCallbackTable : (null)
+0x030 SystemReserved     : [1] 0
+0x034 AtlThunkSListPtr32 : 0
+0x038 FreeList           : (null)
+0x03c TlsExpansionCounter : 0
+0x040 TlsBitmap          : 0x7c97e480
+0x044 TlsBitmapBits      : [2] 1
+0x04c ReadOnlySharedMemoryBase : 0x7f6f0000
+0x050 ReadOnlySharedMemoryHeap : 0x7f6f0000
+0x054 ReadOnlyStaticServerData : 0x7f6f0688  -> (null)
+0x058 AnsiCodePageData   : 0x7ffb0000
+0x05c OemCodePageData    : 0x7ffc1000
+0x060 UnicodeCaseTableData : 0x7ffd2000
+0x064 NumberOfProcessors : 1
+0x068 NtGlobalFlag       : 0
+0x070 CriticalSectionTimeout : _LARGE_INTEGER 0xffffffff`dc3cba00
+0x078 HeapSegmentReserve : 0x100000
+0x07c HeapSegmentCommit  : 0x2000
+0x080 HeapDeCommitTotalFreeThreshold : 0x10000
+0x084 HeapDeCommitFreeBlockThreshold : 0x1000
+0x088 NumberOfHeaps      : 3
+0x08c MaximumNumberOfHeaps : 0x10
+0x090 ProcessHeaps       : 0x7c97de80  -> 0x00080000
+0x094 GdiSharedHandleTable : (null)
+0x098 ProcessStarterHelper : (null)
+0x09c GdiDCAttributeList : 0
+0x0a0 LoaderLock         : 0x7c97c0d8
+0x0a4 OSMajorVersion     : 5
+0x0a8 OSMinorVersion     : 1
+0x0ac OSBuildNumber      : 0xa28
+0x0ae OSCSDVersion       : 0x200
+0x0b0 OSPlatformId       : 2
+0x0b4 ImageSubsystem     : 3
+0x0b8 ImageSubsystemMajorVersion : 4
+0x0bc ImageSubsystemMinorVersion : 0
```

*(continues)*

**Listing 6.2**   Finding the PEB for a process *(continued)*

```
+0x0c0 ImageProcessAffinityMask : 0
+0x0c4 GdiHandleBuffer    : [34] 0
+0x14c PostProcessInitRoutine : (null)
+0x150 TlsExpansionBitmap : 0x7c97e478
+0x154 TlsExpansionBitmapBits : [32] 0
+0x1d4 SessionId          : 0
+0x1d8 AppCompatFlags     : _ULARGE_INTEGER 0x0
+0x1e0 AppCompatFlagsUser : _ULARGE_INTEGER 0x0
+0x1e8 pShimData          : (null)
+0x1ec AppCompatInfo      : (null)
+0x1f0 CSDVersion         : _UNICODE_STRING "Service Pack 2"
+0x1f8 ActivationContextData : (null)
+0x1fc ProcessAssemblyStorageMap : (null)
+0x200 SystemDefaultActivationContextData : 0x00080000
+0x204 SystemAssemblyStorageMap : (null)
+0x208 MinimumStackCommit : 0
```

As you can see, PEB contains quite a lot of information, and you can learn a lot by digging around in this data structure to familiarize yourself with the various components. In this particular exercise, we are specifically interested in the list of process heaps located at offset 0x90. The heap list member of PEB is simply an array of pointers, where each pointer points to a data structure of type _HEAP. Let's dump out the array of heap pointers and see what it contains:

```
0:000> dd 0x7c97de80
7c97de80  00080000 00180000 00190000 00000000
7c97de90  00000000 00000000 00000000 00000000
7c97dea0  00000000 00000000 00000000 00000000
7c97deb0  00000000 00000000 00000000 00000000
7c97dec0  01a801a6 00020498 00000001 7c9b0000
7c97ded0  7ffd2de6 00000000 00000005 00000001
7c97dee0  ffff7e77 00000000 003a0044 0057005c
7c97def0  004e0049 004f0044 00530057 0073005c
```

The dump shows that three heaps are active in our process, and the default process heap pointer is always the first one in the list. Why do we have more than one heap in our process? Even the simplest of applications typically contains more than one heap. Most applications implicitly use components that create their own heaps. A great example is the C runtime, which creates its own heap during initialization.

Because our application works with the default process heap, we will focus our investigation on that heap. Each of the process heap pointers points to a data structure of type _HEAP. Using the dt command, we can very easily dump out the information about the process heap, as shown in Listing 6.3.

**Listing 6.3** Detailed view of the default process heap

```
0:000> dt _HEAP 00080000
   +0x000 Entry             : _HEAP_ENTRY
   +0x008 Signature         : 0xeeffeeff
   +0x00c Flags             : 0x50000062
   +0x010 ForceFlags        : 0x40000060
   +0x014 VirtualMemoryThreshold : 0xfe00
   +0x018 SegmentReserve    : 0x100000
   +0x01c SegmentCommit     : 0x2000
   +0x020 DeCommitFreeBlockThreshold : 0x200
   +0x024 DeCommitTotalFreeThreshold : 0x2000
   +0x028 TotalFreeSize     : 0xcb
   +0x02c MaximumAllocationSize : 0x7ffdefff
   +0x030 ProcessHeapsListIndex : 1
   +0x032 HeaderValidateLength : 0x608
   +0x034 HeaderValidateCopy : (null)
   +0x038 NextAvailableTagIndex : 0
   +0x03a MaximumTagIndex   : 0
   +0x03c TagEntries        : (null)
   +0x040 UCRSegments       : (null)
   +0x044 UnusedUnCommittedRanges : 0x00080598 _HEAP_UNCOMMMTTED_RANGE
   +0x048 AlignRound        : 0x17
   +0x04c AlignMask         : 0xfffffff8
   +0x050 VirtualAllocdBlocks : _LIST_ENTRY [ 0x80050 - 0x80050 ]
   +0x058 Segments          : [64] 0x00080640 _HEAP_SEGMENT
   +0x158 u                 : __unnamed
   +0x168 u2                : __unnamed
   +0x16a AllocatorBackTraceIndex : 0
   +0x16c NonDedicatedListLength : 1
   +0x170 LargeBlocksIndex  : (null)
   +0x174 PseudoTagEntries  : (null)
   +0x178 FreeLists         : [128] _LIST_ENTRY [ 0x829b0 - 0x829b0 ]
   +0x578 LockVariable      : 0x00080608 _HEAP_LOCK
   +0x57c CommitRoutine     : (null)
   +0x580 FrontEndHeap      : 0x00080688
   +0x584 FrontHeapLockCount : 0
   +0x586 FrontEndHeapType  : 0x1 ''
   +0x587 LastSegmentIndex  : 0 ''
```

Once again, you can see that the _HEAP structure is fairly large with a lot of information about the heap. For this exercise, the most important members of the _HEAP structure are located at the following offsets:

```
+0x050 VirtualAllocdBlocks : _LIST_ENTRY
```

Allocations that are greater than the virtual allocation size threshold are not managed as part of the segments and free lists. Rather, these allocations are allocated directly from the virtual memory manager. You track these allocations by keeping a list as part of the _HEAP structure that contains all virtual allocations.

```
+0x058 Segments        : [64]
```

The Segments field is an array of data structures of type _HEAP_SEGMENT. Each heap segment contains a list of heap entries active within that segment. Later on, you will see how we can use this information to walk the entire heap segment and locate allocations of interest.

```
+0x16c NonDedicatedListLength
```

As mentioned earlier, free list[0] contains allocations of size greater than 1016KB and less than the virtual allocation threshold. To efficiently manage this free list, the heap stores the number of allocations in the nondedicates list in this field. This information can come in useful when you want to analyze heap usage and quickly see how many of your allocations fall into the variable sized free list[0] category.

```
+0x178 FreeLists        : [128] _LIST_ENTRY
```

The free lists are stored at offset 0x178 and contain doubly linked lists. Each list contains free heap blocks of a specific size. We will take a closer look at the free lists in a little bit.

```
+0x580 FrontEndHeap
```

The pointer located at offset 0x580 points to the front end allocator. We know the overall architecture and strategy behind the front end allocator, but unfortunately, the public symbol package does not contain definitions for it, making an in-depth investigation impossible. It is also worth noting that Microsoft reserves the right to change the offsets previously described between Windows versions.

Back to our sample application—let's continue stepping through the code in the debugger. The first call of interest is to the `GetProcessHeap` API, which returns a handle to the default process heap. Because we already found this handle/pointer ourselves, we can verify that the explicit call to `GetProcessHeap` returns what we expect. After the call, the `eax` register contains `0x00080000`, which matches our expectations. Next are two calls to the `kernel32!HeapAlloc` API that attempt allocations of sizes 16 and 1500. Will these allocations be satisfied by committing more segment memory or from the free lists? Before stepping over the first `HeapAlloc` call, let's try to find out where the heap manager will find a free heap block to satisfy this allocation. The first step in our investigation is to see if any free blocks of size 16 are available in the free lists. To check the availability of free blocks, we use the following command:

```
dt _LIST_ENTRY 0x00080000+0x178+8
```

This command dumps out the first node in the free list that corresponds to allocations of size 16. The `0x00080000` is the address of our heap. We add an offset of `0x178` to get the start of the free list table. The first entry in the free list table points to free list[0]. Because our allocation is much smaller than the free list[0] size threshold, we simply skip this free list by adding an additional 8 bytes (the size of the _LIST_ENTRY structure), which puts us at free list[1] representing free blocks of size 16.

```
0:000> dt _LIST_ENTRY 0x00080000+0x178+8
 [ 0x80180 - 0x80180 ]
   +0x000 Flink            : 0x00080180 _LIST_ENTRY [ 0x80180 - 0x80180 ]
   +0x004 Blink            : 0x00080180 _LIST_ENTRY [ 0x80180 - 0x80180 ]
```

Remember that the free lists are doubly linked lists; hence the `Flink` and `Blink` fields of the `_LIST_ENTRY` structure are simply pointers to the next and previous allocations. It is critical to note that the pointer listed in the free lists actually points to the user-accessible part of the heap block and not to the start of the heap block itself. As such, if you want to look at the allocation metadata, you need to first subtract 8 bytes from the pointer. Both of these pointers seem to point to `0x00080180`, which in actuality is the address of the list node we were just dumping out (0x00080000+0x178+8=0x00080180). This implies that the free list corresponding to allocations of size 16 is empty. Before we assume that the heap manager must commit more memory in the segment, remember that it will only do so as the absolute last resort. Hence, the heap manager first tries to see if there are any other free blocks of sizes greater than 16 that it could split to satisfy the allocation. In our particular case, free list[0] contains a free heap block:

```
0:000> dt _LIST_ENTRY 0x00080000+0x178
[ 0x82ab0 - 0x82ab0 ]
   +0x000 Flink           : 0x00082ab0 _LIST_ENTRY [ 0x80178 - 0x80178 ]
   +0x004 Blink           : 0x00082ab0 _LIST_ENTRY [ 0x80178 - 0x80178 ]
```

The `Flink` member points to the location in the heap block available to the caller. In order to see the full heap block (including metadata), we must first subtract 8 bytes from the pointer (refer to Figure 6.8).

```
0:000> dt _HEAP_ENTRY 0x00082ab0-0x8
   +0x000 Size            : 0xab
   +0x002 PreviousSize    : 0xb
   +0x000 SubSegmentCode  : 0x000b00ab
   +0x004 SmallTagIndex   : 0xee ''
   +0x005 Flags           : 0x14 ''
   +0x006 UnusedBytes     : 0xee ''
   +0x007 SegmentIndex    : 0 ''
```

It is important to note that the size reported is the true size of the heap block divided by the heap granularity. The heap granularity is easily found by taking the size of the `_HEAP_ENTY_STRUCTURE`. A heap block, the size of which is reported to be 0xab, is in reality 0xa8*8 = 0x558 (1368) bytes.

The free heap block we are looking at definitely seems to be big enough to fit our allocation request of size 16. In the debug session, step over the first instruction that calls `HeapAlloc`. If successful, we can then check free list[0] again and see if the allocation we looked at prior to the call has changed:

```
0:000> dt _LIST_ENTRY 0x00080000+0x178
[ 0x82ad8 - 0x82ad8 ]
   +0x000 Flink           : 0x00082ad8 _LIST_ENTRY [ 0x80178 - 0x80178 ]
   +0x004 Blink           : 0x00082ad8 _LIST_ENTRY [ 0x80178 - 0x80178 ]
0:000> dt _HEAP_ENTRY 0x00082ad8-0x8
   +0x000 Size            : 0xa6
   +0x002 PreviousSize    : 5
   +0x000 SubSegmentCode  : 0x000500a6
   +0x004 SmallTagIndex   : 0xee ''
   +0x005 Flags           : 0x14 ''
   +0x006 UnusedBytes     : 0xee ''
   +0x007 SegmentIndex    : 0 ''
```

Sure enough, what used to be the first entry in free list[0] has now changed. Instead of a free block of size 0xab, we now have a free block of size 0xa6. The difference in size (0x5) is due to our allocation request breaking up the larger free block we saw previously. If we are allocating 16 bytes (0x10), why is the difference in size of the free block before splitting and after only 0x5 bytes? The key is to remember that the size reported must first be multiplied by the heap granularity factor of 0x8. The true size of the new free allocation is then 0x00000530 (0xa6*8), with the true size difference being 0x28. 0x10 of those 0x28 bytes are our allocation size, and the remaining 0x18 bytes are all metadata associated with our heap block.

The next call to `HeapAlloc` attempts to allocate memory of size 1500. We know that free heap blocks of this size must be located in the free list[0]. However, from our previous investigation, we also know that the only free heap block on the free list[0] is too small to accommodate the size we are requesting. With its hands tied, the heap manager is now forced to commit more memory in the heap segment. To get a better picture of the state of our heap segment, it is useful to do a manual walk of the segment. The _HEAP structure contains an array of pointers to all segments currently active in the heap. The array is located at the base _HEAP address plus an offset of 0x58.

```
0:000> dd 0x00080000+0x58 14
00080058    00080640 00000000 00000000 00000000
0:000> dt _HEAP_SEGMENT 0x00080640
   +0x000 Entry            : _HEAP_ENTRY
   +0x008 Signature        : 0xffeeffee
   +0x00c Flags            : 0
   +0x010 Heap             : 0x00080000 _HEAP
   +0x014 LargestUnCommittedRange : 0xfd000
   +0x018 BaseAddress      : 0x00080000
   +0x01c NumberOfPages    : 0x100
   +0x020 FirstEntry       : 0x00080680 _HEAP_ENTRY
   +0x024 LastValidEntry   : 0x00180000 _HEAP_ENTRY
   +0x028 NumberOfUnCommittedPages : 0xfd
   +0x02c NumberOfUnCommittedRanges : 1
   +0x030 UnCommmttedRanges : 0x00080588 _HEAP_UNCOMMMTTED_RANGE
   +0x034 AllocatorBackTraceIndex : 0
   +0x036 Reserved         : 0
   +0x038 LastEntryInSegment : 0x00082ad0 _HEAP_ENTRY
```

The _HEAP_SEGMENT data structure contains a slew of information used by the heap manager to efficiently manage all the active segments in the heap. When walking a segment, the most useful piece of information is the `FirstEntry` field located at the base segment address plus an offset of 0x20. This field represents the first heap block in the segment. If we dump out this block and get the size, we can dump out the next heap block by adding the size to the first heap block's address. If we continue this process, the entire segment can be walked, and each allocation can be investigated for correctness.

```
0:000> dt _HEAP_ENTRY 0x00080680
   +0x000 Size            : 0x303
   +0x002 PreviousSize    : 8
   +0x000 SubSegmentCode  : 0x00080303
   +0x004 SmallTagIndex   : 0x9a ''
   +0x005 Flags           : 0x7 ''
   +0x006 UnusedBytes     : 0x18 ''
   +0x007 SegmentIndex    : 0 ''
0:000> dt _HEAP_ENTRY 0x00080680+(0x303*8)
   +0x000 Size            : 8
   +0x002 PreviousSize    : 0x303
   +0x000 SubSegmentCode  : 0x03030008
   +0x004 SmallTagIndex   : 0x99 ''
   +0x005 Flags           : 0x7 ''
   +0x006 UnusedBytes     : 0x1e ''
   +0x007 SegmentIndex    : 0 ''
0:000> dt _HEAP_ENTRY 0x00080680+(0x303*8)+(8*8)
   +0x000 Size            : 5
   +0x002 PreviousSize    : 8
   +0x000 SubSegmentCode  : 0x00080005
   +0x004 SmallTagIndex   : 0x91 ''
   +0x005 Flags           : 0x7 ''
   +0x006 UnusedBytes     : 0x1a ''
   +0x007 SegmentIndex    : 0 ''
   ...
   ...
   ...
   +0x000 Size            : 0xa6
   +0x002 PreviousSize    : 5
   +0x000 SubSegmentCode  : 0x000500a6
   +0x004 SmallTagIndex   : 0xee ''
   +0x005 Flags           : 0x14 ''
   +0x006 UnusedBytes     : 0xee ''
   +0x007 SegmentIndex    : 0 ''
```

Let's see what the heap manager does to the segment (if anything) to try to satisfy the allocation request of size 1500 bytes. Step over the `HeapAlloc` call and walk the segment again. The heap block of interest is shown next.

```
   +0x000 Size            : 0xbf
   +0x002 PreviousSize    : 5
   +0x000 SubSegmentCode  : 0x000500bf
   +0x004 SmallTagIndex   : 0x10 ''
   +0x005 Flags           : 0x7 ''
   +0x006 UnusedBytes     : 0x1c ''
   +0x007 SegmentIndex    : 0 ''
```

Before we stepped over the call to `HeapAlloc`, the last heap block was marked as free and with a size of 0xa6. After the call, the block status changed to busy with a size of 0xbf (0xbf*8= 0x5f8), indicating that this block is now used to hold our new allocation. Since our allocation was too big to fit into the previous size of 0xa6, the heap manager committed more memory to the segment. Did it commit just enough to hold our allocation? Actually, it committed much more and put the remaining free memory into a new block at address `0x000830c8`. The heap manager is only capable of asking for page sized allocations (4KB on x86 systems) from the virtual memory manager and returns the remainder of that allocation to the free lists.

The next couple of lines in our application simply free the allocations we just made. What do we anticipate the heap manager to do when it executes the first `HeapFree` call? In addition to updating the status of the heap block to free and adding it to the free lists, we expect it to try and coalesce the heap block with other surrounding free blocks. Before we step over the first `HeapFree` call, let's take a look at the heap block associated with that call.

```
0:000> dt _HEAP_ENTRY 0x000830c8-(0xbf*8)-(0x5*8)
   +0x000 Size            : 5
   +0x002 PreviousSize    : 0xb
   +0x000 SubSegmentCode  : 0x000b0005
   +0x004 SmallTagIndex   : 0x1f ''
   +0x005 Flags           : 0x7 ''
   +0x006 UnusedBytes     : 0x18 ''
   +0x007 SegmentIndex    : 0 ''
0:000> dt _HEAP_ENTRY 0x000830c8-(0xbf*8)-(0x5*8)-(0xb*8)
   +0x000 Size            : 0xb
   +0x002 PreviousSize    : 5
   +0x000 SubSegmentCode  : 0x0005000b
   +0x004 SmallTagIndex   : 0 ''
   +0x005 Flags           : 0x7 ''
   +0x006 UnusedBytes     : 0x1c ''
   +0x007 SegmentIndex    : 0 ''
0:000> dt _HEAP_ENTRY 0x000830c8-(0xbf*8)
   +0x000 Size            : 0xbf
   +0x002 PreviousSize    : 5
   +0x000 SubSegmentCode  : 0x000500bf
   +0x004 SmallTagIndex   : 0x10 ''
   +0x005 Flags           : 0x7 ''
   +0x006 UnusedBytes     : 0x1c ''
   +0x007 SegmentIndex    : 0 ''
```

The status of the previous and next heap blocks are both busy (Flags=0x7), which means that the heap manager is not capable of coalescing the memory, and the heap block is simply put on the free lists. More specifically, the heap block will go into free list[1] because the size is 16 bytes. Let's verify our theory—step over the `HeapFree` call and use the same mechanism as previously used to see what happened to the heap block.

```
0:000> dt _HEAP_ENTRY 0x000830c8-(0xbf*8)-(0x5*8)
   +0x000 Size             : 5
   +0x002 PreviousSize     : 0xb
   +0x000 SubSegmentCode   : 0x000b0005
   +0x004 SmallTagIndex    : 0x1f ''
   +0x005 Flags            : 0x4 ''
   +0x006 UnusedBytes      : 0x18 ''
   +0x007 SegmentIndex     : 0 ''
```

As you can see, the heap block status is indeed set to be free, and the size remains the same. Since the size remains the same, it serves as an indicator that the heap manager did not coalesce the heap block with adjacent blocks. Last, we verify that the block made it into the free list[1].

I will leave it as an exercise for the reader to figure out what happens to the segment and heap blocks during the next call to `HeapFree`. Here's a hint: Remember that the size of the heap block being freed is 1500 bytes and that the state of one of the adjacent blocks is set to free.

This concludes our overview of the internal workings of the heap manager. Although it might seem like a daunting task to understand and be able to walk the various heap structures, after a little practice, it all becomes easier. Before we move on to the heap corruption scenarios, one important debugger command can help us be more efficient when debugging heap corruption scenarios. The extension command is called `!heap` and is part of the exts.dll debugger extension. Using this command, you can very easily display all the heap information you could possibly want. Actually, all the information we just manually gathered is outputted by the `!heap` extension command in a split second. But wait—we just spent a lot of time figuring out how to analyze the heap by hand, walk the segments, and verify the heap blocks. Why even bother if we have this beautiful command that does all the work for us? As always, the answer lies in how the debugger arrives at the information it presents. If the state of the heap is intact, the `!heap` extension command shows the heap state in a nice and digestible form. If, however, the state of the heap has been corrupted, it is no longer sufficient to rely on the command to tell us what and how it became corrupted. We need to know how to analyze the various parts of the heap to arrive at sound conclusions and possible culprits.

### *Attaching Versus Starting the Process Under the Debugger*

The debug session you have seen so far has involved running a process under the debugger from start to finish. Another option when debugging processes is attaching the debugger to an already-running process. Typically, using either approach will not dramatically change the way you debug the process. The exception to the rule is when debugging heap-related issues. When starting the process under the debugger, the heap manager modifies all requests to create new heaps and change the heap creation flags to enable debug-friendly heaps (unless the _NO_DEBUG_HEAP environment variable is set to 1). In comparison, attaching to an already-running process, the heaps in the process have already been created using default heap creation flags and will not have the debug-friendly flags set (unless explicitly set by the application). The heap modification flags apply across all heaps in the process, including the default process heap. The biggest difference when starting a process under the debugger is that the heap blocks contain an additional fill pattern field after the user-accessible part (see Figure 6.8). The fill pattern is used by the heap manager to validate the integrity of the heap block during heap operations. When an allocation is successful, the heap manager fills this area of the block with a specific fill pattern. If an application mistakenly writes past the end of the user-accessible part, it overwrites all or portions of this fill pattern field. The next time the application uses that allocation in any calls to the heap manager, the heap manager takes a close look at the fill pattern field to make sure that it hasn't changed. If the fill pattern field was overwritten by the application, the heap manager immediately breaks into the debugger, giving you the opportunity to look at the heap block and try to infer why it was overwritten. Writing to any area of a heap block outside the bounds of the actual user-accessible part is a serious error that can be devastating to the stability of an application.

# Heap Corruptions

Heap corruptions are arguably some of the trickiest problems to figure out. A process can corrupt any given heap in nearly infinite ways. Armed with the knowledge of how the heap manager functions, we now take a look at some of the most common reasons behind heap corruptions. Each scenario is accompanied by sample source code illustrating the type of heap corruption being examined. A detailed debug session is then presented, which takes you from the initial fault to the source of the heap corruption. Along the way, we also introduce invaluable tools that can be used to more easily get to the root cause of the corruption.

## Using Uninitialied State

Uninitialized state is a common programming mistake that can lead to numerous hours of debugging to track down. Fundamentally, uninitialized state refers to a block of memory that has been successfully allocated but not yet initialized to a state in which it is considered valid for use. The memory block can range from simple native data types, such as integers, to complex data blobs. Using an uninitialized memory block results in unpredictable behavior. Listing 6.4 shows a small application that suffers from using uninitialized memory.

**Listing 6.4**　Simple application that uses uninitialized memory

```
#include <windows.h>
#include <stdio.h>
#include <conio.h>

#define ARRAY_SIZE 10

BOOL InitArray(int** pPtrArray);

int __cdecl wmain (int argc, wchar_t* pArgs[])
{
  int iRes=1;

  wprintf(L"Press any key to start...");
  _getch();

  int** pPtrArray=(int**)HeapAlloc(GetProcessHeap(),
                                   0,
                                   sizeof(int*[ARRAY_SIZE]));
  if(pPtrArray!=NULL)
  {
    InitArray(pPtrArray);
    *(pPtrArray[0])=10;
    iRes=0;
    HeapFree(GetProcessHeap(), 0, pPtrArray);
  }
  return iRes;
}

BOOL InitArray(int** pPtrArray)
{
  return FALSE ;
}
```

The source code and binary for Listing 6.4 can be found in the following folders:

Source code: `C:\AWD\Chapter6\Uninit`

Binary: `C:\AWDBIN\WinXP.x86.chk\06Uninit.exe`

The code in Listing 6.4 simply allocates an array of integer pointers. It then calls an `InitArray` function that initializes all elements in the array with valid integer pointers. After the call, the application tries to dereference the first pointer and sets the value to 10. Can this code fail? Absolutely! Because we are not checking the return value of the call to `InitArray`, the function might fail to initialize the array. Subsequently, when we try to dereference the first element, we might incorrectly pick up a random address. The application might experience an access violation if the address is invalid (in the sense that it is not accessible memory), or it might succeed. What happens next depends largely on the random pointer itself. If the pointer is pointing to a valid address used elsewhere, the application continues execution. If, however, the pointer points to inaccessible memory, the application might crash immediately. Suffice it to say that even if the application does not crash immediately, memory is being incorrectly used, and the application will eventually fail.

When the application is executed, we can easily see that a failure does occur. To get a better picture of what is failing, run the application under the debugger, as shown in Listing 6.5.

**Listing 6.5**  Application crash seen under the debugger

```
...
...
...
0:000> g
Press any key to start...(740.5b0): Access violation - code c0000005 (first chance)
First chance exceptions are reported before any exception handling.
This exception may be expected and handled.
eax=00000000 ebx=7ffdb000 ecx=00082ab0 edx=baadf00d esi=7c9118f1 edi=00011970
eip=010011c9 esp=0006ff3c ebp=0006ff44 iopl=0         nv up ei pl zr na pe nc
cs=001b  ss=0023  ds=0023  es=0023  fs=003b  gs=0000            efl=00010246
06uninit!wmain+0x49:
010011c9 c7020a000000    mov     dword ptr [edx],0Ah  ds:0023:baadf00d=????????
0:000> kb
ChildEBP RetAddr  Args to Child
0007ff7c 01001413 00000001 00034ed8 00037118 06uninit!wmain+0x4b
0007ffc0 7c816fd7 00011970 7c9118f1 7ffd4000 06uninit!__wmainCRTStartup+0x102
0007fff0 00000000 01001551 00000000 78746341 kernel32!BaseProcessStart+0x23
```

The instruction that causes the crash corresponds to the line of code in our application that sets the first element in the array to the value 10:

```
mov    dword ptr [edx],0xAh            ;  *(pPtrArray[0])=10;
```

The next logical step is to understand why the access violation occurred. Because we are trying to write to a memory location that equates to the first element in our array, the access violation might be because the memory being written to is inaccessible. Dumping out the contents of the memory in question yields

```
0:000> dd edx
baadf00d  ???????? ???????? ???????? ????????
baadf01d  ???????? ???????? ???????? ????????
baadf02d  ???????? ???????? ???????? ????????
baadf03d  ???????? ???????? ???????? ????????
baadf04d  ???????? ???????? ???????? ????????
baadf05d  ???????? ???????? ???????? ????????
baadf06d  ???????? ???????? ???????? ????????
baadf07d  ???????? ???????? ???????? ????????
```

The pointer located in the edx register has a really strange value (baadf00d) that points to inaccessible memory. Trying to dereference this pointer is what ultimately caused the access violation. Where does this interesting pointer value (baadf00d) come from? Surely, the pointer value is incorrect enough that it wasn't left there by some prior allocation. The bad pointer we are seeing was explicitly placed there by the heap manager. Whenever you start a process under the debugger, the heap manager automatically initializes all memory with a fill pattern. The specifics of the fill pattern depend on the status of the heap block. When a heap block is first returned to the caller, the heap manager fills the user-accessible part of the heap block with a fill pattern consisting of the values baadf00d. This indicates that the heap block is allocated but has not yet been initialized. Should an application (such as ours) dereference this memory block without initializing it first, it will fail. On the other hand, if the application properly initializes the memory block, execution continues. After the heap block is freed, the heap manager once again initializes the user-accessible part of the heap block, this time with the values feeefeee. Again, the free-fill pattern is added by the heap manager to trap any memory accesses to the block after it has been freed. The memory not being initialized prior to use is the reason for our particular failure.

Let's see how the allocated memory differs when the application is not started under the debugger but rather attached to the process. Start the application, and when the Press any key to start prompt appears, attach the debugger. Once attached, set a breakpoint on the instruction that caused the crash and dump out the contents of the edx register.

```
0:000> dd edx
00080178  000830f0 000830f0 00080180 00080180
00080188  00080188 00080188 00080190 00080190
00080198  00080198 00080198 000801a0 000801a0
000801a8  000801a8 000801a8 000801b0 000801b0
000801b8  000801b8 000801b8 000801c0 000801c0
000801c8  000801c8 000801c8 000801d0 000801d0
000801d8  000801d8 000801d8 000801e0 000801e0
000801e8  000801e8 000801e8 000801f0 000801f0
```

This time around, you can see that the edx register contains a pointer value that is pointing to accessible, albeit incorrect, memory. No longer is the array initialized to pointer values that cause an immediate access violation (baadf00d) when dereferenced. As a matter of fact, stepping over the faulting instruction this time around succeeds. Do we know the origins of the pointer value we just used? Not at all. It could be any memory location in the process. The incorrect usage of the pointer value might end up causing serious problems somewhere else in the application in paths that rely on the state of that memory to be intact. If we resume execution of the application, we will notice that an access violation does in fact occur, albeit much later in the execution.

```
0:000> g
(1a8.75c): Access violation - code c0000005 (first chance)
First chance exceptions are reported before any exception handling.
This exception may be expected and handled.
eax=0000000a ebx=00080000 ecx=00080178 edx=00000000 esi=00000002 edi=0000000f
eip=7c911404 esp=0006f77c ebp=0006f99c iopl=0         nv up ei pl nz ac po nc
cs=001b  ss=0023  ds=0023  es=0023  fs=003b  gs=0000            efl=00010212
ntdll!RtlAllocateHeap+0x6c9:
7c911404 0fb70e          movzx   ecx,word ptr [esi]      ds:0023:00000002=????
0:000> g
(1a8.75c): Access violation - code c0000005 (!!! second chance !!!)
eax=0000000a ebx=00080000 ecx=00080178 edx=00000000 esi=00000002 edi=0000000f
eip=7c911404 esp=0006f77c ebp=0006f99c iopl=0         nv up ei pl nz ac po nc
cs=001b  ss=0023  ds=0023  es=0023  fs=003b  gs=0000            efl=00000212
ntdll!RtlAllocateHeap+0x6c9:
7c911404 0fb70e          movzx   ecx,word ptr [esi]      ds:0023:00000002=????
0:000> k
ChildEBP RetAddr
0007f9b0 7c80e323 ntdll!RtlAllocateHeap+0x6c9
0007fa24 7c80e00d kernel32!BasepComputeProcessPath+0xb3
0007fa64 7c80e655 kernel32!BaseComputeProcessDllPath+0xe3
0007faac 7c80e5ab kernel32!GetModuleHandleForUnicodeString+0x28
0007ff30 7c80e45c kernel32!BasepGetModuleHandleExW+0x18e
```

```
0007ff48 7c80b6c0 kernel32!GetModuleHandleW+0x29
0007ff54 77c39d23 kernel32!GetModuleHandleA+0x2d
0007ff60 77c39e78 msvcrt!__crtExitProcess+0x10
0007ff70 77c39e90 msvcrt!_cinit+0xee
0007ff84 01001429 msvcrt!exit+0x12
0007ffc0 7c816fd7 06uninit!__wmainCRTStartup+0x118
0007fff0 00000000 kernel32!BaseProcessStart+0x23
```

As you can see, the stack reporting the access violation has nothing to do with any of our own code. All we really know is that when the process is about to exit, as you can see from the bottommost frame (`msvcrt!__crtExitProcess+0x10`), it tries to allocate memory and fails in the memory manager. Typically, access violations occurring in the heap manager are good indicators that a heap corruption has occurred. Backtracking the source of the corruption from this location can be an excruciatingly difficult process that should be avoided at all costs. From the two previous sample runs, it should be evident that trapping a heap corruption at the point of occurrence is much more desirable than sporadic failures in code paths that we do not directly own. One of the ways we can achieve this is by starting the process under the debugger and letting the heap manager use fill patterns to provide some level of protection. Although the heap manager does provide this mechanism, it is not necessarily the strongest level of protection. The usage of fill patterns requires that a call be made to the heap manager so that it can validate that the fill pattern is still valid. Most of the time, the damage has already been done at the point of validation, and the fault caused by the heap manager still requires us to work backward and figure out what caused the fault to begin with.

In addition to uninitialized state, another very common scenario that results in heap corruptions is a heap overrun.

## Heap Overruns and Underruns

In the introduction to this chapter, we looked at the internal workings of the heap manager and how all heap blocks are laid out. Figure 6.8 illustrated how a heap block is broken down and what auxiliary metadata is kept on a per-block basis for the heap manager to be capable of managing the block. If a faulty piece of code overwrites any of the metadata, the integrity of the heap is compromised and the application will fault. The most common form of metadata overwriting is when the owner of the heap block does not respect the boundaries of the block. This phenomenon is known as a heap overrun or, reciprocally, a heap underrun.

Let's take a look at an example. The application shown in Listing 6.6 simply makes a copy of the string passed in on the command line and prints out the copy.

## Listing 6.6  Heap-based string copy application

```
#include <windows.h>
#include <stdio.h>
#include <conio.h>

#define SZ_MAX_LEN   10

WCHAR* pszCopy = NULL ;

BOOL DupString(WCHAR* psz);

int __cdecl wmain (int argc, wchar_t* pArgs[])
{
    int iRet=0;

    if(argc==2)
    {
        printf("Press any key to start\n");
        _getch();
        DupString(pArgs[1]);
    }
    else
    {
        iRet=1;
    }
    return iRet;
}


BOOL DupString(WCHAR* psz)
{
    BOOL bRet=FALSE;

    if(psz!=NULL)
    {
        pszCopy=(WCHAR*) HeapAlloc(GetProcessHeap(),
                                   0,
                                   SZ_MAX_LEN*sizeof(WCHAR));
        if(pszCopy)
        {
            wcscpy(pszCopy, psz);
            wprintf(L"Copy of string: %s", pszCopy);
            HeapFree(GetProcessHeap(), 0, pszCopy);
            bRet=TRUE;
        }
    }
    return bRet;
}
```

The source code and binary for Listing 6.6 can be found in the following folders:

>  Source code: `C:\AWD\Chapter6\Overrun`
>
>  Binary: `C:\AWDBIN\WinXP.x86.chk\06Overrun.exe`

When you run this application with various input strings, you will quickly notice that input strings of size 10 or less seem to work fine. As soon as you breach the 10-character limit, the application crashes. Let's pick the following string to use in our debug session:

```
C:\AWDBIN\WinXP.x86.chk\06Overrun.exe ThisStringShouldReproTheCrash
```

Run the application and attach the debugger when you see the `Press any key to start` prompt. Once attached, press any key to resume execution and watch how the debugger breaks execution with an access violation.

```
...
...
...
0:001> g
(1b8.334): Access violation - code c0000005 (first chance)
First chance exceptions are reported before any exception handling.
This exception may be expected and handled.
eax=00650052 ebx=00080000 ecx=00720070 edx=00083188 esi=00083180 edi=0000000f
eip=7c91142e esp=0006f77c ebp=0006f99c iopl=0         nv up ei ng nz na po cy
cs=001b  ss=0023  ds=0023  es=0023  fs=003b  gs=0000             efl=00010283
ntdll!RtlAllocateHeap+0x653:
7c91142e 8b39            mov     edi,dword ptr [ecx]  ds:0023:00720070=????????
0:000> k
ChildEBP RetAddr
0007f70c 7c919f5d ntdll!RtlpInsertFreeBlock+0xf3
0007f73c 7c918839 ntdll!RtlpInitializeHeapSegment+0x186
0007f780 7c911c76 ntdll!RtlpExtendHeap+0x1ca
0007f9b0 7c80e323 ntdll!RtlAllocateHeap+0x623
0007fa24 7c80e00d kernel32!BasepComputeProcessPath+0xb3
0007fa64 7c80e655 kernel32!BaseComputeProcessDllPath+0xe3
0007faac 7c80e5ab kernel32!GetModuleHandleForUnicodeString+0x28
0007ff30 7c80e45c kernel32!BasepGetModuleHandleExW+0x18e
0007ff48 7c80b6c0 kernel32!GetModuleHandleW+0x29
0007ff54 77c39d23 kernel32!GetModuleHandleA+0x2d
0007ff60 77c39e78 msvcrt!__crtExitProcess+0x10
0007ff70 77c39e90 msvcrt!_cinit+0xee
0007ff84 010014c2 msvcrt!exit+0x12
0007ffc0 7c816fd7 06overrun!__wmainCRTStartup+0x118
0007fff0 00000000 kernel32!BaseProcessStart+0x23
```

Glancing at the stack, it looks like the application was in the process of shutting down when the access violation occurred. As per our previous discussion, whenever you encounter an access violation in the heap manager code, chances are you are experiencing a heap corruption. The only problem is that our code is nowhere on the stack. Once again, the biggest problem with heap corruptions is that the faulting code is not easily trapped at the point of corruption; rather, the corruption typically shows up later on in the execution. This behavior alone makes it really hard to track down the source of heap corruption. However, with an understanding of how the heap manager works, we can do some preliminary investigation of the heap and see if we can find some clues as to some potential culprits. Without knowing which part of the heap is corrupted, a good starting point is to see if the segments are intact. Instead of manually walking the segments, we use the `!heap` extension command, which saves us a ton of grueling manual heap work. A shortened version of the output for the default process heap is shown in Listing 6.7.

**Listing 6.7**  Heap corruption analysis using the heap debugger command

```
0:000> !heap -s
  Heap      Flags     Reserv  Commit  Virt   Free  List    UCR   Virt   Lock  Fast
                      (k)     (k)     (k)    (k)   length        blocks cont. heap
  ----------------------------------------------
  00080000 00000002   1024    16      16     3     1       1     0      0     L
  00180000 00001002   64      24      24     15    1       1     0      0     L
  00190000 00008000   64      12      12     10    1       1     0      0
  00260000 00001002   64      28      28     7     1       1     0      0     L
  ----------------------------------------------
0:000> !heap -a 00080000
Index   Address   Name      Debugging options enabled
  1:    00080000
    Segment at 00080000 to 00180000 (00004000 bytes committed)
    Flags:                  00000002
    ForceFlags:             00000000
    Granularity:            8 bytes
    Segment Reserve:        00100000
    Segment Commit:         00002000
    DeCommit Block Thres:   00000200
    DeCommit Total Thres:   00002000
    Total Free Size:        000001d0
    Max. Allocation Size:   7ffdefff
    Lock Variable at:       00080608
    Next TagIndex:          0000
    Maximum TagIndex:       0000
    Tag Entries:            00000000
```

*(continues)*

**Listing 6.7**    Heap corruption analysis using the heap debugger command *(continued)*

```
0    PsuedoTag Entries:    00000000
     Virtual Alloc List:   00080050
     UCR FreeList:         00080598
     FreeList Usage:       00000000 00000000 00000000 00000000
     FreeList[ 00 ] at 00080178: 00083188 . 00083188
         00083180: 003a8 . 00378 [00] - free
     Unable to read nt!_HEAP_FREE_ENTRY structure at 0065004a
     Segment00 at 00080640:
         Flags:            00000000
         Base:             00080000
         First Entry:      00080680
         Last Entry:       00180000
         Total Pages:      00000100
         Total UnCommit:   000000fc
         Largest UnCommit:000fc000
         UnCommitted Ranges: (1)
             00084000: 000fc000


     Heap entries for Segment00 in Heap 00080000
         00080000: 00000 . 00640 [01] - busy (640)
         00080640: 00640 . 00040 [01] - busy (40)
         00080680: 00040 . 01808 [01] - busy (1800)
         00081e88: 01808 . 00210 [01] - busy (208)
         00082098: 00210 . 00228 [01] - busy (21a)
         000822c0: 00228 . 00090 [01] - busy (84)
         00082350: 00090 . 00030 [01] - busy (22)
         00082380: 00030 . 00018 [01] - busy (10)
         00082398: 00018 . 00068 [01] - busy (5b)
         00082400: 00068 . 00230 [01] - busy (224)
         00082630: 00230 . 002e0 [01] - busy (2d8)
         00082910: 002e0 . 00320 [01] - busy (314)
         00082c30: 00320 . 00320 [01] - busy (314)
         00082f50: 00320 . 00030 [01] - busy (24)
         00082f80: 00030 . 00030 [01] - busy (24)
         00082fb0: 00030 . 00050 [01] - busy (40)
         00083000: 00050 . 00048 [01] - busy (40)
         00083048: 00048 . 00038 [01] - busy (2a)
         00083080: 00038 . 00010 [01] - busy (1)
         00083090: 00010 . 00050 [01] - busy (44)
         000830e0: 00050 . 00018 [01] - busy (10)
         000830f8: 00018 . 00068 [01] - busy (5b)
         00083160: 00068 . 00020 [01] - busy (14)
         00083180: 003a8 . 00378 [00]
         000834f8: 00000 . 00000 [00]
```

The last heap entry in a segment is typically a free block. In Listing 6.7, however, we have a couple of odd entries at the end. The status of the heap blocks (0) seems to indicate that both blocks are free; however, the size of the blocks does not seem to match up. Let's look at the first free block:

```
00083180: 003a8 . 00378 [00]
```

The heap block states that the size of the previous block is 003a8 and the size of the current block is 00378. Interestingly enough, the prior block is reporting its own size to be 0x20 bytes, which does not match up well. Even worse, the last free block in the segment states that both the previous and current sizes are 0. If we go even further back in the heap segment, we can see that all the heap entries prior to 00083160 make sense (at least in the sense that the heap entry metadata seems intact). One of the potential theories should now start to take shape. The usage of the heap block at location 00083160 seems suspect, and it's possible that the usage of that heap block caused the metadata of the following block to become corrupt. Who allocated the heap block at 00083160? If we take a closer look at the block, we can see if we can recognize the content:

```
0:000> dd 00083160
00083160   000d0004 000c0199 00000000 00730069
00083170   00740053 00690072 0067006e 00680053
00083180   0075006f 0064006c 00650052 00720070
00083190   0054006f 00650068 00720043 00730061
000831a0   00000068 00000000 00000000 00000000
000831b0   00000000 00000000 00000000 00000000
000831c0   00000000 00000000 00000000 00000000
000831d0   00000000 00000000 00000000 00000000
```

Parts of the block seem to resemble a string. If we use the du command on the block starting at address 000830f8+0xc, we see the following:

```
0:000> du 00083160+c
0008316c   "isStringShouldReproTheCrash"
```

The string definitely looks familiar. It is the same string (or part of it) that we passed in on the command line. Furthermore, the string seems to stretch all the way to address 000831a0, which crosses the boundary to the next reported free block at address 00083180. If we dump out the heap entry at address 00083180, we can see the following:

```
0:000> dt _HEAP_ENTRY 00083180
   +0x000 Size             : 0x6f
```

```
+0x002  PreviousSize       : 0x75
+0x000  SubSegmentCode     : 0x0075006
+0x004  SmallTagIndex      : 0x6c 'l'
+0x005  Flags              : 0 ''
+0x006  UnusedBytes        : 0x64 'd'
+0x007  SegmentIndex       : 0 ''
```

The current and previous size fields correspond to part of the string that crossed the boundary of the previous block. Armed with the knowledge of which string seemed to have caused the heap block overwrite, we can turn to code reviewing and figure out relatively easily that the string copy function wrote more than the maximum number of characters allowed in the destination string, causing an overwrite of the next heap block. While the heap manager was unable to detect the overwrite at the exact point it occurred, it definitely detected the heap block overwrite later on in the execution, which resulted in an access violation because the heap was in an inconsistent state.

In the previous simplistic application, analyzing the heap at the point of the access violation yielded a very clear picture of what overwrote the heap block and subsequently, via code reviewing, who the culprit was. Needless to say, it is not always possible to arrive at these conclusions merely by inspecting the contents of the heap blocks. The complexity of the system can dramatically reduce your success when using this approach. Furthermore, even if you do get some clues to what is overwriting the heap blocks, it might be really difficult to find the culprit by merely reviewing code. Ultimately, the easiest way to figure out a heap corruption would be if we could break execution when the memory is being overwritten rather than after. Fortunately, the Application Verifier tool provides a powerful facility that enables this behavior. The application verifier test setting commonly used when tracking down heap corruptions is called the Heaps test setting (also referred to as pageheap). Pageheap works on the basis of surrounding the heap blocks with a protection layer that serves to isolate the heap blocks from one another. If a heap block is overwritten, the protection layer detects the overwrite as close to the source as possible and breaks execution, giving the developer the ability to investigate why the overwrite occurred. Pageheap runs in two different modes: normal pageheap and full pageheap. The primary difference between the two modes is the strength of the protection layer. Normal pageheap uses fill patterns in an attempt to detect heap block corruptions. The utilization of fill patterns requires that another call be made to the heap manager post corruption so that the heap manager has the chance to validate the integrity (check fill patterns) of the heap block and report any inconsistencies. Additionally, normal page heap keeps the stack trace for all allocations, making it easier to understand who allocated the memory. Figure 6.10 illustrates what a heap block looks like when normal page heap is turned on.

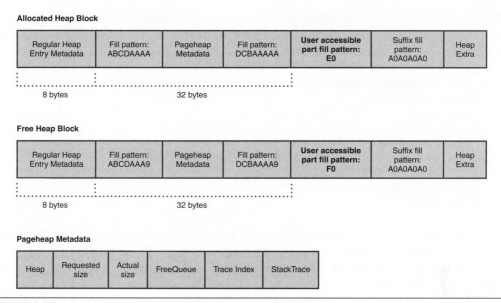

**Figure 6.10** Normal page heap block layout

The primary difference between a regular heap block and a normal page heap block is the addition of pageheap metadata. The pageheap metadata contains information, such as the block requested and actual sizes, but perhaps the most useful member of the metadata is the stack trace. The stack trace member allows the developer to get the full stack trace of the origins of the allocation (that is, where it was allocated). This aids greatly when looking at a corrupt heap block, as it gives you clues to who the owner of the heap block is and affords you the luxury of narrowing down the scope of the code review. Imagine that the `HeapAlloc` call in Listing 6.6 resulted in the following pointer: `0019e260`. To dump out the contents of the pageheap metadata, we must first subtract 32 (`0x20`) bytes from the pointer.

```
0:000> dd 0019e4b8-0x20
0019e498   abcdaaaa 80081000 00000014 0000003c
0019e4a8   00000018 00000000 0028697c dcbaaaaa
0019e4b8   e0e0e0e0 e0e0e0e0 e0e0e0e0 e0e0e0e0
0019e4c8   e0e0e0e0 a0a0a0a0 a0a0a0a0 00000000
0019e4d8   00000000 00000000 000a0164 00001000
0019e4e8   00180178 00180178 00000000 00000000
0019e4f8   00000000 00000000 00000000 00000000
0019e508   00000000 00000000 00000000 00000000
```

Here, we can clearly see the starting (abcdaaaa) and ending (dcbaaaaa) fill patterns that enclose the metadata. To see the pageheap metadata in a more digestible form, we can use the _DPH_BLOCK_INFORMATION data type:

```
0:000> dt _DPH_BLOCK_INFORMATION 0019e4b8-0x20
   +0x000 StartStamp      :
   +0x004 Heap            : 0x80081000
   +0x008 RequestedSize   :
   +0x00c ActualSize      :
   +0x010 FreeQueue       : _LIST_ENTRY 18-0
   +0x010 TraceIndex      : 0x18
   +0x018 StackTrace      : 0x0028697c
   +0x01c EndStamp        :
```

The stack trace member contains the stack trace of the allocation. To see the stack trace, we have to use the dds command, which displays the contents of a range of memory under the assumption that the contents in the range are a series of addresses in the symbol table.

```
0:000> dds 0x0028697c
0028697c  abcdaaaa
00286980  00000001
00286984  00000006
...
...
...
0028699c  7c949d18 ntdll!RtlAllocateHeapSlowly+0x44
002869a0  7c91b298 ntdll!RtlAllocateHeap+0xe64
002869a4  01001224 06overrun!DupString+0x24
002869a8  010011eb 06overrun!wmain+0x2b
002869ac  010013a9 06overrun!wmainCRTStartup+0x12b
002869b0  7c816d4f kernel32!BaseProcessStart+0x23
002869b4  00000000
002869b8  00000000
...
...
...
```

The shortened version of the output of the dds command shows us the stack trace of the allocating code. I cannot stress the usefulness of the recorded stack trace database enough. Whether you are looking at heap corruptions or memory leaks, given any pageheap block, you can very easily get to the stack trace of the allocating code, which in turn allows you to focus your efforts on that area of the code.

Now let's see how the normal pageheap facility can be used to track down the memory corruption shown earlier in Listing 6.6. Enable normal pageheap on the application (see Appendix A, "Application Verifier Test Settings"), and start the process under the debugger using `ThisStringShouldReproTheCrash` as input. Listing 6.8 shows how Application Verifier breaks execution because of a corrupted heap block.

**Listing 6.8**   Application verifier reported heap block corruption

```
...

...

...

0:000> g
Press any key to start
Copy of string: ThisStringShouldReproTheCrash


=======================================
VERIFIER STOP 00000008 : pid 0x640: Corrupted heap block.

      00081000 : Heap handle used in the call.
      001A04D0 : Heap block involved in the operation.
      00000014 : Size of the heap block.
      00000000 : Reserved



=======================================
This verifier stop is not continuable. Process will be terminated
when you use the `go' debugger command.


=======================================

(640.6a8): Break instruction exception - code 80000003 (first chance)
eax=000001ff ebx=0040acac ecx=7c91eb05 edx=0006f949 esi=00000000 edi=000001ff
eip=7c901230 esp=0006f9dc ebp=0006fbdc iopl=0         nv up ei pl nz na po nc
cs=001b  ss=0023  ds=0023  es=0023  fs=003b  gs=0000            efl=00000202
ntdll!DbgBreakPoint:
7c901230 cc              int     3
```

The information presented by Application Verifier gives us the pointer to the heap block that was corrupted. From here, getting the stack trace of the allocating code is trivial.

```
0:000> dt _DPH_BLOCK_INFORMATION 001A04D0-0x20
   +0x000 StartStamp       : 0xabcdaaaa
```

```
   +0x004 Heap            : 0x80081000
   +0x008 RequestedSize   : 0x14
   +0x00c ActualSize      : 0x3c
   +0x010 FreeQueue       : _LIST_ENTRY [ 0x18 - 0x0 ]
   +0x010 TraceIndex      : 0x18
   +0x018 StackTrace      : 0x0028697c
   +0x01c EndStamp        : 0xdcbaaaaa
0:000> dds 0x0028697c
0028697c  abcdaaaa
00286980  00000001
00286984  00000006
00286988  00000001
0028698c  00000014
00286990  00081000
00286994  00000000
00286998  0028699c
0028699c  7c949d18 ntdll!RtlAllocateHeapSlowly+0x44
002869a0  7c91b298 ntdll!RtlAllocateHeap+0xe64
002869a4  01001202 06overrun!DupString+0x22
002869a8  010011c1 06overrun!wmain+0x31
002869ac  0100138d 06overrun!wmainCRTStartup+0x12f
002869b0  7c816fd7 kernel32!BaseProcessStart+0x23
...
...
...
```

Knowing the stack trace allows us to efficiently find the culprit by narrowing down the scope of the code review.

If you compare and contrast the non-Application Verifier-enabled approach of finding out why a process has crashed with the Application Verifier-enabled approach, you will quickly see how much more efficient it is. By using normal pageheap, all the information regarding the corrupted block is given to us, and we can use that to analyze the heap block and get the stack trace of the allocating code. Although normal pageheap breaks execution and gives us all this useful information, it still does so only after a corruption has occurred, and it still requires us to do some backtracking to figure out why it happened. Is there a mechanism to break execution even closer to the corruption? Absolutely! Normal pageheap is only one of the two modes of pageheap that can be enabled. The other mode is known as full pageheap. In addition to its own unique fill patterns, full pageheap adds the notion of a guard page to each heap block. A guard page is a page of inaccessible memory that is placed either at the start or at the end of a heap block. Placing the guard page at the start of the heap block protects against heap block underruns, and placing it at the end protects against heap overruns. Figure 6.11 illustrates the layout of a full pageheap block.

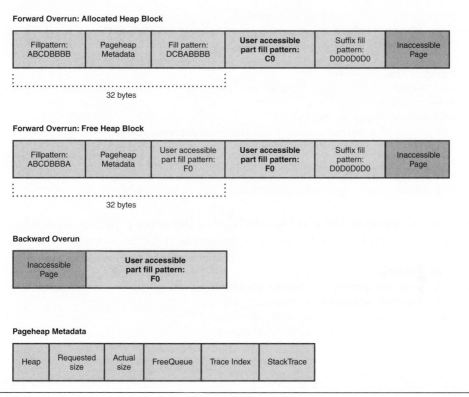

**Figure 6.11**  Full page heap block layout

The inaccessible page is added to protect against heap block overruns or underruns. If a faulty piece of code writes to the inaccessible page, it causes an access violation, and execution breaks on the spot. This allows us to avoid any type of backtracking strategy to figure out the origins of the corruption.

Now we can once again run our sample application, this time with full pageheap enabled (see Appendix A), and see where the debugger breaks execution.

```
...
...
...
0:000> g
Press any key to start
(414.494): Access violation - code c0000005 (first chance)
First chance exceptions are reported before any exception handling.
```

```
This exception may be expected and handled.
eax=006f006f ebx=7ffd7000 ecx=005d5000 edx=006fefd8 esi=7c9118f1 edi=00011970
eip=77c47ea2 esp=0006ff20 ebp=0006ff20 iopl=0         nv up ei pl nz na po nc
cs=001b  ss=0023  ds=0023  es=0023  fs=003b  gs=0000            efl=00010202
msvcrt!wcscpy+0xe:
77c47ea2 668901            mov     word ptr [ecx],ax        ds:0023:005d5000=????
0:000> kb
ChildEBP RetAddr  Args to Child
0006ff20 01001221 005d4fe8 006fefc0 00000000 msvcrt!wcscpy+0xe
0006ff34 010011c1 006fefc0 00000000 0006ffc0 06overrun!DupString+0x41
0006ff44 0100138d 00000002 006fef98 00774f88 06overrun!wmain+0x31
0006ffc0 7c816fd7 00011970 7c9118f1 7ffd7000 06overrun!wmainCRTStartup+0x12f
0006fff0 00000000 0100125e 00000000 78746341 kernel32!BaseProcessStart+0x23
```

This time, an access violation is recorded during the string copy call. If we take a closer look at the heap block at the point of the access violation, we see

```
0:000> dd 005d4fe8
005d4fe8  00680054 00730069 00740053 00690072
005d4ff8  0067006e 00680053 ???????? ????????
005d5008  ???????? ???????? ???????? ????????
005d5018  ???????? ???????? ???????? ????????
005d5028  ???????? ???????? ???????? ????????
005d5038  ???????? ???????? ???????? ????????
005d5048  ???????? ???????? ???????? ????????
005d5058  ???????? ???????? ???????? ????????
0:000> du 005d4fe8
005d4fe8  "ThisStringSh?????????????????????"
005d5028  "??????????????????????????????????"
005d5068  "??????????????????????????????????"
005d50a8  "??????????????????????????????????"
005d50e8  "??????????????????????????????????"
005d5128  "??????????????????????????????????"
005d5168  "??????????????????????????????????"
005d51a8  "??????????????????????????????????"
005d51e8  "??????????????????????????????????"
005d5228  "??????????????????????????????????"
005d5268  "??????????????????????????????????"
005d52a8  "??????????????????????????????????"
```

We can make two important observations about the dumps:

- The string we are copying has overwritten the suffix fill pattern of the block, as well as the heap entry.

- At the point of the access violation, the string copied so far is `ThisStringSh`, which indicates that the string copy function is not yet done and is about to write to the inaccessible page placed at the end of the heap block by Application Verifier.

By enabling full pageheap, we were able to break execution when the corruption occurred rather than after. This can be a huge time-saver, as you have the offending code right in front of you when the corruption occurs, and finding out why the corruption occurred just got a lot easier. One of the questions that might be going through your mind is, "Why not always run with full pageheap enabled?" Well, full pageheap is very resource intensive. Remember that full pageheap places one page of inaccessible memory at the end (or beginning) of each allocation. If the process you are debugging is memory hungry, the usage of pageheap might increase the overall memory consumption by an order of magnitude.

In addition to heap block overruns, we can experience the reciprocal: heap underruns. Although not as common, heap underruns overwrite the part of the heap block prior to the user-accessible part. This can be because of bad pointer arithmetic causing a premature write to the heap block. Because normal pageheap protects the pageheap metadata by using fill patterns, it can trap heap underrun scenarios as well. Full pageheap, by default, places a guard page at the end of the heap block and will not break on heap underruns. Fortunately, using the backward overrun option of full pageheap (see Appendix A), we can tell it to place a guard page at the front of the allocation rather than at the end and trap the underrun class of problems as well.

The `!heap` extension command previously used to analyze heap state can also be used when the process is running under pageheap. By using the –p flag, we can tell the `!heap` extension command that the heap in question is pageheap enabled. The options available for the –p flag are

```
heap -p            Dump all page heaps.
heap -p -h ADDR    Detailed dump of page heap at ADDR.
heap -p -a ADDR    Figure out what heap block is at ADDR.
heap -p -t [N]     Dump N collected traces with heavy heap users.
heap -p -tc [N]    Dump N traces sorted by count usage (eqv. with -t).
heap -p -ts [N]    Dump N traces sorted by size.
heap -p -fi [N]    Dump last N fault injection traces.
```

For example, the heap block returned from the HeapAlloc call in our sample application resembles the following when used with the –p and –a flags:

```
0:000> !heap -p -a 005d4fe8
   address 005d4fe8 found in
```

```
    _DPH_HEAP_ROOT @ 81000
       in busy allocation (  DPH_HEAP_BLOCK:          UserAddr          UserSize -
VirtAddr          VirtSize)
                                            8430c:          5d4fe8                14 -
5d4000              2000
      7c91b298 ntdll!RtlAllocateHeap+0x00000e64
      01001202 06overrun!DupString+0x00000022
      010011c1 06overrun!wmain+0x00000031
      0100138d 06overrun!wmainCRTStartup+0x0000012f
      7c816fd7 kernel32!BaseProcessStart+0x00000023
```

The output shows us the recorded stack trace as well as other auxiliary information, such as which fill pattern is in use. The fill patterns can give us clues to the status of the heap block (allocated or freed). Another useful switch is the −t switch. The −t switch allows us to dump out part of the stack trace database to get more information about all the stacks that have allocated memory. If you are debugging a process that is using up a ton of memory and want to know which part of the process is responsible for the biggest allocations, the heap −p −t command can be used.

## Heap Handle Mismatches

The heap manager keeps a list of active heaps in a process. The heaps are considered separate entities in the sense that the internal per-heap state is only valid within the context of that particular heap. Developers working with the heap manager must take great care to respect this separation by ensuring that the correct heaps are used when allocating and freeing heap memory. The separation is exposed to the developer by using heap handles in the heap API calls. Each heap handle uniquely represents a particular heap in the list of heaps for the process. An example of this is calling the GetProcessHeap API, which returns a unique handle to the default process. Another example is calling the HeapCreate API, which returns a unique handle to the newly created heap.

If the uniqueness is broken, heap corruption will ensue. Listing 6.9 illustrates an application that breaks the uniqueness of heaps.

**Listing 6.9** Example of heap handle mismatch

```
#include <windows.h>
#include <stdio.h>
#include <conio.h>

#define MAX_SMALL_BLOCK_SIZE    20000

HANDLE hSmallHeap=0;
```

```
HANDLE hLargeHeap=0;

VOID* AllocMem(ULONG ulSize);
VOID FreeMem(VOID* pMem, ULONG ulSize);
BOOL InitHeaps();
VOID FreeHeaps();

int __cdecl wmain (int argc, wchar_t* pArgs[])
{
    printf("Press any key to start\n");
    _getch();

    if(InitHeaps())
    {
        BYTE* pBuffer1=(BYTE*) AllocMem(20);
        BYTE* pBuffer2=(BYTE*) AllocMem(20000);

        //
        // Use allocated memory
        //

        FreeMem(pBuffer1, 20);
        FreeMem(pBuffer2, 20000);
        FreeHeaps();
    }

    printf("Done...exiting application\n");
    return 0;
}

BOOL InitHeaps()
{
    BOOL bRet=TRUE ;

    hSmallHeap = GetProcessHeap();
    hLargeHeap = HeapCreate(0, 0, 0);
    if(!hLargeHeap)
    {
        bRet=FALSE;
    }

    return bRet;
}

VOID FreeHeaps()
{
```

*(continues)*

6. MEMORY CORRUPTION PART II—HEAPS

**Listing 6.9**  Example of heap handle mismatch *(continued)*

```
    if(hLargeHeap)
    {
        HeapDestroy(hLargeHeap);
        hLargeHeap=NULL;
    }
}


VOID* AllocMem(ULONG ulSize)
{
    VOID* pAlloc = NULL ;

    if(ulSize<MAX_SMALL_BLOCK_SIZE)
    {
        pAlloc=HeapAlloc(hSmallHeap, 0, ulSize);
    }
    else
    {
        pAlloc=HeapAlloc(hLargeHeap, 0, ulSize);
    }


    return pAlloc;
}


VOID FreeMem(VOID* pAlloc, ULONG ulSize)
{
    if(ulSize<=MAX_SMALL_BLOCK_SIZE)
    {
        HeapFree(hSmallHeap, 0, pAlloc);
    }
    else
    {
        HeapFree(hLargeHeap, 0, pAlloc);
    }
}
```

The source code and binary for Listing 6.9 can be found in the following folders:

Source code: `C:\AWD\Chapter6\Mismatch`

Binary: `C:\AWDBIN\WinXP.x86.chk\06Mismatch.exe`

The application in Listing 6.9 seems pretty straightforward. The main function requests a couple of allocations using the `AllocMem` helper function. Once done with the allocations, it calls the `FreeMem` helper API to free the memory. The allocation helper APIs work with the memory from either the default process heap (if the allocation is below a certain size) or a private heap (created in the `InitHeaps` API) if the size is larger than the threshold. If we run the application, we see that it successfully finishes execution:

```
C:\AWDBIN\WinXP.x86.chk\06Mismatch.exe
Press any key to start
Done...exiting application
```

We might be tempted to conclude that the application works as expected and sign off on it. However, before we do so, let's use Application Verifier and enable full page-heap on the application and rerun it. This time, the application never finished. As a matter of fact, judging from the crash dialog that appears, it looks like we have a crash. In order to get some more information on the crash, we run the application under the debugger:

```
...
...
...
0:000> g
Press any key to start
(118.3c8): Access violation - code c0000005 (first chance)
First chance exceptions are reported before any exception handling.
This exception may be expected and handled.
eax=0006fc54 ebx=00000000 ecx=0211b000 edx=0211b008 esi=021161e0 edi=021161e0
eip=7c96893a esp=0006fbec ebp=0006fc20 iopl=0         nv up ei ng nz ac po cy
cs=001b  ss=0023  ds=0023  es=0023  fs=003b  gs=0000          efl=00010293
ntdll!RtlpDphIsNormalHeapBlock+0x81:
7c96893a 8039a0          cmp     byte ptr [ecx],0A0h        ds:0023:0211b000=??
0:000> kb
ChildEBP RetAddr  Args to Child
0006fc20 7c96ac47 00081000 021161e0 0006fc54 ntdll!RtlpDphIsNormalHeapBlock+0x81
0006fc44 7c96ae5a 00081000 01000002 00000007 ntdll!RtlpDphNormalHeapFree+0x1e
0006fc94 7c96defb 00080000 01000002 021161e0 ntdll!RtlpDebugPageHeapFree+0x79
0006fd08 7c94a5d0 00080000 01000002 021161e0 ntdll!RtlDebugFreeHeap+0x2c
0006fdf0 7c9268ad 00080000 01000002 021161e0 ntdll!RtlFreeHeapSlowly+0x37
0006fec0 003ab9eb 00080000 00000000 021161e0 ntdll!RtlFreeHeap+0xf9
0006ff18 010012cf 00080000 00000000 021161e0 vfbasics!AVrfpRtlFreeHeap+0x16b
0006ff2c 010011d3 021161e0 00004e20 021161e0 06mismatch!FreeMem+0x1f
0006ff44 01001416 00000001 02060fd8 020daf80 06mismatch!wmain+0x53
0006ffc0 7c816fd7 00011970 7c9118f1 7ffdc000 06mismatch!wmainCRTStartup+0x12f
0006fff0 00000000 010012e7 00000000 78746341 kernel32!BaseProcessStart+0x23
```

From the stack trace, we can see that our application was trying to free a block of memory when the heap manager access violated. To find out which of the two memory allocations we were freeing, we unassemble the `06mismatch!wmain` function and see which of the calls correlate to the address located at `06mismatch!wmain+0x55`.

```
0:000> u 06mismatch!wmain+0x53-10
06mismatch!wmain+0x43:
010011c3 0000              add     byte ptr [eax],al
010011c5 68204e0000        push    4E20h
010011ca 8b4df8            mov     ecx,dword ptr [ebp-8]
010011cd 51                push    ecx
010011ce e8dd000000        call    06mismatch!FreeMem (010012b0)
010011d3 e858000000        call    06mismatch!FreeHeaps (01001230)
010011d8 688c100001        push    offset 06mismatch!`string' (0100108c)
010011dd ff1550100001      call    dword ptr [06mismatch!_imp__printf (01001050)]
```

Since the call prior to `06mismatch!FreeHeaps` is a `FreeMem`, we know that the last `FreeMem` call in our code is causing the problem. We can now employ code reviewing to see if anything is wrong. From Listing 6.9, the `FreeMem` function frees memory either on the default process heap or on a private heap. Furthermore, it looks like the decision is dependent on the size of the block. If the block size is less than or equal to 20Kb, it uses the default process heap. Otherwise, the private heap is used. Our allocation was exactly 20Kb, which means that the `FreeMem` function attempted to free the memory from the default process heap. Is this correct? One way to easily find out is dumping out the pageheap block metadata, which has a handle to the owning heap contained inside:

```
0:000> dt _DPH_BLOCK_INFORMATION 021161e0-0x20
   +0x000 StartStamp     : 0xabcdbbbb
   +0x004 Heap           : 0x02111000
   +0x008 RequestedSize  : 0x4e20
   +0x00c ActualSize     : 0x5000
   +0x010 FreeQueue      : _LIST_ENTRY [ 0x21 - 0x0 ]
   +0x010 TraceIndex     : 0x21
   +0x018 StackTrace     : 0x00287510
   +0x01c EndStamp       : 0xdcbabbbb
```

The owning heap for this heap block is `0x02111000`. Next, we find out what the default process heap is:

```
0:000> x 06mismatch!hSmallHeap
01002008 06mismatch!hSmallHeap = 0x00080000
```

The two heaps do not match up, and we are faced with essentially freeing a block of memory owned by heap 0x02111000 on heap 0x00080000. This is also the reason Application Verifier broke execution, because a mismatch in heaps causes serious stability issues. Armed with the knowledge of the reason for the stop, it should now be pretty straightforward to figure out why our application mismatched the two heaps. Because we are relying on size to determine which heaps to allocate and free the memory on, we can quickly see that the AllocMem function uses the following conditional:

```
if(ulSize<MAX_SMALL_BLOCK_SIZE)
{
    pAlloc=HeapAlloc(hSmallHeap, 0, ulSize);
}
```

while the FreeMem function uses:

```
if(ulSize<=MAX_SMALL_BLOCK_SIZE)
{
    HeapFree(hSmallHeap, 0, pAlloc);
}
```

The allocating conditional checks that the allocation size is less than the threshold, whereas the freeing conditional checks that it is *less than or equal*. Hence, when freeing an allocation of size 20Kb, incorrectly uses the default process heap.

In addition to being able to analyze and get to the bottom of heap mismatch problems, another very important lesson can be learned from our exercise: Never assume that the application works correctly just because no errors are reported during a normal noninstrumented run. As you have already seen, heap corruption problems do not always surface during tests that are run without any type of debugging help. Only when a debugger is attached and the application verifier is enabled do the problems surface. The reason is simple. In a nondebugger, non–Application Verifier run, the heap corruption still occurs but might not have enough time to surface in the form of an access violation. Say that the test runs through scenarios A, B, and C, and the heap corruption occurs in scenario C. After the heap has been corrupted, the application exits without any sign of the heap corruption, and you are led to believe that everything is working correctly. Once the application ships and gets in the hands of the customer, they run the same scenarios, albeit in a different order: C, B, and A. The first scenario ran C, immediately causing the heap corruption, but the application does not exit; rather, it continues running with scenario B and A, providing for a much larger window for the heap corruption to actually affect the application.

## Heap Reuse After Deletion

Next to heap overruns, heap reuse after deletion is the second most common source of heap corruptions. As you have already seen, after a heap block has been freed, it is put on the free lists (or look aside list) by the heap manager. From there on, it is considered invalid for use by the application. If an application uses the free block in any way, shape, or form, the state of the block on the free list will most likely be corrupted and the application will crash.

Before we take a look at some practical examples of heap reuse after free, let's review the deletion process. Figure 6.12 shows a hypothetical example of a heap segment.

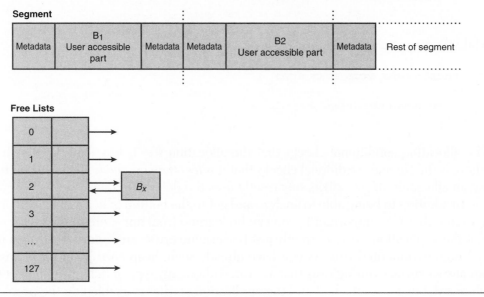

**Figure 6.12**   Hypothetical example of a heap segment

The segment consists of two busy blocks ($B_1$ and $B_2$) whose user-accessible part is surrounded by their associated metadata. Additionally, the free list contains one free block ($B_x$) of size 16. If the application frees block $B_1$, the heap manager, first and foremost, checks to see if the block can be coalesced with any adjacent free blocks. Because there are no adjacent free blocks, the heap manager simply updates the status of the block (flags field of the metadata) to free and updates the corresponding free list to include $B_1$. It is critical to note that the free list consists of a forward link (FLINK) and a backward link (BLINK) that each points to the next and previous free block in the list. Are the FLINK and BLINK pointers part of a separately allocated free list node? Not quite—for efficiency reasons, when a block is freed, the structure of the existing free block changes. More specifically, the user-accessible portion of the heap block is overwritten by the heap manager with the FLINK and BLINK pointers, each pointing to the next and previous free block on the free list. In our hypothetical example in Figure 6.12, $B_1$ is inserted at the beginning of the free list corresponding to size 16. The user-accessible portion of $B_1$ is replaced with a FLINK that points to $B_x$ and a BLINK that points to the start of the list (itself). The existing free block $B_x$ is also updated by the BLINK pointing to $B_1$. Figure 6.13 illustrates the resulting layout after freeing block $B_1$.

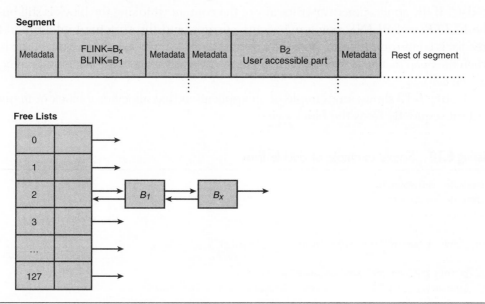

**Figure 6.13**   Heap segment and free lists after freeing $B_1$

Next, when the application frees block $B_2$, the heap manager finds an adjacent free block ($B_1$) and coalesces both blocks into one large free block. As part of the coalescing process, the heap manager must remove block B1 from the free list since it no longer exists and add the new larger block to its corresponding free list. The resulting large block's user-accessible part now contains FLINK and BLINK pointers that are updated according to the state of the free list.

So far, we have assumed that all heap blocks freed make their way to the back end allocator's free lists. Although it's true that some free blocks go directly to the free lists, some of the allocations may end up going to the front end allocator's look aside list. When a heap block goes into the look aside list, the primary differences can be seen in the heap block metadata:

- Heap blocks that go into the look aside list have their status bit set to busy (in comparison to free in free lists)
- The look aside list is a singly linked list (in comparison to the free lists doubly linked), and hence only the FLINK pointer is considered valid.

The most important aspect of freeing memory, as related to heap reuse after free, is the fact that the structure of the heap block changes once it is freed. The user-accessible portion of the heap block is now used for internal bookkeeping to keep the free lists up-to-date. If the application overwrites any of the content (thinking the block is still busy), the FLINK and BLINK pointers become corrupt, and the structural integrity of the free list is compromised. The net result is most likely a crash somewhere down the road when the heap manager tries to manipulate the free list (usually during another allocate or free call).

Listing 6.10 shows an example of an application that allocates a block of memory and subsequently frees the block twice.

**Listing 6.10**   Simple example of double free

```
#include <windows.h>
#include <stdio.h>
#include <conio.h>

int __cdecl wmain (int argc, wchar_t* pArgs[])
{
    printf("Press any key to start\n");
    _getch();

    BYTE* pByte=(BYTE*) HeapAlloc(GetProcessHeap(), 0, 10);
    (*pByte)=10;
    HeapFree(GetProcessHeap(), 0, pByte);

    HeapFree(GetProcessHeap(), 0, pByte);

    printf("Done...exiting application\n");
    return 0;
}
```

The source code and binary for Listing 6.9 can be found in the following folders:

Source code: C:\AWD\Chapter6\DblFree

Binary: C:\AWDBIN\WinXP.x86.chk\06DblFree.exe

Running the application yields no errors:

```
C:\AWDBIN\WinXP.x86.chk\06DblFree.exe
```

To make sure that nothing out of the ordinary is happening, let's start the application under the debugger and make our way to the first heap allocation.

```
...
...
...
0:001> u wmain
06dblfree!wmain:
01001180 55                 push    ebp
01001181 8bec               mov     ebp,esp
01001183 51                 push    ecx
01001184 68a8100001         push    offset 06dblfree!`string' (010010a8)
01001189 ff1548100001       call    dword ptr [06dblfree!_imp__printf (01001048)]
0100118f 83c404             add     esp,4
01001192 ff1550100001       call    dword ptr [06dblfree!_imp___getch (01001050)]
01001198 6a0a               push    0Ah
0:001> u
06dblfree!wmain+0x1a:
0100119a 6a00               push    0
0100119c ff1508100001       call    dword ptr [06dblfree!_imp__GetProcessHeap
(01001008)]
010011a2 50                 push    eax
010011a3 ff1500100001       call    dword ptr [06dblfree!_imp__HeapAlloc (01001000)]
010011a9 8945fc             mov     dword ptr [ebp-4],eax
010011ac 8b45fc             mov     eax,dword ptr [ebp-4]
010011af c6000a             mov     byte ptr [eax],0Ah
010011b2 8b4dfc             mov     ecx,dword ptr [ebp-4]
0:001> g 010011a9
eax=000830c0 ebx=7ffde000 ecx=7c9106eb edx=00080608 esi=01c7078e edi=83485b7a
eip=010011a9 esp=0006ff40 ebp=0006ff44 iopl=0         nv up ei pl zr na pe nc
cs=001b  ss=0023  ds=0023  es=0023  fs=003b  gs=0000              efl=00000246
06dblfree!wmain+0x29:
010011a9 8945fc             mov     dword ptr [ebp-4],eax
ss:0023:0006ff40={msvcrt!__winitenv (77c61a40)}
```

Register eax now contains the pointer to the newly allocated block of memory:

```
0:000> dt _HEAP_ENTRY 000830c0-0x8
   +0x000 Size            : 3
   +0x002 PreviousSize    : 3
   +0x000 SubSegmentCode  : 0x00030003
```

```
+0x004 SmallTagIndex     : 0x21 '!'
+0x005 Flags             : 0x1 ''
+0x006 UnusedBytes       : 0xe ''
+0x007 SegmentIndex      : 0 ''
```

Nothing seems to be out of the ordinary—the size fields all seem reasonable, and the flags field indicates that the block is busy. Now, continue execution past the first call to HeapFree and dump out the same heap block.

```
0:000> dt _HEAP_ENTRY 000830c0-0x8
+0x000 Size              : 3
+0x002 PreviousSize      : 3
+0x000 SubSegmentCode    : 0x00030003
+0x004 SmallTagIndex     : 0x21 '!'
+0x005 Flags             : 0x1 ''
+0x006 UnusedBytes       : 0xe ''
+0x007 SegmentIndex      : 0 ''
```

Even after freeing the block, the metadata looks identical. The flags field even has its busy bit still set, indicating that the block is not freed. The key here is to remember that when a heap block is freed, it can go to one of two places: look aside list or free lists. When a heap block goes on the look aside list, the heap block status is kept as busy. On the free lists, however, the status is set to free.

In our particular free operation, the block seems to have gone on the look aside list. When a block goes onto the look aside list, the first part of the user-accessible portion of the block gets overwritten with the FLINK pointer that points to the next available block on the look aside list. The user-accessible portion of our block resembles

```
0:000> dd 000830c0
000830c0   00000000 00080178 00000000 00000000
000830d0   000301e6 00001000 00080178 00080178
000830e0   00000000 00000000 00000000 00000000
000830f0   00000000 00000000 00000000 00000000
00083100   00000000 00000000 00000000 00000000
00083110   00000000 00000000 00000000 00000000
00083120   00000000 00000000 00000000 00000000
00083130   00000000 00000000 00000000 00000000
```

As you can see, the FLINK pointer in our case is NULL, which means that this is the first free heap block. Next, continue execution until right after the second call to HeapFree (of the same block). Once again, we take a look at the state of the heap block:

```
0:000> dt _HEAP_ENTRY 000830c0-0x8
   +0x000 Size            : 3
   +0x002 PreviousSize    : 3
   +0x000 SubSegmentCode  : 0x00030003
   +0x004 SmallTagIndex   : 0x21 '!'
   +0x005 Flags           : 0x1 ''
   +0x006 UnusedBytes     : 0xe ''
   +0x007 SegmentIndex    : 0 ''
```

Nothing in the metadata seems to have changed. Block is still busy, and the size fields seem to be unchanged. Let's dump out the user-accessible portion and take a look at the FLINK pointer:

```
0:000> dd 000830c0
000830c0   000830c0 00080178 00000000 00000000
000830d0   000301e6 00001000 00080178 00080178
000830e0   00000000 00000000 00000000 00000000
000830f0   00000000 00000000 00000000 00000000
00083100   00000000 00000000 00000000 00000000
00083110   00000000 00000000 00000000 00000000
00083120   00000000 00000000 00000000 00000000
00083130   00000000 00000000 00000000 00000000
```

This time, FLINK points to another free heap block, with the user-accessible portion starting at location 000830c0. The block corresponding to location 000830c0 is the same block that we freed the first time. By double freeing, we have essentially managed to put the look aside list into a circular reference. The consequence of doing so can cause the heap manager to go into an infinite loop when subsequent heap operations force the heap manager to walk the free list with the circular reference.

At this point, if we resume execution, we notice that the application finishes execution. Why did it finish without failing in the heap code? For the look aside list circular reference to be exposed, another call has to be made to the heap manager that would cause it to walk the list and hit the circular link. Our application was finished after the second HeapFree call, and the heap manager never got a chance to fail. Even though the failure did not surface in the few runs we did, it is still a heap corruption, and it should be fixed. Corruption of a heap block on the look aside list (or the free lists) can cause serious problems for an application. Much like the previous types of heap corruptions, double freeing problems typically surface in the form of post corruption crashes when the heap manager needs to walk the look aside list (or free list). Is there a way to use Application Verifier in this case, as well to trap the problem as it is occurring? The same heaps test setting used throughout the chapter also makes a best attempt at catching double free problems. By tagging the heap blocks in a specific way, Application Verifier is able to catch double freeing problems as they occur and break execution, allowing the developer to take a closer look at the code that is trying to free the block the second time. Let's enable full pageheap on our application and rerun it under the debugger. Right away, you will see a first chance access violation occur with the following stack trace:

```
0:000> kb
ChildEBP RetAddr  Args to Child
0007fcc4 7c96ac47 00091000 005e4ff0 0007fcf8 ntdll!RtlpDphIsNormalHeapBlock+0x1c
0007fce8 7c96ae5a 00091000 01000002 00000000 ntdll!RtlpDphNormalHeapFree+0x1e
0007fd38 7c96defb 00090000 01000002 005e4ff0 ntdll!RtlpDebugPageHeapFree+0x79
0007fdac 7c94a5d0 00090000 01000002 005e4ff0 ntdll!RtlDebugFreeHeap+0x2c
0007fe94 7c9268ad 00090000 01000002 005e4ff0 ntdll!RtlFreeHeapSlowly+0x37
0007ff64 0100128a 00090000 00000000 005e4ff0 ntdll!RtlFreeHeap+0xf9
0007ff7c 01001406 00000001 0070cfd8 0079ef68 06DblFree!wmain+0x5a
0007ffc0 7c816fd7 00011970 7c9118f1 7ffd7000 06DblFree!__wmainCRTStartup+0x102
0007fff0 00000000 01001544 00000000 78746341 kernel32!BaseProcessStart+0x23
```

Judging from the stack, we can see that our `wmain` function is making its second call to `HeapFree`, which ends up access violating deep down in the heap manager code. Anytime you have this test setting turned on and experience a crash during a `HeapFree` call, the first thing you should check is whether a heap block is being freed twice. Because a heap block can go on the look aside list when freed (its state might still be set to busy even though it's considered free from a heap manager's perspective), the best way to figure out if it's really free is to use the `!heap -p -a <heap block>` command. Remember that this command dumps out detailed information about a page heap block, including the stack trace of the allocating or freeing code. Find the address of the heap block that we are freeing twice (as per preceding stack trace), and run the `!heap` extension command on it:

```
0:000> !heap -p -a 005d4ff0
    address 005d4ff0 found in
    _DPH_HEAP_ROOT @ 81000
    in free-ed allocation (  DPH_HEAP_BLOCK:        VirtAddr        VirtSize)
                                   8430c:           5d4000            2000
    7c9268ad ntdll!RtlFreeHeap+0x000000f9
    010011c5 06dblfree!wmain+0x00000045
    0100131b 06dblfree!wmainCRTStartup+0x0000012f
    7c816fd7 kernel32!BaseProcessStart+0x00000023
```

As you can see from the output, the heap block status is free. Additionally, the stack shows us the last operation performed on the heap block, which is the first free call made. The stack trace shown corresponds nicely to our first call to `HeapFree` in the wmain function. If we resume execution of the application, we notice several other first-chance access violations until we finally get an Application Verifier stop:

```
0:000> g
(1d4.6d4): Access violation - code c0000005 (first chance)
First chance exceptions are reported before any exception handling.
This exception may be expected and handled.
eax=0006fc7c ebx=00081000 ecx=00000008 edx=00000000 esi=005d4fd0 edi=0006fc4c
eip=7c969a1d esp=0006fc40 ebp=0006fc8c iopl=0         nv up ei pl nz na po cy
cs=001b  ss=0023  ds=0023  es=0023  fs=003b  gs=0000          efl=00010203
ntdll!RtlpDphReportCorruptedBlock+0x25:
7c969a1d f3a5            rep movs dword ptr es:[edi],dword ptr [esi]
es:0023:0006fc4c=00000000 ds:0023:005d4fd0=????????
0:000> g
(1d4.6d4): Access violation - code c0000005 (first chance)
First chance exceptions are reported before any exception handling.
This exception may be expected and handled.
eax=0006fc20 ebx=00000000 ecx=005d4ff0 edx=00000000 esi=00000000 edi=00000000
eip=7c968a84 esp=0006fc08 ebp=0006fc30 iopl=0         nv up ei pl zr na pe nc
cs=001b  ss=0023  ds=0023  es=0023  fs=003b  gs=0000          efl=00010246
ntdll!RtlpDphGetBlockSizeFromCorruptedBlock+0x13:
7c968a84 8b41e0          mov     eax,dword ptr [ecx-20h] ds:0023:005d4fd0=????????
0:000> g


=======================================
VERIFIER STOP 00000008 : pid 0x1D4: Corrupted heap block.

        00081000 : Heap handle used in the call.
        005D4FF0 : Heap block involved in the operation.
        00000000 : Size of the heap block.
        00000000 : Reserved


=======================================
This verifier stop is not continuable. Process will be terminated
when you use the `go' debugger command.

=======================================

(1d4.6d4): Break instruction exception - code 80000003 (first chance)
eax=000001ff ebx=0040acac ecx=7c91eb05 edx=0006f959 esi=00000000 edi=000001ff
eip=7c901230 esp=0006f9ec ebp=0006fbec iopl=0         nv up ei pl nz na po nc
cs=001b  ss=0023  ds=0023  es=0023  fs=003b  gs=0000          efl=00000202
ntdll!DbgBreakPoint:
7c901230 cc              int     3
```

The last-chance Application Verifier stop shown gives some basic information about the corrupted heap block. If you resume execution at this point, the application will simply terminate because this is a nonrecoverable stop.

This concludes our discussion of the problems associated with double freeing memory. As you have seen, the best tool for catching double freeing problems is to use the heaps test setting (full pageheap) available in Application Verifier. Not only does it report the problem at hand, but it also manages to break execution at the point where the problem really occurred rather than at a post corruption stage, making it much easier to figure out why the heap block was being corrupted. Using full pageheap gives you the strongest possible protection level available for memory-related problems in general. The means by which full pageheap is capable of giving you this protection is by separating the heap block metadata from the heap block itself. In a nonfull pageheap scenario, the metadata associated with a heap block is part of the heap block itself. If an application is off by a few bytes, it can very easily overwrite the metadata, corrupting the heap block and making it difficult for the heap manager to immediately report the problem. In contrast, using full pageheap, the metadata is kept in a secondary data structure with a one-way link to the real heap block. By using a one-way link, it is nearly impossible for faulty code to corrupt the heap block metadata, and, as such, full pageheap can almost always be trusted to contain intact information. The separation of metadata from the actual heap block is what gives full pageheap the capability to provide strong heap corruption detection.

## Summary

Heap corruption is a serious error that can wreak havoc on your application. A single, off-by-one byte corruption can cause your application to exhibit all sorts of odd behaviors. The application might crash, it might have unpredictable behavior, or it might even go into infinite loops. To make things worse, the net result of a heap corruption typically does not surface until after the corruption has occurred, making it extremely difficult to figure out the source of the heap corruption. To efficiently track down heap corruptions, you need a solid understanding of the internals of the heap manager. The first part of the chapter discussed the low-level details of how the heap manager works. We took a look at how a heap block travels through the various layers of the heap manager and how the status and block structure changes as it goes from being allocated to freed. We also took a look at some of the most common forms of heap corruptions (uninitialized state, heap over- and underruns, mismatched heap handles, and heap reuse after deletion) and how to manually analyze the heap at the point of a crash to figure out the source of the corruption. Additionally, we discussed how Application Verifier (pageheap) can be used to break execution closer to the source of the corruption, making it much easier to figure out the culprit. As some of the examples in this chapter show, heap corruptions might go undetected while software is being tested, only to surface on the customer's computer when run in a different environment and under different conditions. Making use of Application Verifier (pageheap) at all times is a prerequisite to ensuring that heap corruptions are detected before shipping software and avoiding costly problems on the customer site.

# CHAPTER 7

# SECURITY

Over a relatively short period of time, the attitude toward software security has changed dramatically, both from the developer perspective, as well as from the user perspective. Years ago, computers were mostly disconnected devices, and offline media, mostly floppy disks, was the main source of computer security problems. The big problem at that time was represented by viruses. Today, almost every computer security problem is remotely exploitable because of the high connectivity rate.

Older operating systems, such as Windows 95, provided no support for securing objects stored on the local computer. The advent of the Windows NT code base in consumer markets made a secure C2-compliant kernel available to consumers. Today, the consumer versions of the Windows operation system—namely Windows XP Home and Windows Vista Home—control the access to each object, and, as such, the chance increases for encountering an access denied failure. Another push comes from the security community to always run a process with the least privileged user. In this case, the host computer is isolated from security vulnerabilities that might exist in the applications. How feasible is it to run the application as a nonadministrator? Perhaps it is possible for a few applications, designed with security in mind, while the majority of them will still try to access a registry location or a file system location reserved only to administrators.

Hopefully, object security will become a first-class development pillar. This chapter provides the information required to start the journey toward successful understanding and fixing of software security problems. This chapter focuses primarily on steps executed when a legal operation completes with success of failure and doesn't describe unexpected behavior of code because of code defects (buffer overflow, integer overflow, buffer overrun), currently exploited by viruses, as it is covered very well in several reference books. In this chapter, we explore the following:

- The basics of Windows security and how Windows Security actually works. We summarize the essential information required to understand security-related problems.
- How to inspect various security elements using the debugger extensions. This section introduces several extension commands essential to debugging security aspects.
- How to combine the techniques and information presented so far in the book to resolve problems caused by unexpected security restrictions.

# Windows Security Overview

Any Windows securable object, which can be represented by a handle to it, has security information attached to it, and it is protected using standard Windows security mechanisms. The Windows security model uses three security concepts:

- The discretionary access control list (DACL): Describes what principal can use the object and how
- The identity of the user: Also known as principal
- The Security Reference Monitor (SRM): Uses the information available to restrict the access to the object protected by it

DACLs associated with Windows securable objects are managed by the object creator itself. The DACL is a component within another structure known as the security descriptor, which is a small piece of information stored along with the object in the secured store. The security descriptor is retrieved from the secured store, and it is used every time the object is accessed by a new principal. For example, the files security descriptors are stored in the NTFS file system, the registry keys security descriptors are stored in the registry hives, whereas the kernel objects have the security descriptors stored in the kernel address space.

The Windows SRM runs in the kernel address space, isolated from the user mode code. Most securable objects are created and managed by kernel components that use the address separation to protect the associated security descriptor from the user mode components. Because user mode components cannot use the kernel for implementing their own secure object brokers, several components in Windows implement custom security models using ideas similar to the Windows security mechanisms.

A custom object broker must enforce the mechanism for accessing its object. In other words, when designing a securable objects broker, you must ensure that this object cannot be accessed by using any other mechanism. In those cases, the object broker takes the SRM role and manages the object security descriptors in its proprietary ways. To ensure functional consistency with the rest of the operating system and use the same user interface controls in security settings, the object broker will most likely use the same data structures as Windows SRM.

The other essential component in access control is the security principal, created and certified by the operating system. The security principal is stored in an access token that aggregates the list of group security principals having the principal as a member, the list of special privileges granted by the operating system, plus other information used by the various components in the system.

The access to an object is represented by a collection of bits, each bit representing a right (specific to the object's nature) that can be granted or denied to a principal.

The next section describes all the security structures relevant to debugging Windows applications, and it presents various methods for inspecting them. Readers familiar with those concepts can skip this section. All examples use three new extension commands: `!sd`, `!token`, and `!sid`, available in the default extension loaded by debuggers. This chapter uses the 07sample.exe with the source code and binary located in the following folders:

Source code: `C:\AWD\Chapter7`

Binary: `C:\AWDBIN\WinXP.x86.chk\07sample.exe`

Because the security errors are often encountered in distributed applications, this chapter also uses the sample created for Chapter 8, "Interprocess Communication," consisting of a client application 08cli.exe, a library, 08comps.dll that contains the proxy-stub code, and a server application 08comsrv.exe. The 08comsrv.exe must be registered using the 08comsrv.exe /RegServer command line, and 08comps.dll must be registered using the regsvr32 08comps.dll command line. The source code and the binary files are located in the following folders:

Source code: `C:\AWD\Chapter8`

Binaries: `C:\AWDBIN\WinXP.x86.chk\08cli.exe, 08comps.dll,` and `08comsrv.exe.`

## The Security Identifier

The security identifier, also known as SID, is one of the basic concepts used in Windows Security. The SID identifies a principal or an attribute that is unique relative to the realm of identifiers available in the operating system using that SID. The SID is represented as a simple structure, declared in the winnt.h header file, as shown in Listing 7.1.

**Listing 7.1**  SID structure definition

```
typedef struct _SID_IDENTIFIER_AUTHORITY {
    BYTE   Value[6];
} SID_IDENTIFIER_AUTHORITY;

typedef struct _SID {
    BYTE   Revision;
    BYTE   SubAuthorityCount;
    SID_IDENTIFIER_AUTHORITY IdentifierAuthority;
    DWORD  SubAuthority[1];
} SID;
```

The SID structure is a variable length structure that contains a variable number of SubAuthority entries, designed to represent any principal. The SIDs are grouped based on the IdentifierAuthority. The layout of the SID in memory is trivial, easily understood by the computer, but difficult for humans to interpret. In technical documentation, the SIDs are represented as strings having the form of S-R-I-S-S-S-...-S, where R is the revision level, I identifies the authority controlling the SID, and S is one or more relative subauthority identifiers managed by the authority.

Windows SIDs have the Revision field set to 1 and can have up to six subauthorities. Windows has the IdentifierAuthority equal to five: {0, 0, 0, 0, 0, 5}. For example, Local System, identified as S-1-5-18, is represented in memory by the sequence of bytes shown in the next listing (separated in multiple lines corresponding to each SID component):

```
0:000> db 000840c8 Lc
000840c8  01
          01
             00 00 00 00 00 05-
                               12 00 00 00              . . . . . . . . . . . .
```

The first line represents the SID revision, the second line is the number of RID elements, followed by the Windows authority identifier, and the last one is the RID. This data structure is interpreted and converted to the "S-..." string format by the !sid extension command, as follows:

```
0:000> !sid 000840c8
SID is: S-1-5-18
```

## The Access Control List

The next fundamental structure encountered in debugging Windows security problems is the access control entry (ACE). The ACE indicates what rights are granted to a principal, identified by its SID, over the object protected by that ACE. A collection of ordered ACE forms an Access Control List (ACL), which controls the access rights to the underlying object for all principals.

Structurally, each ACE has a common ACE_HEADER followed by ACE-specific data, an old "C" technique for implementing object polymorphism. All ACE types are very well documented in MSDN, as well as in the winnt.h header file. The current section describes just the ACCESS_ALLOWED_ACE because it is the most used structure. All other ACE types are similar and can be found in the winnt.h header file as well. The ACE structure's header is declared as following:

```
typedef struct _ACE_HEADER {
    BYTE   AceType;
    BYTE   AceFlags;
    WORD   AceSize;
} ACE_HEADER;

typedef struct _ACCESS_ALLOWED_ACE {
    ACE_HEADER Header;
    ACCESS_MASK Mask;
    DWORD SidStart;
} ACCESS_ALLOWED_ACE;
```

The `AceType` field identifies the structure type following the `ACE_HEADER`. The common practice is to cast the generic `ACE_HEADER` structure to the concrete `ACE` type such as `ACCESS_ALLOWED_ACE`, depending on the `AceType` field value. The `Mask` field is a DWORD type combining all the rights granted by this ACE. Each bit has the meaning presented in Table 7.1. From this table, only the least significant 21 bits are effective rights used as such in the ACE; all other bits are used in other contexts in which an access mask is required.

**Table 7.1** The Overall Meaning of the Bits in the Access Mask

| Bits | Meaning |
|---|---|
| 31 | Generic Read |
| 30 | Generic Write |
| 29 | Generic Execute |
| 28 | Generic All |
| 25 to 27 | Reserved |
| 24 | SACL access |
| 21 to 23 | Not defined |
| 20 | Synchronize |
| 19 | Write Owner |
| 18 | Write DAC |
| 17 | Read DAC |
| 16 | Delete |
| 0 to 15 | Object specific rights |

The ACL structure is declared in the winnt.h header file, as follows:

```
typedef struct _ACL {
    BYTE    AclRevision;
    BYTE    Sbz1;
    WORD    AclSize;
    WORD    AceCount;
    WORD    Sbz2;
} ACL;
```

In a real ACL, a variable number of ACEs (as indicated by `AceCount`) follows this structure, using a continuous memory area of `AclSize` bytes. Currently, all ACLs used in the Windows operating system have the revision equal to 2. An ACL can be easily decoded using the `!acl` extension command, as in the following:

```
0:000> !acl 000840ac
ACL is:
ACL is: ->AclRevision: 0x2
ACL is: ->Sbz1       : 0x0
ACL is: ->AclSize    : 0x1c
ACL is: ->AceCount   : 0x1
ACL is: ->Sbz2       : 0x0
ACL is: ->Ace[0]: ->AceType: ACCESS_ALLOWED_ACE_TYPE
ACL is: ->Ace[0]: ->AceFlags: 0x0
ACL is: ->Ace[0]: ->AceSize: 0x14
ACL is: ->Ace[0]: ->Mask : 0x00120089
ACL is: ->Ace[0]: ->SID: S-1-1-0
```

## The Security Descriptor

All structures seen so far are aggregated in the security descriptor (SD) structure, defined in the winnt.h header file as shown here:

```
typedef WORD    SECURITY_DESCRIPTOR_CONTROL;

typedef struct _SECURITY_DESCRIPTOR {
    BYTE   Revision;
    BYTE   Sbz1;
    SECURITY_DESCRIPTOR_CONTROL Control;
    PSID Owner;
    PSID Group;
    PACL Sacl;
    PACL Dacl;
    } SECURITY_DESCRIPTOR;
```

The revision used by the Windows operating systems is set to 1. The `Control` field describes the security descriptor content, such as indicating whether the security descriptor contains a DACL (when SE_DACL_PRESENT flag is set) or a SACL, and much more. All pointers used inside the security descriptor should be treated as offsets from the security descriptor base address when the SE_SELF_RELATIVE bit is set in the Control field; otherwise, the addresses are absolute.

To understand how these structures are laid out in memory, we use the 07sample.exe executable with the option '0,' which exercises security descriptor-related APIs. The source code, shown in Listing 7.2, creates a security descriptor starting from a string using security descriptor definition language (SDDL). The rights of the user accessing the object protected by that security descriptor are obtained using the advapi32!AccessCheck API.

**Listing 7.2**    Sample code exercising the AccessCheck function

```
void Sample0()
{
    LPWSTR stringSD = L"O:SYG:BAD:(A;;FR;;;S-1-1-0)";
    PSECURITY_DESCRIPTOR sd = NULL;
    ...
    if (FALSE == ConvertStringSecurityDescriptorToSecurityDescriptor(
                  stringSD, SDDL_REVISION_1, &sd, NULL))
    { ...  }

    ImpersonateSelf(SecurityIdentification);
    STOP_ON_DEBUGGER;

    HANDLE hToken=NULL;
    if (!OpenThreadToken(
            GetCurrentThread(), TOKEN_QUERY, TRUE, &hToken))
    { ...  }
    RevertToSelf();
    ...
    if (FALSE == AccessCheck(
                  sd,
                  hToken,
                  MAXIMUM_ALLOWED,
                  &rightsMapping,
                  privileges,&privilegesSize ,
                  &grantedAccess,
                  &grantedAccessStatus))
    {
        TRACE(L"AccessCheck failed ");
    }
...
}
```

***Common Sources of Security Descriptors***   The address of a security descriptor is often available in the private symbols. When the private symbols are not available, the security descriptor used for access checks can be discovered as the first parameter to the advapi32!AccessCheck API. The next section interprets the parameter available on the stack after taking into consideration the calling convention used by the API (__stdcall in this case). The function declaration is as follows:

```
WINADVAPI BOOL WINAPI AccessCheck (
    IN PSECURITY_DESCRIPTOR pSecurityDescriptor,
    IN HANDLE ClientToken,
    IN DWORD DesiredAccess,
    IN PGENERIC_MAPPING GenericMapping,
    OUT PPRIVILEGE_SET PrivilegeSet,
    IN LPDWORD PrivilegeSetLength,
    OUT LPDWORD GrantedAccess,
    OUT LPBOOL AccessStatus );
```

We start the 07sample.exe application under a user mode debugger, such as windbg.exe, and set a breakpoint at the API address. The security descriptor is then displayed byte by byte in Listing 7.3.

**Listing 7.3**   Binary representation of a security descriptor

```
0:000> k2
ChildEBP RetAddr
0006fe9c 0100204e ADVAPI32!AccessCheck
0006ff00 01001f33 07sample!Sample0+0x10e
0:000> dc @esp L4
0006fea0   0100204e 00084098 000007bc 02000000   N ...@..........
0:000> db 00084098 L4c
00084098   01 00 04 80 30 00 00 00-3c 00 00 00 00 00 00 00   ....0...<.......
000840a8   14 00 00 00 02 00 1c 00-01 00 00 00 00 00 14 00   ................
000840b8   89 00 12 00 01 01 00 00-00 00 00 01 00 00 00 00   ................
000840c8   01 01 00 00 00 00 00 05-12 00 00 00 01 02 00 00   ................
000840d8   00 00 00 05 20 00 00 00-20 02 00 00               .... ... ...
```

Although the entire security descriptor can be deciphered manually, the best option is to use the provided !sd extension command. The result of using it is shown in Listing 7.4.

**Listing 7.4**   Decoding a security descriptor using the !sd extension command

```
kd> !sd 00084098
->Revision: 0x1
->Sbz1    : 0x0
->Control : 0x8004
            SE_DACL_PRESENT
            SE_SELF_RELATIVE
->Owner   : S-1-5-18
->Group   : S-1-5-32-544
->Dacl    :
->Dacl    : ->AclRevision: 0x2
->Dacl    : ->Sbz1       : 0x0
->Dacl    : ->AclSize    : 0x1c
->Dacl    : ->AceCount   : 0x1
->Dacl    : ->Sbz2       : 0x0
->Dacl    : ->Ace[0]: ->AceType: ACCESS_ALLOWED_ACE_TYPE
->Dacl    : ->Ace[0]: ->AceFlags: 0x0
->Dacl    : ->Ace[0]: ->AceSize: 0x14
->Dacl    : ->Ace[0]: ->Mask : 0x00120089
->Dacl    : ->Ace[0]: ->SID: S-1-1-0

->Sacl    : is NULL
```

The SID and the ACL introduced in the previous sections are part of this security descriptor. Those structure addresses are relative to the security descriptor address and can be easily extracted when the extension does not work because of a symbol mismatch.

## The Access Token

The security descriptor is useful only if we can securely identify the principal requesting access to the secured object protected by the security descriptor. The principal's identity, as well as all privileges granted to it, is encapsulated into a kernel structure called an access token. The access token is used by user mode components by a handle to the token. Those access tokens can be inspected using the !token extension command, which accepts as an argument either the access token address, as normally used in kernel mode debuggers, or a handle to it, as used in user mode debuggers. If the extension is used without an argument, it displays the thread impersonation access token, if present; otherwise, it uses the process token. In Listing 7.5, we use the token passed to the advapi32!AccessCheck function in Listing 7.3. Because we use the –n option, the extension command resolves the name associated with each SID (shown in parenthesis after the SID).

**Listing 7.5** Using the `!token` extension command to display a token in the user mode debugger

```
0:000> * Displays the information for token handle 0x7bc
0:000> !token 7bc -n
TS Session ID: 0
User: S-1-5-21-1060284298-2111687655-1957994488-1003 (User: XP-SP2\TestAdmin)
Groups:
 00 S-1-5-21-1060284298-2111687655-1957994488-513 (Group: XP-SP2\None)
    Attributes - Mandatory Default Enabled
 01 S-1-1-0 (Well Known Group: localhost\Everyone)
    Attributes - Mandatory Default Enabled
 02 S-1-5-32-544 (Alias: BUILTIN\Administrators)
    Attributes - Mandatory Default Enabled Owner
 03 S-1-5-32-545 (Alias: BUILTIN\Users)
    Attributes - Mandatory Default Enabled
 04 S-1-5-4 (Well Known Group: NT AUTHORITY\INTERACTIVE)
    Attributes - Mandatory Default Enabled
 05 S-1-5-11 (Well Known Group: NT AUTHORITY\Authenticated Users)
    Attributes - Mandatory Default Enabled
 06 S-1-5-5-0-35778 (no name mapped)
    Attributes - Mandatory Default Enabled LogonId
 07 S-1-2-0 (Well Known Group: localhost\LOCAL)
    Attributes - Mandatory Default Enabled
Primary Group: S-1-5-21-1060284298-2111687655-1957994488-513 (Group: XP-SP2\None)
Privs:
 00 0x000000017 SeChangeNotifyPrivilege           Attributes - Enabled Default
 01 0x000000008 SeSecurityPrivilege               Attributes -
...
 17 0x000000009 SeTakeOwnershipPrivilege          Attributes -
 18 0x00000001e SeCreateGlobalPrivilege           Attributes - Enabled Default
 19 0x00000001d SeImpersonatePrivilege            Attributes - Enabled Default
Auth ID: 0:1c3a8
Impersonation Level: Identification
TokenType: Impersonation
```

Looking carefully at all SIDs in this token, we can group them in security group principals, user principals, and identifiers, such as the `LogonId`. The SID concept is very flexible because it is just a unique identifier used to represent different entities, such as those shown in Table 7.2.

**Table 7.2**  Example of SID Types

| SID Types | SID Value Examples |
|---|---|
| User identity | S-1-5-21-1060284298-2111687655-1957994488-1003 |
| Group identity | S-1-5-21-1060284298-2111687655-1957994488-513 |
| Logon origin | S-1-5-4 (interactive) |
| User session | S-1-5-5-0- 35778 |
| Attributes | S-1-2-0 (local) |

Several SIDs used as attributes or abstract group's membership encountered everywhere are called Well-Known SIDs. Table 7.3 contains a short list of the most common SIDs. The MSDN, as the authoritative information source, contains the most up-to-date list with Well-Known SIDs used in Windows operating systems.

**Table 7.3**  Well-Known SIDS

| SID Value | SID Usage |
|---|---|
| S-1-1-0 | Special SID representing the Everyone security group |
| S-1-5-18 | Special SID representing the LocalSystem account |
| S-1-5-19 | Special SID representing the LocalService account |
| S-1-5-20 | Special SID representing the NetworkService account |
| S-1-5-6 | User logged as a service |
| S-1-5-2 | User logged on through the network |
| S-1-5-3 | User logged on as a batch account |
| S-1-5-4 | User logged interactively |
| S-1-5-5-X-Y | Identifies the user session |

The extension shows a list of SIDs representing the token principal's identity and the security groups this principal is part of. Afterward, the extension shows a list of privileges granted to this user, some of them being enabled. The token information is established each time the user logs on to the system and remains unchanged for the logon session lifetime. The privileges can be enabled or disabled by the application and can be removed but not added to the token. The same principal authenticated on different systems gets various token information, group membership, or privileges granted to it.

7. SECURITY

The interaction between those concepts can be exemplified by a real-life analogy. The access token is the passport used by travelers, or principals, to identify themselves at different borders. The security descriptor represents the immigration law, used by the immigration officer in the visiting country, that describes the traveler's rights and requirements, based on the country of origin. All information in the passport, such as country of origin or stamps obtained from different consulates, can be mapped to token group memberships and privileges. The immigration agent, the analog of the code performing the access check, trusts the passport issuer—the operating system, in this case—and is sure (harder to achieve in real life) that the passport is not falsified. Depending on the immigration law (security descriptor), the traveler is allowed or denied the right to visit the country (access the object).

In real life, there is no country without an immigration policy, and the software is at least as secure; each object is protected by a security descriptor. In real life, the management of identity documents, the immigration regulation, and travel visa management are performed in small circles under strict control. To achieve the same level of trust in the Windows operating systems, the access token management is done exclusively by the trusted computing base components, known as TCB. Each component running in TCB is trusted by the operating system and implicitly by each user of the security system.

The remainder of this chapter uses the preceding information to explore or resolve various cases in which security plays an important role.

## Source of Security Information

To be able to navigate safely in the vast land of security, the engineers need some clues as far as where to look for security information and what to expect when they find it.

### Access Tokens

Where are the access tokens stored, and how can they be found? The Windows operating system enforces a primary access token for each process in the system. This token identifies the principal creating the logon session hosting the process and is used by default for all object access. The address of the primary access token is available in the nt!EPROCESS structure corresponding to each process. Process access tokens can be displayed from both user mode and kernel mode debuggers, using the !token extension command.

In the user mode debugger, the primary access token is automatically displayed by the !token extension command if the current thread is not impersonating. In the kernel mode debugger, the primary access token address is part of the basic information about the process, displayed by the !process extension command, as shown in Listing 7.6. The listing assumes that the sample process is running on the system.

**Listing 7.6**   Obtaining the process access token

```
kd> * The option 1 displays process basic information (Token, Stats)
kd> !process 0 1 07sample.exe
PROCESS 81136930  SessionId: 0  Cid: 045c    Peb: 7ffd8000  ParentCid: 030c
    DirBase: 0ae64000  ObjectTable: e13e5d38  HandleCount:  18.
    Image: 07sample.exe
    VadRoot 811eaa90 Vads 24 Clone 0 Private 50. Modified 0. Locked 0.
    DeviceMap e164c948
    Token                          e1424030
    ElapsedTime                    00:46:16.327
...
kd> * Token field contains the address of the primary access token
```

In a client-server application, the Windows operating system relies heavily on impersonation. Impersonation is a flexible mechanism by which a thread uses an access token different from the primary access token for accessing all objects from that thread. The thread object, represented in the kernel by the nt!ETHREAD structure, has a reference to the impersonating access token. The basic !thread extension command displays an explicit message when the thread is impersonating, stating the impersonation token and the impersonation level. Listing 7.7 uses the main thread of 07sample.exe immediately after the ImpersonateSelf function returns.

**Listing 7.7**   Displaying the thread impersonation token

### Using the kernel mode debugger
```
kd> * Displays the thread, referred by kernel thread object
kd> !thread ffad3020
THREAD ffad3020  Cid 045c.03f0  Teb: 7ffdf000 Win32Thread: 00000000 RUNNING on
processor 0
Impersonation token:  e1424568 (Level Identification)
...
kd> * Token field contains the address of the impersonation token
```
### Using the user mode debugger
```
0:000> !token -n
TS Session ID: 0
User: S-1-5-21-1060284298-2111687655-1957994488-1003 (User: XP-SP1\TestAdmin)
...
```

When the thread is not impersonating, the impersonation state is clearly shown in the dump in Listing 7.8. All threads in the system start their life in this state, regardless of the impersonating state of the thread creating them.

**Listing 7.8**   Displaying the thread not impersonating

**Using the kernel mode debugger**
```
kd> !thread ffad3020
THREAD ffad3020  Cid 045c.03f0  Teb: 7ffdf000 Win32Thread: 00000000 RUNNING on
processor 0
Not impersonating
...
kd> * Token field is missing. The thread is in Not impersonating state
```
**Using the user mode debugger**
```
0:000> !token
Thread is not impersonating. Using process token
...
```

Last, the access tokens are available as a result of various API calls creating or returning handles to access tokens. If the handle value is known, either from the API output or by other methods, those access tokens can be inspected, as shown in Listing 7.5.

When the thread impersonates an access token, every native API uses that identity to perform the necessary access checks. If the thread is not impersonated, the process access token is to be used instead for each access check test, with one notable exception. In the case of the advapi32!OpenThreadToken API, the developer can choose this identity between the primary access token process and the impersonation access token using the OpenAsSelf parameter. However, we believe that any access token should always be accessible to the process using it.

A user mode application obtains the access token used by Security Reference Monitor by calling the advapi32!OpenThreadToken or the advapi32!OpenProcessToken API. The same APIs are used by the user mode extension, exts.dll, when implementing the !token extension command. When the !token extension command shows no impersonating state for a thread under user mode debugger, the output should be taken with a grain of salt. The extension always falls back to the primary token when it fails to get impersonation information, as we show later in the !token sections.

## Security Descriptors

Where are security descriptors stored? We know that all objects are secured by an attached security descriptor stored in various locations. All kernel objects contain a common header structure, preceding the real object memory address. The header structure, named _OBJECT_HEADER, contains, along with the reference counters and the object type, a pointer to the security descriptor protecting the object. In Listing 7-9, we use a different running instance of the 07sample.exe. The process object is used as a starting point for obtaining the object header that contains the pointer to the security descriptor protecting this object.

**Listing 7.9**   Obtaining the object header for a kernel object

```
kd> !process 0 0 07sample.exe
PROCESS ffbbc818  SessionId: 0  Cid: 01c4    Peb: 7ffde000  ParentCid: 00ac
    DirBase: 0232e000  ObjectTable: e1112e10  HandleCount:   8.
    Image: 07sample.exe

kd> !object ffbbc818
Object: ffbbc818  Type: (812ee900) Process
    ObjectHeader: ffbbc800
    HandleCount: 2  PointerCount: 7
kd> dt _OBJECT_HEADER ffbbc800
    +0x000 PointerCount     : 7
    +0x004 HandleCount      : 2
    +0x004 NextToFree       : 0x00000002
    +0x008 Type             : 0x812ee900 _OBJECT_TYPE
    +0x00c NameInfoOffset   : 0 ''
    +0x00d HandleInfoOffset : 0 ''
    +0x00e QuotaInfoOffset  : 0 ''
    +0x00f Flags            : 0x20 ' '
    +0x010 ObjectCreateInfo : 0x812ca8e8 _OBJECT_CREATE_INFORMATION
    +0x010 QuotaBlockCharged : 0x812ca8e8
    +0x014 SecurityDescriptor : 0xe198bb92
    +0x018 Body             : _QUAD
```

The header contains a pseudo pointer to the object security descriptor. The pseudo pointer uses the last three bits to store state information unrelated to the security descriptor address. This is possible because of the memory alignment used by the security descriptors. After masking the least significant bits, the address points to a valid security descriptor that can be displayed with the !sd extension command, as shown in Listing 7.10.

**Listing 7.10** Obtaining kernel objects security descriptor

```
kd> !sd 0xe198bb92 & 0xFFFFFFF8
->Revision: 0x1
->Sbz1    : 0x0
->Control : 0x8004
            SE_DACL_PRESENT
            SE_SELF_RELATIVE
->Owner   : S-1-5-21-1060284298-2111687655-1957994488-1003
->Group   : S-1-5-21-1060284298-2111687655-1957994488-513
->Dacl    :
->Dacl    : ->AclRevision: 0x2
->Dacl    : ->Sbz1        : 0x0
->Dacl    : ->AclSize     : 0x40
->Dacl    : ->AceCount    : 0x2
->Dacl    : ->Sbz2        : 0x0
->Dacl    : ->Ace[0]: ->AceType: ACCESS_ALLOWED_ACE_TYPE
->Dacl    : ->Ace[0]: ->AceFlags: 0x0
->Dacl    : ->Ace[0]: ->AceSize: 0x24
->Dacl    : ->Ace[0]: ->Mask : 0x001f0fff
->Dacl    : ->Ace[0]: ->SID: S-1-5-21-1060284298-2111687655-1957994488-         1003

->Dacl    : ->Ace[1]: ->AceType: ACCESS_ALLOWED_ACE_TYPE
->Dacl    : ->Ace[1]: ->AceFlags: 0x0
->Dacl    : ->Ace[1]: ->AceSize: 0x14
->Dacl    : ->Ace[1]: ->Mask : 0x001f0fff
->Dacl    : ->Ace[1]: ->SID: S-1-5-18

->Sacl    : is NULL
```

Because the security descriptor address is stored right before the object address, to simplify the operation of getting an object security descriptor, all steps required to get it can be combined in a single line, as follows:

```
!sd poi(<object_address>-4) & FFFFFFF8
```

Not all objects accessible at any given time in the kernel memory have a security descriptor that can be accessed using the method described in Listing 7.10. Persistent kernel objects, such as files or registry keys, keep the security descriptor in a secondary store and manage the security access through their proprietary mechanism. If we are looking at a registry key object, we can see that it has the security descriptor NULL, which does not allow us to statically examine the security descriptor. To demonstrate this case, we used option '4' in the sample, which opens a few registry keys.

**Listing 7.11**   Examining a registry key's object header

```
kd> k4
ChildEBP RetAddr
0006ff00 01001f33 07sample!Sample4Get+0x45
0006ff18 01001e48 07sample!AppInfo::Loop+0xb3
0006ff7c 01002aa6 07sample!wmain+0xa8
0006ffc0 7c816fd7 07sample!__wmainCRTStartup+0x102
kd> dv *key
    softwareKey = 0x000007f4
        bookKey = 0x77c2ed0e
kd> !handle 7f4
processor number 0, process ffbbc818
PROCESS ffbbc818  SessionId: 0  Cid: 01c4    Peb: 7ffde000  ParentCid: 00ac
    DirBase: 0232e000  ObjectTable: e1112e10  HandleCount:    9.
    Image: 07sample.exe

Handle table at e122f000 with 9 Entries in use
07f4: Object: e18cce60  GrantedAccess: 00020019 Entry: e122ffe8
Object: e18cce60  Type: (812e4e70) Key
    ObjectHeader: e18cce48
        HandleCount: 1  PointerCount: 1
        Directory Object: 00000000  Name: \REGISTRY\MACHINE\SOFTWARE

kd> dt _OBJECT_HEADER e18cce48
   +0x000 PointerCount      : 1
   +0x004 HandleCount       : 1
   +0x004 NextToFree        : 0x00000001
   +0x008 Type              : 0x812e4e70 _OBJECT_TYPE
   +0x00c NameInfoOffset    : 0 ''
   +0x00d HandleInfoOffset  : 0 ''
   +0x00e QuotaInfoOffset   : 0 ''
   +0x00f Flags             : 0 ''
   +0x010 ObjectCreateInfo  : 0x812ca8e8 _OBJECT_CREATE_INFORMATION
   +0x010 QuotaBlockCharged : 0x812ca8e8
   +0x014 SecurityDescriptor : (null)
   +0x018 Body              : _QUAD
```

When the security descriptor is not easily available for inspection, its value can be validated at the moment the object broker performs the access check. All other user mode components exposing objects not managed by the kernel (such as Service Control Manager) also use their own mechanism to manage their security descriptors.

# How Is the Security Check Performed?

To ensure consistent access rules across Windows components, the kernel implements a set of security APIs with the signature published in the ntddk.h header file. The central function is the kernel function SeAccessCheck used by the user mode components through the advapi32!AccessCheck API. `SeAccessCheck` takes as parameters the security descriptor, the access token (in the `SubjectSecurityContext` parameter), and the requested access.

```
BOOLEAN SeAccessCheck (
    IN PSECURITY_DESCRIPTOR SecurityDescriptor,
    IN PSECURITY_SUBJECT_CONTEXT SubjectSecurityContext,
    IN BOOLEAN SubjectContextLocked,
    IN ACCESS_MASK DesiredAccess,
    IN ACCESS_MASK PreviouslyGrantedAccess,
    OUT PPRIVILEGE_SET *Privileges OPTIONAL,
    IN PGENERIC_MAPPING GenericMapping,
    IN KPROCESSOR_MODE AccessMode,
    OUT PACCESS_MASK GrantedAccess,
    OUT PNTSTATUS AccessStatus);
```

The access granted by user mode code can be easily identified in the debugger by inspecting the return value and the output parameters filled by the advapi32!AccessCheck API. The access granted by kernel mode code can be identified by inspecting the return from the SeAccessCheck kernel API. To identify access problems caused by improper security settings on various files and registry keys, we can also use tracing tools such as Process Monitor, tools provided free of charge by Microsoft.

# Identity Propagation in Client-Server Applications

Most applications use the primary access token for all operations. Client-server applications often use the impersonation model, in which the server executes most, if not all, of the client requests in the context of an impersonation access token obtained from that client. The impersonation access token is propagated by specific functionality exposed by the interprocess communication infrastructure used to support the client-server conversation. Impersonation functions—such as ntdll!NtImpersonateClientOfPort, exposed by the LPC communication mechanism; rpcrt4!RpcImpersonateClient, implemented by the RPC infrastructure; and advapi32!ImpersonateNamedPipeClient, implemented by the file system redirector—impersonate the caller thread with the client access token used to invoke the server using the respective facilities. In some cases, user credentials are available on the server side, especially in the case of Web-based applications, and the server creates an access token by invoking advapi32!LogonUser(Ex)W directly.

Each protocol uses its proprietary mechanism to propagate the identity of the client. When the client and the server reside on different systems, the Security Server Provider Interface (SSPI) can be used to propagate the security information for client-server applications.

rpcrt4!RpcImpersonateClient is a special "proxy" function that delegates the impersonation request to the underlying communication mechanism used by RPC for that connection. When RPC is used to communicate between two processes residing in the same system, the call uses LPC functions to achieve the result. When the client runs on a different system from the server, RPC uses either the file system redirector functionality, in the case of remote calls using transport security, or SSPI functionality in the vast majority of the cases.

## Remote Authentication and Security Support Provider Interface

The client has a set of credentials that must be presented to the server. These credentials are used to represent the client principal in the server system. SSPI is used to authenticate remote credentials through a variety of security providers, such as NTLM authentication, Kerberos domain-based authentication, or client certificate authentication.

To authenticate to the remote system, the client initiates the call sequence by passing the set of credentials to the secur32!InitializeSecurityContextW API. The opaque blob of data resulting from this call is sent over the wire protocol to the server. The server takes the blob and passes it to the secur32!AcceptSecurityContext API, which generates yet another opaque block of data and tells the server if the authentication is complete. If not, the server-generated block is then sent to the client, which uses it as a parameter to another secure32!InitializeSecurityContextW call. The resultant data blob is sent back to the server, and the process repeats several times until the security package used for the authentication can validate the credential. When the message exchange is complete, the server calls secure32!ImpersonateSecurityContext with the last data blob to impersonate the client. This sequence of calls is often referred to as the ISC/ASC sequence.

Chapter 8 shows how this remote authentication looks on the wire. Listing 7.12 is captured from the server process before the remote client establishes a connection to the server. The return code from every secur32!AcceptSecurityContext call is an important clue for how the ISC/ASC is doing, and each error detected by the respective authentication package is a perfect clue for understanding why the remote authentication fails when it does—a clue often lost by a high-level API using the SSPI.

**Listing 7.12**  Tracing the remote authentication from the server process

```
0:009> bp Secur32!AcceptSecurityContext
0:009> bp Secur32!ImpersonateSecurityContext
0:003> g
...
Breakpoint 0 hit
eax=0009be20 ebx=00000000 ecx=0009722c edx=76f9d1e0 esi=00097220 edi=000000a6
eip=76f949ba esp=005bfe68 ebp=005bfea8 iopl=0         nv up ei pl nz na pe nc
Secur32!AcceptSecurityContext:
76f949ba 55              push    ebp
0:003> k
ChildEBP RetAddr
005bfe64 78023b9f Secur32!AcceptSecurityContext
005bfea8 78023b22 RPCRT4!SECURITY_CONTEXT::AcceptThirdLeg+0x3e
005bff18 78004aed RPCRT4!OSF_SCONNECTION::ProcessReceiveComplete+0x595
005bff28 78001848 RPCRT4!ProcessConnectionServerReceivedEvent+0x20
0:003> * Third Leg is a concept used in NTLM authentication
0:003> g
Breakpoint 1 hit
eax=76f9d1e0 ebx=005bf83c ecx=0009722c edx=75867028 esi=000971e0 edi=005bf848
eip=76f95099 esp=005bf75c ebp=005bf768 iopl=0         nv up ei pl nz na pe nc
Secur32!ImpersonateSecurityContext:
76f95099 55              push    ebp
0:003> k
ChildEBP RetAddr
005bf758 7802372a Secur32!ImpersonateSecurityContext
005bf768 78023701 RPCRT4!SECURITY_CONTEXT::ImpersonateClient+0x39
005bf770 78004443 RPCRT4!OSF_SCONNECTION::ImpersonateClient+0x3b
005bf778 75852a8f RPCRT4!RpcImpersonateClient+0x64
0:003> * The RPCImpersonateClient function uses the SSPI function
```

After all functions shown previously are successfully executed, the calling thread then impersonates the client impersonation access token. The return from the secur32!ImpersonateSecurityContext API is a perfect place to set breakpoints in a security investigation, after the server executes the impersonation function:

```
0:003> gu
eax=00000000 ebx=005bf83c ecx=c000023c edx=7ffe0304 esi=000971e0 edi=005bf848
eip=7802372a esp=005bf764 ebp=005bf768 iopl=0         nv up ei pl zr na po nc
RPCRT4!SECURITY_CONTEXT::ImpersonateClient+0x39:
7802372a 85c0            test    eax,eax
```

After checking the return code, which indicates a successful impersonation according to MSDN, check the thread impersonation access token using the !token extension command, as shown in Listing 7.13.

**Listing 7.13**  Exploring the impersonation token after SSPI impersonation

```
0:003> !token -n
TS Session ID: 0
User: S-1-5-21-1060284298-2111687655-1957994488-1003 (User: XP-SP1\TestAdmin)
...
Auth ID: 0:2780c
Impersonation Level: Impersonation
TokenType: Impersonation
```

After impersonation, the thread can revert to a nonimpersonating state by using a revert function usually matching the impersonation method, both found in MSDN on the same page. Another common impersonation function is advapi32!SetThreadToken, used when the server already has a handle to the client access token obtained through other means. This is commonly used when the server keeps a cache of access tokens and manages their use. advapi32!ImpersonateSelf is another API used in a situation in which a thread needs to use a token similar to the primary access but with a different group membership or a list of enabled privileges.

## Impersonation Level

Another interesting component of the access token, as seen before, is its ImpersonationLevel. The impersonation level is the restriction imposed by the client on the access token usage by the server, a restriction enforced by the operating system. A thread impersonating an access token at an impersonation level less than SecurityImpersonation is incapable of acquiring any secured resource on the system running the server process.

To show the importance of the impersonation level, the example shown in Listing 7.14 makes several calls to GetComputerNameEx API while impersonating the primary access token at different impersonation levels. This function can be exercised by using option '1' in 07sample.exe.

**Listing 7.14** Sample function calling GetComputerNameEx at different impersonation levels

```
void Sample1()
{
    WCHAR computerName[MAX_PATH];
    DWORD arrayLength = MAX_PATH;

    BOOL retCode = TRUE;
    ImpersonateSelf(SecurityAnonymous);

    retCode = GetComputerNameEx(ComputerNameNetBIOS, computerName,     &arrayLength);
    RevertToSelf();
    ...
    ImpersonateSelf(SecurityDelegation);

    retCode = GetComputerNameEx(ComputerNameNetBIOS, computerName,     &arrayLength);
    RevertToSelf();

    if (retCode != TRUE)
    {
        TRACE(L"GetComputerName fails with token @ SecurityDelegation.");
    }
```

The following output shows the results of an execution that fails when the imperson-ation level is set to `SecurityAnonymous` or `SecurityIdentify`:

```
GetComputerName fails with token @ SecurityAnonymous.Last error = 1346
GetComputerName fails with token @ SecurityIdentification.Last error = 1346
```

A quick look in the winerror.h header file reveals the `1346L` error as being the ERROR_BAD_IMPERSONATION_LEVEL error. The error code can also be deci-phered by using the `net helpmsg <error>` command line or the `!error` exten-sion command.

## Security Checks at System Boundaries

Today, even the simpler applications have complicated interactions with the operat-ing system components running in various contexts. For example, when you're test-ing an application in a restricted security context, the application fails to open a file or to log errors in to the Event Log. How will someone start debugging it? In the next section, we evaluate some common scenarios—caused by security checks or encountered in simple applications or in the operating system components—with the goal of creating a debugging framework that can be used in other contexts. Before starting, we need to understand the basic security gates used by the operating system.

Windows has many security boundaries defined and enforced by the operating system, and each transition in and out of those security boundaries is subject to security checks. We can easily identify the common boundaries—such as the file system, Windows registry, each process address space, the kernel address space—whereas others, such as the Windows desktop, are not as clear. The machine is a physical security boundary, but it is a logical security boundary as well. As a result, each API can potentially check the identity of the caller and fail the call according to the security policy implemented in that API. A successful approach to security failure investigations requires a good knowledge of each API, which is hard, if not impossible, to achieve without access to the source code and a lot of time spent to understand that code. In reality, only the API developers understand the code at a level at which they can efficiently pinpoint the problem.

Because it is not practical to know the details of each API, what is the minimum required for successful investigation of security problems? Developers need a bare minimum understanding of the subsystem used and the places where the security checks are most likely to be performed when using the APIs for that subsystem. They also need to know how to probe the results of those checks.

If the code execution does not call into another process, the kernel mode code will be the only resource manager denying access to resources. Please note that many Win32 APIs communicate with different processes to implement their functionality. When the code execution continues into another process, the access gates it must pass by are virtually endless because that call can spawn multiple processes and even multiple systems. For example, a basic three-tier system, with the generic architecture shown in Figure 7.1—using a Web server on the front end, any middleware software in the middle layer, and a database on the back end—has many potential security-related points of failure.

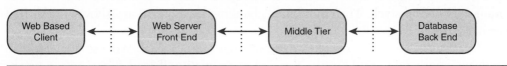

**Figure 7.1**   Typical multitier application

In Figure 7.1, each box can run on one or more systems connected through different communication mechanisms. Each piece involved in this architecture can check the user identity and can reject the call. The next section explores a few failure scenarios encountered in distributed environments in which there are many opportunities for errors.

# Investigating Security Failures

The debugging sessions shown in this section, which are encountered on various systems, are always triggered by access denied errors. Sometimes, the access denied is normal and expected. Other times, the errors are normal but unexpected even in a correctly configured system. Still, it is much easier to debug a failure in a properly configured system than in a misconfigured system, as shown in the last debugging scenario in this section. The first few examples are classic kernel resources denied access followed by more complex distributed scenarios using DCOM as communication infrastructure.

## Local Security Failures

Unexpected failures from various APIs represent one of the biggest sources of frustration in software development, especially when the failure totally contradicts the developer's expectations or experience. Trying to understand why such an API fails always proves to be a challenging task—more difficult than it should be, especially when it is unexpected. A common failure case is encountered when the processes are running under the NetworkService account, identified by S-1-5-20, or under the LocalService account, identified by S-1-5-19.

The example in this section is based on a real situation but was encountered while experimenting with the side effects of invoking advapi32!ImpersonateSelf called by a process running under the NetworkService account. To save time, we decided to use one of the transient processes running under this account, and we attached a debugger to a process running under this identity, identifiable with Task Manager.

In the thread used by the debugger to call `kernel32!DebugBreak`, we change the instruction pointer to the address of `advapi32!ImpersonateSelf` and fill the parameters on the stack. The commands changing the context are shown in the first part of Listing 7.15.

After executing the `advapi32!ImpersonateSelf` API, we use the `!token` extension command to find out the thread impersonation thread. The `!token` extension command indicates that the tread is not impersonating. The last error indicates that the API failed with a completely unexpected access denied error. How can we understand why this function call failed?

**Listing 7.15**   Simulating ImpersonateSelf invocation in the debugger target

```
0:008> |
.  0   id: 650 attach  name: C:\WINDOWS\System32\wbem\wmiprvse.exe
0:008> * set the instruction pointer to the advapi32!ImpersonateSelf
0:008> r $ip=advapi32!ImpersonateSelf
0:008> * enter the argument to the API
0:008> ed esp+4 2
0:008> gu
eax=00000000 ebx=00000001 ecx=00000005 edx=00000015 esi=00000004 edi=00000005
eip=7c9507a8 esp=00a9ffd4 ebp=00a9fff4 iopl=0         nv up ei pl zr na pe nc
cs=001b  ss=0023  ds=0023  es=0023  fs=003b  gs=0000            efl=00000246
ntdll!DbgUiRemoteBreakin+0x2d:
7c9507a8 eb11             jmp      ntdll!DbgUiRemoteBreakin+0x40 (7c9507bb)
0:008> !token
Thread is not impersonating. Using process token...
Error 0xc0000022 getting thread token  !token command failed
0:008> ~.
.  8  Id: 650.334 Suspend: 1 Teb: 7ffd7000 Unfrozen
      Start: ntdll!DbgUiRemoteBreakin (7c95077b)
      Priority: 0  Priority class: 32
0:008> !gle
LastErrorValue: (Win32) 0x5 (5) - Access is denied.
LastStatusValue: (NTSTATUS) 0xc0000022 - {Access Denied}  A process has requested
access to an object, but has not been granted those access rights.
```

As a side note, it is interesting to notice that the same logical error has multiple error codes, depending on the subsystem using it. For example, the unambiguous access denied error can have different values, as shown in Table 7.4.

**Table 7.4**   Different Representations of the Same Logical Error

| Component | Defined In | Symbolic Name | Value |
|---|---|---|---|
| Windows NT Kernel | winnt.h | STATUS_ACCESS_DENIED | ((NTSTATUS)0xC0000022L) |
| Ntdll.dll | winnt.h | STATUS_ACCESS_DENIED | ((NTSTATUS)0xC0000022L) |
| Win32 APIs | winerror.h | ERROR_ACCESS_DENIED | 5L |
| COM APIs | winerror.h | E_ACCESSDENIED | _HRESULT_TYPEDEF_ (0x80070005L) |
| RPC APIs | winerror.h | RPC_E_ACCESS_DENIED | _HRESULT_TYPEDEF_ (0x8001011BL) |

While debugging this scenario, we realized that the `!token` extension command also fails with an access denied error, but apparently the result is correct. We investigate the reason for this failure later in the "!token Extension Command Failure" section.

We should focus on the real problem: figuring out why the `advapi32!ImpersonateSelf` function fails. The first step is to understand what `advapi32!ImpersonateSelf` does under the hood. Based on the explanation found on MSDN, the API creates an impersonation access token by duplicating the primary access token at the requested impersonation level and sets it on the current thread. In pseudo-code, the API functionality resembles the following:

```
ImpersonateSelf(ImpersonationLevel)
{
    processHandle = OpenCurrentProcess()
    processToken = OpenProcessToken(processHandle, TOKEN_DUPLICATE);
    newToken = DuplicateToken(processToken, ImpersonationLevel)
    SetThreadToken(newToken)
}
```

Each step from the pseudo-code shown previously is subject to at least one security check because all objects involved are protected by the Windows kernel. To succeed on the first step, the process object must have been granted the PROCESS_QUERY_INFORMATION to the user making the call—in this case, the NetworkService account. Next, the primary access token must be granted the TOKEN_DUPLICATE right in its security descriptor to the calling user. The last step requires the user to have THREAD_SET_THREAD_TOKEN rights to the thread object. This very simple function tests three security descriptors, as follows:

- Process object security descriptor
- Primary token security descriptor
- Thread object security descriptor

Since the thread is not impersonating at any time, all calls are executed in the context of the primary token, the NetworkService account, which must have access with the specific rights in the corresponding security descriptors described above. Before searching other causes for this failure, we shall investigate each security descriptor taking part in the operation and understand what rights are granted to the user. The simplest way to check them is to start up a kernel mode debugger in local mode and investigate each object. We start by looking at the process object whose process identifier was retrieved in Listing 7.15. The process object security descriptor is explored in Listing 7.16.

## Listing 7.16  Obtaining the process object security descriptor

```
lkd> !process 650 1
Searching for Process with Cid == 650
PROCESS ffacccc8  SessionId: 0  Cid: 0650    Peb: 7ffd5000  ParentCid: 02d0
    DirBase: 0b233000  ObjectTable: e120ddc0  HandleCount: 164.
    Image: wmiprvse.exe
    VadRoot 811c2790 Vads 102 Clone 0 Private 416. Modified 0. Locked 1.
    DeviceMap e15f04a8
    Token                              e1b3db20
...
lkd> !sd poi(ffacccc8-4)&FFFFFFF8
->Revision: 0x1
->Sbz1    : 0x0
->Control : 0x8004
           SE_DACL_PRESENT
           SE_SELF_RELATIVE
->Owner   : S-1-5-20
->Group   : S-1-5-20
->Dacl    :
->Dacl    : ->AclRevision: 0x2
->Dacl    : ->Sbz1       : 0x0
->Dacl    : ->AclSize    : 0x58
->Dacl    : ->AceCount   : 0x3
->Dacl    : ->Sbz2       : 0x0
->Dacl    : ->Ace[0]: ->AceType: ACCESS_ALLOWED_ACE_TYPE
->Dacl    : ->Ace[0]: ->AceFlags: 0x0
->Dacl    : ->Ace[0]: ->AceSize: 0x18
->Dacl    : ->Ace[0]: ->Mask : 0x001f0fff
->Dacl    : ->Ace[0]: ->SID: S-1-5-20

->Dacl    : ->Ace[1]: ->AceType: ACCESS_ALLOWED_ACE_TYPE
->Dacl    : ->Ace[1]: ->AceFlags: 0x0
->Dacl    : ->Ace[1]: ->AceSize: 0x20
->Dacl    : ->Ace[1]: ->Mask : 0x00100201
->Dacl    : ->Ace[1]: ->SID: S-1-5-5-0-32366

->Dacl    : ->Ace[2]: ->AceType: ACCESS_ALLOWED_ACE_TYPE
->Dacl    : ->Ace[2]: ->AceFlags: 0x0
->Dacl    : ->Ace[2]: ->AceSize: 0x18
->Dacl    : ->Ace[2]: ->Mask : 0x00100201
->Dacl    : ->Ace[2]: ->SID: S-1-5-18

->Sacl    : is NULL
```

By interpreting the access bits on the access mask used for the S-1-5-20 user, we conclude that NetworkService has full rights to the process object as expected. The primary access token, obtained in the previous listing, is another object involved in the API implementation and is protected by its security descriptor, as shown in the Listing 7.17.

**Listing 7.17**   Obtaining the primary token object security descriptor

```
lkd> !sd poi(e1b3db20-4)&FFFFFFF8
->Revision: 0x1
->Sbz1     : 0x0
->Control : 0x8004
            SE_DACL_PRESENT
            SE_SELF_RELATIVE
->Owner    : S-1-5-20
->Group    : S-1-5-20
->Dacl     :
->Dacl     : ->AclRevision: 0x2
->Dacl     : ->Sbz1        : 0x0
->Dacl     : ->AclSize     : 0x30
->Dacl     : ->AceCount    : 0x2
->Dacl     : ->Sbz2        : 0x0
->Dacl     : ->Ace[0]: ->AceType: ACCESS_ALLOWED_ACE_TYPE
->Dacl     : ->Ace[0]: ->AceFlags: 0x0
->Dacl     : ->Ace[0]: ->AceSize: 0x14
->Dacl     : ->Ace[0]: ->Mask : 0x000f01ff
->Dacl     : ->Ace[0]: ->SID: S-1-5-18

->Dacl     : ->Ace[1]: ->AceType: ACCESS_ALLOWED_ACE_TYPE
->Dacl     : ->Ace[1]: ->AceFlags: 0x0
->Dacl     : ->Ace[1]: ->AceSize: 0x14
->Dacl     : ->Ace[1]: ->Mask : 0x000f01ff
->Dacl     : ->Ace[1]: ->SID: S-1-5-20

->Sacl     :  is NULL
```

As before, by interpreting the access bits on the access mask used for the S-1-5-20 user, we conclude that NetworkService has full rights to the primary access token, as expected. The thread itself is the last kernel object involved in the operation and follows the same rules governing Windows security. Following the same steps, the security descriptor of the calling thread can be easily obtained. But first we must identify the kernel object representing the failing thread; we match thread identifier 0650.0334 from the user mode debugger with the KTHREAD structure in the kernel mode debugger. The process identifier and the thread identifier were known from the user mode debugger session experiencing this failure.

**Listing 7.18**    Inspecting the security descriptor of the thread object running the failing code

```
lkd> * List all threads running inside the process with 0x0650 PID
lkd> !process 0n1616 4
Searching for Process with Cid == 650
PROCESS ffacccc8  SessionId: 0  Cid: 0650    Peb: 7ffd5000  ParentCid: 02d0
    DirBase: 0b233000  ObjectTable: e120ddc0  HandleCount: 164.
    Image: wmiprvse.exe


        THREAD fface088  Cid 0650.0658  Teb: 7ffdf000 Win32Thread: e1226650 WAIT
        THREAD 8125b020  Cid 0650.04dc  Teb: 7ffde000 Win32Thread: 00000000 WAIT
        THREAD ffadb100  Cid 0650.064c  Teb: 7ffdd000 Win32Thread: e1345138 WAIT
        THREAD ffb25408  Cid 0650.0654  Teb: 7ffdc000 Win32Thread: 00000000 WAIT
        THREAD 811c6b30  Cid 0650.03b4  Teb: 7ffdb000 Win32Thread: e1b4ebf0 WAIT
        THREAD ffb47b18  Cid 0650.05f4  Teb: 7ffda000 Win32Thread: e13482b0 WAIT
        THREAD 811c2da8  Cid 0650.05f8  Teb: 7ffd9000 Win32Thread: 00000000 WAIT
        THREAD ffacaaa0  Cid 0650.0570  Teb: 7ffd8000 Win32Thread: 00000000 WAIT
        THREAD ffb2a020  Cid 0650.0334  Teb: 7ffd7000 Win32Thread: 00000000 WAIT
Lkd> *Inspecting the security descriptor protecting this kernel object
kd> !sd poi(ffb2a020-4)&FFFFFFF8
->Revision: 0x1
->Sbz1    : 0x0
->Control : 0x8004
          SE_DACL_PRESENT
          SE_SELF_RELATIVE
->Owner   : S-1-5-32-544
->Group   : S-1-5-21-1060284298-2111687655-1957994488-513
->Dacl    :
->Dacl    : ->AclRevision: 0x2
->Dacl    : ->Sbz1        : 0x0
->Dacl    : ->AclSize     : 0x34
->Dacl    : ->AceCount    : 0x2
->Dacl    : ->Sbz2        : 0x0
->Dacl    : ->Ace[0]: ->AceType: ACCESS_ALLOWED_ACE_TYPE
->Dacl    : ->Ace[0]: ->AceFlags: 0x0
->Dacl    : ->Ace[0]: ->AceSize: 0x18
->Dacl    : ->Ace[0]: ->Mask : 0x001f03ff
->Dacl    : ->Ace[0]: ->SID: S-1-5-32-544

->Dacl    : ->Ace[1]: ->AceType: ACCESS_ALLOWED_ACE_TYPE
->Dacl    : ->Ace[1]: ->AceFlags: 0x0
->Dacl    : ->Ace[1]: ->AceSize: 0x14
->Dacl    : ->Ace[1]: ->Mask : 0x001f03ff
->Dacl    : ->Ace[1]: ->SID: S-1-5-18

->Sacl    : is NULL
```

Surprisingly, NetworkService has no access to the thread object. After examining it, we can see that only users in the local administrators group, identified by S-1-5-32-544, and the LocalSystem account, identified by S-1-5-18, can change the thread impersonation token, explaining the API failure. In such cases, we often look at similar objects to understand the difference in order to build a theory to explain the failure. We choose another thread in the same process with the address shown in Listing 7.18. The security descriptors shown in Listing 7.18 and Listing 7.19 differ only by one ACE; the failing thread grants all the rights to S-1-5-32-544, whereas the normal thread grants the same rights to S-1-5-20.

**Listing 7.19**   Inspecting the security descriptor of another thread object running in the same process

```
kd> !sd poi(ffacaaa0-4)&FFFFFFF8
->Revision: 0x1
->Sbz1    : 0x0
->Control : 0x8004
            SE_DACL_PRESENT
            SE_SELF_RELATIVE
->Owner   : S-1-5-20
->Group   : S-1-5-20
->Dacl    :
->Dacl    : ->AclRevision: 0x2
->Dacl    : ->Sbz1        : 0x0
->Dacl    : ->AclSize     : 0x30
->Dacl    : ->AceCount    : 0x2
->Dacl    : ->Sbz2        : 0x0
->Dacl    : ->Ace[0]: ->AceType: ACCESS_ALLOWED_ACE_TYPE
->Dacl    : ->Ace[0]: ->AceFlags: 0x0
->Dacl    : ->Ace[0]: ->AceSize: 0x14
->Dacl    : ->Ace[0]: ->Mask : 0x001f03ff
->Dacl    : ->Ace[0]: ->SID: S-1-5-18

->Dacl    : ->Ace[1]: ->AceType: ACCESS_ALLOWED_ACE_TYPE
->Dacl    : ->Ace[1]: ->AceFlags: 0x0
->Dacl    : ->Ace[1]: ->AceSize: 0x14
->Dacl    : ->Ace[1]: ->Mask : 0x001f03ff
->Dacl    : ->Ace[1]: ->SID: S-1-5-20

->Sacl    : is NULL
```

This can be explained by understanding how the security descriptor has been initially assigned to the thread object. It turns out that this thread has been created by a process running under a local administrator identity, and the default security descriptor has been applied to the thread. The thread has been created in the debugger target by the debugger using kernel32!CreateRemoteThread while running under a local administrator account.

Although this example seems unnatural, it can happen very well in any application. It is important to be aware of the complexity of each API and the implications of calling it while impersonating a user different from the primary token user. The next section, "Security Problems During Deferred Initialization," describes other situations generated by similar circumstances.

## Security Problems During Deferred Initialization

The lazy initialization technique defers the initialization of expensive objects as much as possible, with the goal of improving the start-up time while reducing the memory footprint before the component is used. To achieve even greater scalability, the component designers even uninitialize the component after a decay period defined as part of the initial design. They rely on the lazy initialization technique to bring the component back to life when needed. In the client/server application, the lazy initialization phase is triggered by a client request and is subject to all security rules enforced by the operating system. All components involved in the lazy initialization can play a role in the process and must be treated very carefully. The thread impersonation token and its impersonation level, as well as the potential thread impersonation, can affect the overall functionality of the system, or it can introduce subtle functionality bugs that are difficult to find.

The sample simulates the impersonation by creating and impersonating an access token representing a regular user. The user, who has the username Test1 and the password TestUser1, should be creating manually before running the sample and deleted when the sample is no longer used.

Let's analyze the following code that has multiple purposes. It creates a new key in HKLM\Software, it caches the process token for further uses, and it creates a kernel event used to synchronize the access to the same global objects. This code can be exercised using option '2' of 07sample.exe. We use this function to simulate the side effect of executing it while impersonating. This type of functionality is often encountered in the service initialization functions.

**Listing 7.20** *Sample initialization function*

```
void LazyInitialization()
{
    HKEY softwareKey = NULL;
    LONG retCode = RegOpenKeyEx(HKEY_LOCAL_MACHINE, L"Software", 0, MAXIMUM_ALLOWED,
&softwareKey);
    ...
    HKEY bookKey = NULL;
    retCode = RegCreateKey(bookKey, L"Advanced Windows Debugging", &bookKey);
...
    RegCloseKey(bookKey);
    RegCloseKey(softwareKey);

    BOOL otherCode = ImpersonateSelf(SecurityImpersonation);
...
    HANDLE threadToken = NULL;
    otherCode = OpenThreadToken(GetCurrentThread(), TOKEN_QUERY, FALSE, &threadTo-
ken);
...
    if (threadToken) CloseHandle(threadToken);

    HANDLE event = CreateEvent(NULL, FALSE, FALSE, L"07sample");
    CloseHandle(event);

    HANDLE threadTokenAsSelf = NULL;
    otherCode = OpenThreadToken(GetCurrentThread(), TOKEN_QUERY |TOKEN_IMPERSONATE ,
TRUE, &threadTokenAsSelf);
...
    RevertToSelf();
    otherCode = ImpersonateLoggedOnUser(threadTokenAsSelf);
...
    if (threadTokenAsSelf) CloseHandle(threadTokenAsSelf);
    RevertToSelf();
    }
```

Because the product tests are good and no apparent bugs exist in this code, this code is incorporated into a product and then released. Soon after, the customer reports that the application fails with one of the following errors in the log file, printed on the screen by the sample as follows:

```
RegCreateKeyW failed.Last error = 6
ImpersonateSelf failed.Last error = 5
OpenThreadToken failed.Last error = 5
```

Along with the known access denied error code 5, we can see an unexpected invalid handle error 6 coming from the registry API. By correlating all the places where the key is used or created, we figure out the faulting code is in the lazy initialization path. It is triggered by the client request, which executes in the client request thread while the thread impersonates the user. We have simulated the impersonation in a simple client application by logging in a specific user, impersonating it, and calling the LazyInitialization function, as shown in the following:

```
void Sample2()
{
    HANDLE userToken = NULL;
    BOOL retCode =  LogonUser(L"Test1", NULL, L"TestUser1", LOGON32_LOGON_INTERAC-
TIVE, LOGON32_PROVIDER_DEFAULT,  &userToken);
...
    ImpersonateLoggedOnUser(userToken);

    LazyInitialization();

    RevertToSelf();
    CloseHandle(userToken);
}
```

Because the code review does not reveal the failure source, we will run this code under a user mode debugger to fully understand what's going wrong. Immediately after the first failure line executes, that is, the advapi32!RegCreateKey API, we examine the handle value passed in as the first parameter using the !handle extension command. We pick that parameter because the registry API returns 'invalid handle error'.

```
0:000> !handle poi(softwareKey) 7
Handle 58
  Type            Key
  Attributes      0
  GrantedAccess   0x20019:
      ReadControl
      QueryValue,EnumSubKey,Notify
  HandleCount     2
  PointerCount    3
  Name            \REGISTRY\MACHINE\SOFTWARE
0:000> * The !handle command decodes the rights granted to the caller
```

We notice that the registry API was not granting rights to create any new key in the softwareKey. The security manager grants rights to objects when the object is opened, based on its security descriptor and requested access mask. The access granted and stored in the handle table, along with the handle, is checked by every operation using the handle for validity. The access mask associated with the handle is displayed by the !handle extension command, as shown in the previous listing.

In this case, the key was opened while impersonating a low-privilege user. Reading the code once again, we can see the requested mask used to open the registry key as MAXIMUM_ALLOWED, which is a convenient access mask definition that everybody uses. Perhaps the developer had no time or desire to find out the necessary rights, and was not willing to justify the use of GENERIC_ALL. The system indeed returns what the code asks for, but the granted access is different from what the developer intended. As a side note, MAXIMUM_ALLOWED should be used only for probing the object allowed access. Using it anywhere else is a code defect waiting to show up.

After we found one defect, two more errors are waiting. Looking back to the trace log, advapi32!ImpersonateSelf fails with an access denied. As discussed in the earlier section "Local Security Failures," we should first understand the operation and identify the security of all components involved in the operation. It is clear by now that advapi32!ImpersonateSelf opens the process handle, duplicates the primary access token, and sets it on the calling thread. We set a breakpoint at advapi32!ImpersonateSelf in the user mode debugger, but we continue our investigation using a kernel mode debugger while the user mode debugger is stopped at the breakpoint. We start by checking the security information of the process object, as shown in Listing 7.21.

**Listing 7.21**   Examining the process object security descriptor

```
lkd> !process 0 1 07Sample.exe
PROCESS ffb36020  SessionId: 0  Cid: 0784    Peb: 7ffde000  ParentCid: 0284
    DirBase: 0a257000  ObjectTable: e183bbb0  HandleCount:  22.
    Image: 07sample.exe
    VadRoot ffa7c978 Vads 33 Clone 0 Private 66. Modified 0. Locked 0.
    DeviceMap e1798128
    Token                          e196a3f0
...
lkd> !process 0 2 07sample.exe
PROCESS ffb36020  SessionId: 0  Cid: 0784    Peb: 7ffde000  ParentCid: 0284
    DirBase: 0a257000  ObjectTable: e183bbb0  HandleCount:  22.
    Image: 07sample.exe

        THREAD 82f408a8  Cid 0784.04f8  Teb: 7ffdf000 Win32Thread: e17a5d28 WAIT
: (Executive) KernelMode Non-Alertable
SuspendCount 1
        f3ad77d4  SynchronizationEvent
```

```
lkd> !sd poi(ffb36020-4)&FFFFFFF8
->Revision: 0x1
->Sbz1     : 0x0
->Control : 0x8004
             SE_DACL_PRESENT
             SE_SELF_RELATIVE
->Owner    : S-1-5-32-544
->Group    : S-1-5-21-1060284298-2111687655-1957994488-513
->Dacl     :
->Dacl     : ->AclRevision: 0x2
->Dacl     : ->Sbz1        : 0x0
->Dacl     : ->AclSize     : 0x34
->Dacl     : ->AceCount    : 0x2
->Dacl     : ->Sbz2        : 0x0
->Dacl     : ->Ace[0]: ->AceType: ACCESS_ALLOWED_ACE_TYPE
->Dacl     : ->Ace[0]: ->AceFlags: 0x0
->Dacl     : ->Ace[0]: ->AceSize: 0x18
->Dacl     : ->Ace[0]: ->Mask : 0x001f0fff
->Dacl     : ->Ace[0]: ->SID: S-1-5-32-544


->Dacl     : ->Ace[1]: ->AceType: ACCESS_ALLOWED_ACE_TYPE
->Dacl     : ->Ace[1]: ->AceFlags: 0x0
->Dacl     : ->Ace[1]: ->AceSize: 0x14
->Dacl     : ->Ace[1]: ->Mask : 0x001f0fff
->Dacl     : ->Ace[1]: ->SID: S-1-5-18
->Sacl     : is NULL
```

Our thread impersonates the access token, obtained from the `advapi32!LogonUserExW` call, representing user `Test1` who is not a member of any group that can possibly open the process handle for the access requested by `advapi32!ImpersonateSelf`. Listing 7.22 uses the `!thread` extension command to obtain the impersonation access token to be passed as parameter to the `!token` extension command. The thread object address is obtained from Listing 7.21.

**Listing 7.22** Dumping the impersonating token

```
lkd> !thread 82f408a8
THREAD 82f408a8  Cid 0784.07a4  Teb: 7ffdd000 Win32Thread: e189aeb0 WAIT: (Executive)
KernelMode Non-Alertable
SuspendCount 1
    f70687d4  SynchronizationEvent
Impersonation token:  e13fee28 (Level Impersonation)
Owning Process              ffb36020      Image:          07sample.exe
kd> !token e13fee28
```

*(continues)*

**Listing 7.22**    Dumping the impersonating token *(continued)*

```
TS Session ID: 0
User: S-1-5-21-1060284298-2111687655-1957994488-1006
Groups:
 00 S-1-5-21-1060284298-2111687655-1957994488-513
    Attributes - Mandatory Default Enabled
 01 S-1-1-0
    Attributes - Mandatory Default Enabled
 02 S-1-5-32-545
    Attributes - Mandatory Default Enabled
 03 S-1-5-5-0-1757850
    Attributes - Mandatory Default Enabled LogonId
 04 S-1-2-0
    Attributes - Mandatory Default Enabled
 05 S-1-5-4
    Attributes - Mandatory Default Enabled
 06 S-1-5-11
    Attributes - Mandatory Default Enabled
Primary Group: S-1-5-21-1060284298-2111687655-1957994488-513
Privs:
 00 0x000000017 SeChangeNotifyPrivilege        Attributes - Enabled Default
 01 0x000000013 SeShutdownPrivilege            Attributes -
 02 0x000000019 SeUndockPrivilege              Attributes -
Auth ID: 0:1ad29b
Impersonation Level: Impersonation
TokenType: Impersonation
```

With one more code defect understood, it is time to focus on the last one, which is similar to the inability to open the process object.

However, this function has one more problem. The next line in the sample code creates a named event, which, based on default security, grants the impersonating user Test1 full access to it. If the same user can run custom code on the system with the service code having this problem, he can manipulate the event owned by the service. This is a security concern.

Since the application does not set an explicit security descriptor for the newly created event, the system assigns one that is generated using the default security mechanism. The generated security descriptor grants full access to the principal, which is represented by the impersonated access token. In the same function, using the user mode debugger, we can stop after the kernel event creation to inspect its security descriptor. We search the kernel event address of the event handle retrieved in the user mode debugger. The event handle 0x7a8 is used as a parameter to the !handle extension command, along with the process identifier. In Listing 7.23, we retrieve the event security descriptor using the same method as for any other kernel objects.

**Listing 7.23** Dumping the security descriptor for an object created while impersonating

```
kd> !handle 7a8 7 784
processor number 0, process 00000784
Searching for Process with Cid == 784
PROCESS ffb36020  SessionId: 0  Cid: 0784    Peb: 7ffde000  ParentCid: 0284
    DirBase: 0a257000  ObjectTable: e183bbb0  HandleCount:  23.
    Image: 07sample.exe

Handle table at e1910000 with 23 Entries in use
07a8: Object: ffb47ff0  GrantedAccess: 001f0003 Entry: e1910f50
Object: ffb47ff0  Type: (812ed320) Event
    ObjectHeader: ffb47fd8
        HandleCount: 1  PointerCount: 2
        Directory Object: e171d128  Name: 07sample

kd> !sd poi(ffb47ff0-4)&FFFFFFF8
->Revision: 0x1
->Sbz1    : 0x0
->Control : 0x8004
            SE_DACL_PRESENT
            SE_SELF_RELATIVE
->Owner   : S-1-5-21-1060284298-2111687655-1957994488-1006
->Group   : S-1-5-21-1060284298-2111687655-1957994488-513
->Dacl    :
->Dacl    : ->AclRevision: 0x2
->Dacl    : ->Sbz1       : 0x0
->Dacl    : ->AclSize    : 0x40
->Dacl    : ->AceCount   : 0x2
->Dacl    : ->Sbz2       : 0x0
->Dacl    : ->Ace[0]: ->AceType: ACCESS_ALLOWED_ACE_TYPE
->Dacl    : ->Ace[0]: ->AceFlags: 0x0
->Dacl    : ->Ace[0]: ->AceSize: 0x24
->Dacl    : ->Ace[0]: ->Mask : 0x001f0003
->Dacl    : ->Ace[0]: ->SID: S-1-5-21-1060284298-2111687655-1957994488-1006

->Dacl    : ->Ace[1]: ->AceType: ACCESS_ALLOWED_ACE_TYPE
->Dacl    : ->Ace[1]: ->AceFlags: 0x0
->Dacl    : ->Ace[1]: ->AceSize: 0x14
->Dacl    : ->Ace[1]: ->Mask : 0x001f0003
->Dacl    : ->Ace[1]: ->SID: S-1-5-18

->Sacl    :  is NULL
```

The scenarios shown previously might not look familiar to developers not writing a service, not using impersonation, or not explicitly calling the Win32 API directly. But with the advance of Web Services in enterprise software development, it becomes common to make the step into impersonation services. Also, complex libraries with heavy initialization code that is deferred until first use, most likely used inside complex distributed application, are the perfect set-up for the type of problems explored in this section.

## Potential Security Implications of Impersonating

When building the services accepting client requests, we should be aware of how the thread impersonation affects the component used during the service request. Even if the service is not impersonating the user before using the components, each component can potentially impersonate the caller. In such cases, we must be familiar with each component behavior and use this information in deciding to use that component. This is true for components running inside services supporting impersonation sources, such as ASP.NET application, WEB services, RPC, or DCOM servers.

This potential of impersonating is limited only to the thread dispatched as a result of the client invocation. When calling an external component, the developer should understand the implications this impersonating potential can have on the component call and remove it if necessary, using specific techniques for each impersonation source when possible, or delegate the execution to a new thread no longer subject to this potential.

## Distributed COM Errors

As you have seen in Table 7.4, the access denied error can take multiple values depending on the component surfacing the error. We searched the Internet for the error 0x80070005 that is raised by DCOM, and we found more than 7,000 pages with questions and workarounds. We also searched for the decimal form of the error, and we got another 1,500 hits. DCOM access denied errors are hard to investigate because of the  inherent complexity present in any distributed systems. We expect to see a similar level of complexity in distributed applications built on top of other infrastructures.

The access denied errors are raised when the DCOM client has no right to activate the server, when the client is not allowed to invoke the server, when the components are not registered properly, and when the infrastructure encounters an access denied error.

DCOM activation is a good exemplification of user mode systems using custom access checks. DCOM stores the activation and access security descriptors in the registry. All the following scenarios are commonly encountered in operations performed on properly configured systems. At the end of this chapter, we diagnose a system whose configuration has been mistakenly altered and which is failing most DCOM operations, an interesting end-to-end scenario. All scenarios run on a Windows XP SP2 operating system.

### DCOM Activation Checks

A naive approach to debug communication failure, by tracing the client code step-by-step, has a minimal chance of success and should be avoided. Because the DCOM activation is in essence a distributed process, it should be investigated using the model described in Chapter 8, in the section "Breaking the Call Path." Using this model, we first identify the process hosting the binary that returned the original error, and then we try to find out the details of the failure. To use the model, we must understand in greater detail the activation request calling path, which we describe in this section.

Figure 7.2 illustrates all processes involved in DCOM activation. Each box represents a security boundary, and the long vertical gray line represents a system boundary. The client activates a remote COM object by communicating with the local DCOM activation interface implemented by the RPCSS Server service, which delegates the activation request, when necessary, to the remote RPCSS Server service. The remote RPCSS service starts the process hosting the server; it waits for the server process to register as a DCOM server, and finally it calls into the process to obtain the interface requested by caller. Just by looking at all six process boundaries, one also being a machine boundary, it is easy to see how many components must work in perfect harmony to make the activation possible. In a standard enterprise environment, each RPCSS Server service can also talk with the domain controller. To reduce the diagram complexity, the connection to the domain controller was omitted.

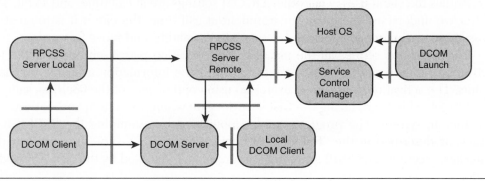

**Figure 7.2**   Processes participating in DCOM activation

According to Figure 7.2, the activation involves the client process, the RPCSS service and the DcomLaunch service on the server side, and the server process. In the case of local activation, the communication from the client-side RPCSS and server-side RPCSS is a shortcut. We start by identifying the processes involved in the activation path and create a mental diagram of the relationship between them. The tlist.exe tool, installed with the Debugging Tools for Windows, is excellent for this. In Listing 7.24, we use `tlist.exe` to find the process identifiers of DcomLaunch and RpcSs services on the server side.

**Listing 7.24** Identifying Rpcss and DcomLaunch services on Windows XP SP2

```
c:\>tlist -s
    0 System Process
    4 System
  300 smss.exe
  432 csrss.exe       Title:
  464 winlogon.exe
  548 services.exe    Svcs:   Eventlog,PlugPlay
  560 lsass.exe       Svcs:   PolicyAgent,ProtectedStorage,SamSs
  716 svchost.exe     Svcs:   DcomLaunch,TermService
  768 svchost.exe     Svcs:   RpcSs
```

After identifying the process used by the execution path, the quickest way to debug is to assume that the activation call reaches the last process in the call chain, attach a user mode debugger to the latest process in the path and stop the process execution, then execute again the failing client call. If the client does not hang, the call path does not reach the process currently stopped in the debugger, and we can detach the debugger by entering the qd command. We repeat the process higher in the call path until the client hangs in the activation call. At that point, we can use this process to identify what credentials the client uses, what other DCOM settings are at call time, and so on. The better we understand the client environment at call time, the easier it is to create a possible scenario for each failure, demonstrate its validity, and move forward.

This section describes all the places in the activation path useful to evaluate the activation progress and explains how to interpret the information available on those points. The activation path can be exercised using option zero of the 08cli.exe sample.

Remote clients are facing the first security gate when the system authenticates to the remote system. The progress can be monitored by examining the SSPI return codes, as described in the "Remote Authentication and Security Support Provider Interface" section. The SSPI authentication request is handled by the RPCSS service code.

After the remote authentication succeeds (local clients are already authenticated by the operating system), the activation code uses the impersonation token representing the client to perform various checks, using the advapi32!AccessCheck in RPCSS service running on the server. As part of the activation, the RPCSS service performs multiple checks, each having its role. Listing 7.25 shows the first check that validates if the caller has the right to access the server using the DCOM protocol. We attach a debugger to RPCSS service and set a breakpoint on the ADVAPI32!AccessCheck, as in the following listing:

**Listing 7.25**   Examine the first AccessCheck performed by RPCSS

```
0:007> bp ADVAPI32!AccessCheck;g
Breakpoint 0 hit
eax=007dfce4 ebx=00000000 ecx=007dfcf8 edx=007dfd08 esi=00000001 edi=00000000
eip=77dd7c11 esp=007dfcb8 ebp=007dfd10 iopl=0         nv up ei pl nz na po nc
cs=001b  ss=0023  ds=0023  es=0023  fs=003b  gs=0000              efl=00000206
ADVAPI32!AccessCheck:
77dd7c11 8bff              mov         edi,edi
0:007> k
ChildEBP RetAddr
007dfcb4 76a822a6 ADVAPI32!AccessCheck
007dfd10 76a824f6 rpcss!CheckForAccess+0x81
007dfd5c 77e7a2c1 rpcss!LocalInterfaceOnlySecCallback+0xb9
007dfdb4 77e7c767 RPCRT4!RPC_INTERFACE::CheckSecurityIfNecessary+0x6f
007dfdcc 77e7bcc9 RPCRT4!LRPC_SBINDING::CheckSecurity+0x4f
007dfdfc 77e7bb6a RPCRT4!LRPC_SCALL::DealWithRequestMessage+0x194
007dfe20 77e76784 RPCRT4!LRPC_ADDRESS::DealWithLRPCRequest+0x16d
007dff80 77e76c22 RPCRT4!LRPC_ADDRESS::ReceiveLotsaCalls+0x28f
007dff88 77e76a3b RPCRT4!RecvLotsaCallsWrapper+0xd
007dffa8 77e76c0a RPCRT4!BaseCachedThreadRoutine+0x79
007dffb4 7c80b50b RPCRT4!ThreadStartRoutine+0x1a
007dffec 00000000 kernel32!BaseThreadStart+0x37
0:007> * !sd extension fails; we grab the ACL directly from the SD
0:007>!acl poi(@esp+4)+poi(poi(@esp+4)+10)
ACL is:
ACL is: ->AclRevision: 0x2
ACL is: ->Sbz1       : 0x0
ACL is: ->AclSize    : 0x30
ACL is: ->AceCount   : 0x2
ACL is: ->Sbz2       : 0x0
ACL is: ->Ace[0]: ->AceType: ACCESS_ALLOWED_ACE_TYPE
ACL is: ->Ace[0]: ->AceFlags: 0x0
ACL is: ->Ace[0]: ->AceSize: 0x14
```

*(continues)*

**Listing 7.25** Examine the first AccessCheck performed by RPCSS *(continued)*

```
ACL is: ->Ace[0]: ->Mask : 0x00000003
ACL is: ->Ace[0]: ->SID: S-1-5-7

ACL is: ->Ace[1]: ->AceType: ACCESS_ALLOWED_ACE_TYPE
ACL is: ->Ace[1]: ->AceFlags: 0x0
ACL is: ->Ace[1]: ->AceSize: 0x14
ACL is: ->Ace[1]: ->Mask : 0x00000007
ACL is: ->Ace[1]: ->SID: S-1-1-0
```

This first checks determines if the user can pass the security limits imposed on the DCOM server machine shown in Figure 7.3. The Component Services security configuration page is started by using the dcomcnfg.exe command line. From the Component Services MMC snap-in, we can configure all security parameters used in DCOM.

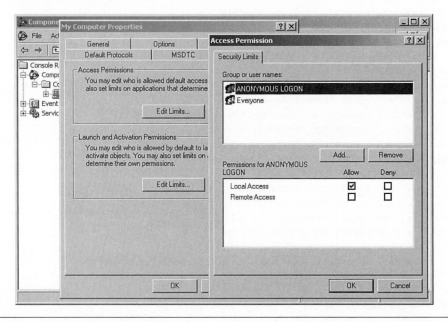

**Figure 7.3** Access permission limits configuration page, differentiating between local and remote clients

After the first check passes, the system validates if the user has the right to activate any DCOM server on the system. Listing 7.26 shows the second access check that is performed against a different security descriptor.

**Listing 7.26**  Examine the second AccessCheck performed by RPCSS

```
0:007> g
Breakpoint 0 hit
eax=007dfce4 ebx=00000000 ecx=007dfcf8 edx=007dfd08 esi=00000001 edi=00000000
eip=77dd7c11 esp=007dfcb8 ebp=007dfd10 iopl=0         nv up ei pl nz na pe nc
cs=001b  ss=0023  ds=0023  es=0023  fs=003b  gs=0000              efl=00000202
ADVAPI32!AccessCheck:
77dd7c11 8bff                mov     edi,edi
0:007> k
ChildEBP RetAddr
007dfcb4 76a822a6 ADVAPI32!AccessCheck
007dfd10 76a8c2e4 rpcss!CheckForAccess+0x81
007dfd5c 77e7a2c1 rpcss!LocalInterfaceOnlySecCallback+0x138
007dfdb4 77e7c767 RPCRT4!RPC_INTERFACE::CheckSecurityIfNecessary+0x6f
007dfdcc 77e7bcc9 RPCRT4!LRPC_SBINDING::CheckSecurity+0x4f
007dfdfc 77e7bb6a RPCRT4!LRPC_SCALL::DealWithRequestMessage+0x194
007dfe20 77e76784 RPCRT4!LRPC_ADDRESS::DealWithLRPCRequest+0x16d
007dff80 77e76c22 RPCRT4!LRPC_ADDRESS::ReceiveLotsaCalls+0x28f
007dff88 77e76a3b RPCRT4!RecvLotsaCallsWrapper+0xd
007dffa8 77e76c0a RPCRT4!BaseCachedThreadRoutine+0x79
007dffb4 7c80b50b RPCRT4!ThreadStartRoutine+0x1a
007dffec 00000000 kernel32!BaseThreadStart+0x37
0:007>!acl poi(@esp+4)+poi(poi(@esp+4)+10)
ACL is:
ACL is: ->AclRevision: 0x2
ACL is: ->Sbz1       : 0x0
ACL is: ->AclSize    : 0x34
ACL is: ->AceCount   : 0x2
ACL is: ->Sbz2       : 0x0
ACL is: ->Ace[0]: ->AceType: ACCESS_ALLOWED_ACE_TYPE
ACL is: ->Ace[0]: ->AceFlags: 0x0
ACL is: ->Ace[0]: ->AceSize: 0x18
ACL is: ->Ace[0]: ->Mask : 0x0000001f
ACL is: ->Ace[0]: ->SID: S-1-5-32-544

ACL is: ->Ace[1]: ->AceType: ACCESS_ALLOWED_ACE_TYPE
ACL is: ->Ace[1]: ->AceFlags: 0x0
ACL is: ->Ace[1]: ->AceSize: 0x14
ACL is: ->Ace[1]: ->Mask : 0x0000000b
ACL is: ->Ace[1]: ->SID: S-1-1-0
```

The security descriptor used in this second check is also a machinewide security limit imposed on the launch and activation of all DCOM servers. It is controlled by another security configuration page shown in Figure 7.4, also part of DCOM configuration.

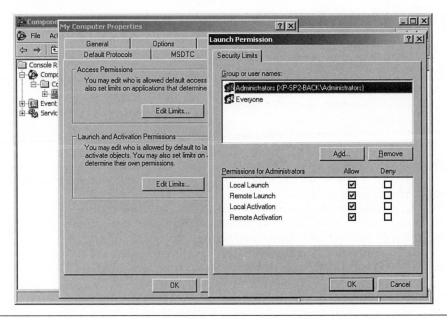

**Figure 7.4** Launch Permission limits configuration page, differentiating between local and remote clients

After those two initial checks—not specific to the component being requested—are successful, the RPCSS server reads from the registry the information pertinent to the component. The component restrictions are finally validated by RPCSS, as shown in Listing 7.27.

**Listing 7.27** Examine the component-specific AccessCheck performed by RPCSS

```
0:007> g
Breakpoint 0 hit
eax=007df59c ebx=0009ade0 ecx=007df5b0 edx=007df5c0 esi=00000001 edi=00000000
eip=77dd7c11 esp=007df570 ebp=007df5c8 iopl=0         nv up ei pl nz na po nc
cs=001b  ss=0023  ds=0023  es=0023  fs=003b  gs=0000            efl=00000206
ADVAPI32!AccessCheck:
77dd7c11 8bff            mov     edi,edi
0:007> k
ChildEBP RetAddr
007df56c 76a822a6 ADVAPI32!AccessCheck
007df5c8 76a8c0cd rpcss!CheckForAccess+0x81
007df5f4 76a8e5fb rpcss!CClsidData::LaunchOrActivationAllowed+0x155
```

```
007df65c 76a8e4ab rpcss!Activation+0x1fb
007df6b8 76a91e12 rpcss!ActivateFromProperties+0x213
007df6c8 76a91e66 rpcss!CScmActivator::CreateInstance+0x10
007df708 76a91e7b rpcss!ActivationPropertiesIn::DelegateCreateInstance+0xf7
007df754 76a8c1d7 rpcss!ActivateFromPropertiesPreamble+0x4c1
007df79c 76a91de7 rpcss!PerformScmStage+0xbb
007df8b0 77e79dc9 rpcss!SCMActivatorCreateInstance+0x97
007df8e0 77ef321a RPCRT4!Invoke+0x30
007dfcf8 77ef36ee RPCRT4!NdrStubCall2+0x297
007dfd14 77e7988c RPCRT4!NdrServerCall2+0x19
007dfd48 77e797f1 RPCRT4!DispatchToStubInC+0x38
007dfd9c 77e7971d RPCRT4!RPC_INTERFACE::DispatchToStubWorker+0x113
007dfdc0 77e7bd0d RPCRT4!RPC_INTERFACE::DispatchToStub+0x84
007dfdfc 77e7bb6a RPCRT4!LRPC_SCALL::DealWithRequestMessage+0x2db
007dfe20 77e76784 RPCRT4!LRPC_ADDRESS::DealWithLRPCRequest+0x16d
007dff80 77e76c22 RPCRT4!LRPC_ADDRESS::ReceiveLotsaCalls+0x28f
007dff88 77e76a3b RPCRT4!RecvLotsaCallsWrapper+0xd
0:007> !acl poi(@esp+4)+poi(poi(@esp+4)+10)
ACL is:
ACL is: ->AclRevision: 0x2
ACL is: ->Sbz1       : 0x0
ACL is: ->AclSize    : 0x50
ACL is: ->AceCount   : 0x3
ACL is: ->Sbz2       : 0x0
ACL is: ->Ace[0]: ->AceType: ACCESS_ALLOWED_ACE_TYPE
ACL is: ->Ace[0]: ->AceFlags: 0x0
ACL is: ->Ace[0]: ->AceSize: 0x18
ACL is: ->Ace[0]: ->Mask : 0x00000001
ACL is: ->Ace[0]: ->SID: S-1-5-18

ACL is: ->Ace[1]: ->AceType: ACCESS_ALLOWED_ACE_TYPE
ACL is: ->Ace[1]: ->AceFlags: 0x0
ACL is: ->Ace[1]: ->AceSize: 0x18
ACL is: ->Ace[1]: ->Mask : 0x00000001
ACL is: ->Ace[1]: ->SID: S-1-5-4

ACL is: ->Ace[2]: ->AceType: ACCESS_ALLOWED_ACE_TYPE
ACL is: ->Ace[2]: ->AceFlags: 0x0
ACL is: ->Ace[2]: ->AceSize: 0x18
ACL is: ->Ace[2]: ->Mask : 0x00000001
ACL is: ->Ace[2]: ->SID: S-1-5-32-544
```

This access check, the last one performed by RPCSS service before it attempts to start the COM server implementing the requested object, is controlled by the component-specific security configuration page shown in Figure 7.5. The configuration page allows the administrator to select between a custom security descriptor and the default security descriptor used for all components. The server-specific configuration page is displayed after selecting the SRV server from the DCOM Config node.

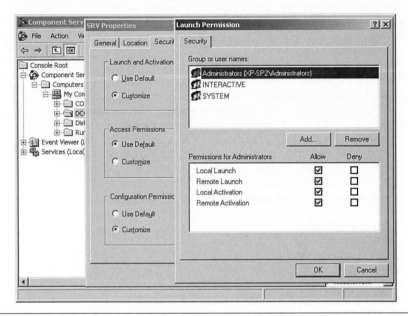

**Figure 7.5** Component specific Launch Permission page, equal to the default Launch Permission

This descriptor shown in Figure 7.5 has the same value as the default Launch Permission. It is easy to observe how restrictive this security descriptor is. To support normal users, it allows all activations originated on the interactive session. At the same time, the activation fails for all nonadministrators logged on from a network authentication, a service authentication, or a batch logon. For example, the code that tries to activate a COM server from an ASP.NET application configured to run under the NetworkService account fails with access denied if the component does not overwrite the default launch permission.

Assuming that the initial gate passed, the activation request is send to the DcomLaunch service, the other service playing a role in the activation process. Prior to Windows XP SP2, this service functionality was part of the RPCSS service. The DcomLauch service rechecks the component-specific permission similarly. Every process spawned by the DCOM Service Control Manager passes through another common gate implemented by the ADVAPI32!CreateProcessAsUserW API called by the DcomLaunch service.

A breakpoint at this function offers the perfect spot for understanding the server command line and the identity under which it will run, as shown in Listing 7.28. We can interpret the parameters from the stack after taking into account the function calling convention. We attach a debugger to the DcomLaunch service and set a breakpoint on the ADVAPI32!CreateProcessAsUserW, as in the following listing.

**Listing 7.28**  Inspecting the command line and the identity of the server about to be started

```
0:010> bp ADVAPI32!CreateProcessAsUserW;g
Breakpoint 0 hit
eax=00000000 ebx=00000410 ecx=0000038c edx=00aff71c esi=00000000 edi=000c2b48
eip=77df7775 esp=00aff690 ebp=00aff7dc iopl=0         nv up ei pl zr na pe nc
cs=001b  ss=0023  ds=0023  es=0023  fs=003b  gs=0000            efl=00000246
ADVAPI32!CreateProcessAsUserW:
77df7775 8bff            mov     edi,edi
0:010> k
ChildEBP RetAddr
00aff68c 76a93acd ADVAPI32!CreateProcessAsUserW
00aff7dc 76a93849 rpcss!CClsidData::PrivilegedLaunchActivatorServer+0x39d
00aff858 77e79dc9 rpcss!_LaunchActivatorServer+0xbc
00aff8b4 77ef321a RPCRT4!Invoke+0x30
...
0:010> * According to MSDN, the command line is the 3rd parameter
0:010> du poi(@esp+c)
000c2750  ""C:\awdbin\WinXP.x86.chk\08comsr"
000c2790  "v.exe" -Embedding"
0:010> * According to MSDN, the primary token is the 1st parameter
0:010> !token poi(@esp+4) -n
TS Session ID: 0
User: S-1-5-21-1060284298-2111687655-1957994488-1003 (User: XP-SP2\TestAdmin)
Groups:
 00 S-1-5-21-1060284298-2111687655-1957994488-513 (Group: XP-SP2\None)
    Attributes - Mandatory Default Enabled
...
...
TokenType: Primary
```

If the activation got to this point, but it fails to create the process, the activation failure is reduced to a process start-up failure in that user context. The failures can be caused by a myriad of factors, but most of the time the user, designated by the token, has no access to the server process files. The environment for the user can be simulated using the runas.exe command, and the process startup should be investigated separately.

If the server is implemented as a Windows Service, the DcomLaunch uses SCM APIs to start the service. Those APIs are perfect for investigating possible errors returned in response to service start-up. If the server is already running and supports multiple activations, the activation path does not even reach this process; it completes in RPCSS.

Almost toward the end of this activation path, when the server process is up and running, the RPCSS makes a final call into the server to create the instance requested by the client. The call is executed while impersonating the user making the original call, and it is handled by the COM server as any other call—subject to all restrictions imposed by call access, which is discussed next.

### DCOM Call Access Checks

Because the DCOM infrastructure processes all client calls before they are dispatched into the server code, it creates a security gate that must be passed by the client before the server executes that request. Those security gates can be initialized explicitly by calling the ole32!CoInitializeSecurity API with the following signature:

```
HRESULT CoInitializeSecurity(
  PSECURITY_DESCRIPTOR pVoid,
  LONG cAuthSvc,
  SOLE_AUTHENTICATION_SERVICE * asAuthSvc,
  void * pReserved1,
  DWORD dwAuthnLevel,
  DWORD dwImpLevel,
  SOLE_AUTHENTICATION_LIST * pAuthList,
  DWORD dwCapabilities,
  void * pReserved3
);
```

The second function parameter represents the minimum accepted authentication level of the inbound call. The first parameter of the API is polymorphic and can be a Windows security descriptor, a NULL value, an AppID string, or a pointer to an object implementing the IAccessControl interface. In reality, this parameter is often NULL and rarely an explicit security descriptor. The NULL value combined with the flag EOAC_APPID in dwCapabilities indicates that the DCOM infrastructure must load the security descriptor from the access permission settings associated with the server application. When EOAC_APPID is not present, the security descriptor used by the DCOM infrastructure allows everyone to make calls into the server, which is not recommended. Figure 7.6 shows how to configure the access permission for inbound calls into the SRV server.

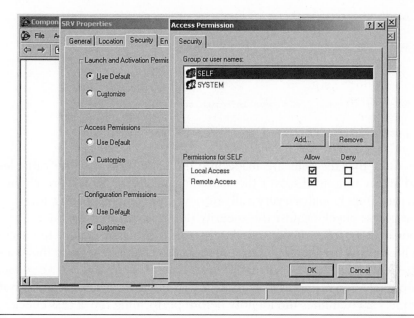

**Figure 7.6**    Component-specific Access Permission page, equal to the default Access Permission

If the application does not explicitly call the ole32!CoInitializeSecurity API, DCOM does it on behalf of the application before exporting the first interface. The default parameters used in this case are NULL for the security descriptor with the EOAC_APPID flag in the dwCapabilities parameter.

---

**NOTE** The server is safer if does not initialize DCOM security rather than initializing it with a weaker restriction, as in the following:

```
CoInitializeSecurity( NULL, -1, NULL, NULL, RPC_C_AUTHN_LEVEL_DEFAULT,
          RPC_C_IMP_LEVEL_IDENTIFY, NULL, EOAC_NONE   , NULL );
```

---

The ole32!CoInitializeSecurity API stores the passed arguments in global variables located inside ole32.dll, having symbolic names similar to argument names. Such values can be interpreted according to their meaning, described in the help page associated with the API initializing them. Their full names are shown in the following:

```
0:000> x ole32!g*
...
772bb20c OLE32!gSecDesc = <no type information>
...
772bb208 OLE32!gAuthnLevel = <no type information>
...
772bbf70 OLE32!gImpLevel = <no type information>
...
772bb05c OLE32!gCapabilities = <no type information>
```

After we know that the calls are made into the server process, the variables can be inspected at any time to discover the source of an access denied error. The DCOM infrastructure impersonates every call, retrieves the impersonating token, and performs the access check against the security descriptor stored in OLE32!gSecDesc. The impersonating token used to make the call is available before the access check function is called. A breakpoint at this function also enables checking the results of the access check. The DCOM infrastructure uses either the advapi32!AccessCheck or the advapi32!AccessCheckByType APIs, depending on the operating system version. Listing 7.29 examines the identity before performing the access check.

**Listing 7.29**   Identifying the caller

```
0:001> k
ChildEBP RetAddr
007efc34 77525505 ADVAPI32!AccessCheckByType
007efc8c 775448c2 ole32!CallAccessCheck+0x9c
007efcec 775387a9 ole32!CheckAcl+0x73
007efd08 77532fe7 ole32!CheckAccess+0x88
007efd5c 77e7a2c1 ole32!ORPCInterfaceSecCallback+0x178
007efdb4 77e7c767 RPCRT4!RPC_INTERFACE::CheckSecurityIfNecessary+0x6f
007efdcc 77e7bcc9 RPCRT4!LRPC_SBINDING::CheckSecurity+0x4f
007efdfc 77e7bb6a RPCRT4!LRPC_SCALL::DealWithRequestMessage+0x194
007efe20 77e76784 RPCRT4!LRPC_ADDRESS::DealWithLRPCRequest+0x16d
007eff80 77e76c22 RPCRT4!LRPC_ADDRESS::ReceiveLotsaCalls+0x28f
007eff88 77e76a3b RPCRT4!RecvLotsaCallsWrapper+0xd
007effa8 77e76c0a RPCRT4!BaseCachedThreadRoutine+0x79
007effb4 7c80b50b RPCRT4!ThreadStartRoutine+0x1a
007effec 00000000 kernel32!BaseThreadStart+0x37
0:001> !token poi(@esp+c)
TS Session ID: 0
User: S-1-5-21-1060284298-2111687655-1957994488-1003
```

```
Groups:
 00 S-1-5-21-1060284298-2111687655-1957994488-513
    Attributes - Mandatory Default Enabled
...
Impersonation Level: Identification
TokenType: Impersonation
```

The impersonation token is not the only reason the DCOM infrastructure denies some calls. All remote calls have an associated authentication level that can vary from RPC_C_AUTHN_LEVEL_NONE, with no client authentication whatsoever, to RPC_C_AUTHN_LEVEL_PKT_PRIVACY, where the client identity is validated at every call and data is encrypted. Server-side DCOM infrastructure rejects all calls made at an authentication level lower than the value passed in ole32!CoInitializeSecurity, which is stored in global variable OLE32!gAuthnLevel. The authentication level has no meaning for calls made between local processes, as those calls are made at the RPC_C_AUTHN_LEVEL_PKT_PRIVACY level, guaranteed by the Windows kernel.

Listing 7.29 is taken from an access check performed before dispatching the client call into the server code, whether it is normal calls or the activation call. The impersonation token provided by the client application has the ImpersonationIdentify level and can cause big problems if the server is not fully initialized. This is one of the potential impersonation access tokens with huge restrictions if it ends up being used in a global initialization, as described in the previous section "Security Problems During Deferred Initialization."

Although it is not very common to implement a full-blown DCOM server, it is common to encounter all those restrictions when writing client code using asynchronous callback paradigms. Each time the client code passes a callback interface to be called from outside the client process, the underlying infrastructure starts a DCOM server, and all checks and settings are applied. In this case, the client code takes the server role and performs all access checks described in this section. Starting with Windows XP SP2, the DCOM infrastructure provides logging for several failures encountered in the normal operation using the NT Event Log, when the following keys are set in the registry:

```
HKEY_LOCAL_MACHINE\SOFTWARE\Microsoft\Ole\CallFailureLoggingLevel
HKEY_LOCAL_MACHINE\SOFTWARE\Microsoft\Ole\ActivationFailureLoggingLevel
HKEY_LOCAL_MACHINE\SOFTWARE\Microsoft\Ole\InvalidSecurityDescriptorLoggingLevel
```

**NOTE** Because RPCSS is a basic service used frequently by the DCOM infrastructure, any breakpoint set in the service is hit very often, and the call source must be checked to avoid wasting time tracing unrelated activation calls. Also, every time one of the system processes is broken under the debugger, the functionality of the machine is impaired.

## !token Extension Command Failure

In the "Local Security Failures" section, the attempt to examine the impersonation token using the !token extension command failed with access denied. Although it is not possible to correct the extension, it is instructive to understand the reason for the failure and the methodology used to find that out. The first step should be to understand the logical execution path leading to this error. The next step is to validate the execution path, using the debugger, by setting breakpoints in the main points from the execution path.

As described in Chapter 2, "Introduction to the Debuggers," in response to the !token extension command, the debugger executes a method named token, implemented in one extension library (in this case exts.dll). Because the extension runs inside the debugger, it is necessary to attach a new debugger to the debugger running the extension. The debugger's debugger can be easily started by entering the .dbgdbg command at the command prompt, or by starting it from the command prompt, commonly used when developing extensions.

Because the impersonation token and the primary token are protected by the kernel, the APIs enabling access to those tokens represent the right place to intercept the extension calls. The extension uses undocumented APIs exposed by ntdll.dll, having similar functionality with the advapi32.dll documented APIs. We learn that by setting breakpoints in the debugger's debugger on all APIs implementing functions having similar names, as in the following:

```
0:000> x *!*OpenProcessToken*
77dd7753 ADVAPI32!OpenProcessToken = <no type information>
77dd1364 ADVAPI32!_imp__NtOpenProcessToken = <no type information>
77e71350 RPCRT4!_imp__OpenProcessToken = <no type information>
7c801434 kernel32!_imp__NtOpenProcessToken = <no type information>
7c90dd90 ntdll!NtOpenProcessToken = <no type information>
7c90dda5 ntdll!NtOpenProcessTokenEx = <no type information>
...
0:000> bp ntdll!NtOpenProcessToken
0:000> bp ntdll!NtOpenThreadToken
0:000> g
```

After invoking the !token extension command again in the debugger, the execution stops into the debugger's debugger. Each API returns an access denied error, explaining the error displayed by the extension. Listing 7.30 shows how to execute the current function after hitting the breakpoint and where to look for the error code.

**Listing 7.30**  Watching the error code returned by OpenThreadToken/OpenProcessToken

```
0:000> g
Breakpoint 1 hit
eax=000007a4 ebx=7ffda000 ecx=00000000 edx=0007dc78 esi=00000000 edi=0007dd04
eip=7c90de0e esp=0007dc5c ebp=0007dc80 iopl=0         nv up ei pl zr na po nc
cs=001b  ss=0023  ds=0023  es=0023  fs=003b  gs=0000          efl=00000246
ntdll!NtOpenThreadToken:
7c90de0e b881000000      mov     eax,0x81
0:000> * Execute the current function, OpenThreadToken and return
0:000> gu
eax=c0000022 ebx=7ffda000 ecx=0007dc58 edx=7c90eb94 esi=00000000 edi=0007dd04
eip=01936cf8 esp=0007dc70 ebp=0007dc80 iopl=0         nv up ei pl zr na po nc
cs=001b  ss=0023  ds=0023  es=0023  fs=003b  gs=0000          efl=00000246
exts!tls+0xbb8:
01936cf8 8945f4          mov     [ebp-0xc],eax    ss:0023:0007dc74=00000000
0:000> * Notice the NT_STATUS access denied error in eax register
0:000> g
Breakpoint 0 hit
eax=00000000 ebx=7ffda000 ecx=0007dc78 edx=0000079c esi=00000000 edi=0007dd04
eip=7c90dd90 esp=0007dc60 ebp=0007dc80 iopl=0         nv up ei pl nz ac pe nc
cs=001b  ss=0023  ds=0023  es=0023  fs=003b  gs=0000          efl=00000246
ntdll!NtOpenProcessToken:
7c90dd90 b87b000000      mov     eax,0x7b
0:000> * Execute the current function, OpenProcessToken
0:000> gu
eax=c0000022 ebx=7ffda000 ecx=0007dc58 edx=7c90eb94 esi=00000000 edi=0007dd04
eip=01936cf8 esp=0007dc70 ebp=0007dc80 iopl=0         nv up ei pl zr na po nc
cs=001b  ss=0023  ds=0023  es=0023  fs=003b  gs=0000          efl=00000246
exts!tls+0xbb8:
01936cf8 8945f4          mov     [ebp-0xc],eax    ss:0023:0007dc74=00000000
0:000> * Notice the NT_STATUS access denied error in eax register
```

Because there is no easy way to identify the security descriptors protecting resources involved in this failure, we start the kernel debugger to examine the access token's security descriptors and the access tokens used by the calling code. Because a full kernel debugger session is not always available, the local kernel debugger is sufficient. The investigation shown in Listing 7.31 focuses on the primary token that is opened by the ntdll!NtOpenProcessToken API.

**Listing 7.31**  Obtaining the token information using local KD

```
lkd> * Finding the token used by the process executing wmiprvse.exe
lkd> !process 0 1 wmiprvse.exe
PROCESS 81a71da0  SessionId: 0  Cid: 03f4    Peb: 7ffd8000  ParentCid: 0320
    DirBase: 0a848000  ObjectTable: e21f59c8  HandleCount: 159.
    Image: wmiprvse.exe
    VadRoot 8203e5b0 Vads 109 Clone 0 Private 377. Modified 89. Locked 0.
    DeviceMap e1881148
    Token                               e18b2a68
...
lkd> * Displaying the token information
lkd> !token e18b2a68 -n
_TOKEN e18b2a68
TS Session ID: 0
User: S-1-5-20 (Well Known Group: NT AUTHORITY\NETWORK SERVICE)
Groups:
 00 S-1-5-20 (Well Known Group: NT AUTHORITY\NETWORK SERVICE)
    Attributes - Mandatory Default Enabled
...
Impersonation Level:       Impersonation
TokenType:                 Primary
Source: Advapi              TokenFlags: 0x81 ( Token in use )
Token ID: 34e00f            ParentToken ID: 0
Modified ID:                (0, 34de7a)
RestrictedSidCount: 0       RestrictedSids: 00000000
```

Because the debugger always has full access to the debugger target process, the only reason for the access failure when opening the primary token can be the primary token security descriptor. Listing 7.32 shows the security descriptor protecting the token obtained from the previous listing.

**Listing 7.32**  Displaying the primary token's security descriptor

```
lkd> !sd poi(e18b2a68-4) & FFFFFFF8
->Revision: 0x1
->Sbz1    : 0x0
->Control : 0x8004
            SE_DACL_PRESENT
            SE_SELF_RELATIVE
->Owner   : S-1-5-20
->Group   : S-1-5-20
->Dacl    :
->Dacl    : ->AclRevision: 0x2
```

```
->Dacl    : ->Sbz1       : 0x0
->Dacl    : ->AclSize    : 0x30
->Dacl    : ->AceCount   : 0x2
->Dacl    : ->Sbz2       : 0x0
->Dacl    : ->Ace[0]: ->AceType: ACCESS_ALLOWED_ACE_TYPE
->Dacl    : ->Ace[0]: ->AceFlags: 0x0
->Dacl    : ->Ace[0]: ->AceSize: 0x14
->Dacl    : ->Ace[0]: ->Mask : 0x000f01ff
->Dacl    : ->Ace[0]: ->SID: S-1-5-18

->Dacl    : ->Ace[1]: ->AceType: ACCESS_ALLOWED_ACE_TYPE
->Dacl    : ->Ace[1]: ->AceFlags: 0x0
->Dacl    : ->Ace[1]: ->AceSize: 0x14
->Dacl    : ->Ace[1]: ->Mask : 0x000f01ff
->Dacl    : ->Ace[1]: ->SID: S-1-5-20

->Sacl    : is NULL
```

The primary token's security descriptor does not allow system administrators to get a handle to it. Because the debugger runs under an administrator principal, different from LocalSystem or NetworkService, the primary token is not accessible to the !token extension command. The failure of opening the impersonating token is caused by a similar incompatibility between the thread object and the administrator account running the debugger.

## DCOM Activation Failure on Windows XP SP2 After Installing an Application

The last debugging example is performed on a previously healthy system running Windows XP SP2 that behaves strangely after the reboot requested by an application installation. The system fails to activate any DCOM server, affecting most administration MMC snap-ins. Even after turning on all DCOM tracing settings, described previously in the "DCOM Call Access Checks" section, no clear message can point to the problem root cause.

We begin debugging by using the model discussed previously of stopping each process that is part of the activation path in the debugger, while retrying the client activation. The first process from the bottom of the call path for which the client hangs is the process hosting the DcomLaunch service. Although this service is stopped in the debugger, no processes that are part of the activation path—namely the client making the activation call, the process hosting the RPCSS service, and the process hosting DcomLaunch—changes and can be investigated.

We expect the client process to have at least one thread with the ole32!CocreateInstanceEx API call on the stack at this time. Therefore, we attach a user mode debugger to the client process and list the stack for all threads. The client activation stack available in Listing 7.33 shows the thread that waits for a reply to a local RPC call, as indicated by the presence of the rpcrt4!LRPC_CALL on the stack. The wait and the visible client hang are caused by the debugger breaks in the process hosting the DcomLaunch service.

**Listing 7.33**   The client stack containing the activation call

```
0:001> ~0 k
ChildEBP RetAddr
0013de30 7c90e3ed ntdll!KiFastSystemCallRet
0013de34 77e7c968 ntdll!NtRequestWaitReplyPort+0xc
0013de80 77e7a716 RPCRT4!LRPC_CCALL::SendReceive+0x228
...
0013e4f0 77545fc8 ole32!CRpcResolver::CreateInstance+0x13d
0013e73c 7752f4f5 ole32!CClientContextActivator::CreateInstance+0xfa
0013e77c 7752f33a ole32!ActivationPropertiesIn::DelegateCreateInstance+0xf7
0013ef2c 77526000 ole32!ICoCreateInstanceEx+0x3c9
0013ef54 77525fcf ole32!CComActivator::DoCreateInstance+0x28
0013ef78 74ef18c1 ole32!CoCreateInstanceEx+0x1e
...
```

Because the error returned to the client has always been an access denied error, the next logical step is identifying the principal that the caller threads run under. As before, we use the !token extension command to obtain the current thread impersonating an access token. Because the extension command acts over the current thread, the first step sets the thread zero as the active thread.

**Listing 7.34**   Identifying the thread identity

```
0:001> ~0s
0:000> !token -n
Thread is not impersonating. Using process token...
TS Session ID: 0
User: S-1-5-21-1060284298-2111687655-1957994488-1003 (User: XP-SP2-BACK\TestAdmin)
Groups:
 00 S-1-5-21-1060284298-2111687655-1957994488-513 (Group: XP-SP2-BACK\None)
    Attributes - Mandatory Default Enabled
 01 S-1-1-0 (Well Known Group: localhost\Everyone)
    Attributes - Mandatory Default Enabled
```

```
 02 S-1-5-32-544 (Alias: BUILTIN\Administrators)
    Attributes - Mandatory Default Enabled Owner
...
Auth ID: 0:45550
Impersonation Level: Anonymous
TokenType: Primary
```

The thread is not impersonating; therefore, it uses the primary token representing a local administrator, powerful enough to do almost anything on this system. We move back to the process hosting the DcomLaunch service to understand what exactly is failing within this process. As seen in Listing 7.34, almost every DCOM call tries to obtain the impersonation access token representing the caller before doing work on the client's behalf, using the underlying protocol impersonation functions. Consequently, we must understand what specific identity makes the call by setting a breakpoint on `rpcrt4!RpcImpersonateClient` and checking the thread impersonation on return, as in Listing 7.35.

**Listing 7.35** Stopping the DcomLaunch code after impersonating the client

```
0:019> bp RPCRT4!RpcImpersonateClient "g @$ra"
0:019> g
eax=00000005 ebx=000c0b78 ecx=0065f7b4 edx=7c90eb94 esi=00000000 edi=0065f854
eip=76a822fc esp=0065f7dc ebp=0065f7f0 iopl=0         nv up ei ng nz na po nc
cs=001b  ss=0023  ds=0023  es=0023  fs=003b  gs=0000          efl=00000286
rpcss!LookupOrCreateTokenForRPCClient+0x24:
76a822fc 8b1d2014a876 mov ebx,[rpcss!_imp__GetCurrentThread
(76a81420)]{kernel32!GetCurrentThread (7c809919)} ds:0023:76a81420=7c809919
0:003> k
ChildEBP RetAddr
0065f7f0 76a95dad rpcss!LookupOrCreateTokenForRPCClient+0x24
0065f858 77e79dc9 rpcss!_LaunchActivatorServer+0x55
0065f8b4 77ef321a RPCRT4!Invoke+0x30
...
0:003> !token
Thread is not impersonating. Using process token...
TS Session ID: 0
User: S-1-5-18
Groups:
 00 S-1-5-32-544
    Attributes - Default Enabled Owner
 01 S-1-1-0
    Attributes - Mandatory Default Enabled
 02 S-1-5-11
```

*(continues)*

**Listing 7.35** Stopping the DcomLaunch code after impersonating the client *(continued)*

```
     Attributes - Mandatory Default Enabled
Primary Group: S-1-5-18
...
Auth ID: 0:3e7
Impersonation Level: Anonymous
TokenType: Primary
0:003> reax
eax=00000005
0:003> !error 5
Error code: (Win32) 0x5 (5) - Access is denied.
```

After the impersonation attempt, the thread is still not impersonating since the API failed with access denied. It is time to look in the execution path closer to the client, in the process hosting the RPCSS service, and identify the thread making this call. A quick scan through the threads reveals the thread from Listing 7.36 with an outstanding RPC call. However, it is not possible to obtain the thread impersonating for the reasons we described in the previous section.

**Listing 7.36** Displaying the thread in the RPCSS service part of the activation path

```
0:008>k
ChildEBP RetAddr
0099f528 7c90e9c0 ntdll!KiFastSystemCallRet
0099f52c 7c8025db ntdll!NtWaitForSingleObject+0xc
0099f590 7c802542 kernel32!WaitForSingleObjectEx+0xa8
0099f5a4 76a92fad kernel32!WaitForSingleObject+0x12
0099f608 76a92a4a rpcss!CClsidData::ServerLaunchMutex+0xce
0099f65c 76a8e4ab rpcss!Activation+0x384
0099f6b8 76a91e12 rpcss!ActivateFromProperties+0x213
0099f6c8 76a91e66 rpcss!CScmActivator::CreateInstance+0x10
0099f708 76a91e7b rpcss!ActivationPropertiesIn::DelegateCreateInstance+0xf7
0099f754 76a8c1d7 rpcss!ActivateFromPropertiesPreamble+0x4c1
0099f79c 76a91de7 rpcss!PerformScmStage+0xbb
0099f8b0 77e79dc9 rpcss!SCMActivatorCreateInstance+0x97
0099f8e0 77ef321a RPCRT4!Invoke+0x30
...
0099fdfc 77e7bb6a RPCRT4!LRPC_SCALL::DealWithRequestMessage+0x2db
0099fe20 77e76784 RPCRT4!LRPC_ADDRESS::DealWithLRPCRequest+0x16d
```

```
0:008> !token
Thread is not impersonating. Using process token...
Error 0xc0000022 getting thread token
```

To obtain the impersonation token, we will use the technique presented in the previous section "!token Extension Command Failure," using the kernel mode debugger in local mode. The result of this step is shown in Listing 7.37.

**Listing 7.37**   Displaying the thread from Listing 7.36 using a kernel mode debugger in local mode

```
lkd> !thread 815aada8
THREAD 815aada8  Cid 035c.0fac  Teb: 7ffd4000 Win32Thread: 00000000 WAIT: (Suspended)
KernelMode Non-Alertable
SuspendCount 1
FreezeCount 1
    815aaf44   Semaphore Limit 0x2
Waiting for reply to LPC MessageId 00015a17:
Current LPC port e1dc2480
Impersonation token:  e23ce530 (Level Identification)
Owning Process            8217a520       Image:          svchost.exe
Wait Start TickCount      657309         Elapsed Ticks: 1362
Context Switch Count      570
UserTime                  00:00:00.0000
KernelTime                00:00:00.0020
Start Address kernel32!BaseThreadStartThunk (0x7c810856)
```

The impersonating token on this thread at the SecurityIdentification level is the actual cause of the failure in the DcomLaunch Server service, as the token at this level cannot be propagated in a sequential remote process. This is in total contradiction to the initial caller access token or to the client code intentions. It looks more like a problem with the impersonation mechanism used by the RPCSS Server service.

After doing some research on the Microsoft MSDN site, we found a reference to a new privilege added in Windows Server 2003 and later to Windows XP SP2, named SeImpersonatePrivilege, that affects the impersonating level obtained after impersonating a client access token. Furthermore, in the Local security Policy shown in Figure 7.7, we see SeImpersonatePrivilege not granted to the NetworkService identity; thus, the error seen before is normal.

Granting the privilege to the SERVICES account, which includes NetworkService, and restarting the system, the system functionality is restored.

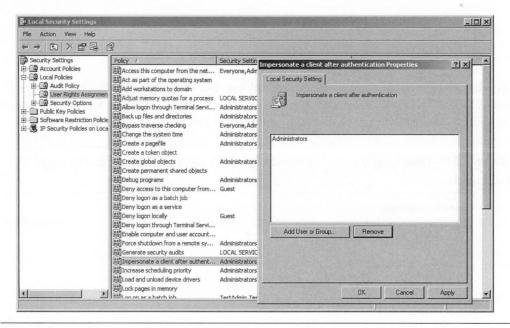

**Figure 7.7**   Impersonate client assignment

## Investigating Security Failures Using Tracing Tools

The common cause of the access denied error cases presented so far in this chapter is the incompatibility between the principal trying to access an object and the security descriptor protecting it. In addition, it is fairly easy to understand what pieces are involved in the operation, and the security information is easily accessible from the Windows debuggers.

On the other end of the spectrum are access denied error cases in complex applications with relatively unknown architecture that encounters errors primarily when accessing protected resources past their security boundary. In those cases, we should start the investigation using various tracing tools to understand what resources are accessed, how they are accessed, and in what order they are accessed.

Process Monitor is such a tool that shows, in real-time, file and registry activity on the local system. When the application interacts with other computer systems, network tracing is the best way to discover the network activity and the access denied error encountered by the application. The next chapter uses a network monitor tool to observe a remote application behavior.

All file system and registry accesses, performed in the "DCOM Activation Checks" section, are easily traceable. For example, the file access operations and their results are clearly exposed by the Process Monitor tool, as shown in Figure 7.8, after hiding the registries and the process activity. In this case, the security descriptor protecting the server image file has been manually changed to deny access to local administrators.

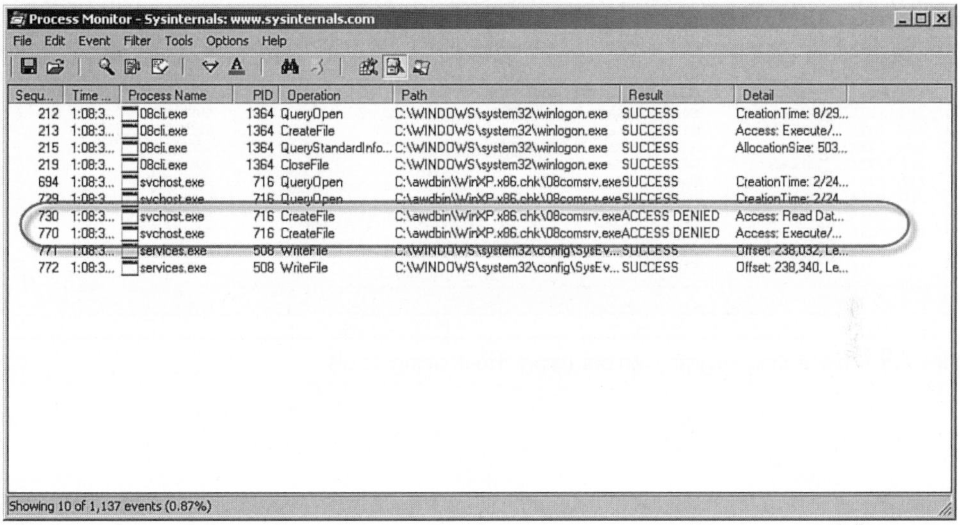

**Figure 7.8**    Detecting file errors using the tracing tools

In Figure 7.8, it is easy to see how the svchost.exe process hosting DcomLaunch tries to open the image file of the server process and fails with access denied errors. This tracing can reveal other file access errors, as well as other errors encountered by the server after process startup. Figure 7.9 shows the errors encountered by the server process when trying to access several registry keys. The registry paths must be correlated with the information available about the component to understand what went wrong. We usually filter the activity by the executable name or by the path of accessed objects.

The errors encountered in Figure 7.9 are caused by an improper registration of the proxy-stub module used by the application when it accesses one interface. Armed with this information and with an overview of the infrastructure, it is very easy to find the solution: reregister the proxy-stub on the system hosting the server process.

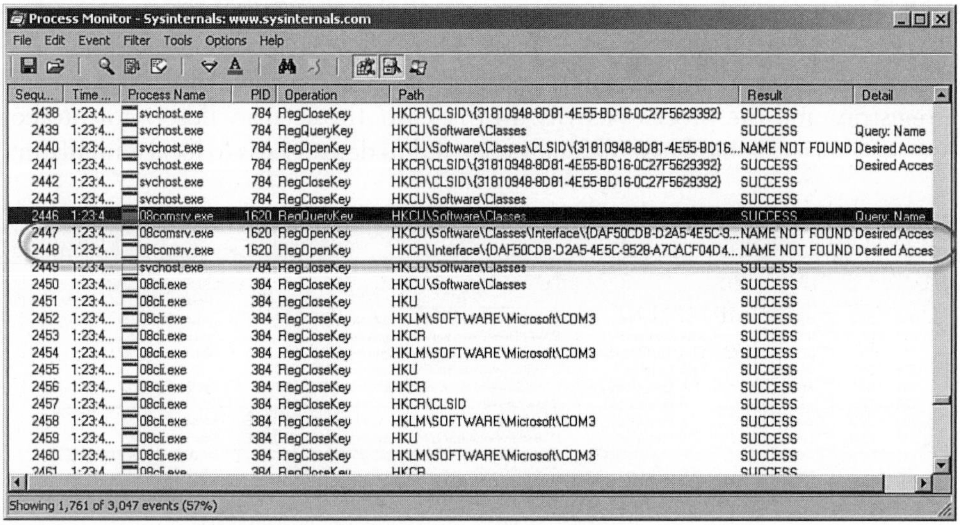

| Sequ... | Time ... | Process Name | PID | Operation | Path | Result | Detail |
|---|---|---|---|---|---|---|---|
| 2438 | 1:23:4... | svchost.exe | 784 | RegCloseKey | HKCR\CLSID\{31810948-8D81-4E55-BD16-0C27F5629392} | SUCCESS | |
| 2439 | 1:23:4... | svchost.exe | 784 | RegQueryKey | HKCU\Software\Classes | SUCCESS | Query: Name |
| 2440 | 1:23:4... | svchost.exe | 784 | RegOpenKey | HKCU\Software\Classes\CLSID\{31810948-8D81-4E55-BD16... | NAME NOT FOUND | Desired Acces |
| 2441 | 1:23:4... | svchost.exe | 784 | RegOpenKey | HKCR\CLSID\{31810948-8D81-4E55-BD16-0C27F5629392} | SUCCESS | Desired Acces |
| 2442 | 1:23:4... | svchost.exe | 784 | RegCloseKey | HKCR\CLSID\{31810948-8D81-4E55-BD16-0C27F5629392} | SUCCESS | |
| 2443 | 1:23:4... | svchost.exe | 784 | RegCloseKey | HKCU\Software\Classes | SUCCESS | |
| 2446 | 1:23:4... | 08comsrv.exe | 1620 | RegQueryKey | HKCU\Software\Classes | SUCCESS | Query: Name |
| 2447 | 1:23:4... | 08comsrv.exe | 1620 | RegOpenKey | HKCU\Software\Classes\Interface\{DAF50CDB-D2A5-4E5C-9... | NAME NOT FOUND | Desired Acces |
| 2448 | 1:23:4... | 08comsrv.exe | 1620 | RegOpenKey | HKCR\Interface\{DAF50CDB-D2A5-4E5C-9528-A7CACF04D4... | NAME NOT FOUND | Desired Acces |
| 2449 | 1:23:4... | svchost.exe | 784 | RegCloseKey | HKCU\Software\Classes | SUCCESS | |
| 2450 | 1:23:4... | 08cli.exe | 384 | RegCloseKey | HKCU\Software\Classes | SUCCESS | |
| 2451 | 1:23:4... | 08cli.exe | 384 | RegCloseKey | HKU | SUCCESS | |
| 2452 | 1:23:4... | 08cli.exe | 384 | RegCloseKey | HKLM\SOFTWARE\Microsoft\COM3 | SUCCESS | |
| 2453 | 1:23:4... | 08cli.exe | 384 | RegCloseKey | HKCR | SUCCESS | |
| 2454 | 1:23:4... | 08cli.exe | 384 | RegCloseKey | HKLM\SOFTWARE\Microsoft\COM3 | SUCCESS | |
| 2455 | 1:23:4... | 08cli.exe | 384 | RegCloseKey | HKU | SUCCESS | |
| 2456 | 1:23:4... | 08cli.exe | 384 | RegCloseKey | HKCR | SUCCESS | |
| 2457 | 1:23:4... | 08cli.exe | 384 | RegCloseKey | HKCR\CLSID | SUCCESS | |
| 2458 | 1:23:4... | 08cli.exe | 384 | RegCloseKey | HKLM\SOFTWARE\Microsoft\COM3 | SUCCESS | |
| 2459 | 1:23:4... | 08cli.exe | 384 | RegCloseKey | HKU | SUCCESS | |
| 2460 | 1:23:4... | 08cli.exe | 384 | RegCloseKey | HKLM\SOFTWARE\Microsoft\COM3 | SUCCESS | |
| 2461 | 1:23:4... | 08cli.exe | 384 | RegCloseKey | HKCR | SUCCESS | |

Showing 1,761 of 3,047 events (57%)

**Figure 7.9**    Detecting registry errors using the tracing tools

## Summary

In this chapter, you learned the basic mechanism used by the operating system to control access to various resources, the mechanism used to identify the principals, and the way to examine each of those elements using the Windows debuggers. In addition, you learned where the security information is stored and how it is propagated from one process to another or from one system to another.

You then used this knowledge to understand several access denied errors encountered in application ranging from a very simple "in the process" access denied error to the complex cases involving distributed COM. Using the same tools and similar heuristics, you can now handle any security failure encountered in the development process or in the deployment phase.

# CHAPTER 8

# INTERPROCESS COMMUNICATION

Years ago, software components were working largely in isolation without much inter-action. The limited interaction was performed using custom mechanisms rarely used by multiple components—mechanisms based on file system operation or network protocols, such as IP or UDP. The ability to understand the communication between components was limited to people who knew the details of the application.

Today, the omnipresent client-server architecture has changed the software land-scape even for simple applications. While MS-DOS applications used to write direct-ly into the video memory buffer to update the visible application state, today's Windows components are making system API calls to have the application state updated. Underneath the system API, Windows calls the process responsible for managing all windows using one of the communication processes described in this chapter. Another application writes an event into the Event Log, which results in an interprocess call to the service responsible for Event Log management.

Today's solutions are using more and more systems running on multiple process-es. Some of them are using this mechanism to provide fault tolerance or security iso-lations, whereas others use this just to achieve scalability levels beyond those provided by the single-process systems. Not knowing how to navigate through this complex infrastructure puts the engineers into a weird situation: They have all the knowledge to tackle the business problem resolved by the software solution, but they are unable to spot the problem easily, as the whole interprocess communication process obstructs them from easily understanding the real problem.

This chapter provides the necessary tools and information required to successful-ly investigate the problems in connected software environments—problems that involve more than one process, or more than one computer. We focus on several com-munication primitives, and we will introduce a few new tools. In this chapter, you will get the answers to several basic questions about a client-server application, such as the following.

■ When the client call fails, how can we find the location and the cause of this failure?

- When the server does not reply in a predictable manner and must be debugged, which thread, process, and system are responsible for blocking the call?
- When the server gets called with invalid parameters, how can we identify the client calling this server method?

We use a new extension command, `!lpc`, available in the Windows debuggers extensions loaded by default. This chapter's sample is a distributed COM application, consisting of a client application, 08cli.exe; a dynamic link library, 08comps.dll, which contains the communication proxy-stub code; and a server application, 08comsrv.exe. The source code and binary are in the following folders:

Source code: `C:\AWD\Chapter8`

Binary: `C:\AWDBIN\WinXP.x86.chk\08cli.exe`, `08comps.dll`, and `08comsrv.exe`.

## Communication Mechanisms

Current Windows operating systems, such as Windows XP and Windows Server 2003, have built-in support for multiple communication protocols. Transport layer protocols, such as connection-based IP or datagram UDP, can be directly used for simple forms of interprocess communication. However, applications might have complex requirements, such as reliable communication or secure communication, requirements that have to be accomplished using the least amount of code. Furthermore, the communication between systems having different architecture—such as a 64-bit processor architecture system communicating with a 32-bit processor architecture system—should work seamlessly. The messages exchanged between heterogeneous systems should be independent from the processor type, the operating system, or the compiler characteristics.

In such cases, developers select session layer communication protocols implementing all the requirements. DCE Remote Procedure Call (DCE/RPC) is such a protocol that satisfies the preceding requirements. RPC is used to implement a familiar call-response communication paradigm between components living in different processes or physical systems. The RPC runtime provides the mechanisms necessary to marshal and unmarshal messages passed between the client and server process used to implement the call-response paradigm. Microsoft's implementation of the RPC protocol, named MSRPC, can use any protocol at the session layer or below that is available between the client and the server, including TPC/IP, Named Pipe, or HTTP. Not surprisingly, most administration tools in the Windows operating system use MSRPC to communicate with the servers managed by them.

With the advent of object-oriented programming practices, developers looked for communication protocols facilitating those practices. Microsoft created the Distributed Common Object Model (DCOM) infrastructure on top of the MSRPC infrastructure. As an added value to MSRPC, the DCOM infrastructure provides the capability to activate, use, and destroy objects implementing multiple interfaces. The lifetime of DCOM objects is explicitly managed by the client application. Accidentally disconnected objects are periodically reclaimed by DCOM's distributed garbage collector.

DCOM objects can be created in virtually every programming language and can be consumed from any language or tools capable of using them. Newer programming languages, based on the .NET runtime, can interact transparently with DCOM objects by exposing the DCOM objects as .NET objects.

The communication between two processes running on the same physical host is natively supported by the Windows kernel in the form of Local Procedure Call (LPC). MSRPC using LPC is often referred to as Local RPC or LRPC. Figure 8.1 shows the relationships between the various communication protocols available in the Windows operating system to aid understanding the entire protocol stack, useful in debugging interprocess communication.

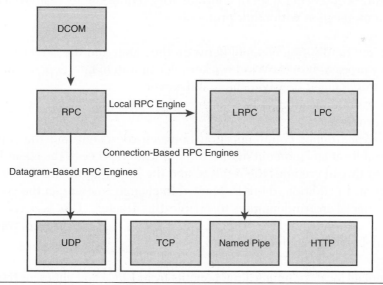

**Figure 8.1**  Relationship between various communication protocols available in Windows operating systems

Most techniques used in debugging a specific protocol are used to debug any protocol derived from it or using it as a communication base. For example, to debug the communication between two processes using DCOM, the developer must also debug the LRPC communication between the client and the server process.

## Troubleshooting Local Communication

The importance of local communication between various processes cannot be ignored. Automation objects, which are exposed or used by all complex applications, are driven by a sequence of DCOM calls against the objects implemented by various servers. Chances are good that sooner or later, an engineer will either provide the service or will consume the service provided by someone else's components. When the client and the server are running in different processes, the calls do not always work as expected. The client can pass the wrong arguments, such as the security context. Likewise, the server can take much longer than expected to process the request. In such cases, the engineer is forced to debug the communication between those processes.

Fortunately, the communication between local components is usually performed using protocols built around the LPC protocol. Mastering this basic protocol, which is the subject of this section, is essential in debugging the Windows operating system. The LPC protocol satisfies a set of contradictory requirements that are hard to meet in local communication with other protocols.

- The communication channel between the client and the server is secured; no other process, besides Windows kernel, can watch, intercept, or alter the messages exchanged between client and server.
- The communication between the client and the server is optimized for performance.
- The synchronous communication between the client and the server is fully traceable; at any moment in the communication process, the client knows what server thread executes the request, and the server knows what client made the request. In addition, there is no need to change anything in the system or add any special instrumentation to enable this tracing. This is a very important aspect of debugging live systems, and it shows that the protocol was built with the debugging capability in mind.

However, not all local communication benefits from LPC capabilities, as there are individual cases in which the local communication is done in unconventional ways. For example, two processes can send windows messages to each other, can use MSRPC over a network protocol, or can even use a transport layer protocol directly. The section "Troubleshooting Remote Communication" is dedicated to debugging the communication using RPC over network protocols. LPC communication is debugged using a kernel mode debugger either connected to the system or running in local mode.

## LPC Background

Despite the fact the protocol is not documented by Microsoft, plenty of references are available to help build a good enough understanding of this protocol to be proficient in debugging it. The history of LPC dates back to the first days of the Windows NT operating system, when the client-server architecture used at the core of the operating system called for a new communication protocol meeting strong performance requirements. The LPC protocol is supported by a suite of APIs implemented directly by the Windows kernel and exposed to user mode code by a series of functions implemented inside ntdll.dll, having the ntdll!Nt[operation]Port form.

To understand how the protocol is used, engineers must have a basic idea about its behavior. The basic communication happens in several important steps, as follows.

1. The server initiates the protocol with the creation of a named port by calling the ntdll!NtCreatePort API. The port is called the connection port.
2. The server listens on that connection port for new communication requests using the ntdll!NtListenPort API. The server must have a thread waiting on the connection port all the time.
3. The client initiates a new connection by sending a connection request to the server by using the ntdll!NtConnectPort API. The request is sent to the port created in step 1.
4. The server examines the connection request and, based on its policies, accepts the connection by using the ntdll!NtAcceptConnectPort API followed by a ntdll!NtCompleteConnectPort call.
5. After the connection has been established, both the client and the server are in possession of a communication port object that can be used for actual communication.
6. The server starts a loop dedicated to the connection port in which it receives a new message, processes the message, and replies to the client using, for example, the ntdll!NtReplyWaitReceivePort API.
7. The client uses ntdll!NtRequestWaitReplyPort to send a new request to the server and waits for the server to process it. Step 6 and step 7 repeat for the duration of the entire conversation between the client and the server.

Each message exchanged between the client and the server has a DWORD unique identifier that is stored in the KTHREAD structure representing the client and the server thread. This identifier is used to track the call path in the kernel mode debugger using the !lpc extension command.

## Debugging LPC Communication

Each thread involved in an LPC conversation maintains a reference to the message that is currently handled by the thread. This reference is listed every time the thread information is displayed. In other words, every time a client thread waits on an LPC request to be processed, the message identifier corresponding to the current request is available after executing the !thread extension command. Likewise, if the server thread processes a message, the message identifier is listed by the !thread extension command. Using the !lpc extension command, all the information about the client connection port, the server connection port, the server communication port, and the server process is obtained using the information associated with the message.

To demonstrate how to use this facility, we examine a call made by the client 08CLI.EXE into the ICalculator::SlowSum method implemented by the 08COMSRV.EXE server that does not return in a timely fashion. Listing 8.1 shows the result of executing the !thread extension command within a kernel mode debugger on the client thread that initiated the request.

**Listing 8.1**   Client's thread waiting on LPC request to complete

```
kd> !thread ffb10020
THREAD ffb10020  Cid 05b4.04f8  Teb: 7ffdd000 Win32Thread: e16e5eb0 WAIT: (WrLpcRe-
ply) UserMode Non-Alertable
    ffb10214  Semaphore Limit 0x1
Waiting for reply to LPC MessageId 00004f99:
Current LPC port e138cd98
Not impersonating
DeviceMap               e1a60398
Owning Process          ffaa62f0      Image:         08cli.exe
Wait Start TickCount    563720        Ticks: 1391 (0:00:00:13.930)
Context Switch Count    98                  LargeStack
UserTime                00:00:00.0000
KernelTime              00:00:00.0530
Start Address kernel32!BaseProcessStartThunk (0x7c810867)
Win32 Start Address 08CLI!ILT+1385(_wmainCRTStartup) (0x0042c56e)
Stack Init f6c05000 Current f6c04c50 Base f6c05000 Limit f6c01000 Call 0
Priority 8 BasePriority 8 PriorityDecrement 0 DecrementCount 16
ChildEBP RetAddr  Args to Child
```

```
f6c04c68 804dc6a6 ffb10090 ffb10020 804dc6f2 nt!KiSwapContext+0x2e
f6c04c74 804dc6f2 ffb10214 ffb101e8 ffb10020 nt!KiSwapThread+0x46
f6c04c9c 805788ef 00000001 00000011 e100da01 nt!KeWaitForSingleObject+0x1c2
f6c04d50 804df06b 000006e0 0015c2b8 0015c2b8 nt!NtRequestWaitReplyPort+0x63d
...
```

The state of the thread holding LPC information is clearly decoded in the third line of the thread information shown in Listing 8.1. The message can be passed to the `!lpc` extension command to extract the associated information, as shown in Listing 8.2. In this case, the command has been used to dump the message information, using the `!lpc message <message_id>` form.

**Listing 8.2**   Using !lpc extension to get message information

```
kd> !lpc message 00004f99
Searching message 4f99 in threads ...
    Server thread ffab41c0 is working on message 4f99
Client thread ffb10020 waiting a reply from 4f99
Searching thread ffb10020 in port rundown queues ...

Server communication port 0xe111b878
    Handles: 1    References: 1
    The LpcDataInfoChainHead queue is empty
        Connected port: 0xe138cd98      Server connection port: 0xe14684f0

Client communication port 0xe138cd98
    Handles: 1    References: 2
    The LpcDataInfoChainHead queue is empty

Server connection port e14684f0  Name: OLE0D6120B10F36435E84795A344064
    Handles: 1    References: 9
    Server process  : ffab3530 (08comsrv.exe)
    Queue semaphore : 8124a248
    Semaphore state 0 (0x0)
    The message queue is empty
    The LpcDataInfoChainHead queue is empty
Done.
```

The extension command extracts the information available about the client-server communication. In the command output, we can find the server process information—

including its image name, the connection port name, plus additional information, such as the message queue length. The queue contains the messages waiting to be served by the process—messages received on both the connection port and the connected port. Listing 8.3 shows a case in which the server process has been stopped in the debugger and the connection requests are pilling up on the connection port. The port address is used as an argument to the !lpc port <port_id> extension command.

**Listing 8.3** Using !lpc extension to get port information

```
kd> !lpc port e13f6878

Server connection port e13f6878  Name: OLE9D3C2AF8298042C9A8D0FACAE0FA
    Handles: 1   References: 10
    Server process  : ffb52020 (08comsrv.exe)
    Queue semaphore : 8124f3d0
    Semaphore state 2 (0x2)
      Messages in queue:
      0000 e13f8528 - Busy  Id=00006dcd  From: 0348.077c  Context=80020000
[e13f6888 . e160a858]
                  Length=0044002c  Type=00380001 (LPC_REQUEST)
                  Data: 00008701 00040342 00007801 000007f4 8f62e1ae 2ee99a5d
      0000 e160a858 - Busy  Id=00006f23  From: 0348.07f0  Context=80020000
[e13f8528 . e13f6888]
                  Length=0044002c  Type=00380001 (LPC_REQUEST)
                  Data: 00005b01 00040342 00007801 000007f4 8f62e1ae 2ee99a5d
    The message queue contains 2 messages
    The LpcDataInfoChainHead queue is empty
```

Another nice feature of the !lpc extension command is the capability of extracting the LPC information from a thread passed in as parameter in the following syntax: !lpc thread <threadid> If the thread identifier is omitted, the extension command  dumps all the LPC activity happening in the system at the time of the execution, as shown in Listing 8.4.

**Listing 8.4** Using !lpc extension to obtain the entire LPC activity on the system

```
kd> !lpc thread
Searching message 0 in threads ...
    Server thread 8118b7b8 is working on message 5ee
Client thread 81129da8 waiting a reply from 88f
    Server thread 81271020 is working on message 1968
    Server thread 8112c168 is working on message 47c7
```

```
    Server thread 81130c98 is working on message 2f35
    Server thread ffb952c8 is working on message 47c4
    Server thread 8120fda8 is working on message 5fe
    Server thread ffbc1c18 is working on message 887
    Server thread ffbcb7f0 is working on message 888
    Server thread ffbc17f0 is working on message 88f
    Server thread 81122768 is working on message 47ca
    Server thread 811323b0 is working on message b6c
    Server thread 81134568 is working on message 2fd1
    Server thread 81206020 is working on message 4b3
    Server thread 81211c58 is working on message 4943
Client thread ffb40da8 waiting a reply from f83
    Server thread 8125d020 is working on message 26ff
    Server thread ffb42da8 is working on message f83
    Server thread ffb06a60 is working on message 2fff
    Server thread ffaba020 is working on message 4d1c
    Server thread ffb096c0 is working on message 29a5
    Server thread ffab1020 is working on message 4e7c
    Server thread ffab41c0 is working on message 4f99
Client thread ffb10020 waiting a reply from 4f99
Done.
```

**NOTE** It is impressive to see how many threads communicate with each other at any given moment, even on an idle machine.

The debugging capabilities of the LPC protocol are wonderful. The client thread is blocked while the server thread processes the message, and it is easily discoverable by inspecting the kernel structures using the !lpc extension command. Knowing these methods, it is not difficult to extend the scope of debugging beyond a single process, used throughout the book, to the entire machine. For example, the synchronization chapter scenarios about detecting deadlocks inside a single process can be extended to a group of processes communicating using LPC-based protocols.

The only caveat to all this is that the LPC information is available only from the kernel mode debugger. That should not be a problem in newer operating systems, such as Windows XP or Windows 2003, because it is very easy to start a kernel debugger in local mode and use it in parallel with the other debuggers. Chapter 2, "Introduction to the Debuggers," is a good reference for the situations in which multiple debuggers must be used simultaneously.

But because the LPC protocol is not documented, it is not used directly outside the Windows core operating system. With only a few exceptions (Windows system

APIs using LPC directly), the developer is exposed to the LPC protocol indirectly through the LRPC protocol or other protocols layered on top of it. Local DCOM invocation is one such protocol, and it is the focus of the next section.

## Debugging Local DCOM and MSRPC Communication

In the most common scenario, the client makes a call into the server that does not return in a reasonable amount of time. The first step of the investigation is identifying the troubled client thread waiting for the server reply. The next step is identifying the server process and the thread processing the respective call, if any, and finding out the thread state. The thread can, for example, wait for another kernel object or user input.

To exemplify this technique, we reuse the client-server sample. The sample calls the server synchronously in a COM multithreaded apartment, which maps directly to synchronous LPC communication. While the server code waits before sending back the response, the client hangs and presents the perfect opportunity for debugging. We start 08CLI.EXE under the debugger and run it freely for a few seconds to complete the initialization sequence. The time window when the communication is not tracked is not relevant since it will wait in hung state much longer. In this case, we realize that the invocation of ICalculator::SlowSum is extremely slow without any explanation (other than the interface method name). The next step is to list all stack threads and identify those threads showing LRPC activity. In Listing 8.5, we can see the first thread having a rpcrt4!LRPC_CCALL object method on the stack. In turn, this method uses LPC APIs directly. The LPC function used in this case, ntdll!NtRequestWaitReplyPort, is a good indicator of a client-initiated call. The client makes a server request and waits for a reply on the LPC port. This technique works for synchronous RPC only.

**Listing 8.5**   Starting the client and listing a partial call stack for each thread

```
C:\>windbg 08CLI.EXE
...
0:003> * The client has been running freely for a few seconds before stopping it
0:003> ~* k2
   0  Id: 5b4.4f8 Suspend: 1 Teb: 7ffdd000 Unfrozen
ChildEBP RetAddr
0012f6e4 7c90e3ed ntdll!KiFastSystemCallRet
0012f6e8 77e7cc55 ntdll!NtRequestWaitReplyPort+0xc
0012f734 77e7aae6 RPCRT4!LRPC_CCALL::SendReceive+0x228
   1  Id: 5b4.1d0 Suspend: 1 Teb: 7ffdc000 Unfrozen
ChildEBP RetAddr
00e9fe18 7c90e399 ntdll!KiFastSystemCallRet
```

```
00e9fe1c 77e76703 ntdll!NtReplyWaitReceivePortEx+0xc
00e9ff80 77e76c1b RPCRT4!LRPC_ADDRESS::ReceiveLotsaCalls+0xf4
   2  Id: 5b4.278 Suspend: 1 Teb: 7ffdb000 Unfrozen
ChildEBP RetAddr
00b0ff1c 7c90d85c ntdll!KiFastSystemCallRet
00b0ff20 7c8023ed ntdll!NtDelayExecution+0xc
00b0ff78 7c802451 kernel32!SleepEx+0x61
#  3  Id: 5b4.bd0 Suspend: 1 Teb: 7ffdb000 Unfrozen
ChildEBP RetAddr
00b6ffc8 7c9507a8 ntdll!DbgBreakPoint
00b6fff4 00000000 ntdll!DbgUiRemoteBreakin+0x2d
```

**NOTE** The naming convention of the CCALL objects is a good indication of the protocol used for interprocess communication. LRPC_CCALL is the client side capable of handling local calls over LPC; OSF_CCALL indicates a communication using a connection-based protocol, such as TCP/IP or named pipes; and DG_CCALL indicates a communication using a datagram-based protocol, such as UDP. The relationship between those protocols can be seen in Figure 8.1.

Examining the entire stack of the thread identified previously helps identify exactly what function call hangs and what layers are involved in handling that call. In the case shown in Listing 8.6, the client call uses DCOM as indicated by the use of the methods in ole32.dll, which in turn uses RPC and, ultimately, LPC to dispatch the call to the server.

**Listing 8.6**  Typical stack of clients using DCOM over LRPC

```
0:003> ~0k
ChildEBP RetAddr
0012f6e4 7c90e3ed ntdll!KiFastSystemCallRet
0012f6e8 77e7cc55 ntdll!NtRequestWaitReplyPort+0xc
0012f734 77e7aae6 RPCRT4!LRPC_CCALL::SendReceive+0x228
0012f740 776016bf RPCRT4!I_RpcSendReceive+0x24
0012f75c 776011b6 ole32!ThreadSendReceive+0xf5
0012f778 7760109a ole32!CRpcChannelBuffer::SwitchAptAndDispatchCall+0x13d
0012f858 7751047c ole32!CRpcChannelBuffer::SendReceive2+0xb9
0012f8c4 77510414 ole32!CAptRpcChnl::SendReceive+0xab
0012f918 77ef3db5 ole32!CCtxComChnl::SendReceive+0x113
0012f934 77ef3ead RPCRT4!NdrProxySendReceive+0x43
0012fd10 77ef3e42 RPCRT4!NdrClientCall2+0x1fa
```

*(continues)*

**Listing 8.6**   Typical stack of clients using DCOM over LRPC   *(continued)*

```
0012fd30 77e8a433 RPCRT4!ObjectStublessClient+0x8b
0012fd40 0042ea5b RPCRT4!ObjectStubless+0xf
0012fe48 0042e7ae 08CLI!MTAClientCall+0x7b
0012ff54 0042f902 08CLI!wmain+0xae
0012ffb8 0042f6bd 08CLI!wmainCRTStartup+0x252
0012ffc0 7c816fd7 08CLI!wmainCRTStartup+0xd
0012fff0 00000000 kernel32!BaseProcessStart+0x23
```

Even if the relevant client thread has been identified, it makes sense to understand why a second thread is waiting on an outstanding LPC call with a stack shown in Listing 8.7. The LPC function used in this case, `ntdll!NtReplyWaitReceivePort`, indicates a server thread waiting to receive a new operation request. Although it might seem a little bit confusing that each DCOM client also has a server role, at the beginning of the chapter, we said that DCOM provides added value functionality to the RPC stack, such as distributed garbage collection. This thread is part of this entire mechanism peculiar to this client process. The client process is notified on this thread when the server goes away, and it cleans up all the structures associated with that server.

**Listing 8.7**   Typical stack of a server thread waiting for a new request on DCOM over LRPC

```
0:003> ~1k
ChildEBP RetAddr
00e9fe18 7c90e399 ntdll!KiFastSystemCallRet
00e9fe1c 77e76703 ntdll!NtReplyWaitReceivePortEx+0xc
00e9ff80 77e76c1b RPCRT4!LRPC_ADDRESS::ReceiveLotsaCalls+0xf4
00e9ff88 77e76a3d RPCRT4!RecvLotsaCallsWrapper+0xd
00e9ffa8 77e76c03 RPCRT4!BaseCachedThreadRoutine+0x79
00e9ffb4 7c80b683 RPCRT4!ThreadStartRoutine+0x1a
00e9ffec 00000000 kernel32!BaseThreadStart+0x37
```

**NOTE** Similar to the naming convention of the CCALL objects, the naming convention for the ADDRESS objects is a good indication of the protocol the process is listening to. LRPC_ADDRESS is the server side waiting to handle local calls over LPC; OSF_ADRESS indicates that the server waits on connection-based protocols, such as TCP/IP or named pipes; and DG_CCALL indicates that the server waits on a datagram-based protocol, such as UDP. The relationship between those protocols can be seen in Figure 8.1.

At this time, there are several ways to find out the server thread that processes the client requests. The first method uses LPC debugging capabilities to track the message being processed, a method requiring kernel mode debugger. In the next step, the engineer hooks the kernel mode debugger to the system or uses it from inside the system in local mode, as described in the Chapter 2. The remaining steps in this section are performed from within the kernel mode debugger.

The LRPC calls can also be tracked by the same methods used in tracking remote calls, methods using RPC troubleshooting state information. This method is documented in the "Troubleshooting Remote Communication" section, and it can be used without a problem in the LRPC communication.

Another option can be to interpret information already available on the client thread and to extract the server information from the MSRPC structures used when making the call. Unfortunately, that method is not possible using public symbols. It also requires a deep knowledge of the internal structures stored inside MSRPC. This method is the least attractive for developers without access to rpcrt4.dll private symbols.

The same instance of the 08cli.exe process started in Listing 8.5 is inspected with the kernel mode debugger. We use the `!process` extension command to list all process threads, as shown in Listing 8.8.

## Listing 8.8  Listing thread summary information

```
kd> !process 5b4 4
Searching for Process with Cid == 5b4
PROCESS ffaa62f0  SessionId: 0  Cid: 05b4    Peb: 7ffde000  ParentCid: 00d8
    DirBase: 0a5d0000  ObjectTable: e10a97d0  HandleCount:  70.
    Image: 08cli.exe

        THREAD ffb10020  Cid 05b4.04f8  Teb: 7ffdd000 Win32Thread: e16e5eb0 WAIT
        THREAD ffafd698  Cid 05b4.01d0  Teb: 7ffdc000 Win32Thread: 00000000 WAIT
        THREAD ffabada8  Cid 05b4.0278  Teb: 7ffdb000 Win32Thread: 00000000 WAIT
```

In addition to the process identifier, we know the client thread's identifier, which is matched against all the threads from Listing 8.8 to obtain the thread ETHREAD structure address. The structure is then used with the `!thread` extension command to confirm the thread validity and obtain the LPC information, as shown in Listing 8-9.

**Listing 8.9** Dumping the kernel thread information

```
kd> !thread ffb10020
THREAD ffb10020  Cid 05b4.04f8  Teb: 7ffdd000 Win32Thread: e16e5eb0 WAIT:
(WrLpcReply) UserMode Non-Alertable
    ffb10214  Semaphore Limit 0x1
Waiting for reply to LPC MessageId 00004f99:
Current LPC port e138cd98
Not impersonating
DeviceMap               e1a60398
Owning Process          ffaa62f0      Image:        08cli.exe
      Wait Start TickCount      563720          Ticks: 1391 (0:00:00:13.930)
Context Switch Count    98                  LargeStack
UserTime                00:00:00.0000
KernelTime              00:00:00.0530
Start Address kernel32!BaseProcessStartThunk (0x7c810867)
Win32 Start Address 08CLI!ILT+1385(_wmainCRTStartup) (0x0042c56e)
Stack Init f6c05000 Current f6c04c50 Base f6c05000 Limit f6c01000 Call 0
Priority 8 BasePriority 8 PriorityDecrement 0 DecrementCount 16
ChildEBP RetAddr  Args to Child
f6c04c68 804dc6a6 ffb10090 ffb10020 804dc6f2 nt!KiSwapContext+0x2e
6c04c74 804dc6f2 ffb10214 ffb101e8 ffb10020 nt!KiSwapThread+0x46
f6c04c9c 805788ef 00000001 00000011 e100da01 nt!KeWaitForSingleObject+0x1c2
f6c04d50 804df06b 000006e0 0015c2b8 0015c2b8 nt!NtRequestWaitReplyPort+0x63d
f6c04d50 7c90eb94 000006e0 0015c2b8 0015c2b8 nt!KiFastCallEntry+0xf8
(TrapFrame @ f6c04d64)
0012f6e4 7c90e3ed 77e7c968 000006e0 0015c2b8 ntdll!KiFastSystemCallRet
0012f6e8 77e7c968 000006e0 0015c2b8 0015c2b8 ntdll!NtRequestWaitReplyPort+0xc
0012f734 77e7a716 0015c2f0 0012f75c 776009c0 RPCRT4!LRPC_CCALL::SendReceive+0x228
0012f740 776009c0 0016149c 0015ecc0 0012f840 RPCRT4!I_RpcSendReceive+0x24
...
0012fe48 0042e7ae a2b35800 01c6e05c 7ffde000 08CLI!MTAClientCall+0x7b
0012ff54 0042f902 00000002 00372e20 00372ea0 08CLI!wmain+0xae
0012ffb8 0042f6bd 0012fff0 7c816d4f a2b35800 08CLI!wmainCRTStartup+0x252
0012ffc0 7c816d4f a2b35800 01c6e05c 7ffde000 08CLI!wmainCRTStartup+0xd
0012fff0 00000000 0042c56e 00000000 78746341 kernel32!BaseProcessStart+0x23
```

The thread information contains the state of this thread decoded as WAIT: (WrLpcReply), as well as the LPC message for which a reply is expected. The message information is used afterward to find out the server thread holding the client execution, as shown in Listing 8.10.

**Listing 8.10**  Finding additional information about the LPC message

```
kd> !lpc message 00004f99
Searching message 4f99 in threads ...
    Server thread ffab41c0 is working on message 4f99
Client thread ffb10020 waiting a reply from 4f99
Searching thread ffb10020 in port rundown queues ...

Server communication port 0xe111b878
    Handles: 1    References: 1
    The LpcDataInfoChainHead queue is empty
        Connected port: 0xe138cd98      Server connection port: 0xe14684f0

Client communication port 0xe138cd98
    Handles: 1    References: 2
    The LpcDataInfoChainHead queue is empty

Server connection port e14684f0   Name: OLE0D6120B10F36435E84795A344064
    Handles: 1    References: 9
    Server process   : ffab3530 (08comsrv.exe)
    Queue semaphore : 8124a248
    Semaphore state 0 (0x0)
    The message queue is empty
    The LpcDataInfoChainHead queue is empty
Done.
```

If present, the second line of Listing 8.10 shows which thread is processing the client request. In a heavy loaded system, it is possible to not find any server thread processing the LPC message. In this case, the developer needs to understand why none of the server threads are picking up the message.

Using the !thread extension command, it is possible to find out everything else about the server process and the thread actively serving the request. This information can be used for further debugging, possibly using a user mode debugger, if desired. In this section, the debugging continues using the kernel mode debugger. Listing 8.11 shows the result of listing the server thread information after switching the debugger view to the server process and reloading the user mode symbols.

## Listing 8.11   Server's thread processing the LPC message

```
kd> .thread /p /r  ffab41c0
Implicit thread is now ffab41c0
Implicit process is now ffab3530
.cache forcedecodeuser done
Loading User Symbols
..............
kd> !thread ffab1020
THREAD ffab1020  Cid 036c.06e0  Teb: 7ffdc000 Win32Thread: 00000000 WAIT: (DelayExe-
cution) UserMode Non-Alertable
    ffab1110  NotificationTimer
Not impersonating
DeviceMap                 e1a60398
Owning Process            ffab3530       Image:        08comsrv.exe
Wait Start TickCount      550275         Ticks: 15038 (0:00:02:30.596)
Context Switch Count      8
UserTime                  00:00:00.0010
KernelTime                00:00:00.0020
Start Address kernel32!BaseThreadStartThunk (0x7c810856)
LPC Server thread working on message Id 4f99
Stack Init f73c1000 Current f73c0cbc Base f73c1000 Limit f73be000 Call 0
Priority 9 BasePriority 8 PriorityDecrement 0 DecrementCount 0
Kernel stack not resident.
ChildEBP RetAddr  Args to Child
f73c0cd4 804dc6a6 ffab10d8 ffab1020 804dc5cb nt!KiSwapContext+0x2e
f73c0ce0 804dc5cb f73c0d64 00e5f428 00e5f448 nt!KiSwapThread+0x46
f73c0d0c 8056603f 00000001 00000000 f73c0d2c nt!KeDelayExecutionThread+0x1c9
f73c0d54 804df06b 00000000 00e5f448 00e5f470 nt!NtDelayExecution+0x87
f73c0d54 7c90eb94 00000000 00e5f448 00e5f470 nt!KiFastCallEntry+0xf8
(TrapFrame @ f73c0d64)
00e5f414 7c90d85c 7c8023ed 00000000 00e5f448 ntdll!KiFastSystemCallRet
00e5f418 7c8023ed 00000000 00e5f448 00e5f558 ntdll!NtDelayExecution+0xc
00e5f470 7c802451 000927c0 00000000 00e5f558 kernel32!SleepEx+0x61
00e5f480 0043ad9b 000927c0 00e5f55c 00e5f58c kernel32!Sleep+0xf
00e5f558 77e79dc9 0092267c 00000001 00000002 SRV!CCalculator::SumSlow+0x2b
00e5f57c 77ef321a 0043857c 00e5f590 00000004 RPCRT4!Invoke+0x30
...
00e5fdfc 77e7bb6a 001625f0 00159360 00165630 RPCRT4!LRPC_SCALL::DealWithRequestMes-
sage+0x2cd
00e5fe20 77e76784 0015939c 00e5fe38 00165630 RPCRT4!LRPC_ADDRESS::DealWithLRPCRe-
quest+0x16d
...
00e5ffec 00000000 77e76bf0 0015e5e8 00000000 kernel32!BaseThreadStart+0x37
```

At this moment, it is very clear why the server thread needs so much time to add a few numbers; one of the sample writers intentionally left a `kernel32!Sleep` function call for debugging purposes.

### Impersonating Local DCOM and LRPC Calls

Impersonation is a fundamental concept used in the current versions of the Windows operating system. It enables a specific thread to execute all the operations under a security context different from the process owning the thread. The impersonation can be enabled or disabled on demand by setting or resetting the impersonation token on the thread.

But what happens from a security perspective when a client thread makes a call into a server using the LPC protocol? The client can specify what impersonation token must be presented to the server, and the kernel stores that information on the server thread. When the server impersonates the client using the RPC function rpcrt4!RpcImpersonateClient or the DCOM function ole32!CoImpersonateClient, the impersonation is performed by another LPC function called ntdll!NtImpersonateClientOfPort. This function uses the impersonation information stored on the thread by the Windows kernel at the moment the message was transferred to the server.

From the user mode debugger, the impersonation information can be checked only after the server makes a call into one of the impersonation functions by checking the token currently set on the thread, the method often used in Chapter 7, "Security."

From the kernel mode debugger, this is much easier; the information is always present in the server thread, as a pointer to _PS_IMPERSONATION_INFORMATION stored in the `ImpersonationInfo` member of the thread structure, _ETHREAD. Along with the impersonation token, there are instructions on how to impersonate the client. In the case shown in Listing 8.12, any impersonation results in a token at identify level.

**Listing 8.12**   Reading ImpersonationInfo stored on the server thread

```
kd> dt _ETHREAD ffab1020 ImpersonationInfo
   +0x20c ImpersonationInfo : 0xe1269038 _PS_IMPERSONATION_INFORMATION
kd> dt 0xe1269038 _PS_IMPERSONATION_INFORMATION
   +0x000 Token            : 0xe1acba08
   +0x004 CopyOnOpen       : 0 ''
   +0x005 EffectiveOnly    : 0 ''
   +0x008 ImpersonationLevel : 1 ( SecurityIdentification )
```

8. INTERPROCESS COMMUNICATION

The information in this section helps when debugging a simple scenario using local LRPC or DCOM calls. More complex scenarios, such as DCOM activation, are, from the perspective of debugging, just a combination of calls and can be handled by following the same simple steps illustrated previously.

# Troubleshooting Remote Communication

MS RPC extends the RPC implementation by providing platform-specific security models and adding support for LPC communication. Although the local communication has excellent debugging support, the remote communication is lacking those facilities. In this section, we explore the option available to developers to compensate for the debugging support missing in this area.

One option is to capture all the knowledge required to debug the main scenarios into a smart extension capable of interpreting all internal structures and the relationship between different structures. The extension can show this information in an easy-to-understand form and can automate the whole process of detecting the call path. Unfortunately, no such extension is currently available.

To answer those challenges, the RPC team introduced a special method of debugging the communication between the client and the server, by using additional tracing information called RPC Troubleshooting State Information. This method is described in the next section.

## Using RPC Troubleshooting State Information

Since this is the only method accessible today, we focus on it for the remainder of this section. Because the information is stored in cells of information used only for debugging purposes, the method using them is also called RPC cell debugging, or cell debugging. The first part of this section describes how to control the RPC runtime behavior regarding the maintenance of the state information; the second part details where this information is stored and how it can be accessed; and the third part describes the tools available to filter and display it. The last part uses those tools to solve a real-case scenario.

Please note that the cell debugging is available starting with Windows XP and Windows 2003.

### Configuring Cell Debugging

Cell debugging is an instrumentation method used by RPC runtime to record the RPC activity. The instrumentation-enabled status, as well as the instrumentation level, can be controlled using a system administrative template available in the Group Policy snap-in. The snap-in can be started using the `gpedit.msc` command, or it can be added to an existing snap-in console by selecting the stand-alone "Group Policy Object Editor" snap-in targeting the local computer. Regardless of how it was started, the policy that controls the Remote Procedure Call behavior can be found under System's Administrative Templates targeting the Computer configuration, as shown in Figure 8.2.

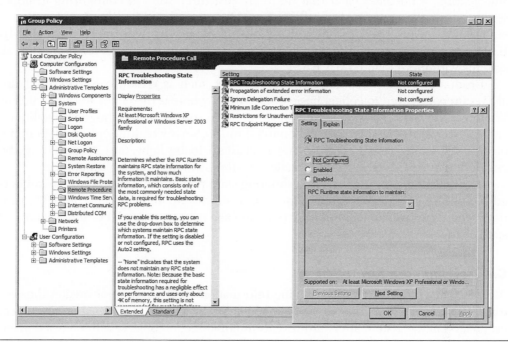

**Figure 8.2** Enabling the RPC troubleshooting state information

RPC Troubleshooting State Information is controlled by the enabled state, which can be in five different states, as follow:

- None state: Instructs the RPC runtime not to collect any information regarding its activity.
- Auto1 state: Instructs the RPC runtime to collect basic information about its activity.
- Auto2 state: Instructs the RPC runtime to collect basic information about its activity, only on systems with more than 128MB of RAM. On a server, this is the default policy, and a direct consequence is that most, if not all, servers have basic information about all RPC calls.

- Server state: Instructs the RPC runtime to collect basic information about its activity, regardless of the system configuration.
- Full state: Instructs the RPC runtime to collect full information about its activity, regardless of the system configuration.

After analyzing all options available for configuring the RCP Troubleshooting Information, it becomes clear that there are just three ways to configuring it: none, server information only, or full information. On a server system, the Auto1 option is equivalent to Auto2 and the Server option for all systems with more than 128MB RAM. On client systems, the Auto1 option is equivalent to the Server option on all systems with more than 64MB RAM.

From a practical perspective, server systems, such as Windows Server 2003, are always preconfigured to collect basic information, whereas the client systems, such as Windows XP, are never configured by default. To use the cell debugging facility on client systems, the facility must be enabled to the Server or Full option, depending on the debugging needs. The tracing is claimed to be light, and it can always be enabled to Server state even on the client system if there is enough memory.

After changing the RPC troubleshooting state policy, the system must be rebooted before the policy takes effect. Once the system is up and running, the RPC runtime records information about its activity in each process using RPC and updates all state changes.

### Cell Debugging Information

After enabling the RPC Troubleshooting Information, the RPC runtime creates the necessary structures to hold the information generated by it. At first glance, the new object list created in the system afterward reveals multiple section objects with names derived from the process identifiers. A snapshot of those handles taken using the Process Explorer tool is shown in Figure 8.3. In the Process Explorer Search dialog box, displayed by selecting the Find menu, we enter the "section" string to search for all objects of the section type. Figure 8.3 shows the sorted result on a system running 08cli.exe.

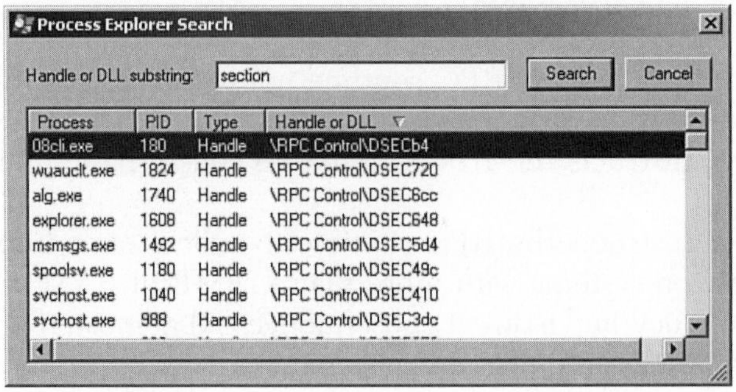

**Figure 8.3**   Debug cell sections

The troubleshooting state sections in Figure 8.3 are accessible to any process running on the local system, a very important aspect when debugging applications spanning multiple processes. Moreover, because the troubleshooting state information is not owned by a specific process and does not require a sophisticated mechanism to get it or update it, we can use the tracing infrastructure even when the system is in really bad shape. Each section object contains multiple cells; each cell contains information about how a specific element is created and maintained, as follows:

- For each new endpoint created in a process, a new cell containing the endpoint information is added to the process's RPC troubleshooting state section.
- For each new thread created by the RPC infrastructure, a new cell containing the thread information is added to the process's RPC troubleshooting state section. This cell is updated each time the thread state changes, and the time stamp of the change is updated.
- Each time the server processes a new connection or communication request, the RPC infrastructure creates a cell representing the server information pertinent to that call.
- For each client-initiated request, a new cell representing the client information pertinent to that call is created. This cell gets created only when the RPC Troubleshooting Information policy is set to Full mode. We use the client information created this way in the section "Getting the Client Call Information."

The next section describes the tools used to extract and filter the information stored in those troubleshooting state sections. It also shows how to interpret and correlate the cell debugging information to solve the problem at hand.

### Accessing Cell Debugging Information

The cell information can be accessed using the stand-alone tool dbgrpc.exe located in the directory in which the debuggers are installed. Alternatively, the rpcexts.dll debugger extension—which is installed by default with the Debugging Tools for Windows—contains a few extension commands for managing the troubleshooting state information. Although the extension is useful to investigate the problem within a debugger, the command-line tool can process the information from a remote machine, calling a RPC interface provided by the RPC infrastructure on that machine, provided that the caller is an administrator on the remote system. The command-line options and the debugger extension command are similar and will be presented side-by-side. Because the information used by the debugger extension is accessible from all processes, the extension works from within any user mode debugger running on the system. The debugger used in this section is attached to the client or the server process.

**NOTE** The extension rpcexts.dll implements multiple extension commands that require access to private symbols. Because we do not have access to private symbols, those commands are not discussed. Also, the extension is not loaded by default, so the extension commands, or at least the first time an extension command is used, we have to prefix it by the rpcexts extension name.

### Getting the Current Time Stamp

The !rpctime extension command shows the time elapsed since the system startup in a <seconds>.<milliseconds> format, as shown in Listing 8.13. The time reference, used in the entire tracing infrastructure, is useful to understand the temporal relationship between cell events. The time stamp is derived from the system time and increases even when the process is stopped in a user mode debugger.

**Listing 8.13**   Using !rpctime to obtain the current time stamp used by troubleshooting infrastructure

```
0:003> !rpctime
Current time is: 002960.857 (0x000b90.359)
```

### Getting Endpoint Information

The !getendpointinfo extension command, used without arguments, lists all endpoints exposed by all processes on the system where the debugger runs. The command output contains five columns in the following order:

- PID: The identifier of the server process hosting the endpoint
- CELL ID: The cell identifier relative to the process PID, identifying the information cell
- ST: The endpoint state telling if the endpoint is active (state equal to one), or if it has been uninstalled
- PROTSEQ: The protocol name
- ENDPOINT: The endpoint name

Listing 8.14 shows a sample result from a system running Windows XP SP2 without additional software installed on it. The output can be used to find out which process owns what endpoints and which protocols are enabled in each process. Protocol names are self-describing, and they enforce the endpoint name format; the TCP protocol can have only numeric endpoints, whereas NMP has the name starting with \pipe\, and so on. Very long endpoint names might be truncated to the size allowed by the cell.

As an observation, all LRPC endpoints with the name starting with OLE are used by the DCOM infrastructure for processes in a client or in a server role.

**Listing 8.14**   Using !getendpointinfo to list all endpoints known by RPC

```
0:005> !getendpointinfo
Searching for endpoint info ...
PID   CELL ID     ST PROTSEQ       ENDPOINT
-----------------------------------------
...
038c  0000.0001  01          LRPC  dhcpcsvc
038c  0000.0003  01          LRPC  wzcsvc
038c  0000.0005  01          LRPC  OLEA0BD1FB22E8E4CB3AED9EA46E
038c  0000.0009  01          NMP   \PIPE\atsvc
038c  0000.000d  01          LRPC  AudioSrv
038c  0000.0010  01          NMP   \PIPE\wkssvc
038c  0000.0013  01          NMP   \pipe\keysvc
038c  0000.0014  01          LRPC  keysvc
038c  0000.0016  01          LRPC  SECLOGON
038c  0000.0017  01          NMP   \pipe\trkwks
038c  0000.0018  01          LRPC  trkwks
038c  0000.001a  01          NMP   \PIPE\srvsvc
038c  0000.0025  01          NMP   \PIPE\browser
038c  0000.0026  01          LRPC  senssvc
038c  0000.0028  01          NMP   \PIPE\W32TIME
...
0240  0000.0001  01          LRPC  OLE9D488805CBAA4A479CDD8DCD0
05cc  0000.0001  01          LRPC  OLE9A35F92EE10245499B5520104
06a0  0000.0001  01          LRPC  OLE71BE2F37F98B4AE5B9E13F5C2
0078  0000.0001  01          LRPC  OLECF2A0CC062794FA78A63DA9A5
0388  0000.0001  01          LRPC  OLE73A51130EAFA4D5AB504E5597
```

The same information can be obtained using the stand-alone dbgrpc.exe tool through the following command line:

```
C:\>dbgrpc -e
```

When we focus on a specific endpoint, the command can be followed by the endpoint name, as in Listing 8.15. The endpoint name acts as a filter for the !getendpointinfo extension command.

**Listing 8.15**   Using !getendpointinfo to list all endpoints known by RPC

```
0:003> !getendpointinfo \PIPE\W32TIME
Searching for endpoint info ...
PID   CELL ID    ST PROTSEQ        ENDPOINT
----------------------------------
038c 0000.0028 01              NMP \PIPE\W32TIME
```

The command-line alternative to obtain the same information passes the endpoint as a parameter to the –E switch, as exemplified in the following:

```
C:\>dbgrpc -e -E \PIPE\W32TIME
```

### Getting Thread Information

Each process with active RPC endpoints must listen on all registered endpoints using one or more threads that are part of the RPC thread pool managed by the RPC runtime. The !getthreadinfo extension command lists all the thread information cells in the following format:

- PID: The identifier of server hosting the thread
- CELL ID: The cell identifier relative to the process PID, identifying the information cell
- ST: The thread state telling whether the thread is idle or it has been dispatched to the server code
- TID: The Win32 thread identifier
- ENDPOINT: The cell containing additional information about the endpoint the thread is listening to
- LASTIME: The time stamp of the last thread state change

The command takes the process identifier as a parameter, as shown in Listing 8.16 where the target process has 0x038c as the process identifier.

**Listing 8.16**   Using !getthreadinfo to list all threads from the RPC thread pool

```
0:005> !getthreadinfo 038c
Searching for thread info ...
PID   CELL ID    ST TID     ENDPOINT   LASTTIME
---------------------------------------------
038c 0000.0004 03 000004a8 0000.0003 0009237f
038c 0000.0006 02 000004b4 <IOCP>     009124dd
```

```
038c 0000.0007 03 000004cc 0000.0005 00958d5d
038c 0000.000a 02 000004c8 <IOCP>    00ac3dc1
038c 0000.000b 03 0000052c 0000.0001 008d7e51
038c 0000.000e 03 0000050c 0000.000d 001320ce
038c 0000.001d 03 00000650 0000.0026 00af1978
038c 0000.0020 03 00000794 0000.0016 000a9d76
038c 0000.0023 03 00000090 <IOCP>    00abc898
038c 0000.0024 03 00000790 0000.0018 000a9d76
038c 0000.0027 03 00000688 0000.0026 00af1978
038c 0000.002c 03 0000078c 0000.0014 000a9d76
038c 0000.002e 03 000007dc 0000.0026 00af196e
```

**ENDPOINT INFORMATION** The cell column does not always contain the endpoint cell information, as is the case for threads having the identifiers b4b, 4c8, and 90. In these cases, the ENDPOINT field has been replaced with the <IOCP> string, indicating that the respective threads are waiting on IO completion ports associated with multiple endpoints.

The command-line alternative to obtain the same information passes the process identifier as a parameter to the –t switch, as exemplified next:

```
C:\> dbgrpc.exe -t -P 38c
```

The output can be filtered further by adding the thread identifier to the command argument list. For example, Listing 8.17 contains the output of the command that filters out a specific thread, having a 0x4a8 identifier in this case, running in the process 38c.

**Listing 8.17**  Using !getthreadinfo to obtain a specific thread RPC information

```
0:005> !getthreadinfo 038c 000004a8
Searching for thread info ...
PID  CELL ID   ST TID      ENDPOINT  LASTTIME
--------------------------------------------
038c 0000.0004 03 000004a8 0000.0003 0009237f
```

The alternative way to obtain the same information is for the user to pass the thread identifier as a parameter to the –T switch, as in the following line:

```
C:\> dbgrpc.exe -t -P 38c -T 4a8
```

*Getting Call Information*

One of the most important pieces of the instrumentation is kept in call info cells. To understand what information is kept there, we provide some background on how RPC runtime works. Similar to the LRPC protocol described in the first section of this chapter, the RPC runtime listens on all endpoints for connection requests and creates the connection object responsible for managing each new connection. The server code in charge of handling the connection later processes all call requests on the connection by creating another transient object generically called SCALL object (more specifically, the call can be served by an LRPC_SCALL, OSF_SCALL, or DG_SCALL class), depending on the protocol serving that connection, created to dispatch that specific call. Each connection object and call object has one associated cell in the list returned by the `!getcallinfo` extension command, as exemplified in Listing 8.18.

The complete listing contains the usual fields—the process hosting that object, the cell identifier, the last update time, and the state of the cell, along with object-specific cells in the following format:

- PID: The identifier of the server process handling the call.
- CELL ID: The cell identifier relative to the process PID, identifying the information cell.
- ST: The thread state telling whether the call is active or it has been completed.
- PNO: The procedure number from the RPC interface that the call is or was made to, also known as an opnum.
- IFSTART: The first 32 bits of the Interface Identifier or IID that the call is or was made to.
- THRDCELL: The identifier of the thread cell containing detailed information about the thread that handles or handled the call.
- CALLFLAG: A combination of flags associated with the call well decoded by the `!getdbgcell` extension command.
- CALLID: The call identifier that can be used to link the call information cell to the client cell information.
- CONN/CLN: The client connection info. For LRPC calls, the column contains in this field the process identifier followed by the thread identifier. The connection-based protocol calls store in this column the cell identifier containing additional information about the connection used on this call.

**Listing 8.18**  Using !getcallinfo to obtain the call information maintained by the server

```
0:005> !getcallinfo
Searching for call info ...
PID  CELL ID    ST PNO IFSTART  THRDCELL  CALLFLAG CALLID    LASTTIME CONN/CLN
--------------------------------------------------------------------------
021c 0000.000e 00 009 00000134 0000.000d 00000009 00000001 0014142a 0348.047c
...
038c 0000.001e 00 003 00000132 0000.0029 00000008 00000000 0004a91f 0348.0628
038c 0000.001f 00 000 d674a233 0000.001d 00000009 00000000 00afb51f 038c.0720
038c 0000.0021 00 004 00000132 0000.000a 00000009 00000000 00870be6 0348.05c0
038c 0000.002a 00 005 fdd384cc 0000.0006 00000009 00000000 0003d03f 0740.0750
038c 0000.002f 00 000 629b9f66 0000.0027 00000009 00000000 0004ad58 021c.00ec
038c 0000.0030 00 007 3faf4738 0000.000e 00000009 00000000 0004c874 021c.00cc
038c 0000.0032 00 009 06bba54a 0000.0027 00000009 004f0044 000521b9 01fc.0208
038c 0000.0037 00 005 00000134 0000.0039 00000009 00000003 00059385 05cc.04c0
038c 0000.003a 00 003 609b9557 0000.0039 00000009 00000004 00059335 05cc.04c0
038c 0000.003b 00 000 63fbe424 0000.0027 00000009 00000000 00afe977 0460.0474
0460 0000.0007 02 009 4b112204 0000.0006 00000009 00000000 0005a9a9 038c.07e8
...
0388 0000.0005 02 004 daf50cdb 0000.0003 00000009 0078006f 008a8023 0078.03ac
```

The command-line alternative to obtain the same information uses the –c switch, as exemplified here:

```
C:\>dbgrpc -c
```

Because the call list gets very large on production servers, it is advisable to filter that information. The extension accepts the call identifier, the first 32 bits of the interface UUID, the procedure number, and the process identifier handling the calls as filter parameters. Each filter parameter has an optional value described in the command help. Listing 8.19 uses default values for all but the process identifier to obtain the call cells available in the process with the 0x38c identifier.

**Listing 8.19**  Using !getcallinfo to filter call information to a specific process

```
0:005> !getcallinfo 0 0 FFFF 38c
Searching for call info ...
PID  CELL ID    ST PNO IFSTART  THRDCELL  CALLFLAG CALLID    LASTTIME CONN/CLN
--------------------------------------------------------------------------
038c 0000.000c 00 000 0a74ef1c 0000.0006 00000009 00000006 008a6272 038c.04e4
038c 0000.000f 00 009 00000134 0000.0007 00000009 0000000c 00908434 0348.047c
```

*(continues)*

**Listing 8.19**   Using !getcallinfo to filter call information to a specific process *(continued)*

```
038c 0000.0012 00 00b 3faf4738 0000.000e 00000009 004f0044 000e17b0 06a0.0780
038c 0000.001b 00 00b 3faf4738 0000.000e 00000009 004f0044 0005467f 0240.0314
038c 0000.001e 00 003 00000132 0000.0029 00000008 00000000 0004a91f 0348.0628
038c 0000.001f 00 000 d674a233 0000.001d 00000009 00000000 00afb51f 038c.0720
038c 0000.0021 00 004 00000132 0000.000a 00000009 00000000 00870be6 0348.05c0
038c 0000.002a 00 005 fdd384cc 0000.0006 00000009 00000000 0003d03f 0740.0750
038c 0000.002f 00 000 629b9f66 0000.0027 00000009 00000000 0004ad58 021c.00ec
038c 0000.0030 00 007 3faf4738 0000.000e 00000009 00000000 0004c874 021c.00cc
038c 0000.0032 00 009 06bba54a 0000.0027 00000009 004f0044 000521b9 01fc.0208
038c 0000.0037 00 005 00000134 0000.0039 00000009 00000003 00059385 05cc.04c0
038c 0000.003a 00 003 609b9557 0000.0039 00000009 00000004 00059335 05cc.04c0
038c 0000.003b 00 000 63fbe424 0000.0027 00000009 00000000 00afe977 0460.0474
```

The command-line alternative to obtain the same information uses the –c parameter, as exemplified here:

```
C:\>dbgrpc -c -P 38c
```

### Getting the Entire Cell Information

Now it is time to look deeper into each cell to decode the cell information not explained or exposed in Listing 8.19. The !getdbgcell extension command understands all cell types and can decode them appropriately. The process and the cell identifier used as parameters in Listing 8.20 are taken from each, obtained after enumerating the cells, as shown in Listing 8.19.

**Listing 8.20**   Using !getdbgcell to obtain the cell information maintained by the server

```
0:005> * Obtaining information about a call cell
0:005> !getdbgcell  038c 0000.000c
Getting cell info ...
Call
Status: Allocated
Procedure Number: 0
Interface UUID start (first DWORD only): A74EF1C
Call ID: 0x6 (6)
Servicing thread identifier: 0x0.6
Call Flags: cached, LRPC
Last update time (in seconds since boot):9069.170 (0x236D.AA)
Caller (PID/TID) is: 38c.4e4 (908.1252)
0:005> * Obtaining information about an endpoint cell obtained in Listing 8.14
```

```
0:005> !getdbgcell 038c 0000.0028
Getting cell info ...
Endpoint
Status: Active
Protocol Sequence: NMP
Endpoint name: \PIPE\W32TIME
```

The command-line alternative to obtain the same information uses the −l switch followed by the cell information, as exemplified by the following:

```
C:\>dbgrpc −l −P 38c −L 0000.000c
```

### Getting the Client Call Information

When the RPC Troubleshooting State Information policy is set to Full, the client call information cell recorded by the RPC runtime can be enumerated using the !getclientcallinfo extension command using the same parameters as the !getcallinfo extension command (see Listing 8.21).

The command output contains the usual fields—the client process identifier, the cell identifier, the last update time, and the state of the cell, along with object-specific cells—in the following format:

- PID: The identifier of the client process originating the call
- CELL ID: The cell identifier relative to the process PID, identifying the information cell
- PNO: The procedure number from the RPC interface that the call is or was made to, also known as opnum
- IFSTART: The first 32 bits of the Interface Identifier or IID that the call is or was made to
- TIDNUMBER: The cell identifier containing detailed information about the thread that initiated the call
- CALLID: The call identifier that can be used to correlate the call information cell to the client cell information
- LASTIME: The time stamp of the last cell update
- PS: A combination of flags associated with the call that can be decoded by the !getdbgcell extension command
- CLTNUMER: The cell identifier of the call target cell that contains additional information about the server handling the call
- ENDPOINT: The name of the server endpoint servicing this call

**Listing 8.21**   Using !getclientcallinfo to obtain the call information maintained by the client

```
0:005> !getclientcallinfo
Searching for call info ...
PID  CELL ID  PNO  IFSTART  TIDNUMBER CALLID   LASTTIME PS CLTNUMBER ENDPOINT
----------------------------------------------------------------------------
038c 0000.003f 0009 4b112204 0000.0000 ffffffff 0005a9a9 09 0000.0040 LRPC00000460
0078 0000.0003 0004 daf50cdb 0000.0000 ffffffff 008a8023 09 0000.0004 OLE73A51130E
```

The command-line alternative to obtain the same information uses the –a switch, as exemplified in the following:

```
C:\>dbrpc -a
```

All this state information can be used in some simple scenarios, where you will learn how to correlate them to get to a resolution faster.

### Using Cell Debugging Information

As in the local client-server scenarios, when debugging remote client-server scenarios, we must often follow the execution path originating from the client process until the call is processed on the server side. This section uses the RPC Troubleshooting State Information collected by the RPC runtime while processing the call to track the execution path.

In this example, the client process 08cli.exe performs a synchronous DCOM call into a remote server, which takes longer than expected to complete. In this specific case, the client and the server system have fixed TPC/IP addresses, 192.168.0.105 and 192.168.0.104, respectively. Both systems are members of the same workgroup, and the list of users is identical between the client and the server, allowing the client to authenticate to our server using pass-through authentication. On the client system, the RPC Troubleshooting State Information policy is set to Full mode, whereas on the server, the policy is set to Server mode. The client starts with the following command line:

```
C:\>08cli.exe server:192.168.0.104
```

The debugging process starts within the client process, where we identified the thread waiting on the call to complete. Listing 8.22 shows the stack zero waiting on the RPC call.

**Listing 8.22**    Typical client stack waiting on remote call made using a connection-based protocol

```
0:003> ~0k50
ChildEBP RetAddr
0012f450 7c90e9c0 ntdll!KiFastSystemCallRet
0012f454 7c8025cb ntdll!NtWaitForSingleObject+0xc
0012f4b8 77e80acb kernel32!WaitForSingleObjectEx+0xa8
0012f4d4 77e80a81 RPCRT4!UTIL_WaitForSyncIO+0x20
0012f4f8 77eeb7ba RPCRT4!UTIL_GetOverlappedResultEx+0x1d
0012f52c 77e8520d RPCRT4!WS_SyncRecv+0xca
0012f54c 77e80e8d RPCRT4!OSF_CCONNECTION::TransSendReceive+0x9d
0012f5c8 77e80e0d RPCRT4!OSF_CCONNECTION::SendFragment+0x226
0012f620 77e80c6f RPCRT4!OSF_CCALL::SendNextFragment+0x1d2
...
0012fccc 0042ead1 RPCRT4!ObjectStubless+0xf
0012fe48 0042e846 08CLI!MTAClientCall+0xc1
0012ff54 00430692 08CLI!wmain+0xb6
0012ffb8 0043044d 08CLI!wmainCRTStartup+0x252
0012ffc0 7c816fd7 08CLI!wmainCRTStartup+0xd
0012fff0 00000000 kernel32!BaseProcessStart+0x23
0:003> |
.  0    id: 63c create  name: 08cli.exe
```

We gather all client information available about that specific thread using the `!getclientcallinfo` extension command. Because there is not much RPC activity on the client system, we can use the command without a filtering option. In Listing 8.23, the PID column is matched against the client's process identifier to obtain the call cell identifier.

**Listing 8.23**    Enumerating all the client call info cells

```
0:002> !rpcexts.getclientcallinfo
Searching for call info ...
PID  CELL ID    PNO  IFSTART  TIDNUMBER CALLID   LASTTIME PS CLTNUMBER ENDPOINT
--------------------------------------------------------------------------------
055c 0000.005b 0009 4b112204 0000.0000 ffffffff 0010a534 09 0000.005c LRPC00000384
0590 0000.0006 0009 4b112204 0000.0000 ffffffff 0000e745 09 0000.0007 LRPC00000384
063c 0000.0003 0004 daf50cdb 0000.0000 00000001 004464bb 07 0000.0004 1359
```

In Listing 8.24, the information about the call is decoded by the `!getdbgcell` extension command. The procedure number is shown in the third line (4 means that the client called the second method of the DCOM interface in which the standard

IUnknown interface uses the first three procedure slots), the target endpoint is shown in the eighth line, and the cell containing additional information about the call target is shown in the seventh line.

**Listing 8.24**   Getting more details from the client cell info

```
0:002> !getdbgcell 063c 0000.0003
Getting cell info ...
Client call info
Procedure number: 4
Interface UUID start (first DWORD only): DAF50CDB
Call ID: 0x1 (1)
Calling thread identifier: 0x0.0
Call target identifier: 0x0.4
Call target endpoint: 1359
```

Because we don't know what system handles the call, we decode and use the call target cell identifier, as shown in Listing 8.25. The current time stamp is useful to understand how long ago this call started—in this case, 004752s − 004482s = 270s, which is almost five minutes.

**Listing 8.25**   Getting more details about the call target

```
0:002> !getdbgcell 063c 0000.0004
Getting cell info ...
Call target info
Protocol Sequence: TCP
Last update time (in seconds since boot): 4482.235 (0x1182.EB)
Target server is: 192.168.0.104
0:002> !rpctime
Current time is: 004752.183 (0x001290.0b7)
```

**NOTE** When the client's information is not available (for example, when it is not enabled), we can use the netstat.exe tool to obtain some of the information required to find the server. In this case, we use the current process 1596(0x63c) to identify the TCP communication connection to the server system. The connection contains both the address of the server and the port number used for the connection.

```
C:\>netstat -o
Active Connections
...
TCP XP-SP2:1734   192.168.0.104:1359 ESTABLISHED 1596
```

After finding the address of the server system and the connection endpoint information, the debugging continues on the server. The first step is to find out which process owns the endpoint used by the client process, using either the dbgrpc.exe tool or the system-provided netstat.exe tool. After identifying the server process, we attach a debugger to that process and identify the pending calls, a process illustrated in Listing 8.26. The process identifier obtained from dbgrpc.exe must be converted from hexadecimal to decimal before using it as a parameter to the debugger command-line option -p.

**Listing 8.26**  Getting the call info from the endpoint information

```
C:\>dbgrpc.exe -e -E 1359
Searching for endpoint info ...
PID   CELL ID    ST PROTSEQ        ENDPOINT
-----------------------------------------
058c 0000.0006 01              TCP 1359
C:\>windgg -p 1420
...
0:007> !getcallinfo 0 0 FFFF 58c
Searching for call info ...
PID   CELL ID    ST PNO IFSTART   THRDCELL   CALLFLAG CALLID     LASTTIME CONN/CLN
---------------------------------------------------------------------------------
058c 0000.0003 00 004 00000132 0000.0005 00000009 00000000 007b30d4 0338.05d4
058c 0000.0004 00 009 00000134 0000.0006 00000009 00000001 0080b279 0338.0710
058c 0000.000a 02 004 daf50cdb 0000.0008 00000001 00000001 007b34c8 0000.0009
```

The active calls from this list are in a state (ST column) different from zero. We focus then on the thread processing those calls. The thread cell identifier is available in the THRDCELL column. The last column indicates the cell identifier for the connection object that contains additional connection properties, such as the authentication level, the authentication service used for this call, and the IP source address, as shown in Listing 8.27.

**Listing 8.27**  Examining the thread and connection object info cell

```
0:000> !getdbgcell 058c 0000.0008
Getting cell info ...
Thread
Status: Dispatched
Thread ID: 0x760 (1888)
Thread is an IO completion thread
Last update time (in seconds since boot): 8074.440 (0x1F8A.1B8)
```

*(continues)*

**Listing 8.27**   Examining the thread and connection object info cell *(continued)*

```
0:000> !getdbgcell 058c 0000.0009
Getting cell info ...
Connection
Connection flags: Exclusive
Authentication Level: Connect
Authentication Service: NTLM
Last Transmit Fragment Size: 144 (0x4CBBA4)
Endpoint for the connection: 0x0.6
Last send time (in seconds since boot): ): 8013.920 (0x1F4D.398)
Last receive time (in seconds since boot): ): 8074.440 (0x1F8A.1B8)
Getting endpoint info ...
Caller is(IPv4): 192.168.0.105
```

We use the thread identifier of the server thread executing the request to obtain the execution stack, as shown in Listing 8.28. Not surprisingly, the thread is executing its long sleep operation, as you saw in the beginning of this chapter.

**Listing 8.28**   The server thread call stack

```
0:000> ~~[760]k
ChildEBP RetAddr
010ef458 7c90d85c ntdll!KiFastSystemCallRet
010ef45c 7c8023ed ntdll!NtDelayExecution+0xc
010ef4b4 7c802451 kernel32!SleepEx+0x61
010ef4c4 0043ad9b kernel32!Sleep+0xf
010ef59c 77e79dc9 SRV!CCalculator::SumSlow+0x2b
010ef5c0 77ef321a RPCRT4!Invoke+0x30
010ef9cc 77ef3bf3 RPCRT4!NdrStubCall2+0x297
...
010efdc0 77e8a067 RPCRT4!RPC_INTERFACE::DispatchToStub+0x84
010efe00 77eac1f4 RPCRT4!RPC_INTERFACE::DispatchToStubWithObject+0xc0
```

The cell information can be used to solve other scenarios involving RPC communication by combining the techniques explained in this section. Because the RPC troubleshooting state information is available globally in the system, there is no overhead when it gets accessed by the command-line tool, making it suitable even for various monitoring scenarios used in the product development phase.

## Analyzing Network Traffic

In the electronic engineering field, the circuits are diagnosed by analyzing the signals circulating inside the troubled devices with various testing gears, from simple scalar meters to sophisticated data analyzers. Because the network traffic is nothing more than an electrical signal over an electronic circuit, the troubleshooting techniques used in electronic engineering can be applied to network communication troubleshooting. The question is, what measuring device can provide the most value?

Although hardware manufacturers use sophisticated tools to measure the electrical characteristics of the networking gear, we can assume that the hardware layer is fully functional. We are interested only in monitoring the logical data flowing over the wires. We can read and analyze the data flowing back and forth between computers using protocol analyzer tools (also known as packet sniffer tools).

In this section, we use Ethereal network analyzer, which is a very powerful, yet easy-to-use tool, available under a GNU General Public License. The tool can be configured to completely capture the traffic going in and out the system running the tool. That is sufficient for analyzing the problems involving just the monitored system. Alternatively, the tool can be configured to capture the entirety of traffic received by a Network Interface Card (NIC) attached to the system, regardless of the source or destination address. This mode, called promiscuous capture mode, requires NIC support. The promiscuous capture mode helps with solving problems involving multiple systems exchanging messages in that network. The capture is controlled from the Capture Interfaces dialog box, obtained by selecting the Interface option in the Capture menu. The dialog box, shown in Figure 8.4, displays real-time statistics for each network interface card and enables starting the capture on any of them. The capture mode used for each NIC can be changed by clicking the corresponding Prepare button.

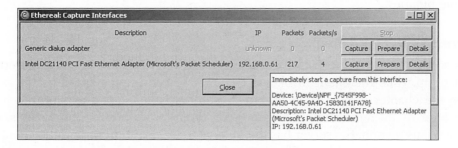

**Figure 8.4**  Capture Interface dialog box used to start capturing the traffic

Regardless of the method of capturing the network traffic, the capture files can then be post processed by various parsers; the traffic can be filtered, or it can be analyzed later. Even if one is not familiar with some of the protocols encountered in the traffic, the decoding performed by the tool is a good guide for further analysis or to clear a resolution.

When the protocol implemented by a specific application is not known, the capture files from a well-behaved installation can be used as reference in analyzing the troubled scenario. In this case, the user focuses on understanding the difference between the capture files of the misbehaving system and the reference capture files. The packet sniffer tools can also be used to learn a system behavior or to verify if the system functionality matches its specification. Questions such as, "Is the network traffic encrypted?" or "How chatty is the protocol?" are answered much faster by analyzing the traffic than by code reviewing the system implementation.

Ethereal shows the packets in an ordered list containing the packet number in the current capture file, the captured time, the source NIC address, the destination NIC address, the protocol name, and additional information decoded from the packet. In a separate window, each packet, interpreted by dissectors, is displayed as a data structure. Because the dissectors are called to interpret the packets hierarchically, the basic information is always decoded. If the higher-level protocols do not provide dissector, this part of the packet is shown as an array of bytes. When the protocol is stateful and the current packet depends on previous packets not captured in the current file, the packet cannot be decoded entirely and the information is presented in the format of a more basic layer. Ethereal also shows a plain dump of the packet content, very useful for a quick visual scan over the packet content.

The capture files used in this section, from 08capture1.cap to 08capture4.cap, are available in the C:\AWDBIN\LOGS folder in the download package containing the sample binaries.

### *Successful DCOM Activation Trace*

This section analyzes the packets exchanged between two systems configured in a workgroup while the client invokes a DCOM method implemented by the server, using the chapter sample code. Figure 8.5 shows Ethereal traffic captured in this case, after removing the additional traffic on the network hosting the systems. As in the previous section, the server has the 192.168.0.104 address, and the client uses the 192.168.0.105 address. The network traffic illustrating this has been captured in the 08capture1.cap file.

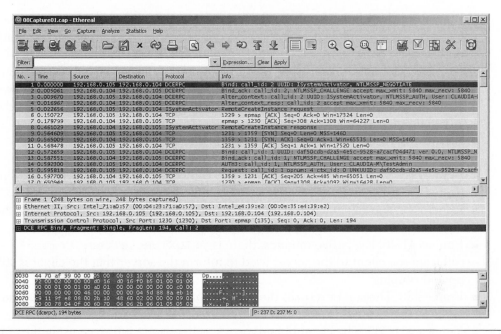

**Figure 8.5** Packets exchanged during a DCOM activation followed by a long-running call

So what are all the packets exchanged in this very simple application? The packets' roles are interpreted as follows:

- Frame 1: The client sends a `Bind` message to bind the `ISystemActivator` interface, identified by the decoder using the {000001A0-0000-0000-C000-000000000046} GUID. This packet also contains the security negotiation message. This message is sent over an existing TPC/IP connection to the DCOM SCM port established before starting the capture operation.

- Frame 2: The server acknowledges the `Bind` with a `Bind_ack` packet. This packet also contains the NTLM challenge message because this is the only common authentication mechanism accepted by both the server and the client.

- Frame 3: The client answers to the challenge with an `Alter_context` message, using information derived from the user `TestAdmin` credentials.

- Frame 4: The server verifies the caller identity and confirms it with an `Alter_context_resp` message. The interface is ready to be used.

- Frame 5: The client invokes `RemoteCreateInstance`, passing the server CLSID as a parameter (the current decoder does not parse this information), in this case `{31810948-8D81-4E55-BD16-0C27F5629392}`.

- Frame 8: The server returns an interface pointer of the requested object, along with the data required to connect to that object instance (information known as the object exporter identifier, or OXID). The OXID returned contains the RPC binding string for the object exporter.

- Frames 9, 10, 11: The client connects to the object exporter managing the interface returned by the activation process.

- Frames 12, 13, 14: The client binds to the `ICalculator` interface and authenticates the user, similar to the process described in frames 2–4.

- Frame 15: The client invokes `IClaculator::SlowSum`, identifiable by the interface IID and the method number or opnum.

- Frames 41-46: Every two minutes, there is an `IOXIDResolver::ComlexPing` call from the client to the server used to inform the server that the client is still up and running.

- Frame 233: The server returns the results from the operation initiated in frame 15.

- Frames 234-235: The client obtains an `IRemUnknown2` interface using the current connection to the server object.

- Frames 234-235: The client executes the `IRemUnknown2::RemRelease` on the interface obtained in frame 235.

### Failing DCOM Activation Trace

Because we use network monitor tools mostly to troubleshoot problems, it is important to know how effective this method is for discovering problems in network communication. What kind of problems can be discovered in this way? This section uses a file capturing a remote DCOM activation failure, which is a fairly common error.

The traffic captured in the failure case shows the deviation from the communication flow characteristic to the successful activation. The differences can lead toward the most likely problem in no time. Figure 8.6 shows the content of the `08capture02.cap` file that contains the whole activity leading to the failure.

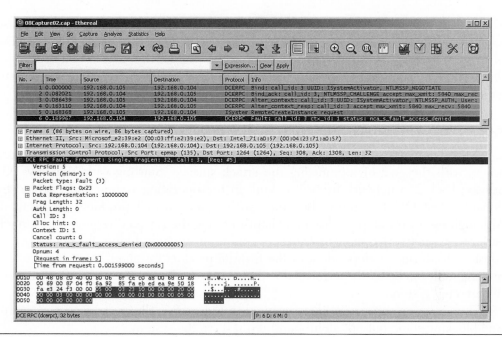

**Figure 8.6**  Packets captured during a failed DCOM activation

The first few packets play similar roles as in the previous section, whereas the last activation packet is completely different. The packet's interpretation is as follows:

- Frame 1: The client sends a bind request to the ISystemActivator interface and also contains the security negotiation message as described.
- Frame 2: The server acknowledges the bind with a Bind_ack packet.
- Frame 3: The client answers to the challenge with an Alter_context message, using information associated with the username TestAdmin, such as the password.
- Frame 4: The server verifies the caller identity with an Alter_context_resp message. The interface is ready to be used.
- Frame 5: The client invokes RemoteCreateInstance.
- Frame 6: The server fails the activation, and the result is sent to the client as a fault frame that contains the access denied error code 0x00000005 nicely extracted by the tool from the error frame.

The username used for this activation request is clearly visible in frame 3. Because frame 4 indicates that the user credentials were accepted by the server, the activation problem is reduced in this case to an authorization problem specific to that user. With the experience acquired from Chapter 7, it is relatively easy to continue the investigation and pinpoint the source of the problem.

### Failing DCOM Activation Trace by Firewall Filtering

Lately, the network security landscape changed toward restricting inbound network access with the goal of minimizing the attack surface. Starting with Windows XP, Service Pack 2, a network firewall is built in the operating system and enabled by default. Most OEM systems also come with other firewall products preinstalled. Although each firewall provides a mechanism to log the rejected requests, it is much easier to use network tracing tools to spot communication problems, facilitated by the consistent interface independent of the firewall product installed. Furthermore, the investigation can be easily performed without making changes to the configuration of the affected system.

The `08capture03.cap` file, displayed in Figure 8.7, illustrates a case of a firewall blocking some but not all inbound requests to the system.

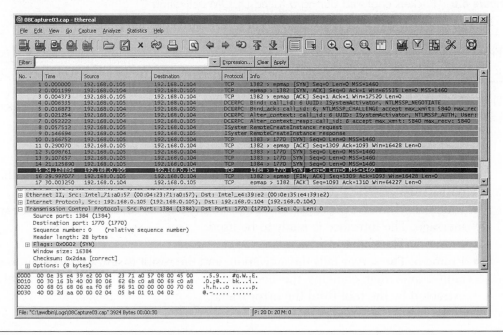

**Figure 8.7**   Packets captured during a DCOM activation blocked by a firewall

The packet's roles are interpreted as follows:

- Frame 1 to Frame 9: The client activates the interface implemented by the server, in this case ICalculator, the same way as in the first trace shown in "Successful DCOM Activation Trace." The server returns the marshaled interface along with the RPC binding information required to connect to it. In this case, the endpoint is a TCP port 1770.
- Frame 10 and beyond: The client tries to establish a TCP connection with the server on port 1770, as shown by the sequence of SYS frames, but there is no reply from the sever. The client tries several times to establish the connection without success. Eventually, the activation call returns a failure in the client process.

In this case, the firewall allows the traffic to the endpoint mapper port 135, but it blocks the traffic to the ports dynamically opened in the server process. From the client code perspective, the DCOM activation request fails with a 0x800706ba error. When the firewall blocks all traffic on the system, even the initial connection to the epmap port fails, as shown in Figure 8.8. The frames illustrated in this example can be found in the 08capture04.cap file.

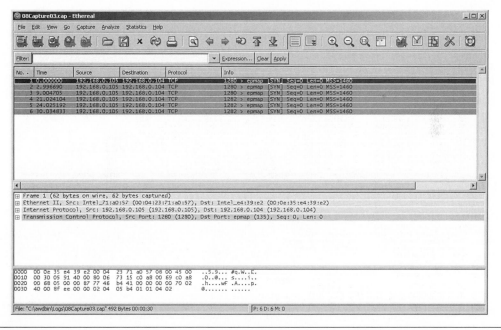

**Figure 8.8**  Packets captured suing a DCOM activation attempt blocked completely by a firewall

### Other Network Protocols

Other communication protocols can be analyzed with the same tools and following the same model. Even if you are not familiar with the wire activity generated by the high-level API calls, common network protocols are usually decoded by network analyzer tools. For those protocols, it is relatively easy to find the relationship between an API call and the associated network activity.

When you design a new protocol, it would be useful for the protocol acceptance to provide your own protocol interpreter to be used within the network analyzer tools. This way, the tools can decode the entire communication between systems. Figure 8.9 shows the traffic capture as a result of opening the registry on a remote machine. In this case, the first protocol decoder is decoding the TCP traffic, the next one in the stack decodes SMB requests, and another one decodes the MSRPC protocol built on the named pipes communications. Because the remote registry operations are fairly common, another protocol decoder interprets the MSRPC traffic generated by the remote registry APIs.

In the `08capture05.cap` capture file, it is easy to get an overview of the message exchanged between the client and the server. For example, the authentication sequence is easily recognized in frames 8 to 13, whereas frames 18 and 21 contain RPC calls made using the SMB protocol.

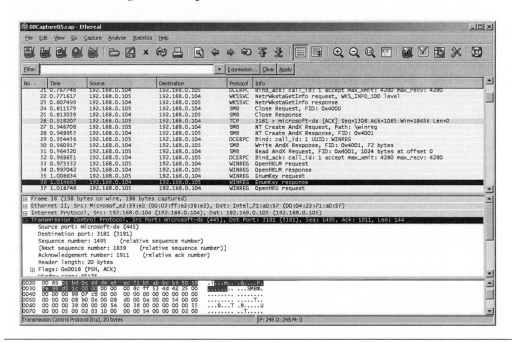

**Figure 8.9**   Packets containing remote registry operations

In other cases, the client and the server are connected with complex networking devices, such as load balancing solutions, and the network tracing is the only way to identify the real cause of the problem. When a packet gets lost in traffic, the network activity captured on the client's network is compared to the traffic on the server's network to prove a mismatch.

## Breaking the Call Path

The previous method of analyzing the network traffic is extremely effective in understanding what is right or wrong in the communication between two computers. Unfortunately, a single wire packet can be the result of a very complex operation, often involving more than one process. Any complex execution path hides the actual source of the error, making it difficult to identify the process in which the error is actually happening and implicitly debug the problem.

What is the most effective way of investigating such a problem? One method is to visualize the call flow as a circuit starting in the client space, passing through several communication layers, and surfacing as a server request in the server process, as illustrated in Figure 8.10. Furthermore, the server can decide to use services provided by yet another server before it returned the information to the client and the circuit extends to the next server. The reverse path is then used to return the results in synchronous calls.

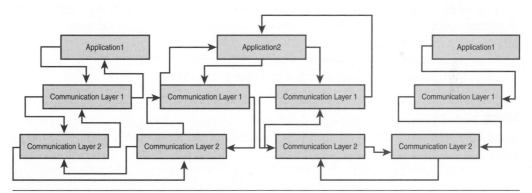

**Figure 8.10**   Sample execution path

We would like to create an analogy between troubleshooting a complicated interprocess communication and an electronic circuit, with the goal to discover what can be borrowed from the latter domain. The electronic circuits have various pins, surfacing signals essential to the good functionality of the circuit board, called test points. To troubleshoot the circuit board, the engineer starts somewhere close to its output and progressively moves toward the circuit input to localize the faulty section. Sometimes he will jump between the input and output to localize the section receiving a proper signal but not generating the expected response, but the majority of the investigation progresses strictly backward.

This pattern can be successfully used in troubleshooting distributed system solutions in which an error is raised somewhere in the middle and we don't know where. The situation is similar to the circuit when the output signal is different from the expected response to the input signal. Any error happening in any of the processes used in the distributed system can be seen as a shortcut in the big circuit that prevents the messages from flowing deeper in the system. Instead of using test points, not available in software, we can use the Windows debuggers. When one component that is part of the communication flow is stopped in the user mode debugger, the whole client-initiated operation cannot proceed, and it hangs. This confirms that this component has an active role in the functional section of the system. In this case, a component closer to the end of the chain is most likely the one raising the error.

One attacks this problem by assuming that the whole scenario works and starts to troubleshoot from the "bottom" of the call stack. Stop the last process of the call chain in the debugger (Application 3 from Figure 8.10) and re-execute the entire operation. If the operation returns with the same failure, that process is not the one generating the failure because it was not even invoked, and we will move up in the stack (Application 3 in this case) and repeat the procedure. When the call does not return, the error must be looked for in that process using the debugging techniques specific to a single-process scenario.

For asynchronous or message-based communication, the procedure must be adapted to the flow of messages within the distributed system.

---

**NOTE** Not surprisingly, debugging a distributed application is labor intensive because on top of the simple-to-use high-level library, we must be aware of the library internal implementation and the system calls used by it.

---

## Additional Technical Information

Debugging interprocess communication is a heuristic process of analyzing the information from multiple sources to understand the problem being debugged. This section describes where to intercept the remote authentication process and how to configure the RPC infrastructure to send additional information for each error encountered while processing a message. The last two tools display information about various interfaces by interrogating the endpoint mapper database.

## Remote Authentication

In the previous chapter, you learned how the remote clients authenticate to the server using SSPI calls. The call stack of the thread executing the call often reveals the authentication mechanism used by the client. In the following example, the client uses NTLM authentication as revealed by its three-leg protocol. The example shown in Listing 8.29 is taken from the RPCSS service, accepting a remote activation call. The network activity shown in Figure 8.5 can be mapped to the SSPI calls. The first `secure32!AcceptSecurityContext` is performed with the data obtained from frame 4, and the second call with the data received from frame 6.

**Listing 8.29**  Server breakpoints encountered using SSPI

```
0:009> bp Secur32!AcceptSecurityContext
0:009> bp Secur32!ImpersonateSecurityContext
0:009> g
Breakpoint 0 hit
eax=0009be20 ebx=00200a03 ecx=76f9d1e0 edx=0009722c esi=000971e0 edi=000af088
\eip=76f949ba esp=005bfd14 ebp=005bfd50 iopl=0         nv up ei pl nz na pe nc
Secur32!AcceptSecurityContext:
76f949ba 55                 push    ebp
0:003> * The first call to AcceptSecurityContext
0:003> k
ChildEBP RetAddr
005bfd10 780239bc Secur32!AcceptSecurityContext
005bfd50 7802389c RPCRT4!SECURITY_CONTEXT::AcceptFirstTime+0xd7
005bfeac 78010000 RPCRT4!OSF_SCONNECTION::AssociationRequested+0x3b8
...
0:003> g
Breakpoint 0 hit
eax=0009be20 ebx=00000000 ecx=0009722c edx=76f9d1e0 esi=00097220 edi=000000a6
eip=76f949ba esp=005bfe68 ebp=005bfea8 iopl=0         nv up ei pl nz na pe nc
Secur32!AcceptSecurityContext:
76f949ba 55                 push    ebp
0:003> * The second call to AcceptSecurityContext
0:003> k
ChildEBP RetAddr
005bfe64 78023b9f Secur32!AcceptSecurityContext
005bfea8 78023b22 RPCRT4!SECURITY_CONTEXT::AcceptThirdLeg+0x3e
```

*(continues)*

**Listing 8.29**   Server breakpoints encountered using SSPI *(continued)*

```
005bff18 78004aed RPCRT4!OSF_SCONNECTION::ProcessReceiveComplete+0x595
005bff28 78001848 RPCRT4!ProcessConnectionServerReceivedEvent+0x20
...
0:003> g
Breakpoint 1 hit
eax=76f9d1e0 ebx=005bf83c ecx=0009722c edx=75867028 esi=000971e0 edi=005bf848
eip=76f95099 esp=005bf75c ebp=005bf768 iopl=0         nv up ei pl nz na pe nc
Secur32!ImpersonateSecurityContext:
76f95099 55              push    ebp
0:003> * The identity of the client is available at the end of the call
0:003> k
ChildEBP RetAddr
005bf758 7802372a Secur32!ImpersonateSecurityContext
005bf768 78023701 RPCRT4!SECURITY_CONTEXT::ImpersonateClient+0x39
005bf770 78004443 RPCRT4!OSF_SCONNECTION::ImpersonateClient+0x3b
005bf778 75852a8f RPCRT4!RpcImpersonateClient+0x64
....
```

## RPC Extended Error Information

The components using RPC-based protocols can benefit from the extended information available in the protocol and controlled by the system policy called "Propagation of Extended Error Information." The policy that controls the propagation of error information can be found under the System's Administrative Templates node targeting the computer configuration, as shown in Figure 8.11.

The policy can be selectively enabled for the processes we are interested in or for all processes. The error information that travels over the wire can then be analyzed with packet sniffer tools. Applications can take advantage of this error information when they encounter errors, if this information is available. Even the simplest approach of logging this extended information helps the debugging process of this application.

## Other Tools

When analyzing RPC failures, there must be a quick way to answer the question, "Is this interface registered or not?" Two tools used for this type of search are rpcdump.exe and ifids.exe, available as free downloads from the company BindView, easily discoverable using an Internet search engine. The Ifids.exe program lists the interfaces registered with the endpoint mapper associated with a specific endpoint. The usage and the tool output are fairly simple, as shown in Listing 8.30.

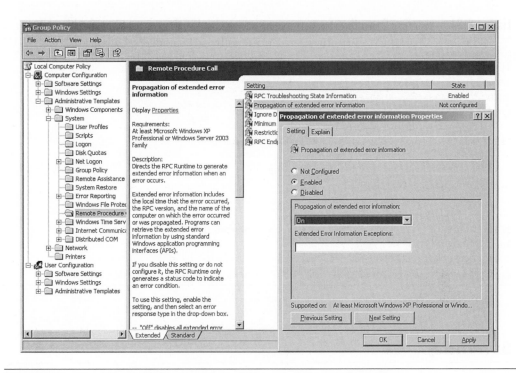

**Figure 8.11** Enabling RPC Propagation of Extended Error Information

**Listing 8.30** Listing all the interfaces registered on the \PIPE\winreg endpoint on the local system

```
C:\>ifids -p ncacn_np -e \PIPE\winreg \\.
Interfaces: 7
  c8cb7687-e6d3-11d2-a958-00c04f682e16 v1.0
  338cd001-2244-31f1-aaaa-900038001003 v1.0
  4b112204-0e19-11d3-b42b-0000f81feb9f v1.0
  00000134-0000-0000-c000-000000000046 v0.0
  18f70770-8e64-11cf-9af1-0020af6e72f4 v0.0
  00000131-0000-0000-c000-000000000046 v0.0
  00000143-0000-0000-c000-000000000046 v0.0
```

rpcdump.exe performs ifids.exe functionality for each endpoint registered on the system. Listing 8.31 shows a simplified output generated when running on a Windows XP SP2 system. The list of registered interfaces is huge and depends on the system configuration.

**Listing 8.31**   Listing all the interfaces registered on the local system, identified by \\.

```
C:\>rpcdump.exe  \\.
IfId: 906b0ce0-c70b-1067-b317-00dd010662da version 1.0
Annotation:
UUID: 705bd495-44aa-4b4d-8e8d-1927d9dd9e8c
Binding: ncalrpc:[LRPC00000fc4.00000001]


IfId: 3c4728c5-f0ab-448b-bda1-6ce01eb0a6d5 version 1.0
Annotation: DHCP Client LRPC Endpoint
UUID: 00000000-0000-0000-0000-000000000000
Binding: ncalrpc:[dhcpcsvc]
...


IfId: 4b112204-0e19-11d3-b42b-0000f81feb9f version 1.0
Annotation:
UUID: 00000000-0000-0000-0000-000000000000
Binding: ncacn_np:\\\\XP-SP2-BACK[\\PIPE\\winreg]
```

# Summary

In this chapter, we focused on troubleshooting distributed services using different tools and techniques with the goal of finding the logical execution path in a client-server application. You learned  the importance of diagnostic capabilities built in a communication protocol, as well as how to use them when debugging secure Windows applications.

Although no general recipe is available, the combination of these techniques can be used practically in any situation. A good overall understanding of the specific distributed system and the underlying communication protocols is a precondition to successful troubleshooting, but it is also the gateway for creating better systems in the future. This chapter also demonstrates the usefulness of using established communication protocols that are supported by the software industry with numerous tools.

# CHAPTER 9

# RESOURCE LEAKS

Without a doubt, resource leaks are one of the main sources of problems that can lead to software instability. One "small" resource leak is all it takes for large corporations to have to restart critical applications and services (and in worst-case scenarios, the entire system) and in the process lose thousands, or sometimes hundreds of thousands, of dollars. Software houses cannot afford to ignore issues such as memory leaks. Serious time and effort has to be scheduled to deal with these problems when they surface during testing. Admittedly, some resource leaks are harder to track down than others, but no questions should be asked concerning whether they should be fixed. Armed with the right thought process, coupled with a set of invaluable tools, a developer can track down these types of problems fairly quickly. This chapter discusses these thought patterns and tools that enable developers to efficiently track down resource leaks.

## What Is a Resource?

In Windows, a resource is any entity that occupies space in the system. Space, in this case, is defined as physical or virtual memory. Examples of such entities include handles, various forms of memory allocations, and COM objects. Although it is true that many of these constructs boil down to a memory allocation, the means by which a developer acquires and releases control of these resources varies. For example, allocating an array of characters using the `new` statement but forgetting to free it using `delete[]` causes a memory leak. (The size of the memory leak is directly proportional to the number of characters.) In the same fashion, instantiating a COM object using `CoCreateInstance` but forgetting to release it also causes a memory leak (and potentially other forms of leaks, depending on what resources the COM object in turn allocates). In many cases, the severity of the resource leak is directly proportional to the abstraction level that you are working with. As is the case with a COM object, it might aggregate other COM objects, which aggregate other COM objects, and so on. The most important aspect with regard to debugging resource leak problems is how the resource is acquired and released.

To effectively debug resource leaks, you must first be able to analyze the problem in front of you. With resource leaks, it simply does not work to sit down and randomly start debugging, hoping to come across a clue that will yield the source of the problem. No, much in the same way a detective has to collect and organize clues and theories, so must the developer. Many times, the theories are proven wrong, and you will find yourself back at the drawing board, looking for other theories on the potential culprit code. By fully understanding the systematic thought process behind analyzing a resource leak, you will be able to tackle any resource leak (whether it is a handle, memory, or a COM object). To aid the developer tackling resource leak problems, there is also a set of tools that you will find invaluable when verifying your theories.

This chapter takes you on the journey of discovering the root cause behind orphaned bits. It discusses the thought process behind your work as a bit detective, as well as explains, in detail, the tools at your disposal to make your work easier. We use two different types of resources as case studies:

- Handles
- Conventional memory allocations

Next, we look at the process of identifying and addressing a resource leak from the 30,000 foot view, and then we start to dig into the details.

# High-Level Process

The process of resolving a resource leak in your code is illustrated in Figure 9.1. In this section, we examine each of the parts of the process in detail.

## Step 1: Identify Potential Resource Leaks

The first step in the resource leak process is convincing yourself that what you are seeing is, in fact, a leak. Many applications will include internal caches that are filled during heavy load and subsequently released when in an idle state, hence leading to a false positive. Another false positive might be that an overall increase in memory usage is observed, but it might not necessarily mean that *your* application is leaking. All good investigations start with the basics, and, as such, the first step should be identifying potentially leaking resources. This is accomplished by a thorough analysis of the state of the machine, paying careful attention to abnormally large amounts of one or more resource types. Only after this has been confirmed can you safely move on to the diagnostics stage. Several different tools are out there that allow you to analyze system health. The most basic tool (part of Windows) is the Task Manager (CTRL+SHIFT+ESC or taskman.exe). Using Task Manager, you get a global view of the system resource consumption, as well as a more granular view for each process running, as shown in Figure 9.2.

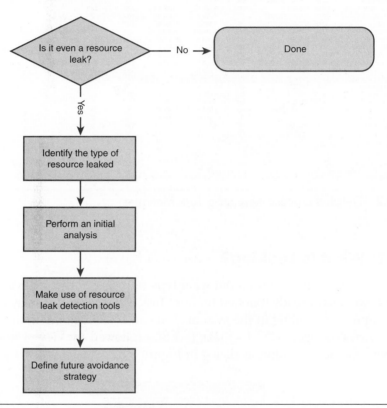

**Figure 9.1**   Resource leak analysis process

Task Manager can be customized to show different types of process data. If the process you are investigating is showing an unusually high amount of resource usage, chances are good that you are seeing a resource leak.

At this point, the first step of the process is completed. You have identified a large amount of resources being consumed by the alleged process by using Task Manager, and it is time to move on to the diagnostics stage.

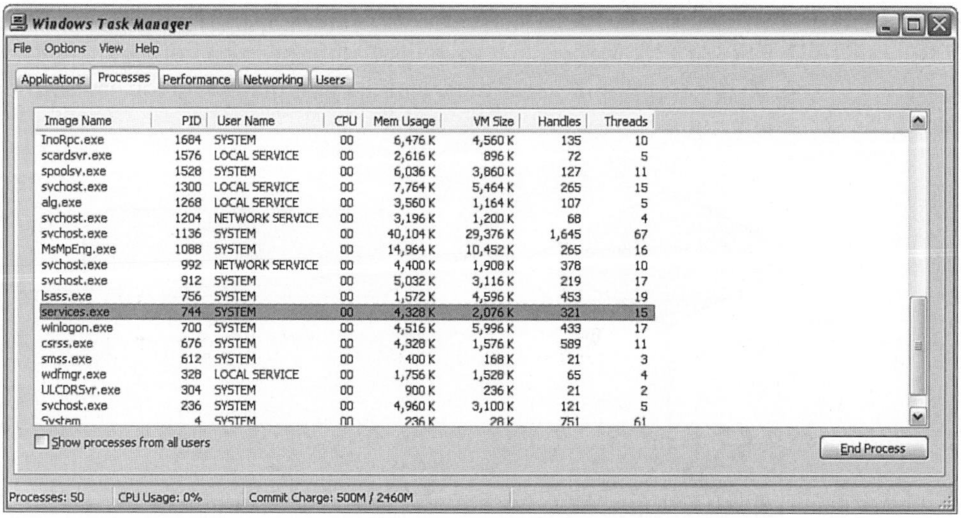

**Figure 9.2**   Detailed process view using Task Manager

## Step 2: What Is Leaking?

The next critical step is figuring out what type of resource the application is leaking. In step 1, we have already touched on how Task Manager can display useful data for any given process running in the system. You can customize the available options by opening Task Manager (CTRL+SHIFT+ESC) followed by View, Choose Columns. This opens the Select Columns dialog in Figure 9.3.

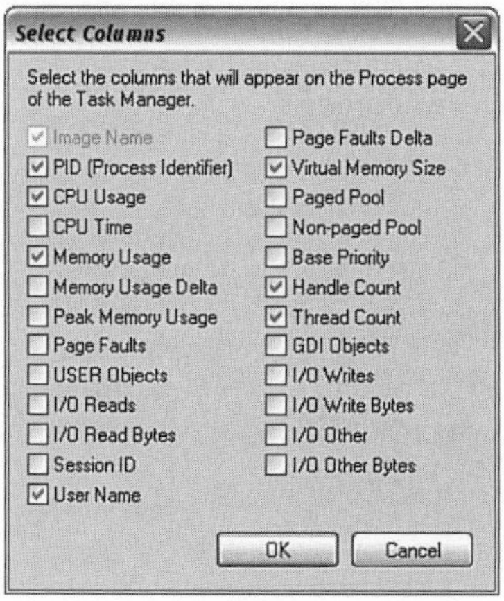

**Figure 9.3**   Customizing the process data in Task Manager

The columns most applicable to resource leaks are

- Memory Usage (working set size)
- Memory Usage Delta
- Peak Memory Usage
- Virtual Memory Size
- Handle Count
- Thread Count
- GDI Objects (if the application uses UI features) and USER Objects

After you've enabled the columns of interest, Task Manager will display the data as new columns in the Processes view.

Another great tool that can be used to track resource leaks is Performance Monitor (Start, Run: perfmon.exe). Performance Monitor has the added benefit of including a ton of memory-related counters that can be used to track leaks over time.

## Step 3: Initial Analysis

Let's say that step 2 showed your process using a large number of handles (more than it should). The next step is to do an initial analysis. Because you are probably familiar with the code you are analyzing, a great starting point is to look at code paths involving handles. It is surprising how many resource leaks can be identified simply by following some basic steps and eyeballing the code that works with the resource in question. What is actually happening to make the resource usage grow in the first place? If you have the answer to that question, you can begin with either code reviewing the paths during those operations or stepping through it in the debugger, paying careful attention to any of those specific resources being used. After you have identified where the resource is opened, finding the missing resource close is fairly trivial. Congratulations! You have just identified and fixed a resource leak at a very low cost.

Unfortunately, not all solutions to resource leaks are as trivial as merely eyeballing the code, and it is sometimes impossible to find the source of the leak that way. Several reasons for this exist:

- The issue is not reproducible all the time. If the resource leak you are debugging happens infrequently (even with the same repro steps), it is very difficult to narrow down where in the code it might be happening.
- The resource leak is identified on a production server that the customer cannot afford to let "sit idle" while it is being debugged. Even worse, a lot of times, restrictions and connectivity issues prevent engineers from even accessing the servers.

- A lot of times, stress testing an application or service yields very nondeterministic results, and the leaks must be debugged on a server that has been heavily used and has had a huge amount of resources leaked.

If you are in any of the previously described situations, your task has just become harder. But fear not; a great number of tools can aid you in identifying and resolving resource leaks that would otherwise be impossible or, at the very least, very expensive to sort out by simple code reviews.

## Step 4: Leak Detection Tools

Let's say that you have developed a service, and it is ready to be included in the nightly stress run. By the sheer definition of stress test code, your service will be hit by thousands of concurrent and different requests, both valid and invalid, for ten hours straight. After being notified that stress testing will commence starting tonight, you go home at the end of the day, expecting the worst. In the morning, the report is published: "No crashes, BUT at the end of the stress run, the memory consumption and handle count of the service had skyrocketed." At the status meeting, the management team looks to you for answers.

Presented with this situation, the best course of action is to take full dumps of the leaking process (see Chapter 13, "Postmortem Debugging") and ask the test team to reproduce the resource leak (that is, run the stress testing overnight again). Prior to starting the new stress run, enable one or more leak detection tools that will allow you to track down the problem much more efficiently. Although the leak is being reproduced, you can analyze the dump files generated earlier (see Chapter 13). If the team is wary about letting this particular resource leak go in hopes of reproducing it again, tell them that without leak detection tools, it might take you weeks of investigation to get to the bottom of it. Really—this is sometimes how long it can take to solve a resource leak postmortem without tools. If they still want you to debug the problem without the leak detection tools, mechanisms are available to make your life a bit easier.

The choice of tools you enable depends entirely on the resource being leaked. Table 9.1 presents the most common options.

**Table 9.1**    Leak Detection Tools

| Name | Resource Leaked | Download |
|------|-----------------|----------|
| htrace | Handles | Debugging Tools for Windows |
| UMDH | Heap Memory | Windows 2003 Server Resource Kit |
| LEAKDIAG | Various forms of memory allocators | ftp://ftp.microsoft.com/PSS/Tools/Developer%20Support%20Tools/LeakDiag/LeakDiag125.msi |

The basic idea behind all these tools is that by enabling them, you are telling Windows that you want to track all resource acquisitions and releases. Windows, in turn, responds by hooking calls to the corresponding resource acquisition/release API(s) and produces a database of all stack traces that acquired and released that particular type of resource. Some of these tools (such as UMDH) query the database for all calls that result in heap memory being allocated and analyze the results to produce a report of potentially leaked memory.

After you have identified the offending stack trace, tracking down the resource leak becomes a much easier task (although not trivial).

Note that some of these tools require support from Windows to work properly and, as such, require the user to enable stack trace recording in the operating system. You will see these tools in action in subsequent parts of the chapter.

### Step 5: Define a Future Avoidance Strategy

At this point, you have identified that there is a resource leak, done an initial analysis, ran the necessary leak detection tools, and finally identified and fixed the offending code. The next step, and perhaps the most crucial, is ensuring that what you just discovered does not happen again; the best way of doing this is to define a future avoidance strategy for that particular problem. As much as we would like to think that we never make the same mistake twice, it happens; and it happens often. By making use of our everyday tools, we can take out part of that human error from our code and let it be "automatically" handled by the system.

## Reproducibility of Resource Leaks

Reproducibility of resource leaks can take on several different shapes. The three main categories of reproductions are

- Sequential and fully reproducible
- Sporadic and reproducible a majority of the time
- Sporadic and reproducible very infrequently

Sequential and fully reproducible resource leaks are typically encountered during development time while running unit tests or an automation test suite. These resource leaks typically surface each time a test is run. Furthermore, running the same test with the same input reproduces the same resource leak. As it turns out, these types of leaks are also the easiest to investigate.

Sporadic resource leaks that are reproducible most of the time might allow for the luxury of enabling leak detection tools and waiting for a few days for the leak to occur again. This assumes that the customer is willing to wait for another occurrence of the problem. If he is not, the scenario turns into the third category of problems and also the toughest form of resource leaks.

If a resource leak reproduces infrequently enough, it is not always feasible to simply tell the customer to enable leak detection tools and then sit back and wait. Customers running your application or service on production machines might be hesitant to install utilities and tools that are not part of the operating system. Furthermore, some leak detection tools slow the processing down and consume more memory than desirable. In these cases, the only two options at your disposal are to either ask for debugging permissions on their servers (hardly ever granted) or to perform postmortem debugging. Postmortem involves taking a snapshot of the process and analyzing the memory snap on a different machine. (For more information on postmortem debugging, see Chapter 13.) Because no leak detection tools were run prior to the process starting, you are now faced with finding a resource leak by merely analyzing the state of the process. These can prove to be daunting tasks that can make the best of software engineers question their abilities. In the following sections, you will see specific examples of resource leaks and how to analyze them. Each of the sections describes a specific type of resource leak. It is important to understand that although we are only covering a few of the possible resource leaks, the five-step resource leak analysis process described can be applied to any type of resource leak.

## Handle Leaks

The Windows kernel defines a set of object *types* that are native to the Windows operating system. Examples of such object types are file objects, process objects, and thread objects. Each object type has an associated set of properties and APIs that work on that particular object type. As an example, consider a file object. A file object has a set of attributes that dictate if a file is hidden, visible, system, and so on. To perform work on an object type, the associated set of APIs must be used. For example, the Win32 API `CreateFile` allows you to create or open a file object. Although the Windows kernel is mostly implemented in C, you can view the object type properties and functions as a method of implementing encapsulation using C. The object types themselves are not exposed directly; rather they require that the developer manipulates the object types via the C APIs, thereby hiding the details of the type and enabling the internals of the type to change over time. Furthermore, the encapsulation model promotes a more robust form of development because the encapsulated data is never manipulated directly by a caller, thereby minimizing the risk of the caller misusing the object data. Most of the APIs are exposed to user mode code via the Win32 APIs. Figure 9.4 depicts the high-level handle architecture.

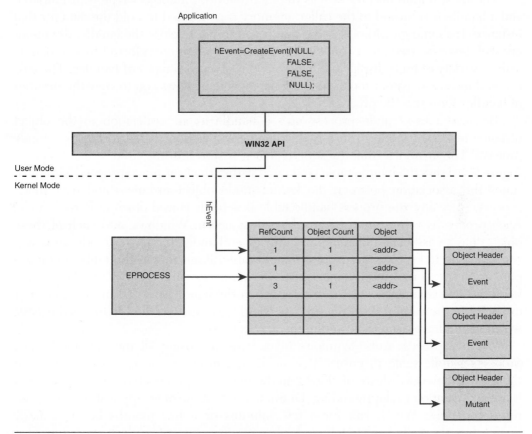

**Figure 9.4** Windows handle architecture overview

In order to work with object types, you must first instantiate an instance of that object type. Let's take a file as an example. The CreateFile API allows you to create or open an existing file. Under the covers, the CreateFile API calls into the kernel, creates an instance of the file object type, and passes back the resulting handle to the client. The handle is what the client uses to refer to the newly created instance in the kernel. If you want to perform other operations on the new file, the handle should always be used when referring to the correct object instance. When you are done with that particular file, you should close the handle so that Windows can properly decrement the reference count on the instance and free the memory when the reference count reaches zero.

The most important takeaway is the fact that after an object type is instantiated and a handle is returned to the caller, memory is consumed to hold the data for that instance. It should go without saying that if you forget to close the handle, the memory will never be freed and you will have what is commonly referred to as a handle leak. A variety of tools display the handle count of various types of handles. The easiest and most convenient tool is Task Manager, which allows you to view the number of handles for a specific process.

Because a user mode process uses a handle as an association to the object instance in kernel mode, where is this handle association stored in the user mode process? The answer to that question is that it is stored in the process handle table. Figure 9.4 shows the handle table contained within the user mode process. This illustrates the association between the kernel mode object instances and user mode process. In reality, the process handle table is actually stored down in kernel mode. Each process is represented by an object instance in Windows, and each of these objects has an associated handle table. Any given handle in the user mode process is really just an index into the process handle table. Each row in the table contains a pointer to the kernel mode object instance, an access mask, and flags. The access mask dictates what access was requested when the handle was first instantiated. For example, in the case of files, the process could have opened the file for read access, which would have been indicated in the access mask.

When a process exits, Windows takes care of closing all the handles in that process's handle table to ensure that no kernel mode instances are leaked. Even though Windows takes care of closing all the handles a process has open upon exit, it is not an invitation to sloppy coding. Defining the lifetime of an application can sometimes be tricky. Will it run for a few minutes or a few months before exited? Sometimes, it's really hard to tell, and relying on process exit to clean up resources is poor programming practice.

## The Leaky Application

Before we jump in and analyze a leaky application, it is important to understand how the application works, as well as the steps that make the leak surface. You might wonder why I would mention something that obvious. The reality is, though, that we are often faced with fixing other engineers' code, and it is important to get a good overview before starting. To illustrate an example of a leaky application, we use a service that exposes a function that allows clients to read text files from the server machine and return the contents of those files. To make life easier, the function is exposed as a static library. The test application displays a prompt allowing the user to type in the filename he is interested in and press Enter. The service call is made followed by a display of the first 1023 characters in that file.

An example of running the application is shown here:

```
C:\AWDBIN\WinXP.x86.chk\09Basichleak.exe
Client application console menu
====================
Enter filename to read > c:\boot.ini

Scheduled request successfully

Data read:
[boot loader]
timeout=30
default=multi(0)disk(0)rdisk(0)partition(1)\WINDOWS
[operating systems]
multi(0)disk(0)rdisk(0)partition(1)\WINDOWS="Microsoft Windows XP Professional"
/fastdetect /NoExecute=OptIn
multi(0)disk(0)rdisk(0)partition(1)\WINXP="Microsoft Windows XP Professional" /fast-
detect
&
Enter filename to read > _
```

The source code and binary for the application can be found in the following folders:

> Source code: `C:\AWD\Chapter9\BasicHLeak\Client` and
> `C:\AWD\Chapter9\BasicHLeak\Server`
> Binary: `C:\AWDBIN\WinXP.x86.chk\09Basichleak.exe`

Now that you have a good understanding of what the code architecture looks like coupled with the QA department's assertion that there is a handle leak, we begin by following the five-step resource leak process. Because we know that we are looking for handle leaks, steps 1 and 2 are combined.

## Steps 1 and 2: Is It Even a Handle Leak?

As always, the first step of investigating a potential resource leak is to confirm that there really is one. Handle leaks can be easily detected by using Task Manager. By default, Task Manager does not display the number of handles for a given process. You can enable this by clicking the Process tab followed by selecting the View and Select

Columns submenu. This brings up a dialog box that displays a host of options that Task Manager is capable of displaying. Check the Handle Count check box, and click OK.

The Processes tab now displays an additional column that shows the number of handles any given process has open. Let's try it with our supposedly leaky application. You can find the leaky application under

```
C:\AWDBIN\WinXP.x86.chk\09Basichleak.exe
```

When the application has started, you are presented with a prompt asking for a filename. Start by entering a valid filename (must include full path), and press Enter. The output shows the first 1023 characters of the file content, followed by another prompt for a filename. Now is a good time to bring up Task Manager and look at the 09Basichleak.exe process in the Processes tab. More specifically, you want to look at the Handles column and see what it shows. It looks like the process at this time has 13 handles open, as shown in Figure 9.5.

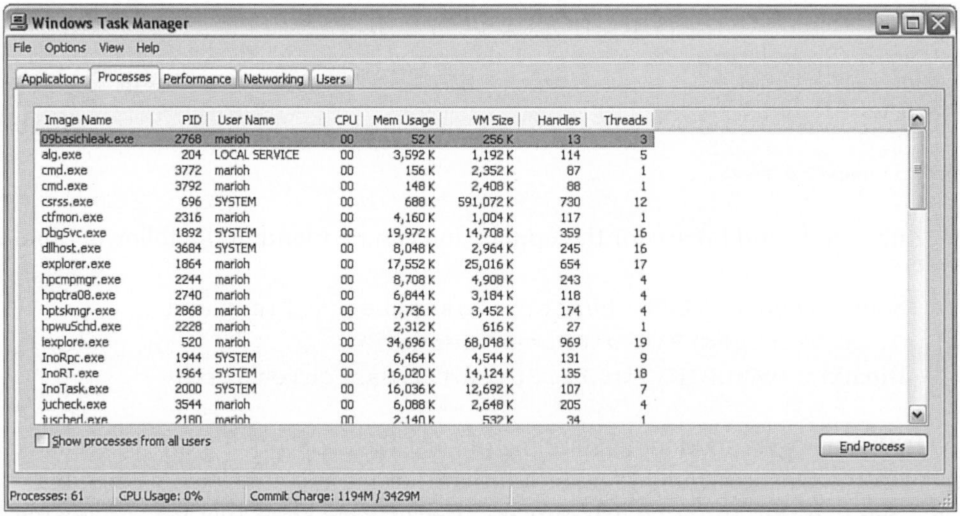

**Figure 9.5** Handle count of the 09Basichleak.exe process after reading the first file

We type in yet another filename and press Enter. Again, we check the handle count, which is now 14. Indeed, this does not look good so far. We continue the process of opening files a dozen or so times, and sure enough, the handle count seems to be going up by one each time a request has executed. Figure 9.6 shows the number of handles opened by the 09Basichleak.exe process after executing the read file request 12 times.

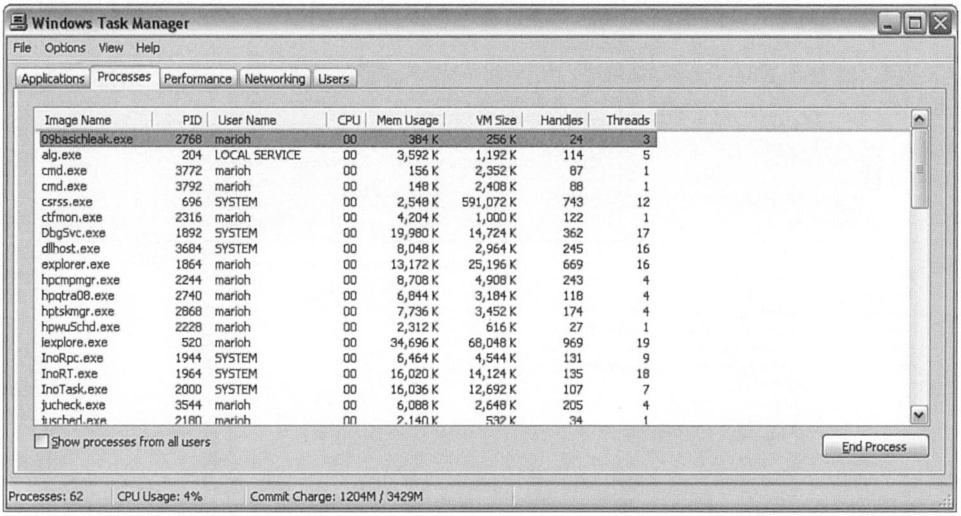

**Windows Task Manager**

File  Options  View  Help

Applications | Processes | Performance | Networking | Users

| Image Name | PID | User Name | CPU | Mem Usage | VM Size | Handles | Threads |
|---|---|---|---|---|---|---|---|
| 09basichleak.exe | 2768 | marioh | 00 | 384 K | 256 K | 24 | 3 |
| alg.exe | 204 | LOCAL SERVICE | 00 | 3,592 K | 1,192 K | 114 | 5 |
| cmd.exe | 3772 | marioh | 00 | 156 K | 2,352 K | 87 | 1 |
| cmd.exe | 3792 | marioh | 00 | 148 K | 2,408 K | 88 | 1 |
| csrss.exe | 696 | SYSTEM | 00 | 2,548 K | 591,072 K | 743 | 12 |
| ctfmon.exe | 2316 | marioh | 00 | 4,204 K | 1,000 K | 122 | 1 |
| DbgSvc.exe | 1892 | SYSTEM | 00 | 19,980 K | 14,724 K | 362 | 17 |
| dllhost.exe | 3684 | SYSTEM | 00 | 8,048 K | 2,964 K | 245 | 16 |
| explorer.exe | 1864 | marioh | 00 | 13,172 K | 25,196 K | 669 | 16 |
| hpcmpmgr.exe | 2244 | marioh | 00 | 8,708 K | 4,908 K | 243 | 4 |
| hpqtra08.exe | 2740 | marioh | 00 | 6,844 K | 3,184 K | 118 | 4 |
| hptskmgr.exe | 2868 | marioh | 00 | 7,736 K | 3,452 K | 174 | 4 |
| hpwuSchd.exe | 2228 | marioh | 00 | 2,312 K | 616 K | 27 | 1 |
| iexplore.exe | 520 | marioh | 00 | 34,696 K | 68,048 K | 969 | 19 |
| InoRpc.exe | 1944 | SYSTEM | 00 | 6,464 K | 4,544 K | 131 | 9 |
| InoRT.exe | 1964 | SYSTEM | 00 | 16,020 K | 14,124 K | 135 | 18 |
| InoTask.exe | 2000 | SYSTEM | 00 | 16,036 K | 12,692 K | 107 | 7 |
| jucheck.exe | 3544 | marioh | 00 | 6,088 K | 2,648 K | 205 | 4 |
| jusched.exe | 2180 | marioh | 00 | 2,140 K | 532 K | 34 | 1 |

☐ Show processes from all users                    [ End Process ]

Processes: 62    CPU Usage: 4%    Commit Charge: 1204M / 3429M

**Figure 9.6**   Handle count of the 09Basichleak.exe process after 12 files have been read

Now, there are times when the handle count can go up due to caching, but after letting the application sit idle for a while, we still don't see the handle count go down. We can fairly safely say that at this point, we are seeing an application that is leaking handles.

## Step 3: Initial Analysis

Because a handle is opaque and can represent any number of object types, how do we go about narrowing down the problem? If we could identify what type of object the handle is associated with, it might give us a better clue to the source of the leak. For example, if all the preceding handles are thread handles, we could focus our efforts in those parts of the code. Unfortunately, Task Manager does not always give us this type of information, and we have to move to a more powerful diagnostics tool.

An excellent tool for this, called Process Explorer, is available free at www.microsoft.com. Process Explorer has the capability to show a lot of useful information about running processes, including the different handles and their associated types. It is well worth your time to play around with this tool, as it has some great exploring capabilities. Figure 9.7 shows Process Explorer when run on our leaky application.

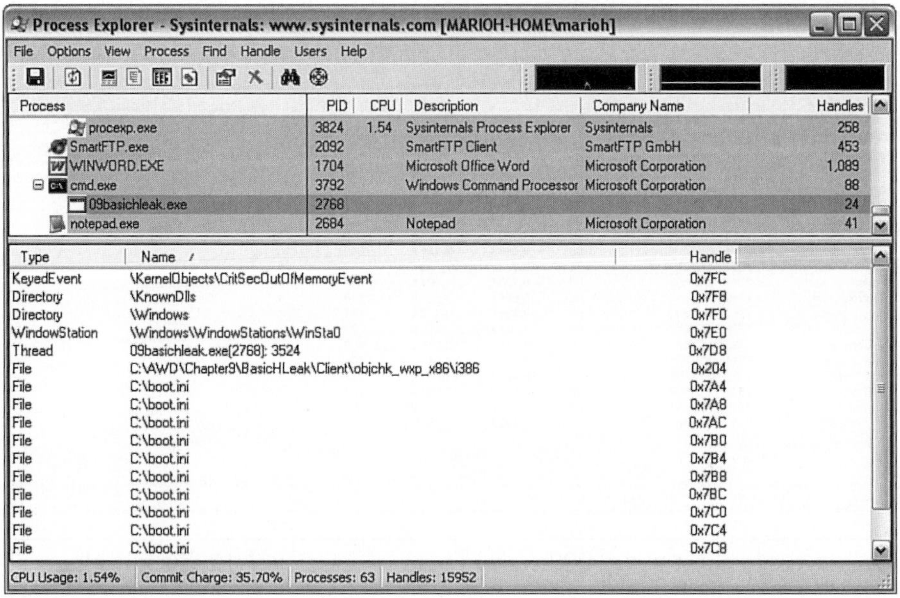

**Figure 9.7** View of 09Basichleak.exe using Process Explorer

As you can tell, what makes this tool so much more powerful than Task Manager is that it is capable of displaying the different types of handles that are opened in the process. But the fanciness does not stop there; it also displays the name of the handle that is opened. In our particular run, we kept opening the same file over and over again (BOOT.INI), and it's clearly shown in the UI of Process Explorer. The number of file handles with the BOOT.INI name corresponds to the number of times we opened that file. It would be a fair statement to say that at this point, we have verified that there is indeed a leak, and the specific handle being leaked is a file handle. Because we know exactly what type of handle is being leaked and it seems that we can reproduce it on every iteration of the command we are executing, the first step we should take is to follow the code path exactly as it happens when we run the operation. The test application we are using makes the following call:

```
CHAR szFiledata[1024];
BOOL bRet=CServer::GetTextFileContents(hCompletionEvent,
                                       pFileName,
                                       szFiledata, 1024 ) ;

if(bRet==FALSE)
{
```

```
    printf("\nFailed to read file\n");
}
else
{
    printf("\nScheduled request successfully\n");
    WaitForSingleObject(hCompletionEvent, INFINITE);
    printf("\nData read:\n");
    printf("%s\n", szFiledata);
}
```

hCompletionEvent is a handle to an event that we created. We use this event as a notification mechanism that the server can signal when the operation is completed. This enables us to perform additional work while the service is doing its work. pFileName in our case is the filename we typed in on the command line (BOOT.INI), and szFileData is a stack allocated string buffer that contains the first 1024 characters of the file content. The last parameter, 1024, simply indicates the number of characters our buffer is capable of storing.

So far, nothing in our code indicates that we are the cause of the file handle leak. We do have a handle, but it's an event handle that does not appear to leak, according to Process Explorer. We continue the investigation by looking at the service implementation of GetTextFileContents:

```
BOOL CServer::GetTextFileContents(HANDLE hEvent,
                                  PWSTR pszFileName,
                                  PSTR pBuffer,
                                  DWORD dwBufferLen)
{
    BOOL bRet=FALSE;

    if(hEvent!=NULL && pszFileName!=NULL && pBuffer!=NULL && dwBufferLen!=0)
    {
        WorkerData* pWorkerData=new WorkerData;
        if(pWorkerData!= NULL)
        {
            pWorkerData->dwBufferLen=dwBufferLen;
            pWorkerData->pBuffer=pBuffer;
            pWorkerData->pszFileName=pszFileName;
            pWorkerData->hCompletionHandle=hEvent;

            bRet=QueueUserWorkItem(RequestWorker,
                            (LPVOID) pWorkerData,
                            WT_EXECUTELONGFUNCTION);
            if(!bRet)
            {
```

```
                delete pWorkerData;
            }
        }
    }


    return bRet;
}
```

A brief glance at this function does not make it clear where the file handle is being opened. A closer look shows that we are using `QueueUserWorkItem` with a callback function called `RequestWorker`. The Win32 `QueueUserWorkItem` API enables an application to queue up a work item on the native Windows thread pool. This means that the application provides a callback function that the operating system invokes using one of its own threads. This seems to make sense because the application calling the service is expected (according to the contract) to give an event handle to the service that is signaled when the request is completed. Based on this information, we continue the investigation by looking at the `RequestWorker` function:

```
DWORD WINAPI CServer::RequestWorker(LPVOID lpParameter)
{
    DWORD dwRet=0;

    WorkerData* pWorkerData=(WorkerData*) lpParameter;

    HANDLE hFile=CreateFile(pWorkerData->pszFileName,
                    FILE_READ_DATA,
                    FILE_SHARE_READ,
                    NULL,
                    OPEN_EXISTING,
                    FILE_ATTRIBUTE_NORMAL,
                    NULL);

    if(hFile!=INVALID_HANDLE_VALUE)
    {
        DWORD dwBytesRead=0;
        BOOL bRet=ReadFile(hFile,
                    (LPVOID) pWorkerData->pBuffer,
                    (pWorkerData->dwBufferLen-1),
                    &dwBytesRead,
                    NULL);
        if(bRet==TRUE)
        {
            dwRet=1;
        }
```

```
    }

    SetEvent(pWorkerData->hCompletionHandle);
    delete pWorkerData;

    return dwRet;
}
```

Now we seem to be getting somewhere. This function manipulates files judging by the `CreateFile` API call, as well as the `ReadFile` API. The `CreateFile` API returns a handle to the opened file, stored in the local variable hFile. Assuming that no failures occur, the code proceeds by calling the `ReadFile` API. After the file has been read, the event handle passed in by the caller is signaled (to indicate that the operation completed), and the function returns. It is important to note that when we say that the function returns, it returns to the Windows thread pool. At this point, it should be clear that we have missed a critical ingredient in this function. We opened the file, which returned a file handle, but we forgot to close the file handle prior to returning. Each time the request is run, we leak one file handle. The solution to this problem is to add a `CloseHandle` call (only if the file was successfully opened) prior to returning from the function. I should also note that it is always beneficial, but often overlooked, that when you find a leak, it is quite useful to look around the same section of code to see if perhaps other leaks are lurking about.

You have followed the five-step leak detection process and managed to find the leak as early as step 3. Finding a leak this early on in the process is very inexpensive. Unfortunately, it is not always the case that you have a fully reproducible problem in which the leak occurs on each operation. Let's make a slight alternation to our code and show how these types of problems can manifest themselves, as well as how to track them down.

## A More Complex Application

If you can track down a handle leak based on only knowing the type of the handle being leaked, consider yourself lucky (or a very skilled code reviewer). Most of the time, further diagnostics is required.

The previous sample shows how you can go about analyzing a fairly simple handle leak and what you can do to get to the bottom of it. Now it's time to look at yet another leaky application with added complexity. The key difference between the last leaky application and this one is that it no longer leaks handles systematically; rather, the occurrence of the leak is sporadic and, at first sight, random. The basic architecture is the same; there is a client application and a server application (implemented as a static library for simplicity sake). The server exposes a set of functions that enable the client to get security-related information about the caller, such as the token privilege count, the group count, and the security indentifier (SID). The client application is called 09hleak.exe and can be found in the following location:

Source code: `C:\AWD\Chapter9\HLeak\Client` and
`C:\AWD\Chapter9\HLeak\Server`
Binary: `C:\AWDBIN\WinXP.x86.chk\09hleak.exe`

The 09hleak.exe binary allows for the following command-line arguments:

```
C:\AWDBIN\WinXP.x86.chk\09hleak.exe /t:<num_threads> /i:<iterations_per_thread>
/s:<sleep_time_per_iteration>
```

```
/t:<num_threads>
```

Specifies the number of concurrent threads that the client uses when invoking operations on the server.

```
/i:<iterations_per_thread>
```

Specifies the number of operations that will be performed by each thread.

```
/s:<sleep_time_per_iteration>
```

Specifies the number of seconds to wait between each operation in each thread.

Once again, for the sake of simplicity, the client stress application links directly against a static library that represents the server. Let's begin by running the application once, specifying that we want 5 threads, 5 iterations per thread, and 0 second sleep time:

```
C:\AWDBIN\WinXP.x86.chk\09hleak.exe /t:5 /i:5 /s:0
```

Let the application run and, at the same time, watch the handle consumption in Process Explorer. Figure 9.8 shows the result of the run in Process Explorer view.

As you can see, our handle count has gone from approximately 8 at the start of the application run to 13 (don't worry if your handle count is different; it's all part of the exercise) at the end of the run. Not a good sign. Now, let's run it again, with the same parameters. Figure 9.9 shows the results in Process Explorer view.

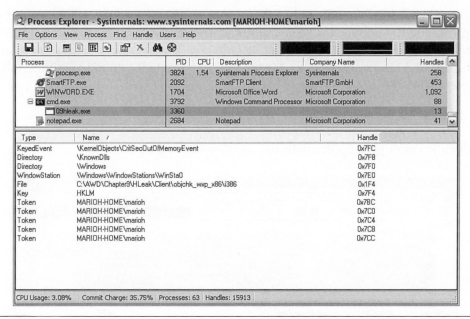

**Figure 9.8**  Handle consumption in the first run of 09hleak.exe

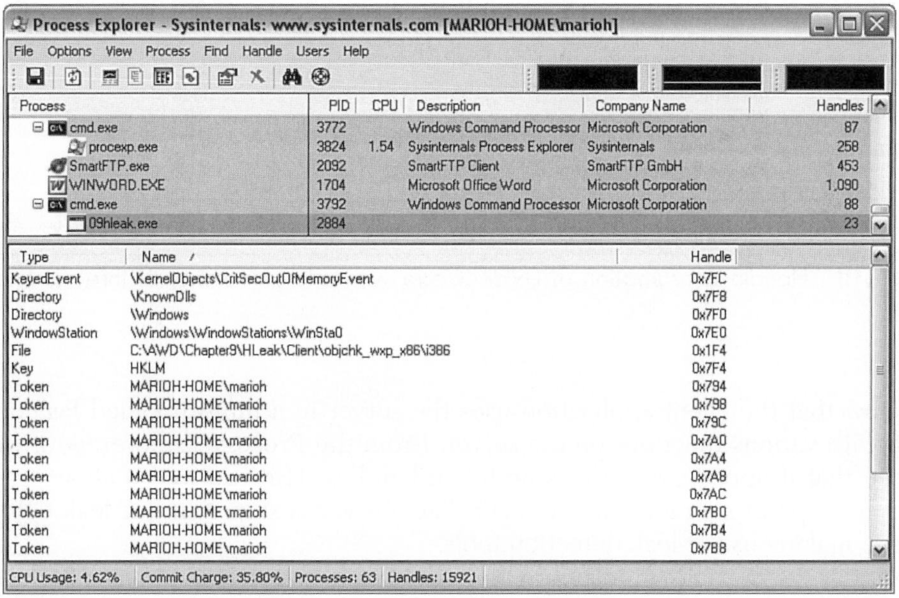

**Figure 9.9**  Handle consumption in the second run of 09hleak.exe

This time, we ended up with 23 handles, even though we used the same input. If you keep running the application, you will notice that there isn't any real pattern to the leak. The only observation that seems to hold true is that if we increase the number of threads and iterations, we see a bigger leak. For example, running with the following command line

```
C:\AWDBIN\WinXP.x86.chk\09hleak.exe /t:20 /i:10 /s:0
```

the handle count goes up dramatically, as shown in Figure 9.10.

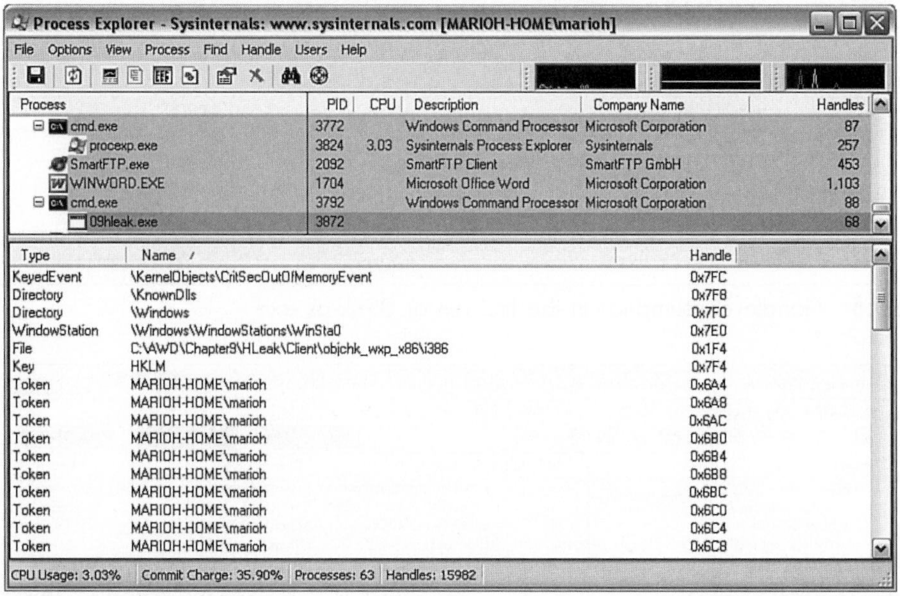

**Figure 9.10**   Handle consumption of 09hleak.exe with a large number of threads and iterations

We know that the client application uses the server in a multithreaded fashion and that it calls various functions on the server. From the Process Explorer view, we can also see that it appears to be leaking token handles. How do we go about tracking down this type of sporadic handle leak? The answer is step 4 in our leak detection process: making use of leak detection tools.

For this exercise, try not to look at the code ahead of time. We are going to show you some of the most important tools of tracking down these types of unpredictable issues. By unpredictable, we mean leaks that do not reproduce consistently and cannot (reasonably) be tracked down via simple code reviews. We will skip steps 1–3 in our five-step leak detection process because we already know that there is a handle leak. We also assume that it cannot be easily spotted by a simple code review.

## Step 4: Make Use of Resource Leak Detection Tools

Okay, we have a sporadic and apparently random handle leak on our hands. Although this might seem like a doomsday scenario, there is some good news. As odd as it might seem, the good news is that the leak appears to surface every time the application is run; it just does not reproduce with the same number of handles being leaked. Why is that good news? Because it is a prime opportunity to leverage an extremely powerful extension command called !htrace that can help you detect where the leak is occurring.

Htrace stands for handle trace, and the basic idea behind the command is to enable the operating system to track all calls (with associated stack traces) that result in handles being opened and closed. When a leak has been identified, you can then use the !htrace extension command to display all the stack traces in the debugger. After all stack traces are shown, you can track down sporadic handle leaks in a much easier fashion. Let's take a look at the available options for the !htrace extension command. First, start our leaky application (with the same command-line options as before):

```
C:\AWDBIN\WinXP.x86.chk\09hleak.exe /t:20 /i:10 /s:0
Press any key to start stress application...
```

Before starting the actual leak reproduction, attach a debugger to the newly created process, set the symbol path, and type !htrace -?:

```
0:001> !htrace -?
!htrace [handle [max_traces]]
!htrace -enable [max_traces]
!htrace -disable
!htrace -snapshot
!htrace -diff
```

The first thing of interest in this help text is the -enable option. Recording all the stack traces for handle open and close calls is not a feature of the !htrace extension command per se; rather, it is an operating system feature. !htrace merely tells the operating system to enable stack tracing for the given process before it can be used. You can do this by using the -enable command. As a matter of fact, if you try to use the other !htrace extension command before stack tracing has been enabled, you will get the following error:

```
0:001> !htrace -snapshot
Handle tracing is not enabled for this process. Use "!htrace -enable" to enable it.
```

Enable stack tracing as shown here:

```
0:001> !htrace -enable
Handle tracing enabled.
Handle tracing information snapshot successfully taken.
```

As you can see, the –enable switch is a two-step operation. First, it enables stack tracing, and second, it takes a snapshot of the current state of the process with regard to handles (as indicated by the second line in the output). As soon as stack tracing has been enabled, Windows starts recording all calls that result in handle creation and deletion. The next time you take a snapshot (using the –snapshot option), the !htrace extension command queries the operating system for all stack traces that result in handle creation and deletion and displays them. If you let your application run a little longer (perhaps leaking some more handles), break in, and take another snapshot, it will, again, show all the stack traces previously shown plus any additional handles created or deleted since the last snapshot was taken. By systematically doing this, you can compare the snapshots and see which portions of your code created and/or deleted handles, or, more interestingly, which parts created handles but did not close them (which might be the culprit of the leak). Back to our leaky application. Because we have just started the process and enabled stack tracing, let the process run to completion. When finished, you can use the !htrace extension command to get a list of all the stacks that have created and deleted handles throughout the duration of the process. Because even "smaller" processes typically create and delete a fairly large number of handles, the following example only shows segments of the output. Also remember that our leaky application leaks handles very sporadically in the sense that no one run is guaranteed to leak the same number of handles even with the same input. Therefore, the output you see in your debug session will more than likely be different from what is listed here.

```
...
...

...

0:001> !htrace -enable
Handle tracing enabled.
Handle tracing information snapshot successfully taken.
0:001> g
(d3c.18c): Break instruction exception - code 80000003 (first chance)
eax=7ffdd000 ebx=00000001 ecx=00000002 edx=00000003 esi=00000004 edi=00000005
eip=7c901230 esp=0028ffcc ebp=0028fff4 iopl=0         nv up ei pl zr na po nc
cs=001b  ss=0023  ds=0023  es=0023  fs=0038  gs=0000             efl=00000246
ntdll!DbgBreakPoint:
```

```
7c901230 cc                    int     3
0:001> !htrace
-------------------
Handle = 0x0000078C - CLOSE
Thread ID = 0x00000410, Process ID = 0x00000D3C

0x0100176A: 09hleak!wmain+0x0000027A
0x01001933: 09hleak!wmainCRTStartup+0x0000012B
0x7C816FD7: kernel32!BaseProcessStart+0x00000023
-------------------
Handle = 0x00000798 - CLOSE
Thread ID = 0x00000410, Process ID = 0x00000D3C

0x0100176A: 09hleak!wmain+0x0000027A
0x01001933: 09hleak!wmainCRTStartup+0x0000012B
0x7C816FD7: kernel32!BaseProcessStart+0x00000023
-------------------
<output truncated>
...
...
...
-------------------
Handle = 0x00000480 - CLOSE
Thread ID = 0x00000C04, Process ID = 0x00000D3C

0x01001E1E: 09hleak!CServer::GetGroupCount+0x000000BE
0x01001499: 09hleak!ThreadWorker+0x000000E9
0x7C80B683: kernel32!BaseThreadStart+0x00000037
-------------------
Handle = 0x00000480 - OPEN
Thread ID = 0x00000C04, Process ID = 0x00000D3C

0x01001E85: 09hleak!CServer::GetToken+0x00000055
0x01001D81: 09hleak!CServer::GetGroupCount+0x00000021
0x01001499: 09hleak!ThreadWorker+0x000000E9
0x7C80B683: kernel32!BaseThreadStart+0x00000037
-------------------
<output truncated>
...
...
...
-------------------
Parsed 0x191 stack traces.
Dumped 0x191 stack traces.
```

The output of the `!htrace` extension command consists of two major sections:

- A list of all stack traces recorded
- A summary section toward the end

The summary section shows how many stack traces were parsed and how many were dumped to the debugger. Let's take a close look at the stack trace section corresponding to the handle `0x480`.

```
Handle = 0x00000480 - OPEN
Thread ID = 0x00000C04, Process ID = 0x00000D3C

0x01001E85: 09hleak!CServer::GetToken+0x00000055
0x01001D81: 09hleak!CServer::GetGroupCount+0x00000021
0x01001499: 09hleak!ThreadWorker+0x000000E9
0x7C80B683: kernel32!BaseThreadStart+0x00000037
```

Each stack trace recorded consists of a header and the stack trace itself. The header consists of the following information:

- Handle value represented as `Handle = <value>`. In our example, the handle value is `0x00000480`.
- Next to the handle value is the type of operation performed. It can be one of the following: `OPEN` or `CLOSE`. Our particular example shows `OPEN`, which means that the stack trace shown is the stack trace that opened the handle.
- Thread ID and Process ID represented as `Thread ID = <value>` and `Process ID = <value>`. These values show which thread the stack trace belongs to, as well as the process ID. One might be inclined to say that the process ID is a waste of space since handles are process relative, and hence the process ID must match the currently running process. This is true most of the time, but as we show later on, there are times when other processes might inject a handle into your process—in which case, the process ID will be different.

The stack trace resembles

```
0x01001E85: 09hleak!CServer::GetToken+0x00000055
0x01001D81: 09hleak!CServer::GetGroupCount+0x00000021
0x01001499: 09hleak!ThreadWorker+0x000000E9
0x7C80B683: kernel32!BaseThreadStart+0x00000037
```

Judging from the stack trace, it looks like 09hleak.exe spawned a new thread. (The clue is the `kernel32!BaseThreadStart` frame.) The main thread entry point is `ThreadWorker`, which calls the server function called `GetGroupCount`, which in turn calls `GetToken`. So it appears that the `GetToken` function in the server caused this handle to be opened. The number next to each frame in the stack trace is the return address for that particular frame. Now that we've identified a stack trace that resulted in opening a handle, there should be a corresponding stack trace that closes the specific handle (`0x00000480`). The easiest way to find this information is to search for the handle value in the output.

```
Handle = 0x00000480 - CLOSE
Thread ID = 0x00000C04, Process ID = 0x00000D3C

0x01001E1E: 09hleak!CServer::GetGroupCount+0x000000BE
0x01001499: 09hleak!ThreadWorker+0x000000E9
0x7C80B683: kernel32!BaseThreadStart+0x00000037
```

The stack trace seems to make perfect sense. The thread ID(s) match, and the stack traces themselves make sense (`GetGroupCount` originally called `GetToken`, which opened the handle. Then `GetGroupCount` closed the handle.) It should be clear that the key to finding the leaking stack traces is to find the ones that have opened handles but have no associated close stack trace. This can be a tedious exercise because it involves checking each opened handle for an associated close in an output that can be pages and pages long. Fortunately, the `!htrace` extension command comes to the rescue. You can use the `-diff` option in `!htrace` to do all that work for you. It basically correlates all paths that resulted in creation and deletion (since the last snapshot) and reports only the stack traces that do not have a delete stack associated. Let's try it.

```
0:001> !htrace -diff
Handle tracing information snapshot successfully taken.
0x191 new stack traces since the previous snapshot.
Ignoring handles that were already closed...
Outstanding handles opened since the previous snapshot:
--------------------
Handle = 0x000004D0 - OPEN
Thread ID = 0x000001B0, Process ID = 0x00000D3C

0x01001E85: 09hleak!CServer::GetToken+0x00000055
0x01001B91: 09hleak!CServer::GetSID+0x00000021
0x0100141B: 09hleak!ThreadWorker+0x0000006B
0x7C80B683: kernel32!BaseThreadStart+0x00000037
--------------------
Handle = 0x000004E0 - OPEN
```

```
Thread ID = 0x00000E64, Process ID = 0x00000D3C

0x01001E85: 09hleak!CServer::GetToken+0x00000055
0x01001B91: 09hleak!CServer::GetSID+0x00000021
0x0100141B: 09hleak!ThreadWorker+0x0000006B
0x7C80B683: kernel32!BaseThreadStart+0x00000037
-------------------
Handle = 0x000004E4 - OPEN
Thread ID = 0x000002D0, Process ID = 0x00000D3C

0x01001E85: 09hleak!CServer::GetToken+0x00000055
0x01001B91: 09hleak!CServer::GetSID+0x00000021
0x0100141B: 09hleak!ThreadWorker+0x0000006B
0x7C80B683: kernel32!BaseThreadStart+0x00000037
-------------------
Handle = 0x000004EC - OPEN
Thread ID = 0x000001B0, Process ID = 0x00000D3C

0x01001E85: 09hleak!CServer::GetToken+0x00000055
0x01001B91: 09hleak!CServer::GetSID+0x00000021
0x0100141B: 09hleak!ThreadWorker+0x0000006B
0x7C80B683: kernel32!BaseThreadStart+0x00000037
-------------------
Handle = 0x000004F0 - OPEN
Thread ID = 0x00000C04, Process ID = 0x00000D3C

0x01001E85: 09hleak!CServer::GetToken+0x00000055
0x01001B91: 09hleak!CServer::GetSID+0x00000021
0x0100141B: 09hleak!ThreadWorker+0x0000006B
0x7C80B683: kernel32!BaseThreadStart+0x00000037
-------------------
Handle = 0x00000504 - OPEN
Thread ID = 0x00000E64, Process ID = 0x00000D3C

0x01001E85: 09hleak!CServer::GetToken+0x00000055
0x01001B91: 09hleak!CServer::GetSID+0x00000021
0x0100141B: 09hleak!ThreadWorker+0x0000006B
0x7C80B683: kernel32!BaseThreadStart+0x00000037
-------------------
Handle = 0x00000508 - OPEN
Thread ID = 0x000002D0, Process ID = 0x00000D3C

0x01001E85: 09hleak!CServer::GetToken+0x00000055
0x01001B91: 09hleak!CServer::GetSID+0x00000021
0x0100141B: 09hleak!ThreadWorker+0x0000006B
0x7C80B683: kernel32!BaseThreadStart+0x00000037
```

```
-------------------
Handle = 0x0000050C - OPEN
Thread ID = 0x00000D18, Process ID = 0x00000D3C

0x01001E85: 09hleak!CServer::GetToken+0x00000055
0x01001B91: 09hleak!CServer::GetSID+0x00000021
0x0100141B: 09hleak!ThreadWorker+0x0000006B
0x7C80B683: kernel32!BaseThreadStart+0x00000037
-------------------
<output truncated>
...

...

-------------------
Handle = 0x00000754 - OPEN
Thread ID = 0x00000EA0, Process ID = 0x00000D3C

0x01001E85: 09hleak!CServer::GetToken+0x00000055
0x01001B91: 09hleak!CServer::GetSID+0x00000021
0x0100141B: 09hleak!ThreadWorker+0x0000006B
0x7C80B683: kernel32!BaseThreadStart+0x00000037
-------------------
Displayed 0x29 stack traces for outstanding handles opened since the previous
snapshot.
```

Interesting, isn't it? It showed 0x29 stack traces that have no associated close handle calls. Even more interesting is the fact that all these stack traces seem to be nearly identical:

```
0x01001E85: 09hleak!CServer::GetToken+0x00000055
0x01001B91: 09hleak!CServer::GetSID+0x00000021
0x0100141B: 09hleak!ThreadWorker+0x0000006B
0x7C80B683: kernel32!BaseThreadStart+0x00000037
```

The server function `GetSID` calls `GetToken`, which opens the handle, but there is no associated close call. Now is the right time to turn to some code reviewing. Looking at the `GetSID` function in the server code, we see the following:

```
PSID CServer::GetSID()
{
    PSID pSid = NULL;
    HANDLE hToken = INVALID_HANDLE_VALUE;
    hToken = GetToken();
    if(hToken!=INVALID_HANDLE_VALUE)
    {
```

```
        DWORD dwNeeded=0;
        BOOL bRes=GetTokenInformation(hToken,
                                      TokenUser,
                                      NULL,
                                      0,
                                      &dwNeeded
                                      );
    if(bRes==FALSE && GetLastError()==ERROR_INSUFFICIENT_BUFFER)
    {
        TOKEN_USER* pBuffer=reinterpret_cast<TOKEN_USER*>(new BYTE[dwNeeded]);
        if(pBuffer!=NULL)
        {
            BOOL bRes=GetTokenInformation(hToken,
                                          TokenUser,
                                          (LPVOID)pBuffer,
                                          dwNeeded,
                                          &dwNeeded
                                          );
            if(bRes==TRUE)
            {
                DWORD dwSidLen=GetLengthSid(pBuffer->User.Sid);
                pSid=static_cast<PSID>(new BYTE[dwSidLen]);
                if(pSid!=NULL)
                {
                    if(CopySid(dwSidLen, pSid, pBuffer->User.Sid)==FALSE)
                    {
                        delete pSid;
                        pSid=NULL;
                    }
                }
            }
            delete pBuffer;
        }
    }
    return pSid;
}
```

The line in bold returns a token to the server GetSID function. The returned handle is located on the stack and is not passed out of the function. Furthermore, there seems to be no CloseHandle call at all in the GetSID function, essentially resulting in a handle leak.

As we have seen, when it comes to sporadic handle leaks that are not easy to track down by solely employing code reviews, the `!htrace` extension command gives invaluable help. It has the capability to show nice and clean stack traces, including deltas of different runs. The general strategy for using `!htrace` is

1. Prior to starting the actual reproducing of the leak, enable handle tracing (using `!htrace -enable`).
2. Run the reproduction and let the process handle leaks.
3. Use `!htrace -diff` to find the offending stacks.

Repeating steps 1–3 will give you enough information to narrow the problem down in the code and find the leak by using code reviews.

The handle tracing mechanism just described works extremely well when tracking down handle leaks. However, there is a caveat to be aware of. The handle tracing uses an array to track all handles. If the array is exhausted, older entries in the array are replaced with new ones. In effect, this means that the longer you run with handle tracing turned on, the greater the chances of the individual array slots being reused; hence, information about older and potentially leaked handles is lost. The best approach when using the handle tracing mechanism is to narrow the problem down to a fairly small and quickly reproducible scenario to ensure that the handle tracing array is not reused.

## Handle Injection and !htrace

As discussed earlier, handles to kernel object instances are process relative and stored in the process handle table. As such, a handle from process A cannot be used in process B because it has no presence of the handle in its handle table. One might be tempted to conclude that all handles in any given process are opened by that process itself. This is true in most cases, but as always, there are exceptions to the rule. It is possible for a process to open a handle and inject that handle into another process, assuming that the injecting process has the right access rights. When that happens, and the injected handle isn't closed by the target process, a handle leak occurs. Even worse, the `!htrace` extension command yields a fairly odd stack trace for that particular handle. Let's look at an example. There are two console applications in this scenario. Console application one is called 09target.exe and is a standard console-based application with the following code:

```
#include <windows.h>
#include <stdio.h>
#include <conio.h>
```

```
int __cdecl wmain (int argc, wchar_t* pArgs[])
{
    printf("Waiting for handles...\n");
    printf("Press any key to exit application...\n");
    _getch();

    return 1;
}
```

The source code and binary for the application can be found in the following folders:

> Source code: `C:\AWD\Chapter9\HInject\Target`
>
> Binary: `C:\AWDBIN\WinXP.x86.chk\09htarget.exe`

As you can see, this code does very little. It simply sits idle and waits for the user to press any key, at which point, it terminates. To illustrate the troubleshooting of handle injection, the source code for the other process in play is not shown. Simply run the application (09hsource.exe).

```
C:\AWDBIN\WinXP.x86.chk\09hsource.exe
Enter process ID to inject handle into: _
```

Using Task Manager, find the process ID of the target process (note the handle count) and enter it in the 09hsource.exe prompt. When it's finished doing its job, it will again present you with the same prompt. Again, bring up Task Manager, and you will see that the handle count has gone up by one. Type the same process ID again and check Task Manager. Again, you will see that the handle count for 09htarget.exe has gone up by one. Keep iterating, and you will see that every time you run through an iteration of the 09hsource.exe application, the handle count goes up by one in the 09htarget.exe process. Furthermore, using the `!htrace` technique described previously, we dump out all the stack traces for the 09htarget.exe process, and we notice that we indeed have a few stack traces that indicate leaked handles. The odd part is that the stack trace looks very convoluted. Here is an example of a stack trace reported by `!htrace` in the 09htarget.exe process:

```
Handle = 0x000007D8 - OPEN
Thread ID = 0x00000854, Process ID = 0x0000093C

0x01001363: 09htarget!XcptFilter+0x00000009
0x010014D3: 09htarget!_NULL_IMPORT_DESCRIPTOR+0x000000CB
0x7C816FD7: kernel32!BaseProcessStart+0x00000023
```

Besides the stack trace itself not making much sense for our 09htarget.exe application, the process ID does not seem to make sense either. As a matter of fact, the process ID listed in the stack trace does not correspond to the 09htarget.exe process ID. Using Task Manager, we can quickly correlate the reported process and find the process that !htrace is reporting. Not surprisingly, the process ID is that of the 09hsource.exe process. Going back to our systematic approach to leak detection, we can safely list the following observations:

- The target process is leaking handles. Furthermore, the target process is leaking handles it is not responsible for.
- Judging by the stack traces given by !htrace in the 09htarget.exe process, the originating process of the handle is 09hsource.exe.

The biggest problem of figuring out the origins of the handle is that the stack we have doesn't seem to make sense. The stack frames point to locations in our binary that do not seem to be in a valid code path. Let's stop and rethink the scenario as a whole. The originating process is 09hsource.exe, and we would expect to see the stack trace of how the handle was obtained in this process when using !htrace. The only problem is that we have attached the debugger to the 09htarget.exe process, and the stack obtained looks odd. The only reason it looks odd is that the debugger is trying to resolve the call frame addresses in the context of 09htarget.exe, but in reality the call frame addresses are only reliable in the context of the 09hsource.exe process. (After all, that process actually opened the handle.) If we tried to resolve the call frame addresses in the context of the 09hsource.exe process, we should be able to get the true stack trace. Let's use the stack trace that didn't seem to make any sense and give it a try. Attach a debugger to the 09hsource.exe process, break in, and resolve each of the addresses listed in the stack trace. We use the ln command to resolve an address to its corresponding symbolic name:

```
...
...
...
0:001> ln 0x7C816FD7
(7c816fb4)   kernel32!BaseProcessStart+0x23   |   (7c816ff1)   kernel32!CsrBasepNlsGe-
tUserInfo
0:001> ln 0x010014D3
(010013a8)   09HSource!wmainCRTStartup+0x12b   |   (0100152e)   09HSource!XcptFilter
0:001> ln 0x01001363
(010012c0)   09HSource!wmain+0xa3   |   (010013a8)   09HSource!wmainCRTStartup
```

The resolution of addresses to possible symbols yields the following potential call stack.

```
09HSource!wmain+0xa3
09HSource!wmainCRTStartup+0x12b
kernel32!BaseProcessStart+0x23
```

This looks very reasonable. The `BaseProcessStart` function in kernel32 calls the `wmainCRTStartup` function in our 09hsource.exe process followed by a call to the actual `wmain` function. So far, nothing indicates that we have opened a handle and injected it into the target process. The key here is to look at the top of the stack:

```
09HSource!wmain+0xa3
```

This frame is making a call to another function. If we unassemble this function at the offset specified, we see the following:

```
0:001> u 09HSource!wmain+0xa3
09HSource!wmain+0xa3:
01001363 8945f0           mov      [ebp-0x10],eax
01001366 837df000         cmp      dword ptr [ebp-0x10],0x0
0100136a 7515             jnz      09HSource!wmain+0xc1 (01001381)
0100136c ff151c100001     call dword ptr [09HSource!_imp__GetLastError (0100101c)]
01001372 50               push     eax
01001373 68ac100001       push     0x10010ac
01001378 ff156c100001     call     dword ptr [09HSource!_imp__printf (0100106c)]
0100137e 83c408           add      esp,0x8
```

Nothing in this unassembled code seems to point to a function call that would open a new handle and inject it. Remember from Chapter 5, "Memory Corruption I—Stacks," that the address listed in the stack trace is the address that the register EIP points to, which also happens to be the address right after a CALL instruction. Let's unassemble again, but this time subtract a few bytes:

```
0:001> u 09HSource!wmain+0xa3-11
09HSource!wmain+0x92:
01001352 8b55ec           mov      edx,[ebp-0x14]
01001355 52               push     edx
01001356 ff1510100001 call dword ptr [09HSource!_imp__GetCurrentProcess (01001010)]
0100135c 50               push     eax
0100135d ff1518100001 call dword ptr [09HSource!_imp__DuplicateHandle (01001018)]
01001363 8945f0           mov      [ebp-0x10],eax
01001366 837df000         cmp      dword ptr [ebp-0x10],0x0
0100136a 7515             jnz      09HSource!wmain+0xc1 (01001381)
```

Now we're getting somewhere. The instruction prior to the current instruction pointer is in fact a CALL instruction. Furthermore, the CALL instruction indicated a call to the `DuplicateHandle` API. If we look up `DuplicateHandle` in MSDN, we see that the API not only allows us to duplicate an existing handle in the current process, but also into a different process. It is now trivial to investigate the parameters sent to the `DuplicateHandle` API and see that we are, in fact, specifying the process ID for the 09htarget.exe process.

## Step 5: Define a Future Avoidance Strategy for Handle Leaks

Last, but not least, we should always make sure that we have learned from our experiences to avoid making the same mistakes twice. One great way of making sure that handles are not lost is to employ an auto acquire/release construct. Very similar to auto pointers, this construct allows you to acquire a handle at any given scope and automatically free it when the auto construct goes out of scope. In our server example, the `GetSID` function could have been altered similar to the following to use an auto handle construct:

```
PSID CServer::GetSID()
{
    PSID pSid = NULL;
    HANDLE hToken = INVALID_HANDLE_VALUE;
    hToken = GetToken();
    AutoHandle autoHandle(hToken);
    ...
    ...
}
```

The `AutoHandle` class takes ownership of the specified handle and closes it when it goes out of scope. Extending the `AutoHandle` class with the following functionality makes it even more flexible:

- Overloading the assignment operator would allow you to write code such as
  `AutoHandle autoHandle=GetToken();`

- Overloading the cast operator to allow casting an `AutoHandle` to a `HANDLE` allows for easier access to the underlying `HANDLE`
- Removing the ownership of the underlying `HANDLE` in cases in which the handle must be passed out of the current scope

This is an example of a very effective way of ensuring that handles are closed properly when they go out of scope. Without a doubt, many ways and alternatives exist for making sure that we make proper use of our tools and code to ensure handle cleanup. Which one you chose depends entirely on your personal preference and coding style.

## Memory Leaks

Whereas the previous section focuses on handle leaks, this section discusses more conventional memory leaks. By conventional, I mean memory leaks that occur while directly allocating and working with memory using any of the memory allocation constructs (such as new and HeapAlloc). Before we dive in and look at how to analyze memory leaks, let us begin by a quick review of how memory is managed in Windows.

The memory manager in Windows can be broken down into several layers, as shown in Figure 9.11.

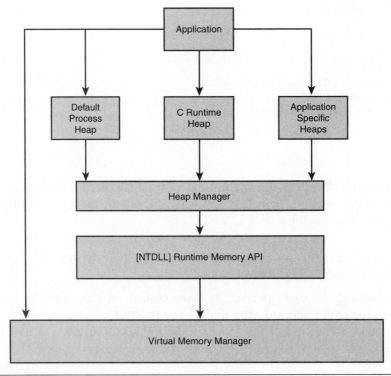

**Figure 9.11** Windows memory architecture overview

The bottom and most low-level component is the Virtual Memory Manager (VMM). The VMM is the last stop for all memory-related requests in the system and works with memory in a much more low-level form than application developers are accustomed to. The VMM operates on the basis of large memory chunks (pages). To make memory allocations of small sizes more efficient, Windows places an abstraction layer on top of the VMM. The abstraction layer is called the heap manager, consisting of an API that application developers can use to allocate memory in a very simple fashion. A heap is best thought of as an isolation layer that enables applications to create separate memory arenas within its address space and work with these arenas (or heaps) in an isolated fashion. Of course, applications are not required to create one or more heaps before they can start manipulating memory. Rather, Windows makes the very logical assumption that any given application will probably need to use at least some memory and create a default process heap when the process is first created. The initial reserved size of the default process heap is 1Mb and grows as needed.

As you can see from Figure 9.11, another layer exists between the VMM and the heap manager, called the Runtime Memory API. It is a very thin layer that simply forwards calls down to the VMM. For example, the heap manager exposes an API called `HeapAlloc`, which is really just a forwarder to the underlying `RtlAllocateHeap` API, which in turn calls the VMM.

On top of the heap manager is the application layer, which uses one or more heaps when allocating memory. The application can choose to use either the default process heap or private heaps (explicitly created by the application). Quite often, applications will make use of multiple heaps unbeknownst to themselves. For example, using the C runtime (such as malloc or new) causes memory to be allocated on the C runtime heap (created during initializing of the C runtime). A note of caution: Careful attention must be paid when working with multiple heaps. Because multiple heaps are treated in an isolated fashion, allocating memory from one heap and deleting that memory on a different heap is undefined behavior (see Chapter 6, "Memory Corruption II—Heaps").

When a process is about to terminate, Windows frees all memory associated with that process and destroys all active heaps.

Now that you have an understanding of how memory is managed in Windows, let's take a look at an example application that leaks memory and see how we can analyze the memory leak and ultimately fix it.

## A Simple Memory Leak

In the "handle leaks" section, we used a client-server paradigm to illustrate a handle leak scenario. Once again, we turn to the same code (slightly modified) to illustrate an example of a memory leak. The server enables the clients to make any of the following calls:

- `GetSID`                  Gets the SID of the caller's token (thread or process token)
- `GetPrivilegeCount`       Gets the privilege count of the caller's token (thread or process token)
- `GetGroupCount`           Gets the group count of the caller's token (thread or process token)

The client application (09basicmleak.exe) spawns a number of threads and randomly picks an operation to perform.

The source code and binary for the application can be found in the following folders:

Source code: `C:\AWD\Chapter9\BasicMLeak\Client` and
`C:\AWD\Chapter9\BasicMLeak\Server`
Binary: `C:\AWDBIN\WinXP.x86.chk\09basicmleak.exe`

Based on initial reports, the application apparently reports an increase in memory usage, and we are now faced with fixing this potential leak. Let's start by following the first two steps of the resource leak process.

## Steps 1 and 2: Is It Even a Leak, and What Is Leaking?

Using Task Manager, memory consumption can be slightly trickier to identify. The primary reason for this is the way that Task Manager reports memory consumption for processes in comparison to, let's say, handles. Let's start by bringing up Task Manager and selecting the Memory Usage and Virtual Memory columns, which tell us how much memory the process is consuming.

Next, start the 09basicmleak.exe process with 5 threads and 50 iterations per thread (0 sleep time) using the following command line:

```
C:\AWDBIN\WinXP.x86.chk\09basicmleak.exe /t:10 /i:50 /s:0
```

Before actually starting the application, bring up Task Manager, find 09basicmleak.exe, and record the Mem Usage and VM Size columns, as shown in Figure 9.12.

From Figure 9.12, we can see that before running any tests, the 09basicmleak.exe process is using 896Kb of memory and 264Kb of virtual memory. Virtual memory indicates how much memory the process is using overall (both in and out of physical memory), whereas the Mem Usage column shows how much physical memory the process is consuming (also known as the process working set). Typically, the best indicator for memory leaks is an increase in virtual memory size and not fluctuations in working set size.

Now, let's allow the 09basicmleak.exe process to run to completion and see what happened with the memory consumption.

**Windows Task Manager**

File  Options  View  Help

Applications | Processes | Performance | Networking | Users

| Image Name | PID | User Name | CPU | Mem Usage | VM Size | Handles | Threads |
|---|---|---|---|---|---|---|---|
| 09BasicMLeak.exe | 2960 | marioh | 00 | 896 K | 264 K | 8 | 1 |
| alg.exe | 204 | LOCAL SERVICE | 00 | 3,592 K | 1,192 K | 114 | 5 |
| cmd.exe | 3772 | marioh | 00 | 976 K | 2,352 K | 87 | 1 |
| cmd.exe | 3792 | marioh | 00 | 1,552 K | 2,420 K | 88 | 1 |
| csrss.exe | 696 | SYSTEM | 00 | 3,724 K | 591,056 K | 733 | 12 |
| ctfmon.exe | 2316 | marioh | 00 | 4,216 K | 1,000 K | 118 | 1 |
| DbgSvc.exe | 1892 | SYSTEM | 00 | 19,992 K | 14,728 K | 361 | 16 |
| dllhost.exe | 3684 | SYSTEM | 00 | 8,048 K | 2,964 K | 245 | 16 |
| explorer.exe | 1864 | marioh | 00 | 13,692 K | 25,148 K | 655 | 14 |
| hpcmpmgr.exe | 2244 | marioh | 00 | 8,708 K | 4,908 K | 243 | 4 |
| hpqtra08.exe | 2740 | marioh | 00 | 6,844 K | 3,184 K | 118 | 4 |
| hptskmgr.exe | 2868 | marioh | 00 | 7,736 K | 3,452 K | 174 | 4 |
| hpwuSchd.exe | 2228 | marioh | 00 | 2,312 K | 616 K | 27 | 1 |
| iexplore.exe | 520 | marioh | 00 | 34,696 K | 68,048 K | 969 | 19 |
| InoRpc.exe | 1944 | SYSTEM | 00 | 6,464 K | 4,544 K | 131 | 9 |
| InoRT.exe | 1964 | SYSTEM | 00 | 16,044 K | 14,128 K | 135 | 18 |
| InoTask.exe | 2000 | SYSTEM | 00 | 16,036 K | 12,692 K | 107 | 7 |
| jucheck.exe | 3544 | marioh | 00 | 6,088 K | 2,648 K | 205 | 4 |
| jusched.exe | 2180 | marioh | 00 | 2,140 K | 532 K | 34 | 1 |

☐ Show processes from all users                                      End Process

Processes: 63        CPU Usage: 0%        Commit Charge: 1232M / 3429M

**Figure 9.12**    Initial memory consumption of 09basicmleak.exe

As you can see from Figure 9.13, both the working set size and the virtual memory size have increased. Not a good sign. Increasing the number of threads and the number of iterations per thread yields the result in Table 9.2.

**Windows Task Manager**

File  Options  View  Help

Applications | Processes | Performance | Networking | Users

| Image Name | PID | User Name | CPU | Mem Usage | VM Size | Handles | Threads |
|---|---|---|---|---|---|---|---|
| 09BasicMLeak.exe | 2960 | marioh | 00 | 924 K | 268 K | 8 | 1 |
| alg.exe | 204 | LOCAL SERVICE | 00 | 3,592 K | 1,192 K | 114 | 5 |
| cmd.exe | 3772 | marioh | 00 | 976 K | 2,352 K | 87 | 1 |
| cmd.exe | 3792 | marioh | 00 | 1,552 K | 2,420 K | 88 | 1 |
| csrss.exe | 696 | SYSTEM | 00 | 3,856 K | 591,056 K | 731 | 12 |
| ctfmon.exe | 2316 | marioh | 00 | 4,216 K | 1,000 K | 118 | 1 |
| DbgSvc.exe | 1892 | SYSTEM | 00 | 19,992 K | 14,728 K | 359 | 16 |
| dllhost.exe | 3684 | SYSTEM | 00 | 8,048 K | 2,964 K | 245 | 16 |
| explorer.exe | 1864 | marioh | 00 | 13,740 K | 25,084 K | 652 | 13 |
| hpcmpmgr.exe | 2244 | marioh | 00 | 8,708 K | 4,908 K | 243 | 4 |
| hpqtra08.exe | 2740 | marioh | 00 | 6,844 K | 3,184 K | 118 | 4 |
| hptskmgr.exe | 2868 | marioh | 00 | 7,736 K | 3,452 K | 174 | 4 |
| hpwuSchd.exe | 2228 | marioh | 00 | 2,312 K | 616 K | 27 | 1 |
| iexplore.exe | 520 | marioh | 00 | 34,696 K | 68,048 K | 969 | 19 |
| InoRpc.exe | 1944 | SYSTEM | 00 | 6,464 K | 4,544 K | 131 | 9 |
| InoRT.exe | 1964 | SYSTEM | 00 | 16,044 K | 14,128 K | 135 | 18 |
| InoTask.exe | 2000 | SYSTEM | 00 | 16,036 K | 12,692 K | 107 | 7 |
| jucheck.exe | 3544 | marioh | 00 | 6,088 K | 2,648 K | 205 | 4 |
| jusched.exe | 2180 | marioh | 00 | 2,140 K | 532 K | 34 | 1 |

☐ Show processes from all users                                      End Process

Processes: 63        CPU Usage: 2%        Commit Charge: 1233M / 3429M

**Figure 9.13**    Memory consumption of 09basicmleak.exe after a complete run

**9. RESOURCE LEAKS**

**Table 9.2**   Memory Consumption for Different Threads and Iterations

| Threads | Iterations | Memory (Kb) | Virtual Memory (Kb) |
|---|---|---|---|
| 10 | 200 | 948 | 292 |
| 10 | 200 | 944 | 288 |
| 10 | 200 | 944 | 288 |
| 20 | 300 | 956 | 300 |
| 20 | 300 | 964 | 308 |
| 20 | 300 | 956 | 300 |

Judging from Table 9.2, the theory of a potential memory leaks is now realized. In addition, the memory leak is not constant with the same number of thread and iterations per thread. This is similar in nature to the handle leak scenario shown earlier. Rather than going to step 3, we assume that the memory leak is expensive to track down through code reviews, so we dive into step 4: use leak detection tools. Tracking down handle leaks proved to be much easier using the incredibly valuable !htrace extension command. Is there something similar for memory leaks? Absolutely! The tool that will save the day is called UMDH.

### Working Set Size Adjustments

The working set size for any process is constantly adjusted by Windows. The adjustments occur because of changes in system load and process priorities. When running the previous memory leak scenario, you might find that the memory consumption reported is slightly different from what we have shown. This is indeed expected. The memory leak is sporadic and (more than likely) doesn't yield the same leak twice. Even though you should see small differences in memory consumption, you should definitely not see large ones. If you do, it might be due to minimizing the command window when looking at the resource consumption. When you minimize a command window, Windows automatically assumes that the window should be put in the background (that is, not being used), and as such trims the working set of any command-line application currently running in the context of that command window. By reducing the amount of physical memory the command shell is using, it can give that memory to other applications that might now be in need of it.

## Step 4: Using Leak Detection Tools

Several tools are available to help efficiently track down memory leaks. In the following sections, we discuss several of the most commonly used tools.

### UMDH

UMDH is a tool that comes as part of the Debugging Tools for Windows installation. The basic idea behind the tool is very similar to the `!htrace` extension command. We begin by simply telling the operating system to store away stack traces for all calls resulting in memory allocations. We take a snapshot of the memory usage before the application begins executing, and when the reproduction is finished, we take another snapshot and compare the results. This yields all stack traces that have not yet been freed, and we can take a more tactical approach to our code review to find the culprit.

First, we need to enable stack traces for memory allocations. To accomplish this, we use the gflags tool and enable 'Create user mode stack trace database' for 09basicmleak.exe. For mode details on how to enable instrumentation using gflags, see Chapter 1, "Introduction to the Tools."

When you have enabled gflags for the 09basicmleak.exe application, run 09basicmleak.exe with the following command line:

```
C:\AWDBIN\WinXP.x86.chk\09basicmleak.exe /t:10 /i:200 /s:0
Press any key to start stress application...
```

Before starting the actual reproduction, we need to run UMDH to take the initial snapshot. UMDH can be run in three modes:

- Mode 1: Creates a dump of the heap allocations grouped by stack traces. This mode tells UMDH to create a dump of all heap allocations. Several options exist for this mode, and most are self-explanatory. The following options are of most interest:

  - `-p` tells UMDH which process ID to record stack traces for.
  - `-l` prints file and line number information as part of stack traces.

- Mode 2: Compares two dumps of heap allocations created in mode 1. This is a very convenient way of analyzing the dumps. Rather than walking the two logs by hand, we can let UMDH do all the work of reporting the difference.
- Mode 3: This mode is a shortcut to using modes 1 and 2.

To illustrate the usage of UMDH, we will show how to use modes 1 and 2 rather than the shortcut mode.

One final note about UMDH before we begin. As with most leak detection tools, to get good stack traces, we must tell the tool where to find symbols. This is required for the tool to be capable of resolving the frames to symbolic information. UMDH expects the symbol path to be set in the _NT_SYMBOL_PATH environment variable.

```
set _NT_SYMBOL_PATH=<path to your symbol store>
```

For more information about symbols, see Chapters 2 and 4.

Now, find the process ID of the newly launched instance of 09basicmleak.exe and type the following on the command line. (UMDH can be found under the root folder of the debugger installation directory.)

```
UMDH.exe -p:<process ID> > firstsnap.txt
```

Run the application to completion and take another snapshot:

```
UMDH.exe -p:<process ID> > secondsnap.txt
```

Now that we have both log files, run the following command to tell UMDH to compare the two log files and pipe the difference to a new file called `diff.txt`:

```
UMDH.exe -v firstsnap.txt secondsnap.txt > diff.txt
```

We now have a file called `diff.txt` that should tell us the source of our leaked allocations. Let's open diff.txt and take a closer look:

```
//
// Each log entry has the following syntax:
//
// + BYTES_DELTA (NEW_BYTES - OLD_BYTES) NEW_COUNT allocs BackTrace TRACEID
// + COUNT_DELTA (NEW_COUNT - OLD_COUNT) BackTrace TRACEID allocations
//      ... stack trace ...
//
// where:
//
//     BYTES_DELTA - increase in bytes between before and after log
//     NEW_BYTES - bytes in after log
//     OLD_BYTES - bytes in before log
//     COUNT_DELTA - increase in allocations between before and after log
//     NEW_COUNT - number of allocations in after log
//     OLD_COUNT - number of allocations in before log
//     TRACEID - decimal index of the stack trace in the trace database
```

```
//          (can be used to search for allocation instances in the original
//          UMDH logs).
//

+    d482 (  d482 -     0)    2a0 allocs   BackTrace00081
+     2a0 (   2a0 -     0)    BackTrace00081    allocations

        ntdll!RtlAllocateHeap+00001292
        09basicmleak!CServer::GetSID+00000115
        09basicmleak!ThreadWorker+0000006E
        kernel32!BaseThreadStart+0000003A


+     bca (  2f28 -  235e)     2 allocs   BackTrace00066

        ntdll!RtlAllocateHeap+00001292
        kernel32!LocalAlloc+00000081
        ADVAPI32!AppmgmtInitialize+00000023
        ADVAPI32!DllInitialize+00000105
        ntdll!LdrpRunInitializeRoutines+000004D7
        ntdll!LdrpInitializeProcess+00001BB6
        ntdll!LdrpInitialize+0000018F
        ntdll!KiUserApcDispatch+00000015
        kernel32!BaseProcessStart+00000000


-      be (  3970 -  3a2e)    65 allocs   BackTrace00068

        ntdll!RtlAllocateHeap+00001292
        msvcrt!malloc+00000060
        msvcrt!malloc_crt+0000002A
        msvcrt!_mbtow_environ+0000005E
        msvcrt!_wgetmainargs+00000079
        09basicmleak!wmainCRTStartup+0000013C
        kernel32!BaseProcessStart+00000029


-      be (  2c30 -  2cee)     2 allocs   BackTrace00072

        ntdll!RtlAllocateHeap+00001292
        msvcrt!malloc+00000060
        msvcrt!malloc_crt+0000002A
        msvcrt!stbuf+00000073
        msvcrt!printf+00000045
        09basicmleak!wmain+0000003E
        09basicmleak!wmainCRTStartup+00000171
        kernel32!BaseProcessStart+00000029


Total increase == ded0
```

The first part of the file contains some very useful and detailed help text on the format of the file. What is really nice about UMDH is that it sorts the stack traces listed according to the size and number of allocations. The stack traces with the biggest and most number of allocations are at the beginning of the file. Let's break down the first stack trace:

```
+    d482 (   d482 -     0)    2a0 allocs    BackTrace00081
+     2a0 (    2a0 -     0)    BackTrace00081    allocations

        ntdll!RtlAllocateHeap+00001292
        09basicmleak!CServer::GetSID+00000115
        09basicmleak!ThreadWorker+0000006E
        kernel32!BaseThreadStart+0000003A
```

The first line tells us that we have a net increase of d482 *bytes* because of the allocations performed by the stack trace shown. It also tells us that that particular stack trace was invoked 2a0 times, resulting in 2a0 allocations. Also shown is the TRACEID for that particular stack trace. This can be useful when you want to coordinate specific stack traces in the original snap files. The second line tells us about the net increase in *allocations* because of the stack trace. In our case, we see that 2a0 allocations have occurred. Finally, we have the stack trace itself, the most interesting piece of information. The first frame (kernel32!BaseThreadStart) is the function that all threads start their execution from. The second frame enters the 09basicmleak.exe function ThreadWorker. This makes perfect sense because the 09basicmleak.exe application spawns threads that in turn call the server. The third frame enters the server function GetSID, which in turn calls AllocateHeap. It seems as if the server is allocating memory, but not freeing it. Looking at the code for GetSID, it is clear that it, in fact, does allocate memory for the SID, but it never releases it. One might be tempted to immediately fix it with a free call in the GetSID function, but is that the correct fix? More careful analysis shows that the server allocated the memory for the SID but passes the SID back to the client expecting the client to free it. Looking at the client code, we quickly see that the client has forgotten to free it. The solution is to simply add the corresponding free call, and the leak is gone. The remainder of the stack traces in the log file show some pretty standard stacks that are not leaks. Remember, the application is still running (albeit ready to terminate), and allocations made by the operating system are only freed when the process exits. For example, the second stack trace shows that the Windows loader allocated memory during initialization of a DLL.

```
+     bca (  2f28 -  235e)      2 allocs    BackTrace00066

        ntdll!RtlAllocateHeap+00001292
        kernel32!LocalAlloc+00000081
        ADVAPI32!AppmgmtInitialize+00000023
        ADVAPI32!DllInitialize+00000105
        ntdll!LdrpRunInitializeRoutines+000004D7
        ntdll!LdrpInitializeProcess+00001BB6
        ntdll!LdrpInitialize+0000018F
        ntdll!KiUserApcDispatch+00000015
        kernel32!BaseProcessStart+00000000
```

This allocation is not something that we were responsible for, and we can safely discard this stack trace.

UMDH is a pretty powerful tool to track down memory leaks. However, it does have some limitations. More specifically, UMDH works best with non-FPO optimized code. Starting with Windows XP SP2, all operating system code is compiled with FPO optimizations turned off, so that should not be a big problem. Another drawback is that UMDH only works with the default Windows heap manager. Customized allocators (such as the C runtime) are not tracked very well using UMDH. To accommodate these shortcomings, another tool was created called LeakDiag, which we examine next.

### UMDH and BSTRs

A BSTR is essentially nothing more than a COM-compatible string (encapsulating the length of the string as well as content). Most of the time, when we're using COM interfaces that accept strings as input, they will be of type BSTR. Allocating BSTRs using the SysAlloc APIs and forgetting to free them leads to a memory leak. These types of memory leaks are not guaranteed to be caught by UMDH. As a matter of fact, most of the time, the stack traces shown by UMDH do not make any sense and can lead you down a long and expensive false path. OLE caches BSTRs to avoid continuous round-trips to the memory manager. As such, allocating a BSTR, freeing it, and then subsequently allocating another BSTR that you forget to free cause UMDH to report the original and nonleaking stack trace to the allocation. If you are ever in a situation in which you suspect that you are leaking BSTRs, there is fortunately a way to turn the caching off. Set the following environment variable, OANOCACHE=1, prior to starting the application, and the caching will be turned off. If you are analyzing a service (not started from a specific command shell), you can set the environment variable in the global system environment table.

### LeakDiag

LeakDiag allows you to track numerous allocations coming from sources other than the default Windows heap manager. For example, if an application calls the VirtualAlloc API directly and forgets to free it, it will not be reported by UMDH; however, LeakDiag will show this leak. In addition, LeakDiag does not require you to enable stack trace recording via gflags. Instead, LeakDdiag uses the Microsoft Detours technology to intercept calls to specified memory allocators.

LeakDiag can be run in two different modes. The first mode is via the command line, and the second mode is via a UI. The former will be demonstrated here. Running LeakDiag is a two-step process:

1. Selecting the target process. This merely tells LeakDiag which process it should intercept memory allocations for, as well as which allocator to intercept:

   ```
   ldcmd.exe /p <processed> /start /a 2
   ```

   The /a option selects the specific allocator you are interested in. In the preceding example, 2 refers to the NT Heap Allocator. As of version 1.25, the following allocators are supported:

   - Virtual Allocator (VirtualAlloc)
   - NT Heap Allocator (HeapAlloc)[DEFAULT]
   - MPHeap Allocator (MPHeap)
   - COM Allocator (CoTask)
   - COM Private Allocator (PrivateMemAlloc)
   - C Runtime Allocator (msvcrt new)

2. Generating log files. Whenever you want to generate a log file for the selected target process, use the /dump switch. For example,

   ```
   ldcmd.exe /p <processed> /dump /a 2
   ```

   The preceding example generates the log file and saves it to the default log file folder. The default log folder is the Logs folder in the installation path of LeakDiag.

Let's return to our 09basicmleak.exe application and use LeakDiag to track down the same memory leak we saw earlier. Start the 09basicmleak.exe application using the following command line:

```
C:\AWDBIN\WinXP.x86.chk\09basicmleak.exe /t:10 /i:200 /s:0
```

Next, find the process ID of the 09basicmleak.exe instance we just started and issue the following command:

```
C:\LeakDiag\Logs>c:\LeakDiag\ldcmd.exe /p 3028 /start /a 2
Sent Start Tracing command for pID 3832
Allocator 1:      TRACING OFF
Allocator 2:      TRACING ON
Allocator 3:      TRACING OFF
Allocator 4:      TRACING OFF
Allocator 5:      TRACING OFF
Allocator 6:      TRACING OFF
```

Remember to specify the process ID relative to your execution. The /start command sends a signal to the process to start intercepting allocation calls, and the /a 2 tells it to intercept all allocations from the heap allocator.

The next step involves dumping all the allocation stack traces. Before issuing a dump command with LeakDiag, you have to make sure that the symbol path is set correctly. Unlike UMDH, LeakDiag does not honor the _NT_SYMBOL_PATH environment variable; rather, it relies on a registry value stored under the following key:

```
HKEY_LOCAL_MACHINE\SOFTWARE\Microsoft\LeakDiag
```

The registry value is named SymPath and needs to be set to the directory containing the symbols. After the symbol path has been set, continue the execution of 09basicmleak.exe and, before exiting, type the following command:

```
C:\LeakDiag\Logs>c:\LeakDiag\ldcmd.exe /p 3028 /dump /a 2
Sent Dump Log command for pID 3832
Allocator 1:      TRACING OFF
Allocator 2:      TRACING ON
Allocator 3:      TRACING OFF
Allocator 4:      TRACING OFF
Allocator 5:      TRACING OFF
Allocator 6:      TRACING OFF
```

This time, we used the /dump switch to tell LeakDiag to produce a log file of all the allocations collected in the process. The actual log filename is a conglomerate of various file attributes (such as filename, date of run, and so on). If you have a lot of log files in the directory, the best way to find the correct one is simply to look at the date and time of the file. In this particular run, the filename corresponding to the run is

```
05/31/2005  03:54 PM   12,631 09basicmleak_2296_WindowsHeapAllocator_050531-
155419_sess_01.xml
```

As you can tell by the `xml` extension, the log file is stored in XML format. A good way to view an XML file is to load it in Internet Explorer. You will also see that the log file comes with the associated schema and is quite large. Rather than listing the entire log file here, we will simply focus on the most important parts, namely how the stack traces are represented. If you want to see the entire log file, it can be found in the following location:

```
C:\AWDBIN\WinXP.x86.chk\09basicmleak_2296_WindowsHeapAllocator_050531-
155419_sess_01.xml
```

The overall structure of the log file resembles the following:

```
<?xml version="1.0" ?>
<logdata>
  <xs:schema id="logdata" xmlns:xs="http://www.w3.org/2001/XMLSchema"
xmlns:msdata="urn:schemas-microsoft-com:xml-msdata"> </xs:schema>
  <LEAKS ver="1.31.03.0915"> </LEAKS>
  <SUMMARY_INFO> </SUMMARY_INFO>
</logdata>
```

Whereas the `schema` section details the structure of the XML data, the `LEAKS` section details allocation history in the application run and finally a summary section that shows information such as LeakDiag settings, modules loaded, overall memory statistics, and so on. The most interesting section is the `LEAKS` section. Expanding the `LEAKS` section reveals a number of `STACK` sections—each one detailing allocations made throughout the lifetime of the application. Looking at the first stack trace yields

```
<STACK numallocs="0710" size="028" totalsize="019880" totalalloccount="0710" totalal-
locsize="019880">
<STACKSTATS>
  <SIZESTAT size="028" numallocs="0710" type="N/A" />
  <HEAPSTAT handle="80000" numallocs="0710" />
  </STACKSTATS>
  <FRAME num="0" dll="09basicmleak.exe" function="CServer__GetSID" offset="0xC8"
filename="c:\zone\pwd\cd\code\resleak\memleak\scenario1\server\srv.cpp" line="42"
addr="0x1001C38" />
  <FRAME num="1" dll="09basicmleak.exe" function="ThreadWorker" offset="0x6B" file-
name="c:\zone\pwd\cd\code\resleak\memleak\scenario1\client\client.cpp" line="36"
addr="0x100142B" />
  <FRAME num="2" dll="kernel32.dll" function="BaseThreadStart" offset="0x37" file-
name="" line="" addr="0x7C80B50B" />
  <STACKID>008E5C88</STACKID>
  </STACK>
```

Although the log file is represented in XML, it yields results very similar to the UMDH logs. The `STACK` element attributes give information, such as number of allocations from the stack trace, size of each allocation, and finally total size. The HEAPSTAT shows which heap the allocation was made on. The final part is a list of frames that make up the stack trace. As we can see, the bottommost frame is the kernel32 function `BaseThreadStart` calling into a `ThreadWorker` function, which calls into the server `GetSID` function, which forgets to release the memory allocated. Although this is essentially the same leak we discovered using UMDH, it should be clear that using LeakDiag can come in handy when you are dealing with leaks that do not originate from the default heap manager.

### The !address Extension Command

The !address extension command comes in very handy when you want to get a quick overview of where the memory in your process is really located. The command gives statistics, such as memory region usage in heaps, stack, free, and so on. To see for yourself, start notepad.exe under the debugger and issue the !address command. The first part of the output gives a more in-depth look at the memory usage, and toward the end of the output, you will see the summary.

```
...
...
---------- Usage SUMMARY -------------
    TotSize     Pct(Tots)  Pct(Busy)   Usage
    001d4000 :  0.09%       10.59%        : RegionUsageIsVAD
    7eeab000 :  99.16%       0.00%        : RegionUsageFree
    00e0d000 :  0.69%       81.36%        : RegionUsageImage
    00040000 :  0.01%        1.45%      : RegionUsageStack
    00001000 :  0.00%        0.02%      : RegionUsageTeb
    00120000 :  0.05%        6.51%      : RegionUsageHeap
    00000000 :  0.00%        0.00%      : RegionUsagePageHeap
    00001000 :  0.00%        0.02%      : RegionUsagePeb
    00001000 :  0.00%        0.02%      : RegionUsageProcessParametrs
    00001000 :  0.00%        0.02%      : RegionUsageEnvironmentBlock
        Tot: 7fff0000 Busy: 01145000

...
...
Largest free region: Base 01014000 - Size 71fec000
```

This can come in quite handy if you are trying to figure out which tool to use to further track down the leak. For example, if you see a large increase in memory usage attributed to a leak, but you do not see any major increase when looking at the `RegionUsageHeap` (in bold), chances are pretty good that the allocations are originating from non-heap-related memory activity (such as calls to `VirtualAlloc`). This eliminates precious time spent on running UMDH (tracks heap allocations only), and you can focus your efforts on running a more suitable tool, such as LeakDiag.

Our example is a simple server for illustrative purposes, but imagine an extremely complex server that has been hammered all day long with client requests and is leaking memory. Where do you begin to look without any tools? Many times, UMDH or LeakDiag can be your answer in these types of situations. But wait, you say! UMDH and LeakDiag assume that we have access to the system and can run these tools. What about the situations in which you simply get a memory dump of the leaked process and are required to analyze the leak postmortem. In this case, runtime leak detection tools are not an option. Fortunately, some powerful commands exist in the debugger that allow you to do some pretty amazing leak analysis.

### The !heap Extension Command

The `!heap` extension command is part of the debugger extension exts.dll and is an extremely powerful command that allows users to get an in-depth look at the memory consumption of a process. For example, the `!heap` extension command is capable of searching the address space for leaked blocks, performing custom searches on all heaps, giving detailed stack traces of allocations, setting breakpoints in the heap manager, and much more. In this section, we use a modified version of the 09basicmleak.exe application used in the previous section. The client code is nearly identical with the exception of the return type. Instead of returning a raw SID structure, the server returns a pointer to a `CIdentity` class instance. The `CIdentity` class instance simply wraps the SID structure in a more programmer-friendly fashion.

```
class CIdentity
{
public:
  virtual BOOL GetUsername(WCHAR** pUserName) { return FALSE; }
  virtual BOOL GetDomain(WCHAR** pUserName) { return FALSE; }

protected:
  CIdentity(PVOID pIdentBlob):m_pIdentityBlob(pIdentBlob){};
  virtual ~CIdentity(){};
  PVOID GetBlob() { return m_pIdentityBlob; }

  PVOID    m_pIdentityBlob;
};
```

The overall idea is for the `CIdentity` class to hold the raw data representing an identity and expose a set of virtual functions that can interpret the data. For example, the virtual function `GetUserName` returns the username of the identity. When a new identity surfaces, a subclass has to be derived from the `CIdentity` class and the appropriate functions overridden. The main point here is that the client always works with instances of the `CIdentity` class, thereby abstracting the specifics of whatever underlying identity might be used at that point. This is a perfect example of the commonly used technique called polymorphism: one interface, multiple implementations. In this particular case, we have a `CSID` class that derives from `CIdentity` to represent the common security identifier used in Windows. For simplicity's sake, the CSID class relies on the default implementation of the functions (returns FALSE).

The client code has changed slightly to work with instances of `CIdentity` instead of the raw SID structures previously used.

As you have probably already guessed, we have a reported memory leak when running the application. Let's take a look at how we can use the `!heap` extension command to analyze the problem.

### Heap Statistics

A very useful trick when looking at resource leaks is to always get a good idea of the overall memory consumption of the leaking process. This includes details, such as how much memory is being consumed, as well as information, such as which heap the memory belongs to. The `!heap` extension command allows you to get a detailed look at the heap summary of the process.

Let's dive right in and take a look at our leaky application.

The source code and binary for the application can be found in the following folders:

Source code: `C:\AWD\Chapter9\MemLeak\Client` and
`C:\AWD\Chapter9\MemLeak\Server`

Binary: `C:\AWDBIN\WinXP.x86.chk\09memleak.exe`

Run the client application with the following command:

```
C:\AWDBIN\WinXP.x86.chk\09memleak.exe /t:64 /i:1000 /s:0
```

After it has finished executing, attach a debugger to the process and use the `!heap` extension command to dump out a summary of all the heaps in the process.

```
0:001> !heap -s
  Heap     Flags      Reserv  Commit  Virt   Free  List   UCR  Virt  Lock  Fast
                       (k)     (k)     (k)    (k)   length      blocks cont. heap
  -----------------------------------------------------------------------------
  00090000 00000002    1024     20      20     3     1      1    0      0    L
  00190000 00001002      64     24      24    15     1      1    0      0    L
  001a0000 00008000      64     12      12    10     1      1    0      0
  00030000 00001002    3136   1232    1232     8     3      1    0      0    L
  -----------------------------------------------------------------------------
```

The -s switch provides some basic information on each heap in the process. The most important data in regards to resource leaks is shown here:

- Heap: The heap address.
- Flags: The flags associated with each heap. Later on, we show a much more readable way of identifying the flags.
- Reserv (k): The amount of memory reserved for the given heap.
- Commit (k): The amount of memory committed for the given heap.
- Virt (k): The amount of virtual memory for the given heap.

The heap overview is always a good starting point when looking at memory leaks, as it gives a breakdown of the activity in each heap in the process. Out of all the heaps, the heap with identifier 00030000 is using up the most memory. More specifically, the amount of reserved memory for the heap is 3136kb, and the amount of committed memory is 1232kb. Confronted with this information, heap 00030000 will be the heap that we start our investigation in. Although seeing this overview allows us to target our leak search, it does not tell us more heap-specific information. For example, it would be really useful to get a list of all the allocations of a particular heap. Fortunately, the !heap extension command allows us to get that information. Using the same command, but specifying a specific heap address, achieves the results we need.

```
0:001> !heap -s 00030000
Walking the heap 00030000 ...
 0: Heap 00030000
    Flags              00001002 - HEAP_GROWABLE
    Reserved           3136 (k)
    Commited           1232 (k)
    Virtual bytes      1232 (k)
    Free space         8 (k)
    External fragmentation         0% (3 free blocks)
    Virtual address fragmentation  0% (1 uncommited ranges)
    Virtual blocks   0
    Lock contention  0
    Segments         3

    Lookaside heap    00030688

                      Default heap   Front heap      Unused bytes
       Range (bytes)  Busy  Free     Busy  Free     Total   Average
    -------------------------------------------------------------
          0 -  1024   43604    1      0     0       438533     10
       1024 -  2048       2    0      0     0            8      4
       2048 -  3072       1    3      0     0            8      8
```

| 4096 | – | 5120 | 1 | 0 | 0 | 0 | 8 | 8 |
|------|---|------|---|---|---|---|---|---|
| 6144 | – | 7168 | 1 | 0 | 0 | 0 | 8 | 8 |
| Total | | | 43609 | 4 | 0 | 0 | 438565 | 10 |

Additional information includes human-readable heap flags, heap fragmentation information, and unused byte count.

This gives us a little more information but certainly not enough to figure out what might be leaking in this heap. If we could use the !heap extension command to get even more detailed information, such as information of each allocation made on the heap, we could get closer to tracking down the leak. The !heap extension command does expose such functionality by using the –a switch. Be warned; the –a switch performs an exhaustive dump of the heap in question. Typically, this can take several seconds or even minutes to finish, and you might end up with so much information that you can't create a console buffer big enough to hold it. Typically, the best thing to do is open a log file using the .logopen <filename> command. Run the !heap extension command and finally close the log file using the .logclose command. Now you can just open the log file and proceed with the analysis. For our example, the log file can be located at the following location:

```
C:\AWDBIN\WinXP.x86.chk\heaplog.txt
```

The log file is split into two sections:

- General information about the heap specified.
- A list of one or more segments with some basic information followed by all heap blocks currently seen in the segment. The heap blocks listed might or might not be in use, as you will see later on.

The first part, overall heap information, is a superset of data gathered by using the !heap –s extension command, as previously explained. The most important part of the log file is the second part: detailed segment information. After the initial segment overview, a long list of heap block information is displayed. Each line of output is organized as follows:

```
<heap block address>: <previous size> . <size> [<Flags>] - <status> (user allocation
size), <debug flags>
```

- Heap block address: The heap block address shows the address of the heap block. Note that the heap block address is not the same as the actual user mode pointer address. It turns out that the address that the !heap extension command shows is the address for the block itself and not the contents (that is, the user allocation) of the allocation. The first 8 bytes of a block structure contains heap block metadata (such as size and flags) kept by Windows to be capable of managing the heapblock. Following that information is the actual data we are interested in. If we wanted to dump out the contents of the user data contained in that block, we would add 8 bytes to the block address.

- Previous size: The size of the previous heap block. The size is in units of allocation granularity and not user data size.

- Size: The size of the allocated block. It is important to note that the size specified is not the same size that the user specified when making the allocation. The reason behind that is simple. The heap manager will allocate memory based on sizes of allocation granularity.

- Flags: The status of the heap block. Examples of status are a free heap block and busy heap block.

- Status: The status field tells you if the block is free or busy. When the block is busy, the allocation is active; when it is free, it is available for use. When it comes to memory leaks, we are typically only concerned with busy allocations.

- User allocation size: This is perhaps the most useful piece of the data when it comes to memory leaks. It tells us the user allocation size that is the cause of the allocation. With this information, we can correlate the size to various allocations we make in the application and see if any of them matches.

- Debug Flags: The heap block flags tell you what type of heap debugging support is enabled. For example, tail fill tells us that the end of the heap block is filled with a well-known pattern.

Presented with this information, how do you actually go about finding a leak? Well, the keyword is patience. The typical strategy employed is to find a pattern in the blocks listed. Most commonly, you will try to find a large number of blocks with the same user allocation size. This is usually a good indicator that they are potentially leaked blocks. In our log file, a few pages down the first segment listing (segment 00), we see the following:

```
0003a4f0: 00028 . 00010 [01] - busy (8)
0003a500: 00010 . 00028 [01] - busy (1c)
0003a528: 00028 . 00010 [01] - busy (8)
0003a538: 00010 . 00028 [01] - busy (1c)
0003a560: 00028 . 00010 [01] - busy (8)
0003a570: 00010 . 00028 [01] - busy (1c)
0003a598: 00028 . 00010 [01] - busy (8)
0003a5a8: 00010 . 00028 [01] - busy (1c)
```

```
0003a5d0:  00028 . 00010 [01] - busy (8)
0003a5e0:  00010 . 00028 [01] - busy (1c)
0003a608:  00028 . 00010 [01] - busy (8)
0003a618:  00010 . 00028 [01] - busy (1c)
0003a640:  00028 . 00010 [01] - busy (8)
0003a650:  00010 . 00028 [01] - busy (1c)
0003a678:  00028 . 00010 [01] - busy (8)
0003a688:  00010 . 00028 [01] - busy (1c)
0003a6b0:  00028 . 00010 [01] - busy (8)
0003a6c0:  00010 . 00028 [01] - busy (1c)
0003a6e8:  00028 . 00010 [01] - busy (8)
0003a6f8:  00010 . 00028 [01] - busy (1c)
0003a720:  00028 . 00010 [01] - busy (8)
0003a730:  00010 . 00028 [01] - busy (1c)
0003a758:  00028 . 00010 [01] - busy (8)
0003a768:  00010 . 00028 [01] - busy (1c)
0003a790:  00028 . 00010 [01] - busy (8)
0003a7a0:  00010 . 00028 [01] - busy (1c)
0003a7c8:  00028 . 00010 [01] - busy (8)
0003a7d8:  00010 . 00028 [01] - busy (1c)
0003a800:  00028 . 00010 [01] - busy (8)
0003a810:  00010 . 00028 [01] - busy (1c)
0003a838:  00028 . 00010 [01] - busy (8)
0003a848:  00010 . 00028 [01] - busy (1c)
```

There appears to be tons and tons of blocks allocated of user sizes 8 and 1c. As a matter of fact, sampling random blocks in the log file yields a fairly large number of these allocated blocks. Considering that the execution is over and the application is about to terminate, chances are good that we have discovered a memory leak.

At this point, we are halfway there. The next step is to find out what these blocks actually contain. If we were leaking memory, it would be reasonable to expect data related to our application contained within those blocks. The tricky and sometimes lengthy part is finding out what the blocks contain. Let's look at the memory of one of these blocks.

```
0:001> dd 0003a7c8+0x8
0003a7d0   010012bc 0003a7a8 00020005 000c01e4
0003a7e0   00000501 05000000 00000015 42f831d9
0003a7f0   125f5219 2b3be507 000003ec 00000000
0003a800   00050002 0008011f 010012bc 0003a7e0
0003a810   00020005 000c011d 00000501 05000000
0003a820   00000015 42f831d9 125f5219 2b3be507
0003a830   000003ec 00000000 00050002 00080118
0003a840   010012bc 0003a818 00020005 000c0116
```

Do the first two DWORDs seem to resemble anything? From this point on, it is a matter of trying to recognize something in the data that can be applicable to your application. Try to use a variety of the different `dump` command flavors to see if you can find anything that makes sense. For example, using the `da` or `du` commands allows you to dump a particular pointer as a string. If that doesn't work, you can try resolving the contents of the allocation. For example, by using the `ln` command on the first DWORD, you get the following result.

```
0:001> ln 010012bc
(010012bc)   09memleak!CSID::`vftable'   |   (010012c8)
09memleak!CIdentity::`vftable'
Exact matches:
```

Now that is too good to be a coincidence. Our test application definitely works with classes of type `CIdentity`. And as we already know, `CSID` is a class derived from `CIdentity`. Because virtual function tables typically come first in the object layout, we can hypothesize

- Judging from the pattern of allocations in the `!heap` extension command output, chances are good one of these heap blocks is leaked.
- Furthermore, by looking around at the heap block contents, we can see that it contains virtual function tables of objects that we are working with.

It can sometimes be a daunting task trying to recognize the contents of leaked heap blocks. Fortunately, after looking at memory leaks for some time, you will learn to recognize certain categories of data by simply using the `dd` command.

### Heap Searching

Before we come to the conclusion that this is in fact a leak (remember—caching can cause objects to stay around even after they are done being used), we should verify the theory. If these potentially leaked blocks were being used (perhaps cached), there would also need to be a reference somewhere in memory that points to that heap block. If there are no references, it means that we definitely have a leak. Once again, the `!heap` extension command provides us the means of finding this out. Using the `-x` and `-v` switches, we can ask the `!heap` extension command to search the entire memory space of the process for the presence of a specified address. In our example, searching for address `0003a7d0` (remember, block address + 0x8 gives the user mode allocation) yields the following:

```
0:001> !heap -x -v 0003a7d0
Entry     User      Heap      Segment      Size  PrevSize  Unused   Flags
-----------------------------------------
0003a7c8  0003a7d0  00030000  00030640      10     28         8     busy

Search VM for address range 0003a7c8 - 0003a7d7 :
```

The search yielded zero results. As stated before, if a currently allocated heap block is not referenced anywhere in memory, we can safely say that we are leaking that block.

Because we know (by code analysis) that we are working with a `CIdentity` class instance (CSID inherits from this class), we can now turn to code reviewing those specific portions of the code. Starting with the client code, we can see that the function called `ThreadWorker` uses the `CIdentity` class.

```
if(dwOperation==GETSID)
{
  CIdentity* pSid=serverInst.GetSID();
  if(pSid==NULL)
  {
    printf("Failed to get SID!\n");
  }
  else
  {
    printf(".");
  }
}
```

The client calls the server function called `GetSID`, which returns an instance of the `CIdentity` class. Because we didn't allocate space in the client code, the server must have been in charge of the allocation and passes it back to the client, if successful. But who is responsible for deleting it? In this case, the answer is that it is the client's responsibility. We can also fairly quickly tell that the code failed that responsibility and is not deleting the memory. The fix is simple; if the server succeeds and passes back an instance, we add the corresponding delete call when we are done with the instance.

After the fix has been made and we rerun the application and go through the same procedure as before using the `!heap` extension command, we notice that all the heap blocks of user allocation size 0x8 are now gone. Interestingly enough, all the reported leaked blocks of sizes 0x8 are gone, but the allocations of size 0x1c still remain. It's time to take a closer look at the first leak we identified and fixed, the `CIdentity` class:

```
class CIdentity
{
public:
  virtual BOOL GetUsername(WCHAR** pUserName) { return FALSE; }
  virtual BOOL GetDomain(WCHAR** pUserName) { return FALSE; }

protected:
  CIdentity(PVOID pIdentBlob):m_pIdentityBlob(pIdentBlob){};
  virtual ~CIdentity(){};
  PVOID GetBlob() { return m_pIdentityBlob; }

  PVOID    m_pIdentityBlob;
};
```

If an instance of this class is allocated, a common allocation layout would contain the virtual function table pointer (because the class contains virtual functions) and any data members. The only data member in this class is a pointer to a VOID (pIdentityBlob). Because both members are pointers (4 bytes each on 32-bit machines), the total size of the object should be 0x8. That matches up with the leaked blocks of user allocation size 0x8 that we saw, but what about the leaked blocks with size 0x1c? The answer is quite simple. We have already determined that we were leaking *instances* of a particular class. As such, if you leak an instance of a class, it means that the destructor will never be called. It is quite common practice for classes to delete any encapsulated data in its destructor. Hence, if you leak the instance, you also leak any data contained within that class. The only data member in the CIdentity class is a PVOID, which we all know is not something we can delete. These observations, coupled with the presence of virtual functions, imply that a derived class might be involved. Let's look at the GetSID server implementation:

```
CIdentity* CServer::GetSID()
{
  PSID pSid = NULL;
  HANDLE hToken = INVALID_HANDLE_VALUE;
  hToken = GetToken();
  if(hToken!=INVALID_HANDLE_VALUE)
  {
    DWORD dwNeeded=0;
    BOOL bRes=GetTokenInformation(hToken,
                                  TokenUser,
                                  NULL,
                                  0,
                                  &dwNeeded
                                  );
```

```
  if(bRes==FALSE && GetLastError()==ERROR_INSUFFICIENT_BUFFER)
  {
    TOKEN_USER* pBuffer=(TOKEN_USER*) new BYTE[dwNeeded];
    if(pBuffer!=NULL)
    {
      BOOL bRes=GetTokenInformation(hToken,
                                    TokenUser,
                                    (LPVOID)pBuffer,
                                    dwNeeded,
                                    &dwNeeded
                                    );
      if(bRes==TRUE)
      {
        DWORD dwSidLen=GetLengthSid(pBuffer->User.Sid);
        pSid=(PSID) new BYTE[dwSidLen];
        if(pSid!=NULL)
        {
          if(CopySid(dwSidLen, pSid, pBuffer->User.Sid)==FALSE)
          {
            delete[] pSid;
            pSid=NULL;
          }
        }
      }
      delete[] pBuffer;
    }
  }
  CloseHandle(hToken);
}

CSID* pIdentity=NULL ;
if(pSid!=NULL)
{
  pIdentity=new CSID(pSid);
  if(pIdentity==NULL)
  {
    delete pSid;
  }
}
return (CIdentity*) pIdentity;
}
```

The code listed is strikingly similar to the GetSID function used earlier in this chapter. The high-level overview shows that the server attempts to get the caller token (thread or process) and retrieves the SID from the token. As part of retrieving this SID, it allocated memory to hold the SID (pSid local variable). At the end of the function, the server code allocates an instance of the CSID class (which derives from CIdentity) and passes this SID pointer to the class constructor. The constructor then assigns ownership of this allocated memory to the class (stores the pointer in the PVOID data member of the CIdentity class). It stands to reason that it is now the responsibility of the class to free the memory associated with the PVOID pointer, but if we look at the code for the CSID class, it does not free the memory it allocated. The fix in this scenario is to add code to the destructor of the CSID class that frees the memory it just took responsibility for.

Now if we run the application once again and go through the same process of using the !heap extension command, we see that all allocations previously leaked are now properly deleted and not shown as busy allocations in the output.

Anytime you work with leaked instances of any kind of encapsulation construct (such as a class), it is also imperative to take a close look at the class itself to make sure that it's freeing the resource it has acquired. It is quite a common programming mistake to forget to release all the resources encapsulated within a particular class.

### Leak Detection

The act of dumping out all heap blocks and systematically searching for any potentially leaked blocks by using the search capabilities takes a toll and can be very expensive. Fortunately, the !heap extension command combines these steps into one by using the -l switch. The -l switch tells the !heap extension command to use a garbage collection algorithm to detect all the active allocations that are not references anywhere in the process. The following debug output shows running the !heap -l extension command on our leaky application (partial output).

```
0:001> !heap -l
Heap 00090000
Heap 00190000
Heap 001a0000
Heap 00030000
Scanning VM ...
Entry     User      Heap      Segment      Size  PrevSize  Unused  Flags
-------------------------------------------
...
...
. . .
012904e8  012904f0  00030000  01280000       28        10       c  busy
01290510  01290518  00030000  01280000       10        28       8  busy
01290520  01290528  00030000  01280000       28        10       c  busy
01290548  01290550  00030000  01280000       10        28       8  busy
01290558  01290560  00030000  01280000       28        10       c  busy
01290580  01290588  00030000  01280000       10        28       8  busy
01290590  01290598  00030000  01280000       28        10       c  busy
```

| 012905b8 | 012905c0 | 00030000 | 01280000 | 10 | 28 | 8 | busy |
| 012905c8 | 012905d0 | 00030000 | 01280000 | 28 | 10 | c | busy |
| 012905f0 | 012905f8 | 00030000 | 01280000 | 10 | 28 | 8 | busy |
| 01290600 | 01290608 | 00030000 | 01280000 | 28 | 10 | c | busy |
| 01290628 | 01290630 | 00030000 | 01280000 | 10 | 28 | 8 | busy |
| 01290638 | 01290640 | 00030000 | 01280000 | 28 | 10 | c | busy |
| 01290660 | 01290668 | 00030000 | 01280000 | 10 | 28 | 8 | busy |
| 01290670 | 01290678 | 00030000 | 01280000 | 28 | 10 | c | busy |
| 01290698 | 012906a0 | 00030000 | 01280000 | 10 | 28 | 8 | busy |
| 012906a8 | 012906b0 | 00030000 | 01280000 | 28 | 10 | c | busy |
| 012906d0 | 012906d8 | 00030000 | 01280000 | 10 | 28 | 8 | busy |
| 012906e0 | 012906e8 | 00030000 | 01280000 | 28 | 10 | c | busy |
| 01290708 | 01290710 | 00030000 | 01280000 | 10 | 28 | 8 | busy |
| 01290718 | 01290720 | 00030000 | 01280000 | 28 | 10 | c | busy |

```
...
...
...
42710 leaks detected.
```

The results of the !heap extension command show a ton of allocations with the block sizes of 28 and 10. (Note that the sizes are heap block sizes and not user allocation sizes.) In addition, the last line of output tells you how many leaks were detected. In this case, 42710 leaked blocks were found. This is an extremely useful feature of the !heap extension command, as it eliminates the need to do a lot of searching by hand.

### Pageheap

The previous example showed a leak that was fairly easy to spot by analyzing the state of the heap and code reviewing. At times, it might not be apparent what is leaking. In those cases, after you have identified a potential leak culprit, it would be useful to see which stack trace made the allocation to begin with. If we had that, we could find out exactly what the code was doing and what it was allocating. The !heap extension command can work in tandem with the stack trace recording capabilities of Windows. To make use of this feature, make sure to enable stack tracing using Application Verifier (see Chapter 1). The applicable switches to the !heap extension command are –p and –a. –p tells the !heap extension command that pageheap information is being requested, and the –a switch allows you to specify an address that you want to see the stack trace for. In the previous section, the address that we thought was leaking was 0026ab88. Issue the following command, and you will see the originating stack trace for that allocation:

```
0:001> !heap -p -a 0003a7c8
    address 0003a7c8 found in
    _HEAP @ 30000
```

```
in HEAP_ENTRY: Size : Prev Flags - UserPtr UserSize - state
    3a7a8: 0007 : N/A  [N/A] - 3a7b0 (1c) - (busy)
    Trace: 003c
    7c96d6dc ntdll!RtlDebugAllocateHeap+0x000000e1
    7c949d18 ntdll!RtlAllocateHeapSlowly+0x00000044
    7c91b298 ntdll!RtlAllocateHeap+0x00000e64
    77c2c3c9 msvcrt!_heap_alloc+0x000000e0
    77c2c3e7 msvcrt!_nh_malloc+0x00000013
    77c29cd4 msvcrt!operator new+0x0000000f
    1001c52 09memleak!CServer::GetSID+0x000000d2
    100143b 09memleak!ThreadWorker+0x0000006b
    7c80b683 kernel32!BaseThreadStart+0x00000037
```

Not only do we see general information about the leaked address (such as which heap it's in and the trace ID), but we also get the full stack trace of the code that made the allocation. From here, it is a trivial exercise to code review and find the culprit code.

It goes without saying that enabling stack tracing—the -p -a option of the !heap extension command—saves you an incredible amount of time.

### Other Heap Extension Command Tricks

If you look at the help for the !heap extension command (by typing !heap -?), you will notice some commands listed that are not documented in the debugger documentation. More specifically, the following commands allow you to do some useful heap filtering and searches. Let's begin with the filtering command. The filtering command allows you to tell the debugger that you are only interested in knowing about allocations that match a specific size (or range). The syntax for the command is

```
!heap -flt s SIZE
```

where SIZE is the size that you are interested in. Alternatively, if you do not know the exact size, rather a range, you can use the following syntax:

```
!heap -flt r SIZEBEGIN SIZEEND
```

where SIZEBEGIN is the starting size, and SIZEEND is the ending size in the range.

Once again, we will use our leaky 09memleak.exe. From prior investigation, we know that the leaked block sizes are 0x8 and 0x1c. Run the 09memleak.exe application with the following command:

```
C:\AWDBIN\WinXP.x86.chk\09memleak.exe /t:64 /i:1000 /s:0
```

After it has finished executing, attach a debugger to the process and execute the
!heap extension command.

```
0:001> !heap -flt s 0x1c
    _HEAP @ 90000
    _HEAP @ 190000
    _HEAP @ 1a0000
    _HEAP @ 30000
      HEAP_ENTRY: Size : Prev Flags - UserPtr  UserSize   - state
        33768: 0007 : N/A  [N/A] - 33770 (1c) - (busy)
        35ae0: 0008 : N/A  [N/A] - 35ae8 (1c) - (busy)
        37ec8: 0007 : N/A  [N/A] - 37ed0 (1c) - (busy)
        37f40: 0007 : N/A  [N/A] - 37f48 (1c) - (busy)
        37f78: 0007 : N/A  [N/A] - 37f80 (1c) - (busy)
        37ff0: 0007 : N/A  [N/A] - 37ff8 (1c) - (busy)
        38028: 0007 : N/A  [N/A] - 38030 (1c) - (busy)
        380a0: 0007 : N/A  [N/A] - 380a8 (1c) - (busy)
        380d8: 0007 : N/A  [N/A] - 380e0 (1c) - (busy)
        38150: 0007 : N/A  [N/A] - 38158 (1c) - (busy)
        38188: 0007 : N/A  [N/A] - 38190 (1c) - (busy)
        38200: 0007 : N/A  [N/A] - 38208 (1c) - (busy)
        38238: 0007 : N/A  [N/A] - 38240 (1c) - (busy)
        382b0: 0007 : N/A  [N/A] - 382b8 (1c) - (busy)
        382e8: 0007 : N/A  [N/A] - 382f0 (1c) - (busy)
        38360: 0007 : N/A  [N/A] - 38368 (1c) - (busy)
        38398: 0007 : N/A  [N/A] - 383a0 (1c) - (busy)
        38410: 0007 : N/A  [N/A] - 38418 (1c) - (busy)
        ...
        ...
        ...
```

The result of the !heap extension command neatly displays all heap blocks of size
0x1c and associated block information. The busy state indicates that the block is currently in use. Even though this information is quite useful for finding out all blocks
with a specific size, we are still left with the task of finding out what those blocks actually contain. As you might have already guessed, the !heap extension command
comes to the rescue. In conjunction with the –p and –h switches, the !heap extension command dumps all heap blocks and tries to resolve the first DWORD. The following debug output shows the result of running the heap –p –h command on the
heap that is supposedly leaking.

```
0:001> !heap -p -h 00030000
    _HEAP @ 30000
      _HEAP_LOOKASIDE @ 30688
```

```
_HEAP_SEGMENT @ 30640
 CommittedRange @ 30680
 HEAP_ENTRY: Size : Prev Flags - UserPtr  UserSize   - state
* 30680: 0303 : N/A  [N/A] - 30688 (1800) - (busy)
  31e98: 0014 : N/A  [N/A] - 31ea0 (88) - (busy)
  31f38: 0093 : N/A  [N/A] - 31f40 (480) - (busy)
  323d0: 0103 : N/A  [N/A] - 323d8 (800) - (busy)
    msvcrt!_iob
  32be8: 0007 : N/A  [N/A] - 32bf0 (20) - (busy)
  32c20: 000b : N/A  [N/A] - 32c28 (3a) - (busy)
  32c78: 000a : N/A  [N/A] - 32c80 (32) - (busy)
  32cc8: 0008 : N/A  [N/A] - 32cd0 (26) - (busy)
  32d08: 000a : N/A  [N/A] - 32d10 (34) - (busy)
  32d58: 000a : N/A  [N/A] - 32d60 (38) - (busy)
  32da8: 0009 : N/A  [N/A] - 32db0 (2e) - (busy)
  32df0: 000a : N/A  [N/A] - 32df8 (36) - (busy)
  32e40: 000b : N/A  [N/A] - 32e48 (3a) - (busy)
  32e98: 000b : N/A  [N/A] - 32ea0 (32) - (busy)
  32ef0: 0011 : N/A  [N/A] - 32ef8 (70) - (busy)
  32f78: 0010 : N/A  [N/A] - 32f80 (62) - (busy)
  32ff8: 0008 : N/A  [N/A] - 33000 (28) - (busy)
  33038: 0004 : N/A  [N/A] - 33040 (8) - (busy)
    09memleak!CSID::`vftable'
  33058: 000c : N/A  [N/A] - 33060 (48) - (busy)
```

As you can see, a lot of allocations with size 1c and 8 are being displayed. What's even more interesting is that all allocations with size 8 have additional information associated with them. More specifically, they show the following:

```
33038: 0004 : N/A  [N/A] - 33040 (8) - (busy)
        09memleak!CSID::`vftable'
```

This is one of the really nice features of using the !heap extension command with the −p switch. Whenever a heap block is encountered, the !heap extension command tries to resolve the first DWORD of that block. In our case, it resolves nicely to our CSID virtual function table (as we discovered earlier).

The next command we will look at is the −srch command. The syntax of the command resembles the following:

```
!heap  -srch [-b|-w|-d|-q] PATTERN
                It scans all heap allocations and it searches
                for the given pattern.
                The size of the pattern can be specified.
```

The -srch command allows a search for particular patterns in all heap allocations. This can come in really handy if we have an idea (or gut feeling) of what might be leaking. Let's say that we wanted to see if any of the leaked blocks in the 09memleak.exe process were leaking CSID instances. The first thing we must do is find out the address to our virtual function table. This can be done by using the X command (see Chapter 2), which allows us to resolve a symbolic name in one or more modules:

```
0:001> X 09memleak!CSID*
01001e20 09memleak!CSID::`scalar deleting destructor' (void)
01001e60 09memleak!CSID::~CSID (void)
01001d40 09memleak!CSID::CSID (void *)
010012bc 09memleak!CSID::`vftable' = <no type information>
```

The * is used as a wildcard. The virtual function table is the last entry shown with an address of 010012bc. Now we can use that address as part of the -srch command:

```
0:001> !heap -srch 010012bc
  _HEAP @ 30000
  in HEAP_ENTRY: Size : Prev Flags - UserPtr UserSize - state
       34f18: 0002 : N/A  [N/A] - 34f20 (8) - (busy)
          09memleak!CSID::`vftable'
  _HEAP @ 30000
  in HEAP_ENTRY: Size : Prev Flags - UserPtr UserSize - state
       3ace0: 0002 : N/A  [N/A] - 3ace8 (8) - (busy)
          09memleak!CSID::`vftable'
  _HEAP @ 30000
  in HEAP_ENTRY: Size : Prev Flags - UserPtr UserSize - state
       3ad18: 0002 : N/A  [N/A] - 3ad20 (8) - (busy)
          09memleak!CSID::`vftable'
  _HEAP @ 30000
  in HEAP_ENTRY: Size : Prev Flags - UserPtr UserSize - state
       3ad50: 0002 : N/A  [N/A] - 3ad58 (8) - (busy)
          09memleak!CSID::`vftable'
  _HEAP @ 30000
  in HEAP_ENTRY: Size : Prev Flags - UserPtr UserSize - state
       3ad88: 0002 : N/A  [N/A] - 3ad90 (8) - (busy)
          09memleak!CSID::`vftable'
  _HEAP @ 30000
  in HEAP_ENTRY: Size : Prev Flags - UserPtr UserSize - state
       3adc0: 0002 : N/A  [N/A] - 3adc8 (8) - (busy)
          09memleak!CSID::`vftable'
  _HEAP @ 30000
  in HEAP_ENTRY: Size : Prev Flags - UserPtr UserSize - state
       3adf8: 0002 : N/A  [N/A] - 3ae00 (8) - (busy)
          09memleak!CSID::`vftable'
```

Judging from the excessive number of CSID virtual function tables left at the end of the application run, this is a good indication that something has forgotten to delete instances of the CSID class.

The final command is the −stat command with the following syntax:

```
!heap -stat [-h HANDLE [-grp A|B|S [MaxDisplay]]]
This command calculates usage statistics on all the heaps (sorting by committed
bytes) or on the given heap.
The -grp A|B|C options specifiy a Group-By criteria.
-grp A groups by Allocation Size
-grp B groups by Block count
-grp S groups by Total Size for each allocation size
If HANDLE is 0, it iterates over all the heaps.
```

The −stat command gives some very nice statistics on the usage of one or more of the heaps by grouping the output by allocation (user) size, the number of blocks with that size, total size of all blocks with that size, and finally the percentage of currently busy blocks. By default, -stat sorts by the biggest totals. Because we know which heap is more than likely leaking in our process (00030000), we select that one for further analysis:

```
0:001> !heap -stat -h 00030000
 heap @ 00030000
group-by: TOTSIZE max-display: 20
    size    #blocks     total     ( %) (percent of total busy bytes)
    1c 52c2 - 90d38   (75.89)
    8 52c2 - 29610   (21.68)
    1000 1 - 1000   (0.52)
    800 1 - 800   (0.26)
    480 1 - 480   (0.15)
    318 1 - 318   (0.10)
    164 2 - 2c8   (0.09)
    220 1 - 220   (0.07)
    58 6 - 210   (0.07)
    54 6 - 1f8   (0.06)
    18c 1 - 18c   (0.05)
    62 4 - 188   (0.05)
    32 7 - 15e   (0.04)
    2a 8 - 150   (0.04)
    2c 7 - 134   (0.04)
    4c 4 - 130   (0.04)
    64 3 - 12c   (0.04)
    5e 3 - 11a   (0.04)
    88 2 - 110   (0.03)
    5a 3 - 10e   (0.03)
```

This can quickly give you an overview of which allocations you should be looking at first. In this case, allocations of size `0x1c` account for 75.89% of all heap usage. The `-grp` sub switch gives you the flexibility to group the information in different ways:

- -grp A: Groups the output by allocation size, showing the biggest allocations first. The top-ranked allocation might be the biggest single allocation but will more than likely not be the biggest user of the heap.
- -grp B: Groups the output by block count, showing the allocations with the largest block count first. If you are in fact looking at a leaked allocation, typically, the top contender in the block count category will match the block size that you are leaking.
- -grp S: Groups by total size. This is the default setting.

I cannot state enough the power that the `!heap` extension command packs. It allows you to see virtually everything you would like to see on heap activity. As a bonus, the search capabilities save a lot of time when looking for culprit leaked objects. It is well worth your time to experiment with this powerful command.

## Step 5: Future Avoidance Strategies

Knowing how to use all these powerful tools is a lifesaver when it comes to tracking down memory leaks. But we would like to avoid using them as much as possible to save us time and frustration during the development process. Much in the same way that we did with handle leaks, now is the time to sit down and think about what we can do in the future to make sure that we don't forget to delete memory when we are done with it. Again, an extremely useful technique is to use an auto construct that automatically deletes memory when the variable goes out of scope. As a matter of fact, it was considered so useful that it was included as part of the standard template library (auto_ptr). Many different flavors of auto constructs are available today. Some do nothing more than a delete at the end of the scope (as with auto_ptr), and some do complicated things (such as reference counting). The bottom line is that you should make use of auto constructs as much as possible when it comes to memory. If one isn't available to suit your needs, write one. It will be well worth your time. Besides merely forgetting to free memory, other things can go wrong in code. Code that isn't exception safe, for example, can very easily cause leaks. Here is a simple example:

```
void myfunc()
{
  BYTE* ptr = new BYTE[255];
```

```
  SomeFunc();

  delete[] ptr;
}
```

If the `SomeFunc` function throws exceptions (that might or might not be caught above you), this function will definitely leak. More specifically, it will leak 255 bytes' worth of memory. If we were to use an auto_ptr, we would be guaranteed that it would not leak—even in the presence of exceptions—because stack unwinding guarantees that all local objects (that is, allocated on the stack) are cleaned up when exiting the function.

Another possibility is to overload the allocation APIs used in your application. This allows for trapping all calls to memory allocations, thereby giving you hooks to all memory allocations performed by your applications. The allocation hooks can then be used to track memory allocations, simulate failures in memory allocations, and much more.

## Summary

Resource leaks are some of the biggest reasons behind software instability and, as such, should be treated as high-priority bugs in any piece of software. In this chapter, we explained the overall process of the leak detection process and two different types of resource leaks (handle and memory leaks), as well as the associated tools to make life much easier when tracking down and fixing leaks. We described how to use UMDH, LeakDiag, and a number of extremely powerful extension commands (`!htrace` and `!heap`) to help more efficiently track down resource leaks. In addition, we have introduced some (but definitely not all) ways of making the tools we use every day (such as the compiler) alleviate the burden of accidentally forgetting to free a resource when you are done using it. The auto construct is a very popular and powerful mechanism to achieve fewer resource leaks in your software.

Armed with the knowledge of the overall resource leak detection process, as well as a good understanding of the most fundamental types of resources, you will be able to tackle any type of resource leak.

# CHAPTER 10

# SYNCHRONIZATION

In this chapter, we take a close look at some very common synchronization problems and how to troubleshoot and find the root cause as efficiently as possible. The chapter starts out by explaining the basic synchronization primitives available in Windows followed by a number of practical debugging scenarios showcasing common synchronization problems and how to use the debuggers to find the root cause.

## Synchronization Basics

The Windows operating system is a preemptive and multithreaded operating system. Multithreading refers to the capability to run any number of threads concurrently. If the system is a single-processor machine, Windows creates the illusion of concurrent thread execution by enabling each thread to run for a short period of time (known as a time quantum). After that time quantum is exhausted, the thread is put into a wait state and the processor switches to another thread (known as a context switch), and so on. On a multiprocessor machine, two or more threads are capable of running concurrently (one thread per physical processor).

By being preemptive, all active threads in the system must be capable of yielding control of the processor to another thread at any point in time. Given that the operating system can take away control from a thread, developers must take care to always be in a state in which control can safely be taken away.

If all applications were single threaded, or if all the threads were running in isolation, synchronization would not be a problem. Alas, for the sake of efficiency, dependent multithreading is the norm today and also the source of a lot of bugs in applications. Dependent multithreading occurs when two or more threads need to work in tandem to complete a task. Code execution for a given task might, for example, be broken up between one or more threads (with or without shared resources), and hence the threads need to "communicate" with each other with regard to the order of thread execution. This communication is referred to as thread synchronization and is crucial to any multithreaded application.

To synchronize threads, Windows provides a set of synchronization primitives.

## Event

The event is a kernel mode primitive accessible in user mode via an opaque handle. An event is a synchronization object that can take on one of two states: signaled or nonsignaled. When an event goes from the non-signaled state to the signaled state (indicating that a particular event has occurred), a thread waiting on that event object will be woken up and allowed to continue execution. Event objects are very commonly used to synchronize code flow execution between multiple threads. For example, the Win32 API ReadFile can read data asynchronously by passing in a pointer to an OVERLAPPED structure. Figure 10.1 illustrates the flow of events.

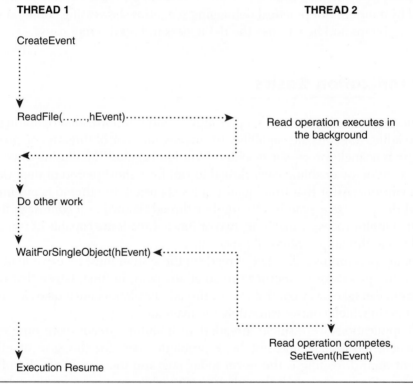

**Figure 10.1**   Asynchronous ReadFile API flow

Part of the OVERLAPPED structure is a handle to an event that the caller passes in. Because the presence of the OVERLAPPED parameter indicates that it is an asynchronous operation, `ReadFile` returns to the caller immediately and processes the read operation in the background. The caller is then free to do other work. When the caller is ready for the results of the read operation, he simply waits (using the `WaitForSingleObject` API) for the state of the event to become signaled. When the background read operations succeeds, the event is set to a signaled state, thereby waking up the calling thread, and allows execution to continue.

There are two forms of event objects: manual reset and auto reset. The key difference between the two is what happens when the event is signaled. In the case of a manual reset event, the event object remains in the signaled state until explicitly reset, thereby allowing any number of threads waiting for the event object to be released. In contrast, the auto reset event only allows one waiting thread to be released before being automatically reset to the nonsignaled state. If no threads are waiting, the event remains in a signaled state until the first thread tries to wait for the event.

In user mode, an event object is represented as an opaque handle to an underlying kernel object. As such, in user mode, looking at how the handle object is laid out in memory is not possible. However, an extension command exists that lets you get some information about a particular handle. The extension command is called `!handle`. To see how the `!handle` extension command works, attach the debugger to an instance of `notepad.exe` and issue the `!handle` command. Listing 10.1 shows the abbreviated output of the `!handle` extension command. (Note that the output might look different, depending on the state Notepad was in when you issued the command.)

**Listing 10.1**    Example of the !handle extension command on an instance of notepad.exe

```
0:001> !handle
Handle 74
  Type          File
Handle 3c8
  Type          Section
Handle 3cc
  Type          Mutant
Handle 3d8
  Type          Mutant
Handle 3dc
  Type          Mutant
Handle 3e0
  Type          Mutant
Handle 3e4
  Type          Mutant
Handle 3e8
  Type          Mutant
```

*(continues)*

**Listing 10.1** Example of the !handle extension command on an instance of notepad.exe *(continued)*

```
Handle 3f0
  Type          Section
Handle 42c
  Type          Key
Handle 438
  Type          Section
Handle 43c
  Type          Port
Handle 47c
  Type          Event
37 Handles
...
...
...
Type          Count
None          1
Event         5
Section       4
File          4
Port          2
Directory     3
Mutant        6
WindowStation 2
Semaphore     5
Key           4
Desktop       1
```

As you can see, the !handle extension command (without parameters) dumps out all the handles opened in the process with abbreviated information. To get more detailed information on a particular handle, you add the handle value to the !handle extension command followed by a value that represents the depth of the information to be displayed. Using a value of f gives you the most exhaustive information. Let's use handle 47c (an event) as an example (see Listing 10.2).

**Listing 10.2** Using the !handle extension command to get detailed information on a handle

```
0:001> !handle 47c f
Handle 614
  Type          Event
  Attributes    0
```

```
GrantedAccess 0x1f0003:
        Delete,ReadControl,WriteDac,WriteOwner,Synch
        QueryState,ModifyState
HandleCount    2
PointerCount   4
Name           <none>
Object Specific Information
  Event Type Auto Reset
  Event is Set
```

Listing 10.2 shows the type of the handle, its attributes, its granted access, its handle counts, and so on. It also gives information on the type of event (auto reset), as well as the state of the event, which in this particular case happens to be set. Another interesting piece of information is the name of the event (set to <none>). As part of the event creation, it is possible to name an event, thereby enabling the event to be used across processes rather than just within a single process. Two or more processes agree on an event name, and when trying to open an event with that particular name, the event will either be created, if it's the first call, or the reference count on the existing event will simply be incremented.

## Critical Section

Critical sections are most commonly used to protect shared resources among threads by guaranteeing exclusive access (that is, only one thread is capable of gaining access to the resource). To illustrate the usage of a critical section, imagine the following piece of pseudo-code:

```
1. Enter Critical Section
...
...
2. Access Shared Resource
...
...
3. Leave Critical Section
```

Furthermore, imagine two threads (T1 and T2) both executing the preceding code, trying to get access to the shared resource. Let's assume that T1 gets to step 1 first. The first thing that happens when T1 tries to enter the critical section is that it checks to see if the critical section is available (that is, that no other thread is currently inside the critical section). Because that is the case, T1 enters the critical section and starts accessing the shared resource in step 2. Now, a context switch occurs, and T2 is allowed to run and gets to step 1 and tries to enter the critical section. Because T1 already owns the critical section, T2 is instructed to wait at the critical section entry point until T1 leaves the critical section. Another context switch occurs, and T1 finishes by executing step 3 and leaves the critical section. At the next context switch, T2 enters the critical section and execution continues.

The way that a thread waits for a critical section to become available is different between single-processor and multiprocessor machines. On single-processor machines, the thread really does go into an efficient wait state (kernel transition), whereas on multiprocessor machines, the thread might try to spin X number of times in hopes that the critical section will become available while spinning. This is to avoid the expense of going into a wait state, which requires a kernel transition and context switch.

Let's take a closer look at the memory layout of a critical section. The underlying critical section data structure is RTL_CRITICAL_SECTION and can be viewed by using the dt command:

```
0:001> dt RTL_CRITICAL_SECTION
   +0x000 DebugInfo        : Ptr32 _RTL_CRITICAL_SECTION_DEBUG
   +0x004 LockCount        : Int4B
   +0x008 RecursionCount   : Int4B
   +0x00c OwningThread     : Ptr32 Void
   +0x010 LockSemaphore    : Ptr32 Void
   +0x014 SpinCount        : Uint4B
```

The individual fields in the RTL_CRITICAL_SECTION structure are discussed in more detail here:

- DebugInfo
  The DebugInfo field is a system-allocated companion structure that contains an assortment of augmented information about the critical section (discussed later).
- LockCount
  This field indicates how many threads are waiting to acquire the critical section. It is by default initialized to –1, which indicates that the critical section has not been acquired. A value of 0 or more indicates that it has been acquired. To find out how many other threads are waiting for the critical section, the following formula can be used:

$$\text{Number of waiting threads} = \text{LockCount} - \text{RecursionCount} + 1$$

In Windows 2003 Server SP1 and later, this field has changed into a bit field to eliminate a very common problem with critical sections known as the lock convoy problem. Later in the chapter, we take a closer look at what a lock convoy is and how to detect it.

- RecursionCount

  It is possible for a thread to acquire a critical section more than once. This field indicates how many times the same thread has acquired the critical section. By default, the value of this field is 0, indicating that there is no thread owning the critical section.

- OwningThread

  If the critical section has been acquired, this field contains the ID of the thread that acquired the critical section.

- LockSemaphore

  This field actually contains a handle to an auto-reset event rather than a semaphore. Its primary usage is to indicate when a critical section is free and ready to be acquired. The event is created whenever an attempt is made to acquire a critical section already acquired by a different thread. To avoid a handle leak, it is critical to call the DeleteCriticalSection API when finished with the critical section.

- SpinCount

  This field is used only on multiprocessor systems. If a thread already owns a critical section and another thread tries to acquire it, that thread will go into a wait state until the critical section is released. Going into this wait state requires a kernel transition, which is an expensive transition. To try and eliminate this transition on multiprocessor systems, rather than immediately going into a wait state, the thread spins SpinCount number of times, trying to acquire the critical section on each spin, improving performance in cases in which the critical section was just about to be released. By default, this value is 0, but it can be changed by using the InitializeCriticalSectionAndSpinCount API.

Now let's take a closer look at the DebugInfo field.

```
0:001> dt RTL_CRITICAL_SECTION_DEBUG
   +0x000 Type              : Uint2B
   +0x002 CreatorBackTraceIndex : Uint2B
   +0x004 CriticalSection   : Ptr32 _RTL_CRITICAL_SECTION
   +0x008 ProcessLocksList  : _LIST_ENTRY
   +0x010 EntryCount        : Uint4B
   +0x014 ContentionCount   : Uint4B
   +0x018 Flags             : Uint4B
   +0x01c Spare             : Uint4B
```

The various parts of the DebugInfo are explained in the following:

- Type
  This field is unused (defaults to 0).
- CreatorBackTraceIndex
  If extended instrumentation has been enabled by running gflags, this field contains the index used while collecting stack trace information.
- CriticalSection
  This field contains a pointer to the critical section associated with this structure, essentially allowing you to backtrack from the debug structure to the critical section.
- ProcessLocksList
  For any given process, a list is maintained by the operating system that contains all the active critical sections in that process. This field represents a node in that list and contains the forward and backward pointers. You can use the FLINK and BLINK pointers of this node to traverse the process-critical section list.
- EntryCount
  This field is incremented anytime a thread goes into a wait state trying to acquire a critical section already owned.
- ContentionCount
  This field is incremented anytime a thread goes into a wait state trying to acquire a critical section already owned.
- Flags
  This field is unused.
- Spare
  This field is unused.

It is important to note that although the RTL_CRITICAL_SECTION_DEBUG seems to contain mainly debugging types of information, it is required by the earlier versions of Windows for a critical section to be considered usable. In fact, if the operating system is unable to allocate memory for this structure during initialization, the API will fail. In Windows Server 2003 SP1 and above, the debug info is no longer necessary for a critical section to function. It is important to note this discrepancy while debugging because a NULL DebugInfo field can make you think that the critical section is in a bad and unusable state.

Rather than having to traverse the critical section list maintained by the operating system by hand, the !cs extension command can be used. Listing 10.3 shows an abbreviated example on a newly started instance of notepad.exe.

10. SYNCHRONIZATION

**Listing 10.3**  Using the !cs command to list all critical sections of a process

```
0:000> !cs
--------------------
DebugInfo           = 0x7c97c420
Critical section    = 0x7c97c0a0 (ntdll!RtlCriticalSectionLock+0x0)
NOT LOCKED
LockSemaphore       = 0x0
SpinCount           = 0x00000000
--------------------
DebugInfo           = 0x7c97c440
Critical section    = 0x7c97c080 (ntdll!DeferedCriticalSection+0x0)
NOT LOCKED
LockSemaphore       = 0x0
SpinCount           = 0x00000000
--------------------
DebugInfo           = 0x7c97c100
Critical section    = 0x7c97c0d8 (ntdll!LdrpLoaderLock+0x0)
LOCKED
LockCount           = 0x0
OwningThread        = 0x00000b48
RecursionCount      = 0x1
LockSemaphore       = 0x0
SpinCount           = 0x00000000
...
...
...
```

As you can see from Listing 10.3, the information displayed is simply a trimmed down version of the actual critical section structure we looked at earlier. If the critical section is acquired, it additionally shows the LockCount, OwningThread, and RecursionCount fields. The !cs extension command can also be used to display information for a single critical section by adding the address of the critical section to the command, as shown here.

```
0:000> !cs 0x7c97c0d8
--------------------
Critical section    = 0x7c97c0d8 (ntdll!LdrpLoaderLock+0x0)
DebugInfo           = 0x7c97c100
LOCKED
LockCount           = 0x0
OwningThread        = 0x00000b48
RecursionCount      = 0x1
LockSemaphore       = 0x0
SpinCount           = 0x00000000
```

Here's one word of caution about the `EnterCriticalSection` API on Windows 2000—it can raise an out of memory exception during low memory conditions. Remember that a critical section uses an event to perform its job, and this event might end up being initialized in the `EnterCriticalSection` API. If the system is low on memory, it will raise the exception. If you want critical sections to work reliably on Windows 2000, you should use the `InitializeCriticalSectionAndSpinCount` API, which allocates the event during initialization of the critical section and doesn't throw any exceptions when subsequently used.

## Mutex

A mutex is a kernel mode synchronization construct that can be used to synchronize threads both within a process as well as across multiple processes (by naming the mutex during creation). Generally speaking, if your synchronization chores are all within the same process, you should use a critical section. If, on the other hand, you need to synchronize across processes, a named mutex is the right approach. Because a mutex is a kernel mode construct, the user mode code accesses the mutex via an opaque handle value. To get more information about a mutex while debugging in user mode, you can use the `!handle` extension command. Attach a debugger to an instance of Notepad and enter `!handle`, as shown in the abbreviated output in Listing 10.4.

**Listing 10.4**   Using the !handle extension command to find a mutex object in notepad.exe

```
0:001> !handle
Handle c
  Type          File
Handle 368
  Type          Section
Handle 36c
  Type          Mutant
Handle 3a4
  Type          Section
Handle 3a8
  Type          Mutant
Handle 3b4
  Type          Mutant
Handle 3b8
  Type          Mutant
Handle 3bc
  Type          Mutant
...
...
```

```
...
39 Handles
Type          Count
Event         5
Section       5
File          4
Port          2
Directory     3
Mutant        7
WindowStation 2
Semaphore     5
Key           4
Desktop       1
KeyedEvent    1
```

The first important thing to notice in Listing 10.4 is that the debugger refers to a mutex as a mutant, and the listing shows that there are seven open mutants. To get extended information for any given mutant, you can issue the !handle extension command, the handle value, and a number that indicates the extent of information to display:

```
0:001> !handle 3b4 f
Handle 3b4
   Type          Mutant
   Attributes    0
   GrantedAccess 0x1f0001:
         Delete,ReadControl,WriteDac,WriteOwner,Synch
         QueryState
   HandleCount   22
   PointerCount  24
   Name          \BaseNamedObjects\CTF.TMD.MutexDefaultS-1-5-21-1123561945-308236825-
725345543-1004
   Object Specific Information
     Mutex is Free
```

In addition to the general kernel object information fields described in the "Event" section of this chapter, the object-specific information shows whether the Mutex is free or busy. (In our case, it's free.) If you dump out extended information for all the mutants in the Notepad instance, you will also see that most of them are named mutants, which indicates that access to that mutant can be made from other processes.

A mutex is considered abandoned if the thread that currently owns it exits without freeing the mutex, thereby preventing any other threads from acquiring it. The operating system detects this scenario and automatically puts the mutex in the signaled state, enabling waiting threads to acquire the mutex. Under this scenario, when a thread wakes up to acquire the mutex, the wait API returns a status code (WAIT_ABANDONED), thereby signaling to the waiting thread that the mutex was abandoned. Typically, a situation such as this indicates a bug in the code, and the scenario should be investigated.

## Semaphore

A semaphore is a kernel mode synchronization object accessible from user mode. It is similar to a critical section and a mutex in the sense that it allows exclusive access to a resource. The main difference, however, is that a semaphore employs resource counting, thereby allowing X number of threads access to the resource. An example of when to use a semaphore is in a system with four USB ports that are accessed by a piece of code. Because there are four USB ports, we would like to allow four threads to concurrently use one of the available USB ports. To accomplish this, we would create a semaphore with a max resource count of 4. As threads try to acquire the semaphore, the reference count (initialized to 4) is checked whether it is greater than 0; if so, it allows the acquisition and decrements the reference count. When the reference count reaches 0, a thread trying to acquire the semaphore will be put to sleep until a thread releases the semaphore and the reference count is incremented. As with events and mutexes, you would use the !handle extension command in the debugger to get extended information on a semaphore. Attach a debugger to an instance of Notepad, and list out all the handles in the process. Find a handle that represents a semaphore, and dump out extended information:

```
0:001> !handle 7f4 f
Handle 7f4
  Type            Semaphore
  Attributes      0
  GrantedAccess 0x100003:
        Synch
        QueryState,ModifyState
  HandleCount     2
  PointerCount    3
  Name            <none>
  Object Specific Information
    Semaphore Count 0
    Semaphore Limit 2147483647
```

The object-specific output shows the state of the semaphore, including the current semaphore count.

# High-Level Process

The process of resolving a synchronization problem in your code is illustrated in Figure 10.2.

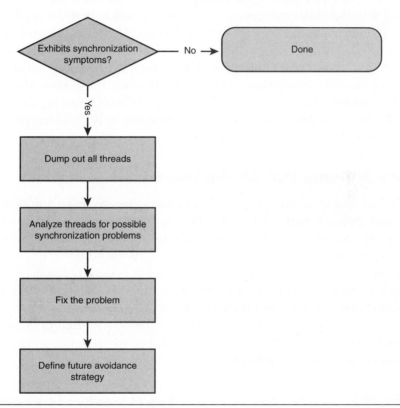

**Figure 10.2**   Synchronization Problem Analysis Process

The process is examined in greater detail in the following sections.

## Step 1: Recognize the Symptoms

The first step in analyzing a possible synchronization problem is learning to recognize the symptoms. Although it is not possible to list all the different symptoms that might surface, it is definitely possible to list a great majority of them. The basic premise of a synchronization problem and corresponding symptom is that progress of an application has halted. This might occur at an easily recognizable level, such as the entire application seeming hung and not responding or when executing specific tasks in the application. A good indicator of a "hanging" application is the CPU usage of the application while performing a task that you know should generate an increase in CPU usage. CPU usage can easily be monitored by using Task Manager (CTRL+SHIFT+ESC). If, for example, your application uses 0% CPU while calculating $\pi$ to the 100,000th decimal, it is quite possible that the application has hung.

Another common symptom of hang is that the CPU has spiked in its usage but does not finish processing within expected time limits. Fundamentally, the application is in a "hung" state, but rather than being hung because two or more threads are waiting on each other using an efficient wait state, these same threads might not be making progress due to spinning viciously and thereby spiking the CPU usage.

If the application is exhibiting the symptoms of not making progress, you should move on to the next step in the process.

## Step 2: Dump Out All the Threads

Okay, so now you have an application that refuses to make any progress on the task at hand. You are fairly certain that you are dealing with a synchronization problem. What do you do next? Situations such as this warrant taking a closer look at the process to see if problems can be identified. Because these types of problems typically involve two or more threads that have not been synchronized properly, the first step is to attach a debugger and list all the threads with their associated stack trace. Looking at the threads and their stacks can give us clues to where to focus our efforts and where the problem might be. The easiest way to dump out all the threads and stack traces is by using the ~*kb command. Listing 10.5 shows the output of the command run on a newly started instance of notepad.exe.

**Listing 10.5**   Using the ~*kb command to dump all threads and associated stacks

```
0:001> ~*kb
0  Id: ea4.e9c Suspend: 1 Teb: 7ffdf000 Unfrozen
ChildEBP RetAddr  Args to Child
0007feb8 77d491be 77d491f1 0007fefc 00000000 ntdll!KiFastSystemCallRet
0007fed8 01002a1b 0007fefc 00000000 00000000 USER32!NtUserGetMessage+0xc
0007ff1c 01007511 01000000 00000000 00bd0ffb notepad!WinMain+0xe5
0007ffc0 7c816fd7 00090000 0007fa0c 7ffd5000 notepad!WinMainCRTStartup+0x174
0007fff0 00000000 0100739d 00000000 78746341 kernel32!BaseProcessStart+0x23

#  1  Id: ea4.974 Suspend: 1 Teb: 7ffde000 Unfrozen
ChildEBP RetAddr  Args to Child
02d5ffc8 7c9507a8 00000005 00000004 00000001 ntdll!DbgBreakPoint
02d5fff4 00000000 00000000 00000000 00000000 ntdll!DbgUiRemoteBreakin+0x2d
```

As can be seen from Listing 10.5, the process has only two threads active. The first thread appears to be the main message pump. (The second frame USER32!NtUserGetMessage+0xc is the clue.) The second thread is the debugger break thread and really has nothing to do with the application itself, as you will always see this type of thread anytime the debugger breaks execution.

After all threads are dumped out, it is time to see if any of them exhibit signs of synchronization problems.

## Step 3: Analyze Threads for Possible Synchronization Problems

A number of scenarios can lead to synchronization problems. This step identifies the offending threads. We defer the process of analyzing the threads to the "Synchronization Scenarios" section of the chapter, where we look at a number of common synchronization problems.

A very common indicator of improper synchronization techniques is when two or more threads are waiting for each other to release some synchronization primitive, but none of the threads are willing to release it until the other thread does so. The key to identifying this scenario is to understand what it means for a thread to "wait." A thread can go into a wait state using a myriad of different techniques. Most commonly, however, a thread will use one of two ways:

- By trying to acquire a synchronization primitive using the primitive's own API(s). A great example of this is when trying to enter a critical section (using the EnterCriticalSection API). A common stack trace in which a thread tries to enter a critical section but is unable to resembles the following:

```
1  Id: 25c.6e0 Suspend: 1 Teb: 7ffde000 Unfrozen
ChildEBP RetAddr  Args to Child
007eff18 7c90e9c0 7c91901b 000007f4 00000000 ntdll!KiFastSystemCallRet
007eff1c 7c91901b 000007f4 00000000 00000000 ntdll!NtWaitForSingleObject+0xc
007effa4 7c90104b 00002008 01001144 01002008 ntdll!RtlpWaitForCriticalSection+
0x132
007effac 01001144 01002008 7c80b683 00000000
ntdll!RtlEnterCriticalSection+0x46
007effb4 7c80b683 00000000 00081000 005cadf8 simple!ThreadProc+0xb
007effec 00000000 01001139 00000000 00000000 kernel32!BaseThreadStart+0x37
```

- If there is no specific API for the synchronization primitive (such is the case with all kernel mode synchronization primitives), the most common APIs used to wait are the WaitForSingleObject(/Ex) or WaitForMultipleObjects(/Ex) APIs. These API(s) take one or more handles to kernel mode synchronization primitives. A common stack trace in this scenario resembles

```
  1  Id: f38.b60 Suspend: 1 Teb: 7ffdd000 Unfrozen
ChildEBP RetAddr  Args to Child
007eff2c 7c90e9c0 7c8025cb 000007e8 00000000 ntdll!KiFastSystemCallRet
007eff30 7c8025cb 000007e8 00000000 00000000 ntdll!NtWaitForSingleObject+0xc
007eff94 7c802532 000007e8 ffffffff 00000000
kernel32!WaitForSingleObjectEx+0xa8
007effa8 01001147 000007e8 ffffffff 7c80b683 kernel32!WaitForSingleObject+0x12
007effb4 7c80b683 00000000 00081000 005cadf8 simple!ThreadProc+0xe
007effec 00000000 01001139 00000000 00000000 kernel32!BaseThreadStart+0x37
```

If any of the threads of interest are in this wait state, the next step is to see which of the threads might potentially not be making progress because of a synchronization problem.

If there are no threads in a wait state or if the threads that were in a wait state were all working fine, the next thing to look for is spinning threads. A number of different ways exist to find out which (if any) threads are spinning. The most basic involves setting breakpoints in suspicious threads at various spots in the call chain and looking to see when and how the breakpoint is hit and under which conditions the thread ends up spinning. This can be a rather time-consuming effort and, fortunately, there is a extension command that makes life simpler. The !runaway extension command lists all the threads according to how much time they have spent executing. An example of the !runaway extension command is shown here:

```
0:001> !runaway
User Mode Time
  Thread      Time
  0:9d8      0 days 0:00:00.046
  1:e48      0 days 0:00:00.000
```

The time shown for each thread is the time the thread has spent in user mode. From the output, we can see that the thread with an ID of 9d8 has been using the most user mode time. If you want a more detailed breakdown of the time the thread has spent executing, you can issue the runaway command and pass in a flags parameter. Specifying parameter 7 yields the most detailed information.

```
0:001> !runaway 7
User Mode Time
  Thread      Time
  0:9d8      0 days 0:00:00.046
  1:e48      0 days 0:00:00.000
Kernel Mode Time
```

```
Thread          Time
  0:9d8         0 days 0:00:00.031
  1:e48         0 days 0:00:00.000
Elapsed Time
Thread          Time
  0:9d8         0 days 0:00:38.000
  1:e48         0 days 0:00:36.734
```

The user mode and kernel mode times specify the amount of time each thread has been executing in that context. The elapsed time shows how long the thread has been executing since it started (independent of whether the thread was utilizing the CPU).

In a scenario in which the application is hung due to one or more threads spinning, this command can very quickly tell you which threads are spinning.

After the culprit threads have been identified and the source of the problem has been found, the next step of the process is to look for an appropriate fix.

## Step 4: Fix the Problem

Depending on the nature of the synchronization problem, there can be several different fixes. For example, deadlocks are fixed by ensuring that the condition in which the deadlock occurs is resolved, orphaned locks are fixed by ensuring that all lock acquisitions are followed by the appropriate release calls, and lock convoys can be fixed by redesigning the code to eliminate contentious locks. We look at a variety of techniques for fixing synchronization problems in more detail in the "Synchronization Scenarios" section of the chapter.

The last step of the process is to define a future avoidance strategy and make sure that the problem diagnosed and fixed does not surface again.

## Step 5: Define Future Avoidance Strategy

As computer scientists, we often pride ourselves on our ability to manage complexity. Just as important as figuring out complex problems, we also need to ensure that similar problems do not reappear in the future. This final step of the process takes what we have learned investigating a synchronization problem and devises a plan for how to avoid similar problems in the future. This might be in the form of changing engineering practices to using tools that can uncover problems early on in the development process.

# Synchronization Scenarios

This part of the chapter shows examples of some of the most common forms of synchronization problems. It shows how to use the debuggers to efficiently track down the problem to find the root cause and what tools and techniques can be used to prevent similar problems in the future.

## Basic Deadlock

Deadlocks are perhaps the most common and frustrating problems that developers encounter when writing multithreaded applications. In essence, a deadlock occurs when two or more threads hold protected resources and refuse to let go of those resources until others have let go of theirs. Because none of threads are willing to release their protected resources, what ultimately happens is that none of the threads will ever make any progress. They simply sit there and wait for the others to make a move, and a deadlock ensues. A deadlock can occur tons of different ways, and we take a look at some common ones throughout this chapter. However, before getting into some of the more complicated cases, we illustrate a simple and simulated deadlock scenario. This will give you a good idea of what a deadlock looks like in the debugger and the commands that can be used to get to the bottom of the deadlock.

The sample application we use to illustrate the deadlock is rather simplistic and is shown in Listing 10.6.

**Listing 10.6**   Sample application that results in a deadlock

```
#include <windows.h>
#include <stdio.h>
#include <conio.h>

CRITICAL_SECTION cs_DB1;
CRITICAL_SECTION cs_DB2;

DWORD WINAPI ThreadProc( LPVOID lpParam )
{
    EnterCriticalSection(&cs_DB1);

    //
    // Do work on stack
    //
    printf("Updating database 1\n");
    Sleep(3000);
```

```
    EnterCriticalSection(&cs_DB2);

    printf("Updating database 2\n");

    LeaveCriticalSection(&cs_DB2);
    LeaveCriticalSection(&cs_DB1);

    return 1;
}

void __cdecl main ( )
{
    HANDLE hThread=NULL;
    DWORD dwId=0;

    InitializeCriticalSection(&cs_DB1);
    InitializeCriticalSection(&cs_DB2);

    hThread = CreateThread(NULL, 0, ThreadProc, NULL, 0, &dwId);
    if(hThread)
    {
        Sleep(2000);
        EnterCriticalSection(&cs_DB2);

        printf("Updating database 2\n");
        Sleep(2000);
        EnterCriticalSection(&cs_DB1);

        printf("Updating database 1\n");

        LeaveCriticalSection(&cs_DB1);
        LeaveCriticalSection(&cs_DB2);

        WaitForSingleObject(hThread, INFINITE);
        CloseHandle(hThread);
    }

    DeleteCriticalSection(&cs_DB1);
    DeleteCriticalSection(&cs_DB2);
}
```

The source code and binary for Listing 10.6 can be found in the following folders:

> Source code: `C:\AWD\Chapter10\DeadLock`
> Binary: `C:\AWDBIN\WinXP.x86.chk\10DeadLock.exe`

The application is a multithreaded application (two threads) that uses two different databases. Each thread needs access to both databases to be capable of performing its work. Because the underlying database access API(s) are not thread safe, the application uses two critical sections, each protecting one database. To avoid polluting the sample code, the code that uses the databases is simulated by simply putting the thread to sleep for a number of milliseconds. When you run this application, you will quickly see that it never finishes. In this simple application, you might have already spotted the problem in the code, but let's attach a debugger to a running instance and see what is actually happening. The first step is to dump out all the threads currently running in the process, which is illustrated in Listing 10.7.

**Listing 10.7**   All thread stacks currently running in the process

```
0:002> ~*kb
   0  Id: 978.960 Suspend: 1 Teb: 7ffde000 Unfrozen
ChildEBP RetAddr  Args to Child
0006fe9c 7c90e9c0 7c91901b 000007dc 00000000 ntdll!KiFastSystemCallRet
0006fea0 7c91901b 000007dc 00000000 00000000 ntdll!NtWaitForSingleObject+0xc
0006ff28 7c90104b 00002008 01001286 01002008 ntdll!RtlpWaitForCriticalSection+0x132
0006ff30 01001286 01002008 000007e8 00001210 ntdll!RtlEnterCriticalSection+0x46
0006ff44 01001406 00000001 00264e20 00263328 10DeadLock!main+0x86
0006ffc0 7c816fd7 00090000 0007fa0c 7ffdf000 10DeadLock!mainCRTStartup+0x12f
0006fff0 00000000 010012d7 00000000 78746341 kernel32!BaseProcessStart+0x23

   1  Id: 978.1210 Suspend: 1 Teb: 7ffdd000 Unfrozen
ChildEBP RetAddr  Args to Child
002bff14 7c90e9c0 7c91901b 000007f4 00000000 ntdll!KiFastSystemCallRet
002bff18 7c91901b 000007f4 00000000 00000000 ntdll!NtWaitForSingleObject+0xc
002bffa0 7c90104b 00002020 010011c4 01002020 ntdll!RtlpWaitForCriticalSection+0x132
002bffa8 010011c4 01002020 002bffec 7c80b683 ntdll!RtlEnterCriticalSection+0x46
002bffb4 7c80b683 00000000 000822c8 02080028 10DeadLock!ThreadProc+0x34
002bffec 00000000 01001190 00000000 00000000 kernel32!BaseThreadStart+0x37

#  2  Id: 978.1074 Suspend: 1 Teb: 7ffdc000 Unfrozen
ChildEBP RetAddr  Args to Child
002fffb4 7c80b683 00000000 00919920 0308f7dc kernel32!CtrlRoutine+0xbd
002fffec 00000000 7c875280 00000000 00000000 kernel32!BaseThreadStart+0x37
```

Albeit simplistic, the threads shown in Listing 10.7 illustrate a very common recognition technique for deadlocks. Two (or more) threads are each waiting to acquire a different critical section, but nothing seems to be happening. To verify that our assumption of a deadlock is indeed correct, we need to take a closer look at the critical sections involved. How do we find the address of the critical section for each thread? From the stacks, we can see that our code is calling the `RtlEnterCriticalSection` API. It seems a bit odd considering that our code is using the `EnterCriticalSection` API. What is going on here is that `EnterCriticalSection` (defined in `kernel32.dll`) is simply an API forwarder to `RtlEnterCriticalSection` (defined in `ntdll.dll`). You can easily detect which API(s) are forwarders by using the linker as illustrated here (abbreviated output):

```
C:\>link /dump /exports %SystemRoot%\system32\kernel32.dll
Microsoft (R) COFF/PE Dumper Version 7.10.4035
Copyright (C) Microsoft Corporation.  All rights reserved.


Dump of file kernel32.dll


File Type: DLL

  Section contains the following exports for KERNEL32.dll

    00000000 characteristics
    44AB7FD3 time date stamp Wed Jul 05 02:01:07 2006
        0.00 version
           1 ordinal base
         949 number of functions
         949 number of names

  ordinal hint RVA       name

          1    0 0000A644 ActivateActCtx
          2    1 000354ED AddAtomA
          3    2 000326C1 AddAtomW
          4    3 00070CBF AddConsoleAliasA
          5    4 00070C81 AddConsoleAliasW
          6    5 00058F26 AddLocalAlternateComputerNameA
          7    6 00058E0A AddLocalAlternateComputerNameW
          8    7 0002BF01 AddRefActCtx
          ...
          ...
          ...
        151   96          EnterCriticalSection (forwarded to NTDLL.RtlEnterCriticalSection)
        152   97 00038211 EnumCalendarInfoA
```

```
153    98 00075749 EnumCalendarInfoExA
   ...
   ...
   ...
```

Because the `EnterCriticalSection` API is just a forwarder, we can also reasonably expect the parameters to the forwarded function to be identical. More specifically, the first parameter to `RtlEnterCriticalSection` should be the address to the critical section. In Listing 10.7, we see that the first thread is calling `RtlEnterCriticalSection`, and the first parameter passed is `01001286`. We can now use the `!cs` extension command to dump out the fields of the critical section:

```
0:002> !cs 01002008
----------------------
Critical section    = 0x01002008 (10DeadLock!cs_DB1+0x0)
DebugInfo           = 0x7c97c8c0
LOCKED
LockCount           = 0x1
OwningThread        = 0x00001210
RecursionCount      = 0x1
LockSemaphore       = 0x7DC
SpinCount           = 0x00000000
```

A lot of information exists in the critical section data structure that we can make use of. Besides the obvious fact that the critical section is in a LOCKED state, the first field, "Critical section," gives us a symbolic reference to the critical section (in our case `10DeadLock!cs_DB1+0x0`). This immediately tells us that the critical section in question relates to the first database in the application. We can also very quickly see which thread is currently holding the critical section—namely thread `0x1210`. But, which thread has an ID of `0x1210`? The top line of each stack trace shows us a number of different IDs. In Listing 10.7, we can see that the top of the stack contains the following:

```
Id: 978.960 Suspend: 1 Teb: 7ffde000 Unfrozen
```

The two numbers in bold serve to identify two entities: The first number identifies the process, and the second the thread. So, the first thread in our process has an ID of `0x960`. Using the same mechanism, we can easily see that the thread corresponding to thread ID `0x1210` is our second thread. Using the same mechanism of dumping out the critical section that the second thread is trying to acquire, we see the following:

```
0:002> !cs 01002020
----------------------
```

```
Critical section    = 0x01002020 (10DeadLock!cs_DB2+0x0)
DebugInfo           = 0x7c97c8e0
LOCKED
LockCount           = 0x1
OwningThread        = 0x00000960
RecursionCount      = 0x1
LockSemaphore       = 0x7F4
SpinCount           = 0x00000000
```

Once again, we see that the lock in question is our second database lock and that the owning thread is a thread with ID of 0x960 (which also happens to be our first thread). The picture should now be clear. The first thread in our process is holding the second database lock while waiting for the first database lock to become available. The second thread holds the critical section associated with the first database lock while waiting for the second to become available. The net result is a deadlocked application.

Now that we know which threads are deadlocking on what, the final step is to do source code analysis to try to break the deadlock. From our simple example, it should be quite evident why the deadlock happened and how it can be broken.

Unfortunately, not a whole lot of help (in the form of tools) is available for developers wanting to more efficiently track down deadlocks. It's mostly a matter of being able to detect the deadlock and manually use the debugger to get the information necessary to resolve it. One potential technique exists that allows you to be notified if the debugger *believes* that a deadlock might be occurring. That technique comes in the form of a registry value located at

```
HKEY_LOCAL_MACHINE\SYSTEM\CurrentControlSet\Control\Session Manager\CriticalSection-
Timeout
```

This value specifies the number of seconds (default is the number of seconds in 30 days) that a critical section is allowed to be held before the debugger displays a warning message. Changing this setting requires a system reboot for the changes to go into effect. Let's try it on our sample application. Start by changing the value to 60 (1 minute), reboot the system, and rerun the application under the debugger. After about 60 seconds, you should see the following debug spew:

```
0:000> g
Updating database 1
Updating database 2
RTL: Enter Critical Section Timeout (60 secs) 0
RTL: Pid.Tid e9c.eb8, owner tid ea0 Critical Section 01002020 - ContentionCount == 1
RTL: Re-Waiting
RTL: Enter Critical Section Timeout (60 secs) 0
```

```
RTL: Pid.Tid e9c.ea0, owner tid eb8 Critical Section 01002008 - ContentionCount == 1
RTL: Re-Waiting
```

What the system is doing is giving the critical section another chance by rewaiting after the expired time period. Eventually, though, the debugger will break execution and display the following:

```
Possible Deadlock in ntdll!RtlInitializeSListHead Lock 10DeadLock!cs_DB2 (01002020)
Possible Deadlock in ntdll!RtlInitializeSListHead Lock 10DeadLock!cs_DB2 (01002020)
!!! second chance !!!
eax=002bff38 ebx=00000000 ecx=7c910833 edx=000000d8 esi=01002020 edi=7c97c140
eip=7c942426 esp=002bff2c ebp=002bffa0 iopl=0         nv up ei pl zr na po nc
cs=001b  ss=0023  ds=0023  es=0023  fs=003b  gs=0000              efl=00000246
ntdll!RtlInitializeSListHead+0x9416:
7c942426 68ca24947c         push    0x7c9424ca
```

If you have very specific lock duration times in your application, this technique can be used to detect *possible* deadlocks.

Although we have shown a deadlock in the context of a critical section, it is important to note that any synchronization primitive can yield a deadlock if not used properly.

## Orphaned Critical Section Scenario 1—Exceptions

Writing well-behaved code in the presence of exceptions can be a daunting task, especially when coupled with multithreading. Although most of the Win32 API(s) are exception free, there are some exceptions, and care must be taken when using them. In this section, we take a look at a scenario involving an application that makes use of C++ exceptions. The application code is shown in Listing 10.8.

**Listing 10.8**   Sample application that utilizes exceptions

```
#include <windows.h>
#include <stdio.h>
#include <conio.h>

CRITICAL_SECTION g_cs;

class InvalidParameterException{};

VOID Call3rdPartyCode(LPVOID lpParam)
{
    if(lpParam==NULL)
    {
```

```
            throw InvalidParameterException();
    }

    //
    // Do some work
    //
}

DWORD WINAPI ThreadProc(LPVOID lpParam)
{
    DWORD dwRet=1;

    try
    {
        EnterCriticalSection(&g_cs);
        Call3rdPartyCode(lpParam);
        LeaveCriticalSection(&g_cs);
    }
    catch(...)
    {
        // Error occured
        dwRet=0;
    }

    return dwRet;
}

void __cdecl main ( )
{
    DWORD dwId=0;
    HANDLE hThread=NULL;

    InitializeCriticalSection(&g_cs);

    hThread = CreateThread(NULL, 0, ThreadProc, NULL, 0, &dwId);
    if(hThread)
    {
        Sleep(500);

        printf("Acquiring critical section\n");

        EnterCriticalSection(&g_cs);

        //
        // Do some work
```

*(continues)*

**Listing 10.8** Sample application that utilizes exceptions *(continued)*

```
    //

    printf("Leaving critical section\n");
    LeaveCriticalSection(&g_cs);

    WaitForSingleObject(hThread, INFINITE);
    CloseHandle(hThread);
    }

    DeleteCriticalSection(&g_cs);
}
```

The source code and binary for Listing 10.8 can be found in the following folders:

> Source code: `C:\AWD\Chapter10\Exceptions`
> Binary: `C:\AWDBIN\WinXP.x86.chk\10Exception.exe`

As you can see, the code in Listing 10.8 is pretty straightforward. The main thread starts by initializing a global critical section followed by the creation of a new thread. After the thread has been successfully created, it then tries to enter the global critical section to perform some work. When done, it leaves the critical section and waits for the worker thread to finish.

The worker thread's job is to call into some third-party code (perhaps a dynamically loaded DLL) under the protection of the global critical section. The code also makes an attempt at being exception safe by wrapping the call with a `try`/`catch` statement, attempting to catch all exceptions thrown, and then it returns a failure code if an exception is thrown.

Although the application is a very poorly designed application, it nevertheless illustrates a very common problem. Before we get into all the different problems with the application, let's run it and see what the final outcome is:

```
 C:\AWDBIN\WinXP.x86.chk\10Exception.exe
Acquiring critical section
```

All that appears to be happening is that the application hangs when trying to acquire a critical section. Let's take a look at the state of the threads in the process by attaching the debugger to the process and dumping out all the threads, illustrated in Listing 10.9.

**Listing 10.9**  Sample application thread state

```
0:001> ~*kb

   0  Id: 424.ba8 Suspend: 1 Teb: 7ffdf000 Unfrozen
ChildEBP RetAddr  Args to Child
0007fe9c 7c90e9c0 7c91901b 000007e8 00000000 ntdll!KiFastSystemCallRet
0007fea0 7c91901b 000007e8 00000000 7c97c140 ntdll!NtWaitForSingleObject+0xc
0007ff28 7c90104b 00002038 010012e5 01002038 ntdll!RtlpWaitForCriticalSection+0x132
0007ff30 010012e5 01002038 000007f4 0000020c ntdll!RtlEnterCriticalSection+0x46
0007ff44 01001459 00000001 00034e50 00033338 10Exception!main+0x65
0007ffc0 7c816fd7 00090000 0007fa0c 7ffd8000 10Exception!mainCRTStartup+0x12f
0007fff0 00000000 0100132a 00000000 78746341 kernel32!BaseProcessStart+0x23


#  1  Id: 424.dfc Suspend: 1 Teb: 7ffde000 Unfrozen
ChildEBP RetAddr  Args to Child
002bffb4 7c80b683 00000000 00000000 00000000 kernel32!CtrlRoutine+0xbd
002bffec 00000000 7c875280 00000000 00000000 kernel32!BaseThreadStart+0x37
```

Listing 10.9 indicates that the main thread is waiting to acquire a critical section but is not capable of doing so. To find out why, we have to dump out the critical section in question and see what information it might provide us:

```
0:001> !cs 01002038
--------------------
Critical section   = 0x01002038 (10Exception!g_cs+0x0)
DebugInfo          = 0x7c97c8c0
LOCKED
LockCount          = 0x1
OwningThread       = 0x0000020c
RecursionCount     = 0x1
LockSemaphore      = 0x7E8
SpinCount          = 0x00000000
```

The critical section is in a locked state, and the owning thread is 0x20c. Because none of the threads in our process has an ID of 0x20c, it stands to reason that at one point, this mysterious thread acquired the critical section but never released it. The only other thread is our worker thread, so could it be the culprit? Possibly, as it definitely tries to acquire a critical section:

```
EnterCriticalSection(&g_cs);
Call3rdPartyCode(lpParam);
LeaveCriticalSection(&g_cs);
```

The only problem is that it also leaves the critical section properly after the call to the third-party code; hence, the critical section should be in a good state. Although that might be our first impression, looking closer at the code reveals the seemingly innocent `try`/`catch` block that surrounds the critical section code. Essentially, because the thread is calling into some third-party code, it wants to do everything it can to protect itself from the code throwing any type of exception; therefore, it tries to catch all exceptions that might come out of it. Although one could argue that this isn't the best way of protecting yourself, there is an even bigger problem looming on the horizon. What actually happens if the third-party code throws an exception? Well, the catch all filter is executed, where it sets the return to indicate an error, and then the thread simply exits. Did we leave the critical section that was acquired prior to calling the third-party code? Absolutely not! The only code that gets executed in this scenario is the catch filter, and we end up with an orphaned critical section. I leave it as an exercise to the reader to verify in the debugger that this is what is actually happening. Hint: Remember the seemingly invalid thread ID that the critical section is owned by from the main thread.

Now we know why the application hung: a worker thread orphaned a critical section while going about its business. In addition to the poor attempt of trying to protect itself by catching all exceptions, the question of holding a lock while calling into some third-party code is brought up. Is that a safe thing to do? Generally speaking, the answer is no. Because you have no idea of what this third-party code might do, holding a critical section while calling it can lead to other devastating problems. Imagine that the third-party code tried to call back on some API that required the same critical section to be acquired. If the API isn't designed to handle a reentry, a deadlock occurs. As a general rule of thumb, developers must exercise extreme caution when dealing with third-party code and trying to protect their code from all the different mishaps that can result.

Say that the developer who wrote the code in Listing 10.9 was set against making any substantial changes to it. Can anything be done to make it at least behave slightly better? Absolutely! The developer can make sure that the critical section is released properly, even in the presence of exceptions, by making sure that it is released in the exception-handling code. If the application becomes more and more complex, scattering calls to `LeaveCriticalSection` all over the place becomes a nightmare. One possible way of more efficiently eliminating the need to scatter these calls is to let the language itself lend you a helping hand. Remember that when an exception is thrown (and not caught), the compiler generates stack unwinding code that enables the exception to percolate down the stack trace. If we can somehow inject the process of releasing the critical section into this stack unwinding process, we could be guaranteed that it will be released. As part of the stack unwinding, the compiler generates code that cleans up any variables defined within the scope. Because a critical section is just a structure with no associated code, the compiler doesn't do anything with it. We can, however, make it do something by wrapping the critical section functionality in a class whose lifetime is tightly coupled to the lifetime of the critical section. Listing 10.10 shows a basic example of a critical section class.

**Listing 10.10**   Critical section class that handles the lifetime of a critical section

```
class CCriticalSection
{
public:
    CCriticalSection(CRITICAL_SECTION* pCs)
    {
        m_pCs = pCs;
        if(m_pCs)
        {
            EnterCriticalSection(m_pCs);
        }
    }

    ~CCriticalSection()
    {
        if(m_pCs)
        {
            LeaveCriticalSection(m_pCs);
        }
    }

private:
    CRITICAL_SECTION* m_pCs;
};
```

The CCriticalSection class in Listing 10.10 is a pretty minimalist version of an auto-critical section class and can easily be extended to provide more advanced functionality, but it serves to illustrate the power of wrapping the act of entering and leaving critical sections in a more automated way. To illustrate how this class can be used, the ThreadProc function can now be rewritten as follows:

```
DWORD WINAPI ThreadProc(LPVOID lpParam)
{
    DWORD dwRet=1;
    CCriticalSection cs(&g_cs);
```

```
try
{
    //EnterCriticalSection(&g_cs);
    Call3rdPartyCode(lpParam);
    //LeaveCriticalSection(&g_cs);
}
catch(...)
{
    // Error occured
    dwRet=0;
}

return dwRet;
}
```

As you can see, the explicit calls to the enter and leave critical sections have now been replaced by an instance of the CCriticalSection class initialized with the critical section of interest. At construction time, the critical section is entered, and at destruction time, it is left. In the presence of exceptions, this works beautifully, as the compiler ensures that any local variables are destroyed as part of the stack unwinding.

In addition to using the language itself, Application Verifier provides a whole set of critical section tests that can be used by enabling the Basics test setting. Run Application Verifier and enable the Basics test setting for the preceding sample application (prior to using the CCriticalSection auto class). When enabled, run the application under the debugger and watch the results:

```
0:000> g
ModLoad: 5cb70000 5cb96000   C:\WINDOWS\system32\ShimEng.dll
(8fc.4bc): C++ EH exception - code e06d7363 (first chance)
=========================================
VERIFIER STOP 00000200 : pid 0x8FC: Thread cannot own a critical section.

        000004BC : Thread ID.
        01002038 : Critical section address.
        7C97CC00 : Critical section debug information address.
        00000000 : Critical section initialization stack trace.


=========================================
This verifier stop is continuable.
After debugging it use `go' to continue.


=========================================
```

```
(8fc.4bc): Break instruction exception - code 80000003 (first chance)
eax=00000000 ebx=003c5638 ecx=7c91eb05 edx=00e6fa9f esi=00000000 edi=000004bc
eip=7c901230 esp=00e6fb58 ebp=00e6fd24 iopl=0         nv up ei pl nz na pe nc
cs=001b  ss=0023  ds=0023  es=0023  fs=003b  gs=0000            efl=00000202
ntdll!DbgBreakPoint:
7c901230 cc              int     3
```

As the thread is about to terminate, Application Verifier tracks down any locked critical sections owned by that thread and breaks execution if any are found. This enables the developer to take a closer look at why a thread that owns a critical section is terminating without releasing it. The good part about enabling Application Verifier is that it catches a lot of synchronization problems when they occur and not afterward, making debugging much, much easier.

## Orphaned Critical Section Scenario 2—Thread Termination

One of the most typical requirements of a multithreaded application is for any given worker thread to be capable of shutting down in a very efficient manner. This might be due to the user cancelling the specific request that the worker thread was servicing or an application shut down, which should quickly stop all the worker threads in the process. One very easy and compelling way of accomplishing this is to call the `TerminateThread` API, which stops a thread dead in its track. If all the threads are independent of each other (that is, share no data and perform very simple work), there should be no harm in doing so, right? The answer is maybe. It all depends on what type of work is being done in the worker thread. Terminating even the simplest of threads can lead to devastating results. To illustrate the point, the application shown in Listing 10.11 creates one worker thread that sits in a tight loop allocating memory, using that memory and deallocating the memory. The main thread then terminates the worker thread (using the `TerminateThread` API) and does some final work before shutting down.

**Listing 10.11**   Simple application utilizing the TerminateThread API

```
#include <windows.h>
#include <stdio.h>
#include <conio.h>


DWORD WINAPI ThreadProc( LPVOID lpParam )
{
    BYTE* pData=NULL;
```

*(continues)*

**Listing 10.11**   Simple application utilizing the TerminateThread API *(continued)*

```
    for(;;)
    {
        pData=(BYTE*) HeapAlloc(GetProcessHeap(), 0, 10000);
        //
        // Use memory
        //
        HeapFree(GetProcessHeap(), 0, pData);
    }

    printf("Exiting thread\n");
    return 1;
}

void __cdecl main ( )
{
    DWORD dwId=0;
    HANDLE hThread=NULL;

    hThread = CreateThread(NULL, 0, ThreadProc, NULL, 0, &dwId);
    if(hThread)
    {
        BYTE* pData=NULL;
        Sleep(500);

        printf("Terminating worker thread...\n");
        TerminateThread(hThread, 0);

        pData = (BYTE*) HeapAlloc(GetProcessHeap(), 0, 10000);
        if(pData)
        {
            //
            // Use memory
            //
            HeapFree(GetProcessHeap(), 0, pData);
        }
        WaitForSingleObject(hThread, INFINITE);
        CloseHandle(hThread);
    }
}
```

The source code and binary for Listing 10.11 can be found in the following folders:

> Source code: `C:\AWD\Chapter10\TerminateThread`
> Binary: `C:\AWDBIN\WinXP.x86.chk\10TermThread.exe`

Execute this application using the following command line:

`C:\AWDBIN\WinXP.x86.chk\10TermThread.exe`

Please note that the application is timing dependent. When you run the application, you might find that it finished execution successfully. If it does, rerun the application a few times, and you will eventually see that the application gets into a state in which it never finishes and simply appears hung. Let's take a closer look by attaching a debugger to the process and dumping out all the threads and associated stacks, as shown in Listing 10.12.

**Listing 10.12**   Thread list and associated stacks of hung application

```
...
...
...
0:001> ~*kb

   0  Id: 404.9dc Suspend: 1 Teb: 7ffdd000 Unfrozen
ChildEBP RetAddr  Args to Child
0006fc64 7c90e9c0 7c91901b 000007f4 00000000 ntdll!KiFastSystemCallRet
0006fc68 7c91901b 000007f4 00000000 00000000 ntdll!NtWaitForSingleObject+0xc
0006fcf0 7c90104b 00080608 7c911320 00080608 ntdll!RtlpWaitForCriticalSection+0x132
0006fcf8 7c911320 00080608 00090000 0007fa0c ntdll!RtlEnterCriticalSection+0x46
0006ff24 01001236 00080000 00000000 00002710 ntdll!RtlAllocateHeap+0x2f0
0006ff44 010013a2 00000001 00263b50 00262bb0 10TermThread!main+0x76
0006ffc0 7c816fd7 00090000 0007fa0c 7ffde000 10TermThread!mainCRTStartup+0x12f
0006fff0 00000000 01001273 00000000 78746341 kernel32!BaseProcessStart+0x23

#  1  Id: 404.870 Suspend: 1 Teb: 7ffdc000 Unfrozen
ChildEBP RetAddr  Args to Child
002fffb4 7c80b683 00000000 77d4882a 00000000 kernel32!CtrlRoutine+0xbd
002fffec 00000000 7c875280 00000000 00000000 kernel32!BaseThreadStart+0x37
```

The first thread in Listing 10.12 definitely looks interesting, as it seems to be waiting for a critical section. Because we don't use any critical sections in our application, you might be inclined to ask why the thread is waiting for one to begin with. To answer this very reasonable question, we need to get some basic information about the thread. Is it one of our threads? If so, what is the thread doing? Looking at the bottommost frames of the thread, we can see that it is indeed our main thread and that it is trying to allocate some memory from the heap. This matches up nicely with our source listing (in bold) in Listing 10.11. Moving up the stack, we see that the `RtlAllocateHeap` function attempts to enter a critical section that ultimately results in a `WaitForSingleObject` call. At this point, a safe assumption is that the critical section is already owned by a different thread, but, as always, we need to make sure that we verify our theories. To find out more detailed information about the critical section in question, we first need to find the address to it. Let's use the `!cs` extension command with that address and see if it resembles a good critical section:

```
0:001> !cs 00080608
--------------------
Critical section    = 0x00080608 (+0x80608)
DebugInfo           = 0x7c97c500
LOCKED
LockCount           = 0x1
OwningThread        = 0x00000224
RecursionCount      = 0x1
LockSemaphore       = 0x7F4
SpinCount           = 0x00000000
```

The `LOCKED` line indicates that the critical section is held. The `OwningThread` field value of `0x224` indicates that a thread with the thread ID of `0x224` is holding the critical section. The `LockSemaphore` field has the value of `0x7F4`. Because we know that `LockSemaphore` corresponds to an event handle, we can use the `!handle` extension command to make sure that it is an event:

```
0:001> !handle 0x7F4
Handle 7f4
  Type          Event
```

At this point, we can safely say that we are working with what looks to be an intact critical section, but the biggest question remains: Which thread is holding this critical section? We only have two threads running in our process, and neither thread has a thread ID of `0x224`. From Listing 10.1, we know that the main thread terminated a worker thread, so it is quite reasonable to assume that our worker thread had a thread ID of `0x224`. To verify this assumption, we can restart the application under the debugger, set a breakpoint at the start of our worker thread procedure (`ThreadProc`), and resume execution. After the breakpoint hits, we check to see what the thread ID is and continue execution until the hang appears again. We then dump the critical section and make sure that the owning thread ID matches the thread ID of the worker thread (see Listing 10.13).

**Listing 10.13**   Identifying the owning thread of the problematic critical section

```
0:000> bp 10TermThread!ThreadProc
0:000> g
Breakpoint 0 hit
eax=00000000 ebx=00000000 ecx=002bffb0 edx=7c90eb94 esi=000822c8 edi=00680066
eip=01001180 esp=002bffb8 ebp=002bffec iopl=0         nv up ei pl zr na po nc
cs=001b  ss=0023  ds=0023  es=0023  fs=003b  gs=0000          efl=00000246
10TermThread!ThreadProc:
01001180 8bff               mov     edi,edi
0:001> ~
   0  Id: ea8.ea0 Suspend: 1 Teb: 7ffdf000 Unfrozen
.  1  Id: ea8.e68 Suspend: 1 Teb: 7ffde000 Unfrozen
0:001> g
Terminating worker thread...
(ea8.fa4): Control-C exception - code 40010005 (first chance)
First chance exceptions are reported before any exception handling.
This exception may be expected and handled.
eax=002fff38 ebx=00000000 ecx=002fff04 edx=7c90eb94 esi=00000000 edi=00000002
eip=7c87533d esp=002fff2c ebp=002fffb4 iopl=0         nv up ei pl zr na po nc
cs=001b  ss=0023  ds=0023  es=0023  fs=003b  gs=0000          efl=00000246
kernel32!CtrlRoutine+0xbd:
7c87533d 834dfcff or dword ptr [ebp-0x4],0xffffffff ss:0023:002fffb0=00000000
0:001> ~*kb

   0  Id: ea8.ea0 Suspend: 1 Teb: 7ffdf000 Unfrozen
ChildEBP RetAddr  Args to Child
0006fc64 7c90e9c0 7c91901b 000007f4 00000000 ntdll!KiFastSystemCallRet
0006fc68 7c91901b 000007f4 00000000 00000000 ntdll!NtWaitForSingleObject+0xc
0006fcf0 7c90104b 00080608 7c911320 00080608 ntdll!RtlpWaitForCriticalSection+0x132
0006fcf8 7c911320 00080608 00090000 0007fa0c ntdll!RtlEnterCriticalSection+0x46
0006ff24 01001236 00080000 00000000 00002710 ntdll!RtlAllocateHeap+0x2f0
0006ff44 010013a2 00000001 00263b78 00262bb0 10TermThread!main+0x76
0006ffc0 7c816fd7 00090000 0007fa0c 7ffd9000 10TermThread!mainCRTStartup+0x12f
0006fff0 00000000 01001273 00000000 78746341 kernel32!BaseProcessStart+0x23

#  1  Id: ea8.fa4 Suspend: 1 Teb: 7ffde000 Unfrozen
ChildEBP RetAddr  Args to Child
002fffb4 7c80b683 00000000 0000000d 0199fe64 kernel32!CtrlRoutine+0xbd
002fffec 00000000 7c875280 00000000 00000000 kernel32!BaseThreadStart+0x37
0:001> !cs 00080608
```

*(continues)*

**Listing 10.13**   Identifying the owning thread of the problematic critical section *(continued)*

```
--------------------
Critical section    = 0x00080608 (+0x80608)
DebugInfo           = 0x7c97c500
LOCKED
LockCount           = 0x1
OwningThread        = 0x00000e68
RecursionCount      = 0x1
LockSemaphore       = 0x7F4
SpinCount           = 0x00000000
```

As you can see from the debug output in Listing 10.13, the worker thread ID has an ID of e68. The critical section being held indefinitely also indicates that the thread that owns the critical section is e68. Because the worker thread was terminated before having a chance to release the critical section, we end up with what is known as an orphaned critical section.

This scenario serves to illustrate that developers have to be extremely cautious when using Win32 API(s). The sample code we just debugged did not have a single critical section in it, yet we managed to stop it dead in its tracks, blocking on a critical section. It turns out that the critical section is owned by the heap manager, and when the main thread terminated the worker thread, the worker thread was in the middle of allocating or deallocating memory. That typically causes the heap manager to acquire the critical section. When the worker thread terminated, the heap manager never had the chance to leave the critical section. Although the tight loop of allocating/deallocating memory in the worker thread is an exaggerated piece of code, it serves to illustrate the importance of understanding your API(s), as well as clearly showing a debugging session for a very common problem. As a general rule of thumb, you should never call `TerminateThread` unless you know *exactly* what the thread is doing.

To make sure that we remember the dangers of calling `TerminateThread`, Application Verifier can be used. By enabling the DangerousAPIs test setting under the Miscellaneous branch on our application, we can rest assured that Application Verifier will trap all calls to the `TerminateThread` API. Enabling this test setting for our sample application and running it under the debugger yields the following:

```
0:000> g
Terminating worker thread...


==========================================
```

```
VERIFIER STOP 00000100 : pid 0x9F8: Dangerous call to TerminateThread.

    00000B28 : Thread ID for the caller of Terminatethread.
    00000000 : Not used.
    00000000 : Not used.
    00000000 : Not used.


=======================================
This verifier stop is continuable.
After debugging it use `go' to continue.


=======================================

(9f8.b28): Break instruction exception - code 80000003 (first chance)
eax=00000000 ebx=003b5470 ecx=7c91eb05 edx=0006fc15 esi=00000000 edi=00000b28
eip=7c901230 esp=0006fd04 ebp=0006fed0 iopl=0         nv up ei pl nz na pe nc
cs=001b  ss=0023  ds=0023  es=0023  fs=003b  gs=0000           efl=00000202
ntdll!DbgBreakPoint:
7c901230 cc              int     3
```

As you can see from the output, the debugger breaks execution immediately after detecting the call to `TerminateThread` and also displays a warning message. Additionally, the thread ID of the offending thread is displayed.

## DllMain Awareness

Dynamic Link Libraries (DLLs) are fundamental constructs in the Windows operating system. At a high level, a DLL is a file that contains executable code and/or data that applications can use. This, in essence, is very similar to a static link library, but rather than forcing the application into linking with a static link library, the application is free to use a DLL dynamically. DLL(s) can be loaded at load time or runtime so that the application can choose what code/data to use, depending on what is being executed in the application. An application can use a DLL in two ways:

- Implicit linking: With implicit linking, the application using the DLL links against an import library provided by the author of the DLL. The DLL is then automatically loaded when the application is loaded. The functions exported by the DLL can be called in the application as if they were part of the application.
- Explicit linking: With explicit linking, the application must make explicit calls to load (LoadLibrary), unload (FreeLibrary), and use the DLL's functions (GetProcAddress). The functions are then called using function pointers.

For a DLL to initialize and uninitialize itself, a special function named DllMain can be exported from the DLL. The function prototype of DllMain resembles the following:

```
BOOL WINAPI DllMain(HINSTANCE hinstDLL, DWORD fdwReason, LPVOID lpvReserved);
```

Each of the arguments is discussed here:

- hinstDLL
  Handle to the DLL module.
- fdwReason
  The DllMain function can be invoked for a number of reasons. It gets invoked when the DLL is loaded into the address space of an application (DLL_PROCESS_ATTACH), when a thread is created in the application (DLL_THREAD_ATTACH), and conversely when a DLL is detached from a process (DLL_PROCESS_DETACH) or a thread is exiting cleanly (DLL_THREAD_DETACH).
- lpvReserved
  Not used.

If the DLL is a relatively simple one that exports a set of functions that do not depend on state, the implementation of DllMain can be omitted. Most of the time, however, an implementation is provided, as the DLL will need to initialize itself (initializing state such as thread local storage). Developers implementing DllMain need to be aware of several limitations of the implementation. Rather than just listing them all, let's take a look at the most common problem encountered when implementing the function.

The DLL we use to illustrate this problem (Listing 10.14) is a simple DLL that performs some DLL initialization. Rather than doing it on the main thread, the code in DllMain creates a new thread that is responsible for the initialization. The main thread simply waits for the worker thread to finish executing and returns from the DllMain function.

**Listing 10.14** Example of a DllMain implementation

```
#include <windows.h>
#include <stdio.h>


DWORD WINAPI InitDllProc( LPVOID lpParam )
{
```

```
    LoadLibrary("xmlprov.dll");
    return 1;
}

BOOL WINAPI DllMain(HINSTANCE hinstDLL, DWORD fdwReason, LPVOID lpvReserved)
{
    BOOL bRet=FALSE;
    switch(fdwReason)
    {
        case DLL_PROCESS_ATTACH:
        {
            DWORD dwId=0;
            HANDLE hThread=NULL;

            hThread = CreateThread(NULL, 0, InitDllProc, NULL, 0, &dwId);
            if(hThread)
            {
                WaitForSingleObject(hThread, INFINITE);
                CloseHandle(hThread);
                bRet=TRUE;
            }
        }
        break;
    }

    return bRet;
}
```

The source code and binary for Listing 10.14 can be found in the following folders:

Source code: `C:\AWD\Chapter10\DllMain\App` and
`C:\AWD\Chapter10\DllMain\ModDll`

Binary: `C:\AWDBIN\WinXP.x86.chk\10dllmain.exe` and
`C:\AWDBIN\WinXP.x86.chk\10moddll.dll`

The application that uses this DLL simply loads the DLL using LoadLibrary. To run the application, use the following command line:

`C:\AWDBIN\WinXP.x86.chk\10dllmain.exe`

Considering the code behind this application, it should finish relatively quickly, but you will notice that the application simply hangs. To get a better idea of what is happening, find the process ID of 10dllmain.exe and attach a debugger to it. The result of attaching the debugger is shown in Listing 10.15.

## Listing 10.15   Attaching a debugger to our DLL sample application

```
...
...
ModLoad: 01000000 01003000   C:\AWDBIN\WinXP.x86.chk\10dllmain.exe
ModLoad: 7c900000 7c9b0000   C:\WINDOWS\system32\ntdll.dll
ModLoad: 7c800000 7c8f4000   C:\WINDOWS\system32\kernel32.dll
ModLoad: 77c10000 77c68000   C:\WINDOWS\system32\msvcrt.dll
ModLoad: 00400000 00404000   C:\AWDBIN\WinXP.x86.chk\10moddll.dll
Break-in sent, waiting 30 seconds...
```

You will immediately notice that the debugger simply sits there and does not break into the process. The last line in Listing 10.15 seems to imply that the debugger tried to send a break-in command but is unable to get a response from the process being debugged. If you wait for the recommended 30 seconds, the debugger eventually breaks in with the following notice:

```
WARNING: Break-in timed out, suspending.
         This is usually caused by another thread holding the loader lock
(498.27c): Wake debugger - code 80000007 (first chance)
eax=0006f8b0 ebx=00400000 ecx=ffffffff edx=000000d8 esi=000007f4 edi=00000000
eip=7c90eb94 esp=0006f770 ebp=0006f7d4 iopl=0         nv up ei pl zr na po nc
cs=001b  ss=0023  ds=0023  es=0023  fs=003b  gs=0000              efl=00000246
*** ERROR: Symbol file could not be found.  Defaulted to export symbols for C:\WIN-
DOWS\system32\ntdll.dll -
ntdll!KiFastSystemCallRet:
7c90eb94 c3              ret
```

The warning is telling us that a loader lock might be held. What is really going on here? The debugger's behavior seems very erratic (does not break in and complains about a loader lock that we never touched in our code). If we turn to our trustworthy troubleshooting process, the next step is to dump out all the threads to see if we can make sense out of the hang. Listing 10.16 shows the threads of our process.

## Listing 10.16   Listing of all threads in the culprit process

```
0:000> ~*kb

.  0  Id: 498.27c Suspend: 1 Teb: 7ffdd000 Unfrozen
ChildEBP RetAddr  Args to Child
0006f76c 7c90e9c0 7c8025cb 000007f4 00000000 ntdll!KiFastSystemCallRet
0006f770 7c8025cb 000007f4 00000000 00000000 ntdll!NtWaitForSingleObject+0xc
0006f7d4 7c802532 000007f4 ffffffff 00000000 kernel32!WaitForSingleObjectEx+0xa8
```

```
0006f7e8 0040113a 000007f4 ffffffff 00000001 kernel32!WaitForSingleObject+0x12
0006f804 00401251 00400000 00000001 00000000 10modDll!DllMain+0x4a
0006f824 7c9011a7 00400000 00000001 00000000 10modDll!_DllMainCRTStartup+0x52
0006f844 7c91cbab 004011ff 00400000 00000001 ntdll!LdrpCallInitRoutine+0x14
0006f94c 7c916178 00000000 c0150008 00000000 ntdll!LdrpRunInitializeRoutines+0x344
0006fbf8 7c9162da 00000000 00083338 0006feec ntdll!LdrpLoadDll+0x3e5
0006fea0 7c801bb9 00083338 0006feec 0006fecc ntdll!LdrLoadDll+0x230
0006ff08 7c801d6e 7ffddc00 00000000 00000000 kernel32!LoadLibraryExW+0x18e
0006ff1c 7c801da4 0100107c 00000000 00000000 kernel32!LoadLibraryExA+0x1f
0006ff38 01001160 0100107c 0006ffc0 01001298 kernel32!LoadLibraryA+0x94
0006ff44 01001298 00000001 00263b08 00262b78 10dllmain!main+0x10
0006ffc0 7c816fd7 5a99c54d 01c6d533 7ffde000 10dllmain!mainCRTStartup+0x12f
0006fff0 00000000 01001169 00000000 78746341 kernel32!BaseProcessStart+0x23


   1  Id: 498.fd4 Suspend: 1 Teb: 7ffdc000 Unfrozen
ChildEBP RetAddr  Args to Child
002bfc10 7c90e9c0 7c91901b 000007e8 00000000 ntdll!KiFastSystemCallRet
002bfc14 7c91901b 000007e8 00000000 00000000 ntdll!NtWaitForSingleObject+0xc
002bfc9c 7c90104b 0197c0d8 7c927357 7c97c0d8 ntdll!RtlpWaitForCriticalSection+0x132
002bfca4 7c927357 7c97c0d8 002bfd30 020a0018 ntdll!RtlEnterCriticalSection+0x46
002bfd1c 7c90eac7 002bfd30 7c900000 00000000 ntdll!_LdrpInitialize+0xf0
00000000 00000000 00000000 00000000 00000000 ntdll!KiUserApcDispatcher+0x7


   2  Id: 498.f90 Suspend: 1 Teb: 7ffdb000 Unfrozen
ChildEBP RetAddr  Args to Child
002cfc0c 7c90e9c0 7c91901b 000007e8 00000000 ntdll!KiFastSystemCallRet
002cfc10 7c91901b 000007e8 00000000 00000000 ntdll!NtWaitForSingleObject+0xc
002cfc98 7c90104b 0197c0d8 7c927357 7c97c0d8 ntdll!RtlpWaitForCriticalSection+0x132
002cfca0 7c927357 7c97c0d8 002cfd2c 00000004 ntdll!RtlEnterCriticalSection+0x46
002cfd18 7c90eac7 002cfd2c 7c900000 00000000 ntdll!_LdrpInitialize+0xf0
00000000 00000000 00000000 00000000 00000000 ntdll!KiUserApcDispatcher+0x7
```

The first thread in Listing 10.16 makes perfect sense. It is our main application thread, where we call LoadLibrary on our sample DLL. The call goes through a myriad of system calls before ending up in our DllMain implementation, as per expectations. The DllMain function finally calls WaitForSingleObject to wait for our worker thread to finish. This wait, however, never seems to be satisfied, implying that our worker thread either did not execute or is hung. Judging from the other threads in the process, we can't see a trace of our worker thread; hence, we draw the conclusion that it never started. So far, the debug session does not seem to make any sense. The last two threads look very strange as well. What we have are two threads that are trying to enter a critical section. Additionally, the bottommost frames of those threads look a bit strange:

```
002cfca0 7c927357 7c97c0d8 002cfd2c 00000004 ntdll!RtlEnterCriticalSection+0x46
002cfd18 7c90eac7 002cfd2c 7c900000 00000000 ntdll!_LdrpInitialize+0xf0
00000000 00000000 00000000 00000000 00000000 ntdll!KiUserApcDispatcher+0x7
```

If we dump the critical section that is being acquired, we can see that it is referred to as a loader lock:

```
0:000> !cs 7c97c0d8
--------------------
Critical section    = 0x7c97c0d8 (ntdll!LdrpLoaderLock+0x0)
DebugInfo           = 0x7c97c100
LOCKED
LockCount           = 0x3
OwningThread        = 0x0000027c
RecursionCount      = 0x2
LockSemaphore       = 0x7E8
SpinCount           = 0x00000000
```

The critical section is in a locked state, and the thread owning the critical section has a thread ID of 0x27c. The thread corresponding to that thread ID happens to be our main thread that is in the process of initializing the DLL we loaded.

Why do we have two threads waiting for the loader lock to be released? Furthermore, why do the thread stacks look so strange? Typically, a user mode thread begins with a frame that resembles the following:

```
kernel32!BaseThreadStart
```

In our case, the thread's starting point seems to be in a frame that resembles

```
ntdll!KiUserApcDispatcher
```

What we are seeing is an example of how a user mode thread actually comes to life in Windows. Figure 10.3 illustrates the high-level process of creating a new thread. Note that many of the details surrounding thread creations are largely undocumented, and, as such, Figure 10.3 should serve as a close high-level approximation.

When a thread is created in Windows, it does not "auto-magically" start executing from the kernel32!BaseThreadStart function, but rather it always begins its life as a user mode APC (Asynchronous Procedure Call). At a high level, when Windows is notified to create a new thread, a user mode APC is queued to the APC queue of the new thread. The APC dispatcher dispatches an APC to the new thread, which in return performs a bunch of initialization work prior to transitioning into a state that we typically associate with being a user mode thread (that is, we see the kernel32!BaseThreadStart in the stack trace). This is exactly what we are seeing with our two threads. They are still in an APC state, performing initialization work.

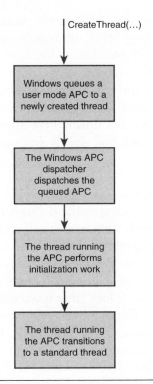

CreateThread(...)

Windows queues a
user mode APC to a
newly created thread

The Windows APC
dispatcher
dispatches the
queued APC

The thread running
the APC performs
initialization work

The thread running
the APC transitions
to a standard thread

**Figure 10.3** High-level overview of the thread creation process

This now explains why at least one of our threads is in the APC state. It seems to be performing initialization work and is getting stuck on trying to acquire the loader lock. Before we go down the route of investigating why it is unable to acquire that lock, we should do due diligence (remember—the more knowledge you have of all the threads in the process, the better the chances of getting to the root cause of whatever might be going wrong); we should also figure out why there is a final third thread stuck in the APC state. After all, our application should have two threads: (1) main thread and (2) worker thread. Remember our earlier discussion of the high-level process and how we will always have a "debugger" thread in our process when we break into the debugger, the thread responsible for issuing the debug break command? Well, the final thread in our process is just that debugger thread. Although, interestingly enough, it also does not seem to look right. The stack trace we expect to see should have a debug break frame in it. Rather than dismissing this thread as "not being ours," let's try to understand where it is coming from. A debugger that is trying to break into the target process can do so in one of two ways:

- Injecting a remote thread into the target process. This thread is then responsible for issuing the debug break, ultimately causing the target process to stop executing. After the remote thread has been injected by the debugger, the debugger simply waits for the thread to finish. The wait time that the debugger specifies is not infinite though, as certain situations might prevent the remote thread from being created. More specifically, the wait time is 30 seconds.
- If the remote thread has not finished creation after 30 seconds, the debugger takes a different approach and simply suspends all the threads in the process and breaks execution.

Now it should start making sense why we are seeing a third thread. The third thread is actually the remote thread injected by the debugger to try to halt execution. Because the thread is stuck in APC mode initializing itself (very similar to our worker thread), the output the debugger displayed (`Break-in send, waiting for 30 seconds...`, and `WARNING: Break-in timed out, suspending`) also makes sense. So, it seems that every thread besides our main thread is getting stuck early on in APC mode because of this mysterious "loader lock" that is wreaking havoc in our process, causing everything to come to a halt. The only remaining question is what this loader lock is and why our main thread appears to be holding it. Earlier, we discussed the overall concept of a DLL and how `DllMain` can be used to initialize the DLL. For Windows to keep the process of loading and unloading DLL(s) structurally intact, it uses a loader lock to serialize all access to `DllMain` functions. It does so to prevent a myriad of issues that would be involved with concurrently executing `DllMain` functions. Windows acquires the lock prior to calling any `DllMain` function and subsequently releases the lock when `DllMain` finishes execution.

Now we have all the pieces to explain what is actually going on. The main thread is executing code in `DllMain`, which indirectly implies that the loader lock is being held. Meanwhile, the worker thread tries to start executing, but it gets stuck while trying to call into `DllMain` (with `DLL_THREAD_ATTACH`), and we end up with a deadlock.

As you have seen, implementing `DllMain` can be quite tricky. In addition to deadlocks, other problems, such as access violations, can surface if the load order isn't respected. As a general rule of thumb, `DllMain` should perform as little work as possible (lazy initialization) and return quickly. What does little work mean? That's a good question. Our implementation can be considered little because it does nothing more than spawn a thread that tries to load another DLL. Microsoft has written a whitepaper on the issue of DLL implementations, and it can be found at the following location:

```
https://www.microsoft.com/whdc/driver/kernel/DLL_bestprac.mspx
```

You can take other precautions to ensure that you won't get into a problematic situation while implementing `DllMain`. First and foremost, be aware of the API(s) that you are calling from `DllMain`. Even though some API(s) might look innocent enough, they might eventually call an API that will cause problems. Unfortunately, there is no set list of dangerous API(s) to avoid; however, there is hope. The hope comes in the form of Application Verifier. Application Verifier has the capability to detect many of the most common problems encountered during `DllMain` implementations. The Application Verifier test setting to use is the Basics test setting. If you enable that test setting for our sample application and rerun the application under the debugger, you will see that the output resembles the following:

```
0:000> g
ModLoad: 00e30000 00e34000   C:\AWDBIN\WinXp.x86.chk\10moddll.dll


=======================================
VERIFIER STOP 00000304 : pid 0x5F4: Waiting on a thread handle in DllMain.

    00000780 : Thread handle.
    00000000 : Not used.
    00000000 : Not used.
    00000000 : Not used.


=======================================
This verifier stop is continuable.
After debugging it use `go' to continue.

=======================================

(5f4.5fc): Break instruction exception - code 80000003 (first chance)
eax=00000000 ebx=003b5c78 ecx=7c91eb05 edx=0006f263 esi=00000000 edi=00000780
eip=7c901230 esp=0006f36c ebp=0006f538 iopl=0         nv up ei pl nz na pe nc
cs=001b  ss=0023  ds=0023  es=0023  fs=003b  gs=0000              efl=00000202
ntdll!DbgBreakPoint:
7c901230 cc              int     3
```

The debugger broke in as soon as it detected a call to `WaitForSingleObject` in the `DllMain` function. It also provides some auxiliary information, such as the thread handle that is being waited on.

Application Verifier has a ton of truly amazing test settings and should be used extensively during development. Trust me—allowing Application Verifier to catch these issues early on will save you a ton of debugging time.

## Lock Contention

Lock contention is an interesting scenario that can dramatically affect the performance and scalability of your application. Lock contention refers to a situation in which a large number of threads compete for a single lock. Depending on how much work is being done in the protected code region, the number of threads waiting to acquire the lock might become larger and larger. Prior to Windows 2003 Server SP1, critical sections employed fair semantics—fair meaning that it observed First-In-First-Out semantics, essentially guaranteeing that the locking order of the critical section would be preserved. The thread that had waited the longest would also be the one that was next in line to acquire the critical section. For a fair locking scheme to work, the act of leaving a critical section must include the transfer of ownership from the owning thread to the thread next in line to acquire it. Transferring ownership increases the time that the owning thread spends in the critical section by an order of magnitude. For example, imagine that a piece of code protected by a critical section did nothing more than increase a reference count:

```
EnterCriticalSection(&cs);
refCount++;
LeaveCriticalSection(&cs);
```

The amount of time spent in the critical section is relatively small because increasing a DWORD by one is a pretty cheap operation. Furthermore, imagine that a ton of threads were waiting on that critical section. Now, as the owning thread leaves the critical section, it must observe the fair semantics of the lock and transfer ownership to the next thread in line. The amount of work required to transfer ownership is pretty large in comparison to the amount of work actually done inside the critical section (incrementing a variable). It potentially has to wake up another thread, resulting in a context switch before the next thread acquires the critical section. The added time required to honor the fair locking semantics results in quite a large overhead, during which even more threads will have an opportunity to get queued up. Figure 10.4 illustrates the work required for a thread to enter, execute the protected region of code, and leave a critical section.

Figure 10.4 shows how a very small region of code is protected by a critical section and what happens when the first thread (T1) enters the critical section, executes the simple increment statement, and leaves the critical section. As can be seen, the amount of time spent executing the relevant increment of the reference count variable is much smaller than the amount of time spent transferring ownership of the critical section.

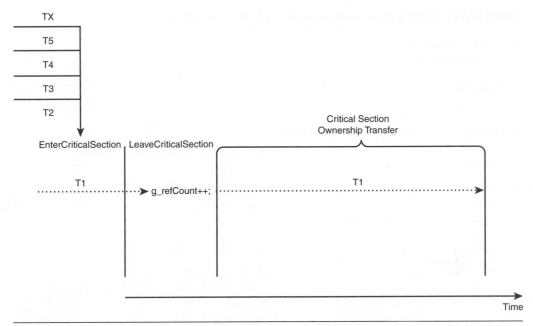

**Figure 10.4** Processing involved with entering and leaving a critical section

The problem being illustrated—the incoming rate of threads trying to acquire the critical section is larger than the amount of time required to enter, process, and leave the critical section (including the work required to transfer ownership)—is known as a lock convoy. Lock convoys can dramatically reduce the performance of an application due to the excessive amount of work required to manage a fair critical section.

How does one recognize if a lock convoy problem is indeed occurring? At a high level, there are a couple of symptoms that are worth looking out for:

- Excessive context switching. Remember that for a critical section to fairly transfer ownership to another critical section, it must wake up that new thread. The act of waking up a thread might result in a context switch.
- Performance degradation on the code path that includes the locking scheme.

If you suspect that a lock convoy might be an issue in your application, the next step is to take a close look at the application using the debuggers and convince yourself that's what's going on. Listing 10.17 shows a sample application that suffers from the lock convoy problem.

**Listing 10.17** Sample application that suffers from lock convoys

```
#include <windows.h>
#include <stdio.h>

CRITICAL_SECTION g_cs;
DWORD g_refCount;

DWORD WINAPI ThreadProc( LPVOID lpParam )
{
    while(true)
    {
        EnterCriticalSection(&g_cs);
        g_refCount++;
        LeaveCriticalSection(&g_cs);
    }
    return 1;
}


void __cdecl main ( )
{
    DWORD dwId=0;
    HANDLE hThread[MAXIMUM_WAIT_OBJECTS];
    DWORD dwRet=0;
    g_refCount=0;

    InitializeCriticalSection(&g_cs);

    for(int i=0; i<MAXIMUM_WAIT_OBJECTS; i++)
    {
        hThread[i] = CreateThread(NULL, 0, ThreadProc, NULL, 0, &dwId);
        if(!hThread[i])
        {
            for(int j=0;j<i;j++)
            {
                CloseHandle(hThread[j]);
            }
            return;
        }
    }

    WaitForMultipleObjects(MAXIMUM_WAIT_OBJECTS, hThread, TRUE, INFINITE);
    for(int i=0; i<MAXIMUM_WAIT_OBJECTS; i++)
    {
        CloseHandle(hThread[i]);
    }
}
```

10. Synchronization

The source code and binary for Listing 10.17 can be found in the following folders:

Source code: `C:\AWD\Chapter10\LockConvoy`

Binary: `C:\AWDBIN\WinXP.x86.chk\10lockconv.exe`

The code in Listing 10.17 is fairly trivial. It creates a number of threads, where each thread sits in a tight loop increasing a reference count variable. The reference count variable increment is protected by a critical section. If we run this application under the debugger, we see that it contains a large number of threads—most of which are waiting to acquire the critical section protecting the reference counter. Note that you have to run this application on a Windows version prior to Windows 2003 Server SP1.

```
  61   Id: a48.a28 Suspend: 1 Teb: 7ff79000 Unfrozen
ChildEBP RetAddr  Args to Child
0128ff14 7c90e9c0 7c91901b 0000073c 00000000 ntdll!KiFastSystemCallRet
0128ff18 7c91901b 0000073c 00000000 7c97c140 ntdll!NtWaitForSingleObject+0xc
0128ffa0 7c90104b 00002008 01001169 01002008 ntdll!RtlpWaitForCriticalSection+0x132
0128ffa8 01001169 01002008 0128ffec 7c80b683 ntdll!RtlEnterCriticalSection+0x46
0128ffb4 7c80b683 00000000 7c910833 00000000 10LockConv!ThreadProc+0x19
0128ffec 00000000 01001150 00000000 00000000 kernel32!BaseThreadStart+0x37
```

So far, so good. We certainly do expect a large number of threads to be waiting on this very contentious lock. Now, let's try to find out which thread owns the critical section. Remember, the first parameter to `RtlEnterCriticalSection` is the address to the critical section in question.

```
0:065> !cs 01002008
--------------------
Critical section   = 0x01002008 (10LockConv!g_cs+0x0)
DebugInfo          = 0x7c97c8c0
LOCKED
LockCount          = 0x1C
OwningThread       = 0x00000000
RecursionCount     = 0x0
LockSemaphore      = 0x73C
SpinCount          = 0x00000000
```

The `LockCount` field seems correct (`0x1C`) and indicates that the critical section is locked and has a large number of threads waiting to acquire it. The `OwningThread` field, on the other hand, seems wrong. It implies that a thread with a thread ID of 0 is holding the critical section. A thread with a thread ID of 0 will never exist in a process. What is going on? What you are seeing is, in essence, a telltale sign that a lock convoy is occurring. Remember that in a lock convoy situation, the owning thread passes ownership of the critical section as it is leaving it. During this time, the critical section is still considered locked, but the releasing code clears the OwningThread field until the new thread enters the critical section—at which point, it gets properly reset.

Because lock convoys can cause serious issues in your code, what are some of the mitigation techniques? Unfortunately, mitigation techniques are not easy to come by for this problem. The best answer is to simply redesign the application and remove the highly contentious lock. Unfortunately, this is not always possible. Another possible mitigation is to rely on spin counts when trying to acquire the critical section. Using this technique can dramatically reduce the amount of time it takes to pass ownership (because a context switch is not required), and the convoy might be broken. Unfortunately, this approach only works on multiprocessor machines.

The problem of lock convoys was deemed important enough that the Windows team decided to make a dramatic change to how critical sections worked in Windows 2003 Server SP1. Because the fundamental problem of lock convoys is that the owning thread has to pass ownership to the next thread in line (to honor the basic design goal of a fair lock), Microsoft decided to make a design change to the critical section and remove the fairness requirement. If a thread does not have to pass ownership, a minimal amount of post-critical section release time would be spent, thereby eliminating the lock convoy problem. A side effect stemming from removing fairness is that a thread that is woken up to enter the critical section would have to compete with brand new incoming threads also trying to compete for it, potentially resulting in thread starvation. Nevertheless, the lock convoy problem was deemed important enough and trumped the potential of thread starvation. To accommodate this change, a change had to be made for how the critical section is structured, and the approach agreed upon was to use the LockCount field to add the additional information required for an unfair lock. More specifically, the LockCount has changed as shown in Figure 10.5.

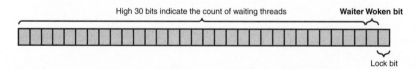

High 30 bits indicate the count of waiting threads          **Waiter Woken bit**

Lock bit

**Figure 10.5**   The LockCount field of the new unfair critical sections

All bits in the new LockCount field are now also stored in an inverted state, so when looking at the LockCount field in the debugger, it is important to flip the bits prior to making assumptions about its state. As Figure 10.5 indicates, the high 30 bits of the LockCount field are pretty straightforward and contain the number of waiting threads.

Bit 1 is the Waiter Woken bit and indicates whether a thread that released the critical section has signaled the event to wake up another thread. If the bit is set, it serves as an indication that another thread leaving the critical section should not set it as well. The least significant bit is the Lock bit, and it indicates whether the critical section is in a locked state.

Let's take a look at a few examples (see Listings 10.18, 10.19, and 10.20) of what the LockCount field resembles with critical sections in various states. (Remember—you must be running on Windows 2003 Server SP1 at a minimum.)

**Listing 10.18**   Unlocked critical section

```
Old Critical Section
   +0x000 DebugInfo         : 0x7c97c8c0
   +0x004 LockCount         : -1
   +0x008 RecursionCount    : 0
   +0x00c OwningThread      : (null)
   +0x010 LockSemaphore     : (null)
   +0x014 SpinCount         : 0


New Critical Section
   +0x000 DebugInfo         : 0x77ca5be0
   +0x004 LockCount         : -1
   +0x008 RecursionCount    : 0
   +0x00c OwningThread      : (null)
   +0x010 LockSemaphore     : (null)
   +0x014 SpinCount         : 0
```

**Listing 10.19**   Locked critical section with no waiters

```
Old Critical Section
   +0x000 DebugInfo         : 0x7c97c8c0
   +0x004 LockCount         : 0
   +0x008 RecursionCount    : 1
   +0x00c OwningThread      : 0x00000b04
   +0x010 LockSemaphore     : (null)
   +0x014 SpinCount         : 0

New Critical Section
   +0x000 DebugInfo         : 0x77ca5be0
   +0x004 LockCount         : -2
   +0x008 RecursionCount    : 1
   +0x00c OwningThread      : 0x00000134
   +0x010 LockSemaphore     : (null)
   +0x014 SpinCount         : 0
```

**Listing 10.20**  Locked critical section with waiters

```
Old Critical Section
   +0x000 DebugInfo       : 0x7c97c8c0
   +0x004 LockCount       : 1
   +0x008 RecursionCount  : 1
   +0x00c OwningThread    : 0x00000b04
   +0x010 LockSemaphore   : 0x000007f4
   +0x014 SpinCount       : 0

New Critical Section
   +0x000 DebugInfo       : 0x77ca5be0
   +0x004 LockCount       : -6
   +0x008 RecursionCount  : 1
   +0x00c OwningThread    : 0x00000134
   +0x010 LockSemaphore   : 0x00000010
   +0x014 SpinCount       : 0
```

To make it easier to understand the LockCount field of the new critical sections, let's look at a binary breakdown of the LockCount field of the critical section in Listing 10.20. To get a binary representation of the LockCount field, we use the dyd command:

```
0:003> dyd 01002008+0x4
                 3        2        1        0
           10987654 32109876 54321098 76543210

0100200c   11111111 11111111 11111111 11111010   fffffffa
01002010   00000000 00000000 00000000 00000001   00000001
01002014   00000000 00000000 00000001 11111000   000001f8
01002018   00000000 00000000 00000000 00010000   00000010
0100201c   00000000 00000000 00000000 00000000   00000000
01002020   00000000 00000000 00000000 00000000   00000000
01002024   00000000 00000000 00000000 00000000   00000000
01002028   00000000 00000000 00000000 00000000   00000000
```

The first thing to remember is that the bits are all inverted, so prior to trying to figure out the lock state, we need to flip the bits again:

```
00000000 00000000 00000000 00000101
```

The Lock Bit (bit 0) is 1, which means that the critical section is locked. The Waiter Woken bit (bit 1) is 0, which means that no waiters have yet been woken. The remaining 30 bits is the number of waiters, which in our case is 1. Fortunately, the !cs extension command has been updated to recognize this change on the affected platforms and can display the information in a friendlier way. For example, if we used the same critical section as preceding as a parameter to the !cs extension command, we would see the following:

```
0:003> !cs 01002008
--------------------
Critical section    = 0x01002008 (10LockConv!g_cs+0x0)
DebugInfo           = 0x77965be0
LOCKED
LockCount           = 0x1
WaiterWoken         = No
OwningThread        = 0x000001f8
RecursionCount      = 0x1
LockSemaphore       = 0x10
SpinCount           = 0x00000000
```

The critical section is in a LOCKED state, has one waiter, and no waiters have been woken.

### Direct Usage of Critical Section Fields

Because the critical section structure is directly available to the developers, there have been cases in which developers make assumptions about the meaning of the fields. One such example is the LockCount field, where application code uses the LockCount field directly to see if the critical section is free or being held. It should go without saying that looking at the critical section fields directly rather than going through the critical section API(s) is a big no-no. Although the structure itself is documented, Microsoft reserves the right to change that structure in any shape it deems necessary. If you have code that directly manipulates the critical section fields, you run the risk of your application not working between Windows versions.

## Managing Critical Sections

Properly managing critical sections is just as important as managing any other form of resource. Mismanagement can lead to devastating situations that are extremely difficult and time-consuming to debug. In this part of the chapter, we take a look at some of the most common problems when managing critical sections.

The four most common types of problems seen when managing critical sections are

- Use of a critical section before initialization
- Use of a critical section after deletion
- Overreleasing the critical section
- Underreleasing the critical section

To understand the first problem, usage of a critical section before initialization, we must first be able to identify what a properly initialized critical section resembles. Listing 10.21 shows the contents of an initialized critical section.

**Listing 10.21**   Properly initialized critical section

```
+0x000 DebugInfo        : 0x7c97c8c0
   +0x000 Type              : 0
   +0x002 CreatorBackTraceIndex : 0
   +0x004 CriticalSection   : 0x0007ff2c
   +0x008 ProcessLocksList : _LIST_ENTRY [ 0x7c97c0c8 - 0x7c97c8a8 ]
   +0x010 EntryCount        : 0
   +0x014 ContentionCount   : 0
   +0x018 Spare             : [2] 0
+0x004 LockCount        : -1
+0x008 RecursionCount   : 0
+0x00c OwningThread     : (null)
+0x010 LockSemaphore    : (null)
+0x014 SpinCount        : 0
```

All fields of the critical section in Listing 10.21 have proper default values, and the `CriticalSection` field of the `DebugInfo` structure points back to the actual critical section structure.

Now, imagine that a thread had managed to call `EnterCriticalSection` before it had been initialized. The net result is most likely an access violation with a stack trace, as follows:

```
ChildEBP RetAddr  Args to Child
0007fe98 7c94243c c0000008 00090000 0007fa0c ntdll!RtlRaiseStatus+0x26
0007ff18 7c90104b 0007ff2c 01001152 0007ff2c ntdll!RtlpWaitForCriticalSection+0x204
0007ff20 01001152 0007ff2c 0007ff50 77c3ac60 ntdll!RtlEnterCriticalSection+0x46
0007ff44 010012a0 00000001 00034e50 00033338 simple!main+0x12
0007ffc0 7c816fd7 00090000 0007fa0c 7ffde000 simple!mainCRTStartup+0x12f
0007fff0 00000000 01001171 00000000 78746341 kernel32!BaseProcessStart+0x23
```

If you encounter a stack trace similar to this, you should first check the structural integrity of the critical section and try to understand if the critical section is in good shape.

```
0:000> dt CRITICAL_SECTION 0007ff2c
   +0x000 DebugInfo        : 0x0007ff50
   +0x004 LockCount        : 2009312352
   +0x008 RecursionCount   : 216660
   +0x00c OwningThread     : 0x0007ff4c
   +0x010 LockSemaphore    : 0x00090000
   +0x014 SpinCount        : 0x7fa0c
```

This seems to be an invalid critical section. All the fields of the critical section have values that do not seem to make sense. Typically, when you are dealing with a critical section that has not yet been initialized, the values you will see are seemingly random and pretty much every field is incorrect.

The second form of mismanaged critical sections is the usage of a critical section after it has been deleted. Once again, it is important to be able to know what a critical section that has been deleted actually resembles:

```
   +0x000 DebugInfo        : (null)
   +0x004 LockCount        : 0
   +0x008 RecursionCount   : 0
   +0x00c OwningThread     : (null)
   +0x010 LockSemaphore    : (null)
   +0x014 SpinCount        : 0
```

Not surprisingly, the fields of the critical section have all been initialized to 0 (or null). Now, if a thread tries to acquire the critical section, you will see an access violation much as you saw in the use before initialization scenario:

```
ChildEBP RetAddr   Args to Child
0007ff18 7c90104b 0007ff2c 01001170 0007ff2c ntdll!RtlpWaitForCriticalSection+0x8c
0007ff20 01001170 0007ff2c 00000000 00000001 ntdll!RtlEnterCriticalSection+0x46
0007ff44 010012aa 00000001 00034e50 00033338 simple!main+0x30
0007ffc0 7c816fd7 00090000 0007fa0c 7ffdd000 simple!mainCRTStartup+0x12f
0007fff0 00000000 0100117b 00000000 78746341 kernel32!BaseProcessStart+0x23
```

The final two problems we will look at fall under the categories of under-and-over releasing critical sections. Both of these problems typically surface as hangs in the application. Let's take a look at the first problem—underreleasing critical sections. This problem is typically easy to spot because you will have a number of threads waiting to acquire a critical section with the following stack trace:

```
   1  Id: 748.d14 Suspend: 1 Teb: 7ffdd000 Unfrozen
ChildEBP RetAddr  Args to Child
002bff14 7c90e9c0 7c91901b 000007e8 00000000 ntdll!KiFastSystemCallRet
002bff18 7c91901b 000007e8 00000000 7c97c140 ntdll!NtWaitForSingleObject+0xc
002bffa0 7c90104b 00002008 010011e0 01002008 ntdll!RtlpWaitForCriticalSection+0x132
002bffa8 010011e0 01002008 002bffec 7c80b683 ntdll!RtlEnterCriticalSection+0x46
...
...
```

From there on, we have all the necessary information in the critical section (such as the owning thread) to backtrack and find out why the critical section was never released.

Similarly, overreleasing a critical section also results in a hang. Imagine that an application executes the following simple piece of code:

```
InitializeCriticalSection(&g_cs);
EnterCriticalSection(&g_cs);
LeaveCriticalSection(&g_cs);
LeaveCriticalSection(&g_cs);
EnterCriticalSection(&g_cs);
```

After the first call to EnterCriticalSection, we would expect the state of critical section to be similar to the following:

```
+0x000 DebugInfo        : 0x7c97c8c0
+0x004 LockCount        : 0
+0x008 RecursionCount   : 1
+0x00c OwningThread     : 0x00000afc
+0x010 LockSemaphore    : (null)
+0x014 SpinCount        : 0
```

Next, the application leaves the critical section, and we expect that the critical section state resembles the following:

```
+0x000 DebugInfo        : 0x7c97c8c0
+0x004 LockCount        : -1
+0x008 RecursionCount   : 0
+0x00c OwningThread     : (null)
+0x010 LockSemaphore    : (null)
+0x014 SpinCount        : 0
```

The next call to leave the critical section causes the overrelease, and the critical section resembles the following:

```
   +0x000 DebugInfo          : 0x7c97c8c0
   +0x004 LockCount          : -2
   +0x008 RecursionCount     : -1
   +0x00c OwningThread       : (null)
   +0x010 LockSemaphore      : (null)
   +0x014 SpinCount          : 0
```

Because the `LockCount` field is not -1 (meaning an unlocked critical section) but rather -2, the next call to `EnterCriticalSection` results in a hang because Windows believes that the critical section is, in fact, locked:

```
  0  Id: 4bc.afc Suspend: 1 Teb: 7ffdf000 Unfrozen
ChildEBP RetAddr  Args to Child
0007fe98 7c90e9c0 7c91901b 000007f4 00000000 ntdll!KiFastSystemCallRet
0007fe9c 7c91901b 000007f4 00000000 7c97c140 ntdll!NtWaitForSingleObject+0xc
0007ff24 7c90104b 00002008 0100118d 01002008 ntdll!RtlpWaitForCriticalSection+0x132
0007ff2c 0100118d 01002008 0007ff4c 00000000 ntdll!RtlEnterCriticalSection+0x46
0007ff44 010012c7 00000001 00034e50 00033338 simple!main+0x4d
0007ffc0 7c816fd7 00090000 0007fa0c 7ffd7000 simple!mainCRTStartup+0x12f
0007fff0 00000000 01001198 00000000 78746341 kernel32!BaseProcessStart+0x23
```

As a last step, we can dump out the critical section to see what happened to it while we attempted to enter it:

```
   +0x000 DebugInfo          : 0x7c97c8c0
   +0x004 LockCount          : -1
   +0x008 RecursionCount     : -1
   +0x00c OwningThread       : (null)
   +0x010 LockSemaphore      : 0x000007f4
   +0x014 SpinCount          : 0
```

The `LockCount` field has now been increased by 1 (-1), which makes sense because we just tried to enter the critical section.

As a general rule of thumb, if you see a hang on a critical section with a negative lock count and the owning thread being `null`, you should consider the source of the problem being an overreleased critical section.

Many more ways exist in which a critical section can get into a nonrecoverable state because of mismanagement. Other such ways include corrupting the critical section, freeing memory containing active critical sections, unloading a DLL with an active critical section, and many more. Rather than having to do a lot of backtracking after the problem surfaces, it would be nice to be able to catch some of these problems when the culprit thread misbehaves rather then when the victim threads either crash or hang. Fortunately, our good old friend Application Verifier comes to our rescue once again. Under the Basics test setting is a setting called Locks, which performs a whole slew of tests while the application runs. It will catch anything from using an uninitialized critical section to freeing a piece of memory that contains an active and not-yet-released critical section. We strongly recommended that you turn on this test setting anytime your application has synchronization code in it, as it catches the culprit code in action rather than as a victim.

## Summary

Multithreading might seem to be a trivial programming exercise. After all, it's pretty simple. You spin up a number of threads and have them work in parallel to accomplish some task. As you've seen throughout the chapter, the area of concurrency and synchronization is far from trivial. One could even argue that it's one of the top areas prone to bugs. Extreme care must be taken to ensure that all threads live and work together in harmony. Small mistakes in this logic can have substantial and devastating consequences.

In this chapter, we took a look at some very common mistakes made when dealing with multithreaded applications and synchronization. We started with a brief overview of the different synchronization primitives available in Windows and the high-level process of troubleshooting a synchronization problem. A number of scenarios, such as deadlocks, orphaned critical sections, API awareness, and managing critical sections were shown, as well as how to find the root cause using the debuggers and tools available. Preventative measures, such as using Application Verifier, show how to find the root cause earlier in the development process, thereby reducing the amount of time spent on debugging complex synchronization problems. Additionally, techniques using the C++ language were shown to decrease the risk of running into synchronization problems.

# PART III

# ADVANCED TOPICS

**Chapter 11**    Writing Custom Debugger Extensions . . . . . . . . . . . . . . . . .553

**Chapter 12**    64-Bit Debugging . . . . . . . . . . . . . . . . . . . . . . . . . . .595

**Chapter 13**    Postmortem Debugging . . . . . . . . . . . . . . . . . . . . . . . .631

**Chapter 14**    Power Tools . . . . . . . . . . . . . . . . . . . . . . . . . . . . . .691

**Chapter 15**    Windows Vista Fundamentals . . . . . . . . . . . . . . . . . . . .709

**Appendix A**    Application Verifier Test Settings . . . . . . . . . . . . . . . . . .747

# CHAPTER 11

# WRITING CUSTOM DEBUGGER EXTENSIONS

As you have seen throughout detailed examples shown so far, the system-level debuggers and tools available to Windows developers provide a range of advanced and powerful techniques to deal with a wide spectrum of problems. Still, there are times when certain aspects of debug sessions become very repetitive and error prone. Examples of this include dumping out custom data structures or finding security settings on kernel objects. Fortunately, the team responsible for the debuggers at Microsoft recognized the pain associated with these tasks and introduced the notion of debugger extensions. At a 50,000 foot level, a debugger extension is a component that enables automation of repetitive and complex tasks for more efficient debugging. This chapter explains the fundamentals behind debugger extensions, discussing the anatomy of a debugger extension. Then it provides a complete walk-through of how to implement a debugger extension that automates the process of dumping the contents of a binary tree data type.

## Introduction to Debugger Extensions

Prior chapters show a variety of useful debugging sessions and associated extension commands. Examples of such include !sid, !token, and !sd. Where do these extension commands come from? Are they implemented in the debugger itself? Most of the debug commands that you have seen so far are implemented as custom debugger extensions. Debugging Tools for Windows includes a core set of debugger extensions that include the most commonly used commands during debug sessions. Table 11.1 lists the core debugger extensions available.

**Table 11.1** Core Debugger Extensions

| Extension | Extension Name | Description |
|---|---|---|
| General Extensions | Ext.dll | General extension commands, such as<br>`error`<br>`cxr`<br>`std_map` |
| User Mode Extensions | Ntsdexts.dll | Extension commands used frequently in user mode debugging, such as<br>`runaway`<br>`critsec`<br>`threadtoken` |
| RPC extensions | rpcexts.dll | Extension commands for debugging RPC, such as<br>`authinfo`<br>`getcallinfo`<br>`rpcheap` |

In its most basic form, a debugger extension is nothing more than a DLL that exports a set of entry points. Each entry point is invoked by the debug engine when the user types the command (same name as the entry point) in a debug session. As an example, consider the following command:

```
0:000> !ext.error 0
Error code: (Win32) 0 (0) - The operation completed successfully.
```

The command states that the error command is part of the ext.DLL extension and that the command should be executed. In this case, the ext.DLL exports a matching 'error' function invoked as a result of the preceding command execution. The command itself simply prints the textual representation of a Windows error code 0 to the debugger console window.

---

### *Examining Debugger Extensions*

Using an SDK tool named dumpbin.exe, you can very easily get a list of all exported functions from any extension DLL (including the ones listed in Table 11.1). For example, running dumpbin.exe against the exts.dll yields the following:

```
C:\>dumpbin /EXPORTS exts.dll
Microsoft (R) COFF/PE Dumper Version 8.00.50727.42
Copyright (C) Microsoft Corporation.  All rights reserved.
```

Dump of file exts.dll

File Type: DLL

  Section contains the following exports for exts.dll

    00000000 characteristics
    44B0109E time date stamp Sat Jul 08 13:07:58 2006
        0.00 version
           1 ordinal base
          32 number of functions
          32 number of names

    ordinal hint RVA      name

        2    0 0002D8F0 DebugExtensionInitialize
        3    1 0002D9B0 DebugExtensionNotify
        4    2 0002DB80 DebugExtensionUninitialize
        1    3 000446E0 _EFN_GetEnvironmentVariable
        5    4 0003FE50 acl
        6    5 0002EC90 atom
        7    6 00024750 avrf
        8    7 00021D50 bitcount
        9    8 000235A0 cs
       10    9 0002ED70 decodeptr
       11    A 0002B250 dlls
       12    B 0002C5E0 dlltree
       13    C 0002ED70 encodeptr
       14    D 00044890 envvar
       15    E 0002E000 gflag
       16    F 0001C850 heap
       17   10 0002DE80 help
       18   11 0002E530 kuser
       19   12 000399E0 mui
       20   13 00045960 peb
       21   14 0003C3D0 psr
       22   15 0003D920 rebase
       23   16 0003F4B0 sd
       24   17 00047260 shipassert
       25   18 0003FD70 sid
       26   19 00040700 slist
       27   1A 00043EC0 stl
       28   1B 00045F70 teb
       29   1C 00047090 tls
       30   1D 00049240 token

```
        31    1E 00050100 tp
        32    1F 00019A40 udeadlock

Summary

        5000 .data
        6000 .reloc
        1000 .rsrc
       54000 .text
```

# Example Debugger Extension

So far, you've seen examples of some small, but very useful, extensions. To illustrate the real power of debugger extensions, let's assume that you have developed a simple version of a binary tree component that allows developers to add items to a binary tree, as well as traverse the tree. (For brevity's sake, other common binary tree operations are omitted.) The binary tree is also limited to storing integers. The code for the binary tree is shown in Listing 11.1 and is fairly self-explanatory.

**Listing 11.1**   Simple C++ binary tree implementation

```cpp
// bstree.h
#ifndef __BSTREE_H
#define __BSTREE_H

#include <windows.h>
#include <strsafe.h>

class CBinaryTree
{
    public:
        CBinaryTree(CHAR* pszDescription);
        BOOL Add(int num);
        VOID Traverse();

    private:
        class _TreeNode
        {
            public:
                _TreeNode(int num)
                    {
                        pLeftChild = NULL; pRightChild = NULL; data=num;
```

```
                }

                int data;
                _TreeNode* pLeftChild;
                _TreeNode* pRightChild;
        };

        BOOL AddNode(_TreeNode* item,
                     _TreeNode* current,
                     DWORD dwRecursiveCount);
        VOID TraverseTree(_TreeNode* current);

        _TreeNode*      m_pHead;
        DWORD      m_dwDepth;
        DWORD         m_dwNumNodes;
};
#endif

// bstree.cpp
#include "bstree.h"
#include <stdio.h>

CBinaryTree::CBinaryTree () : m_pHead(NULL), m_dwDepth(0), m_dwNumNodes(0)
{
}

BOOL CBinaryTree::Add(int num)
{
    BOOL bRet=FALSE;
    _TreeNode* item=new _TreeNode(num);
    if(item!=NULL)
    {
        bRet=AddNode(item, m_pHead, 1);
        if(bRet==TRUE)
        {
            m_dwNumNodes++;
        }
    }

    return bRet;
}

VOID CBinaryTree::Traverse()
{
    TraverseTree(m_pHead);
}
```

*(continues)*

**Listing 11.1** Simple C++ binary tree implementation *(continued)*

```cpp
VOID CBinaryTree::TraverseTree(_TreeNode* current)
{
    if(current==NULL)
    {
        return;
    }

    //
    // Simple left->right subtree traversal
    //
    TraverseTree(current->pLeftChild);
    printf("Item: %d\n", current->data);

    return;
}

BOOL CBinaryTree::AddNode(_TreeNode* item,
                         _TreeNode* current,
                         DWORD dwRecursiveCount)
{
    BOOL bRet=FALSE;

    //
    // Empty tree, initialize the head pointer
    //
    if(current==NULL)
    {
        m_pHead=item;
        m_dwDepth=dwRecursiveCount;
        return TRUE;
    }
    else
    {
        if(item->data>current->data)
        {
            if(current->pRightChild==NULL)
        {
                current->pRightChild=item;
                m_dwDepth=(m_dwDepth<dwRecursiveCount+1) ?
                        dwRecursiveCount+1 : m_dwDepth;
                bRet=TRUE;
            }
            else
```

```
            {
                return AddNode(item,
                                current->pRightChild,
                                dwRecursiveCount+1);
            }
        }
    }
    else if(item->data<current->data)
    {
        if(current->pLeftChild==NULL)
        {
            current->pLeftChild=item;
            m_dwDepth=(m_dwDepth<dwRecursiveCount+1) ?
                    dwRecursiveCount+1 : m_dwDepth;
            bRet=TRUE;
        }
        else
        {
            return AddNode(item,
                            current->pLeftChild,
                            dwRecursiveCount+1);
        }
    }

    return bRet ;
}
```

The source code and binary for the binary tree can be found in the following folders:

Source code: `C:\AWD\Chapter11\bstree`

Binary: `C:\AWDBIN\WinXP.x86.chk\bstree.exe`

Furthermore, a simple test application has been written (bstree.exe) that makes use of the binary tree. The source code for the bstree.exe application is shown in Listing 11.2.

**Listing 11.2**   BSTREE.EXE using the binary tree implementation

```
#include "bstree.h"

void __cdecl main ( )
{
  CBinaryTree* tree = new CBinaryTree();
  if ( tree != NULL )
  {
```

*(continues)*

**Listing 11.2**   BSTREE.EXE using the binary tree implementation *(continued)*

```
    tree->Add (10);
    tree->Add (5);
    tree->Add (15);
    tree->Add (7);
    tree->Add (13);

    tree->Traverse ();
  }
}
```

The output from one application run is as follows:

```
Item: 5
Item: 10
```

Judging from the output, something is going wrong in the application. The code added five nodes to the binary tree, but only two are displayed when traversing the tree. How exactly would you proceed with this debug session? Really only two major portions of this code could have gone wrong:

- The adding of new nodes to the tree
- The traversal code

Since the problem appears to be happening while traversing and displaying the contents of the tree, a good starting point is to set a breakpoint in the `Traverse` function and verify the integrity of the tree by using the `dt` command.

```
0:000> dt this
Local var @ 0x6ff1c Type CBinaryTree*
0x00262c30
   +0x000 m_pHead        : 0x00262c50
```

As you can see, there is not much to the `CBinaryTree` data members. It merely contains a pointer (m_pHead) to the first node of the tree, and the pointer appears, at first sight, to be quite reasonable (that is, non-`null` and within decent range). Because we only have a pointer to the root node of the tree, how can we go about dumping out the contents in the debugger? The good news is that it is possible; the bad news is that it is tedious. As with most binary tree implementations, the head pointer points to a data type that typically contains the data item in the node, as well as a left child/right child item that are yet other pointers to the same data type. Looking at the source code, we can see that the m_pHead pointer is of type _TreeNode, which is shown below:

```
class _TreeNode
{
  public:
    _TreeNode (int num) { pLeftChild=NULL; pRightChild=NULL; data=num; }

    int data;
    _TreeNode* pLeftChild;
    _TreeNode* pRightChild;
};
```

To see the contents of the m_pHead pointer, we again use the dt command on the m_pHead pointer:

```
0:000> dt bstree!CBinaryTree::_TreeNode 0x00262c50
   +0x000 data            : 10
   +0x004 pLeftChild      : 0x00262c78
   +0x008 pRightChild     : 0x00262ca0
```

The data field is set to 10 (which matches the client code's first insertion), and the pointers all seem reasonable. Before we proceed with traversing the entire tree by hand in the debugger, we should take a look at what we expect the tree to look like. Here are the insertions made in the client code:

```
tree->Add(10);
tree->Add(5);
tree->Add(15);
tree->Add(7);
tree->Add(13);
```

The insertions yield a tree shown in Figure 11.1.

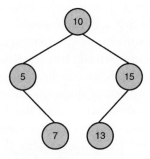

**Figure 11.1**   Tree representation after insertion of 10, 5, 15, 7, and 13

11. WRITING CUSTOM DEBUGGER EXTENSIONS

What we would reasonably expect if we were to dump out the left child pointer is a _TreeNode with the data item set to 5, the left child set to null, and the right child containing yet another valid pointer:

```
0:000> dt bstree!CBinaryTree::_TreeNode 0x00262c78
   +0x000 data              : 5
   +0x004 pLeftChild        : (null)
   +0x008 pRightChild       : 0x00262cc8
```

Continuing this process for the entire tree, we end up with the following debug session:

```
0:000> dt bstree!CBinaryTree::_TreeNode 0x00262cc8
   +0x000 data              : 7
   +0x004 pLeftChild        : (null)
   +0x008 pRightChild       : (null)
0:000> dt bstree!CBinaryTree::_TreeNode 0x00262ca0
   +0x000 data              : 15
   +0x004 pLeftChild        : 0x00262cf0
   +0x008 pRightChild       : (null)
0:000> dt bstree!CBinaryTree::_TreeNode 0x00262cf0
   +0x000 data              : 13
   +0x004 pLeftChild        : (null)
   +0x008 pRightChild       : (null)
```

At this point, we have verified the integrity of the tree (data items were valid, as well as all pointers being dereferenced successfully), which means that the Add function of the tree appears to be working properly and something has to be wrong with the Traverse function. I'll leave it as an exercise to the reader to code review the Traverse function and spot the mistake.

Quite a lot of debugging work, isn't it? And this is only for a tree of size 5. Imagine that this component was used in a system under heavy stress; we could end up with thousands of entries. A much better approach would be if we could tell the debugger how to interpret this data structure by simply issuing a tree command with the head pointer and let the debugger automatically traverse the binary tree instance.

This is a prime scenario in which we can leverage the power of debugger extensions to automate the tedious process of dumping the contents of our tree data type. By creating our own debugger extension, we can implement a command that takes a pointer to the root of the tree and displays the contents. This could save us hours of manual debugging steps. Before we proceed with the technical details of how to implement our debugger extension, we need to look at and understand the two different debugger extension models that the debuggers expose and then decide which would work best for our scenario.

## Debugger Extension Models

The basic idea behind a custom debugger extension is to allow users to automate their debug sessions by typing in specific commands implemented in the debugger extension. How does this actually work? At a high level, it is a four-step process, as illustrated in Figure 11.2.

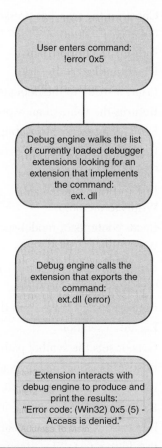

**Figure 11.2** Overview of the debugger extensions process

The most critical part of a debugger extension is how it interacts with the main debug engine (step 4). Three different models exist that define this interaction. The first model, named the WDbgExt model, is the original model, and it has been around for quite some time. Interaction between the debugger extension and main debug engine is done via regular C API(s). Because it is based on C, it provides for a fairly painless programming model, but it is also somewhat limited in what interactions are supported. Table 11.2 shows the currently supported API(s) in the WDbgExts model.

**Table 11.2**    WDbgExts API(s)

| WDbgExts Function | Description |
|---|---|
| GetContext | Returns context of process being debugged. |
| SetContext | Sets the context of the process being debugged. |
| CheckControlC | Checks if the user has pressed CTRL+C. Useful when implementing interruptible commands. |
| GetDebuggerData | Retrieves debugger data. |
| Disasm | Disassembles. |
| Dprintf | Prints a string to the debugger command window. |
| GetExpression | Returns the value of an expression. |
| IoCtl | Entry point for kernel debugger extension routines. |
| GetKdContext | Returns total number of processors and number of current processor. |
| ReadMemory | Reads from memory. |
| WriteMemory | Writes to memory. |
| ReadMsr | Reads contents of model-specific register on Pentiums. |
| WriteMsr | Writes to a model-specific register on Pentiums. |
| ReadPhysical | Reads from physical memory. |
| WritePhysical | Writes to physical memory. |
| StackTrace | Returns a stack trace from the process being debugged. |
| GetSymbol | Locates a symbol. |
| GetSetSympath | Gets or sets the symbol path. |
| ReadControlSpace | Reads processor specific control space. |
| ReadControlSpace64 | Reads the processor-specific control space (64 bit). |
| ReadIoSpace | Reads from system I/O locations. |
| ReadIoSpace64 | Reads from system I/O locations (64 bit). |
| ReadIoSpaceEx | In addition to I/O location reads, reads bus I/O. |
| ReadIoSpaceEx64 | In addition to I/O location reads, reads bus I/O (64 bit). |
| WriteIoSpace | Writes to system I/O locations. |
| WriteIoSpace64 | Writes to system I/O locations (64 bit). |
| WriteIoSpaceEx | In addition to I/O location reads, reads bus I/O. |
| WriteIoSpaceEx64 | In addition to I/O location reads, reads bus I/O (64 bit). |
| SetThreadForOperation | Sets thread to use for next stack trace. |
| SetThreadForOperation64 | Sets thread to use for next stack trace (64 bit). |

A few callbacks functions also enable the debug engine to query the debugger extension for some basic information (such as version), as well as initialization routines called by the debug engine.

- `ExtensionApiVersion`: Returns the version of the extension
- `CheckVersion`: Ensures matching versions between debug engine and extension
- `WinDbgExtensionDllInit`: Initialization routine for WinDbg extensions

The newer and more powerful model is named DbgEng and is based on COM (Component Object Model). Debugger extensions receive COM interface pointers in their implementations that can be used to interact with the main debug engine. The interface pointers are passed to each function exported in the extension DLL. The COM interface model exposes a large API set and enables very fine-grained control over the interaction between the extension and the debug engine. For more detailed information on the available functions for each interface and detailed descriptions, see the SDK documentation (debugext.chm).

The plethora of interfaces and associated functions available for the DbgEng model is substantially larger and more powerful than that of its older sibling (WDbgExts) but also slightly more complex to program against. To bridge the gap between the WDbgExt and DbgEng models, a third model was introduced, called the EngExtCpp model. The EngExtCpp model is a C++ based extension library that is built on top of DbgEng. It provides an abstraction of the DbgEng model that makes programming against it much easier.

It is important to note that the models are not mutually exclusive. A hybrid approach is possible and oftentimes beneficial. In one and the same debugger extension, one can imagine using the C-style API(s) of the WdbgExts model to do simpler tasks while leveraging the power of the DbgEng model for more advanced commands. To make life interesting and educational, we illustrate a hybrid model in the custom debugger extension we are about to implement.

## Requirements for Our Sample Extension

As with any component that we develop, it is important to define the exact requirements. Let's begin our implementation journey by dutifully spending the time to specify exactly what we expect the debugger extension to do.

Our extension DLL is named `sysexts.dll`, and it exports the following commands. (Don't worry about the specific API(s) at the moment; they will be explained later on.)

- ▪ `Help`

  **Description**

  The `help` command displays the syntax of all available commands in the debugger extension as well as a brief description and example of how the command is used.

  **Example**

  **`0:000> !sysexts.help`**

  SYSYEXTS.DLL commands:

  `Help`        = Shows this help

  `DumpTree <address>`      = Dumps out the contents of a CBinaryTree. Address must point to the root node of the tree.

  **Debug Engine API(s)**

  The only debug engine API required in this command is the dprintf API, which allows us to print information to the debug console window (part of the Wdbgexts model).

- ▪ `DumpTree`

  **Description**

  The `DumpTree` command traverses the `CBinaryTree` root pointer passed in and dumps out its contents. The traversal will be done using the standard in-order tree traversal algorithm.

  **Example**

  ```
  0:000> !sysexts.dumptree 0x00262c40
  ** Node **
    Data: 5
    Left child pointer: 0x0
    Right child pointer: 0x262cb8
  ** Node **
    Data: 7
    Left child pointer: 0x0
    Right child pointer: 0x0
  0:000>
  ```

  **Debug Engine API(s)**

  The primary debug engine API required is IDataSpaces::ReadVirtual, which enables an extension to read from virtual memory.

- ▪ Support for custom formatting of our objects when the user types `dt <our-object> <address>`

**Description**

Dumps out an augmented representation of the CBinaryTree contents. The additional information includes the root node of the tree.

**Example**

```
0:000> dt CBinaryTree 0x00262c20
```
  Root Node [Ptr]: 0x262D48
    Root Node data: 10
    Root Node Left Child [Ptr]: 0x262D70
    Root Node Right Child [Ptr]: 0x262D98

  +0x000 m_pHead        : 0x00262d48
  +0x004 m_dwDepth      : 3
  +0x008 m_dwNumNodes   : 5
  +0x00c m_szDescription : [256] "Sample binary tree"

**Debug Engine API(s)**

Implement the KnownStructOutput function.

■ Cancellation support

**Description**

Support for canceling a currently executing command. All debugger extensions that can potentially execute a command for long periods of time should include cancellation logic. Cancellations are normally carried out when the user presses CTRL+C during command execution. Although it is not required to include such support, nothing is more frustrating than having to wait several minutes for a command, which has mistakenly been entered, to finish executing. Since our DumpTree command can potentially take quite some time to finish (if the tree depth is large), we include support for cancellations in our implementation.

**Debug Engine API(s)**

CheckControlC API (part of the Wdbgexts model)

Now that you have a clear understanding of the requirements for our debugger extension, we can begin the implementation journey.

## Required Header Files and Code Organization

To write custom debugger extensions, you must do a custom installation of the Debugging Tools for Windows and select the SDK option. Figure 11.3 shows the directory structure of the SDK folder once installed.

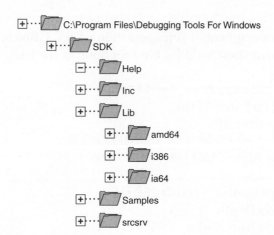

**Figure 11.3** SDK Directory structure

As is the case with any new SDK you encounter, the first thing you must figure out is what header files are required in order to code against it. The choices for which header files can be used are shown in Table 11.3.

**Table 11.3** Available Header Files when Writing Debugger Extensions

| Header File | Description |
|---|---|
| dbgeng.h | Included by all debugger extensions that use the DbgEng model |
| wdbgexts.h | Included by all debugger extensions that use the WDbgExts model |
| engextcpp.hpp | Included by all debugger extensions that use the EngExtCpp model |

If your debugger extension only uses one particular model, including one of the preceding files is sufficient. Because our implementation is a hybrid model, we include both files.

Next, the question of code organization must be addressed. The debugger extension we will be building is laid out as described in Table 11.4.

**Table 11.4**  Files Needed for the Sample Debugger Extension

| Source File | Description |
|---|---|
| Sources | File required by the WDK build environment. This file details how the debugger extension is built (see Compiling and Linking). |
| sysexts.cpp | This file contains the implementation of all the debugger extension commands (including initialization and uninitialization code). |
| sysexts.h | This is the header file that accompanies the main sysexts.cpp file. |
| sysexts.def | This is the file that is referenced from sources and details what functions in the extension DLL are exported. |

Most of the time, the code layout defined in Table 11.4 is perfectly sufficient. If your debugger extension grows in size and the number of implemented commands gets larger and larger, you might consider breaking up the debugger extension source code into separate files to make maintenance easier.

The source code and binary for the sample extension can be found in the following folders:

Source code: `C:\AWD\Chapter11\sysexts`

Binary: `C:\AWDBIN\WinXP.x86.chk\sysexts.dll`

Let's begin by looking at the sysexts.h file:

```
#pragma once
#include <windows.h>

#define KDEXT_64BIT
#define DBG_COMMAND_EXCEPTION          ((DWORD   )0x40010009L)
#include <wdbgexts.h>
#include <dbgeng.h>
WINDBG_EXTENSION_APIS64 ExtensionApis;
```

In addition to including the debug SDK header files as discussed previously, we include `windows.h` to get access to most of the Windows API declarations. The only odd parts of this header file are the following cryptic definitions:

```
#define KDEXT_64BIT
#define DBG_COMMAND_EXCEPTION ((DWORD)0x40010009L)
WINDBG_EXTENSION_APIS64 ExtensionApis;
```

For the first two definitions (`KDEXT_64BIT` and `DBG_COMMAND_EXCEPTION`), if a hybrid model is being implemented (as in our case), the inclusion of both debug header files requires the previous definitions prior to including the wdbgexts.h header file. Without the definitions, you will encounter build errors. If you are implementing a nonhybrid model, the definition is not required.

The third definition also deals with making sure that the wdbgexts model is initialized properly. For an extension to use the WDbgExts API(s), it needs to define a global variable to make sure that it can use the WDbgExts API(s). The global variable needs to be initialized prior to using the debugger extension, and it is typically done in the initialization routine of the extension. (You will see an example of this in the next section "Extension Initialization.")

The last file of importance before we dig into the command implementations is `sysexts.def`:

```
EXPORTS
  help
  dumptree

  DebugExtensionInitialize
  DebugExtensionUninitialize
  KnownStructOutput
```

This file merely tells the build environment which functions in our debugger extension DLL should be considered publicly exported. If we were to add more commands, the name of the function should also be added to this file. We begin our implementation with the extension initialization and uninitialization code.

## Extension Initialization

When a user enters the `.load` command in the debugger, the debug engine responds by loading the extension DLL and executing a sequence of function calls on the debugger extension, enabling the extension to perform some preparatory work before accepting commands. Similarly, when the debugger extension is unloaded, the debug engine calls an exported function on the extension DLL to allow for cleanup. During the debug session, any number of function calls are made by the debug engine to the extension DLL, depending on the action being performed in the debugger. The process of loading and unloading the extension DLL and the corresponding function calls is shown in Figure 11.4.

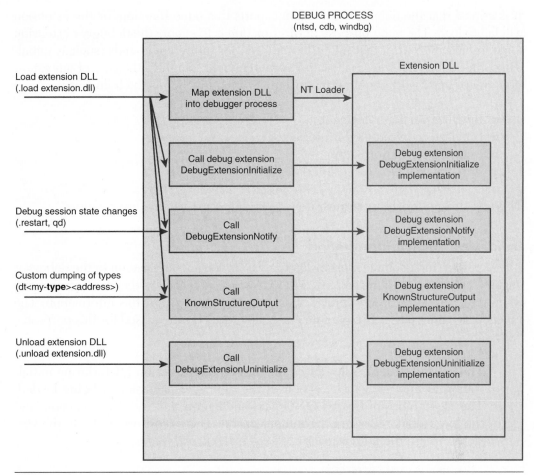

**Figure 11.4**  The process of loading and unloading an extension DLL

When the debugger engine loads an extension in response to the .load command, the debug engine first maps the DLL into the address space of the debugger and subsequently calls the DebugExtensionInitialize function, which must be exported from the custom extension DLL. The exact signature of the function is shown below.

```
HRESULT CALLBACK
DebugExtensionInitialize(OUT PULONG Version, OUT PULONG Flags);
```

It is critical that the debugger extension exports this same function, or the extension will fail to load. The main purpose of this function is to enable the debugger extension to do initialization work that might be required for future commands (such as initializing other debug interfaces, allocating resources, and so on). In the case of our extension, the primary work required in our initialization function is the following.

- Initialize version information.
- Initialize required COM interfaces.
- Initialize type information.
- Initialize WinDbg extension data.

The first thing our extension must do is to initialize the version information.

### Initializing Version Information

It is important for a debugger extension to relay its version information to the debugger engine. The DebugExtensionInitialize function called by the debugger engine when the extension is loaded provides the mechanism to report this information. The function signature passes two parameters—one of which can be used for this purpose.

- Version
  The version structure should be filled in by the extension DLL during initialization to indicate which version of the debugger extension is being loaded. The high 16 bits of this ULONG parameter represent the major version, and the low 16 bits represent the minor version. The easiest way to build the version is to use the helper macro DEBUG_EXTENSION_VERSION:

  ```
  *Version = DEBUG_EXTENSION_VERSION(Major,Minor)
  ```

- Flags
  The flags parameter is reserved and should always be set to 0.

One important issue to note is that when this function is called, it is not guaranteed that there is an active debug session, and the function should not assume that session information is available.

### Initializing COM Interfaces

The next task our initialization code must tackle is to initialize COM debug engine interfaces so that we can effectively interact with the debugger engine to acquire the necessary data structures for the execution of our commands. We will be using the following COM interfaces to dump out our binary tree:

- IDebugClient
- IDebugControl
- IDebugDataSpaces
- IDebugSymbols
- IDebugSymbols3

The very first COM interface that we need access to is the IDebugClient interface. We need this interface so that we can get access to a structure required by the WDbgExts model to function properly, as well as being able to query for all the other interfaces. The way to get an interface pointer to the IDebugClient COM interface is to call the `DebugCreate` API:

```
HRESULT DebugCreate(IN REFIID InterfaceId,OUT PVOID* Interface);
```

The interface ID can be easily retrieved using the `__uuidof` compiler extension that expects the COM interface declaration as part of it. Next, we can use the IDebugClient interface to query for the other COM interfaces that we will be using later on.

The code that initializes the COM interfaces is shown in Listing 11.3.

**Listing 11.3**    Debugger COM interfaces initialization

```
//
// Initialize required COM interface pointers
//
if(FAILED(hRes=DebugCreate(__uuidof(IDebugClient),
                           (void**) &pDebugClient)))
{
    dprintf( "Failed to get required COM interface\n");
    return hRes;
}


if(FAILED(hRes=pDebugClient->QueryInterface(__uuidof(IDebugControl),
                                           (void**) &pDebugControl)))
{
    dprintf( "Failed to get required COM interface\n");
    ReleaseComPointers();
    return hRes;
}


if(FAILED((hRes=pDebugClient->QueryInterface(__uuidof(IDebugDataSpaces),
                                            (void**) &pDataSpaces))))
{
    dprintf( "Failed to get required COM interface\n");
```

*(continues)*

**Listing 11.3** Debugger COM interfaces initialization *(continued)*

```
    ReleaseComPointers();
    return hRes;
}

if(FAILED(hRes=pDebugClient->QueryInterface(__uuidof(IDebugSymbols),
                                    (void**) &pSymbols)))
{
    dprintf( "Failed to get required COM interface\n");
    ReleaseComPointers();
    return hRes;
}

if(FAILED(hRes=pDebugClient->QueryInterface(__uuidof(IDebugSymbols3),
                                    (void**) &pSymbols3)))
{
    dprintf( "Failed to get required COM interface\n");
    ReleaseComPointers();
    return hRes;
}
```

### Initializing Type Information

The next part of the initialization code retrieves type information about the binary tree. To understand why this step is necessary, you must understand how the debugger extension gets the data associated with the binary tree. When the user enters the dumptree command, he specifies an address corresponding to the address of the root node of the tree. The debugger extension's job is to read X number of bytes from that address and interpret the read bytes as if they represented a binary tree. One possible solution is for the debugger extension to include the header for the binary tree and use it as a first class type; however, using this approach has a big drawback. The debugger extension is strongly typed to a particular version of the binary tree, and if the binary tree implementation changes in a future version (such as added data members), you will need to recompile the extension to work against the new binary tree type and keep different versions of the extension. To circumvent this deficiency, the debug engine includes a set of API(s) that enable an extension to query for type information at runtime, thereby minimizing the compile time type dependency. The API(s) is extremely powerful and allows for in-depth type analysis. In our extension, we need to know about the binary tree node type. More specifically, we need to find the offset of each of the data members (right child pointer, left child pointer, and data member) so that we know from where to start reading data relative to the address specified by the user. The in-memory layout of the binary tree node is

```
+0x000 data            : Int4B
+0x004 pLeftChild      : Ptr32 CBinaryTree::_TreeNode
+0x008 pRightChild     : Ptr32 CBinaryTree::_TreeNode
```

Each of the numbers prefixed by a + represents the offset of each of the members in the type. The steps required to programmatically find out about the offsets are as follows:

1. Get the module by using the `IDebugSymbols::GetModuleByModuleName` to be used in subsequent steps. The module of interest is the module where the type is defined. In our case, the module of interest is the bstree module, which contains the `CBinaryTree::_TreeNode` type.
2. Get the type identifier of the type we're interested in (`CBinaryTree::_TreeNode`) using the `IDebugSymbols3::GetTypeId` API. The result of the API call is a type identifier that can be used in subsequent steps.
3. Get the offset for each member using the `IDebugSymbols::GetField Offset` API. The offsets retrieved will be subsequently used by the extension to read the type information.

The code that initializes the type information is shown in Listing 11.4.

**Listing 11.4**   Initialization of type information

```
//
// Initialize type information
//
if(FAILED(hRes=pSymbols->GetModuleByModuleName("bstree",
                                               0,
                                               NULL,
                                               &pBase)))
{
    dprintf("Failed to get module information for bstree.exe\n");
    ReleaseComPointers();
    return hRes;
}
if(FAILED(hRes=pSymbols3->GetTypeId(pBase,
                                    "CBinaryTree::_TreeNode",
                                    &pNodeIndex)))
{
    dprintf("Failed to get type id\n");
    ReleaseComPointers();
    return hRes;
}
if(FAILED(hRes=pSymbols->GetTypeSize(pBase,
```

*(continues)*

**Listing 11.4** Initialization of type information *(continued)*

```
                                        pNodeIndex,
                                        &pSize)))
{
    dprintf("Failed to get type size\n");
    ReleaseComPointers();
    return hRes;
}


if(FAILED(hRes=pSymbols->GetFieldOffset(pBase,
                                        pNodeIndex,
                                        "pLeftChild",
                                        &ulLeftOffset)))
{
    dprintf("Failed to get left child offset\n");
    ReleaseComPointers();
    return hRes;
}


if(FAILED(hRes=pSymbols->GetFieldOffset(pBase,
                                        pNodeIndex,
                                        "pRightChild",
                                        &ulRightOffset)))
{
    dprintf("Failed to get right child offset\n");
    ReleaseComPointers();
    return hRes;
}


if(FAILED(hRes=pSymbols->GetFieldOffset(pBase,
                                        pNodeIndex,
                                        "data",
                                        &ulDataOffset)))
{
    dprintf("Failed to get data offset\n");
    ReleaseComPointers();
    return hRes;
}
```

### Initializing WinDbg Extension Data

The final task that the extension must do is to initialize WinDbg extension data that is required when working with the WinDbg extension model. IDebugControl::

GetWinDbgExtensionApis64 can be used for this purpose and simply accepts a pointer to an instance of WINDBG_EXTENION_APIS64.

The code that initializes the type information is shown in Listing 11.5.

**Listing 11.5**  Initializing the WinDbg extension data

```
//
// Initialize WinDbg extension data
//
ExtensionApis.nSize=sizeof(ExtensionApis);
hRes=pDebugControl->GetWindbgExtensionApis64(&ExtensionApis);
```

## Session State Changes

After the initialization function has been successfully executed, the debug engine calls the DebugExtensionNotify function exported by the extension DLL. This function enables the debug engine to notify the debugger extension of any changes in the session status. If a session ever becomes active or inactive, the debugger extension should make note of this if it needs to suspend certain parts of its code. Similarly, if the debug session ever becomes accessible/nonaccessible, it also should be recorded. The function signature is shown below.

```
void CALLBACK
DebugExtensionNotify ( IN ULONG Notify, IN ULONG64 Argument )
```

The debug engine calls this function (on the extension DLL) and specifies the reason for the notification (see the SDK) in the Notify parameter and 0 for the Argument (reserved). The different notifications are listed in Table 11.5.

**Table 11.5**  Debugger Session States

| State | Description |
| --- | --- |
| DEBUG_NOTIFY_SESSION_ACTIVE | A debugging session is active. The session might not necessarily be halted. |
| DEBUG_NOTIFY_SESSION_INACTIVE | No debugging session is active. |
| DEBUG_NOTIFY_SESSION_ACESSIBLE | The debugging session has halted and is now accessible. |
| DEBUG_NOTIFY_SESSION_INACCESSIBLE | The debugging session has started running and is now inaccessible. |

## KnownStructOutput

The next function call made by the debug engine during load time is to `KnownStructOutput`. The Windows debuggers have a nice feature that enables debugger extensions to support custom displaying of a data type in one single line (such as when the user executes the `dt` command). Rather than calling every extension for every `dt` command issued, the debug engine calls the `KnownStructOutput` function when the DLL first is loaded and asks the extension for the names of data types for which it supports custom formatting. In the load case, it is the responsibility of the debugger extension to return a list of custom data types, if supported. If a call to `dt` is ever issued to the debugger, the debug engine knows to call the correct extension version of the `KnownStructOutput` based on the accumulation of all lists returned during load time. We show an example of a `KnownStructOutput` implementation later in the chapter.

## Uninitializing the Extension

The final function call made by the debug engine is when a user unloads an extension DLL (using the `.unload` command); at this time, the debug engine calls `DebugExtensionUninitialize` on the debugger extension. The function signature is shown below.

```
void CALLBACK DebugExtensionUninitialize(void);
```

A debugger extension should expose this function if it needs to do any cleanup work when the debugger extension is unloaded. An example of cleanup work includes releasing any global resources acquired during initialization (such as releasing any global COM instances or memory).

Because our debugger extension initialization code acquired COM interfaces, it is important that we release the reference count for all the interface pointers to avoid a leak:

```
extern "C" void CALLBACK DebugExtensionUninitialize(void)
{
    ReleaseComPointers();
    return;
}

VOID ReleaseComPointers()
{
    if(pDebugClient) pDebugClient->Release();
    if(pDebugControl) pDebugControl->Release();
    if(pSymbols) pSymbols->Release();
```

```
    if(pSymbols3) pSymbols3->Release();
    if(pDataSpaces) pDataSpaces->Release();
}
```

## Implementing the Help Command

Now that we have the initialization and uninitialization code out of the way, we can move on to the more interesting code of the actual commands we want to implement.

All custom debug commands must adhere to the following signature and must consist of all lowercase letters:

```
HRESULT CALLBACK
(* PDEBUG_EXTENSION_CALL)
(
    IN IDebugClient* Client,
    IN OPTIONAL PCSTR Args
) ;
```

The PDEBUG_EXTENSION_CALL is the function itself and must be named according to the debugger extension command to be implemented. The implementation of our extensions help command is shown in the following:

```
// This function displays help for the debugger extension
HRESULT CALLBACK help ( PDEBUG_CLIENT Client, PCSTR Args )
{
  dprintf ("SYSEXTS.DLL commands:\n"
           "help = Shows this help\n"
           "\tdumptree <address>=Dumps out the contents of a CBinaryTree.  Address
must point to the root node of the tree"
          );

  return S_OK ;
}
```

As you can see, the function is as simple as using the dprintf function to print out the help for the debugger extension. The dprintf function is essentially the equivalent of printf for debugger extensions.

To test the extension, we run an arbitrary application under the debugger. (I typically use notepad.exe.) When you have hit a breakpoint in the debugger, type the following command:

```
.load C:\AWDBIN\WinXP.x86.chk\sysexts.dll
```

At this point, the extension DLL is loaded into the address space of the debugger, and the initialize function is called. If no errors occur, you are presented with the debug symbol. Type `!sysexts.help` to invoke the help command, and you will see the following:

```
0:000> !sysexts.help

SYSYEXTS.DLL commands:


        Help = Shows this help
        dumptree <address> = Dumps out the contents of a CBinaryTree. Address must
point to the root node of the tree
```

If there is an error loading the debugger extension or running the command, such as an exception being thrown, the error will be surfaced as a generic exception in the debug output but will not crash the debug process. The debug engine wraps all calls into the custom debugger extension with an exception handler to avoid any malfunctioning extension from bringing down the entire debug session. Having said that, if the problem is severe enough (such as writing over memory not owned by the extension), chances are that the debug session will fail somewhere down the road. If you suspect that an extension is misbehaving, you need to debug it and find out what is wrong before deploying the extension. The interesting question is how do you go about debugging the extension? Although the answer can seem somewhat odd, it makes perfect sense; simply debug the debugger. Attach the debugger to the debugger, and when the failure occurs, it will break in just like any other debug session.

Now we can move on to implementing the slightly more difficult command, which is that of dumping the contents of our binary tree.

## Implementing the dumptree Command

The fundamental idea behind the `dumptree` command is to enable easy dumping of the contents of a binary tree of type `CBinaryTree`. The command syntax itself is shown below.

```
!sysexts.dumptree <address to root pointer of the binary tree>
```

The function signature and dummy body resemble the following:

```
// This function dumps the CBinaryTree received in the Args
HRESULT CALLBACK dumptree(PDEBUG_CLIENT Client, PCSTR Args)
{
```

```
  HRESULT hRes=S_OK;

  return hRes;
}
```

Before we get too concerned with the implementation details, we will lay out the overall strategy for the `dumptree` command. The algorithm used for this command will be

1. Extract and validate the address passed in by the user.
2. Read the root tree node from memory based on the address specified.
3. Call a recursive in-order `Traverse` function that displays node items until the tree is exhausted.

We need an address to the root node of the tree. This is specified by the user when he enters the command in the debug session, such as

```
!sysexts.dumptree 00181eb4
```

Several questions should arise when looking at the preceding statement. How do we get access to the address specified? How can we be sure that the user has entered a valid address? These questions bring us to the first important part of implementing complex commands: extracting and validating user input.

The parameters that the user enters as part of the command are passed into your function via the `Args` parameter. The `Args` parameter is basically a string that contains the entire command line just entered minus the command name itself. If the user entered the following command

```
!sysexts.dumptree 00181eb4
```

the `Args` parameter would contain

```
00181eb4
```

Because our goal is to be able to read memory at the specified address, we cannot accept this parameter to be of type PCSTR (string pointer); rather, we would ideally want this value to be converted into a pointer that we can pass to the memory access API(s). The API that allows us to achieve this is the `GetExpression` API, which is declared as

```
ULONG_PTR GetExpression ( PCSTR expression )
```

When called, the GetExpression API takes the parameter passed in and tries to evaluate the parameter into a ULONG_PTR. If the evaluation succeeds, the API returns a ULONG_PTR. The pointer can then be used when calling memory access API(s). If the API fails, null is returned.

The dumptree implementations usage of GetExpression is shown below.

```
HRESULT CALLBACK dumptree(PDEBUG_CLIENT pClient, PCSTR szArgs)
{
    HRESULT hRes=S_OK;

    ULONG_PTR pAddress=(ULONG_PTR) GetExpression(szArgs);
    if(!pAddress)
    {
        dprintf("Invalid head pointer address specified: %s\n", szArgs);
        return E_FAIL;
    }

    InOrderTraversal(pAddress);
    return hRes;
}
```

The preceding code is pretty straightforward. We simply pass the szArgs parameter to the GetExpression API. If the return value is non-null, we continue; otherwise, we print out a message to the debug console window stating that an invalid address was specified and returned an error.

Now that we have extracted and verified the address specified as part of our dumptree command, we can proceed by calling the helper function InOrderTraversal, which performs the bulk of the work when traversing and displaying the tree node information.

The InOrderTraversal function recursively traverses the tree and prints out tree node information by using a helper function called GetNodeValues. GetNodeValues performs the interesting work of actually reading the memory contents associated with a tree node. The implementation of GetNodeValues is shown here.

```
HRESULT GetNodeValues(ULONG64 pNode,
                      ULONG* pulData,
                      ULONG* pulLeft,
                      ULONG* pulRight)
{
    if(FAILED(hRes=pDataSpaces->ReadVirtual((ULONG_PTR) pNode+ulDataOffset,
                                 pulData,
```

```
                                         sizeof(ULONG),
                                         NULL)))
{
    dprintf("Failed to read memory at address: 0x%X\n",
            pNode+ulDataOffset);
    return E_FAIL;
}


if(FAILED(hRes=pDataSpaces->ReadVirtual((ULONG_PTR) pNode+ulLeftOffset,
                                         pulLeft,
                                         sizeof(ULONG),
                                         NULL)))
{
    dprintf("Failed to read memory at address: 0x%X\n",
            pNode+ulLeftOffset);
    return E_FAIL;
}


if(FAILED(hRes=pDataSpaces->ReadVirtual((ULONG_PTR) pNode+ulRightOffset,
                                         pulRight,
                                         sizeof(ULONG),
                                         NULL)))
{
    dprintf("Failed to read memory at address: 0x%X\n",
            pNode+ulRightOffset);
    return E_FAIL;
}


    return S_OK;
}
```

At a high level, the function reads in the memory associated with each of the data members by using the `IDataSpaces::ReadVirtual` API. Please note that we are using the offsets previously initialized to get the correct data members. The `ReadVirtual` API is defined as follows. It enables reading memory from the debugger targets virtual address space:

```
HRESULT IDataSpaces::ReadVirtual (
    IN ULONG64 Offset,
    OUT PVOID Buffer,
    IN ULONG BufferSize,
    OUT OPTIONAL PULONG BytesRead
    ) ;
```

The `Offset` parameter is the address we want to read from, the `Buffer` parameter contains the read data upon a successful read, the `BufferSize` parameter indicates the size of the data buffer we passed in, and `BytesRead`, upon completion, contains the actual number of bytes read by the API. If the function is successful, `S_OK` is returned.

The final helper function in our extension is `PrintNode`, which simply prints out the data—the left child pointer and right child pointer members of the tree node.

You can now use the extension to dump trees of arbitrary size in a very simple and convenient fashion. Let's try it out. Run the `bstree.exe` application under the debugger and set the breakpoint at the `Traverse` function. Get the head pointer (as shown previously) and invoke the `dumptree` command:

```
...
...
...
0:000> .load C:\AWDBIN\WinXP.x86.chk\sysexts.dll
0:000> dv
         this = 0x00262c20
0:000> dt this
Local var @ 0x6ff1c Type CBinaryTree*
0x00262c20
   +0x000 m_pHead          : 0x00262c40
   +0x004 m_dwDepth        : 3
   +0x008 m_dwNumNodes     : 5
0:000> !sysexts.dumptree 0x00262c40
** Node **
   Data: 5
   Left child pointer: 0x0
   Right child pointer: 0x262cb8
** Node **
   Data: 7
   Left child pointer: 0x0
   Right child pointer: 0x0
** Node **
   Data: 10
   Left child pointer: 0x262c68
   Right child pointer: 0x262c90
** Node **
   Data: 13
   Left child pointer: 0x0
   Right child pointer: 0x0
** Node **
   Data: 15
   Left child pointer: 0x262ce0
```

```
Right child pointer: 0x0
```

Please note that the example usage of the dumptree command does not include the output from the KnownStructOutput function, which we discuss in the next section.

Here are a couple of notes regarding the dumptree command. If you ever encounter a corrupt tree (that is, one of the pointers in the nodes points to a nonvalid address), the dumptree command records that with an error as per our code. This is usually a perfect indication of a corrupt tree. Further debugging should commence from there (see Chapter 6, "Memory Corruption Part II—Heaps").

## Implementing the KnownStructOutput Function

The KnownStructOutput function is a convenient way of extending the functionality of the regular dt command. By default, the dt command displays the contents of the specified data type (if enough symbolic information is available). If we were to dump an instance of the CBinaryTree::_TreeNode data using the dt command, we would get the following:

```
0:000> dt CBinaryTree::_TreeNode
   +0x000 data            : Int4B
   +0x004 pLeftChild      : Ptr32 CBinaryTree::_TreeNode
   +0x008 pRightChild     : Ptr32 CBinaryTree::_TreeNode
```

It would be nice if we were able to customize the output of the dt command when applied to the CBinaryTree::_TreeNode data type. Providing an implementation of the KnownStructOutput function allows us to add this additional information without much work.

The function prototype for KnownStructOutput is shown below.

```
HRESULT CALLBACK KnownStructOutput (
    IN ULONG Flag,
    IN ULONG64 Address,
    IN PSTR StructName,
    OUT PSTR Buffer,
    IN OUT PULONG BufferSize
    ) ;
```

The function is a dual behavioral function in the sense that, depending on the flag passed, it either returns the names of the types it supports or the result of evaluating a given address for a particular type. The flag possibilities are shown in Table 11.6.

**Table 11.6** Flags for KnownStructOutput

| Flag | Description |
|------|-------------|
| DEBUG_KNOWN_STRUCT_GET_NAMES | Passed to the function when the debug engine first loads the debugger extensions. The extensions implementation should return a list of the structure names it supports custom outputting of information into. |
| DEBUG_KNOWN_STRUCT_GET_ SINGLE_LINE_OUTPUT | Passed to the function when an actual evaluation is to be performed by the debugger extension. |
| DEBUG_KNOWN_STRUCT_ SUPPRESS_TYPE_NAME | Passed to the function to query whether it wants to have the type name automatically printed. |

In our case, the name of the data type we want to provide additional information on is the CBinaryTree::_TreeNode structure. The skeleton code for the KnownStructOutput function is shown below.

```
HRESULT CALLBACK KnownStructOutput (
    IN ULONG  Flag,
    IN ULONG64  Address,
    IN PSTR  StructName,
    OUT PSTR  Buffer,
    IN OUT PULONG  BufferSize
    )
{
  HRESULT hRes=E_FAIL;

  if(Flag==DEBUG_KNOWN_STRUCT_GET_NAMES)
  {
     //
     // Return the list of names of supported data types
     //
  }
  else if(Flag==DEBUG_KNOWN_STRUCT_GET_SINGLE_LINE_OUTPUT)
  {
     //
     // Return the result of evaluating a data type
     //
  }
  else if(Flag==DEBUG_KNOWN_STRUCT_SUPPRESS_TYPE_NAME)
  {
     //
```

```
      // Return S_OK to indicate that we want the type name automatically
      // printed.
      //
      return S_OK;
   }
   else
   {
      dprintf("KnownStructOutput called with invalid flags\n");
   }
   return hRes;
}
```

Let's start with explaining how to go about returning the list of data structure names that we support. The list of names is returned via the OUT Buffer parameter, which is of type PSTR. It is critical to ensure that we have enough room in the Buffer to successfully enter all the data type names. The size of the buffer is passed in via the BufferSize parameter. Here is our implementation of getting the data type names:

```
if(Flag==DEBUG_KNOWN_STRUCT_GET_NAMES)
{
   if ((*BufferSize)<strlen(SYSEXTS_KNOWNSTRUCT_1)+2)
   {
      // Not enough buffer available, return S_FALSE
      (*BufferSize)=strlen(SYSEXTS_KNOWNSTRUCT_1)+2;
      hRes=S_FALSE;
   }
   else
   {
      hRes=StringCchPrintfA(Buffer,
                            (*BufferSize)-2,
                            "%s\0",
                            SYSEXTS_KNOWNSTRUCT_1);
      if (FAILED(hRes))
      {
         dprintf ("Failed to copy the data type name into buffer\n");
      }
   }
}
```

SYSEXTS_KNOWNSTRUCT_1 is defined in the sysexts.cpp file as

```
#define SYSEXTS_KNOWNSTRUCT_1   "CBinaryTree::_TreeNode"
```

Note that we first check to see if the length of the data type name is less than the buffer size passed in. (+2 accounts for both null terminators.) If the size is less, we proceed with filling in the name and returning. If we do not have enough room, we put the required length into the `BufferSize` parameter and return `S_FALSE`, which indicates that the debug engine should allocate a bigger buffer of the size specified and try calling again.

If we supported custom formatting of multiple data types, we would put each name into the buffer separated by NULL terminators and ending the entire string with another `null` terminator.

Now we move on to implementing the evaluator. The debug engine in this case passes us a flag that contains the `DEBUG_KNOWN_STRUCT_GET_SINGLE_LINE_OUTPUT` value and an address to the data structure. The address can be passed to our helper function `GetNodeValues` defined earlier, which reads the node contents at the specified address and returns the node values. After we have successfully read the node values, we can format the output and return to the debug engine. Note that we take extra care not to exceed the buffer size by explicitly checking to make sure that the data will fit:

```
else if(Flag==DEBUG_KNOWN_STRUCT_GET_SINGLE_LINE_OUTPUT)
{
  ULONG ulData=0;
  ULONG ulLeft=0;
  ULONG ulRight=0;

  if(FAILED(hRes=GetNodeValues(Address, &ulData, &ulLeft, &ulRight)))
  {
      return hRes;
  }

  DWORD dwLen=_scprintf(SYSEXTS_KNOWNSTRUCT_OUT,
                        ulData,
                        ulLeft,
                        ulRight)+1;

  if(dwLen>(*BufferSize))
  {
    dprintf("KnownStructOutput unable to fit return data into buffer\n");
    hRes=E_FAIL;
    return hRes;
  }

  hRes=StringCchPrintfA(Buffer,
                        dwLen,
                        SYSEXTS_KNOWNSTRUCT_OUT,
                        ulData,
```

```
                    ulLeft,
                    ulRight);
    if(FAILED(hRes))
    {
        dprintf ("KnownStructOutput unable to write data into buffer\n");
    }
}
```

We have now implemented an augmentation to the standard dt command that allows us to see the root node contents in addition to the data output by the dt command. Let's try it out. Run bstree.exe under the debugger, set a breakpoint in the traverse method, and issue the dt command against the CBinaryTree root node instance:

```
0:000> dt CBinaryTree::_TreeNode 0x000369c8
Binary tree node contents
   Data: 10
   Left Child Pointer: 0x36fb0
   Right Child Pointer: 0x36fd8

   +0x000 data             : 10
   +0x004 pLeftChild       : 0x00036fb0
Binary tree node contents
   Data: 5
   Left Child Pointer: 0x0
   Right Child Pointer: 0x37000

   +0x008 pRightChild      : 0x00036fd8
Binary tree node contents
   Data: 15
   Left Child Pointer: 0x37028
   Right Child Pointer: 0x0
```

## Implementing Command Cancellations

As with any potentially long-running task, the capability to cancel a command comes into play. Imagine that we tried to dump a CBinaryTtree instance with thousands and thousands of nodes and wanted to cancel the command partway through. As it stands now, our dumptree command is not cancelable, which can cause frustration to users of this debugger extension. How can you add cancellation support? The answer is actually quite simple. An API (as part of the WDbgExts model) allows debugger extensions to query for a CTRL+C by the user:

```
ULONG     CheckControlC (VOID);
```

By calling this API at regular intervals in long-running commands, we can make sure to respect the user's wish to cancel. In addition to dutifully respecting the CTRL+C requests by the user, this has the value add of allowing a user to cancel a dumptree command that would potentially never finish (with the exception of a blown stack because of the recursive nature of the implementation). If, for some reason, a bug were to surface in the CBinaryTree implementation that causes the tree to point back to itself, we could potentially recurse endlessly.

In our case, the dumptree command calls a recursive function that keeps printing nodes until the tree is fully exhausted. If we put this check in prior to starting each recursive call, we can simply end the recursion and return to the user:

```
VOID InOrderTraversal(CBinaryTree::_TreeNode* pNode,IDebugDataSpaces* pDataSpaces)
{
  HRESULT hRes;

  if(CheckControlC()==TRUE)
  {
    dprintf("Control C hit, canceling command\n");
    return;
  }

  //
  // Rest of the InOrderTraversal function code
  //
}
```

If we were to modify the client code of the CBinaryTree slightly to add 1,000 nodes to the tree instance and run it under the debugger, followed by a dumptree command, we could press CTRL+C to cancel the command:

```
0:000> !sysexts.dumptree 0x262D48
** Node **
   Data: 0
   Left child pointer: 0x0
   Right child pointer: 0x262d70
** Node **
   Data: 1
   Left child pointer: 0x0
   Right child pointer: 0x262d98
** Node **
   Data: 2
   Left child pointer: 0x0
```

```
   Right child pointer: 0x262dc0
...
...
...
...
** Node **
   Data: 156
   Left child pointer: 0x0
   Right child pointer: 0x265f38
** Node **
   Data: 157
   Left child pointer: 0x0
   Right child pointer: 0x265f60
Control C hit, canceling command
0:000>
```

**A NOTE ON SYMBOLISM** As described in Chapter 4, "Managing Symbol and Source Files," there are essentially two different types of symbol files used during debugging: public symbols (also known as stripped symbols) and private symbols. The main difference between the two different symbol files is the amount of information available to the developer debugging the application. Public symbols provide very limited symbolic information (makes debugging rather hard), and private symbols contain full symbolic information. Every developer would use private symbols any day to debug an application. The problem arises when a product is shipped. Typically, companies allow access (via a symbol server) to limited public symbols to enable at least a rudimentary form of debugging, but it becomes very difficult to do in-depth debugging because of missing symbolic information, such as type information. Custom debugger extensions can be of help in situations in which you do not want to burn a CD with private symbols every time you need to debug an offsite problem. Consider the following scenario in which you have to debug a CBinaryTree with only public symbols. Trying to dump out the contents of the CBinaryTree instance being debugged will fail because public symbols do not offer the data type members as part of its symbolic information. Without private symbols and without knowing the exact layout of the CBinaryTree structure, what do you do? Well, you can deploy the sysexts.dll extension onto that machine and use the augmented information available when typing dt.

The mechanism of supporting extended type information in your debugger extension is a very useful trick to avoid situations when only limited symbolic information is available.

## Versioning

As with any other component, versioning is important in debugger extensions as well. Over the lifetime of an application, the data structures change formats, and debugger extensions will have to be retrofitted to work with the new data structures and versions of applications. To accommodate future changes, a new version of the debugger extension would have to be created (with a new name, such as sysexts20.dll) and used during debugging. Keeping a complete list of these debugger extensions is well worth your time. One could even imagine writing a debugger extension command that queries a global variable for the version of the application and loads the correct version of the debugger extension.

After installing the Windows debuggers, you will notice that the way versioning is handled in the public Windows debuggers is by putting the extension DLL(s) into directories corresponding to each component release. For example, looking at the userexts.dll debugger extension, we can see that it exists in the following subdirectories under the default installation path of the Windows debuggers:

```
C:\Program Files\Debugging Tools for Windows>dir usere* /s
 Volume in drive C has no label.
 Volume Serial Number is 688E-2C02

 Directory of C:\Program Files\Debugging Tools for Windows\nt4chk

04/16/2004  08:59 AM            98,845 userexts.dll
               1 File(s)         98,845 bytes

 Directory of C:\Program Files\Debugging Tools for Windows\nt4fre

04/16/2004  08:59 AM            99,357 userexts.dll
               1 File(s)         99,357 bytes

 Directory of C:\Program Files\Debugging Tools for Windows\w2kchk

04/16/2004  08:59 AM           171,037 userexts.dll
               1 File(s)        171,037 bytes

 Directory of C:\Program Files\Debugging Tools for Windows\w2kfre

04/16/2004  08:59 AM           170,013 userexts.dll
               1 File(s)        170,013 bytes
```

Depending on which operating system version you are debugging, you will need to load the correct version of the userexts.dll debugger extension. You can find out the version of the operating system by running the `!version` debug command.

## Building the Debugger Extension

To compile the extension DLL, we must first ensure that we have added the correct environment variables to the DDK build console. I typically add the following environment variable directly into my systemwide environment settings so that I do not have to worry about setting them on different consoles:

```
DBGSDK_INC_PATH=C:\PROGRA~1\debugg~1\sdk\inc
DBGSDK_LIB_PATH=C:\PROGRA~1\debugg~1\sdk\lib\*
```

Make sure that the paths for the environment variables match the directory structure you have on your machine (as well as platform-specific subdirectories). We have to make a slight adjustment to the sources file and specify the additional paths, as well as make sure that we link to dbgeng.lib:

```
TARGETLIBS= \
    $(CRT_LIB_PATH)\MSVCRT.lib \
    $(SDK_LIB_PATH)\kernel32.lib \
    $(DBGSDK_LIB_PATH)\dbgeng.lib \


INCLUDES= $(DDK_INC_PATH); \
    $(DBGSDK_INC_PATH); \
```

Both of these sections might contain more libraries or include paths depending on the exact nature of the debugger extension, but for the purpose of our custom debugger extension, what is shown in this listing is sufficient. After you have downloaded and installed the source code from the book's Web page, navigate to the C:\AWD\Chapter11\sysexts folder and type

```
build /ZCc
```

Upon success, the resulting sysexts.dll is placed in the output directory. The name of the output directory depends on which type of build environment you opened (checked or free), as well as the operating system. On a WinXP checked build console window (x86), the binary is placed in

```
objchk_wxp_x86\i386\sysexts.dll
```

We can now fire up the debugger, load the extension, and issue any of the commands we just implemented.

## Summary

As you have seen in this chapter, the notion of custom debugger extensions allows the developer to automate the debugging process by developing custom commands to enhance the debugging sessions. This is truly a great tool that every system developer should have in his arsenal. Although we have just scratched the surface of debugger extensions, it is well worth your time to dig into the SDK documentation and familiarize yourself with the large number of API(s) available for developing extensions. The Microsoft debugger team has made a great effort to make the debug API in-depth and enable virtually unlimited possibilities with regard to extending the default debug experience.

# CHAPTER 12

# 64-Bit Debugging

With the advent of 64-bit processors, the need to understand how these processors work and how to debug 64-bit applications is critical. This chapter outlines the fundamentals of 64-bit debugging. The chapter is organized as a complement to all previous chapters in which the debugger listings were captured from systems running a 32-bit version of the operating system. In this chapter, we highlight the difference in behavior when the host systems have a 64-bit architecture. This chapter follows the order in which the concepts are introduced in the book. The chapter focuses on the 64-bit architecture introduced by AMD in 2004. Virtually all computer systems sold today are capable of running 64-bit operating systems. Windows Vista is the first consumer operating system available simultaneously in 64-bit and 32-bit architectures. It is not a question of whether independent software vendors will release native 64-bit applications. It is just a matter of time until they release 64-bit versions of their applications.

This chapter reuses several samples introduced in the previous chapters. The binary files targeted to Windows Vista x64 are available in the C:\AWDBIN\WinLH. AMD64.chk and C:\AWDBIN\WinLH.AMD64.fre folders. If a Windows Vista x64 system is not available, we provide few memory dumps in the C:\AWDBIN\Dumps folder.

## Microsoft 64-Bit Systems

Microsoft officially entered the 64-bit operating system arena with Microsoft Windows XP 64-Bit Edition that could run on systems powered by Intel Itanium processors. As the name indicates, it was based on Windows XP code base, and it was released to the public in 2002, shortly after the 2001 Windows XP (32-Bit Edition) release.

One year later, Microsoft released Windows Server 2003 Enterprise Edition for Itanium-based systems, capable of supporting workloads required by the highest levels of reliability, availability, and scalability provided by Intel Itanium–based systems.

In the same year, Advanced Micro Devices revealed a new 64-bit processor architecture, designed as an extension to the current x86 processor architecture. The new processor's architecture has also been adopted by Intel, marketed under the Intel

Extended Memory 64 Technology name and later under the Intel 64 Architecture name. Because the difference between the implementations is minimal, this architecture is also known as x86–64. Microsoft uses the name x64 to denote the operating system supporting such architectures.

In 2005, Microsoft released the first version of a client and server operating system supporting x64 systems, named Windows XP Professional x64 Edition and Windows Server 2003 SP1 x64 Edition, respectively. Both versions have the same build number, indicating that they were built from the same code base, and they have identical features with the 32-bit version of Windows 2003 SP1.

In the last quarter of 2006, Microsoft released Windows Vista, the next version of the Windows client operating systems with support for both x86 and x64 processors. Starting with the Windows Vista release, the client operating system no longer supports Intel Itanium processors.

Because the Intel Itanium–based system's availability is relatively limited when compared with that of x64-based systems, this chapter focuses on x64 architecture only. The difference between the client and server operating system is relatively small from a debugging perspective; therefore, we will use the Windows x64 term to denote such systems. In this chapter, we also use the term Windows x86 to generically denote the operating system built for 32-bit architecture.

## Operating System Overview

So what exactly is the difference between the Windows x64 operating systems and Windows x86 operating systems? Without a complete analysis of both implementations, it is hard to understand all differences between them. It is highly recommended that you study the book *Microsoft Windows Internals, 4th Edition* (2004, Mark E. Russinovich and David A. Solomon, Redmond, WA: Microsoft Press), which does an excellent job at analyzing in detail each component of the operating system. This chapter provides a very short analysis of the differences and how they impact debugging.

The biggest gain of moving to Windows x64 comes from the processor's capability to access a 64-bit flat virtual address space. Even if a 64-bit pointer can address 16 exabytes, the current Windows x64 implementation limits itself to 16 terabytes of virtual address space shared equally between user mode and kernel mode addresses. This is still a huge improvement compared with the 4-gigabyte limitation imposed by x86 architecture.

To effectively support that virtual address space, Windows x64 is capable of addressing up to one terabyte of physical memory and an additional 512 terabytes in the page file. The physical memory limitation has been chosen based on hardware capabilities available today and in the near future. This limitation can be removed in the future to keep up with the hardware evolution.

As a company, Microsoft has an enormous responsibility to preserve the backward compatibility with existing software running in the enterprises, with each new operating system version. But how compatible is Windows x64 with current applications? Windows x64 can run software applications compiled natively, a process known as targeting, for x64 architecture, as well as software applications targeted at the traditional Windows x86. However, the operating system imposes some restrictions that should be clearly understood and are described next.

The Windows x64 kernel runs strictly 64-bit code and cannot load modules, in general device drivers, designed for the Windows x86 operating systems. Practically, this limitation does not affect mainstream users, as most hardware vendors either provide or are in the process of providing 64-bit drivers for their devices.

All self-contained applications, which depend on nothing but the operating system components, work the same after converting them from a 32-bit target to a 64-bit target. All registry keys and all system file locations are unchanged in Windows x64 as compared with Windows x86. Some might be surprised to find out that most system binaries are still stored in the `%SystemRoot%\system32` folder, even if they are pure 64-bit binaries. All applications are still installed in the `%SystemDrive%\Program Files` folder, as in the Windows x86.

If a native 64-bit application depends on and consumes a component not supplied in the operating system, the application installer must ensure that components compiled for 64-bit are available on the system. In the current Windows x64, it is not possible to load a 32-bit binary into a process running a 64-bit application. For example, a media playback application targeted to Windows x64 that loads various DirectShow filters must find all such filters compiled as 64-bit binaries.

Even if most companies will rerelease their applications as 64-bit versions, most of the existing applications are still targeted to 32-bit only. For enterprises with thousands of 32-bit applications, it is not practical to consider Windows x64 if they have to change or repurchase all those applications. Fortunately, they are supported using the Windows-On-Windows emulation subsystem, known as WOW64. A process running in WOW64 emulation mode is, for all practical purposes, a 32-bit process, as its 64-bit counterpart, and is not capable of loading components targeted to the 64-bit architecture.

Because binaries from different architectures cannot be mixed in the same process, software vendors must understand the market for their applications and choose the target architecture accordingly. Depending on the application, there are several situations that must be treated differently.

Developers supplying components for Windows x64 must also understand who their target audience is and make sure that the component's architecture matches the architecture of the application consuming them. It is not unusual to see the same component available in both architectures on the same system. Windows performance counters libraries are a good example of applying this model.

On the other side of this are the stand-alone applications extensible through a pluggable architecture, such as Internet browsers supporting various add-ons. In this situation, developers must understand the plug-in's availability and perhaps choose to ship their application in both architectures, until the transition to Windows x64 is complete. This approach was taken by the Internet Explorer developers by providing a 32-bit and a 64-bit application. As an alternative, the application can remain in a 32-bit architecture until the whole market makes the transition to 64-bit computing. This solution has been chosen for the Windows Media Player shipped with Windows XP Professional x64.

Native x64 processes run side-by-side with other applications running inside WOW64 processes, and all processes share the same global resources. When the application is a service, it can exist in a single form—either as 64-bit or as 32-bit application. For example, a server cannot run a 64-bit and a 32-bit Web service instance sharing the same port and returning the same Web pages. When this service has a pluggable architecture, the service developers will define what plug-ins can be loaded in their systems, as well as create the mechanism to support the selected mode. It is possible to have a service that can be extended with plug-ins targeted to both 32-bit and 64-bit architecture by loading them in architecture-specific host processes.

Although all this might sound complicated, in reality it isn't that bad. Most problems are encountered when backward compatibility is a must and the applications have multiple dependent components.

In the next section, we briefly analyze how the WOW64 system works to understand what the implications for debugging legacy applications are.

## 32-Bit Application Running in WOW64

Each 32-bit application starts in Windows x64 as a normal 64-bit process. Because all the pointers used in the application, as well as the structures declared by the operating system and used in the application, are restricted to 32-bit, the application cannot run directly. The operating system first loads a few support dynamic link libraries that implement the WOW64 system, as follows:

- ntdll.dll: 64-bit version library that interfaces any user mode process to kernel entry-point functions. The library is the same as the one used natively by any application in Windows x64.
- WOW64.dll: 64-bit library that performs the necessary conversion or thunking of the input parameters, the return values between the 32-bit modules, and the kernel APIs exposed by the 64-bit version ntdll.dll.

■ WOW64Win.dll: 64-bit library that performs the thunking of the 32-bit modules calling into win2k.sys functions as part of the Windows messaging APIs.

■ WOW64Cpu.dll: 64-bit library capable of emulating x86 instruction set. In Windows x64, this library does nothing because the processor is capable of natively executing the x86 instruction stream.

At this point, the process is considered to be created from the operating system point of view; the process initial breakpoint event is sent to the debugger, even if the application is not yet prepared for execution. As a next step, the WOW64 subsystem loads ntdll32.dll, as well as the rest of the 32-bit dynamic link libraries the application depends on. ntdll32.dll is a 32-bit library providing functionality similar to the ntdll.dll. Unlike ntdll.dll, which switches the processor execution from user mode to kernel mode, ntdll32.dll only makes the transition between 32-bit code and the WOW64 system, while remaining in user mode.

Inside a WOW64 process, each thread can execute code in 64-bit mode, called long execution mode, or it can execute code in 32-bit mode, called compatibility mode. The execution mode is determined by the L (long) flag stored in the segment descriptor associated with the current code selector, referred by the cs register. To switch the execution mode, the thread must make a far call through a call gate targeted to a code segment having an opposite execution mode. Applications targeted to 64-bit are referred to as native applications, whereas the applications targeted to 32-bit are referred to as WOW64 applications.

In Listing 12.1, we have a stack for a thread owned by a 32-bit process that executes code in compatibility mode inside the CPU emulator library, WOW64cpu.dll. The stack is taken from a native debugger running, in WOW64 emulation mode, the 32-bit application version of 02sample.exe used in Chapter 2, "Introduction to the Debuggers."

**Listing 12.1**    The native stack on a WOW64 process

```
0:000> k8
Child-SP          RetAddr           Call Site
00000000`0006e508 00000000`78be6866 ntdll!NtTerminateProcess+0xa
00000000`0006e510 00000000`78b83c7d wow64!Wow64SystemServiceEx+0xd6
00000000`0006edd0 00000000`78be6a5a wow64cpu!ServiceNoTurbo+0x28
00000000`0006ee60 00000000`78be5e0d wow64!RunCpuSimulation+0xa
00000000`0006ee90 00000000`78ed8501 wow64!Wow64LdrpInitialize+0x2ed
00000000`0006f6c0 00000000`78ed6416 ntdll!LdrpInitializeProcess+0x17d9
00000000`0006f9d0 00000000`78ef3925 ntdll!LdrpInitialize+0x18f
00000000`0006fab0 00000000`77d59640 ntdll!KiUserApcDispatch+0x15
```

But how can WOW64 applications run side-by-side with the native applications when both are dependent on the same libraries? The separation is achieved by creating a WOW64 virtual environment similar to the environment used by the native applications. Most system resources are shared between the native and WOW64 environment, and Windows APIs retrieve the same value regardless of whether the calling application is a native or a WOW64 application. When a WOW64 application accesses resources that are not common to both environments, the application gets redirected to the WOW64 virtual environment—a mechanism called virtualization.

One component of this virtual environment consists of all registry keys that are part of software configuration and are usually changed when a new application is installed on the system. The virtualized registry keys includes COM registrations, available both systemwide or for specific users. Figure 12.1 uses the regedit.exe, a native application, to show a few registry keys affected by registry redirection.

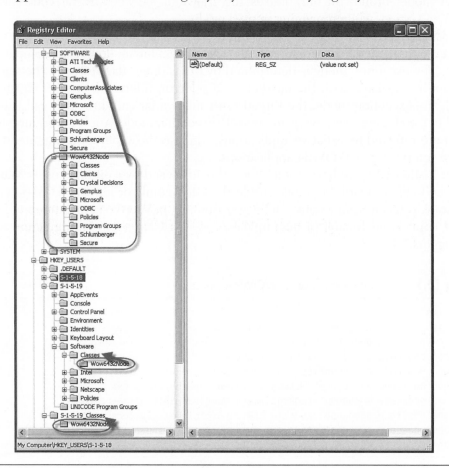

**Figure 12.1** Registries affected by registry redirection

A WOW64 application subject to virtualization observes the content of the HKLM\ Software key from Figure 12.1 replaced by the HKLM\Software\Wow6432Node key, similar to all other keys subject to virtualization. Each registry operation can control the redirection by using the KEY_WOW64_64KEY or KEY_WOW64_32KEY flags.

Similarly, most files under the `%SystemRoot%\system32` folder are virtualized for WOW64 applications. When the application tries to read a file from the `%SystemRoot%\system32` folder, it gets the file from the `%SystemRoot%\sysWOW64` folder instead. The application can disable the file redirection, as needed, using the `Wow64DisableWow64FsRedirection` API.

---

**FILE REDIRECTION SIDE EFFECT** As a side effect of file redirection, WOW64 applications cannot access any file from the real `%SystemRoot%\system32` folder and its subfolders. If a WOW64 application launches an executable provided by the operating system, it will search for the file in `%SystemRoot%\SysWOW64` and its subfolders. This is the reason why most .exe files are duplicated in the `%SystemRoot%\SysWOW64` folder, even if it does not make sense. If necessary, the 32-bit executable is just a launcher for the 64-bit counterpart.

---

Because applications can also use several environment variables to learn about their execution context, several variables are changed to reflect the virtual environment. Few variable environments are added only to the native environment, whereas some are present only in the WOW64 environment. Table 12.1 lists all variables specific to Windows x64 or dependent on the execution mode.

**Table 12.1**  Environment Variables in Windows x64

| Variable Name | Expanded in WOW64 Environment To | Expanded in Native Environment To |
|---|---|---|
| CommonProgramFile(x86) | New in Windows x64, pointing to | %ProgramFiles(x86)%\Common Files |
| CommonProgramFile | % CommonProgramFile(x86)% | %ProgramFiles%\Common Files |
| CommonProgramW6432 | Native % CommonProgramFile% | N/A |
| PROCESSOR_ARCHITECTURE | X86 | AMD64 or IA64 |
| PROCESSOR_ARCHITEW6432 | Native %PROCESSOR_ARCHITECTURE% | N/A |
| ProgramFiles(x86) | New in Windows x64, pointing to | %SystemDrive%\Program Files (x86) |
| ProgramFiles | %ProgramFiles(x86)% | %SystemDrive%\Program Files |
| ProgramW6432 | Native %Program Files% | N/A |

One very common question we have to answer when investigating problems on the Windows x64 platform is whether the process is a native process or a WOW64 process. The answer determines how to debug the process and how to inspect the environment hosting it. When it is possible to access the GUI console, WOW64 applications can be easily recognized in Task Manager by their *32 suffix after the process name. For example, cmd.exe process, shown in Figure 12.2, is running as a WOW64 process.

**Figure 12.2**    32-bit application running in Windows x64

An alternative detection mechanism, more appropriate for debugger users, is identifying the modules loaded in the process. A WOW64 application loads most modules from the %systemroot%\SysWOW64 folder. Because all such modules are targeted to the 32-bit architecture, applications having any of those modules loaded must be a WOW64 process. Furthermore the environment variables used by the respective process can be checked for values specific to the WOW64 environment.

After this short overview of a few new mechanisms employed on Windows x64, we must understand the impact those mechanisms have when debugging applications. The rest of this chapter focuses on the changes imposed by the Windows x64 architecture.

## Windows x64 Changes

In this section, we review all previous chapters, watching for major differences in debugging those scenarios. This is not an exhaustive coverage, rather an introduction to the most important changes to look out for when debugging Windows x64 applications. We recommend that you consult the debugger documentation when a debugging situation requires additional information.

Each subsection has the same title as the previous corresponding chapter and tries to follow the same organization as the chapter itself. The chapters covering topics that do not have differences between Windows x86 and Windows x64 are skipped.

## Chapter 1—Introduction to the Tools

Not all the tools from our toolbox are usable in every situation, especially in an environment that hadn't been envisioned during the tool's creation. Some tools work with limitations, while others do not work at all. This section analyzes the impact Windows x64 has on the tools presented in Chapter 1, "Introduction to the Tools."

### Leak Diagnostic Tool

The Leak Diagnostic tool can be used with some limitations on Windows x64. It installs properly but is not capable of working with processes running in native mode. The good news is that it works just fine when targeted to processes running applications in WOW64 emulation mode. We hope that this limitation will go away in the future as the new Microsoft Detours libraries, that the tool is based on, can intercept APIs on 64-bit platforms.

### Debugging Tools for Windows

Debugging Tools for Windows is available as a native version targeted to Windows x64. Although it is possible to debug native 64-bit processes using a WOW64 debugger tool, for the best result, it is recommended that you use a 64-bit debugger. All tools installed with Debugging Tools for Windows work on Windows x64.

The debugger team recommends using the 32-bit debugger running in WOW64 emulation mode when performing live debugging—in both user and kernel mode—and the debugger target is Windows NT or Windows 2000. The same recommendation is valid for debugging the crash dumps generated on those platforms. A 64-bit user mode process must always be debugged using native 64-bit debuggers. WOW64 processes can be debugged using either native or WOW64 debuggers, but the latter provides an easier experience for those familiar with 32-bit debugging.

All debuggers can be used interchangeable for other situations not mentioned previously. Please look in the debugger help (help topic `Choosing a 32-bit or 64-bit Debugger Package`) for the complete recommendation.

Ideally, you should have both debuggers—a 64-bit version and a 32-bit version—installed side-by-side on the system used for debugging. The right version is then selected based on the debugger target architecture. In this chapter, we assume that you have the 64-bit version of the Debugging Tools for Windows installed in the `c:\debug.x64` folder and the 32-bit version installed in the `c:\debug.x86` folder.

### Microsoft Application Verifier

Microsoft Application Verifier is available as a native application targeted to Windows x64. Because you can also install the 32-bit version on Windows x64, you must choose at times between the native version of the tool and the WOW64 version. To understand what version should be used, we must first understand how Microsoft Application Verifier works.

Each application monitored with Microsoft Application Verifier has an associated registry key identified by the executable name that contains the verifier setting for it. This key is created when the application is configured through the Microsoft Application Verifier tool. The key storing all the verifier settings has the following form:

```
HKEY_LOCAL_MACHINE\SOFTWARE\Microsoft\Windows NT\CurrentVersion\Image File Execution
Options\<Image File Name>
```

But that registry key is subject to the registry redirection as described in the section "32-Bit Application Running in WOW64." As a result, the 64-bit version of Microsoft Application Verifier changes the native registry but does nothing to the virtualized WOW64 registry node, even when the configured application is a 32-bit application. The verifier infrastructure loads two additional libraries in the verified process whose architecture must match the targeted process architecture.

In practice, this means that both versions of the verifier must be installed to test 64-bit and 32-bit applications. The Application Verifier matching the architecture of the process we are interested in must be started from the command line using one of the following commands:

- `%systemroot%\system32\appverif.exe` for 64-bit applications
- `%systemroot%\syswow64\appverif.exe` for 32-bit applications

For example, the first command line can be used to enable Application Verifier for the 64-bit version of notepad.exe, whereas the second will enable it for the 32-bit version of notepad.exe.

### Wireshark

To capture network traffic, Wireshark uses a kernel driver that is currently available only on 32-bit architecture. Because Windows x64 cannot load 32-bit drivers, the tool cannot capture the network traffic. However, the software installs on Windows x64.

Although Wireshark cannot capture any packets passing through the system interfaces, it can be used to visualize and interpret saved capture files. Because Wireshark can capture the network traffic using promiscuous capture mode, it is easy to use another Windows x32 system to perform the capture and move the file for further investigation onto the Windows x64 system for which the capture has been performed.

### Other Tools

All other tools work without problems on the Windows x64 platform.

## Chapter 2—Introduction to the Debuggers

As explained in the previous section, both the 32-bit and 64-bit versions of debuggers can be used to debug dump files or to perform kernel mode debugging. The decision to use one or the other debugger is influenced mainly by the architecture of custom extensions available for the processes subject to debugging. Live debugging should be performed using a debugger that matches the debugger target architecture—the 64-bit debugger for Windows x64 native process and the 32-bit debugger for WOW64 processes. At this time, the 32-bit debugger works better for the WOW64 process because it completely hides the 64-bit aspect of the WOW64 process. Because the experience gained while debugging Windows x86 is fully applicable when debugging a WOW64 process, this section focuses on using a native debugger for both native and WOW64 processes. This configuration is similar to using a kernel mode debugger to debug the processes running on a Windows x64 system.

### Basic Task in Debuggers

The 64-bit pointers and the register values used by Windows x64 architecture represent a major change in interaction mode with the debugger. In the debugger, 64-bit values are represented as two 32-bit numbers, sometimes separated by the grave accent (`) symbol. For example, 0x80000000`00000000 represents the same number as 0x8000000000000000 that is the smallest 64-bit signed integer. This value is equivalent to 0x80000000 on x86 processors.

## What Are the Current Register Values?

Because the pointers have been extended to 64-bit values, all other registers have also been extended to 64 bits. The 64-bit register's names have been changed, and they start with the letter r instead of the letter e. Therefore, the 32-bit eax processor register has been replaced by the 64-bit register rax. The eax mnemonic is still valid and denotes the least significant 32 bits of the native register rax.

The number of general-purpose registers increased with eight more general-purpose registers, identified by r8 through r15. Listing 12.2 shows the result of executing the r command with the default settings.

**Listing 12.2**  x86 64-bit general-purposes register

```
0:000> r
rax=0000000000000000 rbx=0000000000000000 rcx=0000734f67090000
rdx=0000000078ba0002 rsi=0000000000000000 rdi=0000000000000003
rip=0000000078ef3320 rsp=000000000006f6b8 rbp=0000000000080000
 r8=0000000000000002  r9=0000000000000000 r10=0000000000000018
r11=0000000078c108a0 r12=0000000000000000 r13=000000007efdf000
r14=0000000000020000 r15=0000000078ec0000
iopl=0         nv up ei pl nz na pe nc
cs=0033  ss=002b  ds=002b  es=002b  fs=0053  gs=002b          efl=00000202
```

As you saw in the previous chapters, the interoperability between modules or between modules and the operating system is possible because there is a well-defined calling convention of passing the arguments to the calling function and getting back the operation results. The calling convention dictates what registers are preserved across the function calls, how the registers are used to pass the arguments to the called function, and how to return the function results.

The 32-bit compilers use multiple calling conventions, each with its own strengths and weaknesses. In Windows x64, there is a single calling convention having a similar pattern to the __fastcall calling convention used by 32-bit compilers. In the Windows x64 calling convention, the register assignments are the following:

- rcx: Contains the first parameter passed to the function. For example, an object method member invocation in C++ passes the object address or the *this* pointer into the rcx register, similar to the __fastcall calling convention.
- rdx: Contains the second parameter passed to the function.
- r8: Contains the third parameter passed to the function.

- r9: Contains the fourth parameter passed to the function.
- rax: Contains the result of the function call.

Using 64-bit calling convention, most functions receive their argument through registers, and because the number of registers is greater on 64-bit architecture, the stack pointer register is not so volatile. As a result, the rsp register is often used for local variable addressing, decreasing the usage of the stack-frame based address register, rbp, which becomes a general-purpose register in most functions. The functions with more than four parameters use the stack for all parameters beyond the fourth one. Those parameters are stored in the stack from right to left, with the rightmost parameter being stored at the highest address in the stack.

The calling convention does not require to preserve the argument passing registers rcx, rdc, r8 and r9, which can be used as scratch registers. Two more registers, r10 and r11, can also be used by the called function as scratch registers. All other registers maintain the value across the function call. The calling convention is explored in the later section "What Is the Current Call Stack?"

### WOW64 Specific Commands

When debugging a process running an application in a WOW64 system, there are several unique situations not encountered when debugging processes running in long mode. For example, how must you interpret the stack displayed by the debugger in Listing 12.1?

Let's take a WOW64 application that's about to exit, started under native 64-debugger using the following command line:

```
c:\debug.x64\ntsd.exe -g c:\AWDBIN\WinXP.x86.chk\02sample.exe
```

The stack is shown in Listing 12.1, but it has no traces of the debugged process within and does not look right. The process execution is hidden under the WOW64cpu!ServiceNoTurbo function call. The stack information behind this function can be accessed after using the new .effmach command. The .effmach <x86|AMD64|IA64|.> command changes the mode used by the debugger to interpret the debugger target. The command can be used to change the debugger view back and forth between the 32-bit architecture and the native architecture. The dot (.) argument changes the current architecture to the native one.

Listing 12.3 shows the true stack of the same process after the architecture view is changed to 32 bit. The debugger prompt changes into 0:000:x86> to illustrate the alteration from native mode.

**Listing 12.3**   True 32-bit stack in WOW64 process (hidden in Listing 12.1)

```
0:000>.effmach x86
0:000:x86> k
ChildEBP          RetAddr
0014fed0 7d4e80c7 ntdll32!NtTerminateProcess+0x12
0014ff0c 7d4e8072 kernel32!_ExitProcess+0x4b
0014ff20 77bcade4 kernel32!ExitProcess+0x14
0014ff2c 77bcaefb msvcrt!__crtExitProcess+0x32
0014ff5c 77bcaf52 msvcrt!_cinit+0xd2
0014ff70 00401a4f msvcrt!exit+0x11
0014ffc0 7d4e992a 02sample!mainCRTStartup+0x144
0014fff0 00000000 kernel32!BaseProcessStart+0x28
```

In WOW64 emulation mode, each thread has two different contexts: the native context that executes in long mode (used by the WOW64 emulator code) and the 32-bit context visible when the thread execution context switches to compatible mode. Because the code executing in those contexts accesses the thread environment block that contains pointers to other structures, a WOW64 process contains two TEBs for each thread executing 32-bit code. This duplication is also happening with the process environment block; there is one instance for the native code and another one for the code running in compatibility mode inside the WOW64 process. By the same reasoning, the stack used by each thread is duplicated for long and compatibility execution mode.

All that information is returned by the !straddr extension command, implemented in wow64exts.dll, which is installed with the 64-bit Debugging Tools for Windows. The !straddr extension command returns the address of the current thread environment block, the address of the process environment block, and the thread stack used when the processor runs in long and compatibility mode, as shown in Listing 12.4.

**Listing 12.4**   Obtaining WOW64 structures

```
0:000:x86> !wow64exts.straddr

Address of important WOW64 structures:

TEB64: 0x7efdb000
TEB32: 0x7efdd000
PEB64: 0x7efdf000
PEB32: 0x7efde000
STACK64: BASE: 0x70000 LIMIT: 0x6b000 DEALLOC: 0x30000
STACK32: BASE: 0x150000 LIMIT: 0x14e000 DEALLOC: 0x110000
```

These structure addresses can be used as input parameters to other extension commands, as you will see later in this chapter. Most commands or extension commands are aware of the current execution mode and work predictably when the input parameter type matches the execution mode.

### What Code Does the Processor Execute Now?

In Windows x86, the answer is very clear after inspecting the instruction stream from the memory location addressed by the instruction pointer pseudo-register $ip. In Windows x64, the processor execution mode has to be considered as well before answering this question. Listing 12.5 shows the instruction stream interpreted as 64-bit code and later as 32-bit code. Although most instructions share the opcodes between the 32-bit world and the 64-bit world, the interpretation is different, depending on the processor execution mode.

**Listing 12.5**   Unassembly code is dependent on the processor execution mode

```
0:000> .effmach AMD64
Effective machine: x64 (AMD64)
0:000> u ntdll!NtTerminateProcess 14
ntdll!NtTerminateProcess:
00000000`78ef1520 4c8bd1          mov     r10,rcx
00000000`78ef1523 b829000000      mov     eax,29h
00000000`78ef1528 0f05            syscall
00000000`78ef152a c3              ret
0:000> .effmach x86
Effective machine: x86 compatible (x86)
0:000:x86> u ntdll!NtTerminateProcess 14
ntdll!NtTerminateProcess:
00000000`78ef1520 4c              dec     esp
00000000`78ef1521 8bd1            mov     edx,ecx
00000000`78ef1523 b829000000      mov     eax,29h
00000000`78ef1528 0f05            syscall
```

### What Is the Current Call Stack?

In general, the current stack can be easily obtained using any form of the k command. Because there are situations in which the stack pointer is not correct or the local variables cannot be obtained using the standard commands, knowing how the stack is used by x86-64 processors is a requirement for understanding the real problem.

The stack grows toward the lower address, and it must be aligned to 16 bytes before calling into another function. In the "What Are the Current Register Values?"

section, you learned that the first four parameters are always passed through registers (rcx, rdc, r8, and r9), while the rest of them are passed on the stack. To understand the stack management, we use the Function5 function, shown in Listing 12.6, that accepts five 64-bit parameters and calls another function with the same number of parameters. The called function is declared as external to prevent the compiler from inlining it.

**Listing 12.6**   Function with five parameters, calling another function with five parameters

```
extern int CalledFunction5(int a,int b,int c,int d,int e);
int Function5(int a, int b, int c, int d, int e)
{
    CalledFunction5(a,b,c,d,e);
    return 5;
}
```

Listing 12.7 shows the assembly code generated from the source code shown in Listing 12.6 within the Windows Vista Free x64 Build Environment option installed by the WDK. This is generated using the nmake param64.cod command.

**Listing 12.7**   Assembly code representing the Function5 function

```
;       COMDAT ?Function5@@YAHHHHHH@Z
_TEXT      SEGMENT
a$ = 64
b$ = 72
c$ = 80
d$ = 88
e$ = 96
?Function5@@YAHHHHHH@Z PROC NEAR          ; Function5, COMDAT
; 64   : {
$LN3:
  00000    48 83 ec 38     sub     rsp, 56            ; 00000038H
; 65   :     CalledFunction5(a,b,c,d,e);
  00004    8b 44 24 60     mov     eax, DWORD PTR e$[rsp]
  00008    89 44 24 20     mov     DWORD PTR [rsp+32], eax
  0000c    e8 00 00 00 00  call    ?CalledFunction5@@YAHHHHHH@Z ; CalledFunction5
; 66   :     return 5;
  00011    b8 05 00 00 00  mov     eax, 5
; 67   : }
  00016    48 83 c4 38     add     rsp, 56            ; 00000038H
  0001a    c3              ret     0
?Function5@@YAHHHHHH@Z ENDP               ; Function5
_TEXT      ENDS
```

This assembly-generated code starts with the offsets corresponding to all input parameters that can be added to the rsp stack register inside the function to find the parameter address on the stack. These offsets are calculated under the assumption that all parameters are passed through the stack with the rightmost parameter located at the highest address.

The offsets already reflect the first statement in the function that decreases the value of the stack pointer, sub rsp, 56. For example, the offset used to access the last parameter identified by the name e is 0n96—that is, with 0n40 higher than the stack decrement value used in the first instruction. At the beginning of the function call, the offset for the parameter e was 0n40—that is, the offset that would have been used if all parameters were to be passed through the stack.

The calling convention requires that the caller allocates the stack for all parameters passed by registers as they were passed through the stack. The stack space allocated for the parameter passed by registers is neither used nor initialized by the caller but can be used by the called function as temporary storage. Those temporary storage locations are normally used to save the input parameters if any of the registers are needed for other purposes, such as calling another function.

In the case in which the function uses temporary variables, the stack is adjusted to give room to such variables that will be located at the top of the stack area used by the function. The storage allocated before calling another function is similar to the space used for temporary variables. In this specific case, the value used to adjust the stack at the entrance is larger than the space required for those five parameters in order to preserve the stack alignment to 16 bytes. The gap is visible in Figure 12.3.

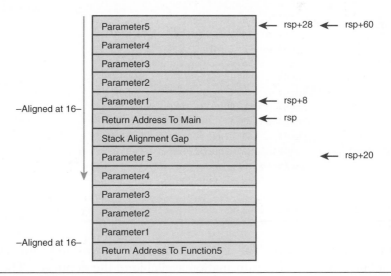

**Figure 12.3** Stack usage on x86-64 calling stack

The rightmost column contains the hexadecimal addresses relative to the `rsp` value used in `Function5`. The next column on the left shows the hexadecimal address relative to the `rsp` value at the `Function5` start, before the adjustment.

So far, the conclusions were based on analyzing the generated code that must be validated in the debugger. The sample can be started under the debugger, using the following command line, which launches the 64-bit version of the sample introduced in Chapter 2 under a 64-bit debugger:

```
C:\>C:\Debug.x64\windbg C:\awdbin\WinLH.AMD64.fre\02sample.exe
```

In this process, we set a breakpoint on the `02sample.exe!CalledFunction5` function that is hit when we select option '5' from the menu. At the breakpoint location, the assumptions described previously can be validated by examining the stack. Listing 12.8 shows the function arguments for each function from the call stack. It might be a surprise to see that most parameters are incorrect. The first four parameters from `Function5` or `CalledFunction5` are random values, while the last one has the correct value.

**Listing 12.8**   *Call-stack function parameter*

```
0:000> kP
Child-SP          RetAddr           Call Site
00000000`000afe98 00000000`00401973 02sample!CalledFunction5(
                  int64 a = 4202800,
                  int64 b = 8793941677150,
                  int64 c = 0,
                  int64 d = 4202020,
                  int64 e = 5)
00000000`000afea0 00000000`0040171a 02sample!Function5(
                  int64 a = 3684256,
                  int64 b = 0,
                  int64 c = 128094338278281250,
                  int64 d = 3684318,
                  int64 e = 5)+0x13
00000000`000afee0 00000000`00401cf1 02sample!main(
                  unsigned long argc = 0,
                  char ** argv = 0x00000000`00000000)+0x12a
00000000`000aff20 00000000`77d5966c 02sample!mainCRTStartup(void)+0x171
00000000`000aff80 00000000`00000000 kernel32!BaseProcessStart+0x2c
```

Why are the values incorrect? This is the unfortunate downside of this calling convention combined with symbol information available to the debugger. The debugger shows the values stored on a stack location corresponding to arguments passed through the registers, and they have random values. Furthermore, if one input parameter is used in a function for something else and it is not needed for the remainder of this function, the parameter value is not stored anywhere. This parameter can't be recovered by the debugger after this point. If it has been stored somewhere, we need to manually find that location and read its value.

For example, when `Function5` in Listing 12.8 starts its execution, the fist parameter is passed into the register `rcx`. When this function calls `CalledFunction5`, the same register, `rcx`, must be filled with the first parameter passed to that function. If `rcx` has not been saved before, and it is not used after the return from `CalledFunction5`, the compiler does not generate code to preserve it. Its value is lost right before the call to `CalledFunction5`.

The situation is a little better for the code compiled using no optimizations, started using the checked build WDK shortcut. In checked builds, each function prefix has special code to save all the input parameters, even if none are used. The checked version of `CalledFunction5` looks much, much better from a debugging perspective, as can be seen in Listing 12.9.

**Listing 12.9**  Unassembled nonoptimized function

```
0:000> uf .
02sample!CalledFunction5:
00000000`00401340 4c894c2420      mov     qword ptr [rsp+20h],r9
00000000`00401345 4c89442418      mov     qword ptr [rsp+18h],r8
00000000`0040134a 4889542410      mov     qword ptr [rsp+10h],rdx
00000000`0040134f 48894c2408      mov     qword ptr [rsp+8],rcx
00000000`00401354 b805000000      mov     eax,5
00000000`00401359 c3              ret
```

The support obtained in the generated checked build from the C/C++ compiler is handy in the development process only. Each application's customers expect that the code released to them is highly optimized. All memory dumps obtained using the Windows Error Reporting feedback loop described in Chapter 13, "Postmortem Debugging," will usually be optimized, without the compiler support.

### What Are the Local Variable's Values?

The display variable command, `dv`, shows the storage holding the local variables. For input parameters, the location is the stack parameter passing area, which is not populated in free or optimized builds. Because `dv` usually shows random values for the input variables, the manual discovery process uses our knowledge about the rules used to generate assembly code, the assembly code itself, and sometimes luck in order to find the right value. Listing 12.10 shows the local variable displayed at the debugger stop used before, at the entrance in CalledFunction5.

**Listing 12.10**    Local variable

```
0:000> dv /V
00000000`000afea0 @rsp+0x08              a = 4202800
00000000`000afea8 @rsp+0x10              b = 8793941677150
00000000`000afeb0 @rsp+0x18              c = 0
00000000`000afeb8 @rsp+0x20              d = 4202020
00000000`000afec0 @rsp+0x28              e = 5
```

What logic must be used to find the right values? Unless the debugger is stopped exactly at the beginning of the function and the input variables have correct values from the register used for parameter passing, the user must question himself whether the values displayed by dv make sense. When a parameter does not look right, the real value must be found by searching the assembly code for the location, if any, where it has been previously stored. That value is then probed to see if it makes sense. If not, the process repeats until the correct value is found.

If necessary, the search for the original of the value must continue into the caller of the current functions. In some cases, the original value is never found, but in most of the cases, the search is successful. It is not acceptable to stop an investigation just because the dv command is not capable of showing the correct information and conclude that the debugger session is corrupted.

There are several ways to search a register name occurrence in one of the assembly instructions in the unassembled function. The debugger support assembly searches using the pound (#) command, which takes as parameters the string pattern to search for, the start address, and the block length in which to search that pattern. The sequential pound (#) command can be repeated without parameters, having as a result the search continuation in the memory block following and adjacent to the last memory block searched. The next listing shows usage of the command and its output when searching for the ebp register, starting at the beginning of the kernel32!CreateProcessW function, with the debugger in x86 mode:

```
0:000> # ebp kernel32!CreateProcessW
kernel32!CreateProcessW+0x2:
771a1d29 55             push    ebp
0:000>
```

## How Do You Inspect the Process Memory?

The familiar commands used to dump memory content work without any change when the processor runs in long mode. The commands, depending on the pointer size to be 32 bits, must be replaced by the 64-bit equivalent or replaced by the commands that take the pointer size into account. For example, instead of the command dds, the newer command dqs must be used—or, even better, the dps command. The following listing shows how to dump the command-line arguments using the dpa command, which replaces the dda command used on the 32-bit architecture.

```
0:000> dpa poi(argv) 12
00000000`003837a0  00000000`003837b8 "WinLH.AMD64.fre\02sample.exe"
```

## Other Exploratory Commands

The process environment block is an important piece of information describing the process currently debugged. Processes running applications in WOW64 emulation mode have two process environment blocks—one associated with the native process and the other provided by the emulator to the code executing 32-bit code. By default, the !peb extension command shows the native process environment block stored at the virtual address pointed to by the $peb pseudo-register. For processes running on a WOW64 system, the !peb extension command tries to find the corresponding 32-bit process environment block and requires the wow64!TEB32 structure symbol. Currently, the symbol is not available in the public symbol file WOW64.pdb, and the command stops its processing at the native process PEB, as shown in Listing 12.11.

**Listing 12.11**   WOW64 applications PEB

```
0:000:x86> !peb
**************************************************************************
***                                                                   ***
***                                                                   ***
***     Your debugger is not using the correct symbols                ***
***                                                                   ***
***     In order for this command to work properly, your symbol path  ***
***     must point to .pdb files that have full type information.      ***
***                                                                   ***
***     Certain .pdb files (such as the public OS symbols) do not      ***
***     contain the required information.  Contact the group that      ***
***     provided you with these symbols if you need this command to    ***
***     work.                                                          ***
```

*(continues)*

**Listing 12.11**   WOW64 applications PEB *(continued)*

```
***                                                              ***
***      Type referenced: wow64!TEB32                           ***
***                                                              ***
***************************************************************************
PEB at 000000007efdf000
    InheritedAddressSpace:    No
    ReadImageFileExecOptions: No
    BeingDebugged:            Yes
    ImageBaseAddress:         0000000000400000
    Ldr                       0000000078fa7ea0
    Ldr.Initialized:          Yes
    Ldr.InInitializationOrderModuleList: 0000000000082e50 . 0000000000082f90
    Ldr.InLoadOrderModuleList:           0000000000082d60 . 0000000000083210
    Ldr.InMemoryOrderModuleList:         0000000000082d70 . 0000000000083220
          Base TimeStamp                     Module
        400000 453bf190 Oct 22 15:32:48 2006 C:\awdbin\WinLH.AMD64.fre\02sample.exe
      78ec0000 42438b79 Mar 24 19:54:33 2005 D:\WINDOWS\system32\ntdll.dll
      78be0000 42438b79 Mar 24 19:54:33 2005 D:\WINDOWS\system32\wow64.dll
      78b90000 42438b79 Mar 24 19:54:33 2005 D:\WINDOWS\system32\wow64win.dll
      78b80000 42438b7a Mar 24 19:54:34 2005 D:\WINDOWS\system32\wow64cpu.dll
    SubSystemData:     0000000000000000
    ProcessHeap:       0000000000080000
    ProcessParameters: 0000000000020000
    WindowTitle:  'C:\awdbin\WinLH.AMD64.fre\02sample.exe'
    ImageFile:    'C:\awdbin\WinLH.AMD64.fre\02sample.exe'
    CommandLine:  'C:\awdbin\WinLH.AMD64.fre\02sample.exe'
    DllPath:      'C:\awdbin\WinLH.AMD64.fre\02sample.exe;D:\WINDOWS\system32;D:\WIN-
DOWS\system;D:\WINDOWS;.; D:\WINDOWS\system32;D:\WINDOWS;D:\WINDOWS\System32\Wbem'

    Environment:  0000000000010000
        =::=::\
        =D:= C:\awdbin\WinLH.AMD64.fre
        =ExitCode=00000000
        ALLUSERSPROFILE=D:\Documents and Settings\All Users
        APPDATA=D:\Documents and Settings\Administrator\Application Data
        CLIENTNAME=Console
        CommonProgramFiles=D:\Program Files (x86)\Common Files
        CommonProgramFiles(x86)=D:\Program Files (x86)\Common Files
        CommonProgramW6432=D:\Program Files\Common Files
        ...
        USERNAME=Administrator
        USERPROFILE=D:\Documents and Settings\Administrator
        windir=D:\WINDOWS
```

This problem can be overcome by using the `!wow64exts.straddr` extension command to obtain the address of the 32-bit PEB and displaying it using the `dt` command. The address is interpreted as the 32-bit PEB using the structure defined in the WOW64 version of ntdll.dll, named ntdll32.dll, as shown in Listing 12.12.

**Listing 12.12**  WOW64 application's PEB using the dt command

```
0:000:x86> !wow64exts.straddr

Address of important WOW64 structures:

TEB64: 0x7efdb000
TEB32: 0x7efdd000
PEB64: 0x7efdf000
PEB32: 0x7efde000
STACK64: BASE: 0x70000 LIMIT: 0x6b000 DEALLOC: 0x30000
STACK32: BASE: 0x150000 LIMIT: 0x14e000 DEALLOC: 0x110000
0:000:x86> dt ntdll32!_PEB 0x7efde000
   +0x000 InheritedAddressSpace : 0 ''
   +0x001 ReadImageFileExecOptions : 0 ''
   +0x002 BeingDebugged     : 0x1 ''
   +0x003 BitField          : 0 ''
   +0x003 ImageUsesLargePages : 0y0
   +0x003 SpareBits         : 0y0000000 (0)
   +0x004 Mutant            : 0xffffffff`ffffffff
   +0x008 ImageBaseAddress  : 0x00000000`00400000
   +0x00c Ldr               : 0x00000000`7d6a01e0 _PEB_LDR_DATA
   +0x010 ProcessParameters : 0x00000000`00100000 _RTL_USER_PROCESS_PARAMETERS
...
   +0x210 FlsListHead       : _LIST_ENTRY [ 0x152f28 - 0x152f28 ]
   +0x218 FlsBitmap         : 0x00000000`7d6a2048
   +0x21c FlsBitmapBits     : [4] 3
   +0x22c FlsHighIndex      : 1
```

From the raw _PEB structure, it is possible to extract the same information that the `!peb` extension command does by traversing the structures referred from _PEB.

Thread environment blocks are yet other useful structures that can be obtained using the `!teb` extension command. The `!teb` extension command suffers from the same drawbacks as the `!peb` extension command when acting on a thread running code through the WOW64 emulator. Listing 12.13 shows the typical result obtained from the `!teb` extension command in this case, as well as what structure must be used as a parameter to the `dt` command in order to visualize the _TEB structure. The address of the thread environment block structure has been obtained from the `!WOW64exts.straddr` extension command shown in Listing 12.12.

## Listing 12.13 WOW64 threads' TEB using !teb extension command and dt commands

```
0:000:x86> !teb
Wow64 TEB32 at 000000007efdd000
*************************************************************************
***                                                                   ***
***                                                                   ***
***     Your debugger is not using the correct symbols               ***
***                                                                   ***
***     In order for this command to work properly, your symbol path ***
***     must point to .pdb files that have full type information.     ***
***                                                                   ***
***     Certain .pdb files (such as the public OS symbols) do not     ***
***     contain the required information.  Contact the group that     ***
***     provided you with these symbols if you need this command to   ***
***     work.                                                         ***
***                                                                   ***
***     Type referenced: wow64!_TEB32                                 ***
***                                                                   ***
*************************************************************************
error InitTypeRead( wow64!_TEB32 )...


Wow64 TEB at 000000007efdb000
        ExceptionList:        000000007efdd000
        StackBase:            0000000000070000
        StackLimit:           000000000006b000
        SubSystemTib:         0000000000000000
        FiberData:            0000000000001e00
        ArbitraryUserPointer: 0000000000152c50
        Self:                 000000007efdb000
        EnvironmentPointer:   0000000000000000
        ClientId:             0000000000000a4c . 0000000000000364
        RpcHandle:            0000000000000000
        Tls Storage:          0000000000000000
        PEB Address:          000000007efdf000
        LastErrorValue:       0
        LastStatusValue:      0
        Count Owned Locks:    0
        HardErrorMode:        0
0:000:x86> dt ntdll32!_TEB 0x7efdd000
   +0x000 NtTib            : _NT_TIB
   +0x01c EnvironmentPointer : (null)
   +0x020 ClientId         : _CLIENT_ID
   +0x028 ActiveRpcHandle  : (null)
   +0x02c ThreadLocalStoragePointer : (null)
   +0x030 ProcessEnvironmentBlock : 0x00000000`7efde000 _PEB
```

. . .

```
  +0xf9c IsImpersonating  : 0
  +0xfa0 NlsCache         : (null)
  +0xfa4 pShimData        : (null)
  +0xfa8 HeapVirtualAffinity : 0
  +0xfac CurrentTransactionHandle : (null)
  +0xfb0 ActiveFrame      : (null)
  +0xfb4 FlsData          : (null)
  +0xfb8 SafeThunkCall    : 0 ''
  +0xfb9 BooleanSpare     : [3]   ""
```

### *Debugger Scenarios*

Chapter 2 describes the mechanism used to start the applications under a debugger, using the Image File Execution Option, known as IFEO. Because this key is in a node subject to registry redirection, we must be careful to change the registry hive used by the architecture of the process we are targeting. Instead of changing the registry directly, we suggest that you use gflags, the tool installed as part of Debugging Tools for Windows.

The 64-bit version of gflags.exe that has been installed by the 64-bit version of Debugging Tools for Windows enables IFEO for a 64-bit process. When the target process runs in WOW64 emulation mode, the change must be done using the 32-bit version of gflags.exe. The following command line enables the IFEO debugger for notepad.exe, 32-bit version.

```
C:\>debug.x86\gflags /p /enable notepad.exe /debug "c:\debug.x86\ntsd.exe -g -G"
```

The next line does the same for the 64-bit version of notepad.exe. Special care must be given to the debugger used as parameter to the IFEO key. If the debugger is a 32-bit debugger, it will be unable to debug the 64-bit application, or, when the application lives in a redirected folder such as %SystemRoot%\system32, it will always load the application from the %SystemRoot%\syswow64 folder instead.

```
C:\>debug.x64\gflags /p /enable notepad.exe /debug "c:\debug.x64\ntsd.exe -g -G"
```

## Chapter 3—Debuggers Uncovered

Chapter 3, "Debuggers Uncovered," focuses on explaining how the debuggers work under the belief that a better knowledge of the tools increases productivity and minimizes the risk of being surprised by their side effects.

### Debugger Events Order

The 03sample.exe used in Chapter 3 worked without any problem in Windows x64 when the command-line parameter pointed to a 64-bit application, but it failed to start any 32-bit applications in WOW64 emulation mode. Because the application writes everything to the console, it isn't hard to figure out the reasons. The operating system raised an exception with a new exception code, 0x4000001C, at application startup. A search in the headers installed with the WDK reveals that new exception code represents the start-up exception for the WOW64 application, raised after the process hosting it has been started.

```
C:\WINDDK\6000\inc>findstr /is 4000001f *.h
api\ntstatus.h:#define STATUS_WX86_BREAKPOINT ((NTSTATUS)0x4000001FL)
```

Because this breakpoint is generated by the operating system each time the application starts under the debugger, it must be handled automatically by the chapter's sample. After adding the handling code, 03sample.exe can start any application, regardless of its architecture. The output generated by the execution of the 32-bit version of xcopy.exe is shown in Listing 12.14. Most of the noninteresting events, which are generated by loading 32-bit DLLs, have been removed to make the listing shorter and easier to understand.

**Listing 12.14**   Debugger events generated a WOW64 process execution (xcopy.exe)

```
D:\AWDBIN\WinLH.AMD64.fre>03sample.exe d:\WINDOWS\SysWOW64\xcopy.exe
PID.TID=2264.3016
CreateProcess PID=2264
PID.TID=2264.3016
ImageName ntdll.dll
PID.TID=2264.3016
ImageName D:\WINDOWS\system32\wow64.dll
PID.TID=2264.3016
ImageName D:\WINDOWS\system32\wow64win.dll
PID.TID=2264.3016
ImageName D:\WINDOWS\system32\wow64cpu.dll
PID.TID=2264.3016
new ExceptionEvent:
        Code = 80000003
        FirstChance = 1
PID.TID=8d8.bc8
ImageName NOT_AN_IMAGE
PID.TID=8d8.bc8
UnloadDll @0000000077D40000
PID.TID=8d8.bc8
ImageName NOT_AN_IMAGE
PID.TID=8d8.bc8
```

```
UnloadDll @000000007D4C0000
PID.TID=8d8.bc8
ImageName D:\WINDOWS\SysWOW64\ntdll32.dll
PID.TID=8d8.bc8
ImageName NOT_AN_IMAGE
PID.TID=8d8.bc8
UnloadDll @0000000077D40000
PID.TID=8d8.bc8
ImageName NOT_AN_IMAGE
PID.TID=8d8.bc8
UnloadDll @0000000078C30000
PID.TID=8d8.bc8
ImageName D:\WINDOWS\syswow64\kernel32.dll
...
PID.TID=8d8.bc8
ImageName D:\WINDOWS\syswow64\MPR.dll
PID.TID=8d8.bc8
new ExceptionEvent:
        Code = 4000001f
        FirstChance = 1
PID.TID=8d8.bc8
ImageName d:\WINDOWS\SysWOW64\ShimEng.dll
PID.TID=8d8.bc8
ImageName d:\WINDOWS\SysWOW64\apphelp.dll
PID.TID=8d8.bc8
UnloadDll @0000000071AF0000
PID.TID=8d8.bc8
UnloadDll @0000000075E60000
Invalid number of parameters
0 File(s) copied
PID.TID=8d8.bc8
ExitProcess ExitCode=4
```

The order of events is very important but relatively predictable after understanding WOW64 implementation details. Immediately after the process creation event, the system loads ntdll.dll and the DLLs used to implement the WOW64 emulation layer. After all the emulation DLLs are loaded, the process is considered started, and the operating system generates the initial breakpoint event.

So far, none of the DLLs required by the application are loaded in the process. The next step loads all the libraries the application depends on, starting with ntdll32.dll. At the end of this process, the operating system generates a second initial breakpoint, signifying the start-up of the 32-bit application running in WOW64 emulation mode. This initial breakpoint has the specific exception code 0x4000001f.

Afterward, the application runs normally. Any breakpoint statement encountered in the application, such as the ones associated with asserts, generates an exception with the same 0x4000001f exception code.

## Exception-Dispatching Mechanism on 64-Bit Operating Systems

Windows x64 offers the same powerful exception-dispatching mechanism used in all Windows operating systems. The mechanism has been specially designed for the 64-bit architecture and benefits from more than ten years of experience with the implementation on x86 processors. The exceptions structures are adjusted to contain the information specific to the new processors and to work in the new model.

### Exception Model on Windows x64

One way to understand the new exception model is to see it in action and compare it to the model supported by Windows x86. The function from the next listing has been used in Chapter 3 to explain the exception model in Windows x86.

```
void try_except()
{
    __try
    {
        *((int *) 0) = 0;
    }
    __except(ex_filter())
    {
    global = 1;
    }
}
```

In 32-bit architecture, the exception-handling mechanism assumes that each function has a block counter associated with it that is updated each time the code execution is transitioning into that block. Listing 12.15 shows the assembly listing generated for the `try_except` function shown previously.

**Listing 12.15** Exception handling code for a very simple function (tryexcept in 02sample.exe)

```
PUBLIC      ?try_except@@YAXXZ                       ; try_except
EXTRN       __C_specific_handler:PROC
;       COMDAT pdata
pdata       SEGMENT
$pdata$?try_except@@YAXXZ DD imagerel $LN9
    DD      imagerel $LN9+32
    DD      imagerel $unwind$?try_except@@YAXXZ
pdata       ENDS
;       COMDAT pdata
pdata       SEGMENT
$pdata$?filt$0@?0??try_except@@YAXXZ@4HA DD imagerel ?filt$0@?0??try_except@@YAXXZ@4HA
    DD      imagerel ?filt$0@?0??try_except@@YAXXZ@4HA+29
    DD      imagerel $unwind$?filt$0@?0??try_except@@YAXXZ@4HA
pdata       ENDS
;       COMDAT xdata
xdata       SEGMENT
$unwind$?filt$0@?0??try_except@@YAXXZ@4HA DD 020f01H
    DD      0500b320fH
```

```
xdata     ENDS
;     COMDAT xdata
xdata     SEGMENT
$unwind$?try_except@@YAXXZ DD 010409H
    DD    04204H
    DD    imagerel __C_specific_handler
    DD    01H
    DD    imagerel $LN9+4
    DD    imagerel $LN9+17
    DD    imagerel ?filt$0@?0??try_except@@YAXXZ@4HA
    DD    imagerel $LN9+17
; Function compile flags: /Odtp
xdata     ENDS
;     COMDAT ?try_except@@YAXXZ
_TEXT     SEGMENT
?try_except@@YAXXZ PROC                     ; try_except, COMDAT
; 28   : {
$LN9:
  00000   48 83 ec 28    sub    rsp, 40             ; 00000028H
; 29   :     __try
; 30   :     {
; 31   :         *((int *) 0) = 0;
  00004   c7 04 25 00 00 00 00 00 00 00 00    mov DWORD PTR ds:0, 0
; 32   :     }
  0000f   eb 0a          jmp    SHORT $LN4@try_except
$LN6@try_except:
; 33   :     __except(ex_filter())
; 34   :     {
; 35   :     global = 1;
  00011   c7 05 00 00 00 00 01 00 00 00  mov DWORD PTR ?global@@3HA, 1
$LN4@try_except:
; 36   :     }
; 37   : }
  0001b   48 83 c4 28    add    rsp, 40             ; 00000028H
  0001f   c3             ret    0
?try_except@@YAXXZ ENDP                     ; try_except
; Function compile flags: /Odtp
?filt$0@?0??try_except@@YAXXZ@4HA PROC           ; `try_except'::`1'::filt$0
  00020   48 89 4c 24 08    mov    QWORD PTR [rsp+8], rcx
  00025   48 89 54 24 10    mov    QWORD PTR [rsp+16], rdx
  0002a   55             push   rbp
  0002b   48 83 ec 20    sub    rsp, 32             ; 00000020H
  0002f   48 8b ea       mov    rbp, rdx
$LN5@filt$0:

; 33   :     __except(ex_filter())

  00032   e8 00 00 00 00    call    ?ex_filter@@YAKXZ    ; rrex_filter
$LN7@filt$0:
  00037   48 83 c4 20    add    rsp, 32             ; 00000020H
  0003b   5d             pop    rbp
  0003c   c3             ret    0
?filt$0@?0??try_except@@YAXXZ@4HA ENDP           ; `try_except'::`1'::filt$0
_TEXT     ENDS
```

The function code, shown in italic characters in Listing 12.15, is as clean as possible. There is no exception bookkeeping code, and only a single nonconditional jump on the line 32 indicates that the code uses exceptions. (No conditional statement is in the function otherwise.)

How does the operating system know what to execute when an exception is generated on a protected block? The first part of the listing, in bold italic font, answers this question. The compiler generates a function information block that contains general information about each function, as well as about each block protected by an exception handler. Each block is identified by an address's range covering the possible values of the instruction pointer while executing that block. The current instruction pointer value is used by the exception-unwinding mechanism implemented in Windows x64 to locate the protected block containing the exception filter and the corresponding exception handler.

In Listing 12.15, the `$pdata$?try_except@@YAXXZ` label contains information for the exception dispatcher that must be used when the function executes code between the `LN9#` and `LN9#+32` addresses, relative to the start of the module. In this case, a single protected block is stored under the `$unwind$?try_except@@YAXXZ#` label.

The block is identified by a range of addresses and contains the address of the exception filter and the location of code continuation after exception handling, as shown in the next listing:

```
DD      @imagerel($LN9#+4)
DD      @imagerel($LN9#+17)
DD      @imagerel(?filt$0@?0??try_except@@YAXXZ@4HA#)
DD      @imagerel($LN9#+17)
```

At the end of the listing, few compiler-generated functions are used to invoke the block filters. Filters are identified with symbols autogenerated and having the following form:

```
`Function Name'::`Function Number'::filt$FilterNumber
```

The generated code is extremely efficient, as it contains just the business logic, neglecting the exceptional code paths entirely. The linker can relocate all exception-related code and information in a separate section of the module and compact all function code in a different section. The resultant module is extremely efficient memory-wise, as it benefits at a maximum from the processor cache. Only one condition must be met: The code should not raise exceptions. In other words, the exception should really be an exception, not an expected error that can be returned over and over.

When the code raises another exception from inside the handler, Windows x64 starts a new exception dispatch that requires a new context to be allocated from the stack. That can use up the available stack fairly easily, and it represents a problem that must be explicitly addressed in highly reliable applications.

The typical C++ exception code exhibiting this problem is shown in the following fragment. We recommend removing any such construct from commercial code and replacing it with other cleanup patterns such as a "Resource Acquisition Is Initialization" pattern.

```
catch(…)
{
    //Cleanup
    throw();
}
```

## Chapter 5—Memory Corruptions Part I—Stacks

Chapter 5, "Memory Corruptions Part I—Stacks," is entirely dependent on the processor architecture. The current chapter is all about the new processor architecture, and most of the time, it covers the differences between x86 and x64 architectures. Most debugging scenarios presented earlier are valid after considering the calling convention used by Windows x64, presented in the section "What Is the Current Call Stack?"

## Chapter 6—Memory Corruptions Part II—Heaps

Chapter 6, "Memory Corruptions Part II—Heaps," uses various commands and techniques dependent on the x86 processor's architecture. As within the previous section, the information presented so far should be enough to investigate most scenarios described in this chapter.

The scenarios in Chapter 6 rely heavily on heap structures that are slightly different in Windows x64. All structures that contain pointers and sizes are adjusted to hold 64-bit values. As an example, the next listing shows the _HEAP_ENTRY structure for 64-bit heaps.

```
0:000> dt ntdll!_HEAP_ENTRY 0000000000080000
   +0x000 PreviousBlockPrivateData : (null)
   +0x008 Size              : 0xc5
   +0x00a PreviousSize      : 0
   +0x00c SmallTagIndex     : 0xb9 ''
   +0x00d Flags             : 0x1 ''
   +0x00e UnusedBytes       : 0 ''
   +0x00f SegmentIndex      : 0 ''
   +0x008 CompactHeader     : 0x1b9`000000c5
```

Note that processes running applications in WOW64 have two types of heaps. The native process contains at least one heap, the process heap, organized as a 64-bit heap, whereas the application itself can have multiple heaps organized as 32-bit heaps.

The !heap extension command, used without parameters, shows the list of heaps created in the process by inspecting the process environment blocks. As with the !peb extension command, the !heap extension command is unable to find 32-bit PEB, and it cannot show the heaps in WOW64 applications when using a native debugger.

Special attention must be paid to enabling the Application Verifier tool, as explained in the section "Chapter 1—Introduction to the Tools," in order to obtain the desired results.

## Chapter 7—Security

All security concepts used in Windows x86 are applicable without any change in Windows x64. Nothing has changed in the way the security principals are identified by the operating system or in the way each object is secured. The access control is performed using the same mechanisms used in Windows x86 but accepting arguments matching the architecture pointer size.

Listing 12.16 shows the typical usage of the most commonly used command in the security area that is different in Windows x64. In this listing, captured from a kernel mode debugger connected to a Windows x64 system, we examine the security descriptor protecting the winlogon.exe process, as well as the token under which the process executes.

**Listing 12.16** Security information on Windows x64

```
1: kd> !process 0 1 winlogon.exe
PROCESS ffffffadfe74010f0
    SessionId: 0  Cid: 02dc    Peb: 7ffffd4000  ParentCid: 0268
    DirBase: 351de000  ObjectTable: fffffa8000b74f90  HandleCount: 691.
    Image: winlogon.exe
    VadRoot ffffffadfe73780f0 Vads 179 Clone 0 Private 3088. Modified 2148. Locked 0.
    DeviceMap fffffa80000027d0
    Token                             fffffa8000742060
    ElapsedTime                       2 Days 12:02:23.296
    UserTime                          00:00:00.546
    KernelTime                        00:00:00.906
    ...
    CommitCharge                      3666

1: kd> !object ffffffadfe74010f0
```

```
Object: fffffadfe74010f0  Type: (fffffadfe7afcd40) Process
    ObjectHeader: fffffadfe74010c0
    HandleCount: 13  PointerCount: 363
1: kd> dt nt!_OBJECT_HEADER fffffadfe74010c0
    +0x000 PointerCount    : 363
    +0x008 HandleCount     : 13
    +0x008 NextToFree      : 0x00000000`0000000d
    +0x010 Type            : 0xfffffadf`e7afcd40 _OBJECT_TYPE
    +0x018 NameInfoOffset  : 0 ''
    +0x019 HandleInfoOffset : 0 ''
    +0x01a QuotaInfoOffset : 0 ''
    +0x01b Flags           : 0x20 ' '
    +0x020 ObjectCreateInfo : 0xfffff800`011d2f00 _OBJECT_CREATE_INFORMATION
    +0x020 QuotaBlockCharged : 0xfffff800`011d2f00
    +0x028 SecurityDescriptor : 0xfffffa80`000037d6
    +0x030 Body            : _QUAD
1: kd> * The address of the security descriptor
1: kd> !sd (poi(fffffadfe74010f0-8)&0xffffffff`fffffff0)
1: kd> !sd (0xfffffa80`000037d6&0xffffffff`fffffff0)
->Revision: 0x1
->Sbz1    : 0x0
->Control : 0x8004
            SE_DACL_PRESENT
            SE_SELF_RELATIVE
->Owner   : S-1-5-32-544
->Group   : S-1-5-18
->Dacl    :
...
->Dacl    : ->Ace[1]: ->SID: S-1-5-32-544

->Sacl    : is NULL

1: kd> !token fffffa8000742060
_TOKEN fffffa8000742060
TS Session ID: 0
User: S-1-5-18
Groups:
 00 S-1-5-32-544
    Attributes - Default Enabled Owner
...
RestrictedSidCount: 0      RestrictedSids: 0000000000000000
OriginatingLogonSession: 0
```

Besides the pointer size, the location of the security descriptor controlling access to kernel objects is also interesting to look for. As in Windows x86, the pointer has least significant bits—four in this case, as the pointers are aligned to sixteen bytes—used for something else, and these must be masked out before using the pointer.

In some situations, the security descriptor associated with a registry key or file subject to WOW64 redirection is different between the native part and the WOW64 part. In such cases, the user experiences asymmetrical behavior for the same application, depending on what version is used. After identifying the component and the environment exhibiting the problem, the security investigation is performed using techniques similar to the ones described in Chapter 7, "Security."

## Chapter 8—Interprocess Communication

The LPC communication between 64-bit processes running 64-bit applications and the processes running applications in WOW64 emulation mode is performed by the Windows kernel, and it is not influenced by the process architecture. However, when data is transferred between the processes without transformation, the application should be aware of marshaling issues. Structure member offsets, member sizes, and the member's alignment is different between those architectures, unless they were carefully crafted to be architecture independent.

What are the options to fix marshaling problems? By far, the best option is to use existing components that can marshal data between architectures without problems. For example, Remote Procedure Call (RPC), as well as newer communication stacks, such as SOAP, has been invented to overcome exactly this problem. Years of work and experience have been put into those protocols that must be leveraged, if possible. If the transition to 64-bit suffers from problems in this area, this is a good opportunity to switch from a handcrafted communication mechanism to protocols used industrywide.

DCOM communication can also show the difference between native processes and WOW64-emulated processes. The DCOM client calls the `ole32!CoCreateInstance` API to obtain a pointer to a server object implementing the requested interface. DCOM uses the registry as the main repository for registration information and loads the respective modules from the file system.

Because DCOM registration is subject to registry redirection, the server component must be properly registered on the architecture making the call. In other words, the component setup must make sure that the registry entries and the files are visible to their client. Out-of-process DCOM servers are subject to another mechanism called "registry reflector."

The registry reflector keeps in sync the 64-bit view and the 32-bit view of several registry keys, including out-of-process DCOM server registration. The registry reflector uses the last writer wins policy when it synchronizes the registry's view. As a result, after registering a 32-bit DCOM server application, its registration shows automatically in the 64-bit registry's view. The 64-bit client will instantiate and use the server, a 32-bit application running in the WOW64 emulation environment.

The communication is possible, as out-of-process servers are isolated from their client, and they can communicate in any architecture combination: 32-bit client calling into a 64-bit or 32-bit server and 64-bit client calling into a 32-bit server or 64-bit server. Despite process isolation, client-server architectures might require proxy-stub modules to be loaded in their processes. Because proxy-stub modules must match the hosting process architecture, the system must contain both a 64-bit version and a 32-bit version of those modules to facilitate the communication across architectures. When a registered proxy-stub on the right architecture cannot be found, the communication fails.

## Chapter 11—Writing Custom Debugger Extensions

Is there any reason to recompile the extension to work on 64-bit debuggers? In most cases, such as debugging using live kernel targets or debugging memory dumps, the existing extension works perfectly inside a 32-bit debugger. For live user mode debugging of native applications, the recommendation is to use only the 64-bit version of the debuggers that are unable to load the 32-bit extensions. The decision to invest some time in creating the 64-bit version of the same extension is influenced by the potential usage of the extension.

## Summary

After reading this chapter, describing what to expect when debugging 64-bit applications, it should be relatively safe for any engineer to move from the comfort zone offered by Windows x86 into the Windows x64 world. The 64-bit code is optimized for performance, causing the tools to have trouble providing reliable information to the user. Therefore, the engineers should be ready to manually interpret the application stack, use the information in this chapter, and solve the problem at hand.

Because all tools are using the same symbols files, the same source files, and basically the same concepts, the right tool must be chosen in order to obtain maximum productivity.

# CHAPTER 13

# POSTMORTEM DEBUGGING

Throughout the book, we have looked at quite a few powerful tools available to developers when troubleshooting problematic code. The ultimate goal is to make sure that these tools become integrated into the development process to ensure high quality. These tools are excellent automated ways to find bugs, but they make no absolute guarantees that the application will be bug free when it ships.

Inevitably, problems surface in the application after it has been shipped. These issues turn up at the most inopportune moments—mainly, while the customer uses it. Depending on the severity of the bug, it can either have devastating effects on the customer or merely be a nuisance. In either case, you can expect a phone call from an upset customer asking why the application is not working properly. To remedy the situation and troubleshoot the problem, one option is to ask the customer for remote access to the computer in question. While it might be feasible, at times, customers typically frown on this, and the answer is in many cases no. The reasons for not granting remote access to a machine vary, but typically they can be because of the following.

- The customer environment or policy does not allow inbound connections.
- Remote debugging requires that a debugger be attached to one or more processes and implies downtime. If the process is running on a critical server, customers will be reluctant to accept downtime.
- Debugging a process via user mode or kernel mode means that developers have full access to the state of the machine, including memory contents. For some customers, this might constitute a privacy issue.

If the customer refuses live access to the machine exhibiting the problem and reproducing the problem locally is not possible, can the problem even be debugged? The answer is yes, and the process of doing so is called postmortem debugging. At a high level, postmortem debugging involves the following steps.

1. Trigger the failure to occur.
2. Take a snapshot of the system state at the point of failure (or even before and after, depending of the type of failure).
3. Send the snapshot to engineers for further analysis.

In this chapter, we take a look at the different ways in which snapshots (also known as dump files) can be generated, the different types of dumps available, and how to analyze them. We also cover two very powerful dump file aggregation services known as Windows Error Reporting and Corporate Error Reporting.

Let's start by looking at some of the fundamental dump file topics.

## Dump File Basics

As we have mentioned, a dump file is an out-of-band representation of the state of a given process. The main purpose behind generating a dump file is to analyze application failures without requiring live debugging access to the computer exhibiting the failures. Once a dump file has been generated, it can be sent to the appropriate engineer, who can then analyze the failure without access to the faulting machine. Instead, he simply loads the dump file on his own computer and analyzes the failure using the postmortem capabilities of the debuggers. What information does a dump file contain? Well, that depends entirely on how the dump file was generated. There are two categories of dump files:

- Full dumps
- Mini dumps

A full dump file contains the entire memory space of a process—the executable image, the handle table, and other information used by the debugger. There is no way of customizing the amount of data collected when using the full dump file. A full dump file can, however, be converted to a mini dump file using the debuggers.

The contents of mini dump files are variable and can be customized by the dump file generator, depending on which generator is used. The information contained within a mini dump file ranges from information on a particular thread to an exhaustive description of the process being dumped. As strange as it might seem, the biggest mini dump file will actually contain more debug information than a full dump file. To that extent, this chapter focuses on the mini dump file construct.

A number of tools are available that will generate dump files, as shown in Table 13.1.

**Table 13.1**  Tools That Generate Dump Files

| Name | Description |
| --- | --- |
| Windows Debuggers | The Windows debuggers can generate dumps of different sizes and enable full control of the dump file generation process. |
| ADPlus | ADPlus is a tool that is part of Debugging Tools for Windows. It acts as a process monitor capable of generating dump files whenever a crash or hang occurs. Additionally, it has a notification mechanism that can notify the user of a crash. |

| Name | Description |
|------|-------------|
| Windows Error Reporting | Windows Error Reporting is a service Microsoft provides that allows customers to register with a live error reporting site. Any time a crash occurs in one of the applications owned by a particular customer, an error report is sent from the crashing machine to the Windows Error Reporting Web site. The crash information (including dump file) can be retrieved from the WER service analyzed by the customer postmortem. |
| Corporate Error Reporting | Corporate Error Reporting works on the same basis as the Windows Error Reporting, although at a corporate server level rather than sending crash information over the Internet. Customers can set up a Corporate Error Server and send crash information to this server. Subsequently, crash information can be sent to the Windows Error Reporting site. |

In this section, we cover how to generate dump files using the Windows Debuggers and ADPlus. Windows Error Reporting and Corporate Error Reporting mechanisms are discussed later in the chapter.

To better illustrate the dump file generation process, we use a simple application that allocates memory on the heap, writes to that memory, and then faults. Listing 13.1 shows the code for the sample application.

**Listing 13.1** Simple crashing application

```
void __cdecl wmain ( )
{
    WCHAR* pszTitle=L"Advanced Windows Debugging";

    wprintf(L"Press any key to start\n");
    WCHAR* pBuffer=(WCHAR*) new WCHAR[wcslen(pszTitle)+1];
    if(pBuffer)
    {
        StringCchCopy(pBuffer, wcslen(pszTitle)+1, pszTitle);
        wprintf(L"Title: %s\n", pBuffer);

        pBuffer=NULL;
        *pBuffer='\0';
    }
    else
    {
```

*(continues)*

**Listing 13.1**   Simple crashing application *(continued)*

```
        wprintf(L"Failed to allocate memory\n");
    }
    wprintf(L"Press any key to end\n");
    __getch();
}
```

The source of the crash should be pretty evident. After we copied the string to the newly allocated heap buffer, the string pointer is reset to `null` and subsequently used when `null` terminating the buffer, leading to a crash. We will start by illustrating how to use the debuggers to generate a dump file.

## Generating Dump Files Using the Debuggers

As noted earlier, the application we will be using is illustrated in Listing 13.1. The compiled version can be found in the following location:

> Source code: `C:\AWD\Chapter13`
>
> Binary: `C:\AWDBIN\WinXP.x86.chk\awdscenario1.exe`

Run the application under the debugger and continue execution until the crash occurs.

```
. . . .
ModLoad: 5cb70000 5cb96000   C:\WINDOWS\system32\ShimEng.dll
Press any key to start
Title: Advanced Windows Debugging
(9d8.f0c): Access violation - code c0000005 (first chance)
First chance exceptions are reported before any exception handling.
This exception may be expected and handled.
eax=00000000 ebx=7ffd5000 ecx=77c418bf edx=77c61b78 esi=7c9118f1 edi=00011970
eip=0100127e esp=0007ff1c ebp=0007ff44 iopl=0         nv up ei pl nz na po nc
cs=001b  ss=0023  ds=0023  es=0023  fs=003b  gs=0000            efl=00010202
awdscenario1!wmain+0xbe:
0100127e c60000          mov     byte ptr [eax],0        ds:0023:00000000=??
0:000> kb
ChildEBP RetAddr  Args to Child
0007ff44 01001495 00000001 00032bf0 00036890 awdscenario1!wmain+0xbe
0007ffc0 7c816fd7 00011970 7c9118f1 7ffd5000 awdscenario1!wmainCRTStartup+0x12f
0007fff0 00000000 01001366 00000000 78746341 kernel32!BaseProcessStart+0x23
```

Not too surprisingly, we crash because of a second-chance access violation. At this point, we would like to generate a dump file for further postmortem analysis. The single biggest question with generating dump files is how much information to include. As a general rule of thumb, the more state that is stored in the dump file, the more information you will have at your disposal when doing postmortem debugging. The biggest limiting factor is the size of the dump file. You might find yourself in environments in which getting a huge dump file from a highly secure server is not feasible, and you might need to work with a stripped down version.

The means by which a dump file is generated is using the .dump command. The .dump /m option indicates to the debugger that it should generate a mini dump file. Additionally, the .dump /m command can take a number of other options, as detailed in Table 13.2.

**Table 13.2**  Options for the .dump Command

| Option | Description |
| --- | --- |
| a | Generates a complete mini dump with all the options enabled. It includes complete memory data, handle information data, module information, basic memory information, and thread information. Equivalent to using /mfFhut. |
| f | Generates a mini dump that contains all accessible and committed pages of the owning process. |
| F | Generates a mini dump that includes all the necessary basic memory information for the debugger to reconstruct the entire virtual memory address space. |
| h | Generates a mini dump that contains handle information. |
| u | Generates a mini dump that includes information on unloaded modules. Note that this is only available on Windows Server 2003. |
| t | Generates a mini dump that includes information on thread times. Thread time information includes created time, as well as user and kernel mode times. |
| i | Generates a mini dump that includes secondary memory information. Secondary memory is any memory (plus a small region surrounding it) that is referenced by a stack pointer or the backing store. |
| p | Generates a mini dump that includes the process and thread environment blocks. |
| w | Generates a mini dump that includes all committed read-write private pages. |
| d | Generates a mini dump that includes all the image data segments. |
| c | Generates a mini dump that includes all image code segments. |
| r | Generates a mini dump that is suited for scenarios in which privacy is of concern. This option erases (replaces with zeroes) any information not needed in order to re-create the stack (including local variables). |
| R | Generates a mini dump that is suited to scenarios in which privacy is of concern. This option removes the full module paths from the mini dump, thereby ensuring the privacy of the user's directory structure. |

In addition to the various options that control the contents of the dump file, the name of the dump file must be specified. When a dump file is generated and a full path is not specified, it will, by default, be generated in the directory from where the debugger was launched. The following example illustrates how to generate a dump file with full memory information using a full path.

```
.dump /mf c:\dumpfile.dmp
```

Let's run the `.dump` command above on our crashing application:

```
0:000> .dump /mf dumpfile.dmp
Creating dumpfile.dmp - mini user dump
Dump successfully written
```

After the debugger is done generating the dump file, you should have a file of approximately 3MB in size. To use the dump file, load it in a new debugger instance using the `/z` switch. For example, to load the dump file we just generated, use the following command.

```
c:\>windbg -z dumpfile.dmp
```

After the debugger has loaded the dump file, you will see the following debug output:

```
...

...

Loading Dump File [C:\dumpfile.dmp]
User Mini Dump File with Full Memory: Only application data is available

Windows XP Version 2600 (Service Pack 2) UP Free x86 compatible
Product: WinNt, suite: SingleUserTS Personal
Debug session time: Thu Nov 16 17:59:25.000 2006 (GMT-8)
System Uptime: 0 days 8:45:08.239
Process Uptime: 0 days 0:01:35.000
...
This dump file has an exception of interest stored in it.
The stored exception information can be accessed via .ecxr.
(9d8.f0c): Access violation - code c0000005 (first/second chance not available)
eax=00000000 ebx=7ffd5000 ecx=77c418bf edx=77c61b78 esi=7c9118f1 edi=00011970
eip=0100127e esp=0007ff1c ebp=0007ff44 iopl=0         nv up ei pl nz na po nc
cs=001b  ss=0023  ds=0023  es=0023  fs=003b  gs=0000            efl=00010202
awdscenario1!wmain+0xbe:
0100127e c60000          mov     byte ptr [eax],0          ds:0023:00000000=??
```

Near the top of the debug output, you will notice that the debugger gives some basic information about the dump file being loaded. Information includes the location of the dump file and the type of dump file, as well as what information is available. The next interesting piece of information is toward the end of the debugger output, where the reason behind the fault is displayed (access violation). Armed with this dump file, you can now debug this failure on any machine that you want without physical access to the faulting machine. We discuss in detail how the postmortem analysis works later in this chapter.

When generating a dump file explicitly using the debugger, one of the difficulties is that a debugger has to be attached to the faulty process at the right time. Although that might not seem like a big hurdle, think about scenarios in which the crash only reproduces every once in a while and the opportunity to attach the debugger is missed. It would be nice to be able to tell Windows to use the debuggers to generate a dump file any time a process crashes. Fortunately, this mechanism exists and is commonly referred to as the postmortem debugger setup. By default, Windows uses Dr. Watson (discussed later in the chapter) as the postmortem debugger. Dr. Watson generates a dump file anytime a process crashes and gives the user the option to send the dump file to Microsoft for further analysis. The postmortem debugger to use can be changed by using the command lines shown in Table 13.3.

**Table 13.3** Postmortem Debugger Setup

| Command Line | Aedebug\Debugger Registry Value | Description |
| --- | --- | --- |
| Windbg -I | windbg.exe -p %ld -e %ld -g | Changes the postmortem debugger to be WinDbg. Note that the -I must be capitalized. |
| cdb -iae | cdb.exe -p %ld -e %ld -g | Changes the postmortem debugger to be cdb. |
| ntsd -iae | ntsd.exe -p %ld -e %ld -g | Changes the postmortem debugger to be ntsd. |
| Drwtsn32 -i | drwtsn32 -p %ld -e %ld -g | Changes the postmortem debugger to be Dr. Watson. |

What happens behind-the-scenes when the command lines in Table 13.3 are executed? The answer is quite simple. They change a few registry values that Windows looks at when it detects a process crash. The registry path used for the postmortem debugger setup is shown here.

```
HKEY_LOCAL_MACHINE\Software\Microsoft\Windows NT\CurrentVersion\AeDebug
```

The AeDebug key contains two values that are critical for the postmortem debugger setup.

### Auto

The auto registry value dictates whether a message box should be displayed whenever a crash occurs and a postmortem debugger is set up. If the value is set to 0, a message box is displayed, and conversely, when set to 1, no message box is displayed. The message box that is displayed is the dreaded "Application X has encountered a problem and needs to close." In that message box, the user can choose to debug the faulting application, send an error report, or skip sending the error report. Figure 13.1 shows an example of the message box when awdscenario1.exe faults and ntsd is set up to be the postmortem debugger.

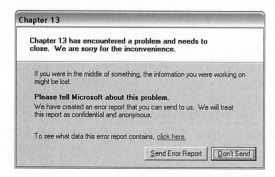

**Figure 13.1**   Example of the Windows fault message when awdscenario1.exe crashes

### Debugger

The debugger registry value dictates which postmortem debugger should be invoked whenever a process faults. This value can either be edited manually to specify a postmortem tool or populated automatically by the debuggers if you configure any of them as the postmortem debugger. As shown in Table 13.3, with the exception of the name of the tool, the rest of the command line resembles the following:

```
-p %ld -e %ld -g
```

The -p %ld part indicates which process the debugger should attach to, and the -e %ld switch specifies an event that is signaled when the attach process is completed. Finally, the -g switch instructs the debugger to ignore the default first breakpoint that always occurs when a debugger is attached to a process. What if you wanted to specify additional options? Ntsd and cdb optionally allow you to specify a key string when you run with the -iaec switch. The key string allows you to add additional options to the Debugger registry value even when using the debugger's own post-mortem registration process. For example, to set ntsd with source line debugging, use the following command line:

```
ntsd -iaec -lines
```

If you check the Debugger registry value, you will see that the -lines switch has been added.

```
ntsd.exe -p %ld -e %ld -g -lines
```

Although the debuggers typically provide more than enough power and flexibility when generating dump files, one additional tool can be used. The tool is called ADPlus.

## Generating Dump Files Using ADPlus

ADPlus is a tool that monitors and automates the generation of dump files for one or more faulty processes and has the capability to notify a user or computer when crashes occur. ADPlus is a command-line-driven script, and Microsoft strongly recommends running ADPlus under the cscript.exe interpreter. As a matter of fact, if the default script interpreter is set to something other than cscript.exe, a dialog appears, asking if you want to change the interpreter to cscript.exe. In addition to the command-line options, ADPlus can work on the basis of configuration files. The configuration files allow for more granular control of the operational flow of ADPlus.

ADPlus can run in one of the following two modes:

- Hang mode is used to troubleshoot processes that exhibit hanging symptoms (such as not making progress or 100% CPU utilization). ADPlus must be started after the process or processes to monitor have already hung.
- Crash mode is used to troubleshoot processes that exhibit crashing behavior. ADPlus must be started before the process crashes.

Let's use crash mode as an example of how to use ADPlus to generate a dump file for awdscenario1.exe. Start by running the awdscenario1.exe application:

```
C:\AWDBIN\WinXP.x86.chk\awdscenario1.exe
```

Before pressing any key to resume execution, run the following command line:

```
C:\>adplus.vbs -crash -pn awdscenario1.exe -y
SRV*c:\Symbols*http://msdl.microsoft.com/download/symbols
```

The −crash switch puts ADPlus into crash mode, the −pn switch tells ADPlus the name of the process to monitor, and the −y sets the symbol path to be used throughout the ADPlus execution. The beauty of using the −pn switch is that it can monitor any number of instances of any given process name by name.

After execution has finished, ADPlus will put the resulting log files under a directory of the Windows debuggers installation path. The name of the directory takes on the following structure:

```
<runtype>_Mode__Date_<date of run>__Time_<time of run>
```

For example, when ADPlus finished executing, the following directory was created:

```
C:\Program Files\Debugging Tools for Windows\Crash_Mode__Date_10-21-2006__Time_10-31-
17AM
```

Note that the default path can be changed by using the −o switch.

In the preceding directory, there are several files, but the most important ones are the *.dmp files, which contain all the dump information from the run. As you can see, several dump files are collected. Why do we have more than one dump file per crash? Well, ADPlus automates the process of collecting dump files and generates dump files when certain preset conditions occur during execution. The name of the dump file gives you the necessary clues to figure out the reason the dump file was generated. For example, in our previous run, ADPlus generated the following dump files:

```
PID-2728__AWDSCENARIO1.EXE__1st_chance_AccessViolation__mini_0BA8_2006-10-21_10-31-
30-671_0AA8.dmp
```

```
PID-2728__AWDSCENARIO1.EXE__1st_chance_Process_Shut_Down__full_0BA8_2006-10-21_10-31-
30-718_0AA8.dmp
```

```
PID-2728__AWDSCENARIO1.EXE__2nd_chance_AccessViolation__full_0BA8_2006-10-21_10-31-
30-687_0AA8.dmp
```

ADPlus generated a mini dump file when the first-chance access violation occurred, followed by a full dump file when the second-chance access occurred, and finally also produced a full dump file when the process was shutting down. Do we need all these dumps for our particular run? No—in our particular case, the most interesting dump file is the second-chance access violation. However, there are situations in which periodic generation of dump files can be very useful, as it can yield a historical perspective of the systematic deterioration of a process. ADPlus even offers a powerful way for the user to configure how often information should be collected and under what conditions, essentially providing a scripting front end for the debuggers. You can learn more about the scripting capabilities of ADPlus in the debugger documentation. It is important to note that ADPlus does not do anything "magical" via its scripting engine. It simply takes a user-friendly way of specifying debugger directives and translates them into pure and automated debugger commands. You can see how the user-friendly configuration actually translates to the debugger commands by looking at the directory called `CDBScripts` located in the same directory as the dump files. In our example, the `CDBScripts` directory contains a file called `PID-2728__ AWDSCENARIO1.EXE.cfg`, which contains all the debugger commands used in that `ADPlus` session.

The last important point about ADPlus is how we can control what type of dump file is generated when a fault occurs. Four command-line switches control this behavior:

- `-FullOnFirst`: This switch causes ADPlus to generate a full dump file when a first-chance exception occurs.
- `-MiniOnSecond`: This switch causes ADPlus to generate a mini dump file when a second-chance exception occurs.
- `-NoDumpOnFirst`: This switch tells ADPlus not to generate a mini dump file when a first-chance exception occurs. This can come in very handy, as applications sometimes generate first-chance exceptions that are gracefully handled.
- `-NoDumpOnSecond`: This switch tells ADPlus not to generate a mini dump file when a second-chance exception occurs.

ADPlus is a convenient, powerful, and flexible tool for monitoring and gathering data from faulty processes. In this section, we covered the basics of the tool, and it is well worth your time to further investigate the other powerful features, such as the scripting capabilities and defining custom exception handlers that allow you to generate dump files when custom exceptions occur.

In addition to creating user mode dump files, kernel mode dump files are also possible. The next section illustrates how to generate kernel mode dump files.

## Creating Kernel Dumps

As with user mode debuggers, you can use any kernel memory dump as the target image. This functionality is used mostly by kernel driver developers to investigate driver failures postmortem. At times, user mode developers can benefit from using kernel dumps—for example, when the system is a critical production system, and we cannot justify down time; when the problem is reported by a customer, and the process dump is not sufficient.

As mentioned earlier, a crash dump file is a dump of the machine state at the time of a serious system exception. This dump file can be analyzed through debugging tools by loading it into the debugger to get information about the state of the machine and eventually arrive at what caused the crash.

Before a crash dump is created, dump creation must be enabled and configured. To configure these settings, go to the Control Panel, click the System icon, select the Advanced tab, go to the Startup and Recovery area, and click on Settings, as shown in Figure 13.2. The desired dump file size must be selected from the Write Debugging Information list. Only one dump file can be created for any given crash. The difference between the different dump files is one of size. The Complete Memory Dump is the largest and contains the most information, the Kernel Memory Dump is somewhat smaller, and the Small Memory Dump is only 64KB in size. The content of those three kinds of kernel mode crash dump files are as follows:

- Complete Memory Dump: This dump file contains all the physical memory for the machine at the time of the fault. This dump file requires a page file on the boot drive that is at least as large as the main system memory: It should be capable of holding a file whose size equals your entire RAM plus one megabyte.
- Kernel Memory: This type of dump contains all the memory in use by the kernel at the time of the crash. This kind of dump file is significantly smaller than the Complete Memory Dump. Typically, the dump file will be around one-third the size of the physical memory on the system. This dump file doesn't include unallocated memory, or any memory allocated to user mode applications. It only includes memory allocated to the Windows kernel and hardware abstraction level (HAL), as well as memory allocated to kernel mode drivers and other kernel mode programs.
- Small Memory dump (Minidump): This is a much smaller file than the other two kinds of kernel-mode crash dumps. It is exactly 64KB in size and requires only 64KB of page file space on the boot drive. This kind of dump file can be useful when space is greatly limited. However, because of the limited amount of information included, errors that were not directly caused by the thread executing at the time of the crash might not be discovered by an analysis of this file.

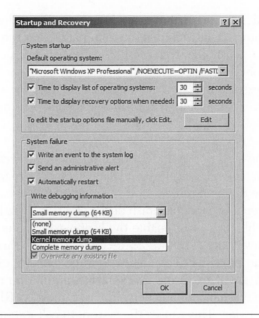

**Figure 13.2**   Configuring an automatic kernel dump

A small memory dump file includes the following:

- The bug check message and parameters, as well as other blue screen data.
- The processor context (PRCB) for the processor that crashed.
- The process information and kernel context (EPROCESS) for the process that crashed.
- The thread information and kernel context (ETHREAD) for the thread that crashed.
- The kernel-mode call stack for the thread that crashed. If this is longer than 16KB, only the topmost 16KB will be included.
- A list of loaded drivers.

In Windows XP and Windows Server 2003, the following items are also included:

- A list of loaded modules and unloaded modules.
- The debugger data block. This contains basic debugging information about the system.

- Any additional memory pages that Windows identifies as being useful in debugging failures. This includes the data pages that the registers were pointing to when the crash occurred, and other pages specifically requested by the faulting component.
- (Itanium processor only) The backing store.
- (Windows Server 2003 only) The Windows type—for example, "Professional" or "Server."

In some situations, the system has not crashed; therefore, a crash dump will not have been created. To debug these cases, it might be advantageous to manually create a crash dump file. This can be done on most systems using a PS2 keyboard. Additional configuration is required to enable a manual crash dump creation. Besides setting the size and location of the dump file, you must enable the keyboard-initiated crash in the registry. In the registry key `HKEY_LOCAL_MACHINE\System\CurrentControlSet\Services\i8042prt\Parameters`, create a value named `CrashOnCtrlScroll`, and set it equal to `REG_DWORD 0x1` (or any nonzero value). After the system has rebooted, you can generate a crash by holding down the rightmost CTRL key and pressing the SCROLL LOCK key twice. This causes the system to call `KeBugCheck()` with a bug check code of `0xE2` (MANUALLY_INITIATED_CRASH).

A common problem encountered in kernel debugger sessions is that some pages are not loaded in physical memory. Because any paged-out memory address is not contained in the dump, in general it is preferable to debug a live machine instead of using the kernel dumps. If the kernel debugger is enabled on the system, the kernel debugger is prompted to investigate the crash. If the kernel debugger is not connected, the system just freezes, waiting for the kernel debugger to connect.

You can generate an explicit dump by using the built-in dump command, `.dump [option] <filename>`, as seen in Listing 13.2. All the dump information is transferred through the communication pipe between debugger and host, and the debugger warns you if the requested dump is large for the communication channel between the kernel debugger host and kernel debugger target. (For example, capturing a full memory dump from a system with 256MB of memory must transfer all that over the channel, and that requires many hours over a serial connection.) During this time, the debugger target system is not operational.

**Listing 13.2**   Creating a kernel mode dump file

```
kd> * .dump without parameters creates a mini kernel dump file
kd> .dump %temp%\mini.dmp
Creating c:\temp\mini.dmp - mini kernel dump
```

```
Dump successfully written
kd> * f parameter generates a full but large dump file
kd> .dump /f %temp%\full.dmp
Creating a full kernel dump over the COM port is a VERY VERY slow opera-
tion.
This command may take many HOURS to complete.  Ctrl-C if you want to ter-
minate the command.
Creating c:\temp\full.dmp - Full kernel dump
Percent written 0
Failed reading target physical memory at 35000, NTSTATUS 0xC000013A
```

Now that we have seen how to generate dump files, it is time to illustrate how dump files can be used in the troubleshooting process

## Using Dump Files

Now that you have been presented with one or more dump files and tasked with the investigation of finding the root cause of the faulty process, what can actually be done using these dump files? Can you dump memory, look at handles, or step through code? Remember that a dump file is simply a static snapshot of the state of a process. As such, setting breakpoints and stepping through code is not possible. Using dump files can be best viewed as manual debugging. By manual, we mean that simply by looking at the state of an application, you will need to manually construct theories about what code has executed to get the application into that state. It should be evident that constructing code execution by state analysis is a much harder proposition than engaging in a live debug session. Nevertheless, plenty of the debugger commands that massage application state into a more digestible form still work when using dump files; and in most cases, with enough patience, the root cause can be found.

Before we take a closer look at the dump files generated in the previous section, one critical piece of information needs to be brought up: symbol files. Dump files contain no symbolic information, and it is critical that symbol files be available when analyzing a dump file. This might seem to be an easy enough task. When an application ships, the symbols are archived; when a dump needs to be analyzed, you simply point the debugger to the archived symbols. This strategy works well if only one version of the application is ever shipped, but alas, applications evolve and typically go through several versions before being retired. Furthermore, applications tend to be patched, which means that individual components of the application be updated, making it harder to manage the versioning of the symbol files. To address these problems, it is strongly recommended that a symbol server be set up so that symbols are archived and can be accessed in a simple and organized fashion. For detailed information on how to set up a symbol server, see Chapter 4, "Managing Symbol and Source Files." Let's start our dump file analysis by looking at a very basic scenario—an access violation.

## Dump File Analysis: Access Violation

In the prior section, we generated a dump file of a faulting application, and we are now tasked with finding the root cause using only the dump file. The dump file that we generated can be found in the following location:

```
C:\AWDBIN\Dumps\dumpfile.dmp
```

To use a dump file, we have to tell the debugger that we want to analyze a dump file by using the –z switch.

```
C:> windbg –z C:\AWDBIN\Dumps\dumpfile.dmp
```

When the debugger has started, the first piece of important information is the access violation output.

```
This dump file has an exception of interest stored in it.
The stored exception information can be accessed via .ecxr.
(9d8.f0c): Access violation - code c0000005 (first/second chance not available)
eax=00000000 ebx=7ffd5000 ecx=77c418bf edx=77c61b78 esi=7c9118f1 edi=00011970
eip=0100127e esp=0007ff1c ebp=0007ff44 iopl=0         nv up ei pl nz na po nc
cs=001b  ss=0023  ds=0023  es=0023  fs=003b  gs=0000            efl=00010202
awdscenario1!wmain+0xbe:
0100127e c60000          mov     byte ptr [eax],0          ds:0023:00000000=??
```

This tells us immediately that the dump file we are investigating was generated because of an access violation. The next logical step is to dump out the stack trace for the offending thread and see what operations were occurring when the access violation occurred.

```
0:000> kb
ChildEBP RetAddr  Args to Child
0007ff44 01001495 00000001 00032bf0 00036890 awdscenario1!wmain+0xbe
0007ffc0 7c816fd7 00011970 7c9118f1 7ffd5000 awdscenario1!wmainCRTStartup+0x12f
0007fff0 00000000 01001366 00000000 78746341 kernel32!BaseProcessStart+0x23
```

Judging from the stack trace, we can see that our application caused an access violation in its main function. To get some more details, we unassemble the top frame and see what was being executed when the access violation occurred.

```
0:000> u awdscenario1!wmain+0xbe
awdscenario1!wmain+0xbe:
0100127e c60000          mov      byte ptr [eax],0
01001281 eb0e            jmp      awdscenario1!wmain+0xd1 (01001291)
01001283 68a4100001      push     offset awdscenario1!`string' (010010a4)
01001288 ff1544100001    call     dword ptr [awdscenario1!_imp__printf (01001044)]
0100128e 83c404          add      esp,4
01001291 688c100001      push     offset awdscenario1!`string' (0100108c)
01001296 ff1544100001    call     dword ptr [awdscenario1!_imp__printf (01001044)]
0100129c 83c404          add      esp,4
```

The offending mov instruction appears to be moving the value 0 to an address specified by the eax register. To find out what the eax register contains, we use the r command.

```
0:000> r
eax=00000000 ebx=7ffd5000 ecx=77c418bf edx=77c61b78 esi=7c9118f1 edi=00011970
eip=0100127e esp=0007ff1c ebp=0007ff44 iopl=0         nv up ei pl nz na po nc
cs=001b  ss=0023  ds=0023  es=0023  fs=003b  gs=0000            efl=00010202
awdscenario1!wmain+0xbe:
0100127e c60000          mov      byte ptr [eax],0           ds:0023:00000000=??
```

The eax register contains a value of 0, which means that the offending mov instruction was trying to store a value of 0 into memory location 0. Suffice it to say that we all know the expected outcome of such an instruction—an access violation. Looking at the code in Listing 13.1, we can also see that it matches perfectly with the debug session. More specifically, the line of code that caused the access violation is *pBuffer='\0';—and the pBuffer pointer value is null.

Now that we have seen how to investigate a simple access violation using the postmortem features of the debugger, we'll take a look at a slightly more complex scenario involving a handle leak.

## Dump File Analysis: Handle Leaks

Crashes are only one category of problems that can be analyzed using dump files. Quite often, resource leaks creep into applications and might need to be analyzed via the dump file mechanism as well. In this section, we use a sample application from Chapter 9, "Resource Leaks," that can be found at

Source code: C:\AWD\Chapter9\HLeak\Client

Binary: C:\AWDBIN\WinXP.x86.chk\09HLeak.exe

We run the application under the debugger with 20 threads, 200 iterations per thread, and 0 sleep time between iterations.

```
C:\AWDBIN\WinXP.x86.chk\09HLeak.exe /t:20 /i:200 /s:0
```

Using task manager, we can see a drastic increase in handle usage. Prior to the application exiting, break into the debugger and generate a dump file using the /mf (full memory) switch.

```
...
...
...
0:000> .dump /mf c:\dumpfile.dmp
Creating c:\dumpfile.dmp - mini user dump
Dump successfully written
```

Once the dump file has been written, exit the current debugger instance, start a new instance with the dump file just generated (or alternatively, the dump file located at C:\AWDBIN\Dumps\dumpfile2.dmp), and issue the !handle extension command to get an idea of the handle usage in the application.

```
0:000> !handle
ERROR: !handle: extension exception 0x80004002.
   "Unable to read handle information"
```

Why is the !handle extension command resulting in an error? The dump file was generated with the full memory dump switch (/mf) and should contain all the necessary information. It turns out that to include handle information in the dump file, a full memory dump is not enough. Dump files that need to include handle information must also add h to the switch. Let's rerun the application under the debugger and issue the following .dump command prior to exiting the application.

```
.dump /mfh c:\dumpfile3.dmp
```

Next, we load the newly generated dump file in the debugger and try to once again use the !handle extension command.

```
0:000> !handle
Handle 00000004
  Type          Token
Handle 00000008
  Type          Token
```

```
Handle 0000000c
    Type          File
Handle 00000010
    Type          Token
Handle 00000014
    Type          Token
Handle 00000018
    Type          Token
Handle 0000001c
    Type          Token
Handle 00000020
    Type          Token
Handle 00000024
    Type          Token
...
...
...
738 Handles
Type          Count
Event         2
File          1
Port          1
Directory     2
WindowStation 1
Key           1
Token         1440
KeyedEvent    1
```

This time, we have complete access to the handle information in the application. We can even get detailed information about any of the listed handles by using the !handle <handle value> command. From the handle statistics at the bottom of the !handle output, we can see that there is an abnormally large number of token handles. We also know from Chapter 9 that a great way of figuring out the allocation sources for handles is to use the !htrace extension command. Enabling htrace on the dump file seems to be the best way to go.

```
00> !htrace -enable
ERROR: Cannot enable handle tracing, status code 0xc0000008.
```

Once again, it seems as if we've hit a snag. Htrace returns an error code when run on a dump file. The bad news is that htrace does not work for dump files, and because of that, getting nice stack traces for each opened handle is not possible. Because htrace information is static in nature, one workaround for this problem is to run `htrace` on the live machine and pipe all the results to a log file. A dump file can be created with associated handle information that can be used to correlate all open handles with the stack traces in the log file. Let's try it on our leaky application and see what can be learned from the log and dump files. Begin by running the leaky application under the debugger. Set the symbol path, enable `htrace`, and open a log file. Resume the application, and prior to exiting, run the `!htrace -diff` command to get the leaked handle stack traces and subsequently close the log file. Last, generate a full memory dump with handle information.

```
...
0:000> !htrace -enable
Handle tracing enabled.
Handle tracing information snapshot successfully taken.
...

...

0:000> .logopen c:\handles.log
Opened log file 'c:\handles.log'
...

...

...

0:000> !htrace -diff
Handle tracing information snapshot successfully taken.
0x1000 new stack traces since the previous snapshot.
Ignoring handles that were already closed...
Outstanding handles opened since the previous snapshot:
--------------------
Handle = 0x00001274 - OPEN
Thread ID = 0x000000e4, Process ID = 0x00000eb8

0x01002939: 09hleak!CServer::GetToken+0x00000049
0x01002651: 09hleak!CServer::GetSID+0x00000021
0x010015f1: 09hleak!ThreadWorker+0x00000081
0x7c80b683: kernel32!BaseThreadStart+0x00000037
--------------------
Handle = 0x00001270 - OPEN
Thread ID = 0x00000fb8, Process ID = 0x00000eb8

0x01002939: 09hleak!CServer::GetToken+0x00000049
0x01002651: 09hleak!CServer::GetSID+0x00000021
0x010015f1: 09hleak!ThreadWorker+0x00000081
0x7c80b683: kernel32!BaseThreadStart+0x00000037
--------------------
Handle = 0x0000126c - OPEN
```

13. POSTMORTEM DEBUGGING

```
Thread ID = 0x00000d68, Process ID = 0x00000eb8

0x01002939: 09hleak!CServer::GetToken+0x00000049
0x01002651: 09hleak!CServer::GetSID+0x00000021
0x010015f1: 09hleak!ThreadWorker+0x00000081
0x7c80b683: kernel32!BaseThreadStart+0x00000037
-------------------
Handle = 0x00001244 - OPEN
Thread ID = 0x00000df0, Process ID = 0x00000eb8

0x01002939: 09hleak!CServer::GetToken+0x00000049
0x01002651: 09hleak!CServer::GetSID+0x00000021
0x010015f1: 09hleak!ThreadWorker+0x00000081
0x7c80b683: kernel32!BaseThreadStart+0x00000037
-------------------
Handle = 0x0000120c - OPEN
Thread ID = 0x00000b78, Process ID = 0x00000eb8

0x01002939: 09hleak!CServer::GetToken+0x00000049
0x01002651: 09hleak!CServer::GetSID+0x00000021
0x010015f1: 09hleak!ThreadWorker+0x00000081
0x7c80b683: kernel32!BaseThreadStart+0x00000037
-------------------
Handle = 0x000011d8 - OPEN
Thread ID = 0x00000bdc, Process ID = 0x00000eb8

0x01002939: 09hleak!CServer::GetToken+0x00000049
0x01002651: 09hleak!CServer::GetSID+0x00000021
0x010015f1: 09hleak!ThreadWorker+0x00000081
0x7c80b683: kernel32!BaseThreadStart+0x00000037
-------------------
Handle = 0x000011ac - OPEN
Thread ID = 0x000009b0, Process ID = 0x00000eb8

0x01002939: 09hleak!CServer::GetToken+0x00000049
0x01002651: 09hleak!CServer::GetSID+0x00000021
0x010015f1: 09hleak!ThreadWorker+0x00000081
0x7c80b683: kernel32!BaseThreadStart+0x00000037
...
...
...
-------------------
Displayed 0x349 stack traces for outstanding handles opened since the previous snap-
shot.
0:000> .logclose
Closing open log file c:\handles.log
```

```
0:000> .dump /mfh c:\dumpfile4.dmp
Creating c:\dumpfile4.dmp - mini user dump
Dump successfully written
```

Next, we load the dump file just generated (or use the dump file at `C:\AWDBIN\Dumps\dumpfile4.dmp`) under the debugger and issue the `!handle` extension command, which tells us exactly which handles are still open in the process. Selecting one of the handles, listed as still open in `dumpfile4.dmp`, is handle:

```
Handle 00001490
  Type          Token
```

To find out the corresponding stack trace that opened this handle, we look into the `htrace.log` file and search for `00001490`.

```
Handle = 0x00001490 - OPEN
Thread ID = 0x000002ac, Process ID = 0x00000eb8

0x01002939: 09hleak!CServer::GetToken+0x00000049
0x01002651: 09hleak!CServer::GetSID+0x00000021
0x010015f1: 09hleak!ThreadWorker+0x00000081
0x7c80b683: kernel32!BaseThreadStart+0x00000037
```

The stack trace shown previously corresponds to the stack trace that resulted in opening the leaked handle. From here, a targeted code review reveals the reason behind the leaked handle. By using some simple correlative and investigative techniques, we are able to arrive at the root cause for the leaked handles.

In this section of the chapter, we looked at how to use the dump files to arrive at the root cause for a particular problem. Generating the correct type of dump file is also of paramount importance. Without the correct information included in the dump file, the critical missing pieces might mean the difference between a successful or failed debug session. As a general rule of thumb, you should always strive to get a dump file that has as much information in it as possible, and the best dump switch for achieving this is the /ma switch.

The importance of postmortem debugging cannot be overstated. Many times, it's impossible to get access to a live debug session, and having the tools and knowledge to properly analyze a bug after the fact is critical. In fact, postmortem debugging using dump files is so important that Microsoft built an entire online service around it, known as the Windows Error Reporting service.

# Windows Error Reporting

Anyone who has been using Windows has come across the message box shown in Figure 13.3 at least once.

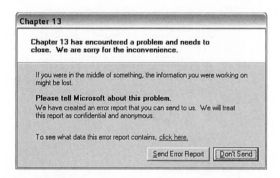

**Figure 13.3**   Dr. Watson message box

Figure 13.3 illustrates the signature UI of a technology known as Dr. Watson. When presented with this message box, the user has the option to send an error report to Microsoft. If the user chooses to send the error report, it is uploaded over a secure channel (HTTPS) to a Microsoft database, where it is categorized (or bucketized) and stored for later analysis. It should come as no surprise that the information sent up as part of the error report includes a dump file that helps the developers looking at the problem find the root cause. The applications that can partake in Windows Error Reporting are not limited to Microsoft products. Any crashing process in Windows will be part of the same mechanism. However, to get access to error reports that correspond to your applications, you must first enroll in the Windows Error Reporting Service. In this section, we take a look at how Windows Error Reporting works, what is sent up as part of the error report, how to enroll in the Windows Error Reporting database, and how to query the service to get the error reports.

## Dr. Watson

Dr. Watson is used in Windows to generate error reporting information that can be sent up to the Windows Error Reporting service. Windows configures Dr. Watson to be the default postmortem debugger. When an application crash occurs, Dr. Watson catches this crash and generates an error report that the user is notified about and can optionally upload to Microsoft. The error collection behavior of Dr. Watson can be customized by running drwtsn32.exe. Figure 13.4 shows the Dr. Watson configuration dialog box.

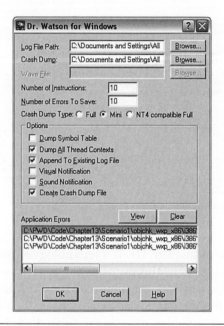

**Figure 13.4**   Dr. Watson configuration dialog box

Each of the configurable options is discussed next.

### Log File Path

The log file path specifies the path where the Dr. Watson log file will be stored. By default, the log file is stored in

```
Documents and Settings\All Users\Application Data\Microsoft\Dr Watson
```

If you change this path, make sure that the specified path grants all users write access.

### Crash Dump

The crash dump specifies the path to the crash dump files that are generated when an application faults. The default file path is

```
Documents and Settings\All Users\Application Data\Microsoft\Dr Watson\user.dmp
```

If you change this path, make sure that the specified path grants all users write access.

### Number of Instructions

This specifies the number of instructions that Dr. Watson will unassemble before and after the current program counter for each thread. By default, the number of instructions to unassemble is 10.

### Number of Errors to Save

This specifies the number of errors that will be saved in the log file. By default, the number of errors logged is 10.

### Crash Dump Type

This specifies the type of crash dump file that is generated by Dr. Watson. By default, a mini dump file is generated that contains only the registers, stack, and portions of memory.

### Options

Table 13.4 describes all the options that can be configured.

**Table 13.4**  Dr. Watson Options

| Option | Description |
|---|---|
| Dump Symbol Table | Dump symbol table for each module. Note that this option can make the log files very large. By default, this option is not enabled. |
| Dump All Thread Contexts | Dumps the state for every thread in the faulting application. By default, this option is not enabled, and Dr. Watson only logs the state of the faulting thread. |
| Append to Existing Log File | Specifies if log information should be appended to the existing log file or if a new log file should be created for each new application fault. By default, this option is enabled. |

*(continues)*

**Table 13.4** Dr. Watson Options *(continued)*

| Option | Description |
|---|---|
| Visual Notification | Specifies if Dr. Watson provides visual notifications about faulting applications. If this is enabled, a dialog box is shown with an OK button. This option is disabled by default. |
| Sound Notification | Specifies if Dr. Watson should provide audible notifications about faulting applications. If enabled, a WAV file can be specified. By default, this option is disabled. |
| Create Crash Dump File | Specifies if Dr. Watson should generate a dump file of the faulting application. By default, this option is enabled and requires that a filename be specified in the Crash Dump field. |

### Application Errors

The application errors option displays all the errors from the various Dr. Watson collections. Let's take the sample awdscenario1.exe used previously in the chapter and see what type of specific information Dr. Watson collects. First, make sure that Dr. Watson is selected as the postmortem debugger by running the following:

```
drwtsn32.exe -i
```

Next, run the awdscenario1.exe application (used earlier in the chapter) using

```
C:\AWDBIN\WinXp.x86.chk\awdscenario1.exe
```

When the Dr. Watson message box is displayed, click Don't Send. To look at the log file generated by Dr. Watson for this crash, we use the following path:

```
Documents and Settings\All Users\Application Data\Microsoft\Dr Watson\ drwtsn32.log
```

The log file is in plaintext, and any text reader or editor (such as Notepad) can be used to open the file.

The log file is organized into one or more `application exception` sections, one section per fault, where each section begins with the following line:

```
Application exception
```

Each `application` `exception` represents a faulting application and contains the following information:

- `App`: The full path to the faulting application followed by the process identifier
- `When`: The date and time of the fault
- `Exception` `number`: The exception number and textual representation of the exception

In our sample run of awdscenario1.exe, the `application` `exception` section of the log file states (if you have had multiple process crashes on the system, you might have to search for the awdscenario1.exe crash)

```
Application exception occurred:
    App: C:\AWDBIN\WinXP.x86.chk\awdscenario1.exe (pid=2276)
    When: 10/19/2006 @ 08:12:41.687
    Exception number: c0000005 (access violation)
```

Each `application` `exception` section is broken down further into the following additional categories.

### System Information

The system information section contains a plethora of information about the system that the faulting application was running on. Our sample run yielded the following system information section:

```
*—> System Information <—*
        Computer Name: MARIOH-HOME
        User Name: marioh
        Terminal Session Id: 0
        Number of Processors: 1
        Processor Type: x86 Family 15 Model 15 Stepping 0
        Windows Version: 5.1
        Current Build: 2600
        Service Pack: 2
        Current Type: Uniprocessor Free
        Registered Organization: The High-tech Avenue
        Registered Owner: Mario Hewardt
```

As you can see, information such as processor count, processor type, and Windows version are all included in this list and can be quite useful when analyzing a problem postmortem. Imagine that a particular crash only occurred when running on Windows XP SP2. The error logs for all the crashes clearly specify that the crash occurred on Windows XP SP2, which helps the developer narrow down the scope of the problem.

## Task List

The task list contains a list of processes running on the system at the point of failure. The list is very similar to the output of the familiar `tlist.exe` command.

## Module List

The module list section contains all the modules (including the address range each module occupies) that were loaded into the faulting process's address space at the point of failure. For our sample run, the module list consists of

```
*—> Module List <—*
(0000000001000000 - 0000000001003000: C:\AWDBIN\WinXP.x86.chk\ awdscenario1.exe
(0000000076390000 - 00000000763ad000: C:\WINDOWS\system32\IMM32.DLL
(0000000077b40000 - 0000000077b62000: C:\WINDOWS\system32\Apphelp.dll
(0000000077c00000 - 0000000077c08000: C:\WINDOWS\system32\VERSION.dll
(0000000077c10000 - 0000000077c68000: C:\WINDOWS\system32\msvcrt.dll
(0000000077d40000 - 0000000077dd0000: C:\WINDOWS\system32\USER32.dll
(0000000077dd0000 - 0000000077e6b000: C:\WINDOWS\system32\ADVAPI32.dll
(0000000077e70000 - 0000000077f01000: C:\WINDOWS\system32\RPCRT4.dll
(0000000077f10000 - 0000000077f57000: C:\WINDOWS\system32\GDI32.dll
(0000000077f60000 - 0000000077fd6000: C:\WINDOWS\system32\SHLWAPI.dll
(000000007c800000 - 000000007c8f4000: C:\WINDOWS\system32\kernel32.dll
(000000007c900000 - 000000007c9b0000: C:\WINDOWS\system32\ntdll.dll
```

## State Dump for Thread ID X

The state dump for the faulty thread includes the processor register state, as well as the unassembly of code prior to and after the faulting instruction. Additionally, the assembly code in this section has one annotation, `FAULT ->`, that helps pinpoint the exact location of the failure.

```
*—> State Dump for Thread Id 0xb6c <—*

eax=00000000 ebx=7ffdf000 ecx=77c418bf edx=77c61b78 esi=01c709ea edi=fcead396
eip=0100127e esp=0007ff1c ebp=0007ff44 iopl=0         nv up ei pl nz na pe nc
cs=001b  ss=0023  ds=0023  es=0023  fs=003b  gs=0000            efl=00000202

function: awdscenario1!wmain
        01001259 8b4dfc          mov     ecx,[ebp-0x4]
        0100125c 51              push    ecx
```

```
0100125d e84e000000        call     awdscenario1!StringCchCopyA (010012b0)
01001262 8b55fc            mov      edx,[ebp-0x4]
01001265 52                push     edx
01001266 68c0100001        push     0x10010c0
0100126b ff1544100001      call dword ptr [awdscenario1!_imp__printf (01001044)]
01001271 83c408            add      esp,0x8
01001274 c745fc00000000    mov      dword ptr [ebp-0x4],0x0
0100127b 8b45fc            mov      eax,[ebp-0x4]
FAULT ->0100127e c60000    mov      byte ptr [eax],0x0     ds:0023:00000000=??
01001281 eb0e              jmp      awdscenario1!wmain+0xd1 (01001291)
01001283 68a4100001        push     0x10010a4
01001288 ff1544100001      call dword ptr [awdscenario1!_imp__printf (01001044)]
0100128e 83c404            add      esp,0x4
01001291 688c100001        push     0x100108c
01001296 ff1544100001      call dword ptr [awdscenario1!_imp__printf (01001044)]
0100129c 83c404            add      esp,0x4
0100129f ff154c100001      call dword ptr [awdscenario1!_imp___getch (0100104c)]
010012a5 33c0              xor      eax,eax
010012a7 8be5              mov      esp,ebp
```

## Stack Back Trace

The stack back trace section contains the stack trace of the faulting thread. Please note that the stack back trace might (and most likely will) contain the incorrect frames, as symbolic information is typically not available. For example, frame 3 in the following shows an incorrect frame for a function in kernel32.dll. The fact that incorrect frames are reported is not an issue, however, because the correct symbols can be loaded when analyzing the fault postmortem using the debuggers.

```
*——> Stack Back Trace <——*
*** ERROR: Symbol file could not be found.  Defaulted to export symbols for C:\WIN-
DOWS\system32\kernel32.dll -
WARNING: Stack unwind information not available. Following frames may be wrong.
ChildEBP RetAddr  Args to Child
0006ff44 01001495 00000001 00262430 00264260 awdscenario1!wmain+0xbe (FPO: [Non-Fpo])
0006ffc0 7c816fd7 20c88c32 01c7a3a2 7ffd7000 awdscenario1!wmainCRTStartup+0x12f (FPO:
[Non-Fpo])
0007fff0 00000000 0100131d 00000000 78746341 kernel32!RegisterWaitForInputIdle+0x49
```

**660** CHAPTER 13 POSTMORTEM DEBUGGING

## Raw Stack Dump

The raw stack dump section contains a raw dump of the stack at the point of failure.

```
*—> Raw Stack Dump <—*
000000000007ff1c  1a 00 00 00 00 00 00 00 - a5 10 00 01 bf 10 00 01   ................
000000000007ff2c  1a 00 00 00 c0 45 03 00 - a5 10 00 01 bf 10 00 01   .....E..........
000000000007ff3c  a4 10 00 01 00 00 00 00 - c0 ff 07 00 48 14 00 01   ............H...
000000000007ff4c  01 00 00 00 70 3b 03 00 - 28 45 03 00 50 10 00 01   ....p;..(E..P...
000000000007ff5c  54 10 00 01 94 ff 07 00 - 98 ff 07 00 a0 ff 07 00   T...............
000000000007ff6c  00 00 00 00 9c ff 07 00 - 58 10 00 01 5c 10 00 01   ........X...\...
000000000007ff7c  a4 5b 64 2d 8f f3 c6 01 - 00 c0 fd 7f 00 dc 31 e4   .[d-..........1.
000000000007ff8c  00 00 00 05 00 00 c0 - 01 00 00 00 70 3b 03 00   ..........p;..
000000000007ff9c  00 00 00 00 28 45 03 00 - 00 00 00 00 7c ff 07 00   ....(E......|...
000000000007ffac  40 fb 07 00 e0 ff 07 00 - 2e 15 00 01 c0 10 00 01   @...............
000000000007ffbc  00 00 00 00 f0 ff 07 00 - d7 6f 81 7c a4 5b 64 2d   .........o.|.[d-
000000000007ffcc  8f f3 c6 01 00 c0 fd 7f - 05 00 00 c0 c8 ff 07 00   ................
000000000007ffdc  40 fb 07 00 ff ff ff ff - a8 9a 83 7c e0 6f 81 7c   @..........|.o.|
000000000007ffec  00 00 00 00 00 00 00 00 - 00 00 00 00 1d 13 00 01   ................
000000000007fffc  00 00 00 00 41 63 74 78 - 20 00 00 00 01 00 00 00   ....Actx .......
000000000008000c  98 24 00 00 c4 00 00 00 - 00 00 00 00 20 00 00 00   .$.......... ...
000000000008001c  00 00 00 00 14 00 00 00 - 01 00 00 00 06 00 00 00   ................
000000000008002c  34 00 00 00 14 01 00 00 - 01 00 00 00 00 00 00 00   4...............
000000000008003c  00 00 00 00 00 00 00 00 - 00 00 00 00 00 00 00 00   ................
000000000008004c  02 00 00 00 00 00 00 00 - 00 00 00 00 00 00 00 00   ................
```

In addition to the wealth of information logged in the Dr. Watson log file, the dump file is perhaps the most important piece of information in the postmortem analysis process. The dump file is located in the same directory as the log file and is named user.dmp (unless the configuration has changed). Let's use the dump file for our awdscenario1.exe run and load it in the debugger (remember to use the –z switch).

```
...
...
...
This dump file has an exception of interest stored in it.
The stored exception information can be accessed via .ecxr.
(bb0.b6c): Access violation - code c0000005 (first/second chance not available)
eax=00000000 ebx=7ffdf000 ecx=77c418bf edx=77c61b78 esi=01c709ea edi=fcead396
eip=0100127e esp=0007ff1c ebp=0007ff44 iopl=0         nv up ei pl nz na po nc
cs=001b  ss=0023  ds=0023  es=0023  fs=003b  gs=0000              efl=00000202
awdscenario1!wmain+0xbe:
0100127e c60000          mov     byte ptr [eax],0          ds:0023:00000000=??
0:000> kb
```

```
ChildEBP RetAddr  Args to Child
0007ff44 01001495 00000001 00032c38 000372c8 awdscenario1!wmain+0xbe
0007ffc0 7c816fd7 fcead396 01c709ea 7ffdf000 awdscenario1!wmainCRTStartup+0x12f
0007fff0 00000000 01001366 00000000 00000000 kernel32!BaseProcessStart+0x23
```

Notice how frame 3 in the stack trace now shows the correct symbolic name. From here on, analyzing the dump file is identical to the exercise shown earlier in the chapter.

Is it possible to turn Dr Watson off? Absolutely! The easiest way to turn off Dr Watson is to right-click on My Computer and select Properties, followed by the Advanced tab. Figure 13.5 shows the dialog displayed.

**Figure 13.5** Controlling Windows Error Reporting

As can be seen from Figure 13.5, two main options are available:

- Disable error reporting: This option disables error reporting but still gives you the option of being notified about critical errors.
- Enable error reporting: You can control which type of error reports to enable by choosing Windows operating system related errors and/or Program errors. If the Programs category is chosen, you can further choose which programs to report errors on by clicking on the Choose Programs button. The process of choosing specific applications is fairly simple and self-explanatory.

The important take-away from this section is how Dr. Watson works, how its configured, what it collects, and where the resulting data is stored.

Although it's useful to be able to configure and debug problems locally, the power of Windows Error Reporting comes from the capability to upload the error information to Microsoft and subsequently extract the error information in a structured fashion. The next section discusses the details of Windows Error Reporting, including the enrollment process, configuration process, feedback loops, and much more.

## Windows Error Reporting Architecture

Windows Error Reporting is a failure data aggregation service that enables Microsoft and ISVs to easily access failure data related to their applications. Figure 13.6 shows the high-level operational flow of the WER service.

Two primary entities are involved in Figure 13.6:

- Computers running applications that exhibit problems and upload error reports to WER
- ISV that monitors for failures related to their applications, reported to WER

Say that a given machine somewhere in the world is running an application (illustrated as Process X in Figure 13.6) produced by company AWD. Furthermore, say that the application crashes and that the user experiencing the crash will be presented with the Dr. Watson UI and asked if he wants to send the error report to Microsoft. The user chooses to do so, and the error report is sent using a secure (HTTPS) channel to the WER service. The WER service, in turn, organizes the error information received into categories (knows as buckets) and stores the error information. To make use of the error reports, a user from company AWD queries the WER service for crashes related to his application and gets the error information reported. If AWD chooses, they can now fix the problem and provide a response so that the next time a user encounters the same crash, Dr. Watson presents him with the response. The response can come in the form of a fix or other helpful information.

As you can see, the WER service is an incredibly powerful mechanism that provides secure aggregation of error reporting information that ISVs can query to actively gauge the health of their applications. Additionally, ISVs can provide responses to known problems and integrate the responses into the WER feedback loop, making it very easy for customers to apply responses when available.

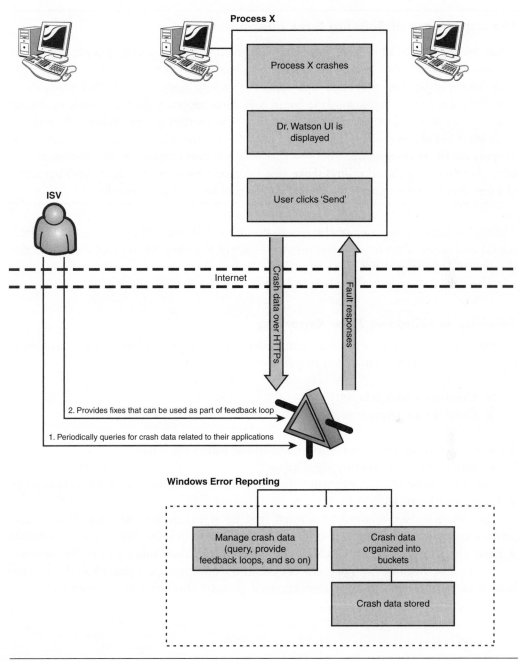

**Figure 13.6**  High-level overview of WER functionality

### The Importance of Sending Error Information

When the Dr. Watson UI rears its head and tells you about an application crash, you might ask yourself: Why bother sending it? Is something ever going to be done about it? The truth of the matter is that Microsoft takes error reporting very seriously. After all, that is why this incredible service was implemented to begin with. Error reporting data is actively monitored and fanned out across the company to the appropriate product groups. When a fix has been identified and is ready to be released (typically via Microsoft Update), users can easily apply the fix. In other words, you—the user—have a direct impact on the visibility of bugs; therefore, you should always make sure to upload the error reports so that Microsoft or other ISVs have the opportunity to analyze the problem and provide a fix.

Throughout the remainder of the discussion of WER, we will be using the awdscenario1.exe application used in the previous part of the chapter to practically illustrate the process of using WER.

The first step in using WER is to enroll, which is described next.

### Enrolling in Windows Error Reporting

To participate in WER, an enrollment process must be completed. The enrollment process is broken down into two steps:

- Creating a user account
- Creating a company account

To start the enrollment process, navigate to the following URL: https://winqual.microsoft.com/SignUp/

After the page has loaded, you will be presented with the account creation page, as shown in Figure 13.7.

To create a user account, you must first have a company account. If you have already created a company account, you can either search for that account or locate it using the drop-down list. Clicking the Next button then takes you to the account creation page. Because we have not yet created a company account, click the expand button next to Create a Company Account to start the company account creation process, as shown in Figure 13.8.

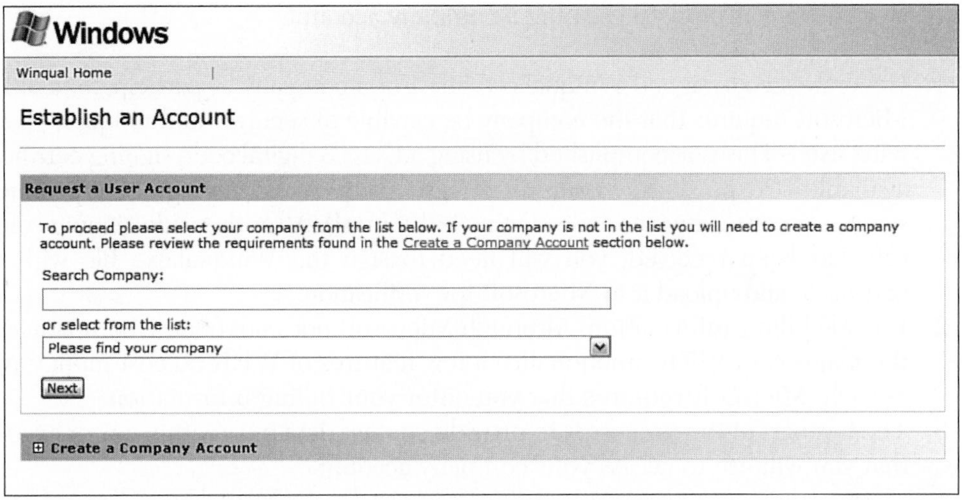

**Figure 13.7** First page of WER signup process

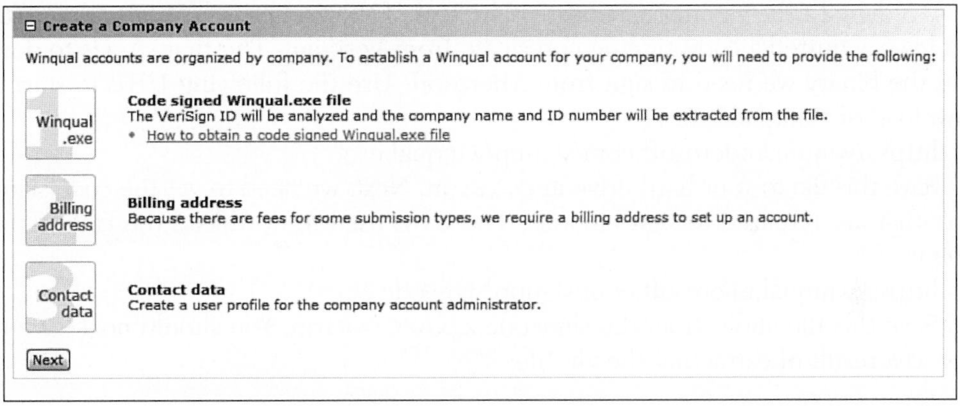

**Figure 13.8** Creating a company account

Three steps are involved with creating a company account.

1. Generate a code signed Winqual.exe file. For a company to participate in WER, Microsoft requires that the company be capable of securely and uniquely identifying itself. This is accomplished by using a Class 3 digital code signing certificate available to purchase from VeriSign (http://www.verisign.com/products-services/security-services/code-signing/index.html). After the code-signing certificate has been received, you will need to sign the Winqual.exe file with the certificate and upload it to Microsoft for verification.
2. Provide billing information. Although Microsoft does not charge companies for the majority of WER functionality, a few features of WER do cost money, and, as such, Microsoft requires that you enter your billing information.
3. The last part of the process is to provide contact data by creating a user account that you will use to access your company account.

Let's start with step 1 (code signing the Winqual.exe file). As mentioned, for security reasons, Microsoft requires that all WER company accounts be identified by using a Class 3 digital code signing certificate. The rest of the sections on WER assume that you have acquired a code signing certificate from VeriSign. The first step is to download the binary we need to sign from Microsoft. Use the following URL to start the download of Winqual.exe:

https://winqual.microsoft.com/signup/winqual.exe

Save this file to your hard drive in `C:\Sign`. Next, we need to get the code signing tools that are required to sign binaries. The URL used to download the code signing tools is

https://winqual.microsoft.com/signup/signcode.zip

Save this file and extract the signcode.zip to `C:\Sign`. You should now have two files as a result of extracting the zip file:

- Readme.rtf: This file contains instructions on how to code sign a binary using the code-signing tools. It also contains a password that must be used when extracting the signcode.exe file (password protected), also located in the zip file.
- Signcode.exe: This is the application that we will use to code sign the Winqual.exe file.

Extract the signcode.exe file (remember to enter the password found in the readme file when extracting) to the same location as the Winqual.exe file (C:\Sign). Also make sure to copy the code-signing certificate file (.spc extension) and the private key (.pvk extension) to the same location. Use the following command line to sign the Winqual.exe file:

```
C:\Sign>signcode.exe /spc myCert.spc /v myKey.pvk -t
http://timestamp.verisign.com/scripts/timstamp.dll winqual.exe
Succeeded
```

You will need to replace mycert.spc and mykey.pvk with the names of your certificate and private key files. During the signing process, you will be asked to enter a private key password. Enter the password provided to you by VeriSign during the certificate purchase process. If the signing succeeds, a Succeeded message is shown. If an error occurs, make sure that you have typed the name of the certificate and private key files properly and that they are located in the same directory as the signcode.exe binary.

The next step in the enrollment process is to take the newly signed Winqual.exe file and upload it to Microsoft for verification purposes. Continuing from the page illustrated in Figure 13.8, click the Next button. The next page enables you to upload your signed Winqual.exe file, as shown in Figure 13.9.

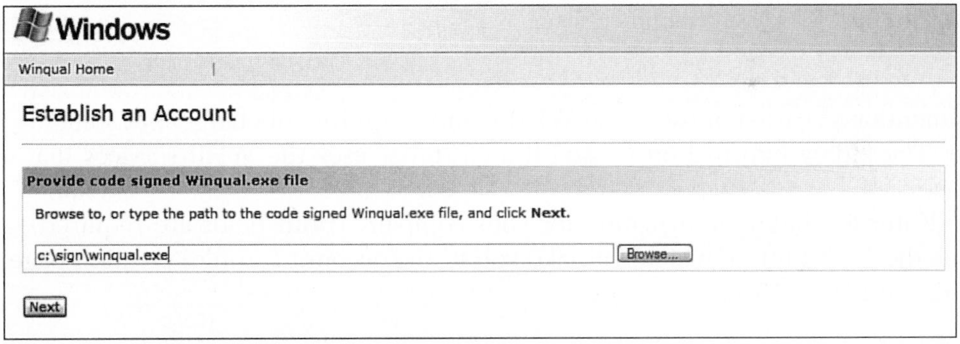

**Figure 13.9**   Uploading the signed Winqual.exe binary

Simply enter the path to the signed Winqual.exe binary and click Next to upload the file. The next page in the process is the Billing information page, as shown in Figure 13.10.

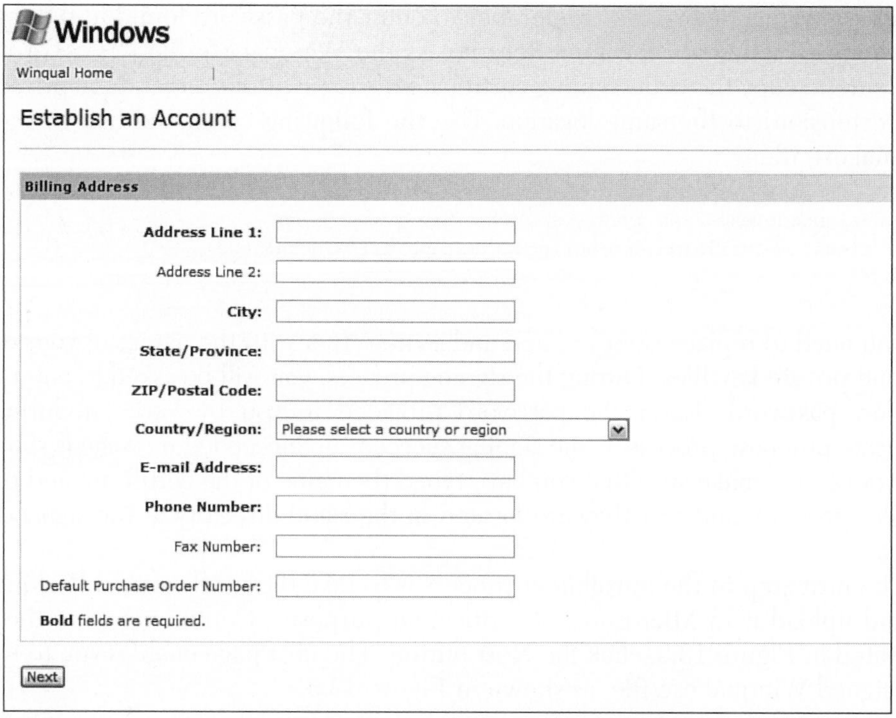

**Figure 13.10**   Billing information page

As mentioned earlier, most of the WER features are free of charge, but some have a fee. The billing information is used if a customer uses the WER services that cost money.

Enter the billing information for your company (**bold** fields are required), and click the Next button, which will take you to the account (profile) creation page, as shown in Figure 13.11.

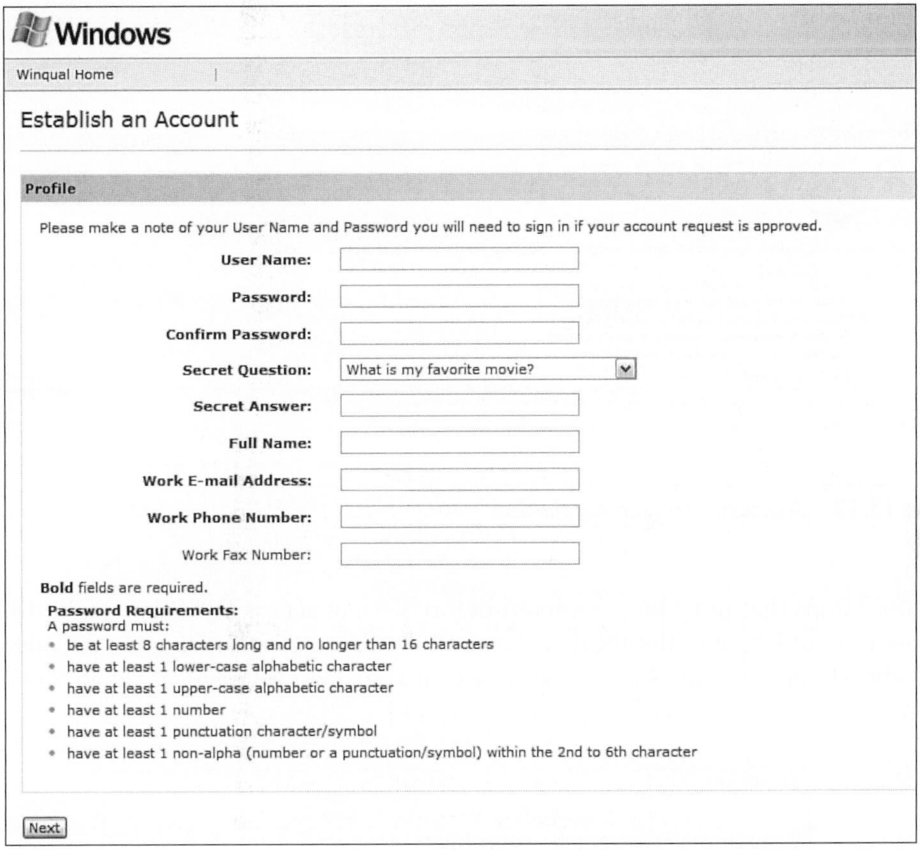

## Windows

Winqual Home |

### Establish an Account

**Profile**

Please make a note of your User Name and Password you will need to sign in if your account request is approved.

| | |
|---:|---|
| **User Name:** | [                    ] |
| **Password:** | [                    ] |
| **Confirm Password:** | [                    ] |
| **Secret Question:** | [ What is my favorite movie?    ▾ ] |
| **Secret Answer:** | [                    ] |
| **Full Name:** | [                    ] |
| **Work E-mail Address:** | [                    ] |
| **Work Phone Number:** | [                    ] |
| Work Fax Number: | [                    ] |

**Bold** fields are required.

**Password Requirements:**
A password must:
* be at least 8 characters long and no longer than 16 characters
* have at least 1 lower-case alphabetic character
* have at least 1 upper-case alphabetic character
* have at least 1 number
* have at least 1 punctuation character/symbol
* have at least 1 non-alpha (number or a punctuation/symbol) within the 2nd to 6th character

[ Next ]

**Figure 13.11**  Profile information page

The User Name and Password fields represent the logon information that you will use when accessing the WER site. Fill in all the information, and pay particular attention to the strong password requirements listed at the bottom. These password requirements are important to ensuring that your company's error information is kept secure.

After all the information has been filled in, click the Next button, and you will be taken to a page indicating that the account has been successfully created, as shown in Figure 13.12.

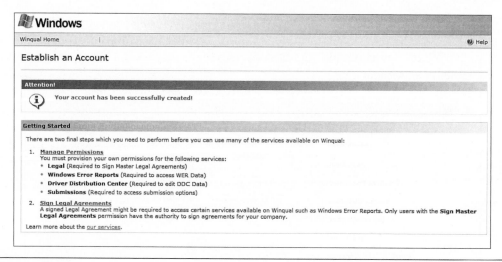

**Figure 13.12** Account creation succeeded

The final steps that must be completed before we can access WER involve setting up permissions and signing the legal agreements. Let's start with managing permissions. Click the Manage Permissions link to access the permissions page, as shown in Figure 13.13.

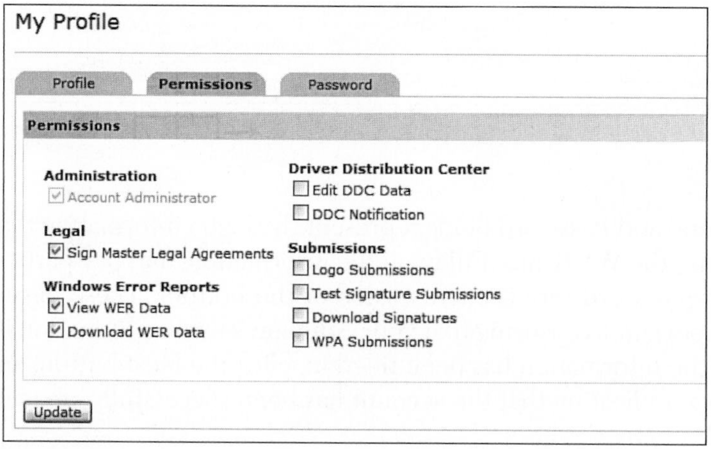

**Figure 13.13** Manage permissions

Make sure that the Sign Master Legal Agreements, View WER Data, and Download WER Data check boxes are enabled for your account, and click the Update button. Note that it is possible to have multiple user accounts associated with one company account in WER. This can be quite useful if you want different users to have varying levels of access (as shown in Figure 13.13). For example, one user can be granted access to the error reports, whereas another user can be granted access to sign legal agreements.

Next, we go back to the page shown in Figure 13.12 to complete the process by signing legal agreements as required by Microsoft. Unfortunately, at the time of this writing, the Sign Legal Agreements link was unavailable, and we must use an alternative URL shown here:

https://winqual.microsoft.com/member/LAC/DocumentDetails.aspx?id=420 &type=0

The URL takes you to the Windows Error Reporting legal agreement page. Carefully read through all the information presented, and if you choose to accept, fill in the information at the bottom of the last page to sign the agreement. If you want a copy of the agreement for your records, you can enter your company information in the form and print a copy.

The signup process is now complete, and you can access the full range of WER features by signing into your account using the following URL:

https://winqual.microsoft.com/default.aspx

### Navigating the WER Web Site

When you log on to the WER Web site, you will be presented with a page that contains recent Winqual announcements. To the left of the announcements is a pane that allows you to navigate to different parts of the site. The three main sections of the navigation pane are

- Windows Logo Programs
- Windows Error Reports
- Driver Distribution Center

In this chapter, we only cover the Windows Error Reports section of the Web site and, more specifically, the Software portion of WER. Figure 13.14 illustrates the options that are available in the Software menu.

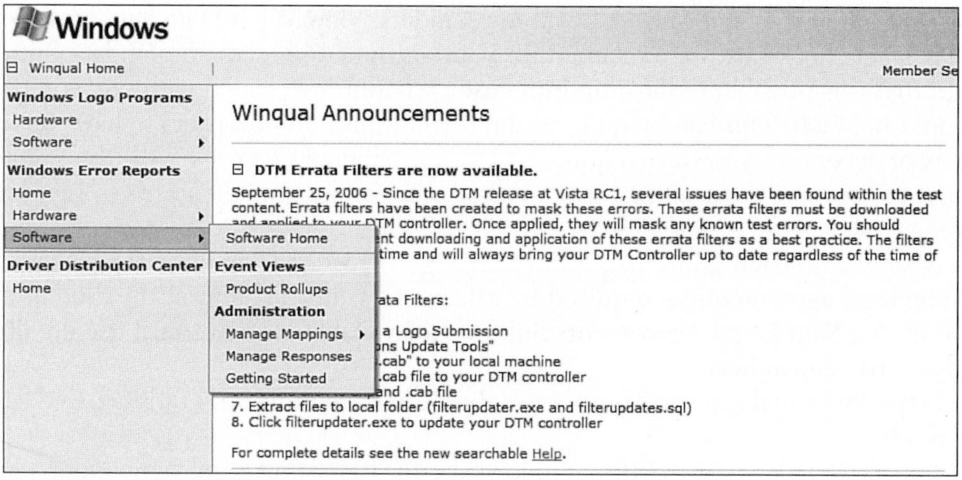

**Figure 13.14** WER Software options

The Product Rollups option under the Event Views category shows a view that organizes the error reports according to product name and version. Figure 13.15 shows an example of the Product Rollup page.

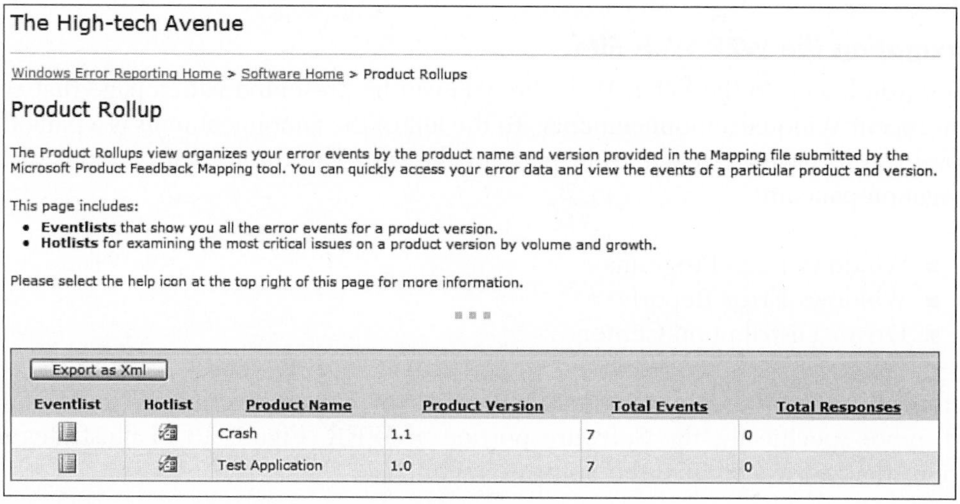

**Figure 13.15** Example of the Product Rollup page

Figure 13.15 shows two products registered: Crash and Test Application. Each of the products has two columns that allow you to dig deeper into any events (crashes or other) that might have been reported for the applications:

- Eventlist: The Eventlist icon takes you to a page that details the complete list of events that have occurred in the application.
- Hotlist: The Hotlist icon takes you to a page that details the biggest hitters for the application over the past 90 days.

The next menu item is the Administrative category. It contains the following options:

- Manage Mappings: This option allows you to map binaries with products so that WER knows which binaries go with which product. We show you how to create a mapping file later in this chapter.
- Manage Responses: This option allows you to define responses to common problems reported by customers and, in essence, create a feedback loop that might contain anything from informative messages to fixes. We look at how to generate a response later in this chapter.
- Getting Started: The Getting Started option takes you to a help page.

Now that we have familiarized ourselves with the general layout of the WER site, it is time to map our product's binaries to a particular product so that WER knows which binary belongs to which product.

### Mapping Binaries to Products

After you've accessed your account, you will need to make sure that any error information reported for your applications is routed to your company account. When an error report is sent to the WER service, it needs to know what about the application identifies it as belonging to a particular company. The key ingredient in this mapping process is the name of the application. As such, companies that sign up with WER need to tell the service the name of the applications (including all binaries) associated with their company. The mapping information is then presented to the WER site using an XML file that the WER service understands. Rather than having customers manually compile this mapping XML file, the WER site has a tool named Microsoft Product Feedback Mapping Tool. The tool can be found at the following URL:

http://www.microsoft.com/downloads/details.aspx?FamilyId=4333E2A2-5EA6-4878-BBE5-60C3DBABC170&displaylang=en

Once installed, run the tool from Start, Programs, Microsoft Product Feedback Mapping Tool, and you are presented with a wizard that guides you through the mapping process. The first page of the wizard is illustrated in Figure 13.16.

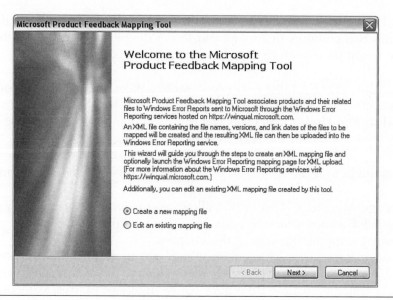

**Figure 13.16**    Microsoft Product Feedback Mapping Tool

To illustrate the process of setting up a mapping file for WER, we will use the awdscenario1.exe application used earlier in the chapter. Make sure that Create a New Mapping File is selected, and click Next. Figure 13.17 shows the Gathering Product Mapping Information page.

The options shown in Figure 13.17 are explained next. Make sure that you enter the information as shown in the figure.

- Product File(s) Directory Path: Specifies the directory path to the application binaries that you want to map.
- Product Name: Specifies the name of the product that you want the binaries to be associated with. Note that the product name is simply a friendly name used on the WER site so that users can more efficiently group and search for error information.
- Product Version: Specifies the product version that you want the binaries to be associated with. Note that the product version is simply a friendly version used on the WER site so that users can more efficiently group and search for error information.

When all information has been entered, click Next, followed by another Next. The wizard now asks you to specify a filename for the mapping file it is about to generate. Enter the following path for the map file and click Next.

```
C:\testmap.xml
```

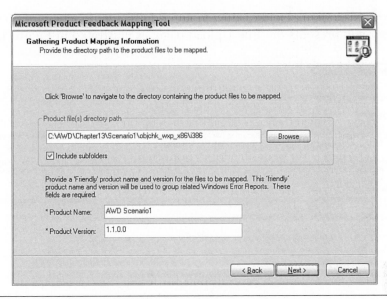

**Figure 13.17**    Gathering Product Mapping Information page

Figure 13.18 shows the last step of the process, which allows you to upload the mapping file to the WER site.

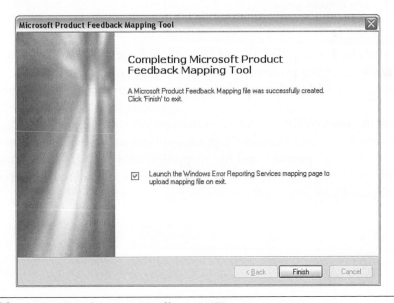

**Figure 13.18**    Uploading the mapping file to WER

Make sure that the check box is checked, and click Finish. The wizard now launches your browser and presents the File Upload page, as illustrated in Figure 13.19.

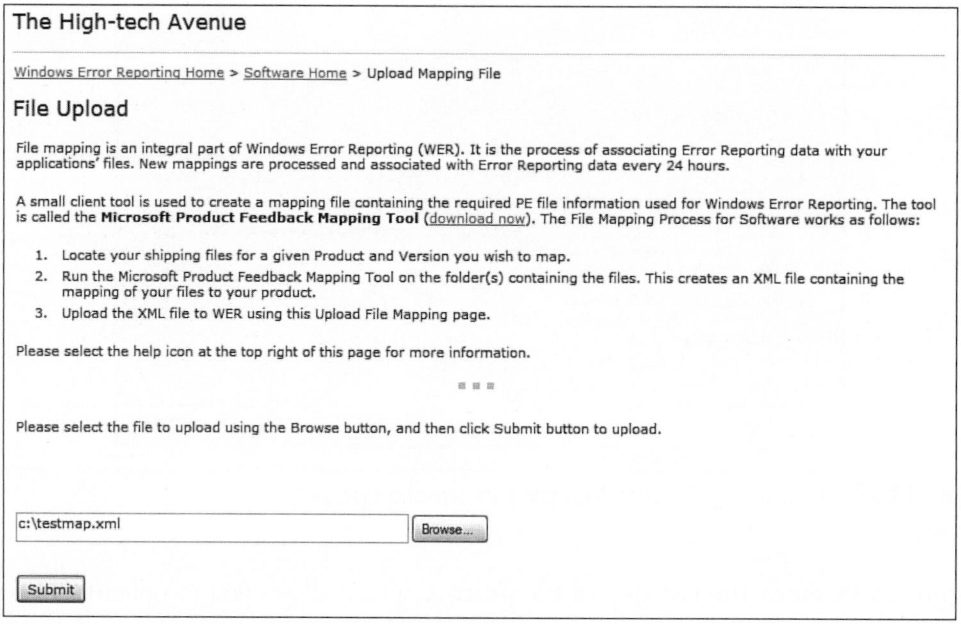

---

**The High-tech Avenue**

Windows Error Reporting Home > Software Home > Upload Mapping File

**File Upload**

File mapping is an integral part of Windows Error Reporting (WER). It is the process of associating Error Reporting data with your applications' files. New mappings are processed and associated with Error Reporting data every 24 hours.

A small client tool is used to create a mapping file containing the required PE file information used for Windows Error Reporting. The tool is called the **Microsoft Product Feedback Mapping Tool** (download now). The File Mapping Process for Software works as follows:

1. Locate your shipping files for a given Product and Version you wish to map.
2. Run the Microsoft Product Feedback Mapping Tool on the folder(s) containing the files. This creates an XML file containing the mapping of your files to your product.
3. Upload the XML file to WER using this Upload File Mapping page.

Please select the help icon at the top right of this page for more information.

■ ■ ■

Please select the file to upload using the Browse button, and then click Submit button to upload.

| c:\testmap.xml | Browse... |

[ Submit ]

---

**Figure 13.19**   File Upload page

Enter the path to the map file we just created and click Submit. Upon a successful upload, the file-mapping process and upload are completed. If you have more than one product, you would go through the whole mapping process again—once for each product.

Back on the main WER site, you can manage your product and file mappings by choosing the Software and Manage Mappings options in the left navigation pane. You can choose to manage product and file mappings, as well as upload a mapping file. For example, selecting the File Mapping link after we uploaded the mapping file is shown in Figure 13.20.

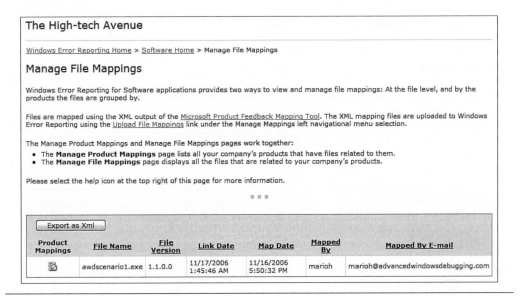

**Figure 13.20**   WER file mappings

From Figure 13.20, you can see that we have one file mapping, where the filename is awdscenario1.exe with specific attributes (such as link date and map date), as well as administrative information, such as who created the mapping and his email address.

Now that we have created a product and file mapping, it is time to look at the report generation aspects of WER. We look at how we can generate reports of the error information sent by customers, as well as delve deeper into each error report (such as crash dumps).

### Querying the Windows Error Reporting Service

Now that we have created an account and mapped our awdscenario1.exe binary to a product, it's time to look at how we can query WER for uploaded error reports. Let's run our awdscenario1.exe application several times, and when it crashes, tell Dr. Watson to upload the error information to the WER site. Note that there is a time delay between the time a user uploads a report and when it becomes available to view. The average delay is typically around 7 days.

After the error reports have been uploaded and made available to you, you will see a table of products on the Product Rollup page, as illustrated in Figure 13.21.

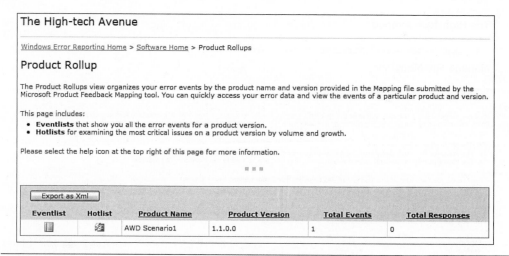

**Figure 13.21**   Product Rollup with error events

Figure 13.21 shows the product we mapped (AWD Scenario1), as well as the total number of events that have been reported. Additionally, the Eventlist and Hotlist columns contain icons that display all the events that have occurred for that particular product, as well as the top error events that have occurred over the past 90 days. The hotlist is a convenient way to identify the top issues with the product. Figure 13.22 illustrates the Event List page displayed when clicking on the Eventlist icon.

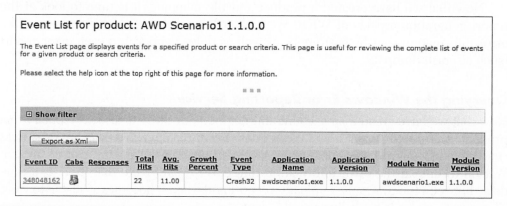

**Figure 13.22**   Event list for AWD Scenario1

The Event List page contains a table in which each row represents a unique error event. In Figure 13.22, we can see that there is only one event with a total hit count of 22. The table also shows what type of event caused the report; in our case, the event type is Crash32, which simply means that the event occurred due to a crash. If you click on the event ID, you will see a breakdown of information related to that particular event. The Event Details page is broken down into three main sections:

- Event Signature: Because one product can have multiple events associated with it, each event must be made unique. The different pieces of information that make an event unique are application name and version, module name and version, and the offset into the module that caused the event to occur. As you can see from Figure 13.23, the offset into the awdscenario1.exe module that caused the crash was 4734.
- Event Time Trending Details: The graph displayed in the Event Time Trending Details section shows how the event manifested itself over time. In Figure 13.23, we can see that our event spiked on November 16 and gradually decreased in frequency over time.
- Platform Details: The last section shows the platform details for the specific event. It shows the operating system breakout, as well as language breakout. This section is critical when trying to identify problems that only occur under certain configurations and can yield clues, such as the event only occurring on non-English versions of the product.

The last important column in the table illustrated in Figure 13.22 is the cabs column. Clicking on the icon gives a list of cabs available for the event. A cab is nothing more than a conglomerate of files that represent the event information (one cab per upload) sent by users who choose to upload the information to Microsoft. One of the most critical files in the cab is the dump file that was generated at the point of failure. This dump file can be used while debugging the problem postmortem, as explained previously. The exact list of files in the cab file is discussed in more detail in the "Corporate Error Reporting" section of the chapter.

Now that we have looked at the various pieces of information accessible through the WER Web site, everything from a high-level overview of the events to a more detailed drilldown using the information the customer uploaded to Microsoft, we next turn our attention to the last critical step in the process—how to provide responses to customers after the issue has been understood.

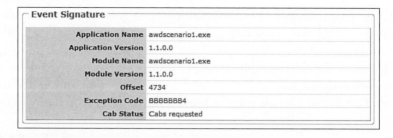

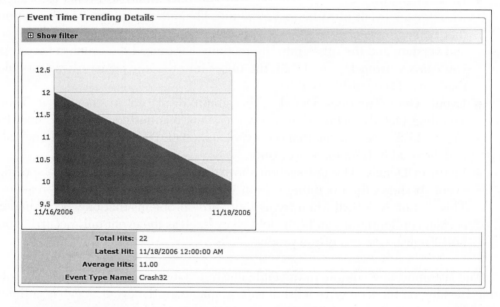

**Figure 13.23**   Event details for AWD Scenario1

## Providing Responses

To provide a response to customers about a particular event, you must navigate to the Event Details page (illustrated in Figure 13.23). If a response has not yet been recorded for the event, the topmost section of the page contains options for registering a response, as illustrated in Figure 13.24.

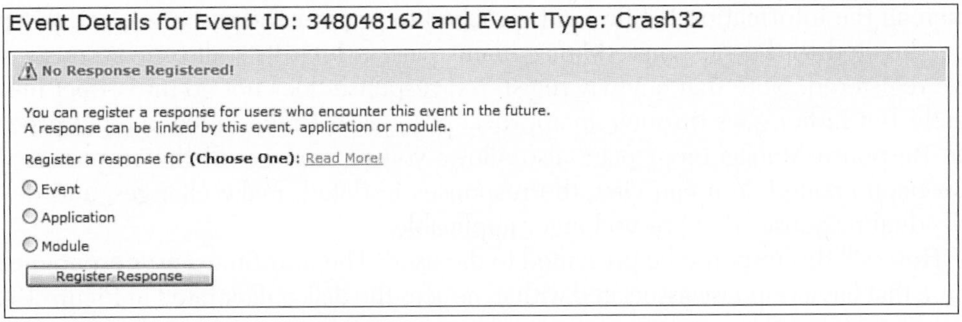

```
Event Details for Event ID: 348048162 and Event Type: Crash32

⚠ No Response Registered!

You can register a response for users who encounter this event in the future.
A response can be linked by this event, application or module.

Register a response for (Choose One): Read More!

○ Event
○ Application
○ Module
   Register Response
```

**Figure 13.24**   Event response options

Responses can be registered at three different levels:

- Event: This is typically used when a fix is very isolated and will not be incorporated into a product update.
- Application: Providing a response at the application level allows you to create a rules-based response that all users with a particular version of your application see. The response can be in the form of an update (such as a new version).
- Module: Providing a response at the module level allows you to create a rules-based response that your users with a particular version of your module see. The response can be in the form of an update (such as a new version).

For our particular scenario, we will choose to use the event-based response registration. Select the Event radio button and click Register Response. The next step is to fill out details about the event response. The following information is required before a response can be registered:

- Products: Enter the name of the product into the Products field.
- URL of Solution/Info: Enter a URL to the response. The URL should point to a page with all the required information for that particular response.
- Response Template: You can choose to use a predefined template for your response or use your own custom template. Examples of predefined templates include the following: System Does Not Meet Minimum Requirements, Product Upgrade, Upgrade to New Version, and more. Depending on which template is chosen in this drop-down, the preview field will change.
- Response Template Preview: This shows a preview of what information will be included in the response.
- Additional Information: Enter any additional information you want to include with the response.

When all the information is filled out, proceed to register the response, and you will be redirected to the Response Management page, which lists all the responses you have registered. Note that a newly registered response does not go into effect immediately, but rather goes through an approval process that takes a few days to process. The Response Management page also allows you to manage all the responses that have been created. You can view the responses in detail, make changes, and delete individual responses that are no longer applicable.

How will this response be presented to the user? The next time a user experiences a failure that has a response associated with it, he sees the dialog illustrated in Figure 13.25.

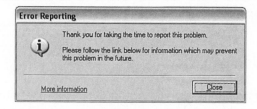

**Figure 13.25**    User experience with an application failure that has a response

If the user clicks on the More Information link, he is taken to a Web page that contains the response to the particular failure with associated information on how to resolve the problem. In our case, he is routed to the page registered as part of the response: http://www.advancedwindowsdebugging.com.

As you can see, WER is an incredibly powerful service that allows you to monitor how well your application behaves in the real world. Allowing customers to send error information that you can analyze and create a response to is an incredible technology that eases the pain customers go through when encountering software problems.

## Corporate Error Reporting

Windows Error Reporting is a great technology to use when gauging the health of your application out in the real world. If a problem ever arises, a fix can be produced and fed to the customer's computer using the response system of WER. The key behind WER is its capability to send error information, which includes information such as general fault information, as well as a mini dump file of the process that crashed. Although the capability to catch and send this error information to Microsoft is the key enabler of WER, it also serves to discourage some ISVs from using the system. More specifically, some ISVs do not want error information sent to Microsoft because of the sensitive nature of the data that might be sent as part of the error information. One example of this is a banking application that contains sensitive information about customer accounts. Because of the strict requirements of some ISVs, Microsoft created what is known as Corporate Error Reporting (CER). CER allows an ISV to enable error reporting across the company and instructs each machine to send information to a file share rather than sending the information to Microsoft. The file share can then be queried periodically to look for any problems that might have surfaced.

In this last part of the chapter, we take a look at how to set up CER, as well as how the data is uploaded and stored on the file share.

## Setting Up Corporate Error Reporting

Group Policy (GP) is a technology in Windows that provides centralized management of computers and users in an Active Directory environment. CER is part of the group policy management capabilities. GP must be used to enable CER either locally (on one machine) or across all company machines. All examples in this part of the chapter are run locally (that is, setting up CER on one machine), but the same principles apply when pushing down policy to all the machines in a company. Note that GP is not available for Windows Home Edition, and you must be running Windows XP Professional Edition or higher when using GP.

To enable CER on a specific machine, the Group Policy edit tool must be used by going to Start, Run and typing `gpedit.msc`. This brings up the GP Microsoft Management Console (MMC) snap-in, as shown in Figure 13.26.

In the navigation pane on the left side, CER settings can be accessed via the following nodes: Local Computer Policy, Computer Configuration, Administrative Templates, System, Error Reporting. Once selected, you can see the available options on the right side. Let's start by taking a look at the Display Error Notification option shown in Figure 13.27. Make sure to enable the settings for each of the configuration dialogs, as shown in figures that follow.

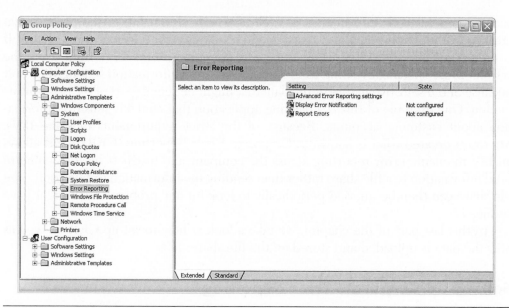

**Figure 13.26**  Group Policy settings for CER

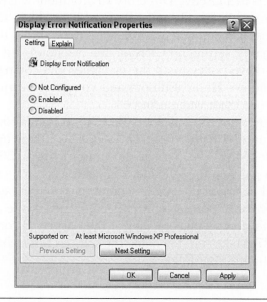

**Figure 13.27**  Display Error Notification settings

The display error notification option allows you to control whether a user who encounters an error will see a UI, giving him the choice to report the error seen. If this option is enabled, the UI that appears to the user gives the user access to the error information. If, furthermore, the configure error reporting is on, the UI will also allow him to send the error report.

If the display error notification is disabled, the user will not be presented with a UI. This does not, however, mean that the error reports are not sent. Whether an error report is sent also depends on the configure error reporting setting.

The next setting is the Configure Error Reporting setting, as shown in Figure 13.28, and it constitutes the main part of CER configuration.

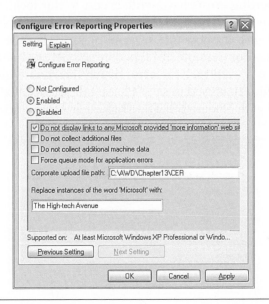

**Figure 13.28**   Configure Error Reporting settings

The Configure Error Reporting settings UI allows you to control how error reporting behaves when encountering errors. The highest-level settings are to enable, disable, or not configure this setting and can be selected through the radio buttons. If you choose to enable error reporting, the following options become configurable:

- Do Not Display Links to Any Microsoft Provided 'More Information' Web Sites: This check box allows you to disable the Microsoft links in the error UI displayed to the user when an error occurs. For example, by default, the UI contains a link to the Microsoft data collection policies.
- Do Not Collect Additional Files: If this check box is checked, the error reports will not collect additional information (files) with the error report.

- Do Not Collect Additional Machine Data: If this check box is checked, additional machine data will not be collected with the error report.
- Force Queue Mode for Application Errors: If this check box is checked, the user will not be able to immediately send error reports; rather, all error reports will be queued so that when the next administrator logs on to the machine, a list of error reports shown, and the administrator can choose which error reports to send.
- Corporate File Path: This field enables CER. Type in the UNC path you want to use for CER. All error reports will be stored at this location, and the administrator can choose which of the error reports to send. Make sure that all the machines reporting errors have write access to this location.
- Replace Instances of the Word 'Microsoft' With: This enables you to customize the error dialogs that show up for users by replacing the word *Microsoft* with something else. For example, if I typed in `The High-tech Avenue` and experienced a crash, I would see the error dialog shown in Figure 13.29. As you can see, the sentence that used to say: "Please tell Microsoft about this problem" is now replaced with "Please tell The High-tech Avenue about this problem."

**Figure 13.29**  Example of customized error reporting UI

In Figure 13.26, the final CER configuration settings that we have not yet discussed are the Advanced Error Reporting settings. These configuration settings are summarized next.

- Default Application Reporting: This setting controls which applications take part in the error reporting infrastructure. You can, for example, configure this option so that all Windows applications are included in error reporting or only Windows components are included.

- List of Applications to Always Report Errors On: This setting allows you to control a list of applications that should always be included in error reporting, regardless of what the default application reporting states.
- List of Applications to Never Report Errors On: This setting allows you to control a list of applications that should never be included in error reporting.
- Report Operating System Errors: This setting controls whether operating system components should be part of error reporting.
- Report Unplanned Shutdown Events: This setting controls whether unplanned shutdown events should be part of error reporting.

Now that we have configured and enabled CER via the error reporting settings, it's time to take a look at a practical example of how the error information for a faulty application shows up in the directory we specified in Figure 13.28. Remember that we are running the faulty application on the same machine that we just configured error reporting on to simulate a domain-enforced group policy.

## Reporting Errors Using Corporate Error Reporting

Now that we have successfully enabled CER, it's time to take a look at what actually happens when an application crashes. We will use our trusty old friend, the awdscenario1.exe application, that we used in previous parts of this chapter. Run the application on the same machine that we used to configure CER using the following path:

```
C:\AWDBIN\WinXP.x86.chk\awdscenario1.exe
```

When you are presented with the Dr. Watson error UI, click the Send button. What happens next is that rather than the error report being sent to the global Windows Error Reporting service, the error report will be stored in the path specified when configuring CER. In our case, we configured the path to be

```
C:\AWD\Chapter13\CER
```

To ensure that error information from multiple sources does not overwrite each other, CER organizes the files under the error reporting folder. Two primary folders are created the first time an error report is generated in the folder:

- Cabs: The Cabs folder contains the actual error information (such as dump files and associated error information).
- Counts: The Counts folder contains the hit count for each fault. The hit count is extremely useful information, as it allows you to focus your efforts on the

faults with the highest hit count. The file stored in the Counts folder is a text file that contains two counts. The first count indicates how many Cabs have been gathered for this fault, and the second count indicates how many hits have been recorded for the particular fault.

Under each of the preceding folders, another nested folder hierarchy is created that uniquely identifies a particular fault. The uniqueness comes from the following properties:

- Image Name: The name of the image that caused the fault. In our example, the folder created would be called awdscenario1.exe.
- Image Version: The version number of the image causing the fault. In our case, the image version number is 1.1.0.0.
- Module Name: The name of the module that caused the fault. In our example, we do not have a separate module (say a DLL), so the name chosen is simply the image name.
- Module Version: The version number of the module causing the fault. In our case, the image version is the same as the module version number 1.1.0.0.
- Offset: The offset in the module that caused the fault to occur (typically the eip register). In our example, the offset was 0000127E.

Figure 13.30 illustrates the folder hierarchy after running the awdscenario1.exe binary.

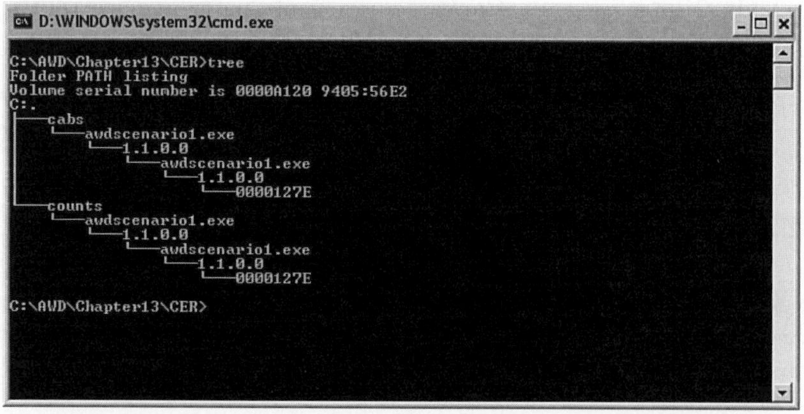

**Figure 13.30** CER folder hierarchy after running awdscenario1.exe

In the leaf folder of any given fault's Cab directory is a compressed cab file. The name of the cab file is chosen at random to avoid multiple failures originating from the same faults overwriting each other's error data. Uncompressing the cab file yields three files:

- Mini dump file: The mini dump file represents the state of the process at the point when the fault happened. Earlier in the chapter, we discussed how to use the dump file to glean more information about the reasons for the fault.
- Version.txt: The version.txt file contains the version of the operating system that the process was running on.
- app compat file: The app compat file is an XML file that contains a list of attributes about the process that failed (such as file description, check sum, and more).

Extract the files in the CAB file generated for our sample run and attach a debugger to the dump file. (Remember to use the –z switch.)

```
...
...
...
This dump file has an exception of interest stored in it.
The stored exception information can be accessed via .ecxr.
(f0f0f0f0.6fc): Access violation - code c0000005 (first/second chance not available)
eax=007b0000 ebx=0006ddec ecx=00001000 edx=7c90eb94 esi=00000000 edi=7ffdd000
eip=7c90eb94 esp=0006ddc4 ebp=0006de60 iopl=0         nv up ei pl zr na pe nc
cs=001b  ss=0023  ds=0023  es=0023  fs=003b  gs=0000          efl=00000246
Unable to load image D:\WINDOWS\system32\ntdll.dll, Win32 error 2
*** WARNING: Unable to verify timestamp for ntdll.dll
*** ERROR: Module load completed but symbols could not be loaded for ntdll.dll
ntdll+0xeb94:
7c90eb94 c3               ret
0:000> .ecxr
eax=00000000 ebx=7ffdd000 ecx=77c418bf edx=77c61b78 esi=01c709ef edi=a32cec54
eip=0100127e esp=0006ff1c ebp=0006ff44 iopl=0         nv up ei pl nz na po nc
cs=001b  ss=0023  ds=0023  es=0023  fs=003b  gs=0000          efl=00010202
awdscenario1!wmain+0xbe:
0100127e c60000           mov     byte ptr [eax],0       ds:0023:00000000=??
0:000> kb
  *** Stack trace for last set context - .thread/.cxr resets it
ChildEBP RetAddr  Args to Child
0006ff44 01001495 00000001 00263798 00264160 awdscenario1!wmain+0xbe
0006ffc0 7c816d4f a32cec54 01c709ef 7ffdd000 awdscenario1!wmainCRTStartup+0x12f
0006fff0 00000000 01001366 00000000 00000000 kernel32!BaseProcessStart+0x23
```

```
0:000> u awdscenario1!wmain+0xbe
awdscenario1!wmain+0xbe:
0100127e c60000              mov       byte ptr [eax],0
01001281 eb0e                jmp       awdscenario1!wmain+0xd1 (01001291)
01001283 68a4100001          push      offset awdscenario1!`string' (010010a4)
01001288 ff1544100001        call      dword ptr [awdscenario1!_imp__printf (01001044)]
0100128e 83c404              add       esp,4
01001291 688c100001          push      offset awdscenario1!`string' (0100108c)
01001296 ff1544100001        call      dword ptr [awdscenario1!_imp__printf (01001044)]
0100129c 83c404              add       esp,4
```

As you can see, the debug session is identical to the previous debug sessions on the same binary.

This concludes our discussion of Corporate Error Reporting. As illustrated, CER is a powerful mechanism that can be enabled via group policy. It enables companies to keep all error reports locally for further analysis, or, alternatively, select error reports can be sent to Microsoft, depending on the configuration of CER.

## Summary

Postmortem debugging is a critical aspect of a software engineer's job. Once an application is shipped to customers, it is usually very difficult to troubleshoot problems. Having the knowledge and ability to respond quickly, accurately, and with as little pain as possible for the customer is key to a company being capable of efficiently managing customer complaints.

In this chapter, we discussed the reasons why it's necessary to sometimes debug a problem postmortem. We looked at what type of debug information is required for postmortem debugging to work and what tools we can use to collect that information. Once the information is in our hands, we also discussed how the debugger can be used to analyze the debug information to arrive at the source of the problem.

A powerful service called Windows Error Reporting was detailed, which gives you the capability to monitor your application's health in the real world and even get access to error information (such as crash dumps) for each particular problem your application might be experiencing, as well as provide a response to the problem.

Corporate Error Reporting was also discussed, which allows you to collect error information and store it on a centralized file share before sending the error reports to Microsoft.

# CHAPTER 14

# POWER TOOLS

Throughout the book, you have seen how various tools and the debuggers work in tandem to ease the software troubleshooting process. We've discussed a wide range of problems, such as memory corruptions, security-related problems, resource leaks, synchronization problems, and much more. Whenever we encountered a problem, we did a basic investigative analysis before diving deeper into a detailed debug session. The more you debug particular categories of problems, the more the initial investigation process starts resembling a generic process. Wouldn't it be nice if we could automate all or parts of the initial investigation and focus our efforts on using the results of the analysis to find the root cause? Fortunately, there are freely available tools that allow us to do just that. In this chapter, we discuss two of these power tools:

- Debug Diagnostics Tool: The Debug Diagnostic Tool automates the process of analyzing crashing, hanging, and leaking processes.
- The `!analyze` extension command: The Debugging Tools for Windows comes with a set of debugger and extension commands that help in the troubleshooting process. One of these commands is called `analyze`, and it automates the initial investigative process.

## Debug Diagnostic Tool

The Debug Diagnostic Tool (also known as DebugDiag) was originally developed as a tool to analyze and debug Internet Information Server (IIS) issues such as crashes, hangs, and memory leaks. While the tool's focus was portrayed as IIS centric, it was designed to be capable of analyzing any process, and it quickly became popular as a general troubleshooting tool. The power of DebugDiag comes in the form of an easy-to-use UI, great analysis capabilities (via analysis scripts), and an extensibility model supported by a large object model that makes writing your own analysis scripts easy.

The DebugDiag tool consists of four primary components.

- Service: The debugger service process (dbgsvc.exe) is the workhorse of DebugDiag. Its responsibilities include controlling the processes being debugged, performance monitoring, enabling memory leak detection, and more.
- Host: The debugger host (dbghost.exe) is the debugger engine of DebugDiag. It allows live debugging of processes through automated scripts and post-mortem debugging.
- User Interface: The UI of the DebugDiag tool.
- Leak tracker: The leak tracker component is responsible for all the work related to tracking memory leaks. It is implemented as a DLL (leaktrack.dll) and is injected into the process being monitored to track memory allocations and their associated call stacks.

Three primary usage scenarios (also known as rules) exist in DebugDiag. Each of the rules focuses on a specific category of problems.

- Crash: The crash rule enables you to analyze a process crash.
- Hang: The hang rule enables you to analyze a hung IIS process.
- Leaks: The leaks rule enables you to analyze leaked resources such as memory and/or handles.

The tool (January 2006 version) can be found at the following location:
http://www.microsoft.com/downloads/details.aspx?familyid=9BFA49BC-376B-4A54-95AA-73C9156706E7&displaylang=en
Installation of the tool is straightforward, and, unless you want to select which specific tools to install, a typical installation is sufficient (installs all the tools).

DebugDiag can be started from Start, All Programs, IIS Diagnostics, Debug Diagnostics Tool, Debug Diagnostics Tool 1.0.

The first time DebugDiag is started, a wizard appears that allows you to select a rule that you are interested in. You can select the crash, hang, or leaks rule. If you don't want to select a rule at that point, clicking Cancel takes you to the main DebugDiag window. In the main window, the Rules tab is selected by default, and the main window displays a list of active rules (initially empty). Every time a new rule is added, it is also added to the rules list. Two other tabs are available: Advanced Analysis and Processes. The Advanced Analysis tab contains a list of analyzer scripts available, as well as a list of data files (dump files) on which the analysis script can be executed. You will see how the Advanced Analysis tab is used in more detail later in the chapter. The Processes tab simply lists all processes running on the system with associated attributes (such as process ID, process name, process identity, and more).

Let's take a look at one of the rules available in conjunction with a buggy application and see how DebugDiag can make our life easier when analyzing the application.

## Analyzing a Memory or Handle Leak

To illustrate how DebugDiag can be used to analyze a leaking application, we will use a scenario from Chapter 9, "Resource Leaks."

Source code: `C:\AWD\Chapter9\BasicMLeak\Client`

Binary: `C:\AWDBIN\WinXP.x86.chk\09BasicMLeak.exe`

The command-line arguments we will use for the test application are as follows:

```
09BasicMLeak.exe /t:50 /i:2000 /s:0
```

The command-line arguments tell the application to run with 50 threads, 2,000 iterations per thread, and 0 sleep time between iterations. When you run this application, you will quickly notice that memory consumption goes up but never comes back down (even when the application is about to terminate). Restart the application and when the `Press any key to start stress application` appears, launch DebugDiag. In the wizard, select the Memory and Handle Leak radio button and click Next. The wizard now allows you to choose which process you want to analyze. Select the 09BasicMLeak.exe process and click Next. The next page in the wizard allows you to configure how memory and handle leak tracking should be performed. The following options are available.

- Warm-Up Time: This option allows you to specify when memory tracking should start. By default, memory tracking will start as soon as the rule is activated. To specify a time limit (in minutes) after which the memory tracking should start, uncheck the check box and specify the time limit in the Edit field.
- Tracking Time: This option allows you to control the time window in which tracking should be performed. By default, this option is set to 60 minutes.
- Auto-Create Crash Rule: If this check box is checked, DebugDiag creates a dump file if an unexpected process exit occurs.
- Auto-Unload: If this check box is selected, DebugDiag automatically unloads the leaktrack.dll when memory tracking completes.

For this exercise, leave the default values intact and click the Next button. The final page of the wizard allows you to name the newly created rule and specify a location where the dump files should be stored. Let's call the rule `Stress` and leave the dump file location as the default. Finally, we can click Finish to save and activate the rule. The main rules window now displays two rules (a leak rule and a crash rule). Proceed with the execution of the sample application and let it terminate. We can now go back to the main window in DebugDiag and click the Analyze button, which brings up a browser to display the results of the memory tracking. The memory tracking report is broken down into two main sections: Analysis Summary and Analysis Details.

The Analysis Summary section contains a table with a summary of problems found during the analysis process. It shows information on all outstanding allocations, including the size of each allocation, as well as the module responsible for the allocation. For each of the problems found, the last column in the table also gives recommendations on actions that can be taken to resolve the problem. Figure 14.1 illustrates the Analysis Summary for the sample run we were investigating.

| Type | Description | Recommendation |
|---|---|---|
| ⚠ Warning | **09BasicMLeak.exe** is responsible for **984.38 KBytes** worth of outstanding allocations. The following are the top 2 memory consuming functions:<br><br>**09BasicMLeak!CServer::GetSID+bd**: 984.38 KBytes worth of outstanding allocations. | If this is unexpected, please contact the vendor of this module, **Advanced Windows Debugging**, for further assistance with this issue. |
| ⚠ Warning | **ntdll.dll** is responsible for **446 Bytes** worth of outstanding allocations. The following are the top 2 memory consuming functions:<br><br>**ntdll!LdrpAllocateDataTableEntry+33**: 160 Bytes worth of outstanding allocations.<br>**ntdll!RtlpAllocateDebugInfo+49**: 160 Bytes worth of outstanding allocations. | If this is unexpected, please contact the vendor of this module, **Microsoft Corporation**, for further assistance with this issue. |
| ⓘ Information | DebugDiag did not detect any known **native heap(unmanaged)** problems in 09BasicMLeak__PID__3372__Date__05_30_2007__Time_05_27_19PM__312__kernel32!ExitProcess.dmp using the current set of scripts. | |

**Figure 14.1**   Analysis summary of 09BasicMLeak.exe run

As you can see, 09BasicMLeak.exe is responsible for approximately 980KB worth of leaked memory. More specifically, the function `GetSID` seems to be the source of the allocation. A row also seems to imply that ntdll.dll is responsible for 446 bytes of outstanding allocations. Normally, rows that show system DLLs do not constitute memory leaks—rather allocations that have not yet had the chance of being freed. The summary section of the report can be quite useful when trying to get an overview of the various components in a process and their corresponding allocation activity.

To get a more detailed picture, consult the analysis details section. This section contains a number of subsections, where each section details specific memory-related information.

- If a dump file was requested at process exit, the first section contains a summary of the information in the dump file.
- Virtual Memory Analysis: This section contains information on the virtual memory activity in the process being analyzed. The section includes information such as virtual memory details, loaded modules, and threads.
- Heap Analysis: The Heap Analysis section contains a top-level overview of heap usage, as well as a detailed breakdown of heap statistics for each heap.
- Leak Analysis: The Leak Analysis section contains the result of the leak analysis performed by DebugDiag. It shows a top-level overview of memory activity, as well as individual heap activity broken down by module.

Let's take a look at the Leak Analysis section of the sample application we just ran. The first part of interest is the overview section, as shown in Figure 14.2.

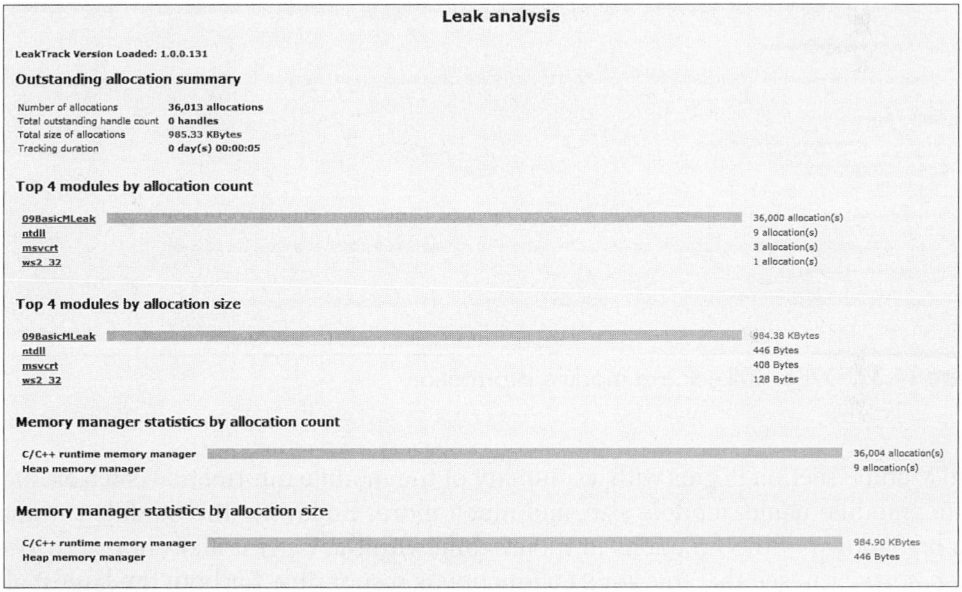

**Leak analysis**

LeakTrack Version Loaded: 1.0.0.131

**Outstanding allocation summary**

| | |
|---|---|
| Number of allocations | 36,013 allocations |
| Total outstanding handle count | 0 handles |
| Total size of allocations | 985.33 KBytes |
| Tracking duration | 0 day(s) 00:00:05 |

**Top 4 modules by allocation count**

| | |
|---|---|
| 09BasicMLeak | 36,000 allocation(s) |
| ntdll | 9 allocation(s) |
| msvcrt | 3 allocation(s) |
| ws2_32 | 1 allocation(s) |

**Top 4 modules by allocation size**

| | |
|---|---|
| 09BasicMLeak | 984.38 KBytes |
| ntdll | 446 Bytes |
| msvcrt | 408 Bytes |
| ws2_32 | 128 Bytes |

**Memory manager statistics by allocation count**

| | |
|---|---|
| C/C++ runtime memory manager | 36,004 allocation(s) |
| Heap memory manager | 9 allocation(s) |

**Memory manager statistics by allocation size**

| | |
|---|---|
| C/C++ runtime memory manager | 984.90 KBytes |
| Heap memory manager | 446 Bytes |

**Figure 14.2**  Leak analysis overview

As you can see from Figure 14.2, 09BasicMLeak.exe is the module that serves as our biggest allocation hog, with a total of 36,000 allocations and 984.38KB total memory. This information allows us to quickly get the information we need in order to focus our troubleshooting efforts in the correct code location. Following the overview section is a detailed drilldown into each module's activity. Because we already know, from the overview section, that 09BasicMLeak.exe seems suspect, we begin by looking at the 09BasicMLeak.exe module section illustrated in Figure 14.3.

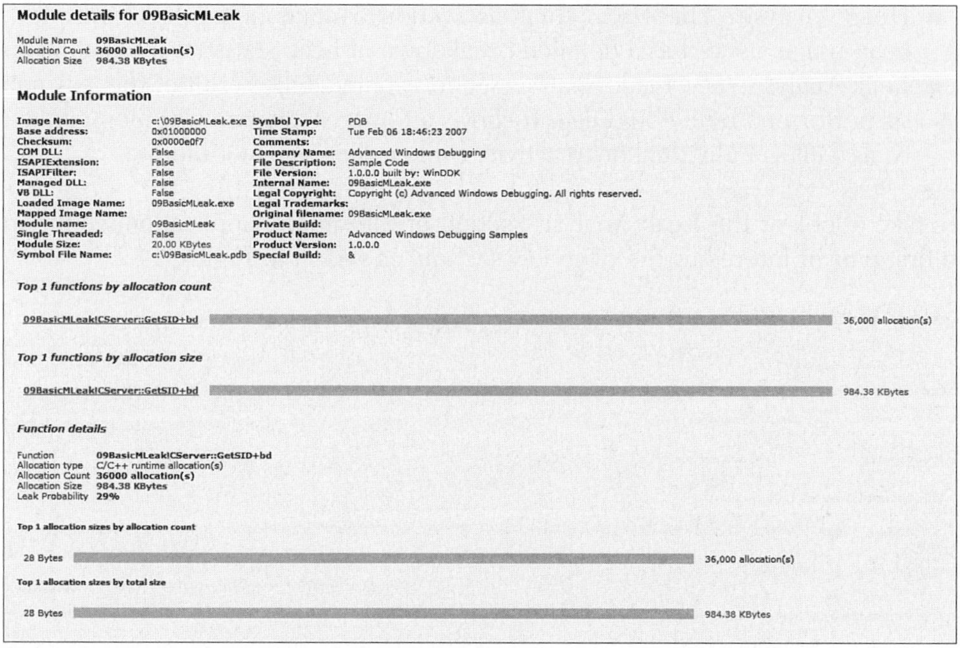

**Module details for 09BasicMLeak**

Module Name   09BasicMLeak
Allocation Count  36000 allocation(s)
Allocation Size   984.38 KBytes

**Module Information**

| | | | | |
|---|---|---|---|---|
| Image Name: | c:\09BasicMLeak.exe | Symbol Type: | PDB | |
| Base address: | 0x01000000 | Time Stamp: | Tue Feb 06 18:46:23 2007 | |
| Checksum: | 0x0000e0f7 | Comments: | | |
| COM DLL: | False | Company Name: | Advanced Windows Debugging | |
| ISAPIExtension: | False | File Description: | Sample Code | |
| ISAPIFilter: | False | File Version: | 1.0.0.0 built by: WinDDK | |
| Managed DLL: | False | Internal Name: | 09BasicMLeak.exe | |
| VB DLL: | False | Legal Copyright: | Copyright (c) Advanced Windows Debugging. All rights reserved. | |
| Loaded Image Name: | 09BasicMLeak.exe | Legal Trademarks: | | |
| Mapped Image Name: | | Original filename: | 09BasicMLeak.exe | |
| Module name: | 09BasicMLeak | Private Build: | | |
| Single Threaded: | False | Product Name: | Advanced Windows Debugging Samples | |
| Module Size: | 20.00 KBytes | Product Version: | 1.0.0.0 | |
| Symbol File Name: | c:\09BasicMLeak.pdb | Special Build: | & | |

*Top 1 functions by allocation count*

09BasicMLeak!CServer::GetSID+bd   36,000 allocation(s)

*Top 1 functions by allocation size*

09BasicMLeak!CServer::GetSID+bd   984.38 KBytes

*Function details*

Function           09BasicMLeak!CServer::GetSID+bd
Allocation type    C/C++ runtime allocation(s)
Allocation Count   36000 allocation(s)
Allocation Size    984.38 KBytes
Leak Probability   29%

Top 1 allocation sizes by allocation count

28 Bytes   36,000 allocation(s)

Top 1 allocation sizes by total size

28 Bytes   984.38 KBytes

**Figure 14.3**   09BasicMLeak.exe module information

The Module section begins with a summary of the module information, such as image name, module name, module size, and much more. Following the module summary is a breakdown of the functions in the module with the biggest allocation activity. In our case, we can see that the GetSID function is responsible for both the largest allocation count and allocation size. The final piece of information is the Function Details section, which details the top allocation functions and gives a breakdown of the different allocations made in the function. For example, Figure 14.3 shows that the GetSID function was responsible for 36,000 allocations of size 28 bytes each.

As you have seen, DebugDiag offers truly amazing analysis capabilities that relieve the developer from having to manually perform costly debug steps. Additionally, DebugDiag shows the outcome of the analysis in an easy-to-read and digestible form. Two other rules are available: crash and hang analysis rules. We strongly encourage you to look into these rules, as they provide information similar to that of the memory and handle leak rules. Both of these rules are backed by powerful analysis scripts. The big question, however, is can this tool be extended and new custom analysis scripts be developed for scenarios that the existing scripts do not cover? The answer is yes, and it involves using the extensibility model of the tool, which we look at next.

## Authoring Custom Analysis Scripts

In addition to providing exciting and powerful analysis scripts out of the box, DebugDiag also exposes powerful scripting access with a rich object model that enables developers to write their own analysis scripts using their favorite scripting language (such as VBScript or JScript). The object model is very extensive and covers a great majority of debugging objects that a developer might need. To get more detailed information on the complete object model, see the DebugDiag documentation.

In this part of the chapter, we illustrate how the scripting capabilities can be used to write your own analysis script that outputs all the locked critical sections in a dump file.

Each script begins with a metadata section that tells the analysis engine the script language used and its category, as well as a description. The metadata section looks very much like an ASP header, as illustrated in Listing 14.1.

**Listing 14.1**   DebugDiag custom analysis script metadata

```
<%@ Language = VBScript %>
<%@ Category = Sample analysis script %>
<%@ Description = Example of a custom analysis script %>
<% script code goes here %>
```

Each of the elements in the metadata (with the exception of the `Language` element) represents the information that will be displayed on the Advanced Analysis tab in the DebugDiag UI.

The goal of our sample script is to be able to dump out all the locked critical sections in the dump file. The perfect object to use for this purpose is the `CritSecInfo` object, which exposes a critical section collection of all the locked critical sections in the dump file. The `CritSecInfo` object has a `Count` property, as well as an `Item` property (among others), that allows you to iterate over all the locked critical sections. Listing 14.2 shows the code required to get access to the critical sections.

14. POWER TOOLS

**Listing 14.2**   Using the CritSec object

```
Set DataFiles = Manager.DataFiles
  For each DataFile in DataFiles
    Manager.Write "<B>Analyzing dump file " & DataFile & "</B><BR>"
    Set Debugger = Manager.GetDebugger(DataFile)
    Set CritSecInfo = Debugger.CritSecInfo
    CritSecCount = CritSecInfo.Count
    if CritSecCount = 0 Then
      Manager.Write "No locked critical sections found<BR>"
    else
      For i = 0 to CritSecCount-1
        Set DbgCritSec = CritSecInfo.Item(i)
        Manager.Write "The owner of critsec: " & DbgCritSec.Address & " is thread: "
        & DbgCritSec.OwnerThreadID & "<BR>"
      Next
    End If
    Set Debugger = Nothing
Next
```

All DebugDiag analysis scripts intrinsically have access to a `Manager` object. The `Manager` object enables the script, for example, to report the results of the analysis, as well as provide access to the data files (that is, dump files) to analyze. The first thing we need to do is get access to all the dump files that the user has chosen to run the script on. The `DumpFiles` property of the `Manager` object returns a collection of user-selected dump files. Because we want to analyze every dump file specified by the user, we next iterate over the returned dump file collection and get a `Debugger` object for each of the dump files in the collection. The `Debugger` object allows the script to get access to a plethora of information about the dump file. (See the DebugDiag documentation for a list of properties.) In our particular case, we are interested in the critical sections of the dump file, and, as such, we use the `CritSecInfo` property of the `Debugger` object. The `CritSecInfo` property returns an instance of the `CritSecInfo` object that can further be used to find all critical sections loaded for that particular dump file. The `CritSecInfo` object has a property called `Count` that returns the number of locked critical sections in the dump file. After the count has been retrieved, you can use the `Item` property to get access to each locked critical section. The `Item` property returns an instance of the `DbgCritSec` object, which contains critical section properties, such as the address of the critical section, the owning thread ID, the spin count, the state, and much more. In our sample script in Listing 14.2, we used the `Address` and `OwnerThreadID` properties to print out the address and owner of the critical section.

As you've noticed in Listing 14.2, the `Write` method of the `Manager` object allows you to write data to the report being prepared for the user. Because the reports are rendered using a browser, we include the proper HTML tags to make sure that the information is formatted properly (that is, using horizontal line breaks).

After the script has been authored, save it with an `.asp` extension and place it in the `Scripts` folder of the installation path for DebugDiag. For example, if the installation drive is `C:\`, place the script file in the following directory:

```
C:\Program Files\IIS Resources\DebugDiag\Scripts
```

After the script has been saved, you can launch DebugDiag, click the Advanced Analysis tab, and select the new and powerful analysis script just created. Notice that you can select multiple dump files, and the new critical section analysis script analyzes each of the selected scripts in turn.

DebugDiag's custom scripting capabilities and rich object model enable engineers to create complex and powerful postmortem analysis scripts that can dramatically reduce the time spent on analyzing the problem. Without this tool, a developer would have to either manually perform all the steps that the script performs (each and every debug session) or, alternatively, write a custom debugger extension that performs the same job as the script. Needless to say, you have already seen in Chapter 11, "Writing Custom Debugger Extensions," that writing custom debug extensions is a slightly more complex endeavor. It is important to note that although the object model exposed by DebugDiag is fairly comprehensive, it is not 100% inclusive, and it is sometimes necessary to write a debug extension that can subsequently be called from a DebugDiag script.

## !analyze Extension Command

The `analyze` extension command was invented as a way of automating failure analysis with the ultimate goal of automatic failure analysis and detection and assignment of known problems. Over time, the breadth and scope of the `!analyze` extension command has grown significantly, and it is now capable of doing automatic analysis of a large range of difficult problems. Examples of such problems include stack smashing, Application Verifier faults, and more. One of the great features of the `!analyze` extension command is its capability to assign failures based on the results of the analysis. For example, you can tell the `!analyze` extension command that any failures that occur within a specific module should be assigned to a particular owner. This can be quite a handy mechanism when failures are automatically analyzed using the

!analyze extension command, and this can reduce the amount of manual time spent doing initial analysis and failure assignments. In this part of the chapter, we take a look at how the !analyze extension command can be used to analyze a failure in one of the applications used in Chapter 10, "Synchronization." Additionally, we show how the automatic failure assignment mechanism can help you reduce the amount of time spent on the analysis and follow-up process.

## The Faulty Application

In Chapter 10, we spent some time investigating a basic deadlock. The initial analysis process involved dumping out all the threads and, for each of them, looking for any locking behavior that might have caused the deadlock to occur. After potential thread culprits had been identified, an in-depth investigation of each of the locking constructs was performed to see if there was a relationship between the threads that might have caused the deadlock. In this section, we take a look at the same deadlock scenario and see how the !analyze extension command can help us become more efficient in the initial analysis. The binary we are investigating can be found in the following location:

Source code: `C:\AWD\Chapter10\Deadlock`

Binary: `C:\AWDBIN\WinXP.x86.chk\10DeadLock.exe`

To begin the automatic analysis process, start 10DeadLock.exe under the debugger and let it run until the deadlock has occurred. Once deadlocked, break into the debugger and dump out all the threads. Next, we need to try to identify a thread that we believe is hung and switch the current thread to the hung thread. In our scenario, thread 0 might be a potential culprit (as can be seen by the attempt to enter a critical section). After you have switched to the potential culprit thread, issue the !analyze extension command as shown here:

```
!analyze -v -hang
```

The -v switch causes the !analyze extension command to output the results in verbose mode, and the -hang switch tells the !analyze extension command that it should perform a hang analysis. The result of executing the command is a slew of information that the command was capable of extrapolating based on the overall state of the process. Let's take a closer look at the output of the command.

## Analyze Results

Listing 14.3 shows the output of the `analyze -hang -v` command we just executed.

**Listing 14.3**   Output of the !analyze extension command

```
0:000> !analyze -hang -v
*******************************************************************************
*                                                                           *
*                      Exception Analysis                                    *
*                                                                           *
*******************************************************************************


FAULTING_IP:
kernel32!CtrlRoutine+bd
7c87533d 834dfcff          or          dword ptr [ebp-4],0FFFFFFFFh


EXCEPTION_RECORD:  ffffffff -- (.exr ffffffffffffffff)
ExceptionAddress: 7c87533d (kernel32!CtrlRoutine+0x000000bd)
   ExceptionCode: 40010005 (Control-C exception)
  ExceptionFlags: 00000000
NumberParameters: 0


FAULTING_THREAD:  00000d08


BUGCHECK_STR:  HANG


PROCESS_NAME:  10DeadLock.exe


ERROR_CODE: (NTSTATUS) 0xcfffffff - <Unable to get error code text>


CRITICAL_SECTION: 01003320 (!cs -s 01003320)


BLOCKING_THREAD:  00000d08


DERIVED_WAIT_CHAIN:

Dl Eid Cid     WaitType
-----------------------
x  0   85c.d08 Critical Section      ->
x  1   85c.8f4 Critical Section      -^
```

*(continues)*

**Listing 14.3** Output of the !analyze extension command *(continued)*

```
WAIT_CHAIN_COMMAND:  ~0s;k;;~1s;k;;

DEFAULT_BUCKET_ID:  APPLICATION_HANG_DEADLOCK

PRIMARY_PROBLEM_CLASS:  APPLICATION_HANG_DEADLOCK

LAST_CONTROL_TRANSFER:  from 7c90e9c0 to 7c90eb94

STACK_TEXT:
0007fed4 7c90e9c0 7c91901b 000007dc 00000000 ntdll!KiFastSystemCallRet
0007fed8 7c91901b 000007dc 00000000 7c97c140 ntdll!NtWaitForSingleObject+0xc
0007ff60 7c90104b 00003320 0100137d 01003320 ntdll!RtlpWaitForCriticalSection+0x132
0007ff68 0100137d 01003320 000007f4 000008f4 ntdll!RtlEnterCriticalSection+0x46
0007ff7c 0100153b 00000001 00032470 00032ce0 10DeadLock!main+0xad
0007ffc0 7c816fd7 00011970 7c9118f1 7ffd6000 10DeadLock!__mainCRTStartup+0x102
0007fff0 00000000 01001679 00000000 78746341 kernel32!BaseProcessStart+0x23


FOLLOWUP_IP:
10DeadLock!main+ad
0100137d 6808110001      push    offset 10DeadLock!`string' (01001108)

SYMBOL_STACK_INDEX:   4

FOLLOWUP_NAME:  MachineOwner

MODULE_NAME: 10DeadLock

IMAGE_NAME:  10DeadLock.exe

DEBUG_FLR_IMAGE_TIMESTAMP:  45c93d82

SYMBOL_NAME:  10DeadLock!main+ad

STACK_COMMAND:  ~0s ; kb

FAILURE_BUCKET_ID:  HANG_10DeadLock!main+ad

BUCKET_ID:  HANG_10DeadLock!main+ad

Followup: MachineOwner
-----
```

A breakdown and detailed description of the output is discussed in the following list.

- FAULTING_IP

  FAULTING_IP shows the value of the instruction pointer when the fault occurred. In our case, the faulting instruction pointer is due to us breaking into the debugger when the deadlock was detected (kernel32!CtrlRoutine).

- EXCEPTION_RECORD

  EXCEPTION_RECORD gives more detail about the exception that occurred in the form of an exception record. From Listing 14.3, we can see that we do not have an exception record recorded with this fault (ffffffff). If an exception record were available, you could use the exr command to display its contents.

- ExceptionAddress

  ExceptionAddress shows the address where the exception occurred. In our scenario, the exception address is 7c87533d, which corresponds to the control routine function in kernel32.dll (kernel32!CtrlRoutine).

- ExceptionCode

  ExceptionCode tells us the exact exception that caused the fault. In our scenario, the exception code is 40010005, which corresponds to a Control-C exception. This exception address is recorded because of breaking into the debugger using Control-C.

- ExceptionFlags

  ExceptionFlags shows the flags associated with the exception. In our case, the flag is set to 00000000.

- NumberParameters

  NumberParameters tells us the number of parameters associated with the exception. In our case, the number of parameters is 0.

- FAULTING_THREAD

  FAULTING_THREAD tells us which thread caused the fault to occur. From the output in Listing 14.3, we can see that the faulting thread is 00000d08. If we look for thread 00000d08 in our thread list, we can see that the faulting thread corresponds to one of the threads waiting for a critical section to become available.

- BUGCHECK_STR

  BUGCHECK_STR represents a textual description of the "bugcheck" that occurred. Note that the name of this field can be misleading because we are in user mode and a bugcheck is typically relevant only in kernel mode faults. Even though the distinction between user mode and kernel mode is not made in the name of this field, the reason behind the fault can still be trusted. In our scenario, the reason for the fault is a HANG.

- PROCESS_NAME

  PROCESS_NAME tells us the name of the process that is exhibiting the fault (10DeadLock.exe).

- ERROR_CODE

  ERROR_CODE tells us the error code (NTSTATUS) that caused the fault.

- CRITICAL_SECTION

  CRITICAL_SECTION shows the address of the critical section that was found and analyzed in the starting thread. Because our starting thread was 0, the critical section address shown is 01003320.

- BLOCKING_THREAD

  BLOCKING_THREAD gives the ID of the thread that is blocking on the critical section shown in the CRITICAL_SECTION field. In our case, the thread that is blocking on the critical section located at address 01003320 is 00000d08.

- DERIVED_WAIT_CHAIN

  DERIVED_WAIT_CHAIN is at the heart of the hang analysis capabilities of the !analyze extension command. When the command was run, it made an attempt to derive how the wait chain looks for each of the threads in the process associated with the critical section listed in the CRITICAL_SECTION field. Let's take a closer look at the output.

```
Dl Eid Cid     WaitType
-  --  ----    -------------
x  0   85c.d08 Critical Section    -->
x  1   85c.8f4 Critical Section    --^
```

From this output, we can see that we have two threads that are associated with the critical section. The most interesting question is what the state of this critical section is (that is, is it locked, and which thread owns it). At the end of each of the threads displayed is a series of characters that denote the state of the critical section in relationship to the thread. The symbols include

- -->: The thread is waiting for the critical section.
- --^: The thread owns the critical section.

From this output, we can very quickly see that the thread with a thread ID of d08 is waiting for a critical section owned by thread 8f4.

- WAIT_CHAIN_COMMAND

  This field shows the commands that can be used to further analyze the wait chain of the problematic lock. In our scenario, the commands to be executed are ~0s;k;;~1s;k;;

- DEFAULT_BUCKET_ID

  DEFAULT_BUCKET_ID details the general category of faults that this particular fault falls under. In our scenario, the fault was determined to be an APPLICA-TION_HANG_DEADLOCK fault.

- PRIMARY_PROBLEM_CLASS

  PRIMARY_PROBLEM_CLASS indicates the primary class of problems that the fault was categorized in. Once again, the primary problem class for our scenario is APPLICATION_HANG_DEADLOCK.

- LAST_CONTROL_TRANSFER

  LAST_CONTROL_TRANSFER shows the last two function calls made on the stack. Listing 14.3 shows the following addresses:

  from 7c90e9c0 to 7c90eb94

  If we use the ln command on these addresses, we can see that the last function call made in our scenario was from ntdll!NtWaitForSingleObject to ntdll!KiFastSystemCallRet.

- STACK_TEXT

  STACK_TEXT shows the full stack trace of the thread. In our case, it shows the stack trace of thread 0.

- FOLLOWUP_IP

  FOLLOWUP_IP shows the instruction that most likely caused the fault. From the output in Listing 14.3, you can see that the call to EnterCritical Section caused a problematic hang in the code.

- SYMBOL_STACK_INDEX

  SYMBOL_STACK_INDEX corresponds to the frame in the thread's stack trace that caused the fault. In our scenario, symbol-stack-index is 4, which corresponds to the frame on the stack that caused the fault:

  10DeadLock!main

- FOLLOWUP_NAME

  FOLLOWUP_NAME shows who should be following up with this particular fault. As you can see, the follow-up in our scenario is said to be MachineOwner, which is typically used when a follow-up directive cannot be found for the particular fault. Later in the chapter, you will see how we can control the contents of this field.

- MODULE_NAME

  This field simply states the module that is exhibiting the fault (10DeadLock).

- IMAGE_NAME

  IMAGE_NAME states the name of the image that the fault occurred in (10DeadLock.exe).

- DEBUG_FLR_IMAGE_TIMESTAMP

  This field shows the image time stamp for the image, where the fault occurred (45c93d82).

- SYMBOL_NAME

  This field shows the symbolic name, where the fault occurred (10DeadLock!main).

- STACK_COMMAND

  STACK_COMMAND shows the commands that were executed to get the stack trace for the faulting thread. In our case, the sequence of commands was ~0s ; kb.

- FAILURE_BUCKET_ID and BUCKET_ID

  The bucket ID fields show the specific category of problems that the fault falls under. This information can be used by the !analyze extension command to determine what additional information to display in the analysis result.

- FOLLOWUP

  FOLLOWUP shows the most appropriate owners for this particular fault. If an owner cannot be found, the default MachineOwner is displayed.

As you have seen, executing the !analyze extension command results in a lot of information that could have otherwise taken quite some time to manually gather. In addition to all this valuable information, another important feature of the !analyze extension command is its capability to assign owners to particular faults. We will take a look at how to customize this capability next.

## Fault Follow-Up

In the previous section, we took a look at the results of running the !analyze extension command on an application that deadlocked. Part of the information we got from the !analyze extension command was the follow-up contact for that particular fault. Because analyze did not have knowledge of who we wanted to assign this particular problem to, it simply defaulted to MachineOwner. We now take a look at how we can customize this behavior to fit our own needs.

For this scenario, we assume that the owner of the 10DeadLock.exe application is named John Anderson (e-mail: johna@fictionous.com). We would like to associate John's name with any failures that occur in the 10DeadLock.exe image. This association is made via a file called the triage.ini file, located under the triage folder in the debugger installation path. By default, the triage.ini file contains a bunch of associations that either ignore the specified faults or assign the faults to a default owner (such as `MachineOwner`). Let's take a look at an example from the `triage.ini` file:

```
nt!Zw*=ignore
```

This line shows that any faults occurring in the `nt` module and starting with the letters `Zw` should be ignored and that no follow-up owner will be displayed by the `!analyze` extension command. As you can see, the `triage.ini` file supports specifying wildcards to make it easier to assign a range of problems to a particular entity.

Let's add a line in the `triage.ini` file that associates John Anderson as the owner of 10DeadLock.exe:

```
10DeadLock!*=John Anderson (johna@fictionous.com)
```

By using only the wildcard character `*`, we can tell the `!analyze` extension command to assign all the faults that occur in the scenario1 module to John. Let's run the application under the debugger again and perform a hang analysis to make sure that the fault does get assigned to John. Listing 14.4 shows an abbreviated version of the result of the `!analyze` extension command.

**Listing 14.4**  Follow-up ownership for scenario1.exe

```
0:000> !analyze -v -hang
***********************************************************************
*                                                                     *
*                        Exception Analysis                           *
*                                                                     *
***********************************************************************


FAULTING_IP:
kernel32!CtrlRoutine+bd
7c87533d 834dfcff        or        dword ptr [ebp-4],0FFFFFFFFh
...
...
...
FOLLOWUP_NAME:   John Anderson (johna@fictionous.com)
...
.
..
...
Followup: John Anderson (johna@fictionous.com)
-----
```

As you can see, the follow-up has now been changed from `MachineOwner` to `John Anderson`, making it easier for the person looking at the analysis to assign the fault to the correct owner.

The capability to specify the owner is incredibly useful when you have a complex system in which a large number of developers are working with many different images and modules. While testing, anytime a fault occurs somewhere in the system, the `!analyze` extension command can be used to glean information about the source of the problem, as well as immediately identify who to contact regarding this failure. One could even imagine a fully automated notification process that automatically parsed the output of the `!analyze` extension command and sent an e-mail to the follow-up specified in the result.

## Summary

In this chapter, we investigated two power tools that can dramatically reduce the amount of time spent on initial failure analysis. The Debug Diagnostics tool introduced a mechanism by which we can automate memory leak detection, crash analysis, and hang analysis, as well as write our own custom analysis scripts. The result of the analysis consists of a well-formatted and easily digestible report with all the relevant information categorized and displayed both in textual, as well as graphical, form. The other tool examined in this chapter came in the form of an extension command called `!analyze`. The `!analyze` extension command has strong analytical capabilities. It has matured over time to be capable of analyzing a large number of difficult problems and performing automatic failure assignments of identified problems.

# CHAPTER 15

# WINDOWS VISTA FUNDAMENTALS

Most applications benefit seamlessly from all the Windows Vista improvements. Most customers using those applications are thrilled by the improvements and are eager to upgrade all computers to Windows Vista. However, some applications crash at random intervals when started under Windows Vista, and the customer demands a new version. The vendor must investigate the root cause of the problem, find a solution, and provide a Vista upgrade for his application.

On previous versions of Windows, crash investigations could be completed in a reasonable time. On Windows Vista, it can take considerably longer. Why is that so?

Although most applications run great in the new environment, Windows Vista security and reliability enhancements affect their functionality. The system is more robust at the expense of applications' compatibility. The Windows Vista operating system is less tolerant of application memory failures and enforces higher security restrictions on system resources. Several familiar system mechanisms redesigned for Windows Vista require some ramp-up time.

This chapter walks through all the scenarios described in the book—scenarios that we consider commonly used in debugging Windows applications with the goal of discovering what is different in Windows Vista. The intent of this chapter is not to be a compressive list of Vista changes; it is limited to the changes with direct implications in the debugging process.

The following sections, each corresponding to a previous chapter, follow the same sequence as the book chapters. Each subheading loosely follows the corresponding chapter organization and focuses only on differences from the previous operating system versions. Chapters not represented here present no significant differences from Windows XP Service Pack 2, and you can assume that nothing specific has been changed. However, it is possible to see slightly different behaviors caused by security improvements.

This chapter reuses several samples introduced in the previous chapters. The binary files targeted to Windows Vista x64 are available in the `C:\AWDBIN\WinLH.AMD64.chk` folder. The binary files targeted to Windows XP are available in the `C:\AWDBIN\WinXP.x86.chk` folder.

# Chapter 1—Introduction to the Tools

Anytime substantial changes are introduced into the core architecture of any operating system, application compatibility becomes an issue. Applications that previously used to work might now need to be changed. Although Microsoft spends an incredible amount of time and resources on ensuring that applications continue working with each operating system version, it is sometimes not feasible or desirable to achieve 100% compatibility. The tools used throughout this book are no exception. Although most of the tools work, some do not work yet on Windows Vista. Table 15.1 shows all the tools used in the book along with their Vista compatibility state.

**Table 15.1**   Tools and Windows Vista

| Tool | Vista Compatible | Alternative Tool |
|------|------------------|------------------|
| WDK | Yes | |
| LeakDiag | No | UMDH |
| UMDH | Yes | |
| Application Verifier | Yes | |
| Global Flags | Yes | |
| Process Monitor | Yes | |
| Ethereal | Yes | |
| DebugDiag | No | None |
| Debugging Tools for Windows | Yes | |

For each of the tools listed as not working in Table 15.1, the Alternative Tool column indicates a suggestion of a different tool to be used instead. Windows Vista security enhancements affect all tools, and the possible change in behavior must be well understood, as exemplified in the section "Registry and File Virtualization."

## Windows Debug Logs

Windows Vista brings huge improvements in the manageability area, especially in the area of managing events raised by various components, which can be used when debugging applications.. The new Event Log system is the central store for all component logs, known as diagnostic logs or debug logs. The debug logs are shown in the Event Viewer after changing the log settings using the Show Analytic and Debug menu item in the View menu. Several channels are disabled by default and may be enabled using the right side panel.

Even if some channels have information useful only to the component designers, the majority of them contain information useful for getting a gut feeling about the machine state. One such log is the Diagnostic-Performance Operational log that contains clear messages about various performance measurements, as shown in Figure 15.1.

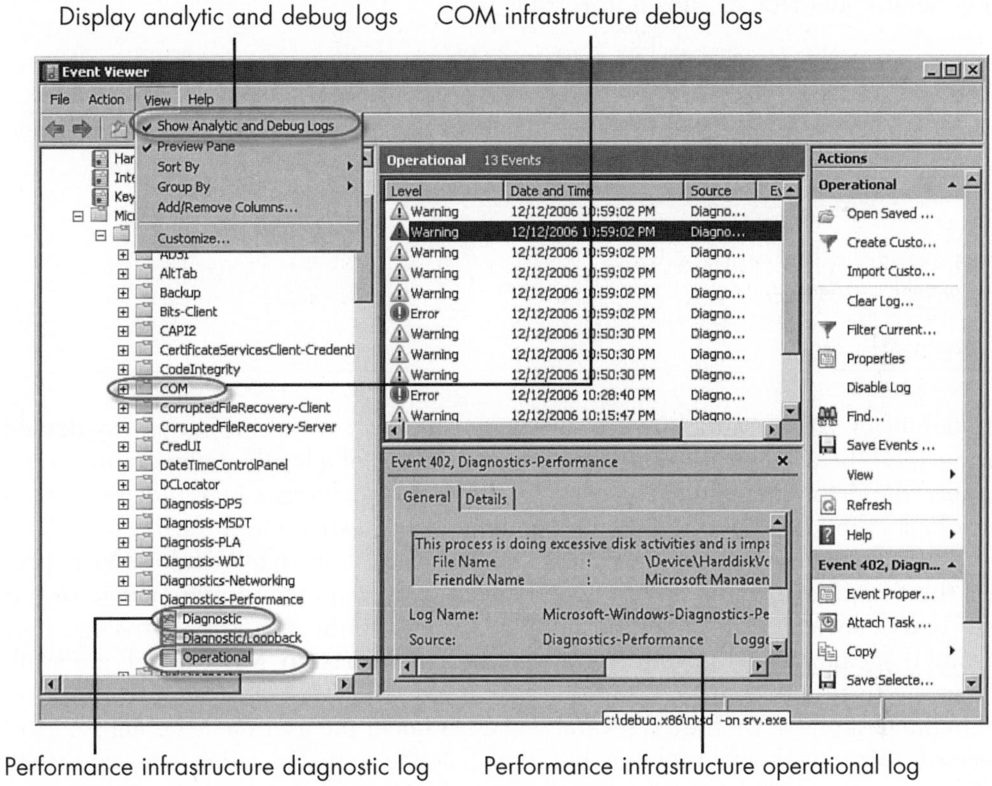

**Figure 15.1**   Operational, analytic, and debug logs stored in Windows Vista Event Log

## Chapter 2—Introduction to the Debuggers

Before deciding if this section is necessary, we did try the scenarios described in Chapter 2, "Introduction to the Debuggers," in all possible configurations. The few problems encountered when establishing the debugging session are discussed in this section.

15. WINDOWS VISTA FUNDAMENTALS

## User Access Control Side Effects

In the beginning, we used the user mode debuggers to start new processes or to attach them to existing ones. The debugger attaches to most running processes without problems, until the target process is a system process. In such cases, the debugger generates an error, as shown in Listing 15.1.

**Listing 15.1**  Debugging a service process from the command prompt

```
C:\>cdb -pn winlogon.exe
Microsoft (R) Windows Debugger Version 6.6.0007.5
Copyright (c) Microsoft Corporation. All rights reserved.

Cannot debug pid 564, Win32 error 5
    "Access is denied."
Debuggee initialization failed, Win32 error 5
    "Access is denied."
```

The debugger fails to attach to the privileged process, returning an access denied error even if the account running the debugger is part of a local administrator group. Because the error seems to be caused by the security changes in Windows Vista, a quick look at the new security features pointed the investigation toward a side effect of the User Account Control (UAC) feature. The UAC feature in Windows Vista protects the computer from unauthorized changes, achieved by multiple means. In this case, UAC converted the powerful administrator account into a low-privilege user account that cannot use the administrative group membership. More details are available in the section that covers Windows Vista security changes.

In the next phase, we started several processes under the user mode debugger. Most processes started without a problem, but some failed to start. The failing ones do so with an error message stating The requested operation requires elevation, as in Listing 15.2. This error happens for all processes that show a UAC elevation prompt.

**Listing 15.2**  Debugging a service process from the normal command prompt

```
C:\>cdb mmc.exe
Microsoft (R) Windows Debugger  Version 6.6.0007.5
Copyright (c) Microsoft Corporation. All rights reserved.

CommandLine: mmc.exe
Cannot execute 'mmc.exe', Win32 error 740
    "The requested operation requires elevation."
Debuggee initialization failed, Win32 error 740
    "The requested operation requires elevation."
```

Next, we start a console in an elevated privilege mode, which has similar rights to those of an administrator account on a down-level platform. Any executable can start under full administrative privileges after selecting the Run as Administrator option from the application shortcut's context menu. Figure 15.2 shows the options available to run the shortcut.

**Figure 15.2**   Running a command prompt under full administrative rights

From the elevated command prompt, the user mode debugger works as expected. It can attach to any running process in the system and can start any application.

We use those two command prompts—one running as a UAC user and one running as an elevated user—to test the kernel mode debugger. The kernel mode debugger running in local mode has proven very useful for investigating access permission problems, deadlocks, or following a series of LPC calls. When started from the normal command prompt, the debugger fails as expected, as shown in Listing 15.3.

**Listing 15.3**   Debugging a service process from the normal command prompt

```
C:\>kd -kl
Microsoft (R) Windows Debugger  Version 6.6.0007.5
Copyright (c) Microsoft Corporation. All rights reserved.

The system does not support local kernel debugging.
Local kernel debugging requires Windows XP, Administrative
privileges, and is not supported by WOW64.
Only a single local kernel debugging session can run at a time.
Debuggee initialization failed, HRESULT 0x80004001
   "Not implemented"
```

There should be no surprise to see the operation failure, as the kernel mode debugger in local mode can do unlimited damage to the system. However, after trying the same operation from an elevated prompt, we were a little bit surprised that the tool is failing with the access denied error shown in Listing 15.4.

**Listing 15.4**   Debugging a service process from an elevated console

```
C:\>kd -kl
Microsoft (R) Windows Debugger  Version 6.6.0007.5
Copyright (c) Microsoft Corporation. All rights reserved.
Debugger can't get KD version information, Win32 error 5
```

To check the kernel mode configuration, we use the kdbgctrl.exe tool, installed with Debugging Tools for Windows. The tool can be used to find out the kernel debugger current state and changing it as needed. The command output tells us that the kernel mode debugger is disabled, as shown in the following listing:

```
C:\>kdbgctrl.exe -c
Kernel debugger is disabled
```

In Windows Vista, as well as in the previous versions of Windows operating systems, the kernel debugger must be enabled at boot time to become active. The next section describes how to configure the kernel debugger's state at the next boot.

## Enabling the Kernel Mode Debugger

Chapter 2 uses bootcfg.exe as the preferred tool to make changes in boot.ini, which controls the kernel mode debugger's state. However, the tool does not exist in Windows Vista because the entire boot loader system changed and the boot configuration moved from boot.ini to a different system store called Boot Configuration Data (BCD). The BCD store can be manipulated using the bcdedit.exe command line. Used without command-line parameters, the command displays all BCD objects from the BCD store with all the configuration parameters or BCD elements, as shown in Listing 15.5.

**Listing 15.5**    Enumerating all BCD objects from an elevated console

```
C:\>bcdedit
Windows Boot Manager
----------
identifier              {bootmgr}
device                  partition=C:
description             Windows Boot Manager
locale                  en-US
inherit                 {globalsettings}
default                 {current}
resumeobject            {b4e45951-b979-11db-b123-967f83be464e}
displayorder            {current}
                        {9556a9b0-7a61-11db-935f-fbbbd349454f}
toolsdisplayorder       {memdiag}
timeout                 3

Windows Boot Loader
----------
identifier              {current}
device                  partition=C:
path                    \Windows\system32\winload.exe
description             Microsoft Windows Vista
locale                  en-US
inherit                 {bootloadersettings}
osdevice                partition=C:
systemroot              \Windows
resumeobject            {b4e45951-b979-11db-b123-967f83be464e}
nx                      OptIn
debug                   Yes
nx                      OptIn
```

The configuration can be changed by passing new values as parameters on the command line. By default, all changes affect the BCD object corresponding to the current running configuration. The changes can be targeted to a different BCD object by specifying it in the command line. Listing 15.6 uses bcdedit.exe to enable the kernel mode debugger on serial port COM1 at a baud rate of 115200.

**Listing 15.6**   Configuring the kernel mode debugger for the running configuration

```
C:\>bcdedit /debug {current} on
The operation completed successfully.
C:\debug.x86>bcdedit /dbgsettings SERIAL DEBUGPORT:1 BAUDRATE:115200
The operation completed successfully.
```

The BCD store, as well as the bcdedit.exe command-line tool, is very well documented on Microsoft's Web site.

After enabling the kernel mode debugger and restarting the system, the kernel debugger works as expected, both in local mode or connected to the host system using a physical cable. Moving on to the next chapter, we are pleasantly surprised to see that the sample used in Chapter 3, "Debuggers Uncovered," works as expected after taking into account UAC restrictions and using an elevated prompt when needed. The mechanism of treating unhandled exceptions is greatly improved in Windows Vista and is described in detail in the section covering Chapter 13, "Postmortem Debugging."

## Address Space Layout Randomization

In some cases, engineers make assumptions about the addresses holding various elements, such as the address of a global variable or a function address. The assumption can be as simple as a note with several commands using virtual addresses to set breakpoints. Such "command notes" are often used by engineers to enter a set of commands faster.

In Windows Vista, the Address Space Layout Randomization (ASLR) feature challenges this assumption. Under ASLR, the system ignores the preferred load address and loads dynamic libraries at different addresses at every system start-up. Listings 15.7 and 15.8 show a fragment from the process environment of the sample 08cli.exe process before and after the system has been restarted.

**Listing 15.7**   DLLs loaded in the 08cli.exe sample (before reboot)

```
0:000> !peb
...
      Base TimeStamp                      Module
    400000 4529f49a Oct 09 00:04:58 2006 c:\AWDBIN\WinXP.x86.chk\08cli.exe
  77570000 4549bdc9 Nov 02 01:43:37 2006 C:\Windows\system32\ntdll.dll
  76d70000 4549bd80 Nov 02 01:42:24 2006 C:\Windows\system32\kernel32.dll
  76e50000 4549bd92 Nov 02 01:42:42 2006 C:\Windows\system32\ole32.dll
...
```

After we restart the system, the same application loads all system dynamic link libraries at different addresses.

**Listing 15.8**   DLLs loaded in the 08cli.exe sample (after reboot)

```
0:003> !peb
...
      Base TimeStamp                    Module
    400000 4529f49a Oct 09 00:04:58 2006 c:\AWDBIN\WinXP.x86.chk\08cli.exe
  774b0000 4549bdc9 Nov 02 01:43:37 2006 C:\Windows\system32\ntdll.dll
  75f40000 4549bd80 Nov 02 01:42:24 2006 C:\Windows\system32\kernel32.dll
  760a0000 4549bd92 Nov 02 01:42:42 2006 C:\Windows\system32\ole32.dll
...
```

The process image is loaded at the same address because it was linked for Windows XP without the /dynamicbase option, the linker option controls the ASLR behavior.

# Chapter 6—Memory Corruptions—Part Heaps

The heap manager in Windows Vista has undergone some major changes. Although the previous versions of the heap manager worked well, rapid advancements in computing hardware have led to new requirements of the heap manager. As development of the operating system moved forward, the three biggest challenges facing the heap manager were those of security, performance, and increased resilience to misbehaving applications. In prior versions of Windows, security attacks became increasingly sophisticated and eventually led to heap-based attacks. While not as frequent as other types of attacks (such as stack-based attacks) and much more complex in nature, the engineers at Microsoft decided to address this very important attack vector in Windows Vista. The other reason for revamping the heap manager dealt with the evolution of hardware. From a historical perspective, computers have gone from having a few megabytes of memory (or kilobytes depending on how far back one goes) to gigabytes and even terabytes of RAM. Additionally, with the advent of multiprocessor systems as standard machine configurations, the requirements on the heap manager changed to be capable of performing well on these types of systems. Finally, the last category of improvement was in the area of increased resilience to misbehaving applications. Mismanaging heap memory has been a constant source of problems in applications, and with Windows Vista, the heap manager now has built-in early detection of several different types of common heap corruptions.

15. WINDOWS VISTA FUNDAMENTALS

To address the new requirements, Windows Vista introduced an updated version of the front end allocator called the low-fragmentation front end. The low-fragmentation heap has been part of Windows since Windows Server 2003 and Windows XP but is now vastly improved and enabled by default in Windows Vista.

Figure 15.3 illustrates the low-fragmentation heap architecture.

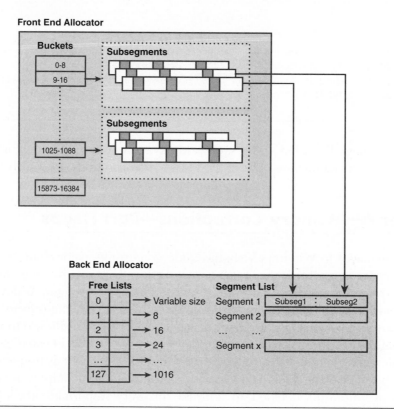

**Figure 15.3**   Low-fragmentation heap architecture

The basic idea behind the low-fragmentation heap is to reduce the amount of fragmentation that could occur with the old look aside list front end. Prior to Windows Vista, the free and busy blocks in any given segment could be interleaved in such a way that there were no free blocks with enough contiguous memory to satisfy the allocation. Figure 15.4 illustrates a hypothetical example of a heap segment that suffers from fragmentation.

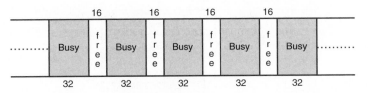

**Figure 15.4**   Fragmentation in a heap segment

The heap segment contains five busy heap blocks of size 32 bytes and four free heap blocks of size 16 bytes. If an allocation of 32 bytes is requested, the allocation would not be satisfied from that segment because the heap manager is unable to find 32 bytes of contiguous memory available (even though more than 32 bytes of total free memory are available).

The low-fragmentation front end allocator in Windows Vista serves to address this problem by maintaining subsegments within each heap segment. Each subsegment can contain only blocks of a predetermined size. For example, Figure 15.3 shows that allocations of size 9–16 bytes have a set of subsegments where each subsegment is housed in the back end allocator's heap segments.

Because each subsegment takes up committed memory from the back end heap segment and is managed by the low-fragmentation front end, how are the heap blocks managed? Say that a heap block of size 16 bytes is freed from one of the subsegments. Who knows that the block is freed? Besides the heap block itself containing flags indicating the status of the heap block (free or busy), the low-fragmentation front end also keeps a singly linked list associated with each subsegment. This singly linked list acts as the free list for the subsegment. When a free heap block becomes available, it is pushed onto the list, and if a subsequent allocation request comes in for that size heap block, the first entry in the list is popped from the list and returned to the caller. The free list for each subsegment can be accessed via a subsegment header that contains some metadata including a pointer to the free list. The subsegments are created when allocation requests arrive at the front end. When a subsegment is created, the heap manager decides the initial size of the subsegment (that is, the number of slots to pre-allocate) based on the history of the heap usage in the application or, if no history is available, a default initial size. If a subsegment ever becomes full, the heap manager can create another subsegment to house allocations.

The layout of a heap block in the low-fragmentation heap is illustrated in Figure 15.5.

15. WINDOWS VISTA FUNDAMENTALS

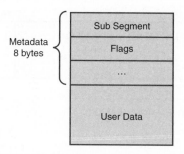

**Figure 15.5** Heap block layout for low-fragmentation heap

At a high level, the major difference between the old heap blocks and the low-fragmentation heap blocks is that of a reference to the subsegment of which the heap block is a part. Additionally, it is important to note that the heap block metadata is now "randomized." The implication of randomizing the metadata is that dumping out the raw contents of the metadata (using, for example, the dc command) no longer yields output that can be easily understood. Fortunately, the !heap extension command has been updated to take the randomization into account, and prior to displaying the contents of the heap block, the !heap extension command decodes the metadata and displays the results. To display low-fragmentation heap blocks using the !heap extension command, the −i switch must be used. For example, if a low-fragmentation heap block resides at address 0x10b25de0, the output of the !heap extension command would be the following:

```
0:028> !heap -i 10b25de0
Detailed information for block entry 10b25de0
Assummed heap      : 0x00100000 (Use !heap -i NewHeapHandle to change)
Header content     : 0x3C67E5EE 0xC2006898
Block flags        : 0x1 LFH (busy )
Total block size   : 0xe units (0x70 bytes)
Requested size     : 0x58 bytes (unused 0x18 bytes)
Subsegment         : 0x05f4dc58

            7710dab4: ntdll!RtlAllocateHeap+0x0000021d
            76eedcaf: ole32!CGIPTable::LazyMarshalGIPEntry+0x00000045
            76eedef2: ole32!CRemoteUnknown::DoCallback+0x0000007a
            76bb6dfe: RPCRT4!Invoke+0x0000002a
            76c303ef: RPCRT4!NdrStubCall2+0x0000027b
            76c321e2: RPCRT4!CStdStubBuffer_Invoke+0x000000a0
            76fd92a0: ole32!SyncStubInvoke+0x0000003c
            76fd923a: ole32!StubInvoke+0x000000b9
```

```
76f025c2: ole32!CCtxComChnl::ContextInvoke+0x000000fa
76f024d3: ole32!MTAInvoke+0x0000001a
76f03403: ole32!STAInvoke+0x00000046
76fd9162: ole32!AppInvoke+0x000000aa
76fd8fdf: ole32!ComInvokeWithLockAndIPID+0x0000032c
76fd9696: ole32!ComInvoke+0x000000c5
76f032d9: ole32!ThreadDispatch+0x00000023
76f0339e: ole32!ThreadWndProc+0x000000f5
77021a10: USER32!InternalCallWinProc+0x00000023
77021ae8: USER32!UserCallWinProcCheckWow+0x0000014b
77022a47: USER32!DispatchMessageWorker+0x00000322
77022a98: USER32!DispatchMessageW+0x0000000f
6f4ce5db: IEFRAME!CTabWindow::_TabWindowThreadProc+0x00000189
767d3833: kernel32!BaseThreadInitThunk+0x0000000e
770da9bd: ntdll!_RtlUserThreadStart+0x00000023
```

## Low Fragmentation Heap and Processor Affinity

In Chapter 6, "Memory Corruptions—Part II" we described how the look aside front end allocator works. As multiprocessor systems became more and more common, the look aside front end suffered a performance hit in the form of cross processor synchronization. If multiple processors accessed the look aside front end, all requesting the same size allocation, access to the look aside front end had to be synchronized (at the bus level), leading to a performance penalty being paid. To address the performance issue, the low fragmentation front end introduced the notion of subsegment processor affinity. The low fragmentation front end keeps a per-processor array of subsegments of specific sizes to avoid contention when manipulating the heap. When multiple processors access heap blocks contained within these subsegments, the heap blocks are managed in isolation; therefore, the chance of multiple processors accessing the same memory locations and cache lines concurrently is reduced.

To illustrate how the debuggers can be used to show information about a low-fragmentation heap, we use the !heap extension command with the −s and −a switches. The output of the !heap extension command when run on an instance of Internet Explorer 7.0 can be found in the following location:

```
C:\AWDBIN\Logs\heap.log
```

In the detailed segment section of the log file, you will find the list of heap blocks available in the segment. Some of the heap blocks with varied sizes are interleaved, whereas some (with the same size) are consecutive. When the output shows a list of same size consecutive heap blocks, the start of the list also shows the subsegment that those blocks are part of (including metadata). An example is shown here:

```
...
...
...
092b95b0   092b95b8   00c50000   09280000      208      208      8   busy
092b97b8   092b97c0   00c50000   09280000      208      208      8   busy
092b99c0   092b99c8   00c50000   09280000      208      208      8   busy
092b9bc8   092b9bd0   00c50000   09280000      208      208      8   busy
092b9dd0   092b9dd8   00c50000   09280000      208      208      8   busy
092b9fd8   092b9fe0   00c50000   09280000      208      208      8   busy
092ba1e0   092ba1e8   00c50000   09280000      208      208      8   busy
092ba3e8   092ba3f0   00c50000   09280000      208      208      8   busy
092ba5f0   092ba5f8   00c50000   09280000      208      208      8   busy
092ba7f8   092ba800   00c50000   09280000      208      208      8   busy
Sub-segment 092dbcd8
    User blocks:        0x092baa08
    Block size:         0x208
    Block count:        15
    Free blocks:        0
    Size index:         48
    Affinity index:     0
    Lock mask:          0x1
    Flags:              0x0
092baa18   092baa20   00c50000   092dbcd8      208      -       8   LFH;busy
092bac20   092bac28   00c50000   092dbcd8      208      -       8   LFH;busy
092bae28   092bae30   00c50000   092dbcd8      208      -       8   LFH;busy
092bb030   092bb038   00c50000   092dbcd8      208      -       8   LFH;busy
092bb238   092bb240   00c50000   092dbcd8      208      -       8   LFH;busy
092bb440   092bb448   00c50000   092dbcd8      208      -       8   LFH;busy
092bb648   092bb650   00c50000   092dbcd8      208      -       8   LFH;busy
092bb850   092bb858   00c50000   092dbcd8      208      -       8   LFH;busy
092bba58   092bba60   00c50000   092dbcd8      208      -       8   LFH;busy
092bbc60   092bbc68   00c50000   092dbcd8      208      -       8   LFH;busy
092bbe68   092bbe70   00c50000   092dbcd8      208      -       8   LFH;busy
092bc070   092bc078   00c50000   092dbcd8      208      -       8   LFH;busy
092bc278   092bc280   00c50000   092dbcd8      208      -       8   LFH;busy
092bc480   092bc488   00c50000   092dbcd8      208      -       8   LFH;busy
092bc688   092bc690   00c50000   092dbcd8      208      -       8   LFH;busy
...
...
...
```

The preceding metadata shows a subsegment with 15 blocks in it of size 0x208 bytes. Following the metadata is the list of heap blocks in that subsegment. As you can see, each block is 0x208 bytes in size and is marked with the LFH to indicate that it is indeed a low-fragmentation heap block.

As you can see, the Windows Vista heap manager has gone through a major face lift. Problems related to security and performance have been greatly improved by the new low-fragmentation front end allocator. The !heap extension command has been updated to work seamlessly with the new heap structures, making it easy to investigate the heap in depth. As more and more applications venture into the Vista space, it will become increasingly important to understand how the new heap works in order to effectively debug applications running on Windows Vista.

# Chapter 7—Security

Without a doubt, Windows Vista introduced unprecedented changes in the security options available to the user. The security model defined in Windows NT has been carried over and enhanced to support the new options, but it remains fully backward compatible. The new security options can be switched on and off, as needed. Windows Vista default settings should meet most application expectations because those defaults are the result of countless hours of application compatibility testing. On rare occasions when one application does not run as expected, the engineers developing a Vista-compatible application should know the significant changes in this space, how to identify them, and their effect on the application. This section is limited to significant changes visible to the engineer debugging an application that has security problems.

The most visible aspect of the new security options is the User Account Control feature already encountered in previous sections. To understand this feature, it is necessary to understand the concepts behind the feature.

Each running process performs at one of the integrity levels shown in Table 15.2, determined based on a multitude of facts. The integrity level is identified by a SID, as is any other principal on Window Vista. The integrity levels use a new identifier authority having the value {0,0,0,0,0,16}. The relative identifiers (RIDs) corresponding to those integrity levels are, starting at low integrity levels, as follows: 0x1000, 0x2000, 0x3000, and 0x4000.

**Table 15.2**   Windows Vista Integrity Levels

| Integrity Level Name | Integrity Level Identifier | Examples of Applications Running at Level |
|---|---|---|
| System | S-1-16-16384 | Svchost.exe<br>Winlogon.exe<br>Windows Kernel |
| High | S-1-16-12288 | mmc.exe<br>setup.exe |
| Medium | S-1-16-8196 | explorer.exe<br>ieuser.exe |
| Low | S-1-16-4096 | iexplore.exe |

What is the purpose of each integrity level, and how does the system decide what integrity level it should choose for each process? Some of the factors used in this evaluation are as follows:

- Windows Vista always runs the Windows services process and the kernel code at the system integrity level.
- The tools requesting administrative privileges are specially recognized by the operating system from their application manifest. An example of the manifest requesting a high integrity level is shown in Listing 15.9. The system also uses other heuristics to determine the required integrity level. For example, any application called setup.exe always starts at a high integrity level.
- The applications used to perform daily tasks, such as word processors, spreadsheet applications, or e-mail software run at the medium integrity level. One way to look at the processes running at the medium integrity level is to consider them as processes started by a normal user, without administrative privileges.
- To prevent the spread of Internet malware, Internet Explorer runs at a low integrity level. Currently, Internet Explorer is the only application using the lowest integrity level.

**Listing 15.9**   The application manifest requesting a high integrity level

```
<?xml version="1.0" encoding="UTF-8" standalone="yes"?>
<assembly xmlns="urn:schemas-microsoft-com:asm.v1" manifestVersion="1.0">
  <assemblyIdentity version="1.0.0.0" processorArchitecture="X86" name="Application"
```

```
type="win32"/>
  <description>Application descriptions</description>
  <trustInfo xmlns="urn:schemas-microsoft-com:asm.v3">
    <security>
      <requestedPrivileges>
        <requestedExecutionLevel level="requireAdministrator" uiAccess="false"/>
      </requestedPrivileges>
      </security>
  </trustInfo>
</assembly>
```

The processes are grouped by their integrity level, and the interaction between two processes running at different integrity levels is controlled by the operating system. The kernel objects created by the processes running at one integrity level cannot be accessed by default by processes running at a lower integrity level.

In addition, the User Interface Privilege Isolation (UIPI) feature controls the flow of Windows messages between processes running at different integrity levels. By default, a process can send Windows messages only to processes running at the same or lower integrity levels.

Both restrictions can be overridden using different techniques. The object creator can adjust the security descriptor protecting the kernel objects to make them accessible by the processes running at lower integrity levels.

An application can demand bypassing UIPI by setting the uiAccess flag to true in the application manifest. Such an application must be Microsoft Authenticode signed and be in a protected location, such as `%systemdrive%\Program Files` and `%systemdrive%\Windows\System32` to start properly.

## User Access Control

User Access Control (UAC) changes how the members of local administrators groups run their applications. UAC can be enabled by using the Local Security Policy snap-in, as shown in Figure 15.6.

In Windows XP, the local administrator members run all their applications under their context, having full administrative privileges. Any vulnerability in any of the applications used by the administrators can be exploited, with severe implications for the whole system. The exploited vulnerability can allow a silent installation of other components on the system, a silent change of the registry and files permission, or performance of administrative tasks.

15. WINDOWS VISTA FUNDAMENTALS

Local security policy snap-in    Local policy    Admin approval policy entry

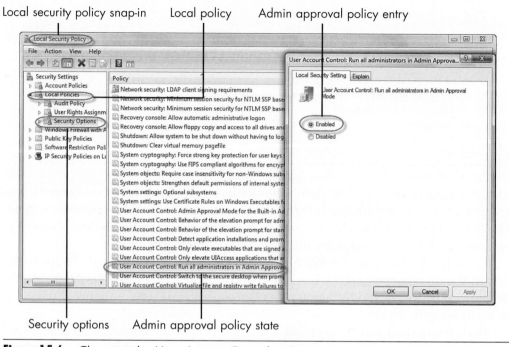

Security options    Admin approval policy state

**Figure 15.6**   Changing the User Access Control setting

In Windows Vista, the local administrator's members run the shell process at the medium integrity level when the UAC policy is set to run all administrators in Admin approval mode and in high integrity level when the policy is disabled.

Unless the administrator starts an application in administrative mode, as shown in Figure 15.2, every new application started from shell inherits shell's integrity level. If the system detects that the application needs additional privileges, as defined in the application manifest or determined by the system heuristics defined in the local security policy, it prompts the administrator for consent in a dialog window similar to the one shown in Figure 15.7.

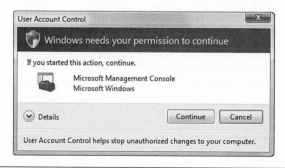

**Figure 15.7**   Elevation consent prompt

After selecting the Continue button, the system starts the application under full administrative privileges, similar to previous operating system versions. Consent behavior is controlled from the same snap-in used to enable UAC.

## UAC in Debugger

When investigating security failures related to UAC, we start by understanding the role of all actors in the failure. As with any other security failure, a UAC failure follows the same pattern: One entity requests access to an object protected by a gatekeeper that uses the object security descriptor to deny access to that object. Listing 15.10 is not a result of debugging a failure case. It displays the security token used by the process running a system process and the security descriptor protecting the process object, illustrating how a mandatory integrity level applies to the kernel object.

**Listing 15.10**   Examine one process running at system integrity level

```
kd> * Use !process extension command to get the process token
kd> !process 0 1 wininit.exe
PROCESS 82e59888  SessionId: 0  Cid: 01cc    Peb: 7ffd5000  ParentCid: 0198
   DirBase: 11d85000  ObjectTable: 8c65ff38  HandleCount:  93.
   Image: wininit.exe
   VadRoot 82efb180 Vads 53 Clone 0 Private 227. Modified 156. Locked 2.
   DeviceMap 84403128
   Token                          8c6651d8
...
   CommitCharge                   294
kd> * Use !token extension command to dump token information.
kd> * Integrity level is the last group in the token
kd> !token 8c6651d8
_TOKEN 8c6651d8
TS Session ID: 0
User: S-1-5-18
Groups:
 00 S-1-5-32-544
    Attributes - Default Enabled Owner
 01 S-1-1-0
    Attributes - Mandatory Default Enabled
 02 S-1-5-11
    Attributes - Mandatory Default Enabled
 03 S-1-16-16384
    Attributes - GroupIntegrity GroupIntegrityEnabled
Primary Group: S-1-5-18
Privs:
 03 0x000000003 SeAssignPrimaryTokenPrivilege    Attributes -
```

*(continues)*

**Listing 15.10** Examine one process running at system integrity level *(continued)*

```
...
 35 0x000000023 SeCreateSymbolicLinkPrivilege    Attributes - Enabled Default
Authentication ID:          (0,3e7)
Impersonation Level:     Anonymous
TokenType:               Primary
Source: *SYSTEM*         TokenFlags: 0x800 ( Token in use )
Token ID: 6c01           ParentToken ID: 0
Modified ID:             (0, 6a7a)
RestrictedSidCount: 0    RestrictedSids: 00000000
OriginatingLogonSession: 0
kd> * What is the security of system-integrity level objects?
kd> * The process object is a perfect example to illustrate it
kd> !sd poi(82e59888-4)&FFFFFFF8
->Revision: 0x1
->Sbz1    : 0x0
->Control : 0x8814
            SE_DACL_PRESENT
            SE_SACL_PRESENT
            SE_SACL_AUTO_INHERITED
            SE_SELF_RELATIVE
->Owner   : S-1-5-32-544
->Group   : S-1-5-18
->Dacl    :
->Dacl    : ->AclRevision: 0x2
->Dacl    : ->Sbz1       : 0x0
->Dacl    : ->AclSize    : 0x3c
->Dacl    : ->AceCount   : 0x2
->Dacl    : ->Sbz2       : 0x0
->Dacl    : ->Ace[0]: ->AceType: ACCESS_ALLOWED_ACE_TYPE
->Dacl    : ->Ace[0]: ->AceFlags: 0x0
->Dacl    : ->Ace[0]: ->AceSize: 0x14
->Dacl    : ->Ace[0]: ->Mask : 0x001fffff
->Dacl    : ->Ace[0]: ->SID: S-1-5-18

...
->Sacl    :
->Sacl    : ->AclRevision: 0x2
->Sacl    : ->Sbz1       : 0x0
->Sacl    : ->AclSize    : 0x1c
->Sacl    : ->AceCount   : 0x1
->Sacl    : ->Sbz2       : 0x0
->Sacl    : ->Ace[0]: ->AceType: SYSTEM_MANDATORY_LABEL_ACE_TYPE
->Sacl    : ->Ace[0]: ->AceFlags: 0x0
->Sacl    : ->Ace[0]: ->AceSize: 0x14
->Sacl    : ->Ace[0]: ->Mask : 0x00000003
->Sacl    : ->Ace[0]: ->SID: S-1-16-16384
```

The integrity level is present in the process token as a special group, the third group having the system-integrity level SID value S-1-16-16384. Each object that must be accessible only to users running at a specific integrity level has the access encoded as an ACE entry in the SACL part of the object security descriptor. Unlike the access checks based on the group membership—where the permission is evaluated by testing each SID from the token against the matching SID from the security descriptor— the mandatory system integrity level is tested taking into account the relative order of mandatory integrity levels. SYSTEM integrity level is highest, followed by HIGH, MEDIUM, and LOW. When the token used to access the resource runs at a lower level than the object integrity level, SYSTEM_MANDATORY_LABEL_ACE_TYPE flags control further access. In Listing 15.10, the flags are interpreted as follows:

```
0x03 = SYSTEM_MANDATORY_LABEL_NO_WRITE_UP | SYSTEM_MANDATORY_LABEL_NO_READ_UP
```

In this case, the object is not accessible to any user on the system except the LocalSystem principal. Listing 15.11 shows the same analysis for a process running under an account part of local administrator group, with UAC policy enabled.

**Listing 15.11**   Examine the explorer.exe process running at medium integrity level (UAC)

```
kd> !process 0 1 explorer.exe
PROCESS 901674f0  SessionId: 1  Cid: 0c04    Peb: 7ffd7000  ParentCid: 09cc
    DirBase: 0a53e000  ObjectTable: 8f55b850  HandleCount: 599.
    Image: explorer.exe
    VadRoot 82ec6428 Vads 337 Clone 0 Private 3112. Modified 27217. Locked 0.
    DeviceMap 927fb4f8
    Token                        9256d890
...
kd> !token 9256d890
_TOKEN 9256d890
TS Session ID: 0x1
User: S-1-5-21-2084298851-3655559499-3523964647-1000
Groups:
 00 S-1-5-21-2084298851-3655559499-3523964647-513
    Attributes - Mandatory Default Enabled
 01 S-1-1-0
    Attributes - Mandatory Default Enabled
 02 S-1-5-32-544
    Attributes - DenyOnly
...
 10 S-1-16-8192
    Attributes - GroupIntegrity GroupIntegrityEnabled
Primary Group: S-1-5-21-2084298851-3655559499-3523964647-513
```

*(continues)*

**Listing 15.11**   Examine the explorer.exe process running at medium integrity level (UAC) *(continued)*

```
Privs:
 19 0x000000013 SeShutdownPrivilege            Attributes -
 23 0x000000017 SeChangeNotifyPrivilege        Attributes - Enabled Default
 25 0x000000019 SeUndockPrivilege              Attributes -
 33 0x000000021 SeIncreaseWorkingSetPrivilege  Attributes -
 34 0x000000022 SeTimeZonePrivilege            Attributes -
Authentication ID:        (0,9ec99)
Impersonation Level:      Anonymous
TokenType:                Primary
Source: User32            TokenFlags: 0xa00 ( Token in use )
Token ID: a2c7b           ParentToken ID: 9ec9c
Modified ID:              (0, 173021)
RestrictedSidCount: 0     RestrictedSids: 00000000
OriginatingLogonSession: 3e7


kd> !sd poi(901674f0-4) & 0xFFFFFFF8
->Revision: 0x1
->Sbz1    : 0x0
->Control : 0x8814
            SE_DACL_PRESENT
            SE_SACL_PRESENT
            SE_SACL_AUTO_INHERITED
            SE_SELF_RELATIVE
->Owner   : S-1-5-21-2084298851-3655559499-3523964647-1000
->Group   : S-1-5-21-2084298851-3655559499-3523964647-513
...

->Sacl    :
->Sacl    : ->AclRevision: 0x2
->Sacl    : ->Sbz1       : 0x0
->Sacl    : ->AclSize    : 0x1c
->Sacl    : ->AceCount   : 0x1
->Sacl    : ->Sbz2       : 0x0
->Sacl    : ->Ace[0]: ->AceType: SYSTEM_MANDATORY_LABEL_ACE_TYPE
->Sacl    : ->Ace[0]: ->AceFlags: 0x0
->Sacl    : ->Ace[0]: ->AceSize: 0x14
->Sacl    : ->Ace[0]: ->Mask : 0x00000003
->Sacl    : ->Ace[0]: ->SID: S-1-16-8192
```

The explorer's process token has a medium integrity level in this case, and the process token is restricted to an integrity level equal to or higher than medium. Furthermore, the third SID in the process token is a restricted SID having the role of denying access to the resources accessible only to that restricted SID, Local Administrators represented by S-1-5-32-544 in this case. It is important to mention that the restricted SID concept is not new. Restricted SIDs are used in down-level platforms by applications using restricted tokens.

The integrity level can be, and is, applied to resources managed by other entities, such as the file system or registry keys. The integrity level is not exposed in the usual places used to change the security on such resources. The operating system installs a new integrity-level-aware tool, icalcs.exe, that supersedes cacls.exe. icacls.exe displays or changes the integrity level of any file by using the setintegritylevel option with the desired integrity level. However, the tool does not allow fine-tuning of the access allowed to lower integrity users, and it always uses the SYSTEM_MANDATORY_LABEL_NO_WRITE_UP flag. Listing 15.12 checks the security on one of the sample files, changes its integrity level, and rechecks its security descriptor. The new mandatory integrity level is set to medium, no write up.

**Listing 15.12**  Changing file integrity level using built in icacls.exe tool

```
C:\>icacls c:\AWDBIN\WinXP.x86.chk\01sample.exe
c:\AWDBIN\WinXP.x86.chk\01sample.exe BUILTIN\Administrators:(I)(F)
                           NT AUTHORITY\SYSTEM:(I)(F)
                           BUILTIN\Users:(I)(RX)


C:\>icacls c:\AWDBIN\WinXP.x86.chk\01sample.exe /setintegritylevel M
processed file: c:\AWDBIN\WinXP.x86.chk\01sample.exe
Successfully processed 1 files; Failed processing 0 files


C:\>icacls c:\AWDBIN\WinXP.x86.chk\01sample.exe
c:\AWDBIN\WinXP.x86.chk\01sample.exe BUILTIN\Administrators:(I)(F)
                           NT AUTHORITY\SYSTEM:(I)(F)
                           BUILTIN\Users:(I)(RX)
                           Mandatory Label\Medium Mandatory Level:(NW)


Successfully processed 1 files; Failed processing 0 files
```

15. WINDOWS VISTA FUNDAMENTALS

## Registry and File Virtualization

This section addresses a more subtle problem encountered when running a nontrivial application in Windows Vista. The sample used in Chapter 7, "Security," demonstrates how the application can fail when moved to the new operating system. The sample has an option to save some data in two protected locations—the HKEY_LOCAL_MACHINE\Software registry key and the C:\Program Files folder—and another option to read this data. The scenario is common for any application that uses global settings, configurable through an MMC snap-in. The application creates the configuration information by pressing the '4' key and verifies the configuration by pressing the '5' key.

The next two listings simulate the preceding situation. Listing 15.13 shows the application that required administrative privileges in Windows XP and now runs flawlessly in the UAC context.

**Listing 15.13**  Setting and retrieving application settings from UAC administrator

```
c:\>c:\AWDBIN\WinXP.x86.chk\07sample.exe
Press:
    0       To use Security Descriptor APIs
    1       To run Impersonation test
    2       To run Default SD test
    3       To run MAXIMUM_ALLOWED test
    4       To set application configuration information
    5       To read application configuration information
    x       To exit
> Creating application settings ...
Registry key HKEY_LOCAL_MACHINE\Software\Advanced Windows Debugging created
Create file C:\Program Files\sample4.test
Creating application done.

> Retrieving application settings ...
Registry key HKEY_LOCAL_MACHINE\Software\Advanced Windows Debugging found
Create file C:\Program Files\sample4.test found
Retrieving application done.
```

Listing 15.14 simulates the application configuration whose functionality is usually hosted within an MMC snap-in. Because MMC.EXE prompts for elevation at startup, the application used in Listing 15.14 has also been started from an elevated prompt, obtained as shown in Figure 15.2.

**Listing 15.14**   Retrieving application settings from an elevated prompt

```
c:\>c:\AWDBIN\WinXP.x86.chk\07sample.exe
Press:
   0      To use Security Descriptor APIs
   1      To run Impersonation test
   2      To run Default SD test
   3      To run MAXIMUM_ALLOWED test
   4      To set application configuration information
   5      To read application configuration information
   x      To exit
> Retrieving application settings ...
RegOpenKeyW failed.Last error = 2
CreateFile failed with:Last error = 2
Retrieving application done.
```

Even if the application can find the configuration while it runs in the UAC context, in Listing 15.14, the application is unable to retrieve any information from the global store.

The registry and file virtualization feature—which has been added to Windows Vista to fix, for a limited time, applications that require administrative privileges—causes the error encountered in this case. This feature is enabled by default, but it can be disabled using the Local Security Policy snap-in used to control UAC behavior, as seen in Figure 15.6. It is not recommended that you disable the virtualization because all existing virtual files or registry keys are lost afterward.

The virtualized files are stored in the user profile, in a folder structure similar to the system folder structure, located in `%USERPROFILE%\AppData\Local\VirtualStore`. This folder tree structure is as follows:

```
C:\>tree %USERPROFILE%\AppData\Local\VirtualStore /a
Folder PATH listing for volume New Volume
Volume serial number is 5C50-0187
C:\USERS\DANIEL\APPDATA\LOCAL\VIRTUALSTORE
+--Program Files
|   +--Common Files
|   \--SmartFTP Client 2.0
|       \--Minidump
\--Windows
    \--Debug
        \--UserMode
```

The virtualized registries are stored in the current user profile in a registry structure similar to the registry hierarchy, under the HKEY_CURRENT_USER\Software\ Classes\VirtualStore key. The command-line tool reg.exe is handy for searching for the key location using a command line as in the following listing:

```
C:\>reg query HKCU /s /k /f "Advanced Debugging"
HKEY_CURRENT_USER\Software\Classes\VirtualStore\MACHINE\SOFTWARE\Advanced Debugging
End of search: 1 match(es) found.
```

Because the applications running at elevated mode are not subject to virtualization, they will have a different view of the system compared to the application running under UAC. Windows Vista virtualization affects all tools using Windows registry as the configuration store. The tool should run elevated or not as needed. For example, to enable Application Verifier on an MMC snap-in, we need to run Application Verifier elevated because MMC.EXE always runs elevated. Otherwise, the configuration tool updates the virtual registry key, which is not used when the application starts in elevated mode. The virtualization state is visible in the Windows Task Manager under the Visualization column in the Processes tab, as shown in Figure 15.8. The column can be enabled using View followed by the Select columns menu command.

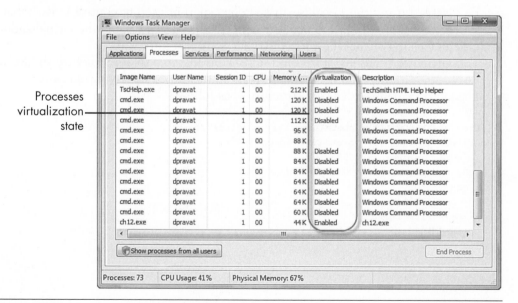

**Figure 15.8**   Viewing process virtualization

Applications such as cmd.exe or reg.exe are not subject to virtualization because they have an application manifest specifying a requestedExecutionLevel in their manifests, as shown in Listing 15.9.

Native x86-64 applications are not virtualized and will fail under a UAC account in the same way they failed on Windows XP, when running under the standard user account. This provides the motivation for writing applications that does not require administrative privileges to work properly. This enforcement has a minimal impact on the applications' compatibility, as the number of x86-64 applications is still small.

**WHY ARE APPLICATIONS NOT WORKING UNDER A STANDARD USER ACCOUNT?** Some applications write on locations protected by the operating system default security settings. To write into those locations, the applications must run under a local administrator account. Applications keeping their configurable setting in the installation folder or in a global registry hive, such as HKEY_LOCAL_MACHINE, are the common failure cases.

The easiest way to find those failures is testing the application under Application Verifier, as described in Chapter 1, "Introduction to the Tools." Another simple tool to evaluate this application behavior is the Microsoft Standard User Analyzer tool, available as a free download on Microsoft's Web site.

Fixing the application, during the development phase is the quickest and the most efficient solution to those problems. As a positive side effect, the application is one step closer to being able to obtain the Certified for Windows Vista logo.

To find out all processes that are not meeting the standards for Windows Vista certification, a simple check of the virtual file and registry locations will most likely reveal them.

Besides the security changes made with the intent of creating the "most secure version of Windows yet," Windows Vista introduced other security changes designed to prevent tampering with so-called protected processes. A protected processes, usually a hosting media playback application, offer a higher degree of protection from tampering, especially when it uses media protected with DRM technologies. Although the changes supporting protected process are implemented deeply in the kernel, they are manifesting themselves in the inability to debug such processes. Microsoft MSDN has several whitepapers describing the protected process and the future of developments in this area.

You learned in this section what is behind security changes implemented in Windows Vista and the effect those changes have on software applications. Furthermore, you learned the mechanisms to extract detailed information from the failing system, failure caused by those security changes.

15. WINDOWS VISTA FUNDAMENTALS

## Chapter 8—Interprocess Communication

The changes introduced by Windows Vista in the interprocess communication area are restricted to the boundaries of a single physical system. Because the computers running Windows Vista must work seamlessly in a heterogeneous network, network-observable behavior is similar to previous operating system behavior, and all techniques based on interpreting the network traffic are still applicable. However, the communication model between various components within the same physical system has been changed. The Lightweight Procedure Call (LPC) protocol has been replaced with the new Advanced Lightweight Procedure Call (ALPC) protocol, which is the foundation for other protocols.

### RPC and DCOM Protocol Changes

All the protocols built on top of ALPC have been changed to take advantage of the new communication paradigms. DCOM and RPC have been also enhanced in the reliability and manageability area.

To improve the RPC debugging capability, its development team introduced two tracing channels. In the Microsoft-Windows-Rpcss-EndpointMapper/Debug channel, the RPC infrastructure records each interface that is registered or unregistered with the EndpointMapper. The Microsoft-Windows-RPC/EEInfo channel collects the error generated by the RPC infrastructure as described in Chapter 8, in the section "RPC Extended Error Information."

As part of management improvements, DCOM has a tracing channel, Microsoft-Windows-COM/Analytic, that can capture events generated by the infrastructure. However, at the time of writing, no information about how to enable this channel or how to interpret the events generated in this log was available.

## Chapter 9—Resource Leaks

In Chapter 9, we discussed a number of different tools and strategies for tracking down resource leaks. Two types of resource leaks were discussed: handles and memory. Handles, as seen from a debugging perspective, behave the same in Windows Vista (that is, the !htrace extension command is fully functional), whereas heap memory has dramatically changed to improve performance and security. Even though the heap manager has changed, some of the leak-detection tools can still be used to track down memory leaks. The two primary tools discussed in Chapter 9 are LeakDiag and UMDH. Unfortunately, at the time of this writing, LeakDiag does not work on Windows Vista, although UMDH can be used as an alternative.

# Chapter 10—Synchronization

In Chapter 10, "Synchronization," we discussed the most commonly used thread synchronization primitives available in Windows. Critical sections, events, mutants, and so on have all been part of the Windows operating system for quite some time. With the advent of Windows Vista, the synchronization capabilities have been extended to include a range of new features. Specifically, the following new synchronization primitives have been introduced:

- Slim reader/writer lock
- Condition variables
- One-time initialization
- Improved thread pool

In this part of the chapter, we take a brief look at the new synchronization features available in Windows Vista.

## Slim Reader/Writer Lock

A reader/writer lock is a synchronization construct commonly used when addressing concurrent access to a shared resource in which multiple concurrent readers are allowed, but writers acquire exclusive ownership of the resource. Although read/write access to a shared resource can be easily solved by using one of the existing synchronization primitives (such as a critical section or a mutex), the benefit of a reader/writer lock is when there is a fairly large number of readers and relatively few writers. In this scenario, using a critical section can be suboptimal because a critical section only allows exclusive access to a shared resource, regardless of whether all the threads trying to get access to the resource are reader threads. The means by which the new reader/writer lock distinguishes between reader and writer lock access is by introducing two lock modes:

- Exclusive: Grants exclusive access to the shared resource. No other thread can access the resource while a thread has exclusive access to a lock. Writer threads typically request exclusive access.
- Shared: Grants shared access to the resource, enabling multiple concurrent threads to read the data protected by the lock. Reader threads typically request shared access.

As with any synchronization construct, fairness is an important aspect. It is important to note that the new reader/writer lock in Windows Vista does not observe fairness.

Table 15.3 lists the new reader/write locks in Windows Vista.

**Table 15.3**   Reader/Writer Lock API(s)

| API | Description |
| --- | --- |
| InitializeSRWLock | Initializes the simple reader/writer lock. The data structure used to represent a reader writer lock is of type SRWLOCK. |
| AcquireSRWLockExclusive | Acquires a reader/writer lock in exclusive mode, indicating that no other threads are allowed to access the lock. An example of this would be for a writer to acquire exclusive access to the lock. |
| AcquireSRWLockShared | Acquires a reader/writer lock in shared mode, indicating that other threads are allowed to access the lock. An example of this would be for a reader to acquire shared access to the lock. |
| ReleaseSRWLockExclusive | Releases a reader/writer lock previously acquired in exclusive mode. |
| ReleaseSRWLockShared | Releases a reader/writer lock previously acquired in shared mode. |

Debugging reader/writer locks can prove to be a challenging task mainly because of the limited amount of bookkeeping associated with the lock. The definition of the SRWLOCK is shown in the following:

```
typedef struct _RTL_SRWLOCK {
        PVOID Ptr;
}
```

As you can see, the contents of the lock are minimal and contain only a pointer to a VOID type. Contrast this definition with that of the critical section, which contains a whole slew of information, such as owning thread, lock count, recursion count, and so on. Even though limited information is available with a reader/writer lock, the debugging process is similar to that of other synchronization constructs.

## Condition Variables

A condition variable is a new synchronization construct introduced in Windows Vista. A condition variable always works in conjunction with either a critical section or a slim reader/writer lock. The basic idea behind a condition variable is that it allows threads to wait until a particular condition occurs. The wait is performed with a three-step atomic operation:

1. Release the lock associated with the condition variable.
2. Enter a wait state.
3. Once woken up, reacquires the lock associated with the condition variable.

The functions associated with condition variables are illustrated in Table 15.4.

**Table 15.4**   Condition Variable API(s)

| API | Description |
| --- | --- |
| InitializeConditionVariable | Initializes a condition variable. |
| SleepConditionVariableCS | Waits on a condition variable and releases the specified critical section as an atomic operation. |
| SleepConditionVariableSRW | Waits on a condition variable and releases the specified slim reader/writer lock as an atomic operation. |
| WakeAllConditionVariable | Wakes up all threads waiting on the specified condition variable. |
| WakeConditionVariable | Wakes a single thread waiting on the specified condition variable. |

Similar to the new slim reader/writer lock, the definition of a condition variable (CONDITION_VARIABLE type) is relatively simple in nature, as shown in the following:

```
typedef struct _RTL_CONDITION_VARIABLE {
        PVOID Ptr;
}
```

15. WINDOWS VISTA FUNDAMENTALS

## One-Time Initialization

It is often necessary for the code to perform one-time initialization work. In a single-threaded environment, it is typically not a difficult chore to achieve, but in a multi-threaded environment, ensuring that the object is constructed only once requires some work. To make it easier for developers requiring one-time initialization in a multi-threaded environment, Windows Vista introduced APIs that help developers take the pain out of the initialization code. Table 15.5 shows the function associated with one-time initialization.

**Table 15.5** One-Time Initialization API(s)

| API | Description |
| --- | --- |
| InitOnceBeginInitialize | Begins one-time initialization. |
| InitOnceComplete | Completes one-time initialization. |
| InitOnceExecuteOnce | Executes the specified initialization function once. No other threads specifying the same one-time initialization structure can execute while the current thread is executing. |
| InitOnceInitialize | Initializes a one-time initialization structure. |

The fundamental data type behind one-time initialization is the INIT_ONCE structure shown in the following:

```
typedef RTL_RUN_ONCE INIT_ONCE;
typedef union _RTL_RUN_ONCE {
    PVOID Ptr;
}
```

## Improved Thread Pool

The thread pool in Windows Vista has gone through a major face-lift. In fact, the thread pool has been rewritten from the ground up to make it more reliable and intrinsically provide many features missing from prior versions of Windows. Here are a few examples of new features added to the Windows Vista thread pool:

- Multiple pools per process
- Cancellation of work
- Automatic cleanup (including releasing of locks)
- Configurable maximum and minimum number of threads

# Chapter 11—Writing Custom Debugger Extensions

Unless you are writing a custom debugger extension that requires Windows Vista specific functionality, you will not need to do anything different. If, however, you are writing a Windows Vista-specific extension, you will need to ensure that the build window in which you choose to build the extension is a Windows Vista build window. This can be done by installing the WDK and choosing the Windows Vista and Windows Longhorn Server build window from the Windows Driver Kits menu item in the Start menu.

In general, it is recommended that debugger extensions are versioned according to the operating system version that they work on. If you look at the debugger extensions that ship with Debugging Tools for Windows, you will see several subdirectories, each representing a particular version of the operating system. Within each of the subdirectories, you can find the debugger extensions requiring that particular Windows version. If, however, you are developing an extension that does not depend on any specific version of Windows, you can simply build one, and the same extension works across multiple Windows versions. The only caveat to this approach is to make sure that the extension is built for the lowest common denominator to ensure that it loads in later versions of Windows.

# Chapter 13—Postmortem Debugging

Postmortem debugging is an important part of an engineer's work. In versions prior to Windows Vista, the fundamental component enabling postmortem data collection was Dr. Watson. Anytime a crash or a hang occurred, Dr. Watson would be invoked to collect postmortem data (in the form of a log file and dump file).

In Windows Vista, Dr. Watson has been retired in favor of a more reliable architecture. Previously, the mechanism by which Dr. Watson was invoked involved an unhandled exception filter that wrapped all the threads executing within a process. When a thread faulted and the exception filter was executed, it launched the Dr. Watson process (via the CreateProcess API) to do error reporting. This approach worked well, but there were certain situations in which complications arose. An example of such a complication was the case when a thread stack has been exhausted or smashed. In that situation, the exception filter might or might not run correctly, depending on the state of the stack. In order to make error reporting in Windows Vista more reliable, the architecture of collecting postmortem data was changed. Figure 15.9 illustrates the new postmortem architecture in Windows Vista.

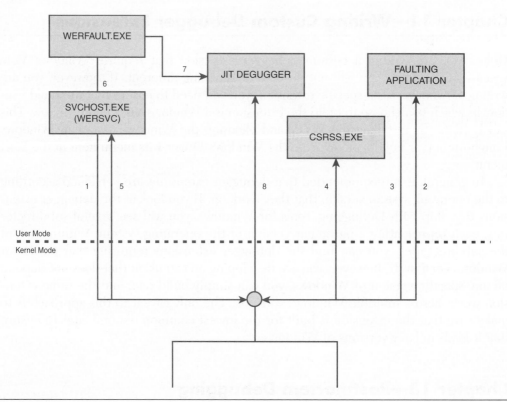

**Figure 15.9** Windows Vista postmortem architecture

When Windows Vista boots, a new service called WERSVC is loaded into a service host and registers a port with the kernel (step 1). The port serves as the communication channel between the kernel and the failures in user mode. When a fault occurs in a user-mode process, the kernel is the first component to see the exception. Because a user-mode application should have the chance of handling first-chance exceptions, the kernel simply routes the exception to the faulting user-mode process (step 2). If the user-mode process cannot handle the exception (an unhandled exception), the try/catch block around the user-mode thread simply returns EXCEPTION_CONTINUE_SEARCH back to the kernel, indicating that it was an unhandled exception (step 3) and that the kernel should continue looking for other components that might be willing to handle the exception. The kernel once again forwards the exception to any associated exception ports for the faulting process. For Win32 processes, all exceptions are routed to the CSRSS process (Win32 subsystem), which in turn returns EXCEPTION_CONTINUE_SEARCH (step 4). At that point, the kernel calls WERSVC service (through an error port in step 5) with associated fault information (such as process identifier, thread identifier, and exception parameters). In turn, the WERSVC component invokes the WERFAULT.EXE process (step 6), which checks to see if it should invoke a Just In Time (JIT) debugger. If a JIT debugger is enabled, the WERFAULT.EXE process launches the debugger and attaches it to the faulting process (step 7). Subsequently, the WERFAULT.EXE process returns a status to kernel mode, indicating that a JIT debugger was launched, and the kernel dispatches the exception to the debugger (step 8). If a JIT debugger was not enabled, the user is presented with an error dialog, allowing him to send an error report to Microsoft or debug the fault.

As you can see, by decoupling and delegating the error-handling responsibilities from the faulting user-mode process to kernel mode, we are no longer at the mercy of user-mode faults (such as stack exhaustion or stack smashing) that might cause the error handling logic to fail. This new architecture and process allow for very reliable error reporting that was previously not possible.

## Dump File Generation

In Chapter 13, we discussed the various ways that dump files can be generated. Windows Vista provides another convenient mechanism available via Task Manager. Right-clicking on a process in the Process tab of Task Manager allows you to select the Create Dump File context-menu item. Creating a dump file using this option creates a mini dump file with full memory information.

Another important change that occurred in Windows Vista is how the error-reporting technology saves dump files locally on the machine. Prior to Windows Vista, Dr. Watson stored generated dump files on the local machine by default. These dump files could be accessed by anyone wanting to debug a particular dump file. In Windows Vista, Dr. Watson has been retired in favor of a more reliable and robust error-reporting mechanism. As part of this change, dump files generated on a machine are not stored on the local machine (by default). To change the default behavior, you can set the ForceQueue registry setting to 1, which forces all dump files to be queued locally prior to being uploaded to Microsoft. The ForceQueue registry value is located in the following registry path:

```
HKEY_LOCAL_MACHINE\SOFTWARE\Microsoft\Windows\Windows Error
Reporting
```

After the ForceQueue registry value is set to 1, all dump files generated will be stored in the following location:

Processes running in system context or elevated:

```
%ALLUSERSPROFILE %\Microsoft\Windows\WER\ [ReportQueue |
ReportArchive]
```

All other processes:

```
%LOCALAPPDATA%\Microsoft\Windows\WER\ [ReportQueue |
ReportArchive]
```

In addition to improved reliability, Windows Vista introduced a set of new API(s) that enable applications to do much more than just trigger the standard error collection mechanism (upload of dump file). More specifically, applications can now programmatically upload custom data in addition to the dump file. The data can come in the form of custom log files, augmented memory dumps, and more. Table 15.6 details the new API(s).

**Table 15.6**  New Windows Error Reporting API(s)

| API Name | Description |
| --- | --- |
| WerAddExcludedApplication | Excludes a specified application from error reporting. |
| WerGetFlags | Retrieves the error by reporting settings for the specified process. |
| WerRegisterFile | Adds a file to the collection of files that can be added to reports generated for the current process. This is a very useful mechanism for adding custom files to the error-reporting process. |
| WerRegisterMemoryBlock | By default, error reporting only collects certain types of memory information. Sometimes it is necessary for processes to augment this information by adding memory dumps of custom memory regions. This API allows the caller to specify the starting address and size of the memory region to be included in the report. |
| WerRemoveExcludedApplication | Removes an application from being excluded from error reporting. |
| WerReportAddDump | Allows the caller to control what is added to the dump file generated during error reporting. |
| WerReportAddFile | Adds a file to the report that is being generated for the fault. |
| WerReportCloseHandle | Closes the specified report. |
| WerReportCreate | Creates a new report. |
| WerReportSetParameter | Sets the parameters of a report. |
| WerReportSetUIOption | Allows the caller to customize the UI that is displayed for a specific report. |
| WerReportSubmit | Submits the specified report. |
| WerSetFlags | Sets the error-reporting settings for the current process. |
| WerUnregisterFile | Removes a file from the collection of files to be added to the reports generated for the current process. |
| WerUnregisterMemoryBlock | Removes a memory block previously registered with the WerRegisterMemoryBlock API. |

The added reliability features as well as new functionality make Windows Vista an extremely powerful platform when it comes to diagnostics and postmortem analysis.

## Summary

Windows Vista represents the latest update to the Windows client family of operating systems. An incredible wealth of new features exist, ranging from exciting new applications to extensively enhanced reliability, robustness, and security features. It should come as no surprise that Windows Vista represents a big milestone in Windows operating system history and enables software developers to use all the new and exciting features when developing software.

Throughout the book, we have discussed specific debugging scenarios, and in this chapter, we detailed each of the scenarios and the differences encountered (as related to debugging) when running with Windows Vista. The discussion started with how the tools work under Windows Vista and then showed specific debugging scenarios related to a specific technology, such as security, heap manager, interprocess communication, and more.

# APPLICATION VERIFIER TEST SETTINGS

Throughout the book, we have used Application Verifier to find problems early in the development phase that otherwise would have been costly to repair. In addition to the test settings that we have used, Application Verifier includes a ton more test settings that can be used, depending on the problem at hand. This appendix serves as a reference to the available test settings.

## Exceptions

The name of this test setting is actually quite misleading. Although you might be led to think that this stop deals with all kinds of exception-related issues, it has only one stop in it. Specifically, it is a stop that allows you to break into the debugger as soon as a first-chance access violation exception occurs. This enables you to catch any first-chance access violations that might have been inadvertently caught by the application.

## Handles

Handles are used as an abstraction model to core operating system objects. One of the most common problems when working with handles is specifying the wrong handle value to the various APIs that accept them. This test setting checks for a variety of different handle problems, as illustrated by Table A.1. By default, all handle-related stop codes cause a break in the debugger if triggered.

**Table A.1**   Handle-Related Stop Codes

| Stop code | Test | Description |
|---|---|---|
| 00000300 | Invalid handles | Causes Application Verifier to stop execution when passing an invalid handle value to system routines. |
| 00000301 | Invalid Thread local storage (TSL) index | To retrieve thread local storage (TLS) data, you must pass in a TLS index value that corresponds to the storage location for the data. If you specify an invalid TLS index, Application Verifier stops execution. |
| 00000302 | Invalid parameters in calls to `WaitForMultipleObjects` | When a call to `WaitForMultipleObjects` is made, the caller needs to specify an array of handles to wait for, as well as the number of handles in the array. If either of those parameters is null or 0, Application Verifier stops execution. |
| 00000303 | null handle values | When a call to a system routine that accepts a handle as input is made with a null handle value, the debugger stops execution. |
| 00000304 | DllMain concurrency problems | If a thread that is currently executing code in DllMain is waiting for another thread handle, Application Verifier stops execution. The error is that the only way for the waiting thread to be signaled is by the executing thread to exit. When the executing thread terminates, it tries to call into the DllMain function with a `DLL_THREAD_DETACH` message. To do so, it must acquire the DLL loader lock. The acquisitions fail due to the first thread already owning the lock. The net result is a deadlock. |
| 00000305 | Invalid handle types | This stop is triggered when code calls into an API that expects a handle of a specific type but passes the wrong handle type instead. For example, calling `SetEvent` with a handle to a semaphore causes this stop to occur. |

# Heaps

The Heaps test setting contains some really powerful instrumentation to make life easier when trying to figure out heap-related problems. In addition to a wide range of verifier stops, the heaps test setting enables instrumentation on a per-heap block basis that includes heap block fill patterns, heap block guard pages, and stack tracing. The stack tracing capabilities are extremely useful, as they provide a historic view (via stack trace recording) of all the allocations and de-allocations made in a process.

The properties that are part of the heaps test setting are quite powerful and extensive. Figure A.1 illustrates the properties available by right-clicking on the heaps test setting and selecting the Properties menu item.

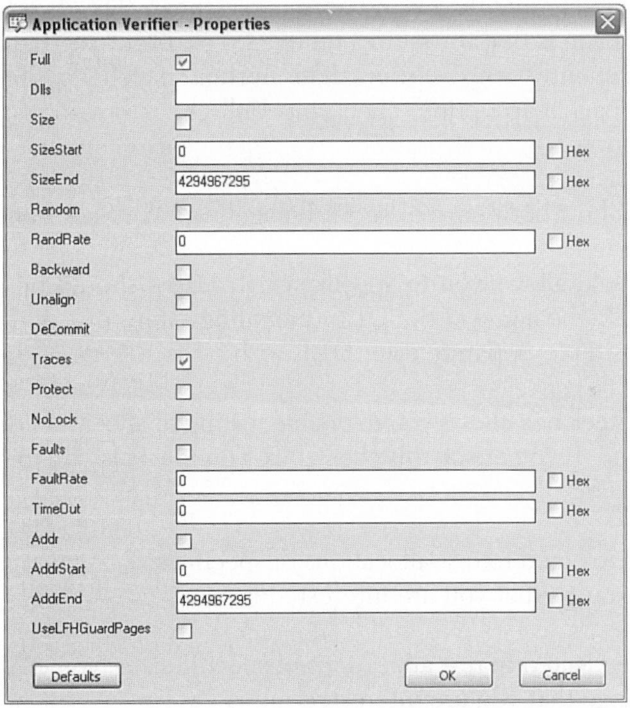

**Figure A.1**    Heaps properties window

Each of the configurable options is discussed in the following list:

- Full
  Heap instrumentation falls into two modes:
    - Normal pageheap: This pageheap option is a lighter version of the full heap instrumentation and does not detect heap-related problems as timely as full pageheap. The benefit in using this mode is that it runs faster and requires fewer resources. To run using normal pageheap, uncheck the Full check box in the Properties window.
    - Full pageheap: Full pageheap is the king of heap instrumentation. It has the capability to detect heap-related problems at the point of occurrence rather than postmortem and typically allows for easier debugging than using normal pageheap. The drawback of full pageheap is that it requires quite a lot of resources (memory) and subsequently runs slower than normal pageheap. To select the full pageheap option, check the Full check box in the Properties window.

  We discuss how both normal and full pageheap work later on this section.
- Dlls
  The Dlls field allows you to specify which DLLs should be part of the heap tests. Specify the name of the DLL (including extension), and if more than one DLL is desirable, separate each DLL with a space.
- Size
  The Size check box allows you to enable testing of allocation of a particular size or size range. If you check this check box, you must also fill in the SizeStart and SizeEnd fields.
- SizeStart
  If you have elected to test allocations of specific sizes, you must enter the start of the size range that you are interested in.
- SizeEnd
  If you have elected to test allocations of specific sizes, you can enter the end of the size range that you are interested in.
- Random
  This check box allows you to select whether to introduce a random factor in which instrumentation model is chosen for allocations. For example, checking this check box allows you to specify that you want some allocations made on the normal pageheap and some allocations made on the full pageheap. If you check this check box, you must also specify the random rate in the RandRate field.

- RandRate
  The RandRate field must be filled in if you also checked the Random check box. In this field, enter a value between 0 and 100 to indicate the probability of making allocations on the normal pageheap versus the full pageheap.
- Backward
  Typically, full pageheap guards against buffer overflows by placing guard pages at the end of each heap block. It is, however, also possible to detect buffer underrun problems by checking the Backward check box.
- Unalign
  Checking the Unalign check box generates allocations that are not aligned with the heap manager's allocation granularity. All heap-based allocations are made at the granularity level of the heap manager, depending on the architecture you are running on (8 bytes on x86 and 16 bytes on x64). Say, for example, that you allocated 5 bytes from the heap. The allocation returned to you is in actuality 8 bytes. The remaining 3 bytes are simply used as padding to align the allocation on the 8-byte allocation granularity. Checking the Unalign check box comes in handy when trapping heap block overruns. Because padding was added, overwriting these padding bytes will not cause an immediate break in the debugger (because a guard page was not there to trap it). To make sure that these overruns surface, the Unalign check box returns allocations that have not been padded to satisfy the heap manager's allocation granularity. Note that some components require that allocations be aligned on the heap manager's allocation granularities and will not work with the Unalign check box checked. (A great example is RPC.)
- DeCommit
  The DeCommit check box, if checked, decommits guard pages when no longer in use, which results in lower memory usage.
- Traces
  Checking the Traces check box causes the test setting to collect stack traces for allocations and deallocations. This check box is on by default and should be left on most of the time, as having the stack traces available when debugging heap-related problems can be a lifesaver.
- Protect
  If this check box is checked, the test setting protects internal heap structures from being corrupted. This can be used to detect random corruptions.
- NoLock
  If this check box is checked, the test setting will not do critical section verification.

- Faults
  If this check box is selected, the test setting enables heap fault injection. If you check this check box, you must also fill in the FaultRate and TimeOut fields.
- FaultRate
  If the Faults check box was checked, you must specify the probability of a fault occurring in the heap manager by specifying a value between 1 and 10,000.
- TimeOut
  If the Faults check box was checked, you can change the time (in milliseconds) during process initialization, where fault injection doesn't occur. This is almost always required, as fault injection during process initialization might prevent the process from starting.
- Addr
  This check box allows you to control the address range in which the test setting works. If you check this check box, you must also specify the AddrStart and AddrEnd fields.
- AddrStart
  The AddrStart field specifies the starting address of the range that the test setting works under.
- AddrEnd
  The AddrEnd field specifies the ending address of the range that the test setting works under.
- UseLFHGuardPages
  This check box, if checked, uses guard pages on the low-fragmentation heap. The low-fragmentation heap is a relatively new heap that was introduced in Windows 2003 Server and turned on by default in Windows Vista.

Before we move on and discuss the various stops available as part of the heap test setting, we need to take a closer look at the difference between normal and full pageheap.

The basic idea behind the normal pageheap setting is to try to catch some categories of heap-related problems by using a fill pattern on the heap blocks. When a heap allocation is made, the heap manager fills the entire allocation with an 'E0' fill pattern. If the allocated memory is not initialized properly and referenced, an access violation will most likely occur, as the application tries to use the contents of the allocated memory (filled with 'E0'). For example, if the allocation is supposed to contain a valid pointer (but does not because of failed initialization), the application might try to dereference 'E0E0,' which is not a valid address, and we will see an access violation. Subsequently, when an allocation is freed, the heap manager fills the allocation with the 'F0' fill pattern. Any attempt to use that allocation after it has been freed most likely also causes an access violation.

Both of these scenarios, memory usage without initialization and memory usage after freeing, are very common problems that plague developers daily.

A final note about fill patterns—in addition to filling the allocation with predefined patterns, Application Verifier prefixes and postfixes each allocated block with a predefined pattern. This can, in certain circumstances, help detect heap under- and overrun problems. Let's say that you had an application that allocated 1Kb of memory. The application populates that memory allocation with what it deems fit, and at times populates more than 1Kb of memory, essentially leading to a scenario in which the allocated block is too small to hold the data. If the application overruns the end of the allocation by a few bytes, the application might generate a fault when trying to use this invalid memory. This is by no means a guarantee to catch all invalid heap usage because you might write to any random memory locations, but it does catch some of the cases. The overall structure of fill patterns used by this test setting is shown in Figure A.2.

| Block Header Start Fill Pattern | BLOCK HEADER | Block Header End Fill Pattern | USER ALLOCATION FILL PATTERN | Post Allocation Fill Pattern |
|---|---|---|---|---|

**Figure A.2**   Fill patterns used by normal pageheap

The various parts of the block in Figure A.2 are shown in Table A.2.

**Table A.2**   Specific Fill Patterns Based on Initialized or Freed Heap Blocks

| Block Portion | Fill Pattern |
|---|---|
| Block Header Start Fill Pattern | If allocation is not initialized, filled with 0xABCDAAAA |
| | If allocation is freed, filled with 0xABCDAAA9 |
| Block Header | None |
| Block Header End Fill Pattern | If allocation is not initialized, filled with 0xDCBAAAAA |
| | If allocation is freed, filled with 0xDCBAAA9 |
| User Allocation Fill Pattern | If allocation is not initialized, filled with 0xE0 |
| | If allocation is freed, filled with 0xF0 |
| Post Allocation Fill Pattern | 0xA0A0A0A0 |

At the point of allocation, the heap manager fills the memory allocation with the correct fill pattern. Usage of the memory that contains fill patterns might or might not fail, depending on how the memory is used. If an application dereferences these fill patterns, an access violation occurs. If it simply overwrites the fill patterns with some data but does not dereference the data, an Application Verifier stop occurs. However, the Application Verifier stop only occurs at the point of deallocation because this is the only chance for Application Verifier to validate the integrity of the fill patterns. Although it's great that it can verify the integrity of the heap block by fill pattern checks, most of the time the damage has already been done, and it can be hard to backtrack and figure out the code path that caused the overwrite. Fortunately, there exists another type of pageheap, known as full pageheap, that is much more aggressive and causes an access violation at the point of misuse, thereby isolating the locality of the code at the point where it is misbehaving.

Full pageheap works by employing what are called guard pages that guard the allocation in question. Every time an allocation is performed, a page of inaccessible memory is added to the end of the allocation, causing any memory access past the end of the allocation to fail (immediately). Similarly, a guard page can also be placed at the beginning of the allocation to catch any memory writes that occur before the actual allocation. In addition, when a memory block is freed, it is not immediately returned to the system; rather, it is kept around for a while (in a pool of protected memory), enabling the system to trap any code that might try to access the allocation after it has been deleted. It shouldn't come as a surprise that using this test setting comes with a great cost. The cost is that of additional memory (because of guard pages) used for each allocation made in the application. Actually, the memory pressure is so high it is recommended that you have at least 256MB of RAM and a 1GB pagefile to make good use of this test. Having said that, when it comes to memory-related problems, this is the most exhaustive test setting one could imagine, and it catches a lot of problems early on. In addition to guard pages, full pageheap uses fill patterns. The layout of the fill pattern is shown in Figure A.3, and the actual fill patterns are shown in Table A.3.

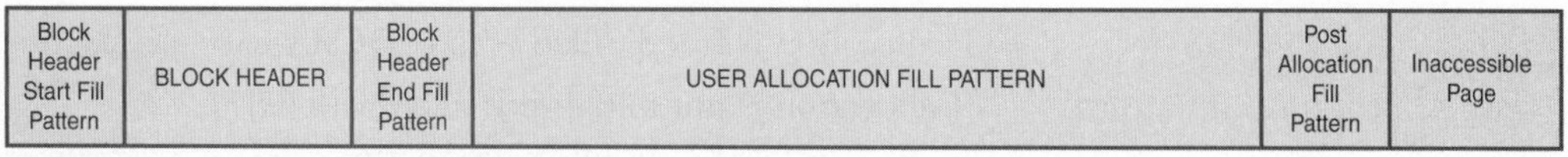

| Block Header Start Fill Pattern | BLOCK HEADER | Block Header End Fill Pattern | USER ALLOCATION FILL PATTERN | Post Allocation Fill Pattern | Inaccessible Page |
|---|---|---|---|---|---|

**Figure A.3**   Fill patterns used by full pageheap

**Table A.3** Specific Fill Patterns Based on Initialized or Freed Heap Blocks

| Block Portion | Fill Pattern |
|---|---|
| Block Header Start Fill Pattern | If allocated, filled with 0xABCDBBBB |
| | If allocation is freed, filled with 0xABCDBBA |
| Block Header | None |
| Block Header End Fill Pattern | If allocated, filled with 0xDCBABBBB |
| | If allocation is freed, filled with 0xDCBABBBA |
| User Allocation Fill Pattern | If allocation is not initialized, filled with 0xC0 |
| | If allocation is freed, filled with 0xF0 |
| Post Allocation Fill Pattern | 0xD0D0D0D0 |

The biggest advantage of this test setting in comparison to the previous one is that the guard pages guarantee that an access violation occurs at the point of memory usage (and not just at memory allocation and freeing). This greatly simplifies tracking down memory-related problems because you catch the code in action rather than post-mortem.

The heap test setting contains a number of stop codes that are monitored during execution of the process. Table A.4 details the different stop codes. By default, all heap-related stop codes cause a break in the debugger if triggered.

**Table A.4** Heap-related Stop Codes

| Stop Code Test | | Description |
|---|---|---|
| 00000001 | Unknown error | This stop triggers when a heap error occurred that cannot be classified in any other way. |
| 00000002 | Buffer overrun | In cases in which full pageheap is enabled, this stop triggers when the application writes past the end of a buffer and hits the guard page. |
| 00000003 | Unserialized heap | Heaps that are not serialized should not be accessed from concurrent threads. This stop triggers if two or more threads access a nonserialized heap at the same time. |
| 00000004 | Large allocations | This stop triggers if the allocation size specified to the `HeapAlloc` and `HeapReAlloc` API(s) is unreasonably high. |

*(continues)*

**Table A.4**   Heap-related Stop Codes   *(continued)*

| Stop Code Test | | Description |
| --- | --- | --- |
| 00000005 | Invalid heap handles | This stop triggers if an invalid handle is specified to one of the heap API(s). |
| 00000006 | Mismatched heaps | This stop triggers if a block of memory allocated in one heap is freed in another heap. |
| 00000007 | Over freed blocks | This stop triggers if a heap block is freed twice. |
| 00000008 | Generic heap corruption | This error is caused by a heap corruption that cannot be categorized. |
| 00000009 | Destroying the default process heap | This stop triggers if an application tries to destroy the default process heap. |
| 0000000A | Heap manager | This stop triggers if the heap manager code raises an access violation. |
| 0000000B | Generic heap corruption | This stop triggers if the source of the heap corruption is undetermined. This can happen when passing an address that points to nonaccessible memory to the heap-free API. |
| 0000000C | Generic heap corruption | This stop triggers if the source of the heap corruption is undetermined. This can happen when passing an address that points to nonaccessible memory to the heap-free API. This can also happen if you are double freeing memory. |
| 0000000D | Use after delete | This stop triggers if a block of memory has been freed and is subsequently written to. |
| 0000000E | Use after delete | This stop triggers if a block of memory has been freed and is subsequently written to. This stop code in comparison to stop code 0000000E typically happens in normal pageheap mode, which uses fill patterns to detect heap problems. |
| 0000000F | Buffer overrun | This stop will be triggered when a buffer overrun occurs in normal pageheap mode by checking the fill patterns employed by normal pageheap. |
| 00000010 | Buffer underrun | This stop is triggered when a buffer underrun occurs and the start stamp of the heap block header is corrupted. |
| 00000011 | Buffer underrun | This stop is triggered when a buffer underrun occurs and the end stamp of the heap block header is corrupted. |

| Stop Code Test | | Description |
|---|---|---|
| 00000012 | Buffer underrun | This stop is triggered when a buffer underrun occurs and the prefix of the heap block header is corrupted. |
| 00000013 | First chance access violation | This stop is trigged when a first-chance access violation occurs. |
| 00000014 | Process heaps | This stop is triggered when a call to `GetProcessHeaps` causes the heap manager to detect inconsistencies in the heap manager structures. |

### *Full Pageheap or Normal Pageheap?*

The pageheap test setting that uses fill patterns only is also referred to as normal pageheap, whereas its more powerful sibling, full pageheap, uses guard pages to trap programming mistakes when they happen. Armed with these two options, when should you choose one over the other? Full pageheap has a much higher chance of catching problems and makes it much easier to track down problems. On the other hand, it uses so much memory that the system can become slow enough that some problems (such as synchronization-related problems) do not even get a chance to occur. Typically, a good strategy is to always have normal pageheap during development, and at regular checkpoints, enable the more exhaustive setting to get coverage. To alleviate some pressure from the more exhaustive test setting, you can also narrow down the source of the potential memory culprit code by setting it to only perform the tests on, for example, a per-DLL basis or allocation-size basis.

## Locks

The Windows operating system is a preemptive operating system, which in essence means that any given thread running in a system must be ready to yield processor control to another thread. This presents a very common dilemma for applications with more than one thread running simultaneously. The dilemma lies in the fact that any resources that threads share between themselves must be strictly controlled to avoid the problem of multiple threads accessing (reading and writing) the resource simultaneously. The process of controlling access to a resource is called synchronization. One very common technique used by applications is to use a built-in synchronization object called a critical section. A critical section ensures that only one thread at a time can access any resource protected by the critical section. Prior to accessing a shared resource, a thread will enter the critical section, use the resource, and then release the critical section. If another thread tries to enter a critical section while it has been entered by another thread, the thread blocks on the critical section until it has been released; at which point, the thread is woken up and allowed to enter it. Before a critical section can be used, it must be initialized; at which point, the operating system allocates the memory required to successfully initialize the object. When the critical section is no longer needed, it must be deleted to avoid memory leaks. A thread that has entered a critical section can reenter it any number of times as long as there is an equivalent call to release the critical section for each time it has been entered. Needless to say, critical sections are very often misused and cause problems, ranging from memory leaks to deadlocks simply due to not following the proper protocol. The Locks test setting provides a range of checks when it comes to critical sections and can save valuable time otherwise spent on debugging concurrency problems. Table A.5 lists all the tests that this test setting provides. By default, all lock-related stop codes cause a break in the debugger if triggered.

**Table A.5**    Lock-Related Stop Codes

| Stop Code | Test | Description |
|---|---|---|
| 00000200 | Thread state does not allow holding critical sections | This stop is triggered when a thread is terminated, suspended, or is in a state in which it cannot hold a critical section. |
| 00000201 | Active critical sections when unloading DLL | If a critical section is found to be active when a DLL is unloaded, Application Verifier stops execution. |
| 00000202 | Freeing of a heap block that contains an active critical section | When a heap allocation is freed and contains an active critical section, Application Verifier stops execution. This test avoids the potential leak of a critical section. |
| 00000203 | Initialize only once | A critical section can be initialized only once. Initializing a critical section more than once is undefined behavior and represents errors in the code. |
| 00000204 | Forgetting to free the critical section | To properly delete or free a critical section, the `DeleteCriticalSection` API must be used. This stop is triggered if a block of memory that contains a critical section has been freed but the critical section was not deleted using the `DeleteCriticalSection` API. |
| 00000205 | Invalid DebugInfo pointer | This stop is triggered if the DebugInfo field of the critical section points to freed memory. |

| Stop Code | Test | Description |
|---|---|---|
| 00000206 | Verify correctness of owner thread ID | Any time a critical section is entered, the thread ID is recorded. If the thread ID is invalid in the current context of execution, Application Verifier stops execution. |
| 00000207 | Verify correctness of the recursion count | Threads that enter a critical section more than once increment the recursion count of a critical section. If the recursion count is not valid in the current context of execution, Application Verifier stops execution. |
| 00000208 | Delete without initialization | If a critical section is deleted without being initialized, Application Verifier stops execution. |
| 00000209 | Release count matches | If a thread releases a critical section more times than it entered it, Application Verifier stops execution. |
| 00000210 | Use prior to initialization | If a critical section is used without being initialized or used after it was deleted, Application Verifier stops execution. |
| 00000211 | Reinitialization | If a critical section is reinitialized by the current thread, Application Verifier stops execution. |
| 00000212 | Invalid deletion of critical section (`VirtualFree`) | When a block of memory containing an active critical section is freed using `VirtualFree`, but the critical section has not been freed via the `DeleteCriticalSection` API, this stop triggers. |
| 00000213 | Invalid deletion of critical section (`UnmapViewOfFile`) | When a block of memory containing an active critical section is unmapped using the `UnmapViewOfFile` API, but the critical section has not been freed via the `DeleteCriticalSection` API, this stop triggers. |
| 00000214 | Leaving an unowned critical section | This stop is triggered when a thread calls `LeaveCriticalSection` on a critical section that it does not own. |
| 00000215 | Private locks usage | This stop is triggered if a thread tries to enter a private critical section defined in a different DLL. |

All the tests listed in Table A.5 are common programming errors that you might encounter when working with critical sections. Without this test setting, most of these errors manifest themselves as memory leaks, dead locks, live locks, and so on and can cause hours of frustrating debugging to figure out. This test setting catches most of the problems at the point when they occur rather than at random points postmortem. Whenever you write code that has to manage synchronization across multiple threads, this test setting should be enabled.

# Memory

The memory test setting traps numerous programming mistakes related to working with memory. Problems, such as passing invalid parameters to the memory API(s), failed object initialization, and module unloading, are all covered in the wide range of stop codes. Table A.6 details all the stop codes available for this test setting. By default, all memory-related stop codes cause a break in the debugger if triggered.

**Table A.6** Memory-Related Stop Codes

| Stop Code | Test | Description |
|-----------|------|-------------|
| 00000600 | VirtualFree or Dll unload | This stop triggers when Application Verifier detects a VirtualFree call with an invalid address or a DLL unload with an invalid start address. |
| 00000601 | VirtualAlloc | This stop triggers when Application Verifier detects a VirtualAlloc call with an invalid start address or size of allocation. |
| 00000602 | MapViewOfFile | This stop triggers when Application Verifier detects a MapViewOfFile call with an invalid base address or size of the mapping. |
| 00000603 | IsBadXXXPtr | This stop triggers when Application Verifier detects an IsBadXXXPtr call with an invalid address. |
| 00000604 | IsBadXXXPtr | This stop triggers when Application Verifier detects an IsBadXXXPtr call with a memory location that is free. |
| 00000605 | IsBadXXXPtr | This stop triggers when Application Verifier detects an IsBadXXXPtr call with a memory address that contains a guard page. This can be especially bad in cases in which the address points to a stack. |
| 00000606 | IsBadXXXPtr | This stop triggers when Application Verifier detects an IsBadXXXPtr call with a null address. |
| 00000607 | IsBadXXXPtr | This stop triggers when Application Verifier detects an IsBadXXXPtr call with an invalid address or size of the memory buffer. |
| 00000608 | Dll unload | This stop triggers when a DLL is being unloaded with an invalid start address. |
| 00000609 | VirtualFree | This stop triggers when a VirtualFree call is used on an address that is actually part of the current thread's stack. |

| Stop codes | Test | Description |
|---|---|---|
| 0000060A | VirtualFree | This stop triggers when VirtualFree is called with an incorrect value for the FreeType parameter. |
| 0000060B | VirtualFree | This stop is triggered when VirtualFree is called with an address that has already been freed. |
| 0000060C | VirtualFree | This stop is triggered when VirtualFree is called with MEM_RELEASE, and the size parameter is greater than 0. |
| 0000060D | DllMain exceptions | This stop is triggered when a DllMain implementation raises an exception. |
| 0000060E | Thread exceptions | This stop is triggered when a thread raises an exception. |
| 0000060F | IsBadXXXPtr | This stop is triggered when a call to IsBadXXXPtr results in an exception being thrown. |
| 00000610 | VirtualFree | This stop is triggered when VirtualFree is called with MEM_RESET and null as the first parameter. |
| 00000612 | HeapFree | This stop is triggered when a HeapFree call is made with a pointer that is part of the current thread's stack. |
| 00000613 | UnmapViewOfFile | This stop is triggered when an UnmapViewOfFile call is made for a block of memory that is part of the current thread's stack. |
| 00000614 | Incorrect address | This stop is triggered if an invalid address is passed to certain API(s). For example, passing null to RtlInitializeResource is incorrect. |
| 00000615 | Incorrect address | This stop is triggered if an invalid address is passed to certain API(s). For example, passing null to EnterCriticalSection is incorrect. |
| 00000616 | Non executable code | This stop is triggered when an application tries to run code from a nonexecutable memory address. |
| 00000617 | Failed buffer initialization | This stop is triggered when an exception is raised while initializing an output parameter passed to the Win32 or CRT API(s). This usually indicates that the associated size parameter is incorrect. |
| 00000618 | HeapSize | This stop is triggered when calling the HeapSize API with an address to a block of memory that has already been freed. |

*(continues)*

**Table A.6**   Memory-Related Stop Codes   *(continued)*

| Stop Code | Test | Description |
|---|---|---|
| 00000619 | VirtualFree | This stop is triggered when a call is made to VirtualFree with an invalid base address. Invalid, in this case, means that the base address specified is not the same as the base address returned from the corresponding VirtualAlloc or VirtualAllocEx API(s). |
| 0000061A | UnmapViewOfFile | This stop is triggered when a call is made to UnmapViewOfFile with an invalid base address. Invalid, in this case, means that the base address specified is not the same as the base address returned from the corresponding MapViewOfFile or MapViewOfFileEx API(s). |
| 0000061B | Thread pool thread exceptions | This stop is triggered when the callback function for a thread pool thread raises an exception. |
| 0000061C | Nonexecutable code | This stop is triggered when an application tries to run code from a nonexecutable memory address. |
| 0000061D | Executable heap | This stop is triggered when an application tries to create an executable heap. |
| 0000061E | Executable memory | This stop is triggered when an application tries to allocate executable memory. |

The memory test setting has one adjustable property called ExecWritePage that allows you to control whether the test setting should check whether an application is creating or allocating executable and writable memory.

# ThreadPool

The native Windows thread pool is a powerful and convenient component to use when an application requires multiple threads. Rather than creating your own thread pool and ensuring that it works optimally, you can let the operating system make decisions on when and how to create threads for you. After all, the operating system has the most knowledge to make these hard decisions. With using the thread pool, however, comes a lot of responsibility. There have been numerous hard-to-track-down bugs stemming from improper usage of the thread pool. For example, changing a thread's state and not resetting it before giving the thread back to the thread pool can lead to serious problems. This test setting traps a lot of these problems and notifies you about potential problems in your code. Table A.7 details the stops that are available for this test setting. By default, all thread pool-related stop codes will cause a break in the debugger if triggered.

**Table A.7**  ThreadPool-Related Stops

| Stop Code | Test | Description |
|-----------|------|-------------|
| 00000700 | Changed thread priority | If an application changes the priority of a thread and does not reset it before handing it back to the thread pool, this stop triggers. |
| 00000701 | Changed thread affinity | If an application changes the affinity of a thread and does not reset it before handing it back to the thread pool, this stop triggers. |
| 00000702 | Unprocessed messages | If a thread has any unprocessed messages left before returning to the thread pool, this stop triggers. |
| 00000703 | Active windows | If a thread has any live and active windows when returned to the thread pool, this stop triggers. |
| 00000704 | Exit or termination of thread | If either `ExitThread` or `TerminateThread` is called on a thread pool thread, this stop triggers. |
| 00000705 | Impersonation | If the thread pool thread impersonates another user but does not revert the impersonation before returning the thread to the thread pool, this stop triggers. |
| 00000706 | Dedicated thread | In some situations, certain API(s) require to be called on a persistent or dedicated thread (for example, the `RegNotifyChangeKeyValue` API), and unless you requested to be given a dedicated thread from the thread pool, this stop triggers. |
| 00000707 | Transaction handle | If an application forgets to reset the transaction handle before returning the thread to the thread pool, this stop triggers. |
| 00000708 | COM initialization | When initializing COM on a thread, care must be taken to uninitialize COM before the thread exits. This stop triggers if there are unbalanced calls to COM initialize and uninitialize. |

The `ThreadPool` test setting also has one associated property named `AsyncCheck`, which enables the verifier to check asynchronous calls that require a persistent thread. To turn this setting on, specify `1`. By default, this property is set to `0` (off).

# TLS

Thread local storage (TLS) is a common mechanism used to allocate local thread-specific data. To allocate TLS data, an application uses the TLS family of API(s). To ensure proper usage of these API(s), this test setting traps calls to the API(s) and stops execution if invalid usage is encountered. Table A.8 details the stops that are part of this test setting. By default, all TLS-related stop codes cause a break in the debugger if triggered.

**Table A.8**   TLS-Related Stop Codes

| Stop Code | Test | Description |
| --- | --- | --- |
| 00000350 | `TlsIndex leak` | If a DLL that allocated a TLS index is unloaded without freeing the index, this stop triggers to avoid TLS index leaks. |
| 00000351 | Corrupted TLS state | If the data structure used to store the TLS slots becomes corrupted, this stop triggers. This is most likely because of a random memory corruption. |
| 00000352 | Invalid TLS index used | If an application uses a TLS index that is considered invalid, this stop triggers. A common source of this problem is to use a TLS index that has already been freed. |

# FilePaths

Applications that make use of system file paths (such as getting the windows directory or the system directory) can suffer problems associated with using the wrong paths. This test setting makes sure that system paths retrieved via the Win32 APIs are correct. The APIs that this test setting hooks are listed in Table A.9. By default, all file path-related stop codes will not cause a break in the debugger if triggered, but rather they will log the stop code in the log file with the offending stack trace.

**Table A.9**   FilePath-Related Stop Codes

| Stop Code | Test | Description |
|---|---|---|
| 00002400 | Common program path | This stop is triggered if the application used a common Program directory path that was not obtained using the proper API(s). |
| 00002401 | Common Start menu directory path | This stop is triggered if the application used a common Start menu directory path that was not obtained using the proper API(s). |
| 00002402 | Programs directory path | This stop is triggered if the application used a program's directory path that was not obtained using the proper API(s). |
| 00002404 | Start Menu directory path | This stop is triggered if the application used a Start Menu Directory Path that was not obtained using the proper API(s). |
| 00002405 | Windows Temp path | This stop is triggered if the application used a Windows Temp path that was not obtained using the proper API(s). |
| 00002406 | Windows directory path | This stop is triggered if the application used a Windows directory path that was not obtained using the proper API(s). |
| 00002407 | System Windows directory path | This stop is triggered if the application used a System Windows directory path that was not obtained using the proper API(s). |
| 00002408 | System directory path | This stop is triggered if the application used a System directory path that was not obtained using the proper API(s). |
| 0000240A | My Documents directory path | This stop is triggered if the application used a My Documents directory path that was not obtained using the proper API(s). |

# HighVersionLie

A very common programming mistake that leads to broken applications is to rely on a hard-coded Windows version number. Far too often, programmers, who require a specific version of Windows for their code to function, check against that version and that version alone. The net result of that approach is that when a new version of Windows ships, the application simply fails because it didn't take into account the increase in version number (although the application would have run just fine). To prevent situations similar to this, this test setting allows the application developer to test his code against "future" versions of Windows. This works by Application Verifier simply hooking calls to the GetVersion and GetVersionEx APIs and returning a version that, by default, supersedes the latest version of Windows. For example, running a simple test application that calls GetVersionEx on the Windows XP Professional Service Pack 2 yields the following results:

```
Local var @ 0x7fea4 Type _OSVERSIONINFOEXA
    +0x000 dwOSVersionInfoSize : 0x9c
    +0x004 dwMajorVersion    : 5
    +0x008 dwMinorVersion    : 1
    +0x00c dwBuildNumber     : 0xa28
    +0x010 dwPlatformId      : 2
    +0x014 szCSDVersion      : [128]   "Service Pack 2"
    +0x094 wServicePackMajor : 2
    +0x096 wServicePackMinor : 0
    +0x098 wSuiteMask        : 0x300
    +0x09a wProductType      : 0x1 `'
    +0x09b wReserved         : 0 `'
```

where the dwMajorVersion (5) and dwMinorVersion (1) indicate Windows XP (see GetVersionEx in MSDN for a list of all Windows versions). Turning the HighVersionLie test on and running the application again yields the following results:

```
Local var @ 0x7fea4 Type _OSVERSIONINFOEXA
    +0x000 dwOSVersionInfoSize : 0x9c
    +0x004 dwMajorVersion    : 7
    +0x008 dwMinorVersion    : 3
    +0x00c dwBuildNumber     : 0xe10
    +0x010 dwPlatformId      : 2
    +0x014 szCSDVersion      : [128]   ""
    +0x094 wServicePackMajor : 2
    +0x096 wServicePackMinor : 0
    +0x098 wSuiteMask        : 0x300
    +0x09a wProductType      : 0x1 `'
    +0x09b wReserved         : 0 `'
```

This time, the major and minor versions are nonexistent Windows versions and the application should handle this situation accordingly.

By default, Application Verifier will use 7 as the Major version, 3 as the minor version, and 0xe10 as the build number. You can very easily configure these settings (and others) by changing the properties for the test setting. Table A.10 explains the available properties.

**Table A.10** HighVersionLie Properties

| Property | Description |
| --- | --- |
| Major version | HighVersionLie uses the value of this property as the major version. |
| Minor version | HighVersionLie uses the value of this property as the minor version. |
| Build number | HighVersionLie uses the value of this property as the build number. |
| Service pack major | HighVersionLie uses the value of this property as the major service pack version. |
| Service pack minor | HighVersionLie uses the value of this property as the minor service pack version. |
| Suite mask | HighVersionLie uses the value of this property as the suite mask. |
| Product type | HighVersionLie uses the value of this property as the product type. |
| CSD version | HighVersionLie uses the value of this property as the CSD version. |

As you can see, in addition to changing the major, minor, and build numbers, you can change a host of other options. Typically, the standard settings are good enough, as most of the time, you want to make sure that your application does not break with new releases of Windows.

The stop codes available for this test setting are all placeholders and serve to indicate that the test setting has been enabled.

# InteractiveServices

Services typically run under an account with high privileges. As such, any security compromises typically have a much bigger effect on the system in comparison to attacks on processes running under less privileged accounts. Attacks can, for example, be carried out using the graphical user interface subsystem of Windows. This type of attack is also known as a shatter attack. One common mechanism is for the less privileged attacking process to send certain Windows messages to a more privileged application and gain unprivileged access (for example, information disclosure or elevation of privilege). Services are allowed to send user interface elements to other interactive applications or simply run as an interactive service themselves. Because special care must be taken to avoid exploits in these types of services, this test setting enables the user to quickly tell if the service is interactive or sends user interface elements (such as Windows messages) to other applications. Table A.11 details the stops that are part of this test setting. By default, all stop codes for this test setting log the results of the test to the log file and include the stack trace.

**Table A.11** InteractiveServices-related Stop Codes

| Stop Code | Test | Description |
|---|---|---|
| 00002800 | Interactive service creation | This stop triggers when an application creates an interactive service using the `CreateService` API. Interactive services can be a security risk. |
| 00002801 | Local system interactive service | The application ran as an interactive service under the local system account, presenting a security risk. |
| 00002802 | Usage of `MessageBox` API | Using the `MessageBox` API to send notifications to the interactive desktop might be a security threat. |
| 00002803 | Usage of `MessageBoxEx` API | Using the `MessageBoxEx` API to send notifications to the interactive desktop might be a security threat. |
| 00002804 | Interactive Desktop | The application called `OpenWindowStation` and `OpenDesktop` to send UI messages to the interactive desktop. This can be a security risk. |
| 00002805 | Interactive Desktop | The application called `OpenDesktop` in order to send UI messages to the interactive desktop. This can be a security risk. |
| 00002806 | Interactive Desktop | The application called `OpenWindowStation` and `OpenInputDesktop` to send UI messages to the interactive desktop. This can be a security risk. |
| 00002807 | Interactive Desktop function pointer | The application tried to get the address of the `OpenDesktop` function in an attempt to send UI messages to it. |

# KernelModeDriverInstall

On Windows, drivers run in kernel mode; therefore, they have access to system-critical data. When drivers fail, it can have a significant impact on the system and, in the worst case, blue screen the system. To make sure that drivers are installed using the proper channels, developers must use the correct API(s). This test setting ensures that applications use the proper API(s) when installing drivers. Table A.12 details the verifier stops that are part of this test setting. By default, all kernel mode driver install-related stop codes will not cause a break in the debugger if triggered; rather, the stop code is logged in the log file with the offending stack trace.

**Table A.12**    KernelModeDriverInstall-Related Stop Codes

| Stop Code | Test | Description |
| --- | --- | --- |
| 00002305 | Driver install | `CreateServiceA` was called to install a kernel mode driver. |
| 00002306 | File system filter driver | `CreateServiceW` was called to install a file system filter driver. |
| 00002307 | File system filter driver | `CreateServiceA` was called to install a file system filter driver. |
| 00002308 | Driver install | `CreateServiceW` was called to install a kernel mode driver. |
| 00002309 | Driver install API | The application installed a driver without using the proper API (`CreateService`). |
| 0000230A | File system driver install | The application installed a file system driver without using the proper API (`CreateService`). |
| 0000230B | Driver install API | The application installed a driver without using the proper API (`CreateService`), and no image path was specified. |
| 0000230C | File system driver install | The application installed a file system driver without using the proper API (`CreateService`), and no image path was specified. |
| 0000230D | Driver install API | The application installed a driver without using the proper API (`CreateService`), and no service type was specified. |

# Low Resource Simulation

To ensure the robustness of an application, the application must not only be capable of running properly under a normal system load, but also when resources are running low. The canonical example of this is ensuring that an application behaves properly when the system it is running on is low on memory. Under these circumstances, one of the problems with ensuring the robustness of an application is simulating an environment in which resources are low. The Low Resource Simulation test setting aids in testing these scenarios by allowing you to define the conditions under which low resource faults should occur during execution. The test setting does not have stops defined for it, but instead allows you to modify a number of test setting parameters. Table A.13 details the various parameters.

**Table A.13** Low Resource Simulation Parameters

| Property | Description |
|---|---|
| Include | Controls which DLLs faults should occur in. DLLs should be specified without their paths and one per row. A * can be used to indicate that all modules should be included in the fault injection. |
| Exclude | A list of DLLs to exclude from the fault injection. DLLs should be specified one per row. |
| Timeout | Indicates how many milliseconds should elapse at process startup before fault injection commences. |
| WAIT | A number between 0 and 100 that indicates the probability that the WaitForXXX API(s) will fail because of fault injection. |
| HEAP_ALLOC | A number between 0 and 100 that indicates the probability that the HEAP_ALLOC API(s) will fail because of fault injection. |
| VIRTUAL_ALLOC | A number between 0 and 100 that indicates the probability that the VIRTUAL_ALLOC API(s) will fail because of fault injection. |
| REGISTRY | A number between 0 and 100 that indicates the probability that the REGISTRY API(s) will fail because of fault injection. |
| FILE | A number between 0 and 100 that indicates the probability that the FILE API(s) will fail because of fault injection. |
| EVENT | A number between 0 and 100 that indicates the probability that the EVENT API(s) will fail because of fault injection. |
| MAP_VIEW | A number between 0 and 100 that indicates the probability that the MAP_VIEW API(s) will fail because of fault injection. |
| OLE_ALLOC | A number between 0 and 100 that indicates the probability that the OLE_ALLOC API(s) will fail because of fault injection. |
| STACKS | If set to TRUE, indicates that the stack growing feature should be disabled to simulate low resources. If set to FALSE, stack growth occurs. |

# LuaPriv

The LuaPriv test setting stands for Limited User Account Predictor and serves two purposes:

- Predicts whether an application is capable of running with a reduced privilege set (such as a normal user).
- Determines possible problems when an application runs with a reduced privilege set (normal user).

Table A.14 lists all the stop codes defined by this test setting. By default, all limited user account-related stop codes don't cause a break in the debugger if triggered. Instead, the stop code is logged in the log file with the offending stack trace.

**Table A.14**  LuaPriv-Related Stop Code

| Stop Code | Test | Description |
| --- | --- | --- |
| 00003300 | Name canonicalization failure | This stop triggers when Application Verifier attempts to canonize the name of an object but fails to do so. |
| 00003301 | Unable to find canonical name | This stop triggers when Application Verifier fails to find the canonical name of an object. |
| 00003302 | Failure to open object | This stop triggers when Application Verifier fails to get information about an object because of errors when attempting to open the object. |
| 00003303 | HKEY_CURRENT_ USER | This stop triggers when Application Verifier is unable to interpret the HKEY_CURRENT_USER registry hive. As a result, registry keys located under that registry hive must be flagged as restrictive. |
| 00003304 | USERPROFILE | This stop is triggered if the USERPROFILE environment variable is not found. This might lead Application Verifier to believe that the current user's profile was not available and therefore list some of the files and directories as being restrictive. |
| 00003305 | Safe object | This stop is triggered due to Application Verifier believing that the object was considered safe. |
| 00003306 | Listed object namespace | This stop is triggered by Application Verifier when an object is encountered that is in the listed namespace. This namespace is not writable by standard users. |

*(continues)*

**Table A.14** LuaPriv-Related Stop Code *(continued)*

| Stop Code Test | | Description |
|---|---|---|
| 00003307 | No namespace | The object was created without specifying a namespace, causing it to be created in a global namespace, which is not writable by standard users. |
| 00003308 | File/directory location | This stop is generated when Application Verifier tries to locate a file or directory but fails in doing so. |
| 00003309 | Failure to open parent object | Application Verified fails to open the parent object in trying to determine if standard users would be able to create child objects. |
| 0000330A | Running as administrator | Application Verifier detects that the application was being run as an administrator. This is simply informative information to make sure that scenarios being tested by running as a standard user are not inadvertently being run as administrators. |
| 0000330B | Failed SID conversion | Application Verifier fails to convert a human-readable form of a security identifier (SID) to the internal Windows form. |
| 0000330C | `GetTokenInformation` | An application calls the `GetTokenInformation` API requesting the listed class of information. Although this might work as a standard user, it generally implies that the application should run as an administrator. |
| 0000330D | Privilege does not exist | The privilege being examined does not exist on the version of Windows that the application is being run on. |
| 0000330E | Privilege lookup failure | Application Verifier fails in looking up a specified privilege (via the LUID). |
| 0000330F | Successful privilege request | The application requests and receives a privilege that is not granted to standard users. |
| 00003310 | Failed privilege request | The application fails in requesting a privilege that is not granted to standard users. |
| 00003311 | Successful access to listed privilege | The application is started as a standard user with access to the listed privilege. |
| 00003312 | Failed access to the listed privilege | The application is started as a user with no access to the listed privilege, although privilege lookup was successful. |
| 00003313 | | The application is started as a user with no access to the listed privilege. |

| Stop Code | Test | Description |
|---|---|---|
| 00003314 | Failed registry query | Application Verifier tries to query a registry value but is unsuccessful. |
| 00003315 | INI file registry mapping | The application uses an INI file that mapped to a registry key, and the syntax of the INI file is unknown. |
| 00003316 | Failed profile access | The application tries to access a given profile but fails. |
| 00003317 | Granted object access | The application is granted access to the specified object. Standard users should be able to access the specified object. |
| 00003318 | Granted object access | The application was granted access to the specified object. Standard users might not be able to access the specified object. |
| 00003319 | Failed security descriptor conversion | Application Verifier attempts to convert a security descriptor to human-readable form but fails in doing so. |
| 0000331A | Object access failure | Application requests access to an object and is denied. |
| 0000331B | Object access | Application requests access to an object that only grants access to trusted users. |
| 0000331C | Object access | Application requests access to an object that only grants access to trusted users. This message is always followed by other messages. |
| 0000331D | Object access | Application requests access to an object that only grants access to privileged users and owners of the object. |
| 0000331E | Object access | Application requests access to an object that only grants access to at least one nonprivileged user. |
| 0000331F | Object access | Application requests access to an object that does not grant access to anyone. |
| 00003320 | Security descriptor analysis | Application Verifier tries to analyze an object's security descriptor by dividing it into individual pieces but fails in doing so. |
| 00003321 | Security descriptor analysis | Application Verifier tries to analyze an ACL in the object's security descriptor discretionary access list but fails in doing so. |
| 00003322 | Object access | The application requests maximum allowed access to the object, and Application Verifier decides to analyze the application as if all object privileges are actually required. |

*(continues)*

**Table A.14** LuaPriv-Related Stop Code *(continued)*

| Stop Code | Test | Description |
|---|---|---|
| 00003323 | Object access | The application requests maximum allowed access to the object Application Verifier attempts to determine which privileges are actually required by the application but fails in doing so. |
| 00003324 | Unknown permissions | The application requested permissions that are unknown to Application Verifier. |
| 00003325 | Profiles | The application is granted access to the profile. |
| 00003326 | Security Identifiers | The application queries Windows whether a listed security identifier is part of a user's token. This operation is normally restricted to users in the listed group. |
| 00003327 | Security Identifiers | The application queries Windows whether a listed security identifier (SID) is part of a user's token although the SID is not identifiable. |
| 00003328 | Profiles | The application called the `WriteProfile` API with input that might fail when run as a standard user. |

# DangerousAPIs

Many of the API(s) in Win32 are extremely powerful. They are powerful to the extent that great care must be taken when using the API(s) to avoid problems that might arise when using them. This test setting checks for calls to these dangerous API(s). Table A.15 details the stops available for this test setting. By default, all dangerous API-related stop codes cause a break in the debugger if triggered.

**Table A.15** DangerousAPIs-Related Stop Codes

| Stop Code | Test | Description |
|---|---|---|
| 00000100 | `TerminateThread` | This stop is triggered if the application terminates a thread using the `TerminateThread` API. `TerminateThread` has a high chance of causing problems, such as deadlocks and data corruption. |

| Stop Code | Test | Description |
|---|---|---|
| 00000101 | Stack commit size | This stop is triggered if the stack size of an application is set to not allow stack growth in cases in which stack overflow exceptions might be raised (low memory conditions). |
| 00000102 | ExitProcess | This stop is triggered if the application terminates a process with several threads running (using the ExitProcess API). ExitProcess internally uses the TerminateThread API, which can cause stability problems (see stop code 00000100). |
| 00000103 | LoadLibrary | This stop is triggered if the application calls LoadLibrary in a DllMain function. Calling this API from the DllMain function can result in crashes or deadlocks. |
| 00000104 | FreeLibrary | This stop is triggered if the application calls FreeLibrary in a DllMain function. Calling this API from the DllMain function can result in crashes or deadlocks. |

The DangerousAPIs test setting has one property (DllMainCheck) that can be changed. If this property is set to TRUE, the test setting traps any calls from DllMain to the LoadLibrary or FreeLibrary APIs.

## DirtyStacks

Uninitialized stack variables are a common source of bugs. This holds especially true for uninitialized stack pointers. To ensure that these types of bugs are caught, this test setting periodically fills the unused portion of the stack with a specific pattern. When the application attempts to use the uninitialized variable, it might result in an access violation due to accessing memory initialized with a fill pattern that is considered an invalid memory access. This test setting results in exceptions being thrown rather than a hard stop.

## TimeRollOver

When working with the GetTickCount and TimeGetTime API(s), it is crucial that the developer handle the cases in which a rollover occurs. In order to test the rollover cases, however, it must be possible to quickly trigger the rollover to occur. This test setting enables you to control when the rollover should occur. No actual stops exist for this test setting. Instead, a test setting property exists (named Delay) that can be set to indicate the number of seconds to delay before a rollover occurs.

## PrintAPI and PrintDriver

Numerous problems can surface when working with the Print API(s). Both the PrintAPI test setting and the PrintDriver test setting enable a slew of tests to ensure proper usage of the API(s).

# INDEX

**Numerics**

32-bit applications, WOW64, running in, 598-602

64-bit debugging, 603-624
  Application Verifyer, 604
  current call stacks, discovering, 609-613
  current register values, finding, 605-607
  custom debugger extensions, writing, 629
  Debugging Tools for Windows, 603-604
  Wireshark, 605
  interprocess communication, 628-629
  Leak Diagnostic tool, 603
  local variable values, discovering, 613-614
  memory corruption, 625-626
  process memory, inspecting, 615
  processors, code processing, 609
  security, 626-628
  WOW64 commands, 607-609

64-bit operating systems, 595-598
  32-bit applications, running in, 598-602

64-bit processors, 595-596

**A**

access, breakpoints, 170-171

access control, Windows Vista, side effects, 712-714

access tokens, 325-330
  client server applications
    *impersonation levels*, 337-338
    *remote authentication*, 335-337
    *security support provider interface support*, 335-337
    *token propagation*, 334-338
  impersonation tokens, dumping, 351
  process access tokens, obtaining, 329
  thread impersonation tokens, displaying, 329

access violation, dump files, analysis, 646-647

Access violation enumerating registry values listing (5-12), 232-234

AccessCheck function, 323-324

accessing cell debugging information, 399-408

ACE (access control entry), 320

ACLs (Access Control Lists), 320-322

activation checks, DCOM, 355-363

activation failures, DCOM, Windows XP2, 371-376

AddEnd option (Heaps test setting), 752

Addr option (Heaps test setting), 752

!address command, 90-91
  listing (2-39), 91

!address debugger command example listing (2-38), 90

!address extension command, 473

ADDRESS objects, naming conventions, 390

address space layout, Windows Vista, 716-717

AddrStart option (Heaps test setting), 752

ADPlus, 632
  dump files, generating, 639-641

AeDebug key, 638
  auto registry value, 638
  debugger registry value, 638-639

agestore.exe, 8

algorithms, LIFO (last in first out) semantics, 209

aliases, events, 134

All thread stacks currently running in the process listing (10-7), 512

allocations
heaps
*back end allocators, 263-270, 272-281*
*front end allocators, 261-263*
memory blocks, 269
allocators, LeakDiag tool, 4-5
analysis
custom analysis scripts, authoring, 697-699
dump files
*access violation, 646-647*
*handle leaks, 647-652*
handle leaks, Debug Diagnostic tool,
693-697
memory leaks, Debug Diagnostic tool,
693-697
network traffic, 413-421
analysis process
memory corruption, 201
*avoidance strategies, 209*
*detection tools, 208*
*instrument source code, 208*
*source code analysis, 202-208*
*state analysis, 201-202*
problem synchronization, 505-509
resource leaks, 428-433
analysis scripts, authoring, Debug
Diagnostic Tool, 697-699
!analyze extension command, 691, 699
fault follow-up, 706-708
faulty applications, analyzing, 700
output, 701, 703
results, analyzing, 701-706
anti-debugging techniques, 159
Application crash seen under the debugger
listing (6-5), 283-286
Application Errors section (Dr. Watson
dialog box), 656-657
Application manifest requesting a high
integrity level listing (15-9), 724
Application option (Dr. Watson dialog box),
656-657
Application that calls a function in a DLL
listing (5-17), 245-247
Application that establishes a connection to
a data source listing (5-9), 223

Application Verifier, 10-16, 604
test settings, 747
*DangerousAPIs, 774-775*
*DirtyStacks, 775*
*Exceptions, 747*
*FilePaths, 764-765*
*Handles, 747-748*
*Heaps, 749-757*
*HighVersionLie, 765-767*
*InteractiveServices, 767-768*
*KernelModeDriverInstall, 768-769*
*Locks, 757-759*
*Low Resource Simulation, 769-770*
*LuaPriv, 771-774*
*Memory, 760-762*
*PrintAPI, 776*
*PrintDriver, 776*
*ThreadPool, 762-763*
*TimeRollOver, 775*
*TSL, 764*
Application verifier reported heap block
corruption listing (6-8), 295-300
Application Verifyer, heap block corruption
reports, 295-299
applications
crashes, 200
deadlocks, 510-516, 519
exceptions, 516-522
handle leaks, 436-460
multithreading, 550
resource leaks, memory leaks, 460-492
unpredictable behavior, 200
architecture, Windows Error Reporting,
662-682
assembly code
ProcA procedure, 214-216
Sum function, 217-219
Assembly code for ProcA listing (5-5),
215-216
Assembly code of the ThreadProcedure
function listing (5-4), 213
Assembly code representing the Function5
function listing (12-7), 610
Assembly instructions right after our call to
Sum listing (5-7), 219

Assembly listing generated for the function
from Listing 324 listing (3-26), 163
asynchronous operations, stack corruptions,
231-240
attaching
debuggers
*to running processes, 35*
*to running processes nonintrusively, 36*
processes to debuggers, 281
Attempt at manually constructing the stack
listing (5-18), 248-255
authentication, remote authentication, 423
client server applications, 335-337
authoring custom analysis scripts, Debug
Diagnostic Tool, 697-699
auto registry value, AeDebug key, 638
avoidance strategies
memory corruption, 209
memory leaks, 491-492
resource leaks, 433
stack corruptions, 255-258

**B**
ba command, 89
back end allocators, heaps, 263-281
Backward option (Heaps test setting), 751
BCD (Boot Configuration Data) objects,
715-716
binary files, debug information,
finding in, 51
Binary folder tree listing (4-3), 182
Binary representation of a security
descriptor listing (7-3), 324
binary trees, C++ binary trees,
implementing, 556, 559-562
Binplace file content listing (4-1), 181
Binplace.exe file, 181
Binplacing the symbol files listing (4-2), 182
blocks (memory)
allocating, 269
freeing, 269
PEB (process environment block), locating,
270-272
boundaries (system), security checks,
338-340

breaking cell paths, 421-422
breakpoints (code), 168-170
access, 170-171
conditional breakpoints, 107
reference releases, detecting, 107
setting, 79-81
*on access, 88-89*
breaks, events
adjusting, 136-140
inspecting, 135
BSTREE.EXE Using the Binary Tree
Implementation listing (11-2), 559-562
BUFFER_OVERFLOW_CHECKS
environment variable, 210
building debugger extensions, 593

**C**
-c parameter, 137
-c2 parameter, 137
C++ binary trees, implementing, 556-562
caches, symbol caches, 54-55
call access checks, DCOM, 364-367
call stacks
current call stacks
*discovering, 609-613*
*displaying, 73-79*
function calls, 210
threads, displaying, 212
Call-stack function parameter
listing (12-8), 612
calling conventions, 243
cdecl, 243
fastcall, 243
functions
*cdecl, 240-243*
*stdcall, 240-243*
stack corruptions, 240-255
stdcall, 243
thiscall, 243
CallProc function, 250-255
calls
client call information, attaining, 407-408
DCOM calls, impersonating, 395-396
information, attaining, 404-407
LRPC calls, impersonating, 395-396

cancellations, commands, implementing, 589-590
CCALL objects, naming conventions, 389
CDB (cdb.exe) tool (Debugging Tools for Windows), 31
cdb.exe, 8
cdecl calling convention, 240-243
cell debugging
  configuring, 396-398
  information, 398-399, 408-412
    *accessing, 399-408*
cell paths, breaking, 421-422
Changing file integrity level using built in icacls.exe tool listing (15-12), 731
Changing kernel flags using command line gflags.exe listing (3-21), 150
Changing the current thread listing (3-36), 176
Changing the default register mask listing (2-20), 69
Client stack containing the activation call listing (7-33), 372
Client's thread waiting on LPC request to complete listing (8-1), 384
code
  execution, 96-97
  Microsoft Detours library, 7
  processors, execution, 72
  source code, Fibonacci, 75-76
code breakpoints
  conditional breakpoints, 107
  reference releases, detecting, 107
  setting, 79-81
code execution, tracing, 94-95
Code exercising the exception dispatching logic listing (3-22), 154
code organization, debugger extensions, 567-570
COM interfaces, initializing, 572-573
Command Line mode (gflags), 19-21
Command to delete the symbol files from the symbol servers listing (4-8), 187
Command to store the symbols on the symbol servers listing (4-6), 184

commands
  !address, 90
  !address extension command, 473
  !analyze extension, 691, 699-701, 703-708
  ba, 89
  cancellations, implementing, 589-590
  !cs, 500
  d, 85
  d*s, 87
  debuggers, 32-33
    *context changing commands, 94-104*
    *entering, 46*
    *exploratory commands, 66-94*
    *helper commands, 104-107*
  dt, 82, 617
  .dump, 635-636
  dumptree command, implementing, 580-585
  dv, 82
  extensions, 553-554
    *building, 593*
    *C++ binary tree implementation, 556-562*
    *code organization, 567-570*
    *command cancellations, 589-590*
    *DebugExtensionNotify function, 577*
    *dumptree command, 580-585*
    *examining, 554*
    *general extensions, 554*
    *header files, 567-570*
    *Help command, 579-580*
    *initialization, 570-576*
    *KnownStructOutput function, 578, 585-589*
    *models, 563, 565*
    *requirements, 565-570*
    *session state changes, 577*
    *uninitializing, 578*
    *user mode extensions, 554*
    *versioning, 592*
  !getcallinfo extension, 404-406
  !getdbgcell extension, 406-407
  !getendpointinfo extension, 400-403
  !handle, 496-497, 502-503
  !heap extension commands, 474-491
  Help command, implementing, 579-580
  !htrace extension command, 455-459

k, 78

.lastevent, 66

!lpc extension, 385-386

p, 95-96

!rpctime extension, 400

!sd extension, 324

.sleep 1000, 44

t, 94-95

!token extension command, failures,
     368-371

u, 72

uf, 215

WOW64 commands, 607-609

wt, 98

communication

     interprocess communication, 379-380
          *64-bit debugging, 628-629*
          *communication mechanisms, 380-382*
          *local communications, 382-393, 395-396*
          *network traffic analysis, 413-421*
          *remote communications, 396-422*
          *RPC extended error information, 424-425*
     remote communication, remote
          authentication, 423
     threads, 387

communication mechanisms, interprocess
     communications, 380-382

communication protocols, LPC protocol,
     382-383
     debugging, 384-388
     development of, 383-384

condition variables, synchronization, 739

conditional breakpoints, 107

configuration
     cell debugging, 396-398
     Corporate Error Reporting, 683-687
          *GP (Group Policy) settings, 683-687*
     debuggers
          *kernel mode debuggers, 37-41*
          *user mode debuggers, 34-36*
     file tree configuration, source servers,
          194-196

Configuring the kernel mode debugger
     for the running configuration
     listing (15-6), 716

connections, kernel debuggers, 39-41

Contents of the stack at the point of crash
     listing (5-13), 235

Context, changing, 98-103

context changing commands, debuggers,
     94-104

CONTEXT structure (exceptions), 146

CONTEXT structure, as defined in MSDN
     listing (3-17), 146

controlling
     events, user mode debuggers, 133-144
     exceptions, user mode debuggers, 144-166
     targets, debuggers, 168-177

Corporate Error Reporting, 633, **682-683**
     configuring, 683-687
     errors, reporting, 687-690
     GP (Group Policy) settings, 683-687

corruption (memory), **199-201, 259**
     application crashes, 200
     detection process, 201
          *avoidance strategies, 209*
          *detection tools, 208*
          *instrument source code, 208*
          *source code analysis, 202-208*
          *state analysis, 201-202*
     heap corruptions, 281
          *handle mismatches, 300-305*
          *heap overruns, 286-300*
          *heap reuse after deletion, 306-314*
          *heap underruns, 286-300*
          *uninitiated state, 282-286*
     stack corruptions, 209-222
          *asynchronous operations, 231-240*
          *avoidance strategies, 255-258*
          *calling conventions mismatch, 240-255*
          *stack overruns, 223-231*
          *stack pointers, 231-240*
     unpredictable behavior, 200

cpr (create a process) event, creating, 141

Crash Dump section (Dr. Watson dialog
     box), 655

Crash Dump Type section (Dr. Watson
     dialog box), 655

Crash reproduced in the debugger
     listing (5-10), 225

crash rule (Debug Diagnostic Tool), 692

Creating a kernel mode dump file listing (13-2), 644
Critical section class that handles the lifetime of a critical section listing (10-10), 521
critical sections
  fields, direct usage, 545
  orphaned critical sections, 516-529
  synchronization, 497-502
    *managing*, 545-550
  unlocked critical sections, 543-545
CritSecInfo object, 697-698
!cs extension command, 500
ct (create a thread) event, creating, 143
current call stacks
  discovering, 609-613
  displaying, 73-79
current register values
  debuggers, displaying, 68-71
  finding, 64-bit debuggers, 605-607
current threads, changing, 175
current time stamps, attaining, 400
custom analysis scripts, authoring with Debug Diagnostic tool, 697-699
custom debugger extensions, writing
  64-bit debuggers, 629
  Windows Vista, 741

**D**
d command, 85
d*s command, 87
DACLs (discretionary access control lists), 318
DangerousAPIs test setting (Application Verifyer), 774-775
dbengprx.exe, 8
dbgrpc.exe, 8
DCE/RPC (DCE Remote Procedure Call), 380
DCOM (Distributed Common Object Model), 381
  activation checks, 355-363
  activation failures, Windows XP SP2, 371-376
  call access checks, 364-367
  calls, impersonating, 395-396

  errors, 354-367
  local communication, debugging, 388-396
deadlocks, 510-516, 519
Debug Diagnostic Tool, 691, 693
  crash rule, 692
  custom analysis scripts, authoring, 697-699
  handle leaks, analyzing, 693-697
  hang rule, 692
  Host component, 692
  leak tracker component, 692
  leaks rule, 692
  memory leaks, analyzing, 693-697
  Service component, 692
  starting, 692
  User Interface component, 692
Debug Diagnostics Tool, 691
Debug directories after bin place operation listing (4-5), 183
Debug directories immediately after building the binaries listing (4-4), 183
Debug Flags field (!heap extension command), 478
debug information, binary files, finding in, 51
Debug registers on a normal processor listing (3-31), 171
debug servers, 110-113
DebugDiag, 27, 697
DebugDiag custom analysis script metadata listing (14-1), 697
DebugExtensionNotify function, 577
Debugger COM interfaces initialization listing (11-3), 573
Debugger events generated a WOW64 process execution (xcopy.exe) listing (12-14), 620-622
Debugger events generated by a simple process execution (xcopy.exe) listing (3-7), 131
debugger extensions, 33
  custom 64-bit debugger extensions, writing, 629
  writing, Windows Vista, 741
debugger registry value, AeDebug key, 638-639

**Debugger Tools for Windows**
  KD (kd.exe) tool, 32
  WinDbg (windbg.exe) tool, 32
debuggers, 30, 45, 123-124
  64-bit debuggers, 605-624
    *code processing, 609*
    *current call stack, 609-613*
    *current register values, 605-607*
    *custom debugger extensions, 629*
    *interprocess communication, 628-629*
    *local variable values, 613-614*
    *memory corruption, 625-626*
    *process memory, 615*
    *security, 626-628*
    *WOW64 commands, 607-609*
  address space layout, Windows Vista,
      716-717
  code breakpoints
    *conditional breakpoints, 107*
    *setting, 79-81, 88-89*
  code execution, 96-97
    *tracing, 94-95*
  commands, 32-33
    *context changing commands, 94-104*
    *entering, 46*
    *exploratory commands, 66-94*
    *helper commands, 104-107*
  context, changing, 98-103
  current call stacks, displaying, 73-79
  current register values, displaying, 68-71
  dump files, generating, 634-639
  events, 140-144
    *cpr (create a process) event, 141*
    *ct (create a thread) event, 143*
    *epr (exit a process) event, 142*
    *et (exit a thread) event, 144*
    *ibp (initial breakpoint) event, 141*
    *ld (load a module) event, 142*
    *ud (unload a module) event, 143*
  exceptions, structured exception dispatching
      mechanism, 144-153
  extensions, 553-554
    *building, 593*
    *C++ binary tree implementation, 556,*
      *559-562*
    *code organization, 567-570*

    *command cancellations, 589-590*
    *DebugExtensionNotify function, 577*
    *dumptree command, 580-585*
    *examining, 554*
    *general extensions, 554*
    *header files, 567-570*
    *Help command, 579-580*
    *initialization, 570-576*
    *KnownStructOutput function, 578,*
      *585-589*
    *models, 563, 565*
    *requirements, 565-570*
    *session state changes, 577*
    *uninitializing, 578*
    *user mode extensions, 554*
    *versioning, 592*
  function execution, stepping over, 95-96
  kernel mode debuggers, 32
    *choosing, 44-45*
    *configuring, 37-41*
    *connecting, 39-41*
    *enabling Virtual PC for, 40*
    *event handling, 166-167*
    *output, 48-49*
    *thread suspension, 176-177*
    *Windows Vista, 715-716*
  last events, displaying, 66
  memory, inspecting, 84-87
  memory locations, contents, 89-90
  postmortem setups, 637
  processes
    *attaching to, 281*
    *starting under, 281*
    *task trees, 34-35*
  prompts, interpreting, 47-49
  reference releases, detecting, 107
  running processes
    *attaching nonintrusively to, 36*
    *attaching to, 35*
  source files, 64-66
  symbols, 49
    *caches, 54-55*
    *loaded modules, 57-60*
    *paths, 52, 55-57*
    *reloading, 60-61*
    *symbol files, 49-51, 57-60*

symbol servers, 52-54
  utilizing, 62-64
  validating, 61
target systems, discovering, 67
targets, controlling, 168-177
user mode debuggers, 30-31, 124
  configuring, 34-36
  event control, 133-144
  event order, 131-133
  event processing, 126-130
  exception control, 144-166
  loops, 125-126
  operating system support, 124-130
  output, 47
  redirecting through kernel debuggers,
    41-44
  starting processes, 125
  target creation, 124-125
  u command, 72
  version output, 67
  Windows Vista, 712-714
value, entering, 103-104
variable values, displaying, 81-84
Windows Vista, 711
Debuggers for Windows, commands, 32-33
debugging
  64-bit debugging, 595-596, 603-624
    Application Verifyer, 604
    custom debugger extensions, 629
    Debugging Tools for Windows, 603-604
    Wireshark, 605
    interprocess communication, 628-629
    Leak Diagnostic tool, 603
    memory corruption, 625-626
    security, 626-628
  Application Verifyer, test settings, 747
  live debugging, thread state management,
    172-176
  LPC communication, 384-388
  memory dumps, 36
  multiple remote systems, 48
  noninteractive processes, 118-119
    without kernel mode debugger, 119-120
  postmortem debugging, 631-632
    Corporate Error Reporting, 682-690
    dump files, 632-641, 645-652

kernel dumps, 642-644
    Windows Error Reporting, 653-682
    Windows Vista, 741-745
  remote debugging, 109
    debug servers, 110-113
    kernel servers, 113-114
    process servers, 113-114
    remote.exe, 109-110
    source resolution, 117
    symbol resolution, 115-116
  scenarios, 117-118
  security failures, 340-378
    deferred initiation problems, 347-354
    local security failures, 340-347
  source files, managing for, 188-196
  symbols, managing, 180-188
  Windows Vista, security, 723-727, 729-735
Debugging a memory dump listing (2-4), 36
Debugging a service non-intrusive
    listing (2-3), 36
Debugging a service process from an
    elevated console listing (15-4), 714
Debugging a service process from the
    command prompt listing (15-1), 712
Debugging a service process from
    the normal command prompt
    listing (15-2), 712
Debugging a service process from
    the normal command prompt
    listing (15-3), 714
Debugging Tools for Windows, 7-9, 29-30,
    123, 603-604
  CDB (cdb.exe) tool, 31
  NTSD (ntsd.exe) tool, 31
  remote.exe, 109-110
  WinDbg (windbg.exe) tool, 31
DebugInfo field (RTL_CRITICAL_
    SECTION structure), 498-500
Deciphering kernel global flags
    listing (3-20), 150
declaring gGlobal variable, 88-89
Decoding a security descriptor using the !sd
    extension command listing (7-4), 325
DeCommit option (Heaps test setting), 751
default process heaps, detailed views,
    273-280

deferred initiation problems, security problems during, 347-354

Detailed view of the default process heap listing (6-3), 273-280

detection process, memory corruption, 201
  avoidance strategies, 209
  detection tools, 208
  instrument source code, 208
  source code analysis, 202-208
  state analysis, 201-202

detection tools, memory corruption, 208

dialog boxes
  Dr. Watson, 653-659
  Options (LeakDialog), 6

Digital Rights Management (DRM) systems, 44, 139

directories, SDK directories, 568

Directory structure on the symbol servers listing (4-7), 185

DirtyStacks test setting (Application Verifyer), 775

discretionary access control lists (DACLs), 318

dispatching exceptions, 149-153

DisplayError function, 240

displaying
  current call stacks, 73-79
  current register values, debuggers, 68-71
  debugger last events, 66
  thread impersonation tokens, 329
  variable values, debuggers, 81-84

Displaying information about a loaded module listing (2-15), 58

Displaying primary token's security descriptor listing (7-32), 370

Displaying the call stack listing (2-24), 76

Displaying the call stack of newly created thread listing (5-3), 212

Displaying the current event handling state listing (3-8), 135

Displaying the first three parameters used by the five functions from the call stack listing (2-26), 77

Displaying the module headers listing (2-16), 59

Displaying the parameters used by the last five functions from the call stack listing (2-25), 76

Displaying the stack size used by the five functions from the call stack listing (2-27), 78

Displaying the thread from listing 736 using a kernel mode debugger in local mode listing (7-37), 375

Displaying the thread impersonation token listing (7-7), 329

Displaying the thread in the RPCSS service part of the activation path listing (7-36), 374

Displaying the thread not impersonating listing (7-8), 330

Distributed Common Object Model (DCOM), 381

DllMain function, 529-537

DLLs (Dynamic Link Libraries), 529, 716-717
  debugger extensions, 33

DLLs loaded in the 08cli.exe sample (after reboot) listing (15-8), 717

DLLs loaded in the 08cli.exe sample (before reboot) listing (15-7), 716

Dlls option (Heaps test setting), 750

double frees, memory blocks, 308-314

Dr. Watson dialog box, 199, 653-654
  Application Errors section, 656-657
  Application option, 656-657
  Crash Dump section, 655
  Crash Dump Type section, 655
  Log File Path section, 654
  Module List section, 658
  Number of Errors to Save section, 655
  Number of Instructions section, 655
  Raw Stack Dump section, 660-662
  Stack Back Trace section, 659
  State Dump for Thread ID X section, 658
  System Information section, 657
  Task List section, 658

DRM (Digital Rights Management) systems, 44, 139

dt command, 82
  WOW 64 applications
    *PEB, 617*
    *TEB, 617*
.dump command, 635-636
dump files, 645-646
  analysis
    *access violation, 646-647*
    *handle leaks, 647-652*
  generating
    *Windows Vista, 743*
    *with ADPlus, 639-641*
    *with debuggers, 634-639*
  postmortem debugging, 632-634
dumpchk.exe, 8
dumping
  impersonation tokens, 351
  kernel thread information, 391
  thread state, 173
  threads, 506-507
Dumping the impersonating token
    listing (7-22), 351
Dumping the kernel thread information
    listing (8-9), 392
Dumping the security descriptor for an
    object created while impersonating
    listing (7-23), 353
Dumping the thread state listing (3-33), 173
dumptree command, implementing, 580-585
dv command, 82

**E**
endpoint information, attaining, 400-402
EnterCriticalSection API, 513-514
entering commands, debuggers, 46
Enumerating all BCD objects from an
    elevated console listing (15-5), 715
Enumerating all the client call info cells
    listing (8-23), 409
environment variables
  BUFFER_OVERFLOW_CHECKS, 210
  Win x64, 601
epr (exit a process) event, creating, 142
error information, sending, importance
    of, 664

errors
  DCOM (Distributed COM) errors, 354-367
  reporting, Corporate Error Reporting,
    687-690
et (exit a thread) event, creating, 144
Wireshark, 26, 605
Evaluating a ct event listing (3-14), 144
Evaluating an et event listing (3-15), 144
Evaluating an ud event listing (3-13), 143
Event Log system, Windows Vista, 710-711
event primitive, synchronization, 494-497
events
  aliases, 134
  breakpoints, 168-170
  breaks
    *adjusting, 136-140*
    *inspecting, 135*
  controlling, user mode debuggers, 133-144
  debuggers, 140-144
    *cpr (create a process) event, 141*
    *ct (create a thread) event, 143*
    *epr (exit a process) event, 142*
    *et (exit a thread) event, 144*
    *ipb (initial breakpoint) event, 141*
    *ld (load a module) event, 142*
    *ud (unload a module) event, 143*
  exceptions, compared, 135
  handling
    *adjusting, 136-140*
    *inspecting, 135*
    *kernel mode debuggers, 166-167*
  last events, displaying, 66
  order, user mode debuggers, 131-133
  processing, user mode debuggers, 126-130
Examine explorer.exe process running
    at medium integrity level (UAC)
    listing (15-11), 729-730
Examine one process running at system
    integrity level listing (15-10), 727, 729
Examine the component specific
    AccessCheck performed by RPCSS
    listing (7-27), 360
Examine the first AccessCheck performed
    by RPCSS listing (7-25), 357
Examine the second AccessCheck per-
    formed by RPCSS listing (7-26), 359

Examining a registry key's object header
listing (7-11), 333
Examining the process memory from a noninvasive debugger listing (3-30), 169
Examining the process object security
descriptor listing (7-21), 350
Examining the thread and connection object
info cell listing (8-27), 411
Example of heap handle mismatch
listing (6-9), 300-305
Example of symbol paths with local cache
listing (2-11), 54
Example of symbol server paths
listing (2-10), 54
Example of the !handle extension command
on an instance of notepad.exe
listing (10-1), 495
Example run of registry enumeration application listing (5-11), 231-232
Examples of using the __cdecl and __stdcall
calling conventions listing (5-15),
240-242
Exception dispatched to the user mode
debugger listing (3-19), 147
exception events, processing, user mode
debuggers, 129-130
exception handlers, frame-based exception
handlers, 159-166
Exception handling code for a very simple
function (tryexcept in 02sample.exe)
listing (12-15), 622-625
exception models, Windows x64, 622-625
exceptions
    applications, utilization, 516-522
    breakpoints, 168-170
    controlling, user mode debuggers, 144-166
    dispatching, 149-153
    events, compared, 135
    life cycles, 147-149
    structured exception dispatching
        mechanisms, 144-153
    structures, 145-146
Exceptions test setting (Application
Verifyer), 747
EXCEPTION_DEBUG_EVENT,
processing, 129-130

EXCEPTION_RECORD structure, 145
EXCEPTION_RECORD structure,
as defined in winnt.h header
listing (3-16), 145
Exception|Event|*, 137
exploratory commands, debuggers, 66-94
Exploring the impersonation token after
SSPI impersonation listing (7-13), 337
extension commands, debuggers, 33
extensions
    custom 64-bit debugger extensions, writing,
    629
    debuggers, 553-554
        building, 593
        C++ binary tree implementation, 556,
        559-562
        code organization, 567-570
        command cancellations, 589-590
        DebugExtensionNotify function, 577
        dumptree command, 580-585
        examining, 554
        general extensions, 554
        header files, 567-570
        Help command, 579-580
        initialization, 570-576
        KnownStructOutput function, 578-589
        models, 563-565
        requirements, 565-570
        session state changes, 577
        uninitializing, 578
        user mode extensions, 554
        versioning, 592

**F**
fastcall calling convention, 243
fault follow-up, !analyze extension command,
706-708
FaultRate option (Heaps test setting), 752
Faults option (Heaps test setting), 752
faulty applications, analyzing, !analyze
extension command, 700
Fibonacci function, source code, 75-76
fields, critical sections, direct usage, 545
file dumps, generating, tools, 632
file redirection, side effects, 601

file tree configuration, source servers, 194-196

file virtualization, Windows Vista, 732-735

FilePaths test setting (Application Verifyer), 764-765

files
  binary files, debug information, 51
  Binplace.exe file, 181
  PDB files, stored information, 191
  source files, 64-66, 179
    *managing, 188-196*
  symbol files, 49-51, 179
    *checking, 57-60*

Final event for any process started under debugger listing (3-11), 142

Finding additional information about the LPC message listing (8-10), 393

Finding the PEB for a process listing (6-2), 270-272

Finding the stack that released a specific handle listing (2-43), 108

flags, KnownStructOutput function, 586

Flags field (!heap extension command), 478

Follow up ownership for scenario1.exe listing (14-4), 707

FPO (frame pointer omission) optimization, 74

frame pointer omission, 217

frame-based exception handlers, 159-166

freeing memory blocks, 269

FreeMem function, 305

freezing threads, 174

front end allocators, heaps, 261-263

Full option (Heaps test setting), 750

full pageheap (Heaps test setting), 750, 754, 757

function calls, call stacks, 210

function execution
  monitoring, 98
  tracing, 98

function prologs, 221

Function with five parameters, calling another function with five parameters listing (12-6), 610

functions
  AccessCheck, 323-324
  calling conventions, 243
    *cdecl, 240-243*
    *fastcall, 243*
    *stdcall, 240-243*
    *thiscall, 243*
  CallProc, 250-255
  DebugExtensionNotify, 577
  DisplayError, 240
  DllMain, 529-537
  execution, stepping over, 95-96
  FreeMem, 305
  InitModule, 245, 250-255
  InOrderTraversal, 582
  KnownStructOutput, 578
  KnownStructOutput function, implementing, 585-589
  Sum, 217, 219
  ThreadProcedure, 212-213

**G**

general extensions, debuggers, 554

Generated code for a simple function using __try/__except support listing (3-25), 162

generating
  dump files
    *Windows Vista, 743*
    *with ADPlus, 639-641*
    *with debuggers, 634-639*
  file dumps, tools, 632
  public symbols, 180-183

Generating annotated assembly file from the source file listing (3-27), 165

!getcallinfo extension command, 404-406

!getdbgcell extension command, 406-407

!getendpointinfo extension command, 400-403

Getting more details about the call target listing (8-25), 410

Getting more details from the client cell info listing (8-24), 410

Getting the call info from the endpoint information listing (8-26), 411

gflags, 16
  Command Line mode, 19-21
  GUI mode, 16-18
  option abbreviations, 19-20
gflags.exe, 8
gGlobal declaration listing (2-36), 88
gGlobal variable, declaring, 88-89
Global Flags, 16
  Command Line mode, 19-21
  GUI mode, 16-18
  option abbreviations, 19-20
GP (Group Policy) settings, Corporate Error
    Reporting, 683-687
GUI mode (gflags), 16-18
GUI view (Process Explorer), 22

**H**
-h parameter, 137
!handle extension command, 496-497,
    502-503
handle leaks
  analyzing, Debug Diagnostic tool, 693-697
  dump files, analysis, 647-652
handles
  handle leaks, 434-460
  injection, 455-459
  mismatches, heaps, 300-305
Handles test setting (Application Verifyer),
    747-748
handling events
  adjusting, 136-140
  inspecting, 135
  kernel mode debuggers, 166-167
hang rule (Debug Diagnostic Tool), 692
header files, debugger extensions, 567-570
headers
  kernel object headers, obtaining, 331
  registry key object headers, examining, 332
Heap block address field (!heap extension
    command), 477
heap coalescing, 268
Heap corruption analysis using the heap
    debugger command listing (6-7),
    289-294

heap corruptions, 281
  handle mismatches, 300-305
  heap overruns, 286-300
  heap reuse after deletion, 306-314
  heap underruns, 286-300
  uninitiated state, 282-286
!heap extension command
  heap searching, 480-484
  heap statistics, 475-480
  leak detection, 484-485
  memory leaks, identifying, 474-491
  Pageheap, 485-486
heap manager (Windows), 261, 717-723
heap searching, !heap extension command,
    480-484
heap statistics, !heap extension command,
    475-480
Heap-based string copy application
    listing (6-6), 287-289
heaps, 259-260
  back end allocators, 263-281
  default process heap, detailed view, 273-280
  front end allocators, 261-263
  heap coalescing, 268
  low fragmentation heaps, 718-721
  memory corruption, 625-626
  segments, layout, 266
  subsegments, 721
Heaps test setting (Application Verifyer),
    749-757
  full pageheap, 750, 754, 757
  normal pageheap, 750, 753, 757
Help command, implementing, 579-580
helper commands, debuggers, 104-107
Heuristic used by debugger to find the
    symbol file listing (2-9), 52
HighVersionLie test setting (Application
    Verifyer), 765-767
Host component (Debug Diagnostic
    Tool), 692
How to Freeze or Unfreeze threads
    listing (3-35), 175
How to suspend and resume threads
    listing (3-34), 174
!htrace extension command, handle
    injection, 455-459

htrace leak detection tool, 432
HTTP servers, public symbols, storing on, 187-188

## I–J

ibp (initial breakpoint) event, creating, 141
identifying
    memory leaks, 462-464
      *leak detection tools, 465-491*
    potential resource leaks, 428-430
Identifying Rpcss and DcomLaunch services on Windows XP SP2 listing (7-24), 356
Identifying the caller listing (7-29), 366
Identifying the owning thread of the problematic critical section listing (10-13), 527
Identifying the thread identity listing (7-34), 372
ImpersonateSelf invocation, debugger targets, simulating, 340-341
impersonation
    DCOM calls, 395-396
    LRPC calls, 395-396
    security implications, 354
impersonation levels, client server applications, 337-338
impersonation tokens, 351
information
    calls, attaining, 404-407
    cell debugging, 398-412
      *accessing, 399-408*
    client calls, attaining, 407-408
    endpoints, attaining, 400-402
    source information
      *gathering, 188-191*
      *using, 192-193*
    threads, attaining, 402-403
information sources (security), 328
    access tokens, 328-330
    SDs (security descriptors), 330-333
Information stored in the PDB file listing (4-8), 191
Initial breakpoint stack trace for any process started under debugger listing (3-10), 141

initialization
    COM interfaces, 572-573
    debugger extensions, 570-576
      *type information, 574-575*
      *version information, 572*
    WinDbg extension, extension data, 576
Initialization of type information listing (11-4), 575
Initializing the WinDbg extension data listing (11-5), 577
InitModule function, 245, 250-255
injection, handles, 455-459
InOrderTraversal function, 582
input parameters, local variables, compared, 84
Inspecting the command line and the identity of the server about to be started listing (7-28), 363
Inspecting the security descriptor of another thread object running in the same process listing (7-19), 346
Inspecting the security descriptor of the thread object running the failing code listing (7-18), 345
installation, WDK (Windows Driver Kit), 24
instrument source code, memory corruption, 208
integrity levels, Windows Vista, 724
InteractiveServices test setting (Application Verifyer), 767-768
interprocess communication
    64-bit debugging, 628-629
    remote authentication, 423
    Windows Vista, 736
interprocess communications, 379-380
    communication mechanisms, 380-382
    local communications, troubleshooting, 382-396
    network traffic, analyzing, 413-421
    remote communications, troubleshooting, 396-422
    RPC extended error information, 424-425
Investigating x86 exception handler list listing (3-23), 160

## K

k command, 78
KD (kd.exe) tool (Debugger Tools for
    Windows), 8, 32
kdbgctrl.exe, 8
kdsrv.exe, 8
kernel, thread information, dumping, 391
kernel dumps, creating, 642-644
kernel mode debuggers, configuring, 37-41
Kernel mode debugger output
    listing (2-7), 48
kernel mode debuggers, 32
    choosing, 44-45
    code breakpoints, setting, 80
    connecting, 39-41
    events, handling, 166-167
    output, 48-49
    threads, suspending, 176-177
    user mode debuggers, redirecting through,
        41-44
    Virtual PC, enabling for, 40
kernel objects
    object headers, obtaining, 331
    SDs (security descriptors), obtaining, 331
kernel servers, remote debugging, 113-114
KernelModeDriverInstall test setting
    (Application Verifyer), 768-769
kill.exe, 8
KnownStructOutput function, 578
    flags, 586
    implementing, 585-589

## L

LAL (look aside list) front end allocator,
    heaps, 261
last events, debuggers, displaying, 66
last in first out (LIFO) semantics,
    algorithms, 209
.lastevent command, 66
.lastevent output listing (2-17), 67
layouts, heap segments, 266
ld (load a module) event, creating, 142
leak detection tools, 432-433, 465
    !heap extension command, 474-491
    LeakDiag, 4-6, 432, 470-474
    UMDH, 465-469

Leak Diagnostic tool, 603
leak tracker component (Debug Diagnostic
    Tool), 692
LeakDiag tool, 4-6, 432
    allocators, 4-5
    memory leaks, identifying, 470-474
    Options dialog box, 6
    Stat screen, 5
    UMDH.exe, 4
leaks
    detecting
        !heap extension command, 484-485
        PUT MEMORY LEAKS and HANDLE
            LEAKS, 693
    resource leaks, 430-431
        analysis process, 428-433
        avoidance strategies, 433
        handle leaks, 434-460
        leak detection tools, 432-433
        memory leaks, 460-466, 468-492
        reproducibility, 433-434
leaks rule (Debug Diagnostic Tool), 692
LF (low fragmentation) front end allocators,
    heaps, 261
libraries, Microsoft Detours, 7
life cycles, exceptions, 147-149
LIFO (last in first out) semantics,
    algorithms, 209
link.exe utility, binary files, finding debug
    information in, 51
listing
    processes, task trees, 34-35
    thread summary information, 391
Listing all processes as task tree
    listing (2-1), 34
Listing all symbol files unused since a
    specific date listing (2-12), 55
Listing all the interfaces registered on
    the local system, identified by \\.
    listing (8-31), 426
Listing all the interfaces registered on
    \PIPE\winreg endpoint on the local
    system listing (8-30), 425
Listing of all threads in the culprit process
    listing (10-16), 532

Listing thread summary information
    listing (8-8), 391
listings
    2-1 (Listing all processes as task tree), 34
    2-2 (Options for attaching the debugger to a running process), 35
    2-3 (Debugging a service non-intrusive), 36
    2-4 (Debugging a memory dump), 36
    2-5 (Switching from user mode to kernel mode debugger), 43
    2-6 (User mode debugger output), 47
    2-7 (Kernel mode debugger output), 48
    2-8 (Using the link.exe utility to find debug information stored in the binary file), 51
    2-9 (Heuristic used by debugger to find the symbol file), 52
    2-10 (Example of symbol server paths), 54
    2-11 (Example of symbol paths with local cache), 54
    2-12 (Listing all symbol files unused since a specific date), 55
    2-13 (Two methods of setting up the symbol path at debugger startup), 55
    2-14 (Using the .sympath and .symfix commands), 56
    2-15 (Displaying information about a loaded module), 58
    2-16 (Displaying the module headers), 59
    2-17 (.lastevent output), 67
    2-18 (Version output from a user mode debugger), 67
    2-19 (Registers value using the default register mask), 69
    2-20 (Changing the default register mask), 69
    2-21 {Pseudo-register used on user mode debugger break (x86)}, 71
    2-22 {u command used in user mode debugger (x86)}, 72
    2-23 (Source of Fibonacci function implemented in the 02sample.exe sample), 75
    2-24 (Displaying the call stack), 76
    2-25 (Displaying the parameters used by the last five functions from the call stack), 76
    2-26 (Displaying the first three parameters used by the five functions from the call stack), 77
    2-27 (Displaying the stack size used by the five functions from the call stack), 78
    2-28 (Manual stack reconstruction using the k command), 78
    2-29 (Using breakpoints in the user mode debugger), 79
    2-30 (Using breakpoints in the kernel mode debugger), 80
    2-31 (Using breakpoints in the user mode debugger), 80
    2-32 (Use of dv command), 82
    2-33 (Use of dt command), 83
    2-34 (Use of d command), 85
    2-35 (Use of d*s command), 87
    2-36 (gGlobal declaration), 88
    2-37 (Typical use of the ba command), 89
    2-38 (!address debugger command example), 90
    2-39 (!address command), 91
    2-40 (Obtaining the process PEB), 92
    2-41 (Obtaining the thread TEB), 93
    2-42 (Trace and watch function execution), 98
    2-43 (Finding the stack that released a specific handle), 108
    2-44 (Remoting the console using remote.exe), 109
    2-45 (Starting the debugger server), 111
    3-1 (Sample code used to start a process under user mode debugger), 125
    3-2 (Standard user mode debugger loop), 126
    3-3 (Simple debugger events processing), 127
    3-4 (Processing output debug string event), 128
    3-5 (Read a specific length string from the debugger target space), 128
    3-6 (Processing exception debug event), 130
    3-7 {Debugger events generated by a simple process execution (xcopy.exe)}, 131
    3-8 (Displaying the current event handling state), 135

3-9 (Tools.ini content), 140

3-10 (Initial breakpoint stack trace for any process started under debugger), 141

3-11 (Final event for any process started under debugger), 142

3-12 (stack trace after loading a dynamic link library), 142

3-13 (Evaluating an ud event), 143

3-14 (Evaluating a ct event), 144

3-15 (Evaluating an et event), 144

3-16 (EXCEPTION_RECORD structure, as defined in winnt.h header), 145

3-17 (CONTEXT structure, as defined in MSDN), 146

3-18 (x86 context flags values), 146

3-19 (Exception dispatched to the user mode debugger), 147

3-20 (Deciphering kernel global flags), 150

3-21 (Changing kernel flags using command line gflags.exe), 150

3-22 (Code exercising the exception dispatching logic), 154

3-23 (Investigating x86 exception handler list), 160

3-24 (Simple function using __try/__except constructs), 162

3-25 (Generated code for a simple function using __try/__except support), 162

3-26 (Assembly listing generated for the function from Listing 324), 163

3-27 (Generating annotated assembly file from the source file), 165

3-28 (Thread environment block on two different threads in the same process), 166

3-29 (Using kls flag for detecting a user mode module mapping), 167

3-30 (Examining the process memory from a noninvasive debugger), 169

3-31 (Debug registers on a normal processor), 171

3-32 (Simulating code tracing after attaching to a running project), 172

3-33 (Dumping the thread state), 173

3-34 (How to suspend and resume threads), 174

3-35 (How to Freeze or Unfreeze threads), 175

3-36 (Changing the current thread), 176

3-37 (Simulating a kernel32!Sleep call), 177

4-1 (Binplace file content), 181

4-2 (Binplacing the symbol files), 182

4-3 (Binary folder tree), 182

4-4 (Debug directories immediately after building the binaries), 183

4-5 (Debug directories after bin place operation), 183

4-6 (Command to store the symbols on the symbol servers), 184

4-7 (Directory structure on the symbol servers), 185

4-8 (Command to delete the symbol files from the symbol servers), 187

4-9 (Information stored in the PDB file), 191

4-10 (SourceServer information stored in the PDB file), 191

4-11 (Source server file tree configuration), 194

5-1 (Simple console-based application that simulates a memory corruption), 203-207

5-2 (Sample application showing the creation of a new thread), 210-211

5-3 (Displaying the call stack of newly created thread), 212

5-4 (Assembly code of the ThreadProcedure function), 213

5-5 (Assembly code for ProcA), 215-216

5-6 (Preamble assembly code for calling the Sum function), 217

5-7 (Assembly instructions right after our call to Sum), 219

5-8 (ProcA function epilog), 220

5-9 (Application that establishes a connection to a data source), 223

5-10 (Crash reproduced in the debugger), 225

5-11 (Example run of registry enumeration application), 231-232

5-12 (Access violation enumerating registry values), 232-234

5-13 (Contents of the stack at the point of crash), 235

5-14 (Walking the stack back in time), 236-239

5-15 (Examples of using the __cdecl and __stdcall calling conventions), 240-242

5-16 (Simple application that declares a number of functions), 244-245

5-17 (Application that calls a function in a DLL), 245-247

5-18 (Attempt at manually constructing the stack), 248-255

6-1 (Simple application that performs heap allocations), 270

6-2 (Finding the PEB for a process), 270, 272

6-3 (Detailed view of the default process heap), 273-280

6-4 (Simple application that uses uninitialized memory), 282-283

6-5 (Application crash seen under the debugger), 283-286

6-6 (Heap-based string copy application), 287-289

6-7 (Heap corruption analysis using the heap debugger command), 289-294

6-8 (Application verifier reported heap block corruption), 295-300

6-9 (Example of heap handle mismatch), 300, 302-305

6-10 (Simple example of double free), 308-312, 314

7-1 (SID structure definition), 319

7-2 (Sample code exercising the AccessCheck function), 323-324

7-3 (Binary representation of a security descriptor), 324

7-4 (Decoding a security descriptor using the !sd extension command), 325

7-5 (Using the !token extension command to display a token in the user mode debugger), 326

7-6 (Obtaining the process access token), 329

7-7 (Displaying the thread impersonation token), 329

7-8 (Displaying the thread not impersonating), 330

7-9 (Obtaining the object header for a kernel object), 331

7-10 (Obtaining kernel objects security descriptor), 332

7-11 (Examining a registry key's object header), 333

7-12 (Tracing the remote authentication from the server process), 336

7-13 (Exploring the impersonation token after SSPI impersonation), 337

7-14 (Sample function calling GetComputerNameEx at different impersonation levels), 338

7-15 (Simulating ImpersonateSelf invocation in the debugger target), 341

7-16 (Obtaining the process object security descriptor), 343

7-17 (Obtaining the primary token object security descriptor), 344

7-18 (Inspecting the security descriptor of the thread object running the failing code), 345

7-19 (Inspecting the security descriptor of another thread object running in the same process), 346

7-20 (Sample initialization function), 348

7-21 (Examining the process object security descriptor), 350

7-22 (Dumping the impersonating token), 351

7-23 (Dumping the security descriptor for an object created while impersonating), 353

7-24 (Identifying Rpcss and DcomLaunch services on Windows XP SP2), 356

7-25 (Examine the first AccessCheck performed by RPCSS), 357

7-26 (Examine the second AccessCheck performed by RPCSS), 359

7-27 (Examine the component specific AccessCheck performed by RPCSS), 360

7-28 (Inspecting the command line and the identity of the server about to be started), 363

7-29 (Identifying the caller), 366

7-30 (Watching the error code returned by OpenThreadToken/ OpenProcessToken, 369

7-31 (Obtaining the token information using local KD), 370

7-32 (Displaying primary token's security descriptor), 370

7-33 (client stack containing the activation call), 372

7-34 (Identifying the thread identity), 372

7-35 (Stopping the DcomLaunch code after impersonating the client), 373

7-36 (Displaying the thread in the RPCSS service part of the activation path), 374

7-37 (Displaying the thread from Listing 736 using a kernel mode debugger in local mode), 375

8-1 (Client's thread waiting on LPC request to complete), 384

8-2 (Using !lpc extension to get message information), 385

8-3 (Using !lpc extension to get port information), 386

8-4 (Using !lpc extension to obtain the entire LPC activity on the system), 386

8-5 (Starting the client and listing a partial call stack for each thread), 388

8-6 (Typical stack of clients using DCOM over LRPC), 389

8-7 (Typical stack of a server thread waiting for a new request on DCOM over LRPC), 390

8-8 (Listing thread summary information), 391

8-9 (Dumping the kernel thread information), 392

8-10 (Finding additional information about the LPC message), 393

8-11 (Server's thread processing the LPC message), 394

8-12 (Reading ImpersonationInfo ImpersonationInfo stored on the server thread), 395

8-13 (Using !rpctime to obtain the current time stamp used by troubleshooting infrastructure), 400

8-14 (Using !getendpointinfo to list all endpoints known by RPC), 401

8-15 (Using !getendpointinfo to list all endpoint known by RPC), 402

8-16 (Using !getthreadinfo to list all thread from RPC thread pool), 402

8-17 (Using !getthreadinfo to obtain a specific thread RPC information), 403

8-18 (Using !getcallinfo to obtain the call information maintained by the server), 405

8-19 (Using !getcallinfo to filter call information to a specific process), 405

8-20 (Using !getdbgcell to obtain the cell information maintained by the server), 406

8-21 (Using !getclientcallinfo to obtain the call information maintained by the client), 408

8-22 (Typical client stack waiting on remote call made using a connection-based protocol), 409

8-23 (Enumerating all the client call info cells), 409

8-24 (Getting more details from the client cell info), 410

8-25 (Getting more details about the call target), 410

8-26 (Getting the call info from the endpoint information), 411

8-27 (Examining the thread and connection object info cell), 411

8-28 (Server thread call stack), 412

8-29 (Server breakpoints encountered using SSPI), 423

8-30 (Listing all the interfaces registered on \PIPE\winreg endpoint on the local system), 425

8-31 (Listing all the interfaces registered on the local system, identified by \\.), 426

10-1 (Example of the !handle extension command on an instance of notepad.exe), 495

10-3 (Using the !cs command to list all critical sections of a process), 501

10-4 (Using the !handle extension command to find mutex object in notepad.exe), 502

10-5 (Using the °kb command to Dump all threads and associated stacks), 506

10-6 (Sample application that results in a deadlock), 510

10-7 (All thread stacks currently running in the process), 512

10-8 (Sample application that utilizes exceptions), 516

10-9 (Sample application thread state), 519

10-10 (Critical section class that handles the lifetime of a critical section), 521

10-11 (Simple application utilizing the TerminateThread API), 523

10-12 (Thread list and associated stacks of hung application), 525

10-13 (Identifying the owning thread of the problematic critical section), 527

10-16 (Listing of all threads in the culprit process), 532

10-17 (Sample application that suffers from lock convoys), 540

10-18 (Unlocked Critical Section), 543

10-19 (Locked Critical Section with no Waiters), 543

10-20 (Locked Critical Section with Waiters), 544

10-21 (Properly initialized critical section), 546

11-1 (Simple C++ Binary Tree Implementation), 556, 559

11-2 (BSTREE.EXE Using the Binary Tree Implementation), 559-562

11-3 (Debugger COM interfaces initialization), 573

11-4 (Initialization of type information), 575

11-5 (Initializing the WinDbg extension data), 577

12-1 (Native stack on a WOW64 process), 599

12-2 (x86-64-bit general purposes register), 606

12-3 {True 32 bit Stack in WOW64 Process (hidden in Listing 121)}, 608

12-4 (Obtaining WOW64 structures), 608

12-5 (Unassembly code is dependent on the processor execution mode), 609

12-6 (Function with five parameters, calling another function with five parameters), 610

12-7 (Assembly code representing the Function5 function), 610

12-8 (Call-stack function parameter), 612

12-9 (Unassembled non-optimized function), 613

12-10 (Local variable), 614

12-11 (WOW64 applications PEB), 615, 617

12-12 (WOW64 application's PEB using the dt command), 617

12-13 (WOW64 threads' TEB using !teb extension command and dt commands), 618

12-14 {Debugger events generated a WOW64 process execution (xcopy.exe)}, 620-622

12-15 {Exception handling code for a very simple function (tryexcept in 02sample.exe)}, 622, 624-625

12-16 (Security information on Windows x64), 626

13-1 (Simple crashing application), 633

13-2 (Creating a kernel mode dump file), 644

14-1 (DebugDiag custom analysis script metadata), 697

14-2 (Using the CritSec object), 698

14-3 (Output of the !analyze extension command), 701-703

14-4 (Follow up ownership for scenario1.exe), 707

15-1 (Debugging a service process from the command prompt), 712

15-2 (Debugging a service process from the normal command prompt), 712

15-3 (Debugging a service process from the normal command prompt), 714

15-4 (Debugging a service process from an elevated console), 714

15-5 (Enumerating all BCD objects from an elevated console), 715

15-6 (Configuring the kernel mode debugger for the running configuration), 716

15-7 {DLLs loaded in the 08cli.exe sample (before reboot)}, 716

15-8 {DLLs loaded in the 08cli.exe sample (after reboot)}, 717

15-9 (Application manifest requesting a high integrity level), 724

15-10 (Examine one process running at system integrity level), 727, 729

15-11 {Examine explorer.exe process running at medium integrity level (UAC)}, 729-730

15-12 (Changing file integrity level using built in icacls.exe tool), 731

15-13 (Setting and retrieving application settings from UAC administrator), 732

15-14 (Retrieving application settings from an elevated prompt), 733

live debugging, thread state management, 172-176

loaded modules, checking, 57-60

local communication, troubleshooting, 382-396

Local Procedure Call (LPC), 381

local security failures, investigating, 340-344, 347

Local variable listing (12-10), 614

local variables

  input parameters, compared, 84

  values, discovering, 613-614

lock contention, synchronization, 538-545

LockCount field (RTL_CRITICAL_ SECTION structure), 498

Locked Critical Section with no Waiters listing (10-19), 543

Locked Critical Section with Waiters listing (10-20), 544

Locks test setting (Application Verifyer), 757-759

LockSemaphore field (RTL_CRITICAL_ SECTION structure), 499

Log File Path section (Dr. Watson dialog box), 654

logger.exe, 8

logviewer.exe, 8

look aside list (LAL) front end allocators, heaps, 261

loops, user mode debuggers, 125-126

low fragmentation (LF) front end allocator, heaps, 261

low fragmentation heaps, 718-721

Low Resource Simulation test setting (Application Verifyer), 769-770

LPC (Local Procedure Call), 381

!lpc extension command, 385-386

LPC protocol, 382-383

  debugging communication, 384-388

  development of, 383-384

LRPC calls, impersonating, 395-396

LuaPriv test setting (Application Verifyer), 771-774

**M**

managing critical sections, 545-550

Manual stack reconstruction using the k command listing (2-28), 78

manually constructing, stacks, 247, 249-252

mapping binaries to products, Windows Error Reporting, 673-677

memory

  heaps

    *back end allocators, 263-281*

    *front end allocators, 261-263*

  inspecting, 84-87

  kernel dumps, creating, 642-644

  memory leaks, 460-492

    *avoidance strategies, 491-492*

    *identifying, 462-464*

    *leak detection tools, 465-491*

  process memory, inspecting, 615

memory blocks

  allocating, 269

  double frees, 308-314

  freeing, 269

memory corruption, 199-201, 259

  application crashes, 200

  detection process, 201

    *avoidance strategies, 209*

    *detection tools, 208*

    *instrument source code, 208*

    *source code analysis, 202-208*

    *state analysis, 201-202*

heap corruptions, 281
 *handle mismatches, 300-305*
 *heap overruns, 286-300*
 *heap reuse after deletion, 306-314*
 *heap underruns, 286-300*
 *uninitiated state, 282-286*
 heaps, 625-626
 stack corruptions, 209-222
  *asynchronous operations, 231-240*
  *avoidance strategies, 255-258*
  *calling conventions mismatch, 240-255*
  *stack overruns, 223-231*
  *stack pointers, 231-240*
 stacks, 625
 unpredictable behavior, 200
memory dumps, debugging, 36
memory leak detection
 LeakDiag (Leak Diagnosis) tool, 4-6
 UMDH, 9
memory leaks, 460-492
 analyzing, Debug Diagnostic tool, 693-697
 avoidance strategies, 491-492
 identifying, 462-464
 leak detection tools, 465
  *!heap extension command, 474-491*
  *LeakDiag, 470-474*
  *UMDH, 465-469*
memory locations, contents, displaying, 89-90
Memory test setting (Application Verifyer), 760-762
Microsoft Application Verifier, 10-16
Microsoft Detours, 7
mismatches, handles, heaps, 300-305
models, debugger extensions, 563-565
Module List section (Dr. Watson dialog box), 658
modules, loaded modules, checking, 57-60
monitoring function execution, 98
mov edi,edi instruction, 222
MSRPC, communication, debugging, 388-396
multiple remote systems, debugging, 48
multithreading, 493, 550
mutex kernel mode synchronization construct, 502-504

**N**
naming conventions
 ADDRESS objects, 390
 CCALL objects, 389
Native stack on a WOW64 process listing (12-1), 599
network protocols, analyzing, Wireshark, 26
network traffic, analyzing, 413-421
NoLock option (Heaps test setting), 751
noninteractive processes, debugging, 118-119
 without kernel mode debugger, 119-120
normal pageheap (Heaps test setting), 750-753, 757
npipe protocol, 111
NTSD (ntsd.exe) tool (Debugging Tools for Windows), 31
ntsd.exe, 8
Number of Errors to Save section (Dr. Watson dialog box), 655
Number of Instructions section (Dr. Watson dialog box), 655
NX enabled systems, Windows support for, 255

**O**
object headers
 kernel objects, obtaining, 331
 registry keys, examining, 332
object security, 317-319
 access tokens, 325-328
 ACLs (Access Control Lists), 320-322
 client server applications
  *impersonation levels, 337-338*
  *remote authentication, 335-337*
  *security support provider interface support, 335-337*
  *token propagation, 334-338*
 SDs (security descriptors), 322-325
 security checks, 334
  *system boundaries, 338-340*
 security failures
  *deferred initiation problems, 347-354*
  *investigating, 340-378*
  *local security failures, 340-347*

security information sources, 328
  *access tokens, 328-330*
  *SDs (security descriptors), 330-333*
  SIDs (security identifiers), 319-320, 325-328
  *types, 327*
  *well-known SIDs, 327*
object security descriptors, process object
  security descriptors, 342-344
objects
  ADDRESS objects, naming
    conventions, 390
  BCD (Boot Configuration Data), 715-716
  CCALL objects, naming conventions, 389
  CritSecInfo, 697-698
Obtaining kernel objects security descriptor
  listing (7-10), 332
Obtaining the object header for a kernel
  object listing (7-9), 331
Obtaining the primary token object security
  descriptor listing (7-17), 344
Obtaining the process access token
  listing (7-6), 329
Obtaining the process object security
  descriptor listing (7-16), 343
Obtaining the process PEB listing (2-40), 92
Obtaining the thread TEB listing (2-41), 93
Obtaining the token information using local
  KD listing (7-31), 370
Obtaining WOW64 structures
  listing (12-4), 608
one-time initialization APIs,
  synchronization, 740
operating systems
  64-bit operating systems, 595-598
  user mode debuggers, support, 124-130
  Windows Vista, 709
    *custom debugger extensions, 741*
    *debuggers, 711-717*
    *debugging security, 723-735*
    *Event Log system, 710-711*
    *heap manager, 717-723*
    *interprocess communication, 736*
    *one-time initialization, 740*
    *postmortem debugging, 741-745*
    *resource leaks, 736*
    *synchronization, 737-740*
    *tools, 710*
    *user access control side effects, 712-714*
Options dialog box (LeakDialog), 6
Options for attaching the debugger to a
  running process listing (2-2), 35
order, events, user mode debuggers, 131-133
orphaned critical sections, 516-529
output
  !analyze extension command, 701-703
  kernel mode debuggers, 48-49
  user mode debuggers, 47
  *version output, 67*
Output of the !analyze extension command
  listing (14-3), 701-703
OUTPUT_DEBUG_STRING_EVENT,
  processing, 127-129
overruns
  heaps, 286-300
  stacks, 223-231
OwningThread field (RTL_CRITICAL_
  SECTION structure), 499

**P**
p command, 95-96
Pageheap, !heap extension command,
  485-486
paths, symbols, 52
  setting, 55-57
PDB files, stored information, 191
PEB (process environment block)
  locating, 270, 272
  obtaining, 93
  WOW64 applications, 615
    *dt command, 617*
pointers (stacks), 231-240
postmortem debugging, 631-632
  Corporate Error Reporting, 682-683
    *configuring, 683-687*
    *error reporting, 687-690*
    *GP (Group Policy) settings, 683-687*
  dump files, 632-634, 645-646
    *access violation analysis, 646-647*
    *generating, 634-641*
    *handle leak analysis, 647-652*
  kernel dumps, creating, 642-644

Windows Error Reporting, 653-662
  *architecture, 662-682*
Windows Vista, 741-745
Preamble assembly code for calling the Sum
  function listing (5-6), 217
Previous size field (!heap extension
  command), 478
primary token object security descriptor,
  obtaining, 344
primitives, synchronization, event primitive,
  494-497
PrintAPI test setting (Application
  Verifyer), 776
PrintDriver test setting (Application
  Verifyer), 776
private symbols, 591
ProcA function epilog listing (5-8), 220
ProcA procedure, 214, 220
  assembly code, 214-216
procedures, ProcA, 214, 220
  assembly code, 214-216
process access tokens, obtaining, 329
Process Explorer, 22-23
process health, analyzing, Process Explorer,
  22-23
process memory, inspecting, 615
Process Monitor, 23
process object security descriptors
  examining, 350
  obtaining, 342-344
process servers, remote debugging, 113-114
processes
  64-bit processes, 595-596
  debuggers, attaching to, 281
  interprocess communication
    *64-bit debugging, 628-629*
    *Windows Vista, 736*
  interprocess communications, 379-380
    *communication mechanisms, 380-382*
    *local communications, 382-396*
    *network traffic analysis, 413-421*
    *remote communications, 396-422*
    *RPC extended error information, 424-425*
  listing task trees, 34-35
  noninteractive processes, 118-119
    *without kernel mode debugger, 119-120*

PEB (process environment block)
  *locating, 270, 272*
  *obtaining, 93*
running processes
  *attaching debuggers nonintrusively to, 36*
  *attaching debuggers to, 35*
starting under debuggers, 281
user mode debuggers, starting, 125
Processing exception debug event
  listing (3-6), 130
Processing output debug string event
  listing (3-4), 128
processors
  code execution, 72
  code processing, discovering, 609
  tracing, 172
product rollup page, Windows Error
  Reporting, 672
programming errors, memory corruption,
  199-200
  application crashes, 200
  detection process, 201-209
  stack corruptions, 209-258
  unpredictable behavior, 200
prologs, functions, 221
prompts, debuggers, interpreting, 47-49
propagation, token propagation, client server
  applications, 334-338
Properly initialized critical section
  listing (10-21), 546
Protect option (Heaps test setting), 751
protocols
  communication protocols, 380-382
    *LPC protocol, 382-384*
  npipe protocol, 111
  TCP, 112-113
Pseudo-register used on user mode
  debugger break (x86) listing (2-21), 71
public symbols, 591
  generating, 180-183
  HTTP servers, storing on, 187-188

**Q–R**
Random option (Heaps test setting), 750
RandRate option (Heaps test setting), 751
Raw Stack Dump section (Dr. Watson dialog
  box), 660-662

Read a specific length string from the debugger target space listing (3-5), 128

reader/writer locks, synchronization, 737-738

Reading ImpersonationInfo ImpersonationInfo stored on the server thread listing (8-12), 395

RecursionCount field (RTL_CRITICAL_SECTION structure), 499

redirecting user mode debuggers through kernel debuggers, 41-44

redirection, files, side effects, 601

reference releases, detecting, 107

register values
  current register values, finding, 605-607
  debuggers, displaying, 68-71

Registers value using the default register mask listing (2-19), 69

registry keys, object headers, examining, 332

registry virtualization, Windows Vista, 732-735

reloading symbols, 60-61

remote authentication, 423
  client server applications, 335-337

remote communication
  cell paths, breaking, 421-422
  remote authentication, 423
  RPC extended error information, 424-425
  troubleshooting, 396-422

remote debugging, 109
  debug servers, 110-113
  kernel servers, 113-114
  process servers, 113-114
  remote.exe, 109-110
  source resolution, 117
  symbol resolution, 115-116

remote systems, multiple remote systems, debugging, 48

remote.exe, 8

remote.exe utility, remote debugging, 109-110

Remoting the console using remote.exe listing (2-44), 109

reporting errors, Corporate Error Reporting, 687-690

reproducibility, resource leaks, 433-434

requirements, debugger extensions, 565-570

resolving
  sources, remote debugging, 117
  symbols, remote debugging, 115-116

resource leaks, 427, 430-431
  analysis process, 428-433
  avoidance strategies, defining, 433
  handle leaks, 434-460
  leak detection tools, 432-433
  memory leaks, 460-492
    *avoidance strategies, 491-492*
    *identifying, 462-464*
    *leak detection tools, 465-491*
  potential resource leaks, identifying, 428-430
  PUT MEMORY LEAKS and HANDLE LEAKS, 693
  reproducibility, 433-434
  Windows Vista, 736

resources, 427-428

results, analyzing, !analyze extension command, 701, 703-706

resuming threads, 174

Retrieving application settings from an elevated prompt listing (15-14), 733

reuse, heaps after deletion, 306-314

rollup page, Windows Error Reporting, 672

RPC troubleshooting state information, 396
  cell debugging
    *configuring, 396-398*
    *information, 398-412*
  extended error information, 424-425

!rpctime extension command, 400

rtlist.exe, 8

RTL_CRITICAL_SECTION structure, 498

running processes, debuggers
  attaching nonintrusively to, 36
  attaching to, 35


**S**

Sample application showing the creation of a new thread listing (5-2), 210-211

Sample application that results in a deadlock listing (10-6), 510

Sample application that suffers from lock convoys listing (10-17), 540

Sample application that utilizes exceptions listing (10-8), 516
Sample application thread state listing (10-9), 519
Sample code exercising the AccessCheck function listing (7-2), 323-324
Sample code used to start a process under user mode debugger listing (3-1), 125
Sample function calling GetComputerNameEx at different impersonation levels listing (7-14), 338
Sample initialization function listing (7-20), 348
scenarios, debugging scenarios, 117-118
scripts, custom analysis scripts, authoring, 697-699
!sd extension command, 324
SDDL (security descriptor definition language), 323
SDK directories, 568
SDs (security descriptors), 322-325, 330-333
   kernel object SD, obtaining, 331
   primary token object security descriptor, obtaining, 344
   process object security descriptors
      *examining, 350*
      *obtaining, 342-344*
security, 317
   !token extension commands, failures, 368-371
   64-bit debugging, 626, 628
   client server applications
      *impersonation levels, 337-338*
      *remote authentication, 335-337*
      *security support provider interface support, 335-337*
      *token propagation, 334-338*
   DCOM (Distributed COM) errors, 354-367
   debugging, Windows Vista, 723-735
   impersonation, implications, 354
   information sources, 328
      *access tokens, 328-330*
      *SDs (security descriptors), 330-333*
   object security, 317-319
      *access tokens, 325-328*
      *ACLs (Access Control Lists), 320-322*

*SDs (security descriptors), 322-325*
*SIDs (security identifiers), 319-320, 325-328*
security checks, system boundaries, 338-340
security failures
   *deferred initiation problems, 347-354*
   *investigating, 340-378*
   *local security failures, 340-344, 347*
security checks, 334
security checks, 334
   system boundaries, 338-340
security descriptor definition language (SDDL), 323
security failures, investigating, 340-378
   deferred initiation problems, 347-354
   local security failures, 340-347
Security information on Windows x64 listing (12-16), 626
Security Reference Monitor. *See* SRM (Security Reference Monitor)
security support provider interface support, client server applications, 335-337
segments, heaps, layout, 266
semaphore kernel mode synchronization object, 504
sending error information, importance of, 664
Server breakpoints encountered using SSPI listing (8-29), 423
Server thread call stack listing (8-28), 412
Server's thread processing the LPC message listing (8-11), 394
servers
   debug servers, 110-113
   kernel servers, remote debugging, 113-114
   process servers, remote debugging, 113-114
   symbol servers, 52-54
Service component (Debug Diagnostic Tool), 692
session states, debuggers
   changes, 577
   DebugExtensionNotify function, 577
setting code breakpoints, 88-89
Setting and retrieving application settings from UAC administrator listing (15-13), 732

SID structure definition listing (7-1), 319
side effects
    access control, Windows Vista, 712-714
    file redirection, 601
SIDs (security identifiers), 319-320, 325-328
    types, 327
    well-known SIDs, 327
Simple application that declares a number of
    functions listing (5-16), 244-245
Simple application that performs heap
    allocations listing (6-1), 270
Simple application that uses uninitialized
    memory listing (6-4), 282-283
Simple application utilizing the
    TerminateThread API
    listing (10-11), 523
Simple C++ Binary Tree Implementation
    listing (11-1), 556, 559
Simple console-based application that
    simulates a memory corruption
    listing (5-1), 203-207
Simple crashing application
    listing (13-1), 633
Simple debugger events processing
    listing (3-3), 127
Simple example of double free
    listing (6-10), 308-312, 314
Simple function using __try/__except
    constructs listing (3-24), 162
simulating ImpersonateSelf invocation,
    debugger targets, 340-341
Simulating a kernel32!Sleep call
    listing (3-37), 177
Simulating code tracing after attaching to a
    running project listing (3-32), 172
Simulating ImpersonateSelf invocation in
    the debugger target listing (7-15), 341
Size field (!heap extension command), 478
Size option (Heaps test setting), 750
SizeEnd option (Heaps test setting), 750
SizeStart option (Heaps test setting), 750
.sleep 1000 command, 44
source code
    Fibonacci function, 75-76
    instrument source code, memory corruption
        analysis, 208

source code analysis, memory corruption,
    202-208
source files, 64-66, 179
    information
        *gathering, 188-191*
        *using, 192-193*
    managing for debugging, 188-196
Source of Fibonacci function implemented
    in the 02sample.exe sample
    listing (2-23), 75
Source server file tree configuration
    listing (4-10), 194
source servers
    file tree configuration, 194-196
    without source revision control, 194-196
sources (security information), 328
    access tokens, 328-330
    resolving, remote debugging, 117
    SDs (security descriptors), 330-333
SourceServer information stored in the PDB
    file listing (4-9), 191
SpinCount field (RTL_CRITICAL_
    SECTION structure), 499
SRM (Security Reference Monitor), 318
sse (single step exception), 138
ssec (single step exception
    continuation), 138
Stack Back Trace section (Dr. Watson dialog
    box), 659
stack corruptions, 209-222
    asynchronous operations, 231-240
    avoidance strategies, 255-258
    calling conventions mismatch, 240-255
    stack overruns, 223-231
    stack pointers, 231-240
stack overruns, 223-231
stack pointers, stack corruptions, 231-240
Stack trace after loading a dynamic link
    library listing (3-12), 142
stacks
    call stacks
        *displaying, 212*
        *function calls, 210*
    manually constructing, 247-252
    memory corruption, 625
    ProcA procedure, 214
        *assembly code, 214-216*

Standard user mode debugger loop
  listing (3-2), 126
starting
  Debug Diagnostic Tool, 692
  processes under debuggers, 281
Starting the client and listing a partial call
  stack for each thread listing (8-5), 388
Starting the debugger server
  listing (2-45), 111
Stat screen (LeakDiag), 5
state analysis, memory corruption, 201-202
State Dump for Thread ID X section (Dr.
  Watson dialog box), 658
state transition, kernel mode prompts, 42
Status field (!heap extension command), 478
stdcall calling convention, 240-243
stepping over, function execution, 95-96
stop codes
  DangerousAPIs test setting, 774
  FilePath test setting, 765
  Handles test setting, 748
  Heaps test setting, 756
  Locks test setting, 758-759
  LuaPriv test setting, 772-774
  Memory test setting, 761-762
  ThreadPool test setting, 763
  TLS test setting, 764
Stopping the DcomLaunch code
  after impersonating the client
  listing (7-35), 373
storing
  public symbols, HTTP servers, 187-188
  symbols in symbol stores, 184-186
string events, processing, user mode
  debuggers, 127-129
stripped symbols. *See* symbols
structured exception dispatching methods,
  144-153
structures
  exceptions, 145-146
  WOW64 structures, obtaining, 608
subsegments, 721
Sum function, assembly code, 217-219
summary information, threads, listing, 391
suspending threads, 174
  kernel mode debuggers, 176-177

Switching from user mode to kernel mode
  debugger listing (2-5), 43
sxd (set exceptions disable), 136
sxe (set exceptions enable), 136
sxi (set exceptions ignore), 137
sxn (set exceptions notify), 137
symbol caches, 54-55
symbol files, 49-51, 179
  checking, 57-60
symbol servers, 52-54
symbol stores, 184-186
symbols, 591
  debuggers, 49
    *caches, 54-55*
    *loaded modules, 57-60*
    *paths, 52, 55-57*
    *reloading, 60-61*
    *symbol files, 49-51, 57-60*
    *symbol servers, 52-54*
    *utilizing, 62-64*
    *validating, 61*
  managing, 180-188
  private symbols, 591
  public symbols, 591
    *generating, 180-183*
    *sharing on HTTP servers, 187-188*
  resolving, remote debugging, 115-116
  symbol stores, storing in, 184-186
symchk.exe, 8
symstore.exe, 8
synchronization, 493
  critical sections
    *managing, 545-550*
    *orphaned critical sections, 516-529*
    *unlocked, 543-545*
  deadlocks, 510-519
  DllMain function, 529-537
  lock contention, 538-545
  problem analysis process, 505-509
  threads, 493
    *critical sections, 497-502*
    *event primitive, 494-497*
    *mutex, 502-504*
    *problem analysis, 507-509*
    *semaphore, 504*

Windows Vista, 737
   *condition variables, 739*
   *one-time initialization, 740*
   *reader/writer locks, 737-738*
   *thread pools, 740*
system boundaries, security checks, 338-340
system health, analyzing, Process Explorer,
   22-23
System Information section (Dr. Watson
   dialog box), 657
system targets, controlling, debuggers,
   168-177

**T**
t command, 94-95
target systems
   debuggers, discovering, 67
   kernel debuggers, connecting to, 39-41
targets
   controlling, debuggers, 168-177
   ImpersonateSelf invocation, simulating,
     340-341
   user mode debuggers, creating, 124-125
Task List section (Dr. Watson dialog
   box), 658
task trees, processes, listing in, 34-35
TCP (Transmission Control Protocol),
   112-113
TEB (thread environment block)
   obtaining, 93
   WOW64 applications, dt command, 617
TerminateThread API, 523, 525-528
termination, threads, 523-529
test settings, Application Verifyer, 747
   DangerousAPIs, 774-775
   DirtyStacks, 775
   Exceptions, 747
   FilePaths, 764-765
   Handles, 747-748
   Heaps, 749-757
   HighVersionLie, 765-767
   InteractiveServices, 767-768
   KernelModeDriverInstall, 768-769
   Locks, 757-759
   Low Resource Simulation, 769-770
   LuaPriv, 771-774

Memory, 760-762
PrintAPI, 776
PrintDriver, 776
ThreadPool, 762-763
TimeRollOver, 775
TSL, 764
thiscall calling convention, 243
Thread environment block on two
   different threads in the same
   process listing (3-28), 166
thread impersonation tokens, displaying, 329
Thread list and associated stacks of hung
   application listing (10-12), 525
thread local storage (TLS), 764
thread pools, synchronization, 740
thread state, dumping, 173
thread state management, live debugging,
   172-176
ThreadPool test setting (Application
   Verifyer), 762-763
ThreadProcedure function, 212-213
threads
   call stacks, displaying, 212
   communication, 387
   current threads, changing, 175
   dumping out, 506-507
   freezing, 174
   information, attaining, 402-403
   kernel threads, dumping, 391
   multithreading, 493, 550
   resuming, 174
   summary information, listing, 391
   suspending, 174
     *kernel mode debuggers, 176-177*
   synchronization, 493
     *critical sections, 497-502*
     *event primitive, 494-497*
     *mutex, 502-504*
     *semaphore, 504*
   synchronization problems, analyzing,
     507-509
   TEB (thread environment block),
     obtaining, 93
   termination, 523-529
   unfreezing, 174

time stamps, current time stamps,
attaining, 400
TimeOut option (Heaps test setting), 752
TimeRollOver test setting (Application
Verifyer), 775
tlist.exe, 8
TLS (thread local storage), 764
!token extension command, failures, 368-371
token propagation, client server applications,
334-338
impersonation levels, 337-338
remote authentication, 335-337
security support provider, 335-337
tools, 3-4
!analyze extension command, 691, 699-708
Application Verifier, 10-16
Debug Diagnostic Tool, 691-693
*crash rule, 692*
*custom analysis script analysis, 697-699*
*handle leak analysis, 693-697*
*hang rule, 692*
*Host component, 692*
*leak tracker component, 692*
*leaks rule, 692*
*memory leak analysis, 693-697*
*Service component, 692*
*starting, 692*
*User Interface component, 692*
Debug Diagnostics Tool, 691
DebugDiag, 27
Debugging Tools for Windows, 7-9, 29-30
*CDB (cdb.exe) tool, 31*
*commands, 32-33*
*KD (kd.exe) tool, 32*
*NTSD (ntsd.exe) tool, 31*
*WinDbg (windbg.exe) tool, 31-32*
Wireshark, 26
for Windows Vista, 710
Global Flags, 16
*Command Line mode, 19-21*
*GUI mode, 16-18*
*option abbreviations, 19-20*
leak detection tools, 432-433
LeakDiag (Leak Diagnosis) tool, 4-6
Process Explorer, 22-23

Process Monitor, 23
UMDH, 9
WDK (Windows Driver Kit), 23-26
*installing, 24*
Tools.ini content listing (3-9), 140
Trace and watch function execution
listing (2-42), 98
Traces option (Heaps test setting), 751
tracing
code execution, 94-95
function execution, 98
processors, 172
Tracing the remote authentication from the
server process listing (7-12), 336
tracing tools, security failures, investigating,
376-378
traffic (network), analyzing, 413-421
troubleshooting
local communication, 382-396
remote communication, 396-422
RPC troubleshooting state information, 396
*cell debugging, 396-412*
True 32 bit Stack in WOW64 Process (hidden in Listing 121) listing (12-3), 608
TSL test setting (Application Verifyer), 764
Two methods of setting up the symbol path
at debugger startup listing (2-13), 55
type information, debugger extensions,
initializing, 574-575
Typical client stack waiting on remote call
made using a connection-based
protocol listing (8-22), 409
Typical stack of a server thread waiting for a
new request on DCOM over LRPC
listing (8-7), 390
Typical stack of clients using DCOM over
LRPC listing (8-6), 389
Typical use of the ba command
listing (2-37), 89

**U**
u command, 72
u command used in user mode debugger
(x86) listing (2-22), 72
UAC (User Access Control), Windows Vista,
725-731

uf command, 215
uld (unload a module) event, creating, 143
UMDH leak detection tool, 9, 432
  BSTRs, 469
  memory leaks, identifying, 465-469
UMDH.exe LeakDiag tool, 4, 8
Unalign option (Heaps test setting), 751
Unassembled non-optimized function
    listing (12-9), 613
Unassembly code is dependent on
    the processor execution mode
    listing (12-5), 609
underruns, heaps, 286-300
unfreezing threads, 174
uninitializing debugger extensions, 578
uninitiated state, heap corruptions, 282-286
Unlocked Critical Section
    listing (10-18), 543
unlocked critical sections, 543-545
Use of d command listing (2-34), 85
Use of d*s command listing (2-35), 87
Use of dt command listing (2-33), 83
Use of dv command listing (2-32), 82
UseLFHGuardPages option (Heaps test
    setting), 752
User allocation size field (!heap extension
    command), 478
User Interface (Debug Diagnostic Tool), 692
user mode debuggers, configuring, 34-36
User mode debugger output listing (2-6), 47
user mode debuggers, 30-31, 124
  code breakpoints, setting, 79-81
  event processing, 126-130
  events
    controlling, 133-144
    order, 131, 133
  exceptions
    controlling, 144-166
    structured exception dispatching
      mechanism, 144-153
  kernel debuggers, redirecting through,
    41-44
  loops, 125-126
  operating systems, support for, 124-130
  output, 47
  processes, starting, 125

targets, creating, 124-125
u command, 72
version output, 67
Windows Vista, 712-716
user mode extensions, debuggers, 554
Using !getcallinfo to filter call information to
    a specific process listing (8-19), 405
Using !getcallinfo to obtain the call
    information maintained by the server
    listing (8-18), 405
Using !getclientcallinfo to obtain the call
    information maintained by the client
    listing (8-21), 408
Using !getdbgcell to obtain the cell
    information maintained by the server
    listing (8-20), 406
Using !getendpointinfo to list all endpoint
    known by RPC listing (8-15), 402
Using !getendpointinfo to list all endpoints
    known by RPC listing (8-14), 401
Using !getthreadinfo to list all thread from
    RPC thread pool listing (8-16), 402
Using !getthreadinfo to obtain a
    specific thread RPC information
    listing (8-17), 403
Using !lpc extension to get message
    information listing (8-2), 385
Using !lpc extension to get port information
    listing (8-3), 386
Using !lpc extension to obtain the
    entire LPC activity on the system
    listing (8-4), 386
Using !rpctime to obtain the current time
    stamp used by troubleshooting
    infrastructure listing (8-13), 400
Using breakpoints in the kernel mode
    debugger listing (2-30), 80
Using breakpoints in the user mode
    debugger listing (2-29), 79
Using breakpoints in the user mode
    debugger listing (2-31), 80
Using kls flag for detecting a user mode
    module mapping listing (3-29), 167
Using the !cs command to list all critical
    sections of a process listing (10-3), 501

Using the !handle extension command to find mutex object in notepad.exe listing (10-4), 502

Using the !token extension command to display a token in the user mode debugger listing (7-5), 326

Using the *kb command to Dump all threads and associated stacks listing (10-5), 506

Using the .sympath and .symfix commands listing (2-14), 56

Using the CritSec object listing (14-2), 698

Using the link.exe utility to find debug information stored in the binary file listing (2-8), 51

**V**

validating symbols, 61

values
   entering, 103-104
   local variables, discovering, 613-614

variable values, debuggers, displaying, 81-84

variables
   condition variables, synchronization, 739
   environment variables
      *BUFFER_OVERFLOW_CHECKS environment variable, 210*
      *Windows x64, 601*
   gGlobal variable, declaring, 88-89
   local variables, discovering, 613-614

version information, debugger extensions, initializing, 572

version output, user mode debuggers, 67

Version output from a user mode debugger listing (2-18), 67

versioning debugger extensions, 592

Virtual Memory Manager (VMM). *See* VMM (Virtual Memory Manager)

Virtual PC, kernel debugger, enabling for, 40

VMM (Virtual Memory Manager), 461

**W**

Walking the stack back in time listing (5-14), 236-239

Watching the error code returned by OpenThreadToken/OpenProcessToken listing (7-30), 369

WDbgExts APIs, 564-565

WDbgExts extension, 563-565
   APIs, 564
   code organization, 567-570
   header files, 567-570
   initialization, 570-575
      *COM interfaces, 572-573*
      *extension data, 576*
      *type information, 574-575*
      *version information, 572*
   requirements, 565-570

WDK (Windows Driver Kit), 23-26
   installing, 24

well-known SIDs, 327

WinDbg (windbg.exe) tool (Debugging Tools for Windows), 31-32

Windbg GUI
   event breaks, adjusting, 138
   event handling, adjusting, 138

windbg.exe, 8

Windows Advanced Option menu, 38

Windows Driver Kit (WDK). *See* WDK (Windows Driver Kit)

Windows Error Reporting, 633
   architecture, 662-682
   binaries, mapping to products, 673-677
   Dr. Watson dialog box, 653-654
      *Application Errors section, 656-657*
      *Application option, 656-657*
      *Crash Dump section, 655*
      *Crash Dump Type section, 655*
      *Log File Path section, 654*
      *Module List section, 658*
      *Number of Errors to Save section, 655*

*Number of Instructions section, 655*
*Raw Stack Dump section, 660-662*
*Stack Back Trace section, 659*
*State Dump for Thread ID X section, 658*
*System Information section, 657*
*Task List section, 658*
postmortem debugging, 653-662
product rollup page, 672
software options, 672
web site, navigating, 671
**Windows heap manager, 261**
**Windows Vista, 709**
custom debugger extensions, writing, 741
debuggers, 711
*access control side effects, 712-714*
*address space layout, 716-717*
*kernel mode debuggers, 715-716*
*user mode debuggers, 712-714*
debugging, postmortem debugging, 741-745
debugging security, 723-725
*file virtualization, 732-735*
*registry virtualization, 732-735*
*UAC (User Access Control), 725-731*
dump files, generating, 743
Event Log system, 710-711
heap manager, 717-723
integrity levels, 724
interprocess communication, 736
resource leaks, 736
synchronization, 737
*condition variables, 739*
*one-time initialization, 740*
*reader/writer locks, 737-738*
*thread pools, 740*
tools, 710
**Windows x64**
Application Verifier, 604
changes to, 602-605
Debugging Tools for Windows, 603-604
environment variables, 601

Wireshark, 605
exception models, 622-625
Leak Diagnostic tool, 603
**working set sizes, adjustments, 464**
**WOW64**
32-bit applications, running in, 598-602
applications, 615-617
commands, 607-609
structures, obtaining, 608
**WOW64 application's PEB using the dt command listing (12-12), 617**
**WOW64 applications PEB listing (12-11), 615-617**
**WOW64 threads' TEB using !teb extension command and dt commands listing (12-13), 618**
**writing custom 64-bit debugger extensions, 629**
**wt command, 98**

**X-Z**
x86 context flags values listing (3-18), 146
x86-64-bit general purposes register listing (12-2), 606

**BOOKS ONLINE**
**ENABLED**

# THIS BOOK IS SAFARI ENABLED

## INCLUDES FREE 45-DAY ACCESS TO THE ONLINE EDITION

The Safari® Enabled icon on the cover of your favorite technology book means the book is available through Safari Bookshelf. When you buy this book, you get free access to the online edition for 45 days.

Safari Bookshelf is an electronic reference library that lets you easily search thousands of technical books, find code samples, download chapters, and access technical information whenever and wherever you need it.

**TO GAIN 45-DAY SAFARI ENABLED ACCESS TO THIS BOOK:**

- Go to **http://www.awprofessional.com/safarienabled**
- Complete the brief registration form
- Enter the coupon code found in the front of this book on the "Copyright" page

Addison
Wesley

If you have difficulty registering on Safari Bookshelf or accessing the online edition, please e-mail customer-service@safaribooksonline.com.